MAPPING
AMERICA'S PAST
A Historical Atlas

MARK C. CARNES AND JOHN A. GARRATY

WITH PATRICK WILLIAMS

A HENRY HOLT REFERENCE BOOK
HENRY HOLT AND COMPANY NEW YORK

A Henry Holt Reference Book
Henry Holt and Company, Inc.
Publishers since 1866
115 West 18th Street
New York, New York 10011

Henry Holt ® is a registered trademark
of Henry Holt and Company, Inc.

Published in Canada by Fitzhenry & Whiteside Ltd.,
195 Allstate Parkway, Markham, Ontario L3R 4T8.

Library of Congress Cataloging-in-Publication Data

Carnes, Mark C. (Mark Christopher).
Mapping America's past : a historical atlas / Mark C. Carnes and John A. Garraty with Patrick Willliams.
p. cm.
Includes bibliographical references and index.
1. United States—Historical geography—Maps. I. Garraty, John Arthur. II. Williams, Patrick. III. Title.
G1201.S1 C3 1996 <G&M>
No prev. ed. ddc—DC20 96–34030
CIP
MAPS

ISBN 0-8050-4927-4

Henry Holt books are available for special promotions and premiums.
For details contact: Director, Special Markets.

First Edition—1996

Designed by Arcadia Editions Limited

Printed in United States of America
All first editions are printed on acid-free paper.∞

10 9 8 7 6 5 4 3 2 1

A good historical atlas, like all good historical writing, condenses the fog of the past into streams of meaning. This clear distillate reveals not just what happened, but what mattered: troops that clashed in battle rather than those who lost their way; towns that mushroomed into cities rather than those that dwindled; emigrants who chanced the long journey rather than their relatives who remained behind. This filtering of the gritty ambiguities of the past is what makes historical atlases so appealing, and the reason why we agreed to design and write one ourselves. The task, we thought, would be as clear as the maps we had always enjoyed. But clarity, we discovered in the first map we attempted, can be the murkiest of illusions.

We chose what we thought would be a fairly simple subject: the Underground Railroad—the network of volunteers who helped runaway slaves. Most historical atlases, indeed, most U.S. history texts, have included maps of the subject. We consulted the original source, Wilbur G. Siebert's *The Underground Railroad*, published in 1898. Siebert had interviewed hundreds of runaways and those who helped them escape, and from these anecdotal reports he prepared a map, similar in appearance to the railway maps of his day, showing a thick web of escape routes to freedom. Mapmakers in recent years have retained Siebert's information but replaced the static routes with broad arrows sweeping up from the plantation regions of the deep South, neatly conveying the image of a massive slave exodus.

It's an effective map, but poor history. Part of the problem rests with Siebert himself, whose express purpose was to prove that the Underground Railroad was "one of the greatest forces" leading to the destruction of slavery; his informants shared his desire to magnify their accomplishments. Furthermore, the use of railroad as metaphor and railway map as representation fostered the common misconception that the Underground Railroad functioned as an extensive and well-organized system. During the 1850s, however, fewer than one slave in 400 managed to escape. The South did not secede so as to staunch the hemorrhaging loss of slaves via the Underground Railroad. On the contrary, it was the *inability* of slaves to escape that required their liberation by force. This, we concluded, was the real story of slavery and the Underground Railroad. We therefore designed a map of the Myth of the Underground—juxtaposed with another showing the actual escape routes of a half-dozen runaway slaves, whose unusual circumstances illustrated the hopeless plight of the great majority.

As we turned to other subjects, we found similar distortions: maps portraying the U.S. Army's one-sided slaughter of the Indians as the convergence of tidy (and apparently evenly matched) rectangles; maps delineating the "boundaries" of Indian "nations"; maps rendering the back and forth shuttle of slave ships as a "triangular slave trade"; maps outlining the crazy tangle of incompatible trackage after the Civil War as an "integrated railway network"; maps purporting to describe variations in the "intelligence" of races and regions; and on and on.

To be sure, no atlas is free of distortion. Historical maps are interpretations, mere glimpses into the gloaming haze. Rather than scrub the gritty complexities out of the past, we have chosen to focus on them: the vote of the Maryland legislature over paper money in 1785; the cholera epidemic in Nashville, Tennessee in 1873; the debate over Prohibition in Grand Rapids, Michigan; the activities of the Works Progress Administration in Erie, Pennsylvania; the rise of racially segregated housing in post–World War II St. Louis; the failure of the strategic hamlet program in Duc Lap, Vietnam. We moved in closer still to show the voyage of a single slave ship in 1773, and to indicate how architecture expressed religious views in colonial churches, or controlled sexual behavior in 19th-century utopian communes.

If some historical maps efface the complicating details, others present the details as indigested masses of statistical information. Such maps commonly assume that information constitutes meaning, or can serve as its substitute. For example, a staple of nearly every U.S. historical atlas is the map sequence of population density (1 dot = x-thousand people) over time. This shows that the nation's population had increased and spread, a defensible conclusion that contributes little to historical understanding.

We have instead incorporated statistical information to examine public or scholarly debates: maps of population density to consider the impact of frontier conditions on human fertility; maps of immigrant settlement to outline the growth of the Socialist Party in the Midwest or the appeal of isolationist legislation during the 1930s; maps of canals and railroads to explore the hypothesis that the nation's economy would have been better served by a reallocation of investment in its transportation infrastructure. We chose topics that struck us as especially important or illustrative and then sought ways to illuminate them.

The decision to spotlight one theme ensures that others will be cast into shadows. Our own perspective has been influenced by the tremendous expansion of social and cultural history during the past thirty years. We have devoted more space to gender and sexuality than to the American Revolution; to disease and health than to state formation and boundary disputes; and to language, education, religion and publishing than to voyages of exploration. We also included layouts on work and labor, crime and punishment, and the emergence of social classes. In 1944, the condition of African-Americans was the central "dilemma" of the American experience, Swedish economist Gunnar Myrdal observed, and his words remain true. African Americans accordingly figure prominently in fully thirty of our layouts—about a quarter of the atlas. While social and cultural history add color and depth to the historical landscape, they can never overshadow the political and military struggles that often carve its contours. Nearly 200 maps consider these matters.

This atlas is about America—by which we expansively mean the inhabitants of the United States and its geographical antecedents—but we have included nearly 100 maps of other countries. The United States is a nation of immigrants, and our history derives from many societies and cultures. We have therefore included maps of religious and economic forces of 17th-century England; the slave trade in 18th-century West Africa; famine in 1840s and 1850s Ireland; poverty in 19th-century rural Japan; persecution in a 20th-century Lithuanian shtetl. Massive human migrations speak powerfully of this nation's ties to the rest of the world.

Throughout, we have adhered to the conviction that an historical atlas does not chart fixed landmarks of the past but instead provides a momentary sounding of its shifting meanings. Having conceded this, we nevertheless persist in the belief that this mapping of America's past may better help us discern where we have been and where we are, and perhaps even allow a glimpse of the journey ahead.

Mark C. Carnes,
for the authors

CONTENTS

PART 7: POST-WAR AMERICA 202

PART 8: AMERICA AND THE WORLD AFTER WORLD WAR II 226

PART 1: PRE-COLUMBIAN AMERICA

They came in search—literally—of a better life, seeking a herd of wooly mammoths just beyond the frozen horizon. They unknowingly crossed into a different continent, and a new world. They pushed south, beckoned by the sun and by the game that flourished in dense forests and vast grasslands. They endured mountain enclaves and forbidding deserts, they ranged along broad plains, still in search of big, furred beasts; they scavenged limitless woodlands for nuts and berries; they learned to plant. Their numbers increased and they built villages and towns. And, as humans always do, they tried to make sense of the peculiarities of land and climate, and of the riddles of life and death. They were the earliest Americans, separated by tens of thousands of years and thousands of miles from their human relations in Africa, Europe and Asia.

A CONTINENT ADRIFT
TENSIONS IN THE EARTH'S CRUST

Baseball fans from Maine to Japan were settling in for the third game of the 1989 World Series at San Francisco's Candlestick Park when their television pictures began to shudder. ABC sportscaster Al Michaels shouted, "We're having an earth—." Then the screens went black. At the stadium, people heard a sound like rolling thunder. The stands swayed, the foul poles lurched, the lights went out, and pieces of concrete broke loose from the roof. Across the bay, an elevated highway collapsed, crushing scores of motorists, and a section of the San Francisco-Oakland Bay Bridge toppled into the water. It was over in 15 seconds, leaving 60 dead and thousands more injured, victims of California's most recent earthquake.

After the TV crews had switched to auxiliary power, millions of Americans became witnesses to the aftermath of an unsettling geological reality that Californians take in their stride, something they evade with black humor or attenuate with "quake-proof" buildings but from which they cannot escape. Each year, the state is rocked by thousands of tremors. The 1989 earthquake, although worse than most, measuring 6.9 on the Richter scale, did not approach the destruction of the 1906 San Francisco earthquake, which scientists have fixed at 8.3, 25 times more powerful than the one in 1989. (The Richter scale, which is logarithmic, represents factors of ten.)

Reasons for Earthquakes

California is particularly vulnerable to earthquakes because it is located astride the San Andreas Fault, the major north-south seam between the Pacific Plate and the North American Plate, two rigid slabs of the earth's surface. About 50 miles thick and thousands of miles in diameter, these plates "float" upon hot, partially molten matter. About 200 million years ago, all of the continental plates were joined in a single supercontinent, termed Pangaea, "all land."

Since then, they have gradually been drifting apart, and occasionally back into contact with each other.

The North American Plate moved steadily westward, pushed by the molten rock that welled up through rifts in the floor of the Atlantic Ocean. It eventually collided with the Pacific Plate, which was moving in a northwesterly direction. The force of the collision, accumulating and intensifying over millions of years, crumpled the western edges of the North American Plate, forming the western mountain ranges; further north, the Pacific Plate pushed beneath the North American Plate, enabling the molten rock in the interior to rise through the earth's surface as volcanic eruptions.

The Appalachian mountain range had been formed still earlier, when the North American continental shelf extended to the eastern edge of the North American Plate. The shelf bumped into another continent—perhaps western Africa—and its crust buckled. These wrinkles, worn down by erosion, became the Appalachian Mountains. The central portion of the continent is relatively stable.

The North American Plate is expected to maintain its westerly course, grinding into the Pacific Plate and causing more earthquakes along the San Andreas Fault. Meanwhile, the northern drift of the Pacific Plate may in 10 million years carry Los Angeles into the neighborhood of San Francisco.

Bemused citizens of San Francisco, far right, watch their city ablaze on the morning of the 1906 earthquake. The earthquake reduced the woodframe buildings to heaps of kindling that ignited when stoves overturned. Over 500 city blocks burned down, leaving 250,000 homeless. The smiling people shown here were presumably not among the 700 who perished.

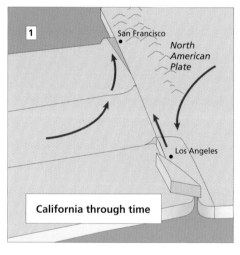
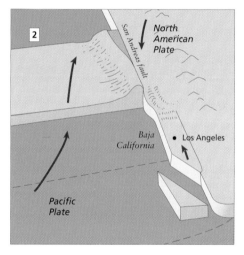
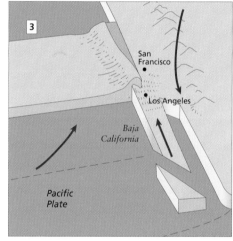

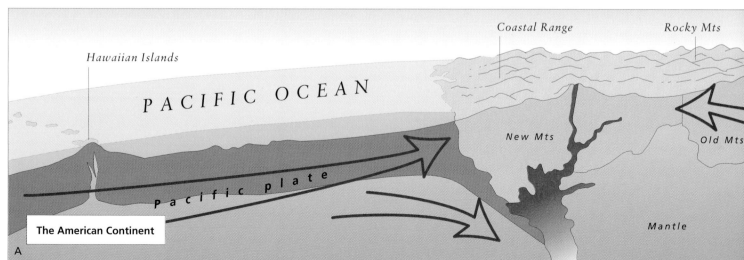

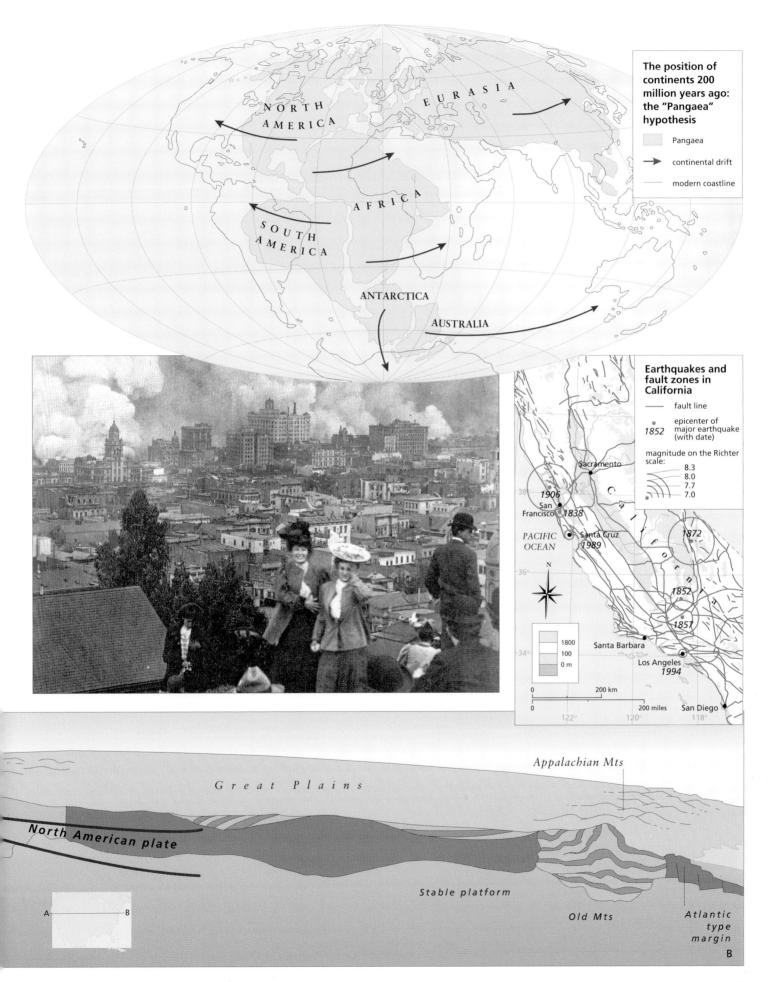

The position of continents 200 million years ago: the "Pangaea" hypothesis

- Pangaea
- ➔ continental drift
- — modern coastline

NORTH AMERICA

EURASIA

AFRICA

SOUTH AMERICA

ANTARCTICA

AUSTRALIA

Earthquakes and fault zones in California

- — fault line
- *1852* epicenter of major earthquake (with date)

magnitude on the Richter scale:
- 8.3
- 8.0
- 7.7
- 7.0

Sacramento

1906
San Francisco *1838*

PACIFIC OCEAN

Santa Cruz *1989*

N

1872

1852

1857

Santa Barbara

Los Angeles *1994*

1800
100
0 m

0   200 km

0   200 miles

San Diego

122°   120°   118°

Great Plains

Appalachian Mts

North American plate

Stable platform

A   B

Old Mts

Atlantic type margin

B

13

THE CLIMATIC CHALLENGE
CLIMATE IN AMERICAN HISTORY

The extremes of the New World climate continually caught settlers from the Old World by surprise. The first Massachusetts Puritans, after sweating through a summer unlike anything they had known in England, were stunned by the frigid winter gales that struck in December. When backers in London got word of the harsh New England climate, they advised Governor John Winthrop not to waste money "building where you are" but to find instead "some fitter place more to the South." However, Winthrop and his companions remained, planting the seeds of a vibrant civilization that took root throughout much of North America. Historian Arnold Toynbee cited this as proof that civilizations thrive in the face of adversity.

Toynbee observed that New England, "the hardest country of all," far out-distanced its colonial rivals. He argued, conversely, that "ease is inimical to civilization," that the South, though favored with a "relatively genial soil and climate," was subjugated during the Civil War by the North, whose people had acquired habits of industry and resourcefulness through generations of struggle with a hostile environment.

Toynbee failed to recognize that nearly every region of the country posed a tremendous challenge to immigrants. New England winters are indeed bitter, but its coast is washed by the warm breezes from the Gulf Stream. Midwestern winters are much more severe. Deep in the interior of a large continent, the Midwest is deprived of the moderating influence of nearby oceans and is chilled by the cold, dry air masses that form over Canada and descend far south. Daunting snow storms are often followed by long summer droughts. (*See The Dust Bowl, Drought and despair on the Great Plains, p 178–179*).

The climate of the South also offers bracing challenges, especially a sweltering humidity that ascends from the tropics and periodically coalesces as hurricanes.

Westerners, on the other hand, have had to contend with extreme aridity, as the winds of the Pacific rise over the mountain ranges and deposit their moisture as rain along the coast.

Toynbee was wrong to believe that a single region of America (New England) possessed an "optimum climatic area" for generating vital civilizations. Rather, nearly everyone who settled in the United States had to adapt to unfamiliar—and extreme—weather conditions.

In their long quest for new crops and new methods of cultivating them, new types of housing and clothing, and new ways of understanding the capriciousness of nature, they slowly acquired many of the traits that we now think of as American.

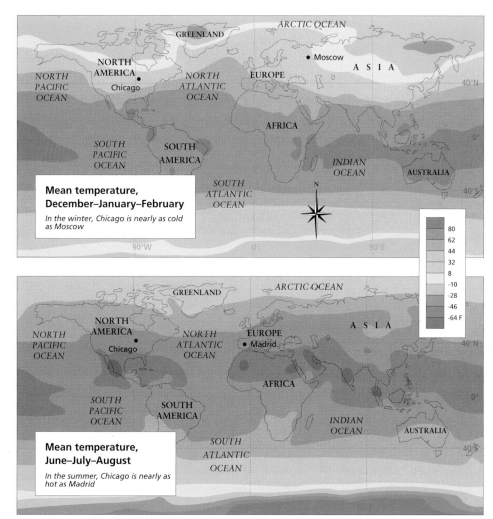

Mean temperature, December–January–February

In the winter, Chicago is nearly as cold as Moscow

	80
	62
	44
	32
	8
	-10
	-28
	-46
	-64 F

Mean temperature, June–July–August

In the summer, Chicago is nearly as hot as Madrid

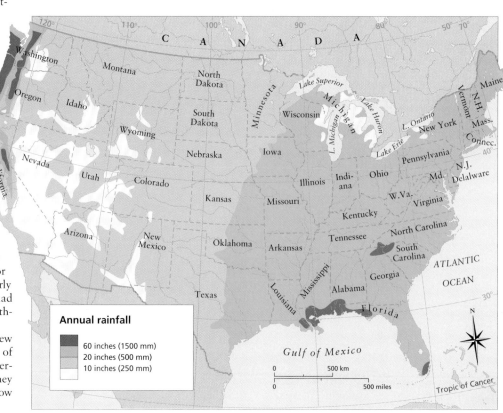

Annual rainfall

60 inches (1500 mm)
20 inches (500 mm)
10 inches (250 mm)

0   500 km

0   500 miles

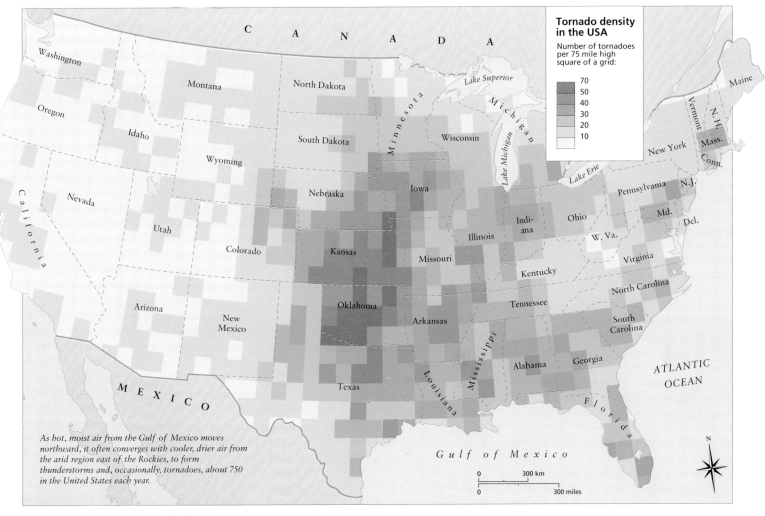

Tornado density in the USA

Number of tornadoes per 75 mile high square of a grid:

- 70
- 50
- 40
- 30
- 20
- 10

As hot, moist air from the Gulf of Mexico moves northward, it often converges with cooler, drier air from the arid region east of the Rockies, to form thunderstorms and, occasionally, tornadoes, about 750 in the United States each year.

0   300 km

0   300 miles

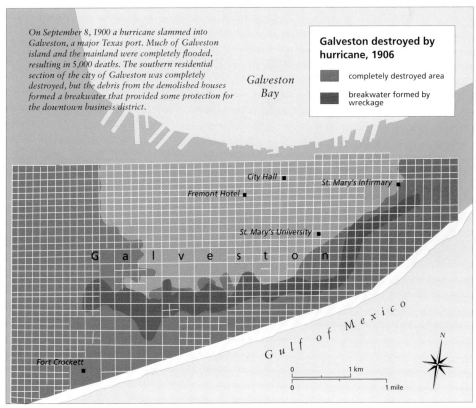

On September 8, 1900 a hurricane slammed into Galveston, a major Texas port. Much of Galveston island and the mainland were completely flooded, resulting in 5,000 deaths. The southern residential section of the city of Galveston was completely destroyed, but the debris from the demolished houses formed a breakwater that provided some protection for the downtown business district.

Galveston destroyed by hurricane, 1906

- completely destroyed area
- breakwater formed by wreckage

Galveston Bay

City Hall ■

Fremont Hotel ■

St. Mary's Infirmary ■

St. Mary's University ■

G a l v e s t o n

Fort Crockett ■

Gulf of Mexico

0   1 km

0   1 mile

GLOBAL WARMING
ATMOSPHERIC CHANGE OVER THE LAST 18,000 YEARS

The earth's atmosphere is getting warmer, and has been doing so for nearly 18,000 years. Around 16,000 BC, when the last ice age began to wane, the mean global temperature was about nine degrees Fahrenheit cooler than today. The atmosphere began to warm gradually, about five-hundredths of a degree every hundred years, until the 20th century, when it rose by more than a degree. The Environmental Protection Agency (EPA) estimates that by the year 2100 global temperatures may soar another nine degrees. If this happens, agricultural regions will be transformed entirely and the polar ice caps will begin to melt, raising sea levels and inundating huge stretches of low-lying land, especially in the Southeast.

At the peak of the last major glaciation 18,000 years ago, most of what is now Canada was covered by enormous mounds of ice, and the continental United States by thick forests.

As global temperatures began to climb, the glaciers receded, the forests west of the Mississippi gave way to grasslands and deserts, and, as the ice caps melted, the Atlantic Ocean washed over low lying sections of the continental shelf.

Causes of Global Warming

What brought about the close of the last ice age and commenced the subsequent warming trend is still disputed. Scientists point to an intensified luminosity of the sun; to a cyclical wobble in the earth's axis; and to an upwelling of decaying plant and animal matter from the ocean floor, increasing the concentration of carbon dioxide (CO_2) in the atmosphere.

There is greater agreement on the reasons for the intensification of the warming trend during the 20th century. For thousands of years, the earth's atmosphere contained a concentration of carbon dioxide that ranged from 200 to 300 parts per million. During the last half of the 19th century it was about 280, but by 1958 had increased to 315, and by 1990, to 345. This exacerbated the normal "greenhouse effect," a phenomenon caused by the fact that atmospheric CO_2 allows sunlight to pass through it freely, but absorbs the heat radiated from the earth's surface.

Carbon dioxide is pumped into the air when fossil fuels are burned, or when forests, which absorb carbon dioxide and release oxygen, are destroyed. Of special concern is the retreat of the lush tropical forests, which have been hacked down or burned by loggers, farmers, and ranchers. These short-sighted practices are tolerated and even condoned by governments of developing nations. The United States, which early in its history sacrificed its woodlands in order to achieve economic growth, now finds it difficult to preach a doctrine of conservation to developing nations.

Consequences

Because it seems doubtful that fossil fuel consumption can be checked (*See , Energy versus the Environment, p 260–261*), or the assault on the forests stayed, carbon dioxide concentrations will therfore likely double during the 21st century. The American Association for the Advancement of Science has predicted that a doubling of CO_2 would raise the average global temperature four to nine degrees F.

Mathematical models, though much in dispute, indicate that warming on this scale would result in extraordinary climatic, environmental and geographical transformations. The great northern forests that cover Canada would virtually disappear; the dry grasslands of the Midwest would extend far to the north; and much of the Gulf coast will be covered by tropical forests. The EPA further predicted that by 2100 melting ice caps will "most likely" raise sea levels five to seven feet, and perhaps as much as 11 feet. This would greatly alter the U.S. coastline, leaving most of southern Florida underwater.

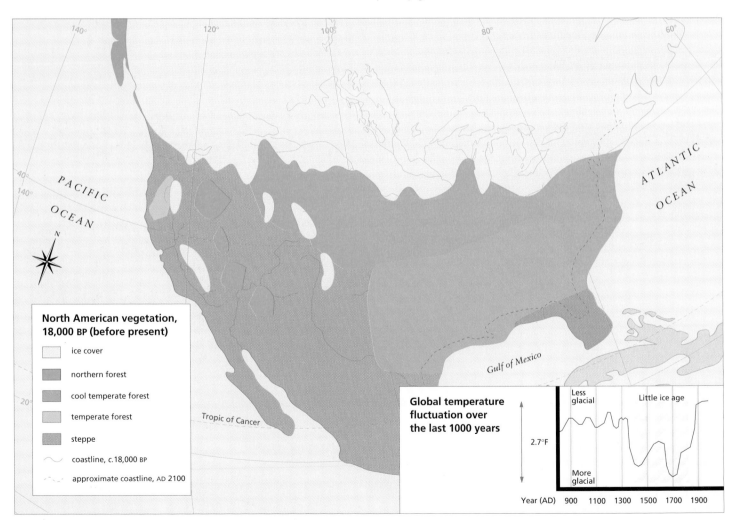

North American vegetation, 18,000 BP (before present)

- ice cover
- northern forest
- cool temperate forest
- temperate forest
- steppe
- coastline, c.18,000 BP
- approximate coastline, AD 2100

Global temperature fluctuation over the last 1000 years

2.7°F

Less glacial

Little ice age

More glacial

Year (AD) 900 1100 1300 1500 1700 1900

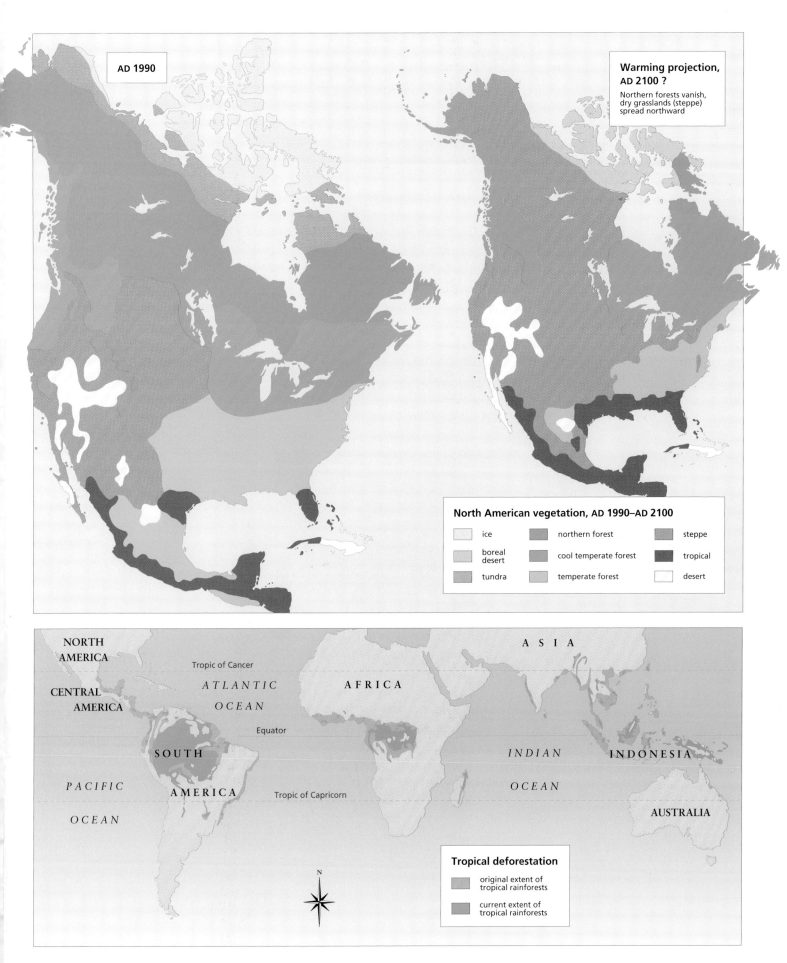

AD 1990

Warming projection, AD 2100 ?
Northern forests vanish, dry grasslands (steppe) spread northward

North American vegetation, AD 1990–AD 2100

- ice
- boreal desert
- tundra
- northern forest
- cool temperate forest
- temperate forest
- steppe
- tropical
- desert

NORTH AMERICA

CENTRAL AMERICA

Tropic of Cancer

ATLANTIC OCEAN

AFRICA

ASIA

Equator

SOUTH AMERICA

PACIFIC OCEAN

Tropic of Capricorn

INDIAN OCEAN

INDONESIA

AUSTRALIA

N

Tropical deforestation
- original extent of tropical rainforests
- current extent of tropical rainforests

FIRST PEOPLES OF NORTH AMERICA
ORIGINS OF THE FIRST AMERICANS

Tens of thousands of years ago, human beings first walked from Siberia into North America along a land bridge over what is now the Bering Strait. Drawn onward by hunger, or by the recollection of it, they slogged through the arctic expanses, eyes fastened on the eastern horizon, straining to catch sight of the woolly mammoths whose flesh would feed them, whose huge bones would frame their huts, whose hides would be sewn together to cover their bodies, and whose fat would burn to warm them at night. These travelers from Asia were unaware that they had set foot upon another continent, much less that they had begun a new era in the diffusion of human beings throughout the world.

Thus commenced the first chapter in the peopling of North America, or so most scientists now believe. But if there is broad agreement on how the first inhabitants arrived, other issues remain sources of debate. Who were these people and where did they come from? When did they first set foot on North American soil? What routes did they follow as they pushed east and south ?

The bones or artifacts of the low-browed, squat-framed Neanderthals or other pre-mod-

winter remained impenetrable.

About 35,000 years ago, Neanderthals were everywhere being replaced by a new type of *Homo sapiens*—people physiologically much like ourselves. After another 10,000 years or so, modern humans had established settlements at Mal'ta and Afontova Gorna in the Lake Baikal region of Siberia. Somewhat later, perhaps 18,000 years ago, these people may have made their way eastward to the upper Lena and Aldan rivers and eventually crossed from Asia into North America.

Some scientists, however, believe that the first North Americans evolved from a racial stock originating in northern China. Paleolithic (stone age) skulls found along China's Yellow River contain distinct tooth shapes common to American Indians but different from paleolithic skulls in the Lake Baikal region. Perhaps these northern Chinese, after migrating into northeastern Siberia, were the first to cross into North America.

Crossing into the Americas
Asia and Alaska are now separated by the Bering Strait, 53 miles across at its narrowest point. That early peoples possessed the skill to navigate this stretch of frigid water seems doubtful. During the bitterest extremes of the ice ages, however, atmospheric moisture con-

densing as snow fed the great sheets of ice that descended from the poles. The withdrawal of this enormous volume of water caused ocean levels to fall hundreds of feet, exposing more and more of the continental shelves. For 10,000 years after 60,000 BP (before the present), and again after 25,000 BP, Asia and North America were joined by a land bridge.

Did humans cross during the first or second era? Because there is little persuasive archeological evidence that human beings had inhabited eastern Asia or the New World during the earlier ice age, it seems likely that they first moved into North America during the second cold period, probably about 15,000 years ago, several thousand years after arriving on the banks of the Lena and Aldan rivers in Siberia.

Once they had roamed into Alaska, these early peoples confronted a new obstacle. Great sheets of ice had congealed into a large mass covering most of Canada. One huge glacier jutted out along southern Alaska and across the Aleutians. Another extended northward along the Brooks Range. Together they blocked migration east and south. But the earth's rising temperature melted the edges of the glaciers, leaving an ice-free corridor east of the Mackenzie Mountains and extending to the open plains in the south.

The early inhabitants of Alaska may have passed through the corridor and continued east of the Rockies until they reached the heart of the continent. Within the following several thousand years, they had extended their range throughout the Americas, adapting to the varying habitats they found, from tundra, steppe grassland, desert to forest.

"Newspaper Rock" (left) at Holbrook, Navajo County, Arizona, an example of ancient pictograms, possibly denoting events and seasonal records important to the people of the region.

Paleoindian America

- Ancient ice cover
- Steppe
- Forestation
- Paleoindian Site Concentrations
- Ancient coastline
- Modern coastline

ern humans have not been found in the New World, leading most scientists to believe that human beings originated in the Old World, probably Africa or other regions where food was plentiful and the climate hospitable. Neanderthals eventually learned to control fire and improved their hunting techniques and tools, skills that enabled them to wander further north. About 50,000 years ago, some reached the Don River near Volgograd in eastern Russia. For these peoples, northern Siberia with its extreme cold and nine long months of

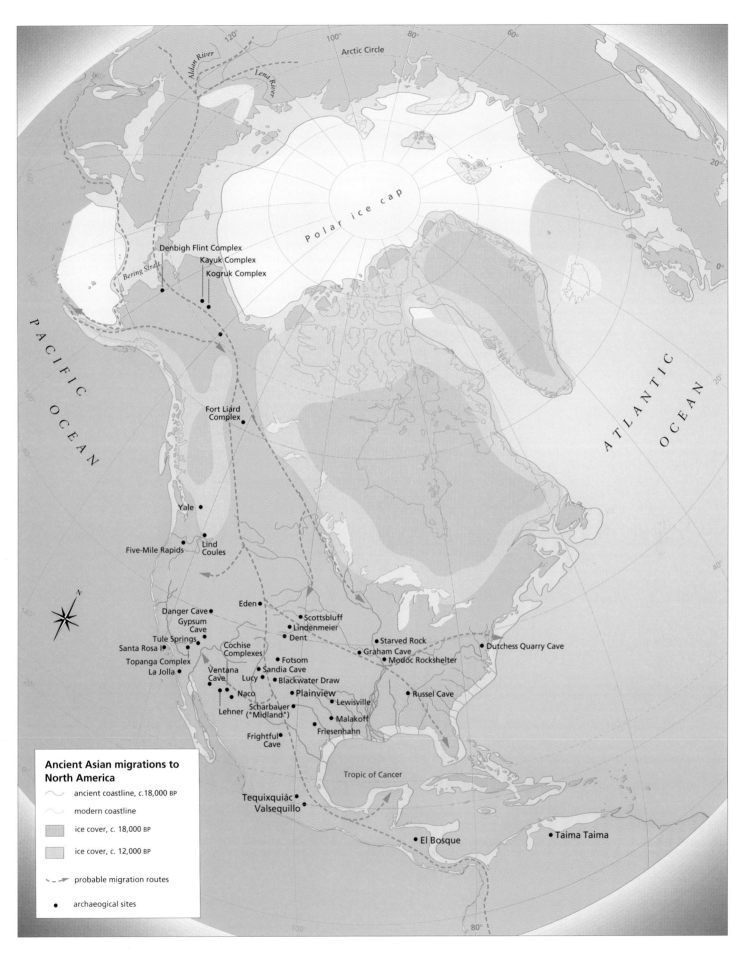

120° Aldan River
100° Arctic Circle
80°
60°
20°
Lena River

Polar ice cap

Bering Strait

Denbigh Flint Complex
Kayuk Complex
Kogruk Complex

PACIFIC OCEAN

ATLANTIC OCEAN

Fort Liard Complex

Yale •

Five-Mile Rapids • Lind Coules •

N

Eden •
Danger Cave •
Gypsum Cave •
Tule Springs •
Santa Rosa I •
Topanga Complex •
La Jolla •
Ventana Cave •
Cochise Complexes
Lucy •
Naco •
Lehner •
Scharbauer ("Midland") •
Frightful Cave •

Scottsbluff •
Lindenmeier •
Dent •
Fotsom •
Sandia Cave •
Blackwater Draw •
Plainview •
Lewisville •
Malakoff •
Friesenhahn •

Starved Rock •
Graham Cave •
Modoc Rockshelter •
Russel Cave •

Dutchess Quarry Cave •

Tropic of Cancer

Tequixquiác •
Valsequillo •

El Bosque •

Taima Taima •

Ancient Asian migrations to North America

〰 ancient coastline, c.18,000 BP

〰 modern coastline

▨ ice cover, c. 18,000 BP

▨ ice cover, c. 12,000 BP

- - ➤ probable migration routes

• archaeogical sites

MYTH OF THE MOUND BUILDERS
COMPLEX STRUCTURES ERECTED BY NATIVE AMERICANS

As settlers spilled across the Appalachians and into the Ohio Valley after the Revolutionary War, they came upon thousands of huge earthen heaps. Some were hundreds of feet high; some looked like pyramids, but with the apex lopped off; some, viewed from above, were shaped like regular circles or polygons, and others, like serpents or animals. Many contained human skeletons and finely-wrought copper and mica artifacts. Such sustained and sophisticated enterprise, most settlers assumed, could not have been the work of the indolent and nomadic savages, who also professed ignorance as to mound origins. America must have once been inhabited by a highly-advanced race of white mound builders, or so many Americans believed.

Fantastic hypotheses abounded. Some conjectured that the mound builders had come from the lost continent of Atlantis. Others, citing Biblical references to Hebrews worshipping in "high places," identified the mound builders as descendants of the Ten Lost Tribes of Israel. In 1811 De Witt Clinton, destined to become governor of New York, maintained that the mounds in the western part of his state had been constructed by wayward Vikings. William Henry Harrison, several years before assuming the Presidency, speculated that the mounds had been erected as defensive fortifications by a race of advanced agricultural peoples.

The most important variant of this theme was propounded by the Mormon prophet Joseph Smith, who received from the angel Moroni golden plates bearing the writings of the "former inhabitants of this continent." These he translated from the "ancient Egyptian" and published as the *Book of Mormon* (1830). This described how peoples much like those in the Bible had repeatedly contended for control of North America. It told of a barbarous race of red-skinned Lamanites that destroyed the cities of the highly-civilized Nephites—the mound builders. In AD 401, at the climactic battle at the hill Cumorah, the Nephites were wiped out. Mormon, the sole survivor, inscribed on the golden tablets the tale of his people.

During the 1880s, John Wesley Powell, the first director of the Smithsonian Institution's Bureau of Ethnology, organized a systematic study of the mounds. Some fantastic stories were easily put to rest. Hand-made artifacts, which some enthusiasts claimed to show long-extinct animals, had been improperly analyzed. Some artifacts were outright frauds.

In 1894 Powell released a report that demolished the notion that the "Moundbuilders" were a long-lost race distinct from and superior to the Indians. That the Indians had forgotten their mound-building forebears, the report noted, was not inconceivable, for even the memory of modern peoples had proven deficient. Why else had so many scholars neglected Hernando de Soto's reports of mound building Indians during his explorations of the southeastern United States in the 16th century?

De Soto, who had sailed into Tampa Bay in June 1539, touched shore and pushed inland seeking gold and silver. The first Indian town he came upon was blistered with strange earthen mounds. De Soto wrote that the chief's house stood "up a very high mount made by hand for defense." During subsequent travels through the southeast, he found similar mounds in virtually every Indian village. The Indians, he concluded, "always try to dwell on high places." They built the mounds "with the strength of their arms, piling up very large quantities of earth and stamping on it with great force until they have formed a mound from 28 to 42 feet in height." Only after de Soto had crossed the Mississippi and ventured onto the edges of the Great Plains did evidence of mound-building Indians fade.

Scholars now believe that the mounds were constructed during a 3,000-year period that ended with the white conquest of the Ohio and Mississippi valleys. The earlier mounds, dating from 1000 BC to about AD 1000, were used chiefly for burial. They were built by tribes that supplemented their diet of nuts, berries, small animals, and fowl by cultivating maize and other crops. This cultural complex is known as Adena and, during the later period, Hopewell. The Hopewell culture began to decline around AD 700, possibly when population growth overstrained the economic base.

About this time a new and more complex cultural and economic structure emerged along the Mississippi Valley. "Mississippian" Indians were highly adaptable. They excelled at hunting, foraging, fishing, and agriculture. In addition to maize, they cultivated beans, squash, and sunflowers in the fertile soils of the Mississippi floodplain.

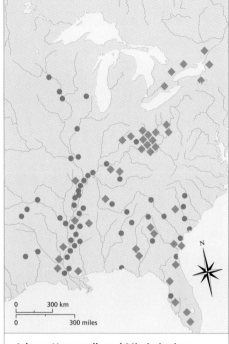

Adena, Hopewell, and Mississippian mounds

◆ major Adena or Hopewell mounds 1000 BC to AD 1000

● major Mississippian mounds AD 700 to 1700

Right: a "cremation scene tablet" from an "ancient plate," "proof" of the existence of a long-lost civilazation in the Mound Builder country. In fact, this tablet was a hoax, one of the many that had surfaced in connection with the growing myth surrouding the Mound Builders.

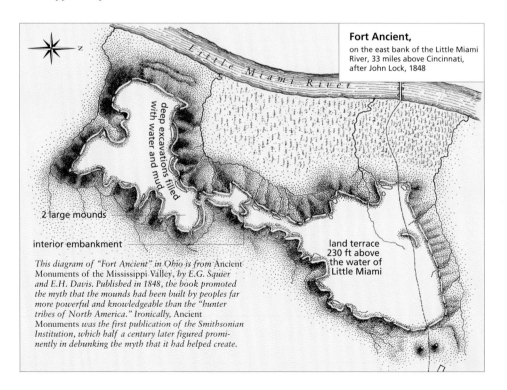

Fort Ancient,
on the east bank of the Little Miami River, 33 miles above Cincinnati, after John Lock, 1848

Little Miami River

deep excavations filled with water and mud

2 large mounds

interior embankment

land terrace 230 ft above the water of Little Miami

This diagram of "Fort Ancient" in Ohio is from Ancient Monuments of the Mississippi Valley, *by E.G. Squier and E.H. Davis. Published in 1848, the book promoted the myth that the mounds had been built by peoples far more powerful and knowledgeable than the "hunter tribes of North America." Ironically,* Ancient Monuments *was the first publication of the Smithsonian Institution, which half a century later figured prominently in debunking the myth that it had helped create.*

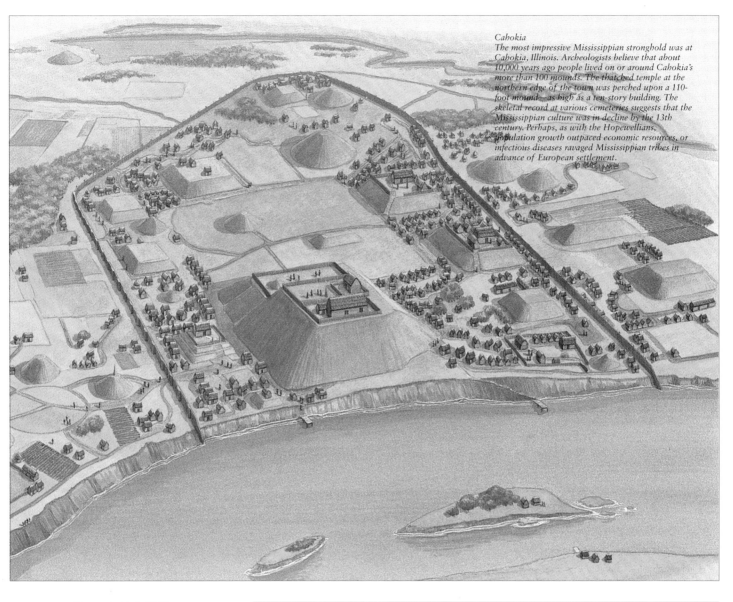

Cahokia
The most impressive Mississippian stronghold was at Cahokia, Illinois. Archeologists believe that about 10,000 years ago people lived on or around Cahokia's more than 100 mounds. The thatched temple at the northern edge of the town was perched upon a 110-foot mound—as high as a ten-story building. The skeletal record at various cemeteries suggests that the Mississippian culture was in decline by the 13th century. Perhaps, as with the Hopewellians, population growth outpaced economic resources, or infectious diseases ravaged Mississippian tribes in advance of European settlement.

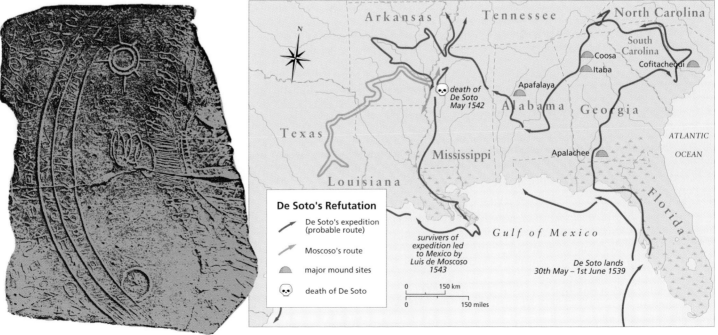

De Soto's Refutation

↗ De Soto's expedition (probable route)

↗ Moscoso's route

◖ major mound sites

☠ death of De Soto

ORIGINS OF INDIAN LANGUAGES
TWO THOUSAND TONGUES OR THREE ?

The dark-hued peoples to whom Columbus applied a single label spoke a multitude of languages. Even his "Indian" guides were bewildered by the strange tongues of the tribesmen they encountered and were obliged to resort to pantomime to make their meaning clear. The linguistic diversity of North American Indians—the number of languages and dialects once exceeded 2,000— has proven a source of consternation to missionaries and soldiers, and to modern linguists. Why did native Americans speak so many languages? Where did these languages originate and how were they related? More important still, what clues on the origins of Indian culture are imbedded in their words and linguistic structures?

Powell's Classification (1891)
The first major attempt to impose order upon the chaos of Indian linguistics was undertaken by John Wesley Powell, Director of the Bureau of American Ethnology of the Smithsonian Institution. Powell collected and compared vocabulary lists of North American tribes from missionaries, army officers, and adventurers. In 1891, he concluded that the hundreds of Indians languages and dialects had evolved from some 58 distinct linguistic stocks, each of which was as distinct from one another as "from the Aryan or the Scythian families."

Only a handful of stocks were spoken by Indian peoples living east of the Mississippi. Among these, the most important were Algonquian, Siouan, Muskogean, and Iroquian. Among the tribes of the Southeast, many Indians, such as the Apache and Navaho, spoke Athabascan (also called Na-Dene), a linguistic stock they shared with the Indians of eastern Alaska and the Yukon Territory of northern Canada. The Comanche, Ute, and Hopi spoke languages that Powell classified as Uto-Aztecan.

The greatest diversity—nearly 40 stocks— was found west of the Rockies. One western state, California, with almost 30 distinct languages, exhibited more linguistic diversity than all of Europe.

Sapir's Speculation (1929)
Powell conceded that his classification was "only a beginning," and that "some of the families may in future be united to other families," but he thought this unlikely. In 1929, however, anthropologist Edward Sapir suggested that many of Powell's "genetically" unrelated stocks had originated from the same source. The North American Indian languages had evolved not from 58 stocks, as Powell contended, but from perhaps as few as six basic groups.

Where Powell maintained the linguistic distinctiveness of the Iroquian, Siouan, Caddoan, and Muskogean stocks, Sapir found that they shared enough words and grammatical structures to be lumped into a "superstock" that he called "Hokan-

Siouan." He further proposed that the Algonquian languages of the east were related to the Salishan and Wakashan languages of the Pacific Northwest. He also combined many of the languages of California and Oregon into another superstock—"Penutian."

Some of Sapir's speculations were accurate. Most astonishing was his contention—eventually confirmed—that Yurok and Wiyot, languages spoken by isolated tribes in coastal California, were related to the Algonquian language that prevailed among Indians of the Atlantic coast.

But scholars spotted some technical errors in his analysis, and skeptics rejected his linking of Hokan and Siouan, languages that most experts considered to be unrelated. Sapir himself had doubts about this category, which he eventually called his "waste-paper basket stock." Most linguists had also questioned his fusion of Algonquian and Wakashan stocks.

Later linguists generally emulated the skepticism of Sapir's critics, preferring intensive analyses of a single language to speculation on the origins of linguistic "superstocks."

Greenberg's Hypothesis
American Indian linguistics subsequently drifted from the more synthetic approach of European historical linguistics. This tradition had been founded by Sir William Jones, who in 1786 advanced the startling hypothesis that Latin, Greek, and Sanskrit had "sprung from some common source." This claim, though

ridiculed at the time, was confirmed a century later. During the 1950s, linguist Joseph Greenberg similarly proposed that the hundreds of African languages had stemmed from only four basic linguistic groups. Despite initial criticism, his classification became the basis for most subsequent work in the field.

Greenberg then turned to North America and threw American Indian linguists into turmoil by hypothesizing that Indian languages of the western hemisphere had evolved from only three stocks. Sapir's error, he wrote, was not in lumping too many groups together, but in failing to combine enough. Thus Hokan and Siouan were indeed related to each other, as Sapir had surmised, but they were also related to the Muskogean, Iroquian, Algonquian, Penutian, Uto-Aztecan and to all but two of Powell's 58 "genetically" distinct languages. Greenberg termed this truly seminal superstock "Amerind" and speculated further that it had been spoken by the first peoples to cross from Siberia into the Americas. Eskimo and Athabascan, the only two stocks unrelated to super-group Amerind, were the products of later migrations.

Critics contended that the similarities among the Amerind languages were due to chance, or to the inevitable cultural borrowings that occur among neighboring peoples. They pointed out that the Tuscarora word for "tooth" sounds much like the English—hardly proof of the languages' common origin. Predictably, partisans on both sides have called

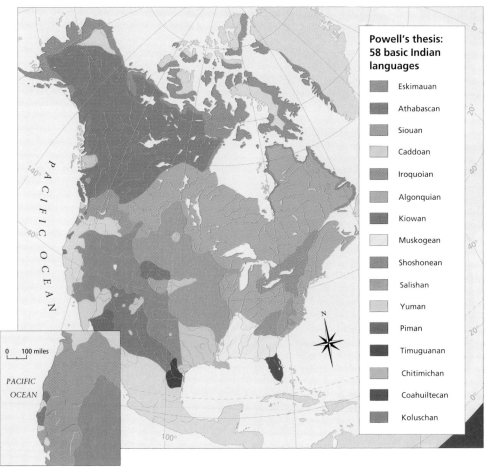

Powell's thesis: 58 basic Indian languages

- Eskimauan
- Athabascan
- Siouan
- Caddoan
- Iroquoian
- Algonquian
- Kiowan
- Muskogean
- Shoshonean
- Salishan
- Yuman
- Piman
- Timuguanan
- Chitimichan
- Coahuiltecan
- Koluschan

PACIFIC OCEAN

PACIFIC OCEAN

0   100 miles

for further research, which is the only certain outcome of this debate.

Language and Culture

The mapping of Indian cultural areas is almost as problematic as mapping their linguistic stocks. The map at right shows the differing economic basis for different regions. Indians in the woodland areas east of the Mississippi River subsisted on wild plants or they grew their own crops, while Indians on the Great Plains relied on hunting.

But the map of economic areas and linguistic stocks are strikingly different. Although the Indians of the Great Plains and those of the Mississippi had markedly different economics and cultures, their languages were closely related. And the economically similar tribes of the Atlantic coast spoke less similar languages.

This suggests that language is the basic element of human culture—and endures far longer than other cultural expressions.

Indian shell gorget (far right) excavated by students of the University of Oklahoma, Spiro Mound, LeFlore County. The shell shows borrowings from many Native American cultures, evidence of the malleability of culture, as opposed to the stability of grammatical structure and vocabulary.

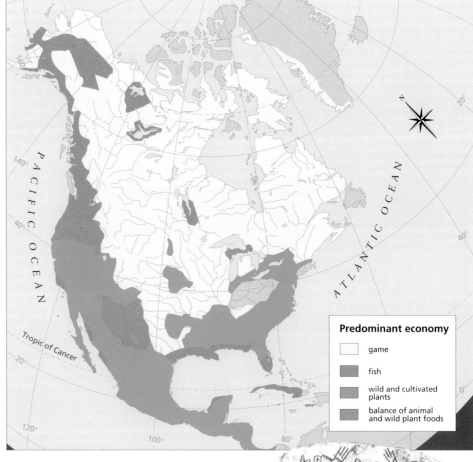

Predominant economy

- game
- fish
- wild and cultivated plants
- balance of animal and wild plant foods

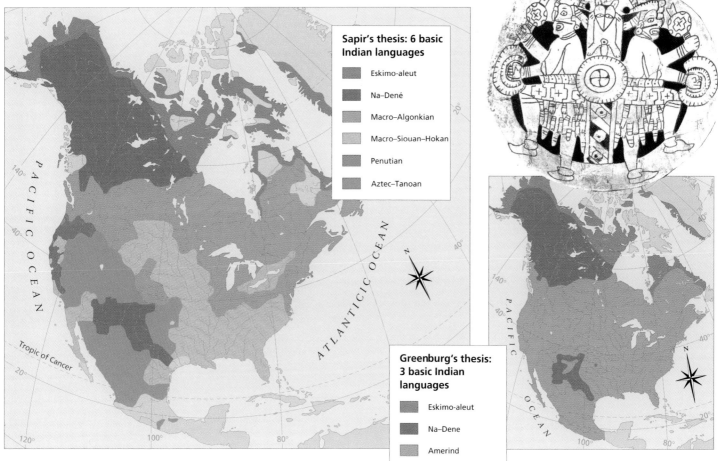

Sapir's thesis: 6 basic Indian languages

- Eskimo-aleut
- Na–Dené
- Macro–Algonkian
- Macro–Siouan–Hokan
- Penutian
- Aztec–Tanoan

Greenburg's thesis: 3 basic Indian languages

- Eskimo-aleut
- Na–Dene
- Amerind

SAVAGE TRIBES OR SOVEREIGN NATIONS?
CONTRASTING VIEWS OF EUROPEAN COLONISTS

European colonists held two views of the native peoples whose land they were appropriating. Some maintained that the Indians were childlike creatures, who had no rights to the lands they occupied. As the Reverend Robert Cushman told potential Puritan emigrants, Massachusetts Bay Colony was "spacious and void," for its natives "do but run over the grass, as do also the foxes and wild beasts." This "vast and empty chaos" would rightfully belong to those who made use of it. Other whites conceived of Indian land claims in quite the opposite way. To them, Indian tribes were sovereign nations, and as such possessed legal title to tribal land, including the right to relinquish it by treaty.

Neither view bore much resemblance to reality, no Indian tribe was devoid of economic organization or government; however none approached European standards in such matters. Most tribes varied in social and political organization, land utilization, and attitudes toward property. For example, individual Plains Indians "owned" their tipis but not the land on which they rested. Among some tribes of the Southwest, women held title to the farm plots, even when their husbands were chiefly responsible for working the fields. Among Northwest Coast Indians, rights to fish in particular spots could be bought, sold, or passed down to a son.

Indian Territoriality: Tribes as Nation States?
Westerners have commonly imposed their own notions of fixed boundaries and political sovereignty upon the Indians. Maps such as the one below imply an analogy with European nation-states, each of which occupied an area with fixed boundaries. Tribal boundaries, when they existed at all, were neither spelled out in deeds or treaties nor marked by fences or any other sign of occupation.

Indians therefore moved freely from one habitat to another in search of food, unconstrained by fears of crossing abstract political boundaries. Particularly when they were decimated by disease, neighboring tribes would combine to form more effective hunting and war parties. In the Northwestern Plains, the Assiniboin, Ojibwa, and Cree ranged over the same hunting grounds. Often they camped together, intermarried, and established military and trading alliances.

Indian Trading Relations, c. 1650
Indian tribes shared hunting grounds, and cultivated trade relationships, sometimes over great distances. Trade was especially common east of the Mississippi, where rivers and streams facilitated travel. But even in the West, where formidable deserts and mountain ranges separated the tribes, Indians developed extensive trading networks.

Well before the arrival of the Europeans, permanent trade centers had evolved along the seams of different environments. At the Mandan-Hidatsa and Arikara trade centers along the Missouri River, furs and dried meat from the Great Plains were traded for garden crops and woodland products from the Mississippi River region.

At the Dallas trade center, fish, cooking oils, and seashells from the Pacific Northwest were traded for furs, stones, and metals from the Great Plateau. At the Pecos and Zuni centers of the Southwest, products from the Pacific, the Southwest, the Plains, and even the eastern woodlands, were all exchanged.

The small Native American town of Pomeiockt at the mouth of Gibbs Creek, situated in what later became the state of North Carolina (above). This watercolor was made by John White between 1585 and 1587, during his time in the colony of Virginia.

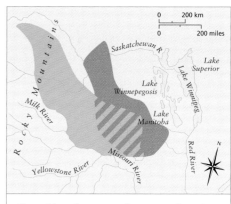

Shared hunting grounds among the Northern Great Plains Indians, c. 1840

Assiniboin　　Plains Ojibwa (Chippewa)

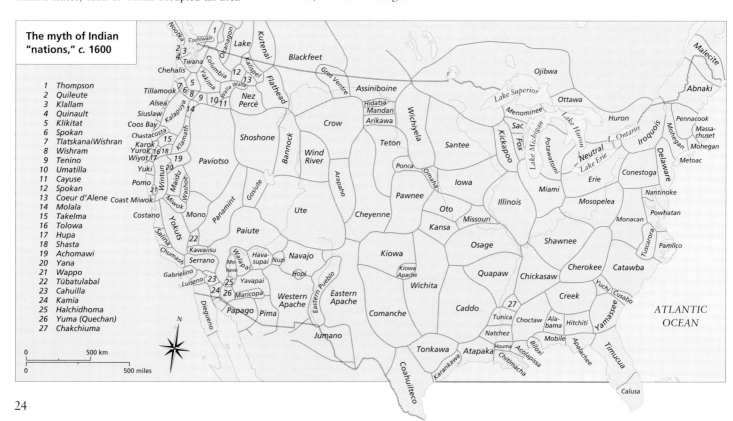

The myth of Indian "nations," c. 1600

1 Thompson
2 Quileute
3 Klallam
4 Quinault
5 Klikitat
6 Spokan
7 TlatskanaiWishran
8 Wishram
9 Tenino
10 Umatilla
11 Cayuse
12 Spokan
13 Coeur d'Alene
14 Molala
15 Takelma
16 Tolowa
17 Hupa
18 Shasta
19 Achomawi
20 Yana
21 Wappo
22 Tübatulabal
23 Cahuilla
24 Kamia
25 Halchidhoma
26 Yuma (Quechan)
27 Chakchiuma

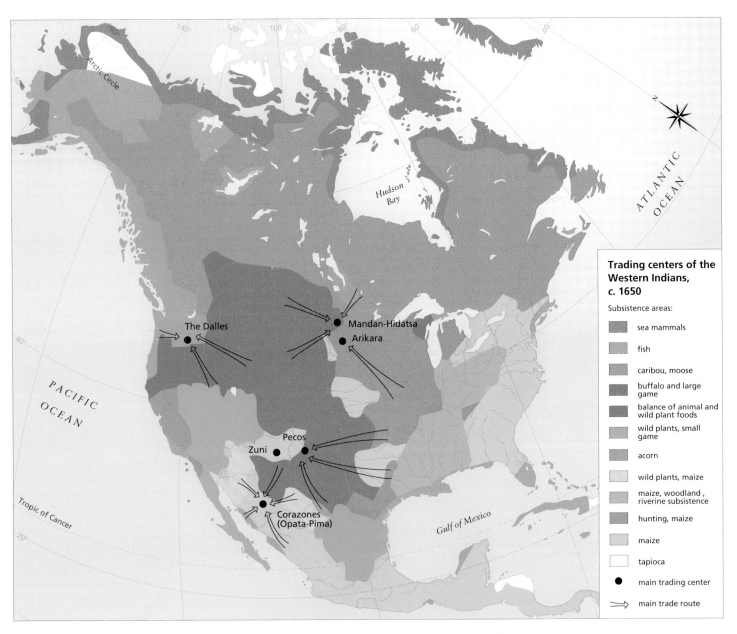

Trading centers of the Western Indians, c. 1650

Subsistence areas:

- sea mammals
- fish
- caribou, moose
- buffalo and large game
- balance of animal and wild plant foods
- wild plants, small game
- acorn
- wild plants, maize
- maize, woodland , riverine subsistence
- hunting, maize
- maize
- tapioca
- ● main trading center
- ⟶ main trade route

An Indian map (right)

By the 16th century European cartography had evolved to assist rulers in determining the boundaries of nation states, and landholders in determining the extent of their domains, as well as to provide explorers with points of reference as they ventured across the open seas. None of these purposes mattered to the Indians, whose maps were elaborations of their mental representations of the world.

One example is the map of Lean Wolf, a Hidatsa warrior. Lean Wolf, whose village was near Fort Berthold, raided a Sioux village near Fort Buford to steal horses. He represented himself as a wolf and drew circles to indicate the lodges of his Hidatsa tribe. The dots within the circles stood for the number of pillars supporting each roof and thus suggested the relative size of the families dwelling therein. The Sioux lodges were indicated by crosses, and the dwellings of whites by squares. Crosses combined with circles denoted Hidatsa-Sioux intermarriages, and the cross within a square indicated a house where a white man and Sioux woman cohabited. Lean Wolf's journey to the village was indicated with a dotted line, and his return route with hoofprints, testimony to the raid's success. Clearly, Lean Wolf's interest lay not in tribal boundaries or property lines, but in kinship and residential patterns.

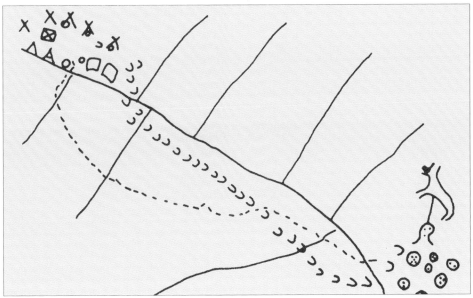

THE WORLD IN 1500 I

PEOPLES AND LIVELIHOODS

In 1500 the population of the world was probably between 400 million and 450 million, although population estimates for these early years are problematic, (*see Disease Devastates the Indians, p 38–39,*) especially for the New World. China and India each had over 100 million people, most of whom lived adjacent to the Huang Ho (Yellow), Yangtze, or Ganges rivers. Europe, ravaged intermittently by the bubonic plague during the 14th and 15th centuries, contained about 80 million inhabitants, approximately as many as in 1300. France, the Lowland countries, the British Isles, and the area roughly encompassing modern Germany were growing more rapidly than the populations in the states of the Mediterranean basin. The Americas were thinly settled, with the exceptions of the American empires of the Aztecs, 5 million, and Incas, 3 million.

Few people lived in the Sahara or Gobi deserts, the Amazon jungle, the Arctic tundra, or the steppes of Siberia. In areas with a less forboding climate or geography, however, varying population levels reflected the extent to which societies had mastered farming and animal husbandry. Primitive societies that depend on hunting and food-gathering cannot feed more than two people per square mile. But by 3,000 BC, most Europeans and Asians ensured a dependable supply of food by cultivating cereal grains, which could be stored for long periods. They also domesticated large mammals and used plows or hoes to till the soil. By 1500, China supported large populations by developing a strain of rice, imported from Southeast Asia, that yielded three crops a year, and by building elaborate irrigation and flood control systems.

Aztecs and Incas

Aztecs and Incas lagged behind the Chinese. They did not grow cereals, nor had they domesticated cattle or pigs. But the Americans nevertheless sustained relatively large populations—and established impressive cities—by improving an indigenous crop, maize, that required relatively little water and produced large yields. Despite these advantages, maize nevertheless contributed to the region's economic backwardness. The failure to domesticate large animals not only deprived the Meso-Americans of a stable supply of protein, but also forced them to rely on slave gangs to do work commonly performed in Europe and Asia by draught animals.

The Growth of Cities

Agricultural surpluses enabled the growth of cities and thus of civilization itself. In 1500, although few cities contained more than 10,000 people, Venice had about 115,000, Milan had 100,000, and London had 70,000. In the late 13th century Marco Polo reported that Hangchow, China had 3 million inhabitants, an estimate that some demographers think is

much too low. Edo, Japan probably had over 500,000 people, and Tenochtitlan, the capital of the Aztec empire, had over 300,000.

Consequences for the Americas

These economic and demographic patterns affected the development of America in several ways. The vast, fertile lands of the western hemisphere were ideally suited for the type of agriculture then practiced throughout Europe. But in 1500 there were too few people east of the Mississippi to provide the requisite labor to exploit the area's potential. Moreover, the peoples of the Aztec and Incan empires, though substantial in number, were quickly depopulated by smallpox and measles epidemics attending the arrival of the Spaniards. In the absence of a sufficiently large indigenous population, the European colonists increasingly chose to import to the New World black slaves from sub-Saharan Africa.

A native American family (above) near Roanoke Island, as depicted John White, c. 1585. The mixed economy reflected a division in gender roles: the man, with bow and arrows in hand, hunted, while the woman, baby in arms, cultivated by simple means the corn and vegetables seen at their feet.

European peasants enjoying May Day festivities (below), which probably originated as ancient agricultural celebrations. Such rituals centered (here, literally) on trees and other emblems of agriculture, seeking to promote crop fertility and, as the map shows, the human fecundity associated with plow cultivation.

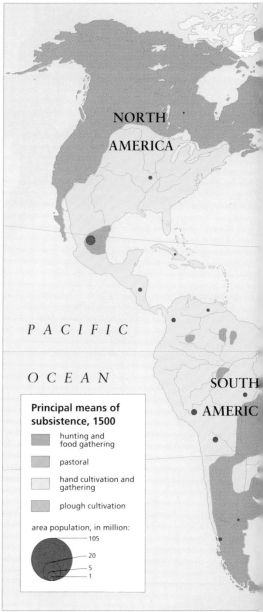

NORTH AMERICA

PACIFIC

OCEAN

SOUTH AMERICA

Principal means of subsistence, 1500

- hunting and food gathering
- pastoral
- hand cultivation and gathering
- plough cultivation

area population, in million:
- 105
- 20
- 5
- 1

A street scene from London (left) depicting the coronation procession of King Edward VI in 1547. Like most early 16th-century cities, London, a city of 70,000, existed as a place where the surplus food from the countryside was exchanged for artisanal goods and, increasingly, products from abroad.

Although ocean-going Chinese vessels plied the Indian Ocean and South China Sea during the 15th century (right), European governments and traders more aggressively sought long-distance opportunities because they desired ready access to the huge populations and wealth of the Far East.

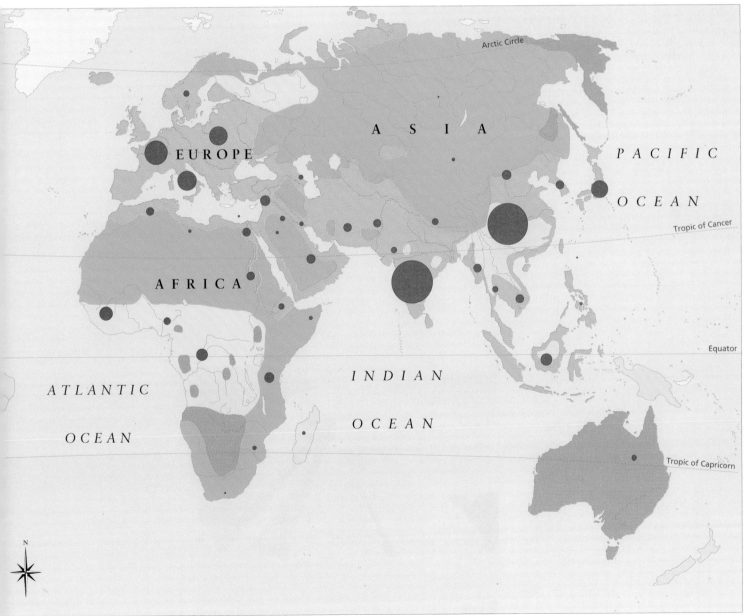

THE WORLD IN 1500 II
POLITICS AND RELIGION

Towards the close of the 15th century, as the Incas, Mayas, Aztecs, and other peoples of the New World unknowingly awaited their "discovery" by Europeans, Christendom and the Islamic world contended for mastery of the Mediterranean. Although each civilization was composed of various religious sects and political factions, Christians still looked to the Italian city-states for economic leadership and to Rome for ecclesiastical authority; and Moslems increasingly found inspiration in the resurgent Ottoman Turks. But if the contest between Christian and Islamic worlds was fought on the waters or shores of the Mediterranean, the prize was control of trade with distant China, the richest and most advanced empire in the world.

The Islamic world was situated literally at the center of the Old World: the major blocks of population—the Europeans, sub-Saharan Africans, Chinese, and Indians—were located around its periphery. Moslem sultans commanded strategic mountain passes and ocean straits, and Moslem traders exacted huge profits along the long trade routes.

Then as now, the most important potential market, with its 100 million inhabitants, was China. But the Ming emperors closed their borders to foreigners and chose to live in splendid ignorance of the "barbarians" beyond the Great Wall. The island empire of Japan, isolated and hopelessly rent by rival warlords, and India, also in chaos, were of limited worldwide trading significance.

Not surprisingly, the great struggle pitted Moslems against Christians. In the western Mediterranean, Isabella of Castile, in marital alliance with Ferdinand of Aragon, united Spain and drove the Moors from the Iberian peninsula in 1492. Early in the 1500s, Spain crossed the Strait of Gibraltar and resumed its leisurely advance against the Moslems. In the eastern Mediterranean, however, Mohammad the Conqueror, founder of the Ottoman Empire, inspired a "Second Islam" that thundered northward against the Byzantine Christians. In 1453, the Turks captured Constantinople, renamed it Istanbul, and proclaimed it the capital of the Ottoman Empire. They then pushed into the Balkans and up the Danube. Meanwhile, the Turkish navy battled the Venetians and in 1477 raided the outskirts of Venice. Two years later, the chastened Venetians agreed to pay the Turks huge annual subsidies to retain trading rights in the eastern Mediterranean.

Many contemporaries explained the Turkish advance as divine retribution for the moral degeneracy of the Christian Church. In 1492, when a corrupt ecclesiastical politician, Rodrigo Borgia, was elected to the throne of Saint Peter as Alexander VI, the authors of the *Nuremberg Chronicle* of human history, bemoaned the "calamity of our time." They left several blank pages at the end of the tome to record events between 1493 and the Day of Judgment.

Historians, though, often err at prophecy. The Christian world, though poised to experience momentous changes, was not in decline. Moreover, the Islamic pre-occupation with the eastern Mediterranean was unwise. Portugal and Spain decided to circumvent the Islamic stranglehold rather than challenge it. Henry the Navigator of Portugal dispatched captains to sail south and then east around Africa to the Far East. A Genoese mapmaker proposed to attain the same result by sailing due west across the Atlantic. After negotiating with both Portugal and Spain, he finally persuaded Ferdinand and Isabella to finance his enterprise. With three now-famous ships, Christopher Columbus set sail for China and the Indies.

An English Puritan family discussing the Bible (above right), a potentially subsersive activity that threatened European monarchs whose power was sanctified by the authority of the Pope. During the 16th century, the Christian world would be rent by the Great Reformation; but competition between Catholic and Protestant monarchs only spurred the outward thrust of Europe.

A pyramid, or Castillo (below) on the plaza at Chichén Itza in Yucatan. Modern scholars once regarded the Mayans as peaceful people whose priests made use of pyramids such as this one to contemplate the heavens. But recently deciphered Mayan hieroglyphs reveal that priests sacrificed prisoners atop pyramids such as this one so as to propitiate the gods—and to ensure political stability.

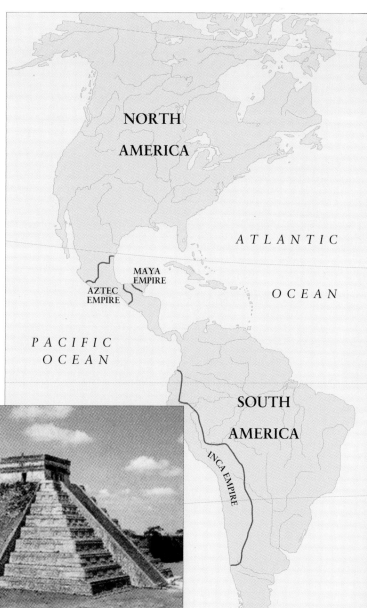

Church and State

Nearly everywhere, religion was an inescapable aspect of life in 1500; its common values, language, and institutions ensured the cohesion of far-flung civilizations. Agriculture provided the economic basis for most of these civilizations, and people who till the soil tend to be more receptive to the mediation with the divine provided by priests and prophets.

The great religions of the world, though initially effective at channeling the potentially revolutionary resentments of the masses, had by the late 15th century established vast ecclesiastical bureaucracies and become accommodated to political authority. (The exception is Judaism, which endured for many centuries without the benefit of a state.)

The 14th-century Islamic philosopher Kbn-Khaldun described the secular benefits of "the

love of God," noting that it inspired men to forget their differences and willingly sacrifice themselves for the glory of a "great and powerful empire." The gentle Confucius advanced the interests of the state less militantly: "Let the ruler be a ruler and the subject a subject; let the father be a father and the son a son."

By the 1500s the ecclesiastical bureaucracies were often surfeited with wealth but malnourished with faith. Having lost much of their power to inspire the masses, they sought to overawe them with displays of wealth, or intimidate them with expressions of power.

A graveyard on the outskirts of Mecca (left), the final resting place for many of the pilgrims who journeyed from all parts of the Islamic world to visit the birthplace of Muhammad. Religious pilgrimages helped unify the far-flung Islamic world, much as the Crusades had promoted cultural interaction among the Christian monarchies of western Europe.

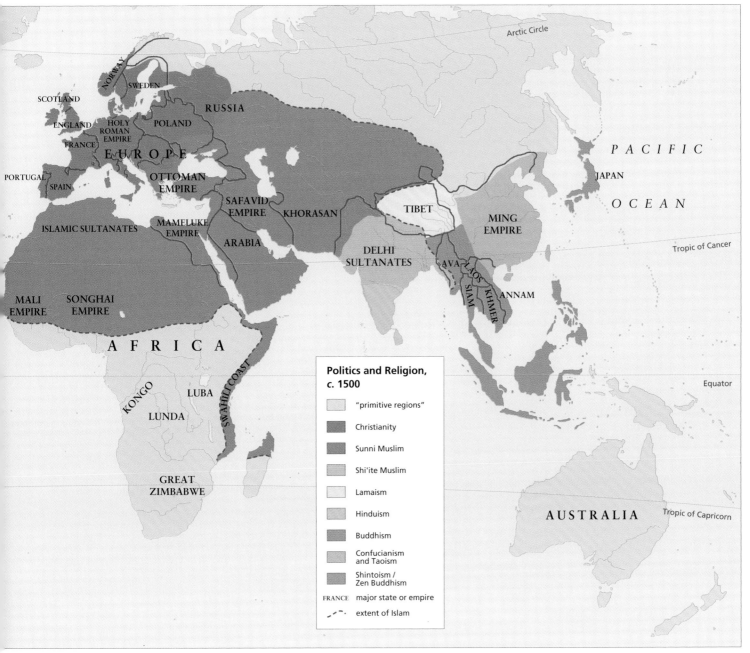

Politics and Religion, c. 1500

- "primitive regions"
- Christianity
- Sunni Muslim
- Shi'ite Muslim
- Lamaism
- Hinduism
- Buddhism
- Confucianism and Taoism
- Shintoism / Zen Buddhism
- FRANCE major state or empire
- ⌐ ⌐ ⌐ extent of Islam

PART 2: COLONIAL AMERICA

In 1782 Crevecoeur, a Frenchman who settled in rural New York, defined "the American" as a "new man," someone who in "leaving behind all his ancient prejudices and manners, receives new ones." For many years, historians regarded the exceptional character of American society as its distinguishing trait. Some stressed the settlers' liberation from the tight fetters of European society; and others, the freedom afforded by North America's seemingly inexhaustible land and resources. As Europe slipped into an abyss of revolution and war during the late 19th and early 20th centuries, the United States stood out all the more as a beacon of social cohesion and democracy. In recent decades, however, two factors have led to a reconsideration of American exceptionalism. Historians of ethnicity have been struck by how much of the Old World the immigrants brought to the New; and historians intent on explaining the remarkable ascent of Europe during the 15th and 16th centuries have realized the American colonies did not represent a repudiation of Europe, but instead served as the most spectactular manifestation of its genius at modernization and prowess at warfare.

COLUMBUS NAVIGATES TO A "NEW" WORLD

CONCEIT, COURAGE, AND NAVIGATION

In 1488 the Portuguese explorer Bartholomeu Dias sailed along the west coast of Africa, rounded its tip at the Cape of Good Hope, ventured upon the waters of the Indian Ocean, and then raced back to Lisbon to report his discovery of a probable sea route to India. Two years later Henricus Matellus, a German cartographer working in Italy, prepared a world map, centered upon the Indian Ocean, that incorporated Dias's discoveries. But Germanus's map also suggested that Europeans could even more readily reach the Far East by sailing west across the "Oceanus Occidental." Many explorers had proposed such a venture, but in early 1492 the most persistent of them—Cristoforo Colombo of Genoa—found a backer in Queen Isabella of Spain.

We now know that centuries before Columbus, Norsemen had sailed from Iceland along the coasts of Greenland, Newfoundland, and Labrador nearly as far as New England. Where Columbus differed from these men, and from most of the sailors of his day, was his willingness to strike out across the aimless wastes of the Atlantic—a conceit borne of undeniable courage and considerable vanity, but also of a confidence in new navigational techniques.

Calculating Latitude

Columbus knew that if his ships wandered off course, they would be likely to run out of food or water. He therefore charted a route along the coast of Africa to the Canary Islands, then westward along the 28th parallel to Antilia, a large (albeit non-existent) island that had appeared on many charts. He would continue along the parallel until he attained landfall at the island of Cipangu (Japan).

Columbus apparently used an astrolabe to reckon his course. The astrolabe, which indicated the angle of elevation of the sun, was suspended from a knob by one man while another sighted the noontime sun. Latitude was determined by comparing this angle with charts indicating its elevation for that date at the equator. For example, if the sun's elevation at the equator on August 1 was known to be ten degrees, and the shipboard astrolabe showed the sun's elevation at 60 degrees, the ship's latitude would have been calculated by subtracting ten degrees, representing the seasonal variation in the sun's position, from the reading of 60, leaving a seasonally adjusted elevation of 50 degrees. Because the elevation of the sun is inversely proportional to latitude (at the North Pole, where the latitude is 90 percent, the elevation of the sun approaches zero), the seasonally adjusted elevation would have been subtracted from 90. In this case, the ship's latitude was 40 degrees.

Calculating Longitude

Calculating longitude in the 15th century was more problematic. This was no small matter insofar as Columbus did not know how far

west he would have to travel. Martellus's map placed Cipangu about 90 degrees of longitude west of the Canary Islands. Columbus, who overestimated the width of Asia and underestimated the circumference of the earth, assumed this distance to be 2,400 miles. (The actual distance is 10,600 miles.) Because his ships could travel more than 150 miles a day with a strong wind, he believed that the journey would take little more than a month.

On August 3, 1492, Columbus set out from Palos with his fleet, the *Santa Maria*, the *Pinta*, and the *Nina*. At the Canary Islands he made repairs and gathered more provisions. On September 6, Columbus boarded the *Santa Maria*, his flagship, gave the order to weigh anchor and then shouted the course: "West; nothing to the north, nothing to the south."

During the first ten days, a steady easterly wind pushed his tiny fleet, by his reckoning, at least 1,000 miles westward. The winds then abated and at times vanished. Lest his crew grow nervous about sailing so far from land, and impatient about failing to reach their destination, Columbus intentionally understated their progress. By early October, Columbus was becoming uneasy; he knew they had traveled more than 2,400 miles. On October 9, with Cipangu nowhere in sight, he promised

his anxious men that he would turn back if land was not sighted within three days. At 2.00 a.m. on October 12, under a nearly full moon, the lookout on the *Pinta* shouted "*Tierra! Tierra!*" A grateful Columbus named the island San Salvador, "Holy Saviour." Searching for treasure, he pushed on to Cuba. When the natives spoke of a gold-rich place called *Cubanocan*, meaning "middle of Cuba," he assumed that they had referred to *El gran can*—Marco Polo's Great Khan of China. Columbus returned to Spain certain that he had explored the edge of Asia. Three later voyages failed to shake his conviction.

Subsequent explorers persisted in his error. In 1497 John Cabot, an Italian sailing for King Henry VII of England, took a northerly route across the Atlantic, landed in Newfoundland, and pronounced it a "New Island" off Eurasia. In 1507, mapmaker Johan Ruysch depicted Greenland and Newfoundland as eastern promontories of Asia. Cathay and Tibet were several hundred miles further west. Ruysch included the legendary but non-existent island of Antilia, and omitted the elusive Cipangu, claiming that it had probably been mistaken for Spagnola Island (now Haiti/Dominican Republic). Southeast of Asia was Mundus Novus, the South American continent.

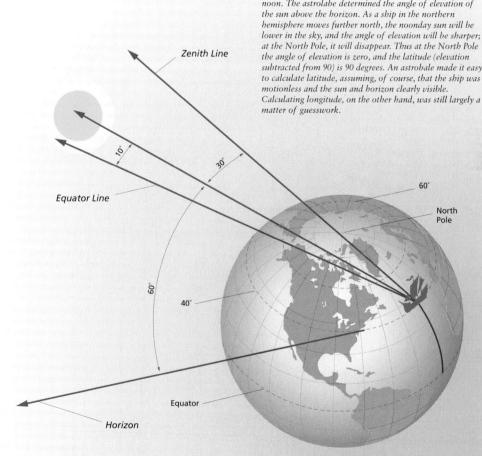

Taking a latitude reading.
Columbus resolved to hold a westward course along the 28th parallel while crossing the Atlantic. To do this he no doubt used an astrolabe to calculate latitude every day at noon. The astrolabe determined the angle of elevation of the sun above the horizon. As a ship in the northern hemisphere moves further north, the noonday sun will be lower in the sky, and the angle of elevation will be sharper; at the North Pole, it will disappear. Thus at the North Pole the angle of elevation is zero, and the latitude (elevation subtracted from 90) is 90 degrees. An astrobale made it easy to calculate latitude, assuming, of course, that the ship was motionless and the sun and horizon clearly visible. Calculating longitude, on the other hand, was still largely a matter of guesswork.

Zenith Line

Equator Line

10°

30°

60°

North Pole

60°

40°

Equator

Horizon

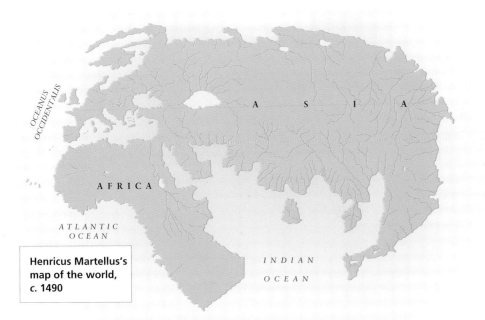

Henricus Martellus's map of the world, c. 1490

Christopher Columbus's encounter with Native Americans, as portrayed by Théodore de Bry (1528–98) in Les Grands Voyages (above). The Native Americans bring food, and Columbus plants a crucifix. The raising of the crucifix was part of a set ritual by which Columbus claimed each "new island" as a "possession" of the King and Queen of Spain.

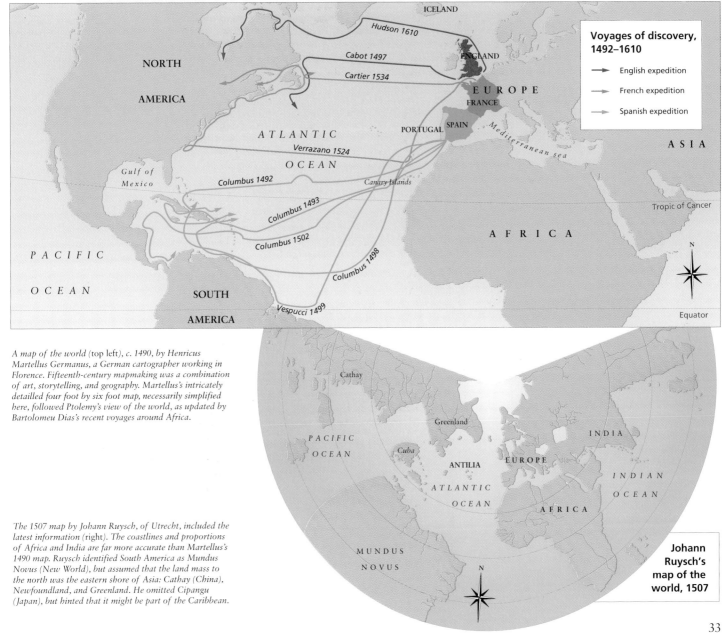

Voyages of discovery, 1492–1610

→ English expedition
→ French expedition
→ Spanish expedition

A map of the world (top left), c. 1490, by Henricus Martellus Germanus, a German cartographer working in Florence. Fifteenth-century mapmaking was a combination of art, storytelling, and geography. Martellus's intricately detailed four foot by six foot map, necessarily simplified here, followed Ptolemy's view of the world, as updated by Bartolomeu Dias's recent voyages around Africa.

The 1507 map by Johann Ruysch, of Utrecht, included the latest information (right). The coastlines and proportions of Africa and India are far more accurate than Martellus's 1490 map. Ruysch identified South America as Mundus Novus (New World), but assumed that the land mass to the north was the eastern shore of Asia: Cathay (China), Newfoundland, and Greenland. He omitted Cipangu (Japan), but hinted that it might be part of the Caribbean.

Johann Ruysch's map of the world, 1507

EUROPEAN ECOLOGICAL IMPERIALISM
PLANTS AND ANIMALS FROM THE OLD WORLD THRIVE IN THE NEW

In 1493, on his second voyage across the Atlantic, Columbus commanded a flotilla of 17 ships, 1,200 men, hundreds of cattle, pigs, and horses, and countless seeds for wheat, melons, onions, salad greens, grapes, and sugar cane. This journey proved more significant than its celebrated precursor in some respects, for it inaugurated the European conquest of the ecological system of North America. Although Columbus did not know it, the true wealth of the "New World" was not to be found in its position athwart the sea route to the silks and spices of China, nor in its virtually untapped deposits of gold and silver, but in its extraordinary susceptibility to European flora and fauna.

During the 15th and 16th centuries, Spanish explorers and settlers often released pigs into the dense tropical undergrowth of the Caribbean. There, far removed from their natural enemies, the animals thrived and multiplied. Ship-wrecked sailors, upon rescue, commonly attibuted their survival to the abundant supply of pigs. The meat-loving Spaniards also brought cattle to the New World, along with horses, which intimidated the Indians and allowed the rancheros to keep track of their unfenced herds.

After the cattle had eaten through the dry stubble of the Mexican plateau, the rancheros drove their herds northward. Eventually, they came upon the grasslands along the edges of the Great Western plains. This proved an ideal habitat for both the cattle and horses, though it was shared, at least for a time, with vast herds of buffalo.

English colonists also brought to the Americas pigs and cattle, which they set loose in the forests. Many fell to cougars and wolves, or succumbed to the cold winters. Numbers nevertheless grew almost geometrically; with remarkably little effort, these colonists ate far more meat than their counterparts left back in England.

The pigs and cattle, by chewing through the undergrowth of the virgin forests, cleared the way for the farmers, who cut down the trees, ploughed the land, and planted crops. The most important crop was wheat, the staple of the European diet.

Wheat yields in the Delaware and Hudson valleys were astonishingly high, and diseases such as the Hessian fly, which posed a constant threat to the crop in Europe, did not arrive upon North American shores until late in the 18th century.

During the 18th century, cotton was grown chiefly along the coast of the Carolinas; after

1793, when Eli Whitney devised a machine to separate the seed from the cotton fibers, cotton cultivation spread throughout the Deep South.

Why did European plants and animals almost always supplant the indigenous species of the western hemisphere? And why were the yields of the same crops and animals so much higher in the New World than in Europe? Historian Alfred W. Crosby has argued that when North and South America broke from Pangaea millions of years ago, *(see A Continent Adrift, p 12–13)*, the organisms on those continents evolved in a less competitive environment than those that remained linked to Europe, Africa and Asia, where unremitting biological warfare swept from Spain to China, and from Scandinavia to the southern tip of Africa. For millions of years, the species of the western hemisphere were shielded from this lethal conflict by the Pacific and Atlantic oceans. With the arrival of Columbus, that was forever changed.

Not all indigenous plants succumbed to competition from European organisms. Maize, or corn, an Indian crop, was adopted by European colonists as a feed for pigs and cattle; new strains were developed and by the middle of the 19th century the crop had become a staple part of the American diet, and has since become a crop utilized across the world.

Left: European rancheros and Plains Indians, mounted upon horses, reduced and eventually exterminated the gigantic herds of buffalo, whose chief protection had been their swiftness.

Below: European explorers and settlers introduced pigs into the New World where, in the absence of their usual predators, the animals proliferated. Cattle, too, thrived in the New World. Largely because of pigs and cattle, Americans have nearly always consumed more meat than Europeans.

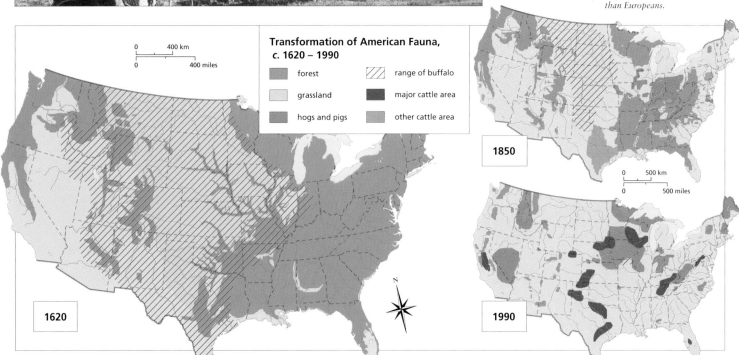

Transformation of American Fauna, c. 1620 – 1990

- forest
- grassland
- hogs and pigs
- range of buffalo
- major cattle area
- other cattle area

0   400 km
0   400 miles

1620

1850

0   500 km
0   500 miles

1990

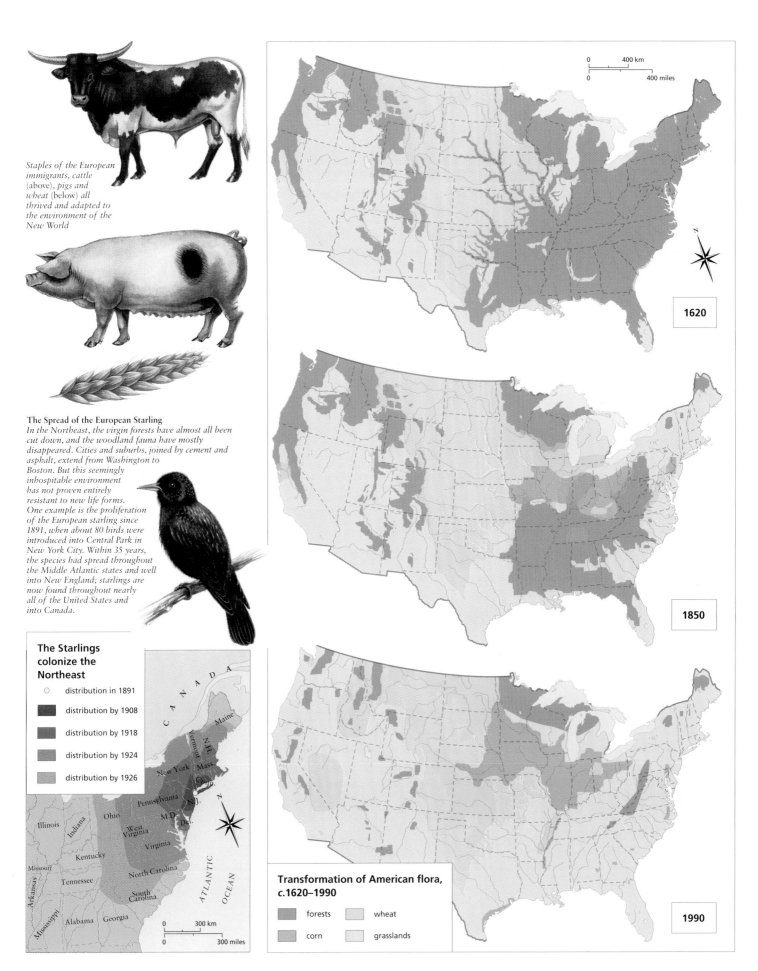

Staples of the European immigrants, cattle (above), pigs and wheat (below) all thrived and adapted to the environment of the New World

The Spread of the European Starling
In the Northeast, the virgin forests have almost all been cut down, and the woodland fauna have mostly disappeared. Cities and suburbs, joined by cement and asphalt, extend from Washington to Boston. But this seemingly inhospitable environment has not proven entirely resistant to new life forms. One example is the proliferation of the European starling since 1891, when about 80 birds were introduced into Central Park in New York City. Within 35 years, the species had spread throughout the Middle Atlantic states and well into New England; starlings are now found throughout nearly all of the United States and into Canada.

The Starlings colonize the Northeast

○ distribution in 1891

■ distribution by 1908

■ distribution by 1918

■ distribution by 1924

distribution by 1926

Transformation of American flora, c.1620–1990

■ forests   wheat

■ corn   grasslands

1620

1850

1990

35

EUROPEAN FOOTHOLDS ALONG THE ATLANTIC
THE EARLY STRUGGLE FOR SURVIVAL

Much as most Americans nowadays rely on the automobile, the early colonists depended on boats and settled along the navigable bays and rivers of the Atlantic seaboard. As late as 1650, hardly a colonist had planted his home more than a dozen miles from deep water. Jamestown (1607), the first permanent English settlement, was located on a swampy fist of land on the James River; Virginians subsequently hugged the banks of the lower Chesapeake and its tributaries. English Puritans founded Plymouth Colony (1620) and Massachusetts Bay Colony (1630) along the Massachusetts Bay. Roger Williams, expelled from Massachusetts for preaching religious toleration, established Rhode Island (1636) on the shores of the Narragansett Bay. Massachusetts colonists pushed down the Connecticut Valley and founded settlements at Hartford (1636) and New Haven (1638). In 1624, Dutch fur traders built Fort Orange (now Albany) at the confluence of the Mohawk and Hudson rivers. The Dutch colony of New Netherlands extended to New Amsterdam (now Manhattan) at the mouth of the Hudson. Swedish merchants constructed Fort

Christina (1638) as a trading outpost on the Delaware River.

Although promoters of colonial enterprises emphasized patriotic and religious benefits, particularly when appealing for government assistance, most of the colonies were conceived as private business ventures. European monarchs, preoccupied with matters of defense closer to home, usually offered little more than a title to New World lands.

The problems inherent in private commercial settlement were evident from the start. In 1587, Sir Walter Raleigh and his backers, holding a charter from Queen Elizabeth I to search and settle the entire continent south of Newfoundland, deposited an underfunded and unprepared contingent of 117 men, women, and children on Roanoke Island. Three years later, when the first relief ship arrived, the settlers had vanished without a trace. Subsequent ventures fared little better.

The quest for quick profits left the colonists ill-prepared to grow their own food. They were forced to barter for it with the Indians, who at first offered little resistance to the bearded newcomers in huge canoes. Mighty tribes such as the Powhatans, with 9,000 people, had little apparent reason to fear the starving settlers in

Jamestown. The Indians also responded favorably to the hospitality of the traders, who offered valuable metal tools and cloth in return for plentiful trifles such as animal pelts.

But relations with the settlers carried a hidden price. European diseases soon devastated many tribes. Probably half the Algonquians of southern New England, and three-quarters of the Abnaki were killed by the "plague" of 1616–18. Many of the survivors were demoralized by the impotence of their medicine men, and by the power of the white god, who seemingly spared his people. Trade further destabilized the Indian economy and culture. Prior to the arrival of Dutch traders, the Delaware Indians lived in longhouses and farmed, but spurred by a craving for guns and alcohol, the men of the tribe wandered increasingly long distances in search of furs. Eventually they came to blows with the Susquehanna Indians. Competition for fur also prompted the Iroquois, armed with European firearms, to wage a war of genocide against the Hurons.

As long as relations centered on trade, Europeans and Indians co-existed in relative peace. But in the 1620s two factors led to the successful colonization of the New World, and to the removal of the Indians. In 1625, Charles I launched a crackdown on the Puritans. This

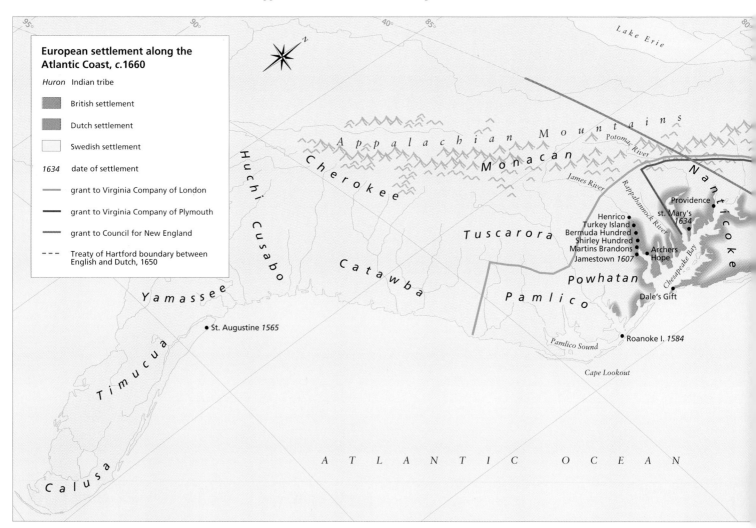

precipitated the Great Migration of the 1630s, which in one decade brought over 10,000 Puritans to Massachusetts. Meanwhile, Virginia colonists discovered that tobacco flourished along the tidewater and could be profitably sold in London. During the 1620s, English immigrants fanned out along the James and York rivers, and pushed northward along the Chesapeake.

The swelling English populations overwhelmed the Swedish and Dutch colonies, occupied Indian lands, and chopped down the forests on which Indians depended for game and berries. On March 22, 1622, the Powhatans ended their truce and slaughtered hundreds of settlers. After the attack, an English leader rightly predicted: "Now their cleared grounds in all their villages shall be inhabited by us." The Algonquian tribes of southern New England were similarly squeezed between the English settlers and the Iroquois, their traditional enemies to the west. Unable to forge an alliance with the Narragansett Indians, who sided with the settlers, the aggressive Pequots chose to fight alone. During the misnamed Pequot War of 1636–37, they were virtually exterminated. The pattern would become more familiar as English and other European settlers pushed further westward.

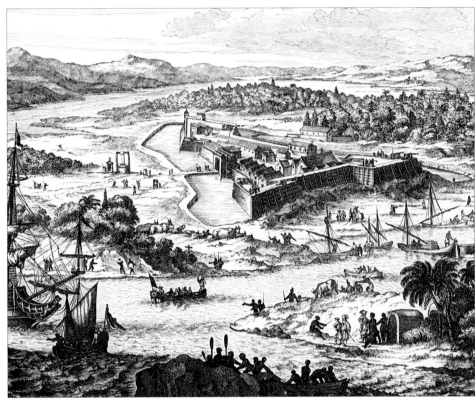

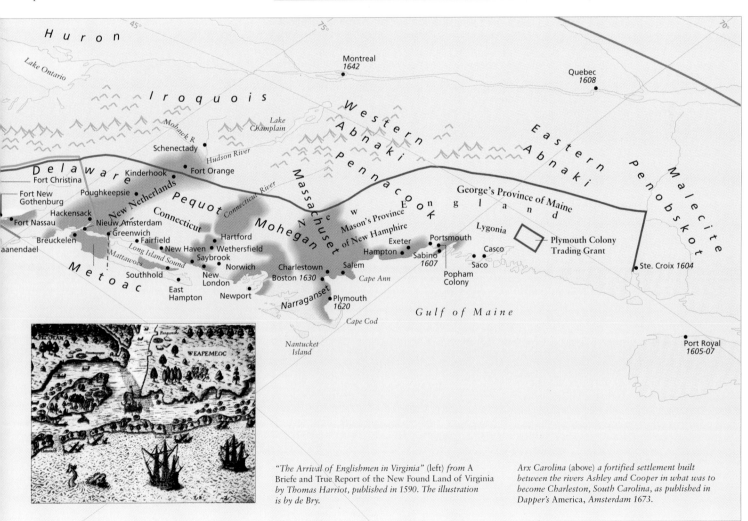

"The Arrival of Englishmen in Virginia" (left) from A Briefe and True Report of the New Found Land of Virginia by Thomas Harriot, published in 1590. The illustration is by de Bry.

Arx Carolina (above) a fortified settlement built between the rivers Ashley and Cooper in what was to become Charleston, South Carolina, as published in Dapper's America, Amsterdam 1673.

DISEASE DEVASTATES THE INDIANS
SMALLPOX AND TYPHUS WIPE OUT ENTIRE TRIBES

The Indians of the New World were sub-
dued by relatively few Spanish conquistadors and English and French colonists.
The Indians succumbed not for want of
military skill—often they resisted with
cunning and ferocity. Nor was it
because their stone tools and bows and
arrows were no match for the con-
querors' steel, iron, and gunpowder; the
tribes of sub-Saharan Africa, with no better weapons than the Indians, resisted the
European advance for centuries. The critical difference was that the Europeans were
aided by lethal but entirely unseen allies—
microbes to which the Indians had no
resistance. Smallpox, measles, typhus, and
other diseases wiped out entire Indian
tribes and enfeebled many others.

The debilitating effect of disease upon New
World Indians was apparent almost from the
start of European colonization.

In 1520, the Aztecs expelled Cortez and his
600 soldiers from Tenochtitlan. The Spaniards
laid siege to the city, little expecting that their
tiny band could bring down an empire of millions. But a Spanish soldier, infected with
smallpox, had unknowingly left behind the
microbes that swept through its Indian population. Within two months, Montezuma, the
Aztec emperor, was dead, and resistance had
collapsed. When Cortez re-entered Tenochtitlan, he found that "The street squares, houses
and courts were filled with bodies, so that it
was almost impossible to pass." During the
next 80 years, scores of epidemics devastated
the Aztecs and, further south, the Incas.

English and French germs were as deadly as
the Spanish. In 1585, Sir Francis Drake, preparing for a raid against Spanish possessions,
stopped at the Cape Verde Islands. There some
of his men contracted a fever—probably
typhus—but he sailed for Florida undaunted by
their discomfort. When they landed at St.
Augustine, the disease spread to the natives, who,
according to Drake, "died verie fast and said
amongst themselves, it was the Englisshe God
that made them die so faste." Some 30 years later
an outbreak of smallpox almost wiped out the
Indians of Plymouth Bay, prompting the Puritan
divine, Cotton Mather, to offer thanks to God
for having cleared the lands "of those pernicious
creatures, to make room for better growth."

Population Losses
The depopulation of the New World Indians
was a human calamity of seemingly unprecedented proportions. Their suffering cannot be
imagined, nor the number of fatalities calculated with any precision. Estimates of the
death toll depend upon the size of the Indian

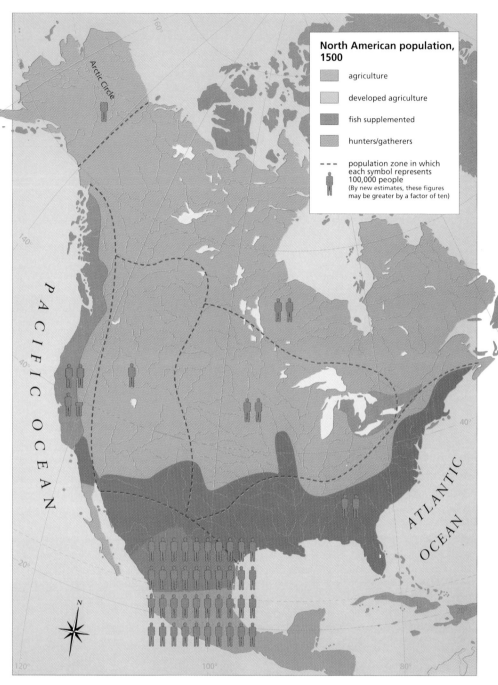

North American population, 1500

- agriculture
- developed agriculture
- fish supplemented
- hunters/gatherers
- - - population zone in which
each symbol represents
100,000 people
(By new estimates, these figures
may be greater by a factor of ten)

PACIFIC OCEAN

ATLANTIC OCEAN

Arctic Circle

Native Americans, probably Seminole Indians of Florida,
leaving offerings of food and gifts at the foot of a column
erected by the French explorer Jean Ribaut in 1562. The
Indians, isolated from the infectious diseases that had long
ravaged the Old World, often contracted fatal diseases from
contact such as this. This illustration was painted by
Jacques Le Moyne in 1564.

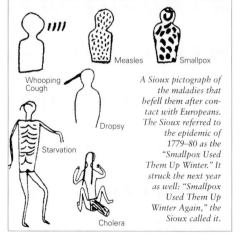

Measles   Smallpox

Whooping
Cough

Dropsy

Starvation

Cholera

A Sioux pictograph of
the maladies that
befell them after con-
tact with Europeans.
The Sioux referred to
the epidemic of
1779–80 as the
"Smallpox Used
Them Up Winter." It
struck the next year
as well: "Smallpox
Used Them Up
Winter Again," the
Sioux called it.

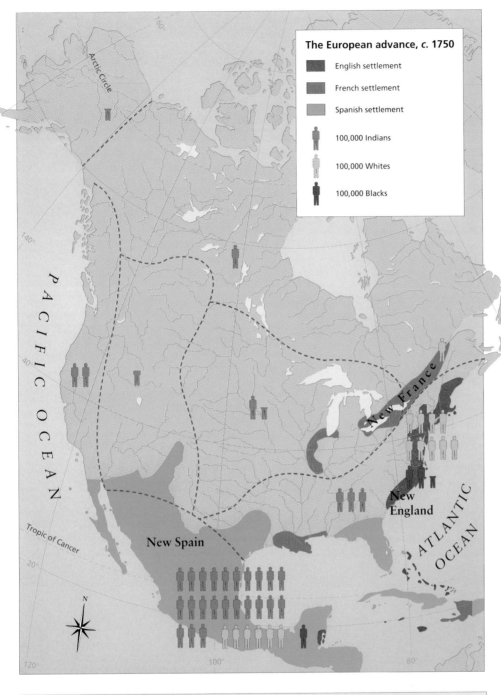

The European advance, c. 1750

- English settlement
- French settlement
- Spanish settlement

- 100,000 Indians
- 100,000 Whites
- 100,000 Blacks

PACIFIC OCEAN

Arctic Circle

New France

New England

ATLANTIC OCEAN

New Spain

Tropic of Cancer

Genetic sameness :
The distribution of the
O-blood type among native
peoples of the world

Percentage:
- 90
- 80
- 70
- 60

PACIFIC OCEAN

NORTH AMERICA

EUROPE

ASIA

PACIFIC OCEAN

ATLANTIC OCEAN

AFRICA

Tropic of Cancer

INDIAN OCEAN

Equator

SOUTH AMERICA

Tropic of Capricorn

population at the time of European contact.

Well into the 20th century, anthropologists had agreed that the pre-Columbian Amerindian population numbered approximately 14 million, most of whom lived within the realm of the Aztecs and the Incas. Perhaps 1 million Indians lived north of the Rio Grande. The most densely populated region of what is now the United States was the coast of California, Oregon, and Washington, where fish provided an unusually abundant source of protein. The southern regions, with the cultivation of maize and other forms of horticulture, were the next most populated areas.

By 1600, when some population records are available, the Amerindians of the western hemisphere numbered around 11 million, 80 percent of the pre-contact total. This percentage was consistent with fatality rates during other human epidemics.

Since World War II, however, scholars have proposed far higher pre-Columbian population levels, and thus far higher fatality rates due to disease. If, as some state, the Amerindians of the Old World numbered 100 million prior to Columbus, then 90 percent of the population had disappeared by 1600. Mexico, which by these estimates had a population of 25–30 million, was reduced to 3 million by 1568, and to 1.6 million by 1620. Estimates of population north of the Rio Grande rose from 1 million to 4 to 18 million.

By 1750, the European domination of North America was assured. In addition to New Spain, which had fallen to the Spaniards early, some 900,000 English colonists, and their nearly 250,000 African slaves with them, had taken possession of the Atlantic seaboard. Another 70,000 French had settled New France. The Indian populations of North America had been reduced to around 600,000.

The New World: An Enormous Island

Was it possible that where 20 Indians had lived in 1500, only one remained a century later? Could 100 million Amerindians have perished of European diseases? Skeptics point out that such a loss of life was unprecedented in history.

But the Amerindians had evolved in a relatively isolated environment for many thousands of years. Around 8000 BC, rising ocean levels flooded the land bridge connecting North America with Asia.

From that point on, new peoples and germs arrived in the western hemisphere infrequently. The New World, historian William McNeill has written, became "no more than an enormous island," whose peoples had become deprived of (or, others might say, spared from) the biological scourges that strengthened the immunological systems of Old World peoples.

Evidence of the extraordinary biological uniformity (and vulnerability) of Amerindians (left.) The distribution of the blood group O gene was far higher among aboriginal populations in North and South America than anywhere else in the world. This confirms the Indians' protracted isolation from the people (and microbes) of the Old World.

THE GREAT ENGLISH MIGRATION
RELIGIOUS ZEAL OR ECONOMIC DESIRE?

On April 8, 1630, 400 men, women, and children boarded the Arbella and a few other ships docked at Southampton, England and set sail for the New World, beginning a general exodus that lasted nearly two decades. During these years, over 50,000 English emigrated to the Americas. Most were young, unmarried men who made their way to the tobacco and sugar plantations of the South and the Caribbean. Of the nearly 15,000 emigrants who departed for the rocky shores of New England, however, the majority were mature men and their families. Statistically indistinguishable from those who remained behind, these colonists impressed historian Virginia Anderson as "overwhelmingly ordinary." Why, then, did they choose to leave?

Geographical Variations
One clue to the motivations of the New England colonists was that most left the same region of England, apparently departing from Yarmouth and Ipswich in the southeast of England, or from Southampton, Weymouth, Plymouth, and Bristol in the south. Genealogical information confirms the impression that most emigrants came from the southeast and the south, a flat area of rich soil and dry climate known as the lowlands. Within the region, East Anglia, comprising the counties of Norfolk, Suffolk, and Essex, provided a disproportionate share of New England colonists.

Religious Factors
During the late 16th and early 17th centuries, the lowlands, and East Anglia in particular, were ablaze with Puritan religious fervor. Essex, Suffolk, Norfolk, Northamptonshire, and Rutland provided a disproportionately high number of Puritan ministers. Moreover, when Puritans in Parliament rose up against King Charles I in 1642, Norfolk, Suffolk, Essex, Cambridgeshire, Hertfordshire, and Huntingdonshire formed an Eastern Association to raise an army, entrusted to the Puritan zealot Oliver Cromwell, against the King. The area initially controlled by the Parliamentarians during the Civil War roughly encompassed the region of the greatest English migration to New England.

However, if the emigrants fled England for religious reasons—to escape, as one settler put it, the *"multitude of irreligious lascivious and popish affected persons"* in league with the King—why did so few colonists become members of churches once they had arrived in New England? (*See Church Membership, p 50–51.*)

Economic Factors
In light of this and related arguments, some historians have insisted that the emigrants were motivated less by religious enthusiasm than by economic necessity. The revisionists note that although the lowlands were a center of religious dissent, it was also buffeted by economic calamities. About a quarter of the New England colonists had worked in the cloth industry, also located chiefly in south and southeastern England, which was severely depressed during these years. The lowlands was also wracked by a spate of disastrous crop failures after 1621. In this view, English clothworkers, farmers, and the tradesmen who attended to the needs of both, left for the New World because they could no longer make a living in the Old.

Causation and Complexity
But English clothworkers had little reason to believe that their skills would command greater profits in the wilds of New England, where the requisite raw materials for their trades were almost non-existent. Nor could hungry English farmers, having heard the appalling reports of starvation and disease among the colonists, have set sail for the New World expecting to fill their bellies. The safest conclusion—and the one favored by many recent historians—is that no single reason sufficiently explains human behavior. Religious enthusiasm, the prospect of eventual economic advancement, and a vague longing for change together prompted the Great Migration.

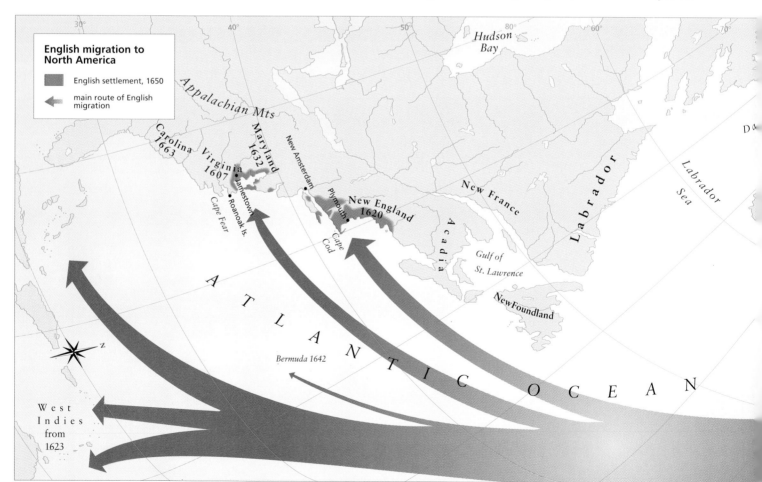

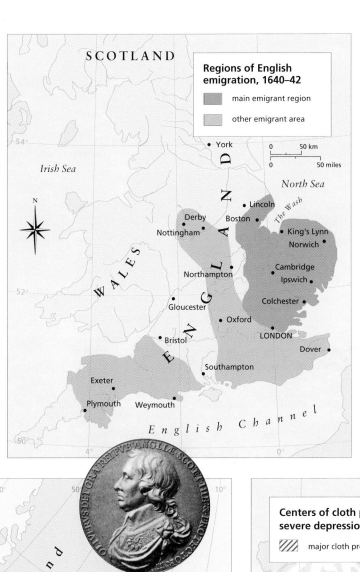

Regions of English emigration, 1640–42

- main emigrant region
- other emigrant area

SCOTLAND

Irish Sea

North Sea

WALES

ENGLAND

The Wash

- York
- Lincoln
- Derby
- Boston
- Nottingham
- King's Lynn
- Norwich
- Northampton
- Cambridge
- Ipswich
- Gloucester
- Colchester
- Oxford
- LONDON
- Bristol
- Dover
- Southampton
- Exeter
- Plymouth
- Weymouth

English Channel

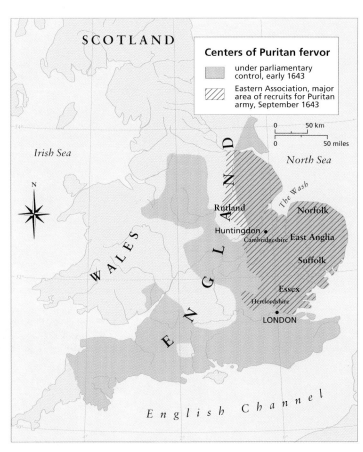

Centers of Puritan fervor

- under parliamentary control, early 1643
- Eastern Association, major area of recruits for Puritan army, September 1643

SCOTLAND

Irish Sea

North Sea

WALES

ENGLAND

The Wash

- Rutland
- Norfolk
- Huntingdon
- East Anglia
- Cambridgeshire
- Suffolk
- Essex
- Hertfordshire
- LONDON

English Channel

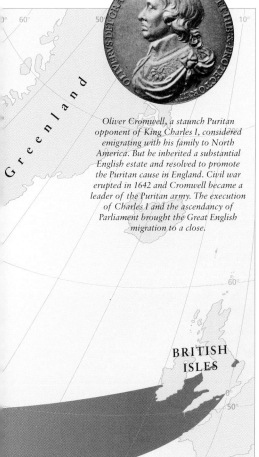

Oliver Cromwell, a staunch Puritan opponent of King Charles I, considered emigrating with his family to North America. But he inherited a substantial English estate and resolved to promote the Puritan cause in England. Civil war erupted in 1642 and Cromwell became a leader of the Puritan army. The execution of Charles I and the ascendancy of Parliament brought the Great English migration to a close.

Greenland

BRITISH ISLES

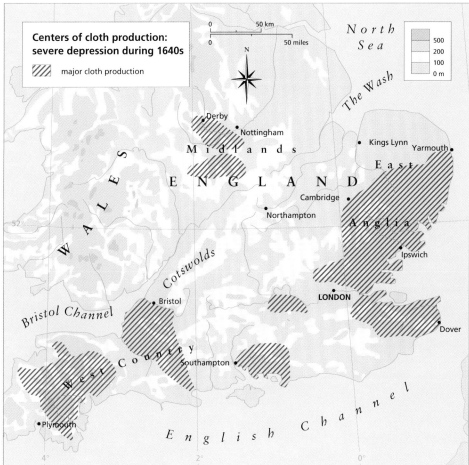

Centers of cloth production: severe depression during 1640s

- major cloth production

North Sea

The Wash

- Derby
- Nottingham
- Kings Lynn
- Yarmouth

Midlands

East

WALES

ENGLAND

Anglia

- Cambridge
- Northampton
- Ipswich

Cotswolds

- Bristol
- LONDON
- Dover

Bristol Channel

West Country

- Southampton

- Plymouth

English Channel

- 500
- 200
- 100
- 0 m

SPAIN'S NORTH AMERICAN FRONTIER
THE WORK OF CHURCH AND STATE

In North America, Spain's reach far exceeded its grasp. By the end of the 18th century, it claimed a large part of what would become the western United States, but, after three centuries of New World colonization, its sparse northern settlements were spread thin. The rich mining centers and large haciendas of early Mexican frontiers could hardly be found. The Spanish presence, such that it was, was less the product of a northward movement of population than an effort of Church and state, of soldiers and Franciscan missionaries, to secure the borderlands and pacify, Catholicize, and Hispanicize their native populations. Though largely unsuccessful, the Spaniards, as well as both their Indian converts and their Indian antagonists, left an imprint on the Southwest and Florida so distinct that it would survive subsequent American conquest and settlement.

By 1550, the Spanish had explored what would become the southern and western United States but had not found precious metals or native populations that could be forced to yield up wealth or labor as readily as those of central Mexico and Peru. Settlement of these areas was therefore delayed by decades, even centuries. Their eventual colonization would be the work not so much of conquistadors as of Church and state, eager to solidify their hold

on indigenous peoples and prevent European rivals from encroaching on Catholic Spain's American claims. Spain established military garrisons (presidios) in Florida in the 1560s in response to English raiding and French settlement; in Texas nearly 150 years later as France expanded in the Mississippi Valley; and in California in the late 18th century to contain Russian advances on the West Coast.

Although settlers followed in the army's wake, Spain possessed neither enough soldiers to subdue Northern tribes nor enough colonists to overwhelm them. Neither Spain nor central Mexico was so overcrowded, nor the northern frontier so attractive, as to stimulate mass migration. In effect, Spain hoped instead to colonize its frontier with Hispanicized natives. Mission outposts were established not only to convert, but to pacify and culturally assimilate the Indians.

Throughout the 17th and 18th centuries native Americans were gathered into Franciscan communities. They were catechized, and taught to labor in ways useful to the Spanish. Their labor was expropriated by the missions themselves, by government officials, by private landowners, and, in some cases, by individuals officially entitled to tributes of produce or personal service. Yet the Pueblo Revolt of 1680, which drove Spanish settlers from almost all of New Mexico for over a decade, graphically illustrated how tentative and incomplete Spain's hold on the Indians, and thus on its borderlands, remained. Even

the relatively accommodating Pueblo Indians revealed a determination to cling on to their distinctive culture.

The larger contours of the North American frontier illustrated this insecurity. Spain effectively controlled only isolated enclaves, separated from one another by vast expanses of rugged territory and by unreduced peoples like the Apache and the Comanche. Though Spain established a string of settlements and missions anchored by St. Augustine, its grasp on Florida remained tenuous, effectively slipping away with the Seven Years War. Spain never established its pre-eminence in New Mexico very much beyond the river valley of the upper part of the Rio Grande.

In Texas, colonists clustered near the San Antonio River from the presidio and missions of San Antonio east of the Gulf of Mexico and in settlements bordering French Louisiana. Their attempts to pacify or assimilate Indians yielded relatively little, and the province itself lost its strategic importance with the temporary cession of Louisiana to Spain in 1762. Spanish settlement in present-day Arizona never extended farther north than Tuscon, and Spain's effort to settle California remained confined to a long but narrow strip of the coastline.

The Spanish presence in the far-flung footholds took various forms. Among sedentary agricultural people like the Pueblo Indians, the Spanish planted their missions amidst existing settlements. For instance, they simply appended a mission complex to the southern end of the fortress-village of Cicuye, later known as Pecos, which long had been a center of trade between the Plains and the Pueblo tribes.

Elsewhere, such as in California and Texas, the Spanish gathered, or forced nomadic hunter-gatherers into mission communities, imposing entirely new forms of economic and social life on them. Indian communities did not thrive under either circumstance, and were decimated by European disease. As their numbers diminished, the settler population increased. Presidios and their soldiers often formed the core of civil settlements, and population increasingly spread out from towns into the surrounding countryside. This "Spanish" population, however, was rarely exclusively European in origin. Spanish, Indian, and African blood mixed freely on the Mexican frontier, with ethnic, classification often reflecting an individual's social position or manner of living.

The rise of this mixed population provides an important clue to Spain's legacy in North America. It had failed both in its larger design of making the borderlands secure and in many of the details—the attempt to ensure that frontier trade flowed exclusively to the south or that towns were laid out according to officially approved design, for example. Despite these failures, and despite arrogance and cruelty in its dealings with Indians, Spain's colonizing, its attempt to assimilate rather than displace non-

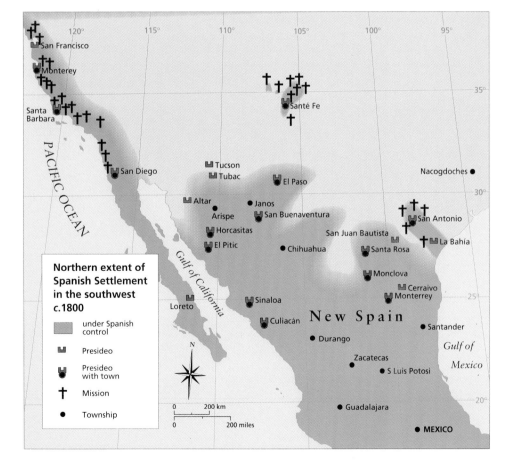

Northern extent of Spanish Settlement in the southwest c.1800

under Spanish control
Presideo
Presideo with town
Mission
Township

PACIFIC OCEAN
San Francisco
Monterey
Santa Barbara
San Diego
Gulf of California
Loreto
Tucson
Tubac
El Paso
Altar
Janos
Arispe
San Buenaventura
Horcasitas
El Pitic
Chihuahua
Sinaloa
Culiacán
Durango
Zacatecas
S Luis Potosi
Guadalajara
Santé Fe
Nacogdoches
San Antonio
San Juan Bautista
Santa Rosa
La Bahía
Monclova
Cerraivo
Monterrey
Santander
New Spain
Gulf of Mexico
MEXICO

hostile Indians, and the Indians resistance to these efforts, shaped the Southwest in profound ways. Its people, its geography (from the sites of its great cities to the names of its mountains and rivers), its architecture, its cuisine, even its jurisprudence, bore the mark of the clash and confluence of Spanish and native American cultures.

Pecos, New Mexico, a pueblo site transformed by the Spanish into a mission, viewed from the North in the reconstruction. The quadrangle is in the middle foreground, with the south pueblo in the background, where the convent and mission was adapted and rebuilt from existing structures

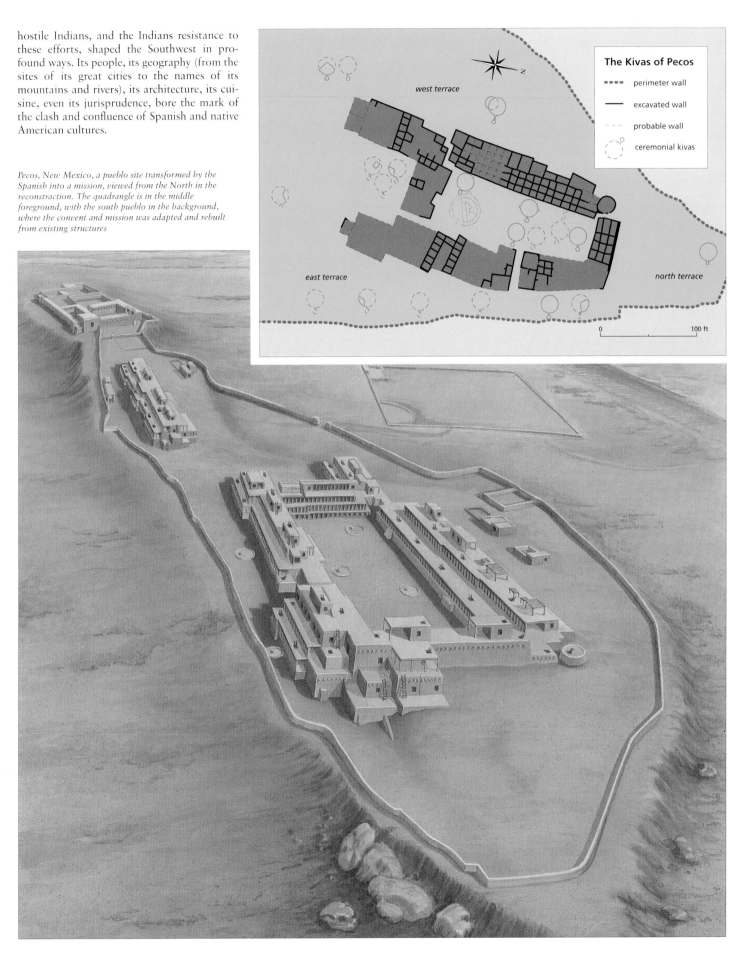

The Kivas of Pecos

• • • • perimeter wall

—— excavated wall

‐ ‐ ‐ probable wall

◯ ceremonial kivas

west terrace

east terrace

north terrace

0   100 ft

AFRICAN SLAVE TRADE
THE VOYAGE OF THE SLOOP "ADVENTURE"

From 1619, when a Dutch frigate sold 20 blacks to English colonists at Jamestown, until 1808, when Congress abolished the African slave trade, nearly 400,000 Africans were brought against their will to British North America. Approximately 8 million more were taken to the sugar or coffee plantations in Brazil and the Caribbean and to the mines of Spanish America, many of which had been established in the 16th and 17th centuries. Few slaves were imported to British America until the early 18th century, when a shortage of labor, an increased demand for staple crop, and a plentiful supply of Africans prompted Southern planters to rely almost exclusively on slaves.

There were few English colonists in the North or the South who opposed slavery on principle. Slaves could be found working on the docks and in the warehouses of the Northern cities, in foundries in Pennsylvania, and on small farms in the North. But far more slaves were purchased in the South, where climate and geography favored the cultivation of cash crops—tobacco in Virginia and Maryland, rice in the Carolinas, and the rapidly expanding cotton in Georgia and elsewhere.

Most of the slaves brought to British North America came from three stretches of West Africa: the Windward Coast of Senegambia and Sierra Leone; the Leeward Coast, comprising the Gold Coast, the Bight of Benin, and the Bight of Biafra; and Angola, much further south. Virginia planters favored the Ibo tribesmen of Biafra, while planters from South Carolina, North Carolina, and Georgia, who viewed the Ibo as too short and too fragile emotionally, preferred the Senegambians, especially those of the Bambara and Malinke tribes, and the Angolans.

Slaving along the Gold Coast:
The Voyage of the Sloop Adventure

On October 25, 1773, the *Adventure,* laden with 15,000 gallons of Newport-made rum, departed that city, setting course for West Africa. The enterprise was financed by Christopher and George Champlain, Newport merchants, and their brother Robert captained the ship and its crew of ten.

In early December the *Adventure* arrived at Sierra Leone and purchased rice. But Robert Champlain bought no slaves, for he had been told that the slaves there were inferior to those to be found further south on the Gold Coast and at Wyhdah.

He reached the Gold Coast in January and set course for the Dutch castle of Elmina, a major slave station. Unfortunately for Champlain, the slave holds were nearly depleted and prices high. He finally traded 250 gallons of rum for his first slave, a woman, and six ounces of gold. Because this was an exceptionally high price, he resolved to deal directly with the local chiefs from then on.

Champlain spent most of February searching for slaves along the Gold Coast, but with little success. (He refused to look in the Bight of Biafra, whose slaves he regarded as utterly unfit.) By late March, having acquired only five of the 70 slaves necessary for a full cargo, he stopped at the Cape Coast Castle and purchased 16 males and 14 females at the unusually high price of 225 gallons of rum for the males, 205 for the females.

In April, Champlain put in to a smaller English fort at Annamabu, ten miles east of the Cape Coast Castle, and purchased 17 males and 10 females at prices slightly lower than before. Then he set sail for the West Indies, anxious to depart from the coast before the summer heat and diseases decimated crew and slaves alike.

In June the *Adventure* arrived at Grenada, with only four of its 66 slaves dying en route; the remainder sold for about 37 pounds sterling each. By this calculation, the *Adventure*, despite paying exceptionally high prices for its slaves, probably yielded a profit of about 400 pounds sterling, a return of about 23 percent on the original investment.

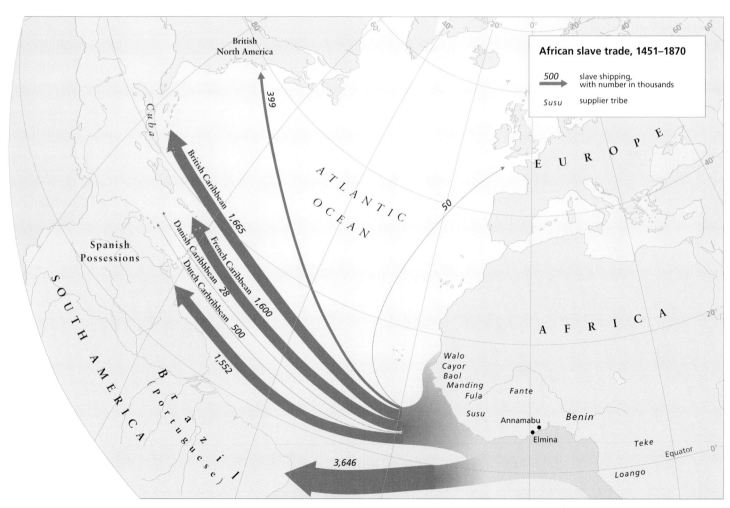

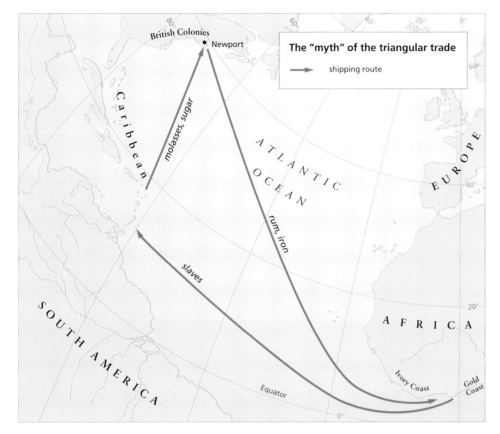

The "myth" of the triangular trade

→ shipping route

The "Myth" of the Triangular Trade?

How did the African slaves get to the British colonies of North America? Generations of children were taught that merchants from Newport and Boston sent ships laden with rum and iron bars to West Africa, where they were exchanged for slaves. The ships then sailed to the West Indies, traded the slaves for molasses and sugar, and returned to New England carrying the basic ingredients of rum. Repeatedly historians cited the example of the voyage of the brigantine *Sanderson*, which departed Newport, Rhode Island, in 1753.

Some historians have questioned the significance of the triangle trade. They note that during the 18th century, trade with Africa involved less than one percent of all American exports. Moreover, most colonial ships shuttled back and forth between coastal ports, rarely attempting the long middle passage to Africa. Although the triangular trade was not crucial to the colonies as a whole, it mattered enormously to tiny Rhode Island, whose rocky soil and meager farms no longer sustained the port cities of Newport, Bristol, and Providence. On the eve of the American Revolution, the Governor of Rhode Island observed that the rum distilleries in these cities were "the main hinge upon which the trade of the colony turns." Most of the rum was exported, mainly to West Africa in return for slaves.

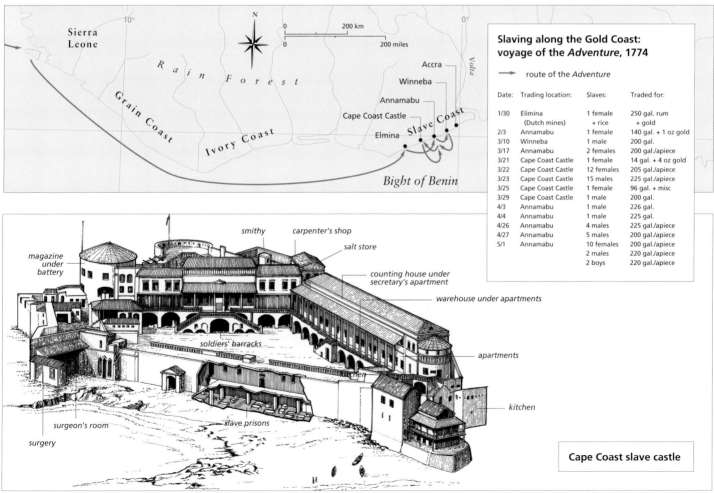

Slaving along the Gold Coast: voyage of the *Adventure*, 1774

→ route of the *Adventure*

Date:	Trading location:	Slaves:	Traded for:
1/30	Elimina (Dutch mines)	1 female + rice	250 gal. rum + gold
2/3	Annamabu	1 female	140 gal. + 1 oz gold
3/10	Winneba	1 male	200 gal.
3/17	Annamabu	2 females	200 gal./apiece
3/21	Cape Coast Castle	1 female	14 gal. + 4 oz gold
3/22	Cape Coast Castle	12 females	205 gal./apiece
3/23	Cape Coast Castle	15 males	225 gal./apiece
3/25	Cape Coast Castle	1 female	96 gal. + misc
3/29	Cape Coast Castle	1 male	200 gal.
4/3	Annamabu	1 male	226 gal.
4/4	Annamabu	1 male	225 gal.
4/26	Annamabu	4 males	225 gal./apiece
4/27	Annamabu	5 males	200 gal./apiece
5/1	Annamabu	10 females	200 gal./apiece
		2 males	220 gal./apiece
		2 boys	220 gal./apiece

Cape Coast slave castle

CHURCH FORMATION IN COLONIAL AMERICA
ERA OF EXPANSION: 1680–1770

Americans usually think of the 17th century as the great age of religion and American churches. This is not true. Aside from the special example of New England between about 1630 and 1660, the century that witnessed the greatest increase in churches and established America's denominational pluralism and regional peculiarities was the 18th.

Before 1680, America's churches were overwhelmingly Protestant and narrowly English. Two churches, the Congregational and the Church of England, or "Anglican," accounted for more than 90 percent of the congregations in the British colonies. They reflected the persistence rather than the demise of the traditional European state-church relationship in America. Congregational churches of New England and the Anglican churches of Virginia received their principal financial support from taxes and enjoyed a legal monopoly over religious activity. Where governments failed to support churches, churches hardly existed, as in Maryland, where anti-Catholic mobs desecrated Catholic chapels during the colony's frequent political turmoil yet where only two or three Anglican congregations and one or two Quaker meetings existed through the 1680s.

Congregations formed after 1680 transformed organized religion in America. Above all, they quickly outnumbered their 17th-century predecessors. Fully 85 percent of the colonial churches existing on the eve of the American Revolution had been founded after 1700, and no less than 60 percent of them were founded after 1740 in the 30 years before the Revolution. As a result, the old Congregationalist and Anglican churches formed before 1680 comprised only 15 percent of the congregations existing in the 1770s.

Pre-Revolutionary colonial church expansion occurred in two waves: 1680 to 1710 and 1740 to 1770. In the first, both Congregationalists and Anglicans strengthened the state-church patterns begun in the previous century. Anglican campaigns for legal establishment created nearly 90 congregations between 1680 and 1710, most of them in Maryland, North Carolina, South Carolina, and New York, where English-speaking residents had often been without effective organized religious worship of any kind. Congregationalists established some 60 new congregations in New England between 1680 and 1710, most in new towns but others in older towns where churches divided in response to new settlement patterns.

The second period of congregational growth, from 1740 to 1770, stemmed from two causes. Some of it benefited from Calvinistic revivalism in New England and the middle colonies (1740–1755) and in the southern colonies (1755–1770). Dissenting evangelical Baptist and Congregationalist churches benefited most clearly from this revivalism, although perhaps a third of the new congregations survived for less than a decade.

At least as many new churches resulted from proselytizing by increasingly powerful and numerous colonial denominations. The Society for the Propagation of the Gospel in Foreign Parts (SPG), the Church of England's missionary organization for English settlers, established nearly 150 congregations between 1740 and 1770. The Synod of Philadelphia and its constituent presbyteries established more than 200 Presbyterian churches, and the several Baptist associations, including those of Philadelphia, Charleston, and Rhode Island, established 200 Baptist congregations. Together with these, the German Lutheran and German Reformed denominations accounted for most of the 1,200 congregations formed in the colonies between 1740 and 1770.

Eighteenth-century church expansion brought modern religious heterogeneity to the colonies, except for New England which remained remarkably homogeneous however. In the 1770s, 75 percent of its churches were Congregationalist; only about 13 percent were Baptist, 8 percent were Anglican, and 3 or 4 percent were Presbyterian. Heterogeneity was much more important in the southern colonies. In the 1770s, a third of all congregations there were Anglican, 30 percent were Baptist, and 25

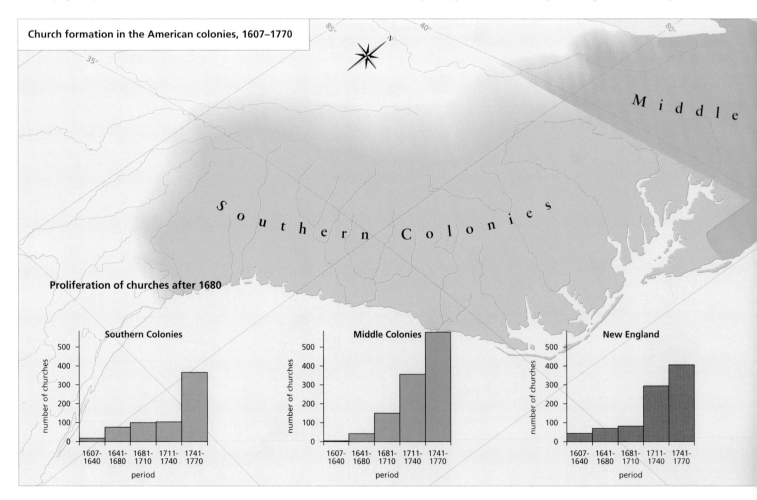

Church formation in the American colonies, 1607–1770

Middle

Southern Colonies

Proliferation of churches after 1680

Southern Colonies

number of churches — period
1607-1640, 1641-1680, 1681-1710, 1711-1740, 1741-1770

Middle Colonies

number of churches — period
1607-1640, 1641-1680, 1681-1710, 1711-1740, 1741-1770

New England

number of churches — period
1607-1640, 1641-1680, 1681-1710, 1711-1740, 1741-1770

George Whitefield, a young English preacher whose visits to America after 1739 attracted huge audiences and helped draw thousands into organized religion. Though himself a Calvinist, Whitefield contributed to the growth of all denominations. "Don't tell me you are a Baptist, an Independent, a Presbyterian, a dissenter, tell me you are a Christian. That is all I want," he preached.

percent were Presbyterian, many of the latter being recently- arrived Scottish immigrants.

Yet no region equalled the diversity of the middle colonies. By the 1770s, German-speaking congregations accounted for nearly a third of the region's churches, and they were divided into two major groups (German Lutheran and German Reformed or Calvinist) and four minor groups (Amish, Mennonite, Moravian, and German Baptist). Among English-speaking colonists, Presbyterians accounted for a quarter of the region's churches, followed by Baptist, Quaker, and Anglican churches. Perhaps most indicative of the heterogeneity was the establishment of 12 Catholic churches in the region by the 1770s. Accounting for only one percent of all churches there, they were solidly established and forecast the expansion of Catholicism in the next half-century.

Thus, the 30 years before the Revolution transformed early America's religious landscape. The early government-supported Congregationalist and Anglican churches of New England and Virginia gave way to rapidly increasing Presbyterian, Baptist, Lutheran, and German Reformed churches, as well as numerous sects and even Catholicism. Together, they created the vigorous ethnic and theological mix that subsequently characterized much of 19th-century American religion and society.

Jon Butler

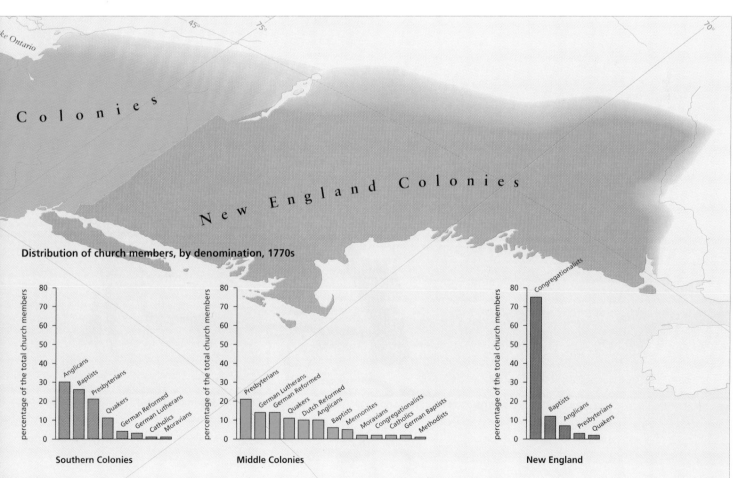

Distribution of church members, by denomination, 1770s

Southern Colonies

percentage of the total church members

Anglicans, Baptists, Presbyterians, Quakers, German Reformed, German Lutherans, Catholics, Moravians

Middle Colonies

percentage of the total church members

Presbyterians, German Lutherans, German Reformed, Quakers, Dutch Reformed, Anglicans, Baptists, Mennonites, Moravians, Congregationalists, Catholics, German Baptists, Methodists

New England

percentage of the total church members

Congregationalists, Baptists, Anglicans, Presbyterians, Quakers

SACRALIZING THE LANDSCAPE
TOWARD ECCLESIASTICAL SPLENDOR

The rapid formation of congregations after 1680 transformed the location and appearance of churches. By the time of the Revolution, almost all church buildings constructed before 1680 had been destroyed. Of the two or three early churches that still survive, each had been extensively remodeled and enlarged. The buildings constructed after 1680 were far more ornate and larger than their predecessors. In fact, the buildings that today pass for our "colonial" church heritage actually represent only the mature 18th-century colonial period and would have startled the earliest colonists, whose small church buildings are lost to us.

Deeds and archaeological excavations suggest that most pre-1680 colonial churches could easily be described in two words: small and crude. Few were larger than 20 by 40 or 50 feet. They were usually constructed in wood, rather than the brick and stone commonly used in England, and they were sparsely furnished and decorated. Many Virginia parishes constructed no church buildings at all before 1680 and those that did often erected small, bare buildings that deteriorated quickly. The first church in Sudbury, Massachusetts, erected in 1643, was a wooden building with a thatched roof and rough-hewn interior that measured only 20 by 30 feet. Not until a third church was constructed in 1688 could the town claim a church with a permanent roof and finished interior.

Colonial American church architecture changed dramatically after 1680. First, the number of congregations multiplied significantly, so that church buildings interrupted the European-settled landscape more frequently than before 1680. Though no more than five church buildings were standing in Maryland in 1680, for example, more than 40 could be found by 1720 and more than 70 by 1770.

Second, the post-1680 churches of all denominations reflected the growing wealth of the colonies. Now buildings might measure 50 by 60 or more and accommodate 150 to 300 persons. They also were more substantial. New England's largely wooden churches were now built on deep foundations by master craftsmen who could span significant lengths and raise buildings to staggering heights, often to striking visual effect. Churches in the middle and southern colonies were equally large, though more often constructed of brick, stone, and stucco.

Regional variations increasingly typified church construction. The churches of post-1680 Virginia and Maryland tended to be long and narrow, and their masons often introduced English and Flemish bond styles into the brickwork, as they did at Virginia's Stration Major parish church (1720s). South Carolina craftsmen more often erected square stucco churches, like that at St. James Goose Creek parish (1706), and though the buildings looked squat, they were often as tall as the Virginia churches. Before 1740, few rural churches had steeples, and congregations that could afford bells placed them in wooden stands on the ground, usually building the steeples a decade or more later.

America's post-1680 churches reflected the colonists' concern for material display. As early as 1692, newly formed Maryland parishes of the Church of England used local craftsmen to construct and furnish their new church buildings and imported far more raw materials to be transformed into pews and pulpits on site than finished products from London or elsewhere.

New England's 18th-century churches, "simple" and "sparce" only by 19th-century standards, grew increasingly large. They featured substantial subtle interior decoration—smoothly polished pews, finely carved pulpits, mahogany baptismal fonts, and silver communion goblets—created by local furniture makers and silversmiths. South Carolina's St. James Goose Creek church, also constructed by local craftsmen, contained a Royal Coat of Arms, carved cherubs gilded with gold paint, and a cantilevered pulpit with a mahogany sounding board. From their carefully laid-out boxed-pews, the St. James Goose Creek parishioners and slaves could both admire local handiwork and hear their minister's new sermon.

Between 1680 and 1770, the colonial cities became centers of ecclesiastical splendor. Though New York City lacked a single church steeple in the 1670s, four pierced the skyline by 1720 and more were added in the next decade. In Philadelphia, the Anglican, Presbyterian, and German Lutheran and German Reformed churches constructed between 1720 and 1750 transformed the skyline of a city previously known for only modest Quaker meeting houses. Yet no city, not even Boston, possessed two such fine examples of architectural splendor as Charles Town, whose first large Anglican church, St. Phillips (1720), was joined six blocks to the south in 1751 by St. Michaels. Both had an organ, steeples, bells, hanging lamps, embroidered seat cushions, finely carved pews, and massive columns, all reflecting the wealth generated in colonies seeking to emulate rather than reject still-familiar European patterns in church architecture and conspicuous consumption.

Jon Butler

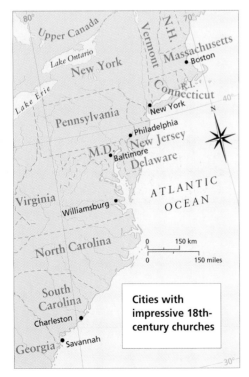

The First Sudbury Meetinghouse, 1643, a rough and rude building characteristic of 17th-century New England houses of worship. Did the simplicity of such structures reflect a disdain for the trappings of worship, or did they represent the impoverished condition of the congregation?

Cities with impressive 18th-century churches

Views of the interior (above) and exterior (left) of St. James Church in Groose Greek, South Carolina. Built in 1708, the church featured elaborate windows and woodwork and demanded highly skilled craftsmanship. The house of God became a place of opulent beauty.

Top: *St. Michael's Church (1751), Charleston, South Carolina. An early example of the ornate and richly elegant architecture that became common in urban churches later in the century.*

Bottom: *Seven church steeples and the tower of Fort George dominate the sky line, an inescapably visible symbol of organized religion's newfound affluence and cultural domination. Drawing is based on a contemporary engraving.*

CHURCH MEMBERSHIP

LESS THAN GOD-FEARING

Most colonists did not belong to or attend church in the colonial period, a pattern that conflicts with modern myths about early American religion but which was well known at the time. Moreover, this pattern changed little down to the time of the Revolution. The formation of congregations and construction of church buildings that so dramatically altered the colonial landscape between 1680 and 1770 helped Christianity to survive in rapidly expanding colonial settlements, but, on the eve of the Revolution, fewer than 20 percent of American adults adhered to a church in any significant way, a far cry from the 60 percent who do so in the late 20th century.

Only in the earliest years of the Puritan experiment did churches command the loyalty of most New Englanders. Between 1630 and 1660, adult church membership in most New England towns approached 70 or 80 percent. Membership was never universal, however, and ominous patterns in Boston and Salem suggest that the impending decline occurred not only because the churches were strict and concerned only with current members—"tribal," as the historian Edmund Morgan describes it—but also because increasing numbers of New Englanders were indifferent about organized worship. By 1650, fewer than 50 percent of Boston's adults were church members. By the 1680s, many New England towns reported church membership rates of no more than 10 to 25 percent. By 1690, on the eve of the witch trials, Salem's churches could claim only 15 percent of its adults as members, including only half of the town's well-to-do selectmen.

Church membership rates in the middle and southern colonies were even lower than in New England. Although the slack church participation in the former New Netherlands picked up somewhat after 1690, when Dutch Reformed congregations became centers for Dutch ethnic expression, low church adherence among English settlers kept New York's general membership rates low throughout the colonial period. In Pennsylvania, high church membership rates occurred only in the earliest years of Quaker settlement, between 1682 and 1695, then fell off quickly as non-Quakers arrived. The small number of churches in early Virginia and their remarkable absence in early Maryland necessitated low church involvement through the early Chesapeake. Even when churches existed, attachment could prove erratic, as in New England. In Virginia's Charles Parish, 85 percent of newborn Caucasian children went unbaptized between 1650 and 1680, although the parish supported a clergyman and sustained regular worship throughout the period.

Local and regional differences also characterized church adherence in the 18th-century colonies. The growing splendor and increasing number of churches in the colonial cities actually masked low church membership rates. In 1780, Samuel Mather guessed that scarcely a sixth of Boston's adults attended church, and in New York City and Philadelphia, church membership probably did not approach 10 percent. Rural church membership rates could be equally low, although there were important and puzzling variations. Ministers responding to a Church of England survey in 1724 claimed sabbath attendance of several hundred persons (probably an exaggeration) but usually reported fewer than 20 or 30 persons taking communion. In Newcastle, Delaware, Anglican congregation-eligible persons taking communion actually declined from about 20 percent in the 1740s to between 8 and 12 percent in the 1770s, with no compensating rise in adherence to other churches, and despite an increase in the parish's population. Relatively low participation characterized other Anglican congregations as well.

Church membership did not reflect society. Among European colonists, most members were women, and few African slaves or native Americans adopted Christianity in the colonial era. After 1680, women comprised about 60 percent of church members in most congregations. Married women usually joined congregations long before their husbands, especially in New England, and their husbands often did not become members until they were in their fifties, sometimes on the eve of their election to local office. Revivals temporarily brought more men into congregations, especially in the 1740s, but the women's numerical majority surfaced again when the revivals faded. Though conversion rhetoric was important to early colonization and prompted some proselytizing among both native Americans and, later, African slaves, most missionary work proved feeble and ineffective. Native Americans resisted conversion until well into the

19th century, and not until the 1760s, at the earliest, did African slaves turn to Christianity in any signficant number.

At the time of the Revolution, then, between 70 and 90 percent of all European colonists in America remained unattached to any church. The southern colonies contained both extremes. South Carolina tied New Hampshire for the highest church membership rate (about 16 percent), and North Carolina had the lowest rate (about four percent). However, if slaves, who accounted for nearly 50 percent of the population, are counted, the church membership rates of the southern colonies fell by half in most places, while New England's rate of church membership rose, at least relative to the total population. In short, although Christianity survived in the New World wilderness, in part through a dramatic congregational expansion from 1680 to 1770, the great age of American religious prosperity would wait for the next two centuries.

Jon Butler

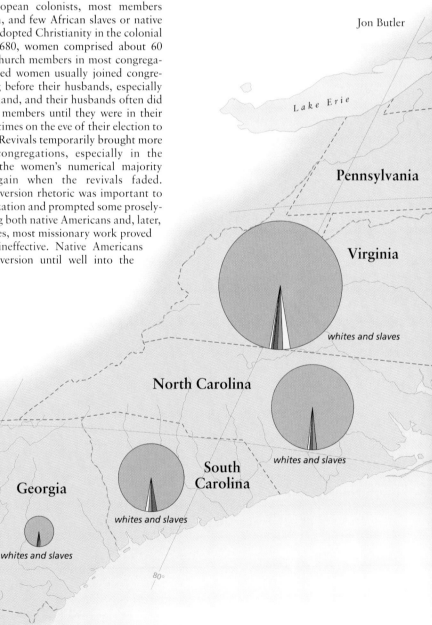

whites and slaves

whites and slaves

whites and slaves

whites and slaves

whites and slaves

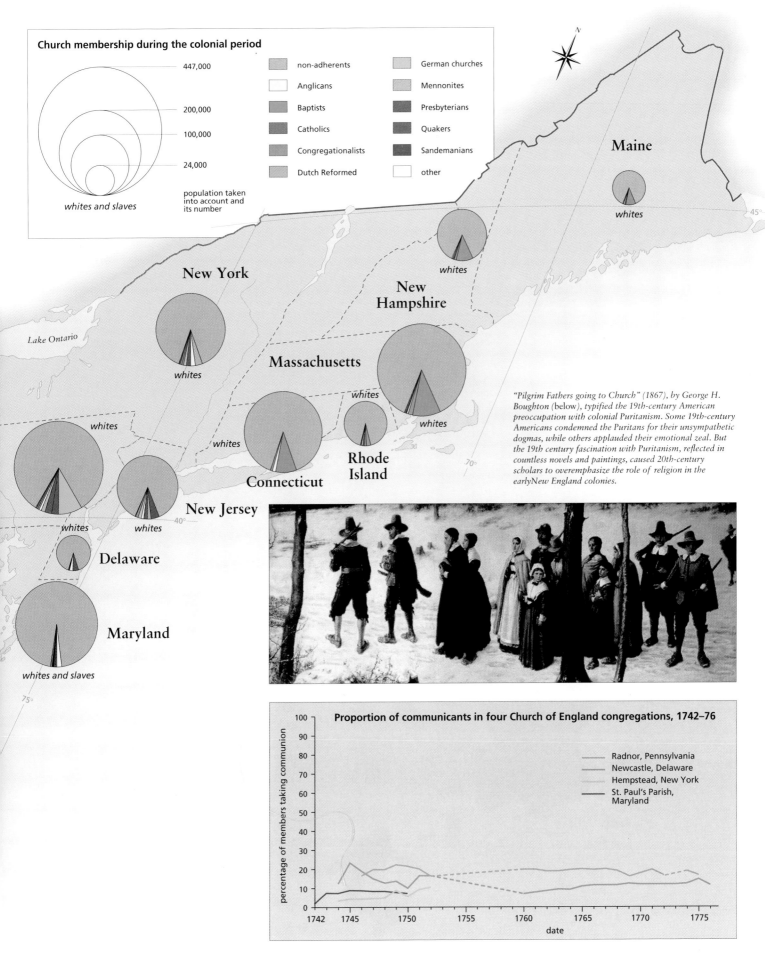

Church membership during the colonial period

447,000
200,000
100,000
24,000

whites and slaves

population taken into account and its number

non-adherents
Anglicans
Baptists
Catholics
Congregationalists
Dutch Reformed

German churches
Mennonites
Presbyterians
Quakers
Sandemanians
other

Maine
whites

New York
whites

Lake Ontario

New Hampshire
whites

Massachusetts
whites

whites

Connecticut
whites

Rhode Island
whites

New Jersey
whites

whites

Delaware
whites

Maryland
whites and slaves

"Pilgrim Fathers going to Church" (1867), by George H. Boughton (below), typified the 19th-century American preoccupation with colonial Puritanism. Some 19th-century Americans condemned the Puritans for their unsympathetic dogmas, while others applauded their emotional zeal. But the 19th century fascination with Puritanism, reflected in countless novels and paintings, caused 20th-century scholars to overemphasize the role of religion in the earlyNew England colonies.

Proportion of communicants in four Church of England congregations, 1742–76

percentage of members taking communion

100
90
80
70
60
50
40
30
20
10
0

1742   1745   1750   1755   1760   1765   1770   1775

date

Radnor, Pennsylvania
Newcastle, Delaware
Hempstead, New York
St. Paul's Parish, Maryland

THE CONTAINMENT OF FRANCE
THE COLONIES, PAWNS OF EUROPEAN POLITICS

The question of which European power would win North America was a subject of much debate in the late 17th century. If the matter were to be decided solely by the colonists, the English, whose settlements along the Atlantic Coast were thriving, would likely prevail east of the Mississippi, and the Spanish in the Southwest. By contrast, France's few and widely scattered settlements were vulnerable. But the colonists did not control the destiny of the continent, for statesmen in Europe readily exchanged or sacrificed colonial possessions to achieve compelling objectives in Europe. There, France was supreme.

France's power derived from a strong central government and a population of 20 million—four times that of Spain or England. King Louis XIV awed Europe by keeping some 200,000 men in arms even in peacetime. France's influence was magnified by the debilities of its neighbors. Spain had long squandered its dwindling resources and was wasting yet more in an effort to recover Portugal. The Netherlands and England had emptied each other's treasuries in wars over colonial trade. The Holy Roman Empire continued to disintegrate, and Austria struggled simultaneously to fend off the Turks and to keep intact its polyglot empire.

British statesmen increasingly recognized that their overseas commercial empire would not be secure until the continental states had joined to oppose France. "France will outdo us at sea when they have nothing to fear on land," the Duke of Newcastle explained. Britain accordingly devised and for several generations pursued a grand strategy of supporting a coalition of states to bottle up France on the continent. The strategy was first implemented in 1689 when Britain, which had often sided with France against the Netherlands or Spain, joined the League of Augsburg. The League, which comprised the Holy Roman Empire, Spain, Sweden, Bavaria, Saxony, the Palatinate, and the Dutch Republic, was at war with France. During the War of the League of Augsburg (known in English colonies as King William's War), the French won the land battles, but failed to drive coalition forces from the field. At sea, combined British and Dutch fleets held France in check. Fighting continued intermittently until 1696, when France and England, treasures exhausted, agreed to peace. Though the treaty terms were inconclusive, the British had managed to stall French ambitions.

The soldiers had scarcely returned to their homes when war broke out again. In 1700 Charles II, King of Spain, was approaching death. Because he was childless, it was unclear who was his rightful successor. On October 1,

Charles bequeathed the whole of Spain and its territories to a relative, Philip, grandson of Louis of France. A month later Charles died and Philip became king. The Emperor of Austria, who also claimed the Spanish throne, called for a resumption of the Grand Alliance against France. Louis played into the hands of the allies by persuading Philip to grant French merchants exclusive rights to supply slaves to the Spanish Americas. English and Dutch merchants howled in protest and their governments, fearful of the combined might of France and Spain, joined the coalition.

The main battles of the War of the Spanish Succession (Queen Anne's War in the Americas) were fought in Europe, where allied forces led by the Duke of Marlborough won a series of tactical victories and achieved supremacy at sea. The Treaty of Utrecht (1713) ended France's ambitions in Spain, and France also yielded Nova Scotia, Newfoundland, and Hudson's Bay to Britain. Negotiators failed to set the boundaries between European colonies in the vast region south of the St. Lawrence river. This would await the outcome of the Great War for the Empire.

In 1720, French statesmen had sought to break free of their isolation by negotiating a marriage of the 10-year-old Louis XV, King of France (far right), to the Spanish infanta. English statesmen countered with unsuccessful plans for the marriage of Louis to the Prince of Wales' daughter.

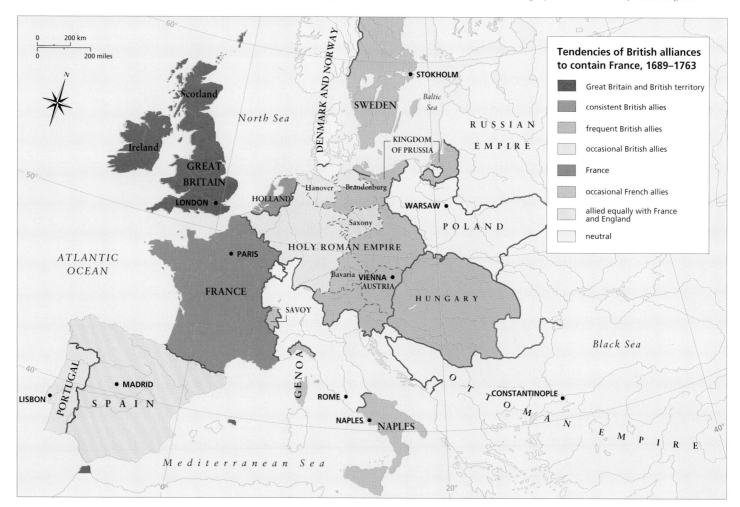

Tendencies of British alliances to contain France, 1689–1763

- Great Britain and British territory
- consistent British allies
- frequent British allies
- occasional British allies
- France
- occasional French allies
- allied equally with France and England
- neutral

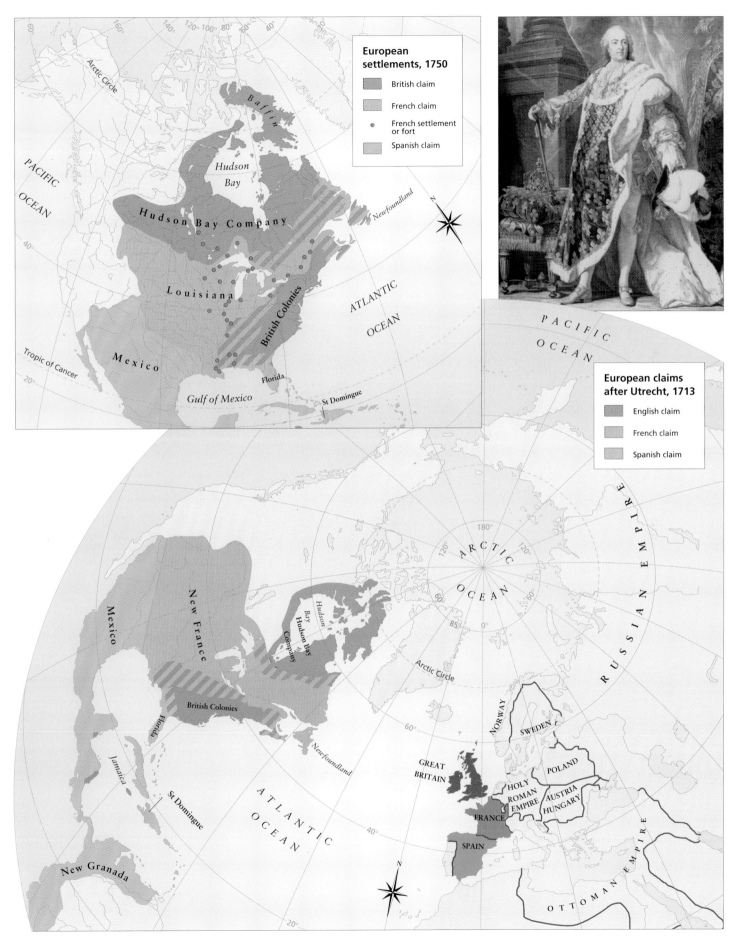

European settlements, 1750

- British claim
- French claim
- French settlement or fort
- Spanish claim

PACIFIC OCEAN

Arctic Circle

Baffin

Hudson Bay

Hudson Bay Company

Newfoundland

N

Louisiana

British Colonies

ATLANTIC OCEAN

Tropic of Cancer

Mexico

Florida

St Domingue

Gulf of Mexico

European claims after Utrecht, 1713

- English claim
- French claim
- Spanish claim

PACIFIC OCEAN

ARCTIC OCEAN

RUSSIAN EMPIRE

Mexico

New France

Hudson Bay

Hudson Bay Company

Arctic Circle

British Colonies

Florida

Newfoundland

Jamaica

St Domingue

ATLANTIC OCEAN

New Granada

N

NORWAY

SWEDEN

GREAT BRITAIN

POLAND

HOLY ROMAN EMPIRE

AUSTRIA HUNGARY

FRANCE

SPAIN

OTTOMAN EMPIRE

EIGHTEENTH-CENTURY WARFARE
THE STRATEGY OF DEFENSE

Military science was revolutionized in the second half of the 17th century. Advances in gunpowder and smooth-barreled musketry rendered infantrymen, formerly armed with pikes, far more effective. Artillery, too, acquired greater range and accuracy. But these potent new technologies led to an arms race that drained royal treasuries throughout Europe; and monarchs, having spent enormous sums on equipping and maintaining their armies, now became reluctant to risk them in bloody encounters. Strategists favored defense over offense, and military art was chiefly concerned with the design and construction of fortifications. Its consummate practitioner was Vauban, the chief engineer of Louis XIV, who ringed France with 60 formidable fortresses.

New World Fortifications
In the early 1700s, French strategists reasoned that if Vauban's fortifications had rendered France almost invulnerable, a string of fortresses would also protect New France from the encroachments of its more prolific English neighbors. Fortifications, moreover, could also serve as supply depots from which offensive forces could suddenly strike at the enemy. By mid-century, both French and English forts dotted the frontier.

But military doctrines devised in the Old World were often of limited application in the New. North American fortresses, most of which were constructed with timber, rarely approached Vauban's standards. And even stone and earthen fortifications were more vulnerable in the Americas. The distances to be defended were so great, and the frontier regions so thinly populated, that a besieged fort could relatively easily be cut off and starved into submission. Moreover, European powers, always more attentive to nearby dangers than more distant ones, often failed to provide the New World strongholds with adequate garrisons. Throughout the 18th century, enterprising colonists, though unpracticed in the highly stylized arts of 18th-century warfare and siegecraft, devised ways to force professional European armies to abandon their forts and surrender.

The Siege of Louisbourg
An example of this strategy occurred during King George's War (1744–48). France and England, although technically at peace following the Treaty of Utrecht in 1713, continued to wrangle over the boundaries of Acadia (Nova Scotia), northern New England, and the territory along the Ohio River. In 1744, these and other tensions in Europe caused France and England to go to war.

When news of hostilities reached Governor William Shirley of Massachusetts in June, he devised a plan to seize Louisbourg, the seemingly impregnable French fortress guarding Quebec and the approaches to the St. Lawrence river. It was the work of hundreds of men

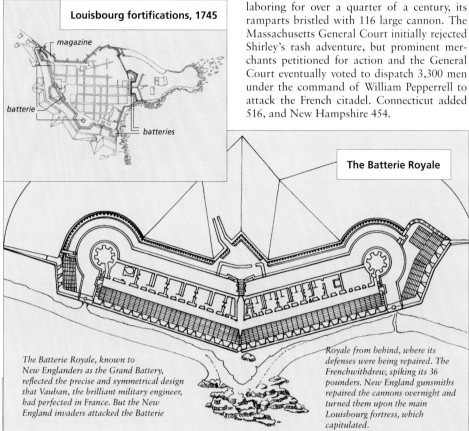

Louisbourg fortifications, 1745

magazine

batterie

batteries

laboring for over a quarter of a century, its ramparts bristled with 116 large cannon. The Massachusetts General Court initially rejected Shirley's rash adventure, but prominent merchants petitioned for action and the General Court eventually voted to dispatch 3,300 men under the command of William Pepperrell to attack the French citadel. Connecticut added 516, and New Hampshire 454.

The Batterie Royale

The Batterie Royale, known to New Englanders as the Grand Battery, reflected the precise and symmetrical design that Vauban, the brilliant military engineer, had perfected in France. But the New England invaders attacked the Batterie Royale from behind, where its defenses were being repaired. The French withdrew, spiking its 36 pounders. New England gunsmiths repaired the cannons overnight and turned them upon the main Louisbourg fortress, which capitulated.

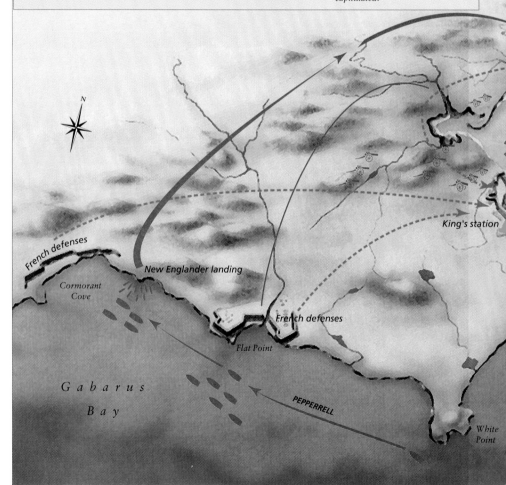

N

French defenses

Cormorant Cove

New Englander landing

French defenses

Flat Point

King's station

Gabarus Bay

PEPPERRELL

White Point

Within a few weeks, the invasion force set sail for Louisbourg. It could not enter the harbor, which was guarded by three separate installations: the fortress on the west bank, a Grand Battery of 28 heavy cannon at the center of the harbor, and a smaller battery on an island near the harbor entrance. Pepperrell chose to land against a weakly defended position on Gabarus Bay to the west of the harbor.

Once ashore, the attackers spent weeks hauling their cannon across a marsh toward the fortress. Meanwhile, a small contingent attacked the Grand Battery and seized it without a fight. (The French, believing that uncompleted renovations had left the battery indefensible, had abandoned it. In their haste to get out, they neglected to effectivly put out of action its 36-pound cannons.)

The New Englanders hauled the captured guns to both sides of the harbor, demolished the island battery and punched holes through the fortress walls. British warships now moved close enough to join in the bombardment. Its position hopeless, the French garrison surrendered. The New Englanders, ironically, were denied the fruits of their campaign when Louisbourg was returned to the French in 1749 after the war.

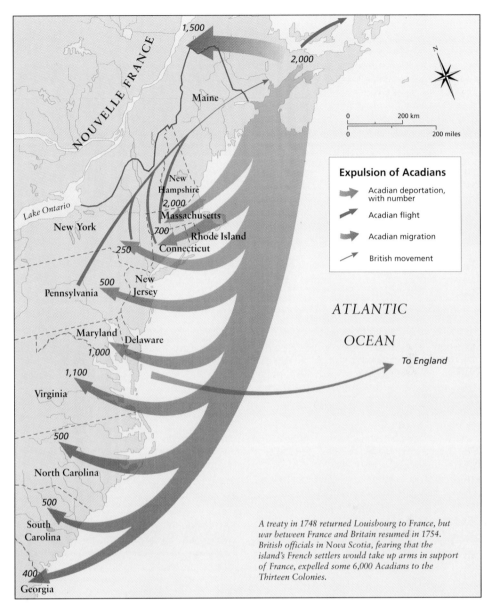

Expulsion of Acadians

⮕ Acadian deportation, with number

➤ Acadian flight

➡ Acadian migration

➚ British movement

A treaty in 1748 returned Louisbourg to France, but war between France and Britain resumed in 1754. British officials in Nova Scotia, fearing that the island's French settlers would take up arms in support of France, expelled some 6,000 Acadians to the Thirteen Colonies.

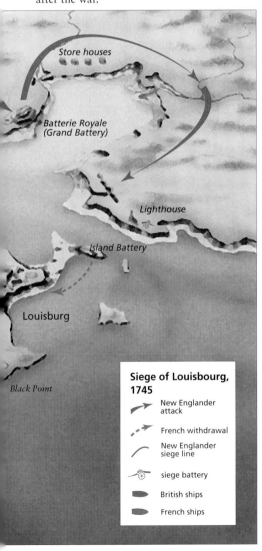

Siege of Louisbourg, 1745

➤ New Englander attack

⌁ French withdrawal

⌒ New Englander siege line

⊕ siege battery

▬ British ships

▬ French ships

New Englanders landing at Gabarus Bay, 1745 (below). A mid-18th-century engraving of the landing at Gabarus Bay. The mighty guns of the Louisbourg fortress, in the distance, failed to prevent the landing. The New Englanders, commanded by William Pepperrell, first took the Grand Battery, whose guns forced the main fortress into submission.

GEORGE WASHINGTON IN THE WEST
THE FIRST BLOW FOR CONTROL OF AMERICA

We tend to think of George Washington as a great planter and military leader, and then as a noble statesman—the father of his country—dignified, reserved, public-spirited, and possessed not so much of extraordinary intelligence as wisdom. He was all of these things and more. But what first brought him to the attention of his fellow Americans was his reputation as a man of action, a bold frontiersman, a veteran of the war with France for control of the West that became the French and Indian War, and what historian Lawrence Henry Gipson called the Great War for the Empire. Indeed, it can be said that Washington almost singlehandedly started that war.

Washington made four trips into the wild land beyond the upper reaches of the Potomac River, the first as an apprentice surveyor in 1748, when he was a lad of 16. In that year he was living at Mount Vernon, the plantation of his half brother Lawrence, who had inherited it on the death of their father in 1743. Nearby was Belvoir, the seat of the great Lord Thomas Fairfax, who owned vast tracts in the as yet unsettled Shenandoah valley. When Fairfax dispatched a team of surveyors to the southern branch of the Potomac, he allowed George to go along. This was his first wilderness experience, sleeping on vermin-infested straw, slogging through raw March rainstorms, and coming into contact with "wild" Indians. He returned after a month with a taste for the western country and an awareness of its rich potential. He was soon making a good income as a surveyor, and he began to invest his earnings in land in the region.

In 1747, a group of Virginians, one of whom was Lawrence Washington, had formed the Ohio Company and obtained a large land grant south of the Ohio River. But the territory was also claimed by the French in Canada. In 1753, the French built a series of forts running south from Lake Erie in what is now west-

George Washington (right), *in the uniform of a colonel in the Virginia militia, the first of Charles Willson Peale's seven paintings of Washington, who was made a colonel at the age of 23 in 1755. Washington sat for this painting in 1772 at Mount Vernon.*

ern Pennsylvania. Alarmed, the governor of Virginia, Robert Dinwiddie, an investor in the Ohio Company, commissioned Washington, now a major in the Virginia militia, to go to the area to warn the French invaders that they were trespassing on Virginian territory and should therefore withdraw.

In October 1753, Washington set out from Fort Cumberland on the upper Potomac accompanied by Jacob Van Braam, a Hollander who could speak French, along with Christopher Gist, a frontiersman familiar with the region, and four "servitors." In late November they reached the junction where the Monongahela and Allegheny meet to form the Ohio River. After conferring with the pro-British Iroquois chief known as the "Half-King" at Logstown, an Indian settlement about 20 miles west of the forks, Washington pushed north to the new French post on the Allegheny, Fort Venango, then on to Fort Le Boeuf, where on December 9 he delivered Dinwiddie's message to the commandant, Legardeur de St. Pierre, who agreed to send it on to the Marquis Duquesne, the governor of Canada. But St. Pierre refused to withdraw from the new forts.

The trip back in blinding snowstorms across ice-choked streams through hostile Indian country almost cost Washington his life on several occasions. He did not reach Fort Cumberland until January 7, 1754, whence he hastened on to Williamsburg to report to Governor Dinwiddie.

Dinwiddie promoted Washington to lieu-

tenant colonel and sent him off in March with 150 soldiers and a few cannon to seize the strategic forks of the Ohio. But before they had reached the forks, they learned that the French had already constructed Fort Duquesne on the site and manned it with a large force. Instead of turning back, Washington built a fortified camp in a clearing and pressed onward. His force surprised a small French reconnaissance party, killing ten and capturing 22 more. After his first experience under enemy fire, Washington wrote: "*I heard the bullets whistle, and, believe me, there is something charming in the sound.*"

This "victory" brought down upon the Virginians the wrath of the French. Washington fell back to his base, aptly named Fort Necessity, but was soon surrounded and compelled to surrender. After tricking Washington into signing a statement written in French admitting that he had "assassinated" what were described not as soldiers but as "emissaries," the French allowed the Virginians to withdraw safely. Washington later claimed to have been misinformed by his interpreter, Van Braam, who was "little acquainted with the English tongue," but this lame excuse was scarcely necessary. Despite his "confession" and the ignominious defeat he had suffered, he returned to Virginia a hero. He had struck the first blow against the French and precipitated a war that, as it turned out, was to determine who was to control not merely the Ohio country but the whole of North America.

Mount Vernon (above), the home of George Washington. On the death of his father the plantation was inherited by his half brother Lawrence in 1743.

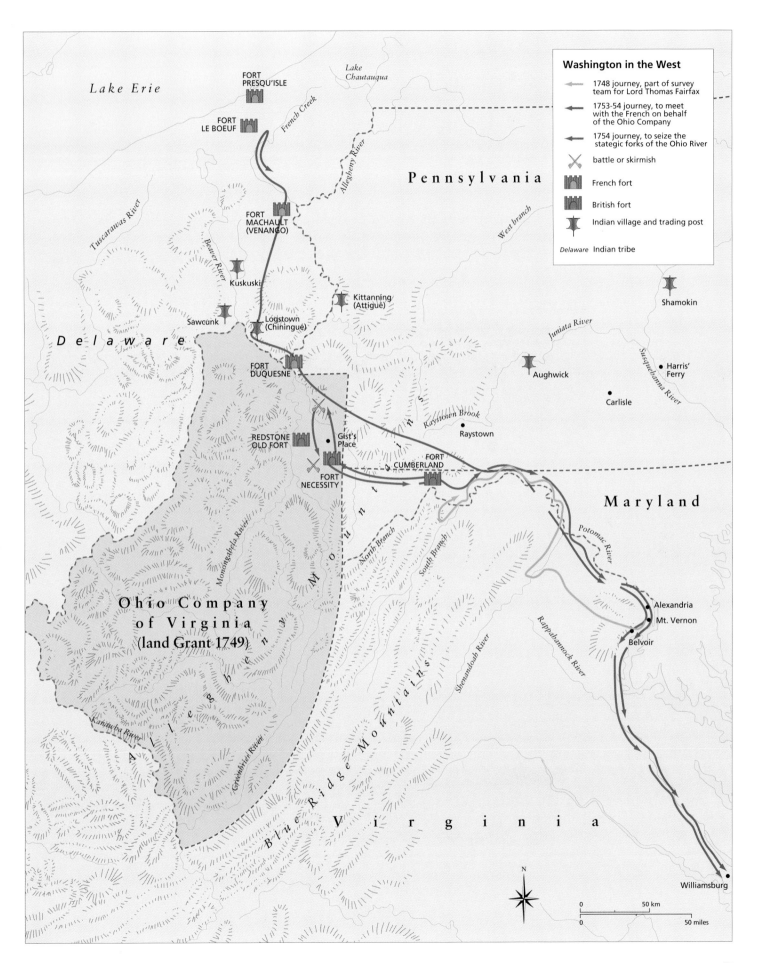

Lake Erie

FORT PRESQU'ISLE

FORT LE BOEUF

French Creek

Lake Chautauqua

Allegheny River

Pennsylvania

West branch

Tuscarawas River

FORT MACHAULT (VENANGO)

Beaver River

Kuskuski

Sawcunk

Kittanning (Attigué)

Logstown (Chiningué)

Delaware

FORT DUQUESNE

Shamokin

Juniata River

Susquehanna River

Aughwick

Harris' Ferry

REDSTONE OLD FORT

Gist's Place

Raystown Brook

Raystown

Carlisle

FORT CUMBERLAND

FORT NECESSITY

Monongahela River

Maryland

North Branch

South Branch

Potomac River

Ohio Company of Virginia (land Grant 1749)

Kanawha River

Greenbrier River

Alexandria

Mt. Vernon

Belvoir

Rappahannock River

Shenandoah River

Blue Ridge Mountains

Allegheny Mountains

Virginia

N

Williamsburg

0   50 km

0   50 miles

Washington in the West

1748 journey, part of survey team for Lord Thomas Fairfax

1753-54 journey, to meet with the French on behalf of the Ohio Company

1754 journey, to seize the stategic forks of the Ohio River

battle or skirmish

French fort

British fort

Indian village and trading post

Delaware Indian tribe

THE GREAT WAR FOR THE EMPIRE

THE FIRST GLOBAL WAR

The shots exchanged by the French from Fort Duquesne and Washington's men began not only the French and Indian War but the far larger Seven Year's War, which raged in Europe and in the West Indies and parts of Asia between 1756 and 1763. "A cannon shot fired in America," Voltaire later wrote, "set Europe in a blaze." When news of the fighting reached England, the government sent Major General Edward Braddock, an officer in the elite Coldstream Guards, to America with two regiments of Redcoats and orders to drive the French from Fort Duquesne. One of Braddock's first actions was to invite Washington to join his staff.

After conferring with five colonial governors in Alexandria, Virginia, a stone's throw from Mount Vernon, Braddock set out in May 1755 from Fort Cumberland at the head of 1,400 British regulars, 700 militiamen from Maryland, Virginia, and the Carolinas, and various Indian allies. Building a road capable of supporting wagons and cannon as they went, the British army advanced at the stately pace of about two miles a day, following the path Washington had blazed the previous spring.

Finally, Braddock decided to press ahead with his foot soldiers, leaving most of his cannon and supply wagons to make their way as best they could. He passed the ruins of Fort Necessity and the site where Washington had surprised the French reconnaissance party and forded the Monongahela River about 10 miles south of Fort Duquesne.

On July 9, the army was only eight miles from Fort Duquesne. By this time, however, Braddock's Indian allies, whom he had counted on to serve as scouts and flankers, had deserted him. Braddock had, Washington noted years later, "absolute contempt" for Indians, and they responded by leaving him to his own devices. As a result, his advance guard was ambushed by French and Indian forces while passing through a narrow path in a dense forest. The withering fire of unseen sharpshooters engulfed the close-packed soldiers. They fell back in panic, running into the main body of infantrymen, who in the confusion were unable to deploy properly.

The result was catastrophic. Washington, striving to rally the troops, had two horses shot out from under him, and a bullet carried off his hat. He was unscathed, but most of the other officers were not so lucky. Towering over the

milling footsoldiers, swords flashing as they tried to bring order from the chaos, they made easy targets. Nearly three-quarters of them were casualties. After losing four horses, General Braddock fell, mortally wounded by a bullet in his lung. It was left to Washington to lead the remnants of the shattered Anglo-American army back to the safety of Virginia.

For a time after the ambush of Braddock's army, British arms staggered from disaster to disaster. Now in total command of the west, pro-French Indians ravaged frontier settlements in Pennsylvania and Maryland. British and colonial attempts to capture Fort Niagara, the fall of which would have cut off all the western French forts from supplies and reinforcements, and against Crown Point, the gateway to Montreal at the southern end of Lake Champlain, got nowhere. In 1756, French general Montcalm destroyed forts Oswego and George on Lake Ontario. The following year, he smashed Fort William Henry, south of Crown Point.

By this time the war had spread to Europe, and there too, French forces were in the ascendant. But finally, in 1757, when William Pitt had become British prime minister, the tide turned. Pitt was committed to an all-out

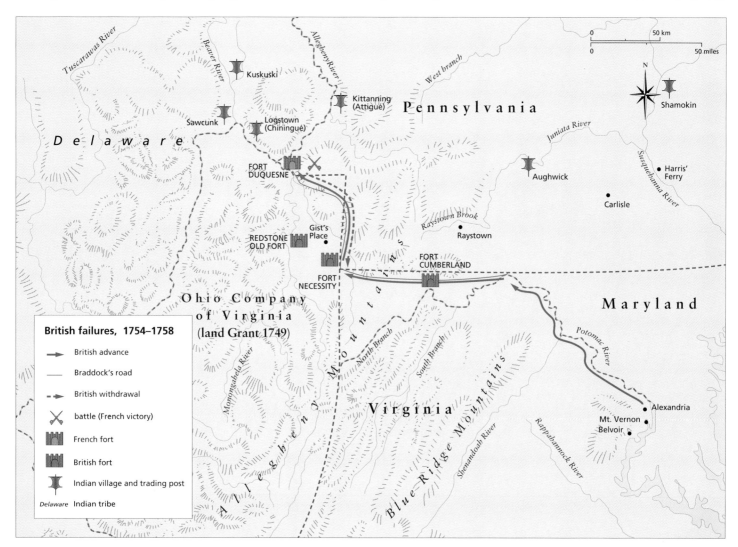

British failures, 1754–1758

→ British advance

— Braddock's road

- ‑ ‑ British withdrawal

✗ battle (French victory)

🏰 French fort

🏰 British fort

⚜ Indian village and trading post

Delaware Indian tribe

The British seizure of Quebec on September 13, 1759 (above). British General James Wolfe conquered the fortress by landing an army under cover of darkness. The British scaled the nearly undefended cliffs and advanced across the Plains of Abraham. The French general, Louis Montcalm, *who had captured Fort Ontario at Oswego (1756), Fort William Henry on Lake George (1757), and held off a furious attack on Fort Ticonderoga (1758), led his army out to meet the British in open battle. The British won; both generals were killed.*

defense of the North American empire. When the colonial assemblies failed to provide needed men and money, he raised British taxes, borrowed heavily, and dispatched thousands of Redcoats to America. He used powerful and talented officers like James Wolfe and Jeffrey Amherst without regard for seniority. In July 1758 Amherst and Wolfe, backed by a 40-ship flotilla, captured Louisbourg on Cape Breton Island, the gateway to the St. Lawrence River, then blockaded by the fleet. Far to the west in Pennsylvania, General John Forbes led an enormous British and colonial force of more than 6,000 men, assisted this time by friendly Indians, to attack Fort Duquesne. Washington, in command of a Virginia regiment, led the advance party, eager to avenge Braddock's defeat. On Christmas Day he reached the fort, only to find it a smoking ruin, fired and abandoned by the French defenders.

In July 1759, Fort Niagara was overrun. In August, General Amherst took Crown Point. In September, General Wolfe captured Quebec, although both he and General Montcalm were killed in the fight. The following year, Amherst led a three-pronged assault on Montreal, which fell in September. All of French North America was in British hands.

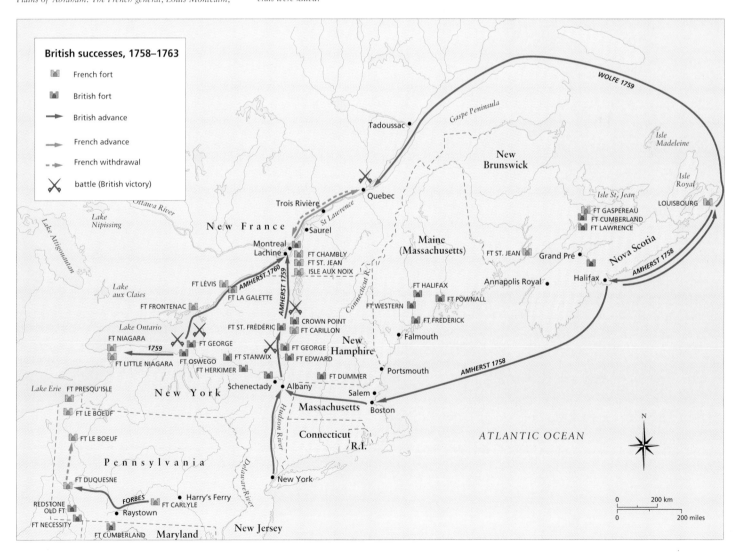

PART 3: A NEW NATION

Gentlemen in wigs and satin knee-britches composing philosophical tracts—the Founding Fathers (and their equally quaintly bedecked spouses) little resemble the 20th-century image of revolutionaries: Lenin atop a cannon rallying the sailors at Kronstadt, or Mao in peasant garb haranguing the troops on the Long March. But the American Revolution was no misnomer. It irreparably shattered the twin pillars of tradition: monarchical authority and hereditary privilege, it revivified an ancient experiment in democracy, conferring political form on a fractious people; and it loosened the bonds of society, giving free rein to acquisitive, religious, and reforming energies. More than its topographical constituents—mountains and farmlands, forests and towns—the new nation was an amalgam of ideas, extracted from classical Greece and Rome, from the Old and New Testaments, from peasant culture and Enlightenment philosophy, fused in the heat of war and invasion, and then poured, white hot, over much of North America, whose borders it eventually overspilled.

THE AMERICAN REVOLUTION
A SHOT IS HEARD AROUND THE WORLD

The American Revolution was caused by irreconcilable disagreements that had developed between the colonies and the government in London, but it broke out because of specific events that took place in and around the town of Boston. One thing led to another: an angry crowd of "Indians" dumped British owned tea in the harbor; Parliament ordered the port sealed until Massachusetts paid for the tea, and drastically revised the colony's liberal charter in order to reduce local autonomy; Minutemen outside Boston began to drill and collect weapons; General Gage sent Redcoats to forestall them and shots were fired—a few Minute men died at Lexington, more (and many more Redcoats) were killed at Concord.

Although greatly outnumbered by the British in terms of population, manufacturing capacity, and wealth, the colonists had important advantages in the war that broke out in 1775. They already had what they wanted—their lands (except for the small areas where British troops were based) and the power to govern themselves. For their part, the British had to fight the war far from their source of supplies in Britain. At the start, the British also suffered from overconfidence. Many of their officers had commanded colonial militia during the

French and Indian war. That experience had convinced them that colonials were dirty, undisciplined, and cowardly. One such officer, General James Grant, boasted that with the help of no more than a 1,000 Redcoats he could "geld" all the men in America, "partly by force and partly by a little coaxing." In addition, British public opinion was divided. Many influential people thought it wrong to spill the blood of what they considered fellow countrymen. Others worried that sending more troops to America might open Great Britain to attack by France or some other European power. American opinion was also divided, but when British troops invaded a region, these differences tended to disappear and local militiamen flocked in force to resist the invasion of their neighborhoods.

As time passed it became clear that because of the Royal Navy, the British could control the seaport towns and their environs, but that when they advanced any distance into the interior, the going was much more difficult. In the end, it was the futility of the struggle rather than any particular defeat that led the British to give up the fight and recognize American independence.

Lexington and Concord
With Minutemen gathering in increasing numbers around Boston, General Thomas

Gage became concerned about munitions being accumulated at Concord. He therefore sent 700 Redcoats commanded by Lt. Col. Francis Smith under cover of darkness to take control of the munitions and to arrest the Patriot leaders, Samuel Adams and John Hancock, who were known to be in Lexington. Forewarned, the Patriot leader, Paul Revere, and a second courier, William Dawes, galloped to Lexington in time to alert Adams and Hancock. Revere was apprehended by the British on the way to Concord and forced to return to Boston without his horse. Dawes turned back, but Dr. Samuel Prescott, who had joined them at Lexington, continued on to Concord.

What happened on the Lexington common when the Redcoats were confronted by 70 Minutemen may have been "the shot heard round the world," but there was no real battle. Eight Americans were killed and a number of others, along with one Redcoat, were wounded. But when the British reached Concord the fighting was serious enough to force the British to withdraw. Along with reinforcements sent out by Gage, they suffered heavy losses to sniper fire on their retreat to Boston.

Breed's Hill
After Lexington and Concord, armed colonials gathered around Boston in steadily

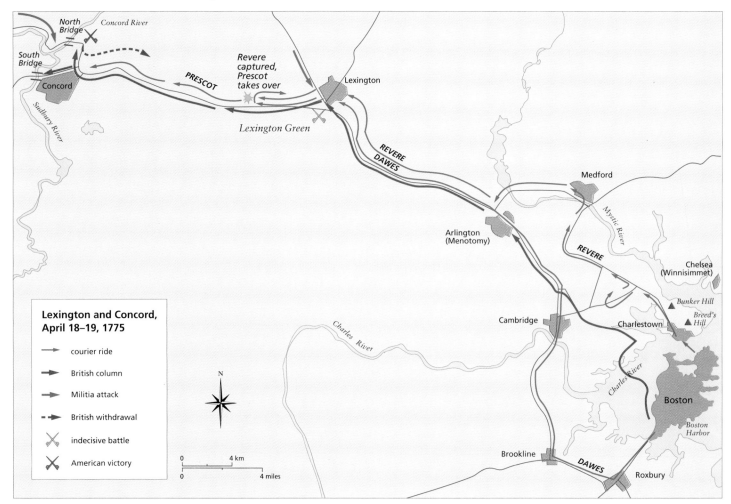

Lexington and Concord, April 18–19, 1775

→ courier ride

➤ British column

➤ Militia attack

- -➤ British withdrawal

⚔ indecisive battle

⚔ American victory

0 — 4 km
0 — 4 miles

John Trumbull, the "painter of the Revolution," only 20 years old at the outbreak of hostilities, served in the war for a year and took up art at 21. When he complained that artists in America failed to receive the honors accorded artists in antiquity, his father responded: "You appear to forget, sir, that Connecticut is not Athens." Trumbull's Death of General Warren at Breed's Hill shows dramatically—but inaccurately—Joseph Warren being bayonetted. The physician-turned-military leader was in fact shot while trying to rally the militia.

increasing numbers. The city was subjected to what amounted to an informal and unorganized siege. In June 1775, militiamen occupied the high ground on the Charlestown peninsula within artillery range of Boston. As the historian W. J. Wood has written, the British generals "were fed up to the teeth with their situation." Their troops, the cream of the British army, were "surrounded by hordes of peasants armed with old muskets and fowling pieces." Gage therefore ordered 2,500 Redcoats commanded by General Sir William Howe to cross over to Charlestown and drive them off. The first British attack sought to outflank the Americans on Breed's Hill. It was stopped by troops commanded by John Stark. To ensure that his men did not fire their inaccurate muskets too soon, Stark drove a stake into the ground 50 yards from the defence and ordered the men not to fire until the Redcoats reached that point. The second British attack, a direct assault on the hill, was driven back with terrible losses. Their third assault succeeded, but only because the defenders had exhausted their ammunition. The British regulars suffered more than 1,000 casualties, the colonial force only about 400. As a result of this costly "victory," Gage was removed from command, and replaced by Howe.

On June 15, the Continental Congress in Philadelphia had named George Washington commander in chief of the American army. He proceeded at once to Boston. It took time to gather supplies, but early in 1776, when his force was strengthened by the arrival of 50 cannon captured from the British at Fort Ticonderoga, on Lake Champlain, he fortified Dorchester Heights, south of Boston. Having no desire to make another assault on a fortified hill, General Howe ordered his troops back aboard ship and sailed off to Halifax, Nova Scotia.

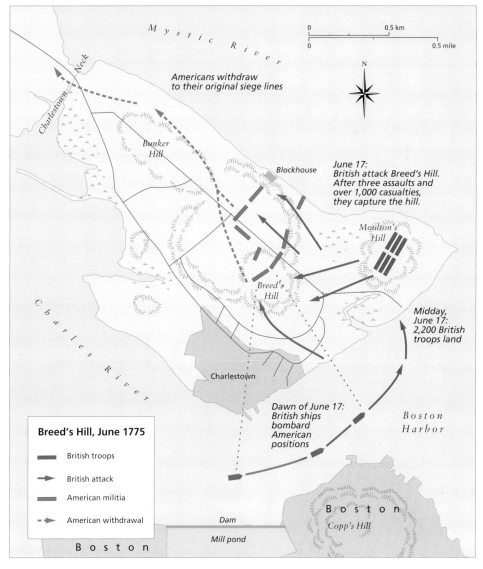

Mystic River

0   0.5 km
0   0.5 mile

N

Charlestown Neck

Americans withdraw to their original siege lines

Bunker Hill

Blockhouse

June 17:
British attack Breed's Hill.
After three assaults and over 1,000 casualties, they capture the hill.

Moulton's Hill

Breed's Hill

Midday,
June 17:
2,200 British troops land

Charles River

Charlestown

Boston Harbor

Dawn of June 17:
British ships bombard American positions

Breed's Hill, June 1775

▬ British troops

➤ British attack

▬ American militia

⇢ American withdrawal

Dam

Mill pond

Boston

Boston

Copp's Hill

FROM NEW YORK TO PRINCETON
VICTORIES IN THE MIDST OF RETREAT

Getting the British out of Boston, the so-called "cockpit of the Revolution," had been a good start, but it did not mean that independence would be easily won. By the time the Declaration of Independence was signed in Philadelphia, British troops were back in force on Staten Island in New York harbor. New York had enormous strategic importance because Redcoat control of the city and the Hudson River would split the rebellious colonies in two. Great Britain therefore used its command of the sea to concentrate the largest army it had ever sent overseas to seize New York and put an end to the revolt.

By the end of July, General Sir William Howe had landed 32,000 soldiers on Staten Island. They were backed by a veritable armada of 73 warships manned by 13,000 sailors, and commanded by Howe's brother, Admiral Richard Howe. General Washington had hurried an army of 19,000 men, many inexperienced militia, to New York. On August 22, General Howe crossed to Long Island and administered a stinging defeat to the Americans. However, he failed either to continue the attack or to interpose British warships between the Americans and Manhattan Island. After two days, Washington managed to withdraw his troops to Manhattan.

Being still on an island and thus subject to amphibious attack from every side, Washington's army was in grave danger. But instead of following in quick pursuit, Sir William delayed, hoping to negotiate a general peace. By the time he crossed to Manhattan in mid September, Washington had retreated to the forested northern part of the island, where he held off a strong British attack at the Battle of Harlem Heights. Howe then transported his men by sea to a point south of New Rochelle, in an effort to outflank the Americans, and at White Plains on October 28 won a hard fought battle. At this point, Washington finally decided to abandon the defense of New York and get out of range of the Royal Navy. He crossed the Hudson to the mainland and retreated southward through New Jersey. Howe dispatched troops under General Charles Cornwallis in pursuit. Washington's army slogged slowly southward, weakened by desertions, hampered by muddy roads and ice-clogged streams.

But in the course of his retreat, Washington won two brilliant battles. First, after his famous crossing of the Delaware River in a sleet storm on Christmas night, he overwhelmed 1,400 sleepy Hessian mercenary troops garrisoned at Trenton in a dawn attack, taking more than 900 prisoners. Next, after circling around Cornwallis's pursuing troops, again in the dead of night, he struck the British base at Princeton. These victories had little strategic significance, because both armies ceased fighting and went into winter quarters. More important, Howe remained in control of New York and the Hudson Valley. But the two victories, coming after the defeats in and around New York, gave a vital boost to American morale. As for the British reaction, one colonel put it this way: *"Though it was once the fashion of this army to treat [the Americans] in the most contemptible light, they are now become a formidable enemy."*

New York patriots pull down the gilded statue of George III at Bowling Green on June 9, 1776 (above). The British had the next laugh, if not the last one, for within weeks General Howe's army had driven Washington and his army from New York City. Painting by William Walcott, in 1854.

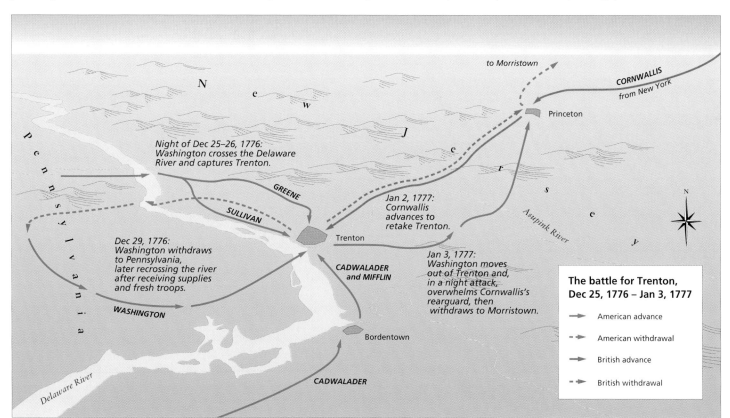

Night of Dec 25–26, 1776: Washington crosses the Delaware River and captures Trenton.

Dec 29, 1776: Washington withdraws to Pennsylvania, later recrossing the river after receiving supplies and fresh troops.

Jan 2, 1777: Cornwallis advances to retake Trenton.

Jan 3, 1777: Washington moves out of Trenton and, in a night attack, overwhelms Cornwallis's rearguard, then withdraws to Morristown.

GREENE

SULLIVAN

WASHINGTON

CADWALADER and MIFFLIN

CADWALADER

Trenton

Bordentown

Princeton

to Morristown

CORNWALLIS from New York

Aspink River

Delaware River

Pennsylvania

N e w   J e r s e y

The battle for Trenton, Dec 25, 1776 – Jan 3, 1777

→ American advance

⇢ American withdrawal

→ British advance

⇢ British withdrawal

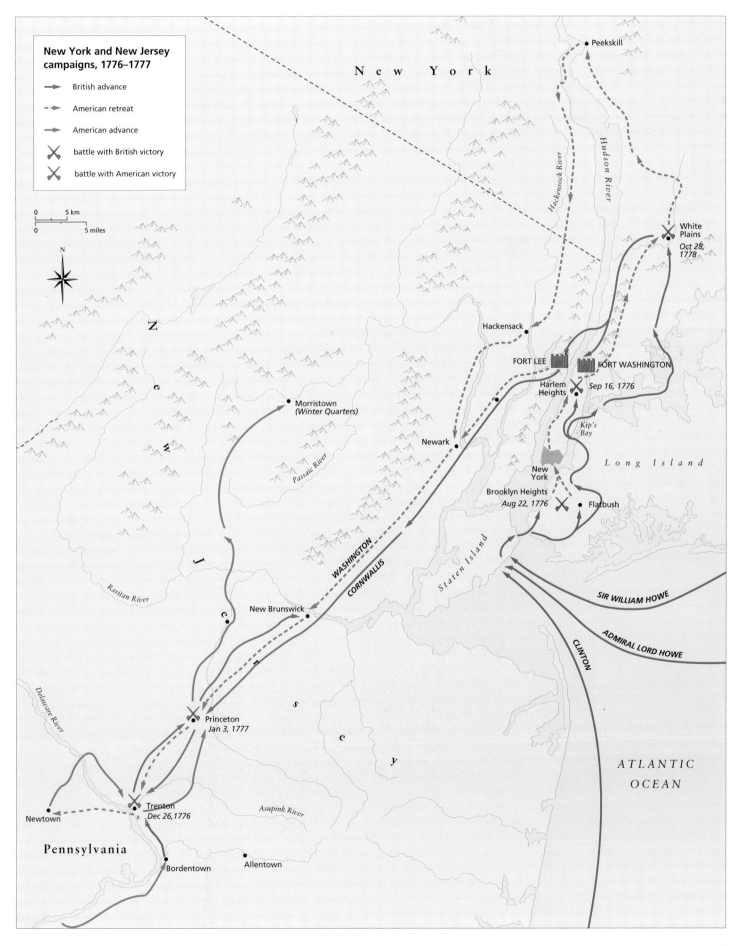

New York and New Jersey campaigns, 1776–1777

→ British advance

⇢ American retreat

→ American advance

✕ battle with British victory

✕ battle with American victory

0   5 km

0   5 miles

N

New York

Peekskill

White Plains
Oct 28, 1778

Hackensack

FORT LEE   FORT WASHINGTON

Harlem Heights   *Sep 16, 1776*

Kip's Bay

Long Island

New York

Brooklyn Heights
Aug 22, 1776   Flatbush

Staten Island

SIR WILLIAM HOWE

ADMIRAL LORD HOWE

CLINTON

ATLANTIC OCEAN

Morristown
(Winter Quarters)

Newark

Passaic River

Raritan River

New Brunswick

WASHINGTON

CORNWALLIS

Delaware River

Princeton
Jan 3, 1777

Newtown

Trenton
Dec 26, 1776

Asupink River

Pennsylvania

Bordentown   Allentown

Hackensack River   Hudson River

THE BATTLE OF SARATOGA

FRANCE RECOGNIZES THE INDEPENDENCE OF THE UNITED STATES

During the winter of 1776–1777, the British high command in London adopted a complicated plan for separating New England from the rest of the United States. It was based on General John Burgoyne's paper, "My Thoughts on Conducting the War from the Side of Canada." One army, led by Burgoyne, was to drive south from Canada though Lake Champlain to capture Fort Ticonderoga. Burgoyne would then march southward past Saratoga to the Albany area. A smaller force commanded by Colonel Barry St. Leger was to march east toward Albany from Lake Ontario. A third, under General Howe, would either advance up the Hudson River from New York or be left free to strike south in force to attack Philadelphia.

The scheme got off to a promising start. Burgoyne, at the head of an army consisting of 650 Loyalists, 500 Indians, 3,000 German mercenaries, 3,000 Redcoats, and 138 cannons left Fort St. Johns on the Richelieu river in mid-June. By the second week of July, the expedition had sailed down Lake Champlain, forced the evacuation of Fort Ticonderoga without losing a man, and driven off small American units southeast of the fort. Soon thereafter, the invaders entered heavily forested country, criss-crossed by deep ravines. They were burdened by an enormous baggage train. Eighteenth-century European armies were accustomed to bringing as many of the comforts of home with them on campaigns as possible. Burgoyne's personal equipage included, besides his mistress, his dress uniforms and a large supply of champagne. The commander of the German mercenaries, Baron von Riedesel, was accompanied by his wife and three children under the age of seven. Progress was slow. Retreating Patriots dammed streams and felled great trees across forest paths. Burgoyne's force was harassed by militia attacks as local residents exchanged plows, axes, and saws for muskets in order to protect their homes. Apparently oblivious of the increasing danger, Burgoyne proceeded southward (at an average rate of less than one mile per day for the better part of the month). After reaching Saratoga he was forced on the defensive by the arrival of ever-mounting numbers of militiamen. On September 19, at Bemis Heights near the town of Stillwater, he made a desperate attack on the entrenched Patriot army under General Horatio Gates, only to be thrown back with heavy losses.

Meanwhile, St. Leger had advanced from Fort Oswego on Lake Ontario as far as Fort Stanwix, which he placed under siege. He defeated one relief expedition at the Battle of Oriskany on August 6, but when an American army under Benedict Arnold arrived on the scene, he abandoned the siege and retreated to Fort Oswego.

As for General Howe, who was never one to hurry (his biographer notes that "a single-minded devotion to business" was not one of Howe's strong points), he decided to attack Philadelphia rather than Albany and set off for that purpose by sea.

It was not until October that a small British force under Sir Henry Clinton headed north to help Burgoyne, but before Clinton could get anywhere near the beleaguered Burgoyne, it was too late. On October 7 Burgoyne again tried to advance in the direction of Stillwater, only to be thrown back. He then retreated to Saratoga, where he was soon surrounded. On October 17 he surrendered. Some 5,700 soldiers, all that remained of his army, were marched off as prisoners of war.

When the news of Saratoga reached Europe, France, which was already supplying financial aid to the Americans, recognized the independence of the United States and signed a commercial treaty and an alliance guaranteeing the "independence absolute and unlimited" of the United States.

Surrender of General Burgoyne at Saratoga, by John Trumbull (above), a painting commissioned by Congress in 1817. The failure of two of the three components of the British pincer attack on Abany left Burgoyne vulnerable to the heavily reinforced Americans. After several weeks of fighting north of Albany, Burgoyne on October 17 surrendered his entire army to General Horatio Gates.

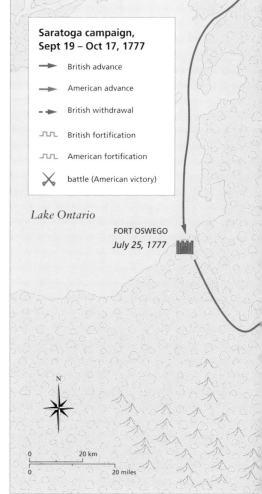

**Saratoga campaign,
Sept 19 – Oct 17, 1777**

→ British advance

→ American advance

⇢ British withdrawal

⎍ British fortification

⎍ American fortification

✕ battle (American victory)

Lake Ontario

FORT OSWEGO
July 25, 1777

0   20 km

0   20 miles

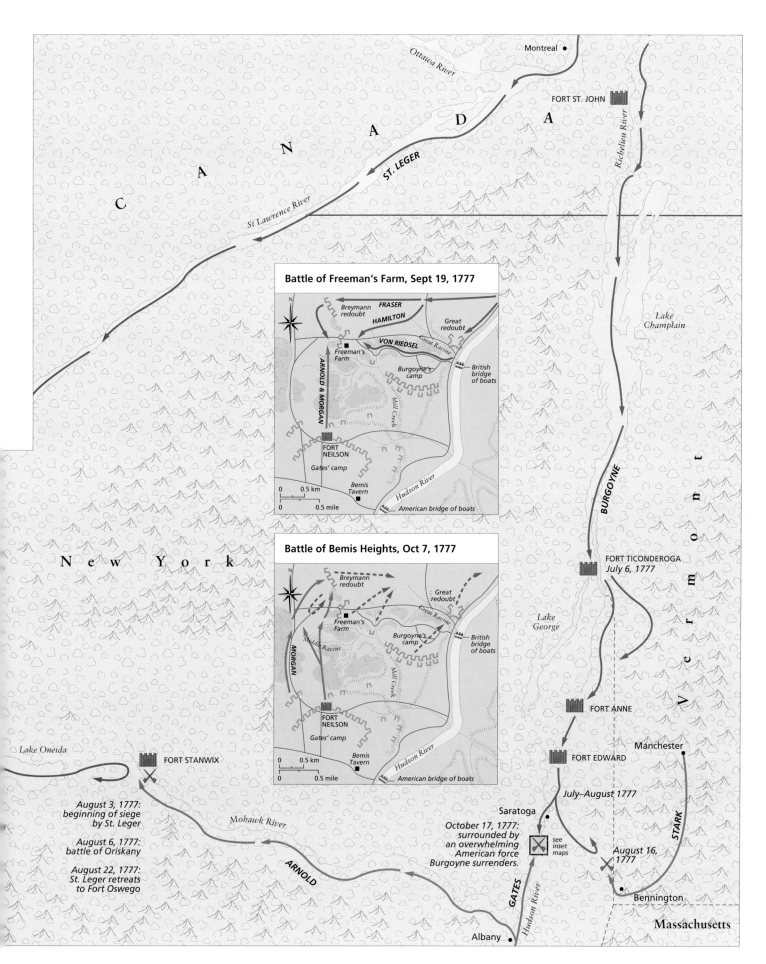

Montreal

FORT ST. JOHN

Ottawa River

ST. LEGER

St Lawrence River

C A N A D A

Richelieu River

Lake Champlain

BURGOYNE

FORT TICONDEROGA
July 6, 1777

Lake George

V e r m o n t

Battle of Freeman's Farm, Sept 19, 1777

N

Breymann redoubt   FRASER
HAMILTON
Great redoubt
ARNOLD & MORGAN
VON RIEDSEL
Great Ravine
■ *Freeman's Farm*
British bridge of boats
Burgoyne's camp
Mill Creek
FORT NEILSON
Gates' camp
Bemis Tavern
Hudson River
0   0.5 km
0   0.5 mile
American bridge of boats

Battle of Bemis Heights, Oct 7, 1777

N

Breymann redoubt
Great redoubt
Great Ravine
MORGAN
■ *Freeman's Farm*
British bridge of boats
Middle Ravine
Burgoyne's camp
Mill Creek
FORT NEILSON
Gates' camp
Bemis Tavern
Hudson River
0   0.5 km
0   0.5 mile
American bridge of boats

FORT ANNE

Manchester

FORT EDWARD

July–August 1777

STARK

N e w   Y o r k

Lake Oneida

FORT STANWIX

August 3, 1777:
beginning of siege
by St. Leger

August 6, 1777:
battle of Oriskany

August 22, 1777:
St. Leger retreats
to Fort Oswego

Mohawk River

ARNOLD

GATES

Hudson River

Saratoga

October 17, 1777:
surrounded by
an overwhelming
American force
Burgoyne surrenders.

see
inset
maps

August 16,
1777

Bennington

Massachusetts

Albany

67

THE WAR MOVES SOUTH
BRITISH INCURSIONS INTO THE CAROLINAS AND VIRGINIA

After the catastrophe at Saratoga, the British made no further effort to subdue the northern states. Instead they turned their attention to the Carolinas, where large numbers of Loyalists were thought to be ready to take up arms in support of the Crown. In December 1779, Sir Henry Clinton, who had replaced General Howe as commander-in-chief, left New York by sea with 8,500 troops and a formidable fleet. By March he had placed Charleston under siege and on May 12 the city surrendered. More than 5,000 Americans were taken prisoner. Clinton then returned to New York, leaving General Cornwallis to subdue the back country.

Cornwallis was confronted by a mixed force of Continentals and militia under General Horatio Gates, who had won an undeserved reputation for military acumen at Saratoga. At Camden, in north-central South Carolina, the two forces clashed, and in a matter of hours Gates's reputation had evaporated. Instead of relying on his veterans to bear the brunt of the British attack, he put raw militia in the front line. When the Redcoats attacked, bayonets fixed, the militiamen "ran like a torrent," most without firing a shot, and the battle was lost.

Fortunately for the Americans, Washington then replaced Gates with Nathanael Greene, who displayed a real talent both for hit-and-run warfare and the proper use of irregular troops, qualities that Cornwallis lacked. Militiamen were excellent shots, but tended to run when determined infantrymen continued to advance after enduring their volleys. Greene quickly learned to put them in the center of his

General Nathanael Greene, a young capable Rhode Islander, in a series of well planned engagements, sapped the strength of the British forces, finally obliging Cornwallis to withdraw to the coast.

fatigable Sumpter." The most important of these took place at King's Mountain in North Carolina, where only two months after the disaster at Camden a horde of "backwater men" had smashed the left wing of Cornwallis' army; at Cowpens in central South Carolina, where Continentals and militia units commanded by Brigadier General Daniel Morgan destroyed a Loyalist army the following January; and at Guilford Court House in

north-central North Carolina in March 1781, where Greene administered a thrashing to Cornwallis in a classic set-piece engagement.

After the battle of Guilford Court House, Cornwallis retreated to Wilmington, North Carolina, where he could be resupplied by sea. Greene, Marion, Sumter, and other local commanders were thus left free to regain control of South Carolina, which they did, though not without difficulty, in a series of attacks on British posts. By autumn only the Charleston area was still in British hands.

Cornwallis, however, did not long remain in Wilmington. In late April, reinforced and resupplied, he marched north into Virginia, where he received still more reinforcements, sent south by sea from New York. He conducted a series of raids deep into Virginia and one of his raiding parties almost captured Governor Thomas Jefferson and members of the state legislature that Jefferson was entertaining at his home at Monticello. New Patriot units commanded by the Marquis de Lafayette and General von Steuben checked Cornwallis' advance, and he retreated to his Yorktown base, near the mouth of Chesapeake Bay.

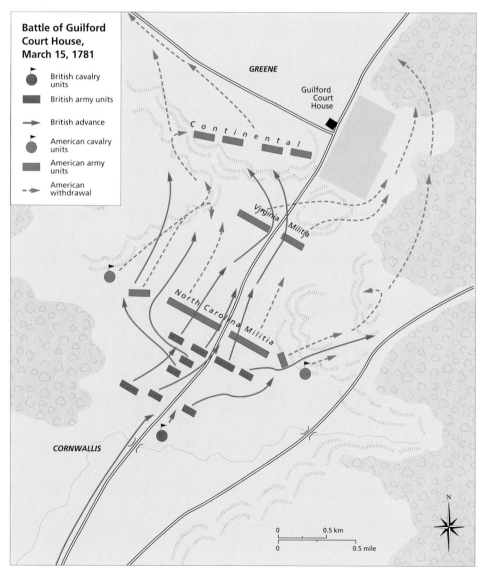

Battle of Guilford Court House, March 15, 1781

- 🔴 British cavalry units
- ▬ British army units
- → British advance
- ▸ American cavalry units
- ▬ American army units
- ⇢ American withdrawal

GREENE

Guilford Court House

Continental

Virginia Militia

North Carolina Militia

CORNWALLIS

0   0.5 km
0   0.5 mile

N

General, the Lord Cornwallis (above), commander of the British field force in the last campaign of the war.

force, have them fire a volley or two, and then fall back behind the more reliable regulars.

There followed an almost untrackable series of skirmishes and set battles, many extremely bloody. Nearly all of these clashes were won by the Americans. Some were commanded by Greene, others by guerrilla leaders such as the "Swamp Fox" Francis Marion, and Thomas Sumter, described by Cornwallis as *"the inde-*

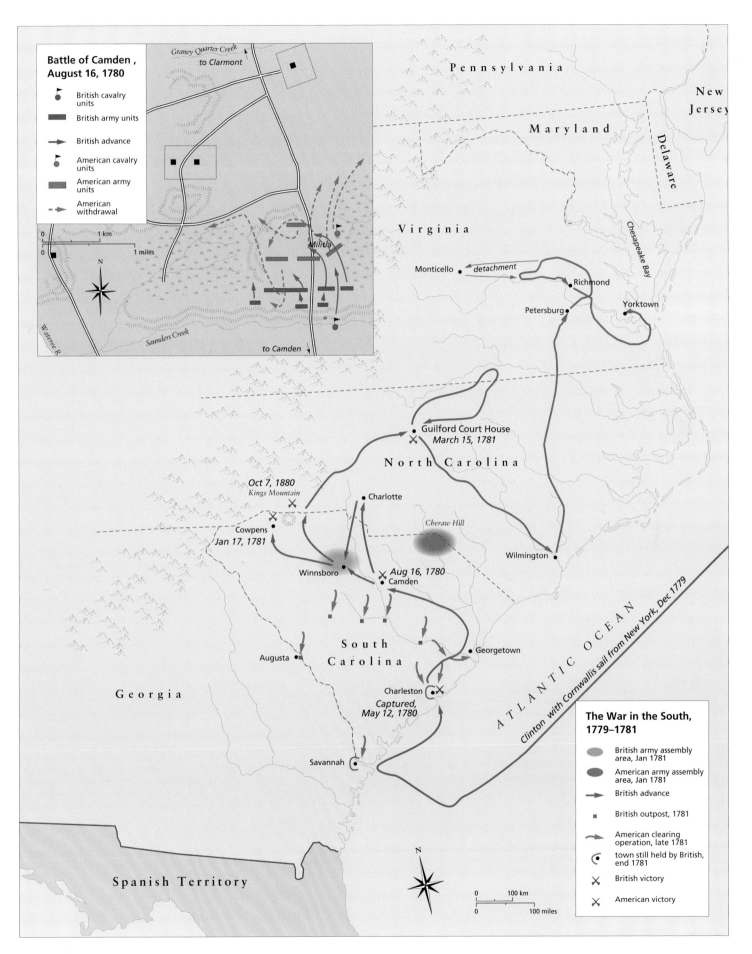

**Battle of Camden ,
August 16, 1780**

- British cavalry units
- British army units
- British advance
- American cavalry units
- American army units
- American withdrawal

Graney Quarter Creek

to Clarmont

Militia

Saunders Creek

Wateree R.

0   1 km
0   1 miles

N

to Camden

**The War in the South,
1779–1781**

- British army assembly area, Jan 1781
- American army assembly area, Jan 1781
- British advance
- British outpost, 1781
- American clearing operation, late 1781
- town still held by British, end 1781
- British victory
- American victory

P e n n s y l v a n i a

New Jersey

M a r y l a n d

Delaware

V i r g i n i a

Chesapeake Bay

Monticello   *detachment*   Richmond

Petersburg   Yorktown

Guilford Court House
March 15, 1781

N o r t h   C a r o l i n a

Oct 7, 1880
Kings Mountain

Charlotte

Cheraw Hill

Cowpens
Jan 17, 1781

Winnsboro

Wilmington

Aug 16, 1780
Camden

S o u t h
C a r o l i n a

Augusta

Georgetown

G e o r g i a

Charleston
*Captured,
May 12, 1780*

A T L A N T I C   O C E A N

Clinton with Cornwallis sail from New York, Dec 1779

Savannah

S p a n i s h   T e r r i t o r y

N

0   100 km
0   100 miles

THE BATTLE OF YORKTOWN

A FIERCE BOMBARDMENT LEADS TO BRITISH SURRENDER

The Battle of Yorktown was the last significant engagement of the War for Independence. It was in every sense a Franco-American operation, the only significant military engagement undertaken by the two nations as a result of the treaty of alliance signed in 1778. The campaign was complex by 18th-century standards, but it was extremely well coordinated, involving the cooperation of French troops commanded by the Comte de Rochambeau stationed at Newport, Rhode Island; Washington's army in the New York area; other American units confronting General Cornwallis in Virginia; and two French fleets, one at Newport, the other in the West Indies.

Washington was eager to attack General Clinton in New York City, and in May 1781, at a meeting with Rochambeau in Connecticut, he persuaded the Frenchman to join in the effort. The plan called for the support of the French West Indian fleet commanded by Admiral de Grasse, who was currently en route to the islands from France. In preparation for the assault on New York, Rochambeau's troops had joined with the Americans north of the city in early July. But before an attack could be mounted, Washington learned that de Grasse had left the Indies not for New York but for the Yorktown area.

Washington immediately decided to bypass New York and hurry to Virginia. Leaving a skeleton force outside New York in the hope of convincing Clinton that an attack was imminent, he and Rochambeau marched off on August 21 with 9,000 men. At the same time, the French squadron at Newport, commanded by the Comte de Barras, slipped out of the harbor, evaded blockading British vessels, and sailed for Chesapeake Bay laden with French siege guns.

De Grasse left Haiti on August 5, but sailed first to Cuba, partly to deceive the British

The Yorktown campaign, April – September 1781

English maneuvers:

→ Cornwallis

→ Graves

US maneuvers:

→ Washington

French maneuvers:

→ De Barras

→ Lafayette

→ De Grasse

→ Rochambeau

about his eventual destination. A few days later British Admiral Sir Samuel Hood sailed directly for Yorktown, but when he arrived on August 25 there were no French warships in sight, so he went on to New York. The very next day, August 29, de Grasse arrived and quickly landed 3,000 soldiers to join with American units commanded by the Marquis de Lafayette and General von Steuben, who were hemming in Cornwallis. De Grasse then deployed his ships to blockade Yorktown.

Events now unfolded in rapid-fire order. On September 5, 19 British warships, under Admiral Thomas Graves and Admiral Hood, arrived off the Chesapeake. De Grasse gave battle at once. The fight was inconclusive, but the British suffered much heavier damage, and in the course of the struggle, during which the fleets moved in a southeasterly direction to a point nearly a hundred miles from Yorktown, de Barras's squadron from Newport reached the mouth of the Chesapeake. Admiral Graves, battered and now badly outnumbered, gave up all hope of relieving Cornwallis and sailed back to New York. The French thus obtained total command of the seas around Yorktown.

Next, de Grasse dispatched transports to bring Washington's army, which was waiting at the head of the Chesapeake, to the scene, and Barras unloaded the French artillery. Cornwallis was doomed. Washington had at his disposal nearly 17,000 men, and a force almost as large was also at hand on the French warships. French and American batteries pounded the defenses of Yorktown incessantly. Advancing through the trenches that had been dug to protect them from British fire, the allied army drew closer and closer to the British lines.

Back in New York, General Clinton prepared a new relief expedition consisting of 7,000 soldiers and a fleet of 25 ships of the line. It sailed off on October 19, but was already too late. Cornwallis, his position subject to continuous bombardment so heavy that, as he put it, "we dare not show a gun," asked for terms on October 17. Two days later, while Clinton's fleet was leaving New York harbor, Cornwallis formally surrendered.

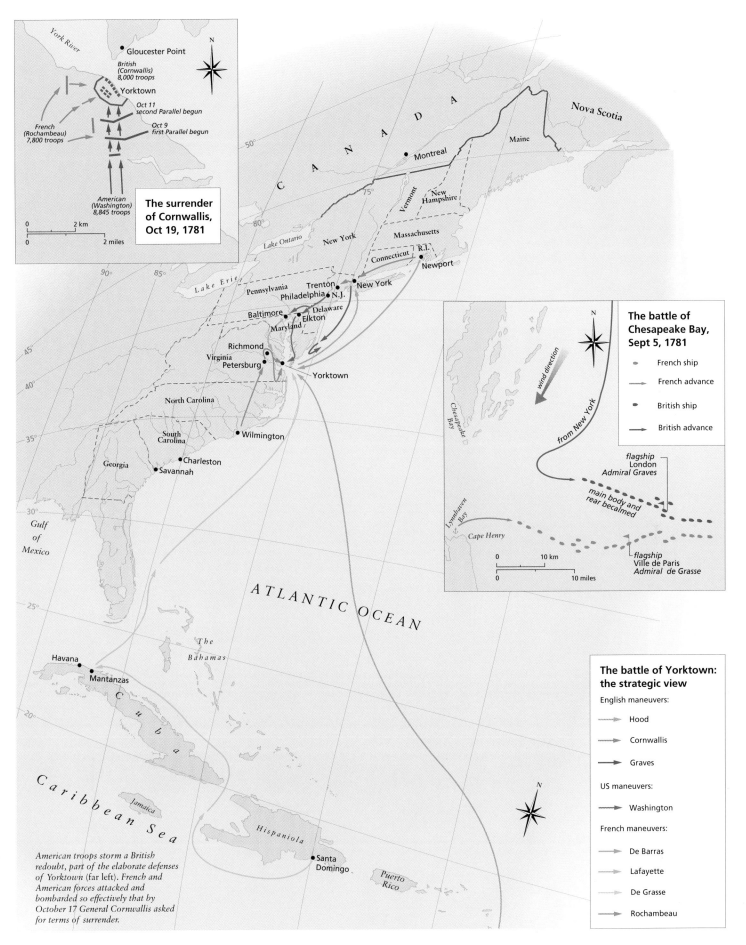

The surrender of Cornwallis, Oct 19, 1781

York River

● Gloucester Point

British (Cornwallis) 8,000 troops

Yorktown

Oct 11 second Parallel begun

Oct 9 first Parallel begun

French (Rochambeau) 7,800 troops

American (Washington) 8,845 troops

N

| 0 | | 2 km |
| 0 | | 2 miles |

The battle of Chesapeake Bay, Sept 5, 1781

N

- ● French ship
- → French advance
- ● British ship
- → British advance

wind direction

from New York

flagship London Admiral Graves

main body and rear becalmed

Chesapeake Bay

Lynnhaven Bay

Cape Henry

flagship Ville de Paris Admiral de Grasse

| 0 | 10 km |
| 0 | 10 miles |

CANADA

Nova Scotia

Montreal

Maine

Lake Ontario

New York

Vermont

New Hampshire

Massachusetts

R.I.

Connecticut

Newport

Lake Erie

Pennsylvania

Trenton

New York

Philadelphia

N.J.

Baltimore

Delaware

Elkton

Maryland

Richmond

Virginia

Petersburg

Yorktown

North Carolina

South Carolina

Wilmington

Georgia

Charleston

Savannah

Gulf of Mexico

ATLANTIC OCEAN

The Bahamas

Havana

Mantanzas

Cuba

Jamaica

Caribbean Sea

Hispaniola

Santa Domingo

Puerto Rico

50°

75°

80°

90°

85°

45°

40°

35°

30°

25°

20°

The battle of Yorktown: the strategic view

English maneuvers:

- → Hood
- → Cornwallis
- → Graves

US maneuvers:

- → Washington

French maneuvers:

- → De Barras
- → Lafayette
- → De Grasse
- → Rochambeau

American troops storm a British redoubt, part of the elaborate defenses of Yorktown (far left). French and American forces attacked and bombarded so effectively that by October 17 General Cornwallis asked for terms of surrender.

PEOPLE OF THE NEW NATION
THE COMPLEXITY OF NATIONAL IDENTITY

In 1790, the year after George Washington took office as the first president of the United States, Congress, as required by the Constitution, undertook a census for the purpose of apportioning representation and direct taxes among the states. The result was the first "snapshot" of the population of the United States. It provides important insights into who Americans were and where they lived. Census statistics, subdivided by race, age, and gender help to determine the amount of labor available, the kinds of institutions that a community needs and can support, and political choices about who exercises power and for what ends.

The 1790 census sheds light on all these topics, but it does have limits. Because it was to be used for apportionment, Congress saw no need for the detailed questions that became standard in the 19th century, and had been common in colonial censuses. Slaves, for example, were counted separately, but no effort was made to distinguish them by age or sex, because they were considered only three-fifths of a free person for the purposes of apportionment. Among whites, women, who had no political or military power or responsibilities, were counted with girls. Only white males were divided at 16, when taxes were levied and militia duty expected. Thus the map of age and sex composition is for whites, and age is for males.

By 1790, the scattered and isolated settlements of the early years of colonization had grown to almost 4 million people along most of the Atlantic seaboard and well inland. Individual state populations ranged from 59,000 in Delaware to 748,000 in Virginia. As the figure on the growth of the colonial and English population shows, the colonial population experienced one of the first population explosions, with increases averaging about three percent per year after 1700. This meant that the population doubled in about 25 years. Only the spurt of growth in England after 1740 prevented the colonial population from catching that of the mother country by 1800. Much of America's growth after 1700 was the result of large families, which meant that the population was very young. Immigration, however, also contributed to the increase. Generally, immigrants were older males, and so affected the age and gender composition of regions where they were common.

Within the country, different regions have quite different types of people. The maps here show, for each of the 285 counties in the United States, three of the most important demographic characteristics: race, age, and sex.

The map of the proportion of the population that was black shows that the racial make-up of counties was subject to wide variation. In 1790, the national population was 19.3 percent black, but many counties diverged markedly from the norm. Generally, the proportion of blacks increased from north to south, in spite of the fact that slavery had been present in all the northern states before 1780. Although all the counties with black majorities were in the south, and most were in the lowlands near the Atlantic, not all southern counties had a large proportion of slaves. But with the exception of four Virginia counties that eventually became part of West Virginia, all the counties that were less than 5 percent black were from Pennsylvania and north. Of the counties with under 10 percent blacks, 25 were in the south, though, as the map demonstrates, many were in the interior. The contrast between the interior of North Carolina and the coastal regions of South Carolina and Georgia was dramatic. Slave labor was an important economic and social structure of that part of the country, almost unknown elsewhere.

To put the figures for 1790 in proper perspective, age and gender pyramids for 1770 (estimated) and 1980 have been included. It is clear that the early population was much more youthful, and hence the proportion of people in the labor force was much lower, even though children could contribute some work on farms. Less obvious is that women were a majority in 1980, a situation that first occurred in 1950.

The white population was relatively homogeneous in terms of age and gender. In 240 counties, between 45 and 55 percent of the people were under 16. To the extent that counties deviated from national standards, it was often

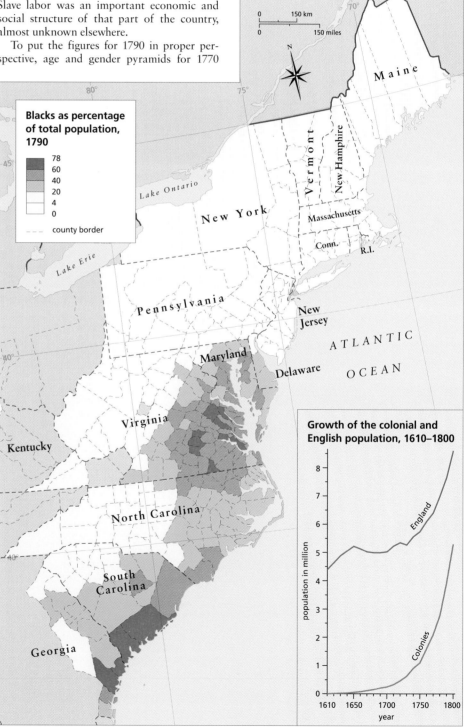

Blacks as percentage of total population, 1790

78
60
40
20
4
0

county border

Growth of the colonial and English population, 1610–1800

on an east–west axis. Of the 27 counties in which more than 55 percent of the white males were under 16, many were in the southern backcountry, with two in Pennsylvania and one in Rhode Island. Some of the lowest proportions of young people were also in the south, along the coast. In the north, two types of counties had relatively few children. On the frontier of Vermont and New York, the process of settlement was still dominated by adult males. The 1,074 residents of Ontario County, New York were 75 percent adult and 68 percent male; there were only ten blacks. Cities such as Boston, New York City, and Philadelphia tended to have more adults than average.

The range of variation in the gender ratio (here the percent male) was very small. The national population was 51 percent male, as 204 counties fell within the range of 50 to 52

percent male, and only 47 had a female majority of any kind. Surprisingly, a number of them were in the south. Traditionally, eastern New England was seen as the place of female surpluses, because of migration to the west. The extreme frontier areas of Vermont and New York were among the counties with more than 55 percent male, but there were similar regions in South Carolina and Georgia. Often, a high gender ratio meant low proportion of children. As is evident from the map, the relationship was not perfect.

Robert V. Wells

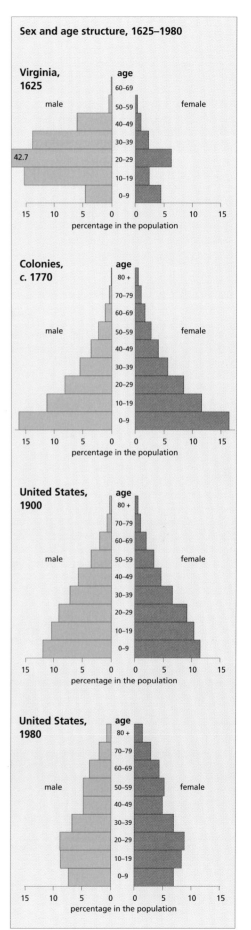

Sex and age structure, 1625–1980

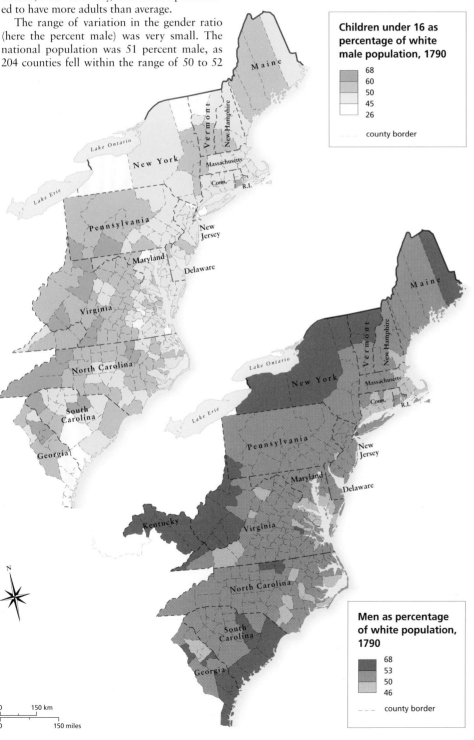

Children under 16 as percentage of white male population, 1790

68
60
50
45
26

county border

Men as percentage of white population, 1790

68
53
50
46

county border

0   150 km

0   150 miles

73

POLITICAL CONFLICT IN THE NEW NATION

FRONTIERSMEN VERSUS EASTERNERS

Although all the British colonies in America developed separately, and although social and economic conditions differed greatly from one to another, a common pattern of political development occurred in all: representation in the legislatures was based on geography. The legislators were elected by voters from particular townships or counties. This had the obvious democratic advantage of assuring that each political unit had a voice in the colonial government and that the lawmakers were under considerable pressure to act in accordance with their best judgment of how "the people" of their district felt about the matter at hand when they voted. However, this decentralized system often caused problems.

The chief flaw in the system was that in the rapidly developing colonies people were constantly moving westward into territory beyond existing towns and counties. Inevitably, settlers in frontier districts had interests that conflicted with those in older regions. Settlers wanted land to be cheap and readily available, whereas the inhabitants of coastal areas tended to think that cheap, fertile land in the west would depress the value of their already developed property. Westerners wanted the legislatures to provide men and money to help them in their conflicts with Indians. They also wanted the colonial government to spend money building and repairing roads and making other "internal improvements" in order to make it easier and cheaper for them to get their furs and farm products to market. In most instances, easterners objected to such expenditures, at least on the scale that the westerners desired.

These conflicts were inherent in the situation. But they were much exacerbated by the fact that in many colonies, westerners were not fairly represented in the colonial legislatures. Existing lawmakers (voting in the interests of their constituents) tended either not to create new districts at all or to make them so large that people living in them were badly underrepresented in the legislature. As early as the 1670s, representation in the oldest colonial legislature, the Virginia House of Burgesses, was so skewed in favor of the tidewater planters (there had not even been an election in 15 years) that frontier settlers took up arms, marched eastward, burned Jamestown to the ground, and forced the royal governor to flee.

In the New England colonies, where western lands were settled by the movement of whole communities to townships authorized by the legislature, the size of each unit was essentially the same, so the distribution of voting power was much fairer. East–west conflicts of interest with their resulting resentments existed, but the settlement of disagreements was achieved by something approaching majority rule. But at the time of the Revolution in every colony

south of New England, the seaboard districts dominated the government to a far greater extent than their population warranted.

The votes in the separate states on the ratification of the new Constitution reflect the different interests of eastern and western citizens to some extent, though of course there were other reasons why people favored or supported the new frame of government. Geographical factors were less important in New England for the reason just stated, but they nonetheless affected how people felt about the new, more powerful central government that they were asked to consider. In general, what the historian Jackson Turner Main (a grandson of the author of the "frontier thesis," Frederick Jackson Turner) calls "cosmopolitans" tended to support the Constitution, while "localists" opposed it. There were a great number of exceptions, but the preponderance of merchants and eastern people of wealth were pro-Constitution. The typical small farmer opposed it, principally, it seems, out of fear that "outsiders" would be able to restrict their

liberty the way the British had, before independence had been won.

To an extent this was true also in New York, though in that state rival groups within the cosmopolitan elite took sides for reasons that had little to do with economic or geographic factors. In Pennsylvania, however, and throughout most of the South, east–west divisions remained strong, as the map (below) makes clear. Indeed there were western districts where people seem to have voted for or against the Constitution simply to oppose the position taken by the tidewater planters.

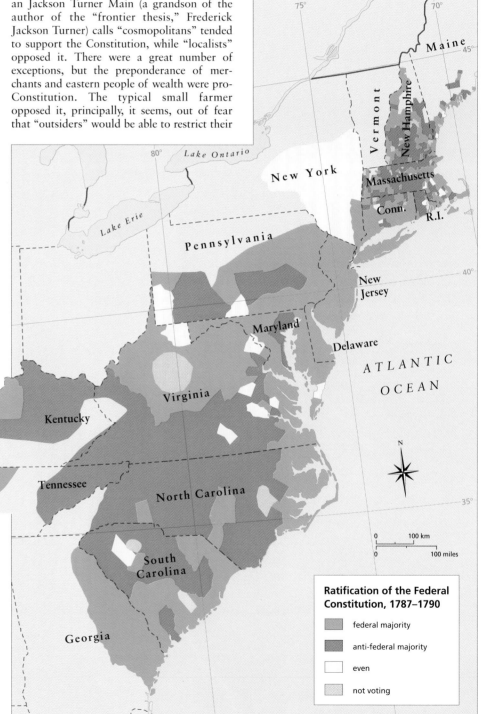

Ratification of the Federal Constitution, 1787–1790

- federal majority
- anti-federal majority
- even
- not voting

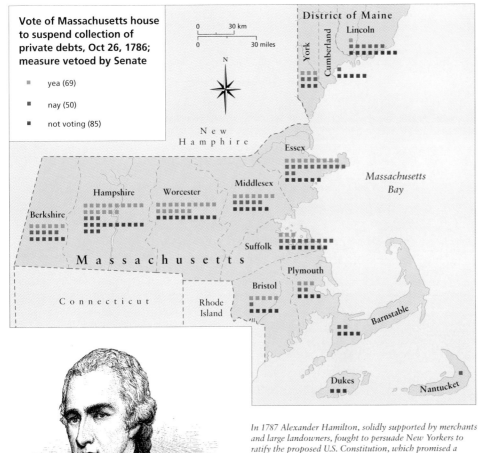

Vote of Massachusetts house to suspend collection of private debts, Oct 26, 1786; measure vetoed by Senate

- yea (69)
- nay (50)
- not voting (85)

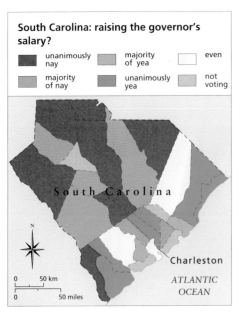

In 1787 Alexander Hamilton, solidly supported by merchants and large landowners, fought to persuade New Yorkers to ratify the proposed U.S. Constitution, which promised a strong federal government. His most important contribution was a set of essays called The Federalist. In 1788, Hamilton's oratory helped persuade the New York State convention to vote for ratification: New York City delegates generally favored ratification, and rural upstate voters opposed it.

South Carolina: raising the governor's salary?

- unanimously nay
- majority of nay
- majority of yea
- unanimously yea
- even
- not voting

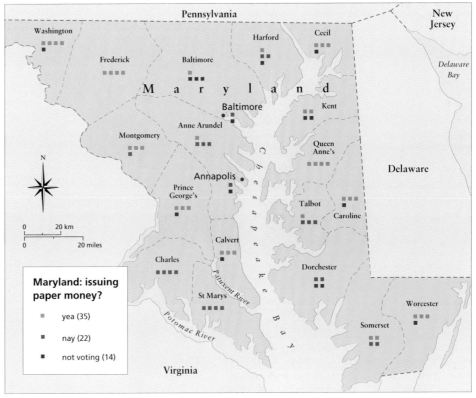

Maryland: issuing paper money?

- yea (35)
- nay (22)
- not voting (14)

Shays' Rebellion

In 1786, the Massachusetts Supreme Court voted down a bill suspending the collection of debts. A postwar depression, combined with steep property taxes, had hit debt-ridden western farmers hard. When the legislature refused to provide them with "relief," westerners, led by Daniel Shays, staged the "rebellion" that bears his name. The division in the legislature on debt relief was clear-cut: the easterners were against the westerners. Troops were dispatched, the rebels were routed, and Shays fled to Vermont.

In 1787, only months after the collapse of Shays' Rebellion, a similar issue divided South Carolinians. Again the issue was money, in this case a bill fixing the salary of the governor at the princely sum of £1,000. Here the rural, "loyalist" interests were against the measure, while the tidewater delegates, representing the well-to-do planters, supported it. In this instance the "have-nots" carried the day when the bill was defeated by 54 yeas to 63 nays. The legislators then voted to pay the governor a more modest sum, £800.

The same type of east–west division that led to Shays' Rebellion in Massachusetts occurred in 1785 in Maryland, the particular issue in this case being a bill requiring the state to issue paper money in the form of "bills of credit." A majority of the legislators from the older counties on lower Chesapeake Bay opposed the measure, but elsewhere support of the bill was strong; it passed by 38 to 22, with the "inland" counties of Washington, Frederick, Montgomery, and Prince George's backing it by 13 to 1. It was defeated, however, in the Maryland upper house.

CLAIMING THE WEST
STATE-MAKING AND SPECULATION ALONG THE FRONTIER

America's great attraction for European settlers was its enormous expanse of undeveloped land. The forests, furs, and perhaps gold and silver of the land promised quick wealth, but ultimately land as a place to build homes, grow crops, or raise livestock was at the heart of its appeal. There was far more land than the first settlers could possibly use, more even than they could imagine, but many obstacles blocked their access to it. Not the least of these were the Indians, whose land it already was. Much of colonial history resulted from the settlers' efforts to gain control of the unknown wealth that lay, in their minds, over the next hill.

The first English "owners" of land in America were the rulers in whose names the land had been claimed by various explorers. The kings later granted portions of their American domain to individuals and groups, either as a form of royal largesse, or in exchange for a share of the future product of the area or past services of one kind or another. James I, for example, gave Virginia to the founders of the Virginia Company in exchange for one-fifth of the gold and silver and one-fifteenth of the copper "to be gotten or had" in that colony, and Charles II presented William Penn with Pennsylvania as payment of a debt of £16,000 he owed Penn's late father.

All grants spelled out the boundaries of such properties, but no one in England had ever seen, much less mapped or surveyed, anything in America more than a few miles from the coastline. The charter granted by Charles I to the founders of Massachusetts Bay precisely defined the northern and southern borders of the colony and then added, "in Length and Longitude ... from the Atlantick ... on the East Parte, to the South Sea [*i.e.*, the Pacific Ocean] on the West Parte."

In 1629, when Charles made this grant, and for decades thereafter, no one had any idea how far west the South Sea was. At the time it did not matter because 17th-century settlers had all the land they could handle right where they were. But as grant after grant was made over the years, overlapping occurred. The most confusing of all was one of the first, which defined the boundaries of Virginia as running from 200 miles north and south of Point Comfort, on the Atlantic, "*throughout from Sea to Sea, West, and Northwest.*" This was eventually interpreted by the Virginians to mean most of North America north of North Carolina, even (had they known of its existence) Alaska.

Massachusetts and Connecticut had rival claims to parts of what later became Ohio, as did Pennsylvania. The boundaries of Georgia, South Carolina, and North Carolina overlapped. Spain further complicated matters by insisting that Florida extended far into these English "possessions." France had set up trading posts on land that Virginia and the New England colonies considered theirs.

So long as no one tried to occupy these lands, the conflicting claims were not important. East of the Appalachians, where the English colonists actually lived during the first 100 years of settlement, there were some boundary disputes, but they remained relatively insignificant.

Transylvania

In 1775 a group of North Carolina speculators employed Daniel Boone to lead a party of settlers into what they hoped would become Transylvania, in what is now eastern Kentucky and Tennessee. The following year other settlers from Pennsylvania proposed creating a vaguely defined state of Westsylvania. Neither of these efforts at state-making succeeded.

During and after the American Revolution, all states with trans-Appalachian claims ceded them to Congress, but federal ownership of the land did not determine who would occupy it or how it would be governed. In 1784 another group of settlers founded the State of Franklin and elected John Sevier governor, but it was not recognized by the federal government and eventually disintegrated.

Cartright and Jefferson

However ill-conceived Transylvania, Franklin, and other such "governments" were, they

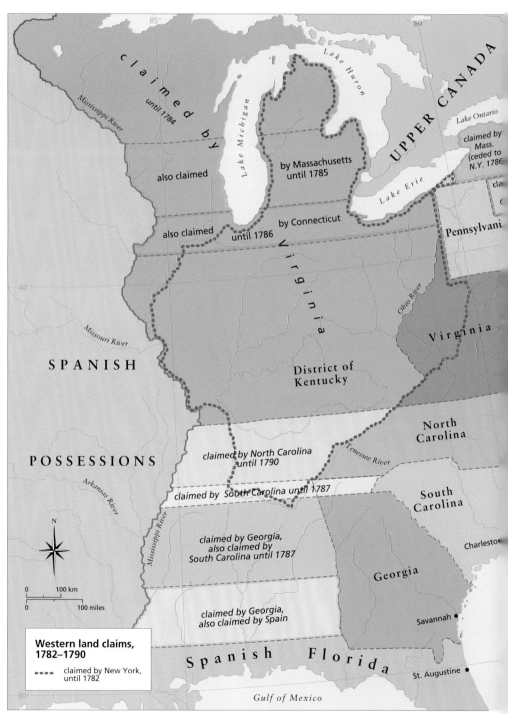

Western land claims, 1782–1790

···· claimed by New York, until 1782

reflected actual conditions. "Lawless" frontier communities badly needed governments and their inhabitants would willingly supply them if a better-established authority did not make the effort.

Actually, this had been obvious from the start; as early as 1774 an English radical, John Cartright, had proposed turning the 13 colonies and the area east of the Mississippi River into self-governing, but not independent, states. Cartright drew an inaccurate but revealing map of American colonies showing western states with names like Chicasawria and Mansisipia, and Erieland.

In 1784 Thomas Jefferson drafted a more accurate plan neatly divided by north–south and east–west lines.

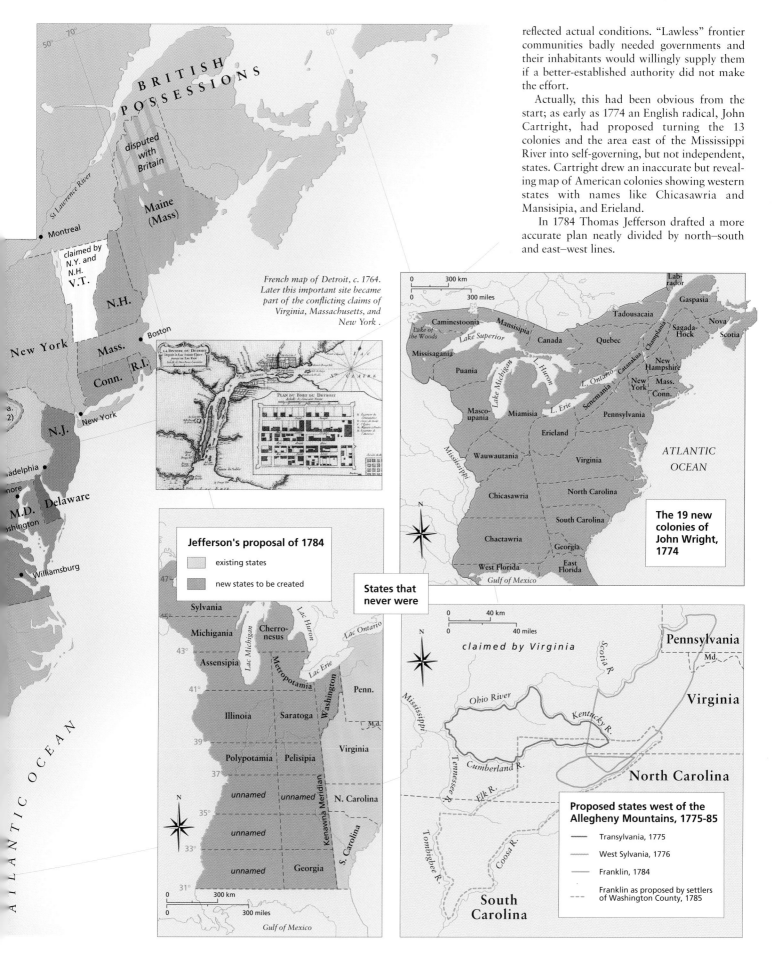

French map of Detroit, c. 1764. Later this important site became part of the conflicting claims of Virginia, Massachusetts, and New York .

Jefferson's proposal of 1784

existing states

new states to be created

States that never were

The 19 new colonies of John Wright, 1774

Proposed states west of the Allegheny Mountains, 1775-85

Transylvania, 1775

West Sylvania, 1776

Franklin, 1784

Franklin as proposed by settlers of Washington County, 1785

LEWIS AND CLARK
SHATTERED DREAMS OF A WATER ROUTE ACROSS THE CONTINENT

In 1803 President Thomas Jefferson dispatched Robert R. Livingston to Paris to negotiate the purchase of New Orleans and Florida. On April 10, Napoleon Bonaparte, preoccupied with new campaigns in Europe, instructed Foreign Minister Talleyrand to sell the entire province of Louisiana. Livingston, thunderstruck by the proposal, asked for a few days to think it over. When James Monroe, also representing the president, arrived the next day, the two negotiators agreed to buy Louisiana for $15 million. What exactly they had purchased, however, was unclear. When Livingston asked about the province's boundaries, Talleyrand replied: "I can give you no direction. You have made a noble bargain for yourselves, and I suppose you will make the most of it."

For centuries, European explorers assumed the existence of a water passage through the North Ameriacan continent to a western sea. When explorers of New France happened upon the Missouri River, which originated beyond the western horizon, they thought that they had found the solution to what historian Bernard DeVoto has termed the "Northwestern Mystery." Generations of French, British, and Spanish geographers, explorers, and empire builders marshalled the fragmentary reports of fur traders and Indians to confirm their optimism about the possibility of an all-water passage through the trans-Missouri region.

One of the earliest representations of a possible northwest passage appeared in a map, published in 1758, by a French traveler, Simon le Page du Pratz. He cited an Indian, Moncacht-Ape, who claimed to have followed the Missouri nearly to its source. Then he took a brief portage northward to a "Beautiful River" that emptied into a western ocean. Du Pratz assumed that both the Missouri and the "Beautiful River" traversed a wide plain bordered by a northern mountain range terminating at the 42nd parallel, and a southern range terminating at the 37th parallel.

In 1784 Peter Pond, an employee of the Northwest Company, depicted the "Stony Mountains" as a single, unbroken ridge that extended as far south as the 39th parallel. But most assumed that these "Stony Mountains" were comparable in size to the Blue Ridge Mountains of Virginia, and thus posed no formidable barrier. Moreover, Pond located the headwaters of the Missouri near what he called the Naberkistagen River, which led to a "South Sea." The two rivers might be linked by a short portage, or conceivably, by a canal.

The Rockies were missing entirely from Jedediah Morse's map of 1797. Like du Pratz, Morse depicted the trans-Missouri as consisting of "very extensive plains" and added a "River of the West" originating near the Missouri and flowing into the Pacific. Aaron Arrowsmith's 1802 map more accurately located the Rockies, but he also assumed a short

portage between the headwaters of the Missouri and a tributary to the Oregon River. The following year, Nicholas King modified Arrowsmith's map in several significant ways. He placed the "River of the West," renamed the Great Lake River, still closer to the Missouri and, even more important, he assumed that the Rocky Mountain chain terminated at about the 45th or 46th parallel. Through the "conjectural" plains to the south, he posited another Pacific-draining river, represented as a dotted line, originating near the Missouri. Samuel Lewis' map of 1804 pushed the Rockies almost to the West Coast, and depicted them as a broken range that would little impede westward settlement or commerce. All assumed that the Missouri and some westward-flowing river were separated by little more than a short portage.

Lewis and Clark
President Jefferson, who had long been interested in exploring the Missouri, had acquired many maps of the region. Upon learning that Livingston and Monroe had bought all of Louisiana, he despatched Meriwether Lewis, his private secretary, on an expedition to ascertain whether the Missouri would provide "water communication across this continent for the purposes of commerce." Lewis chose as his companion officer William Clark.

In the spring of 1804, Lewis and Clark led a group of 48 men up the Missouri. By late fall they had reached what is now North Dakota, where they built a small station, Fort Mandan, and spent the winter. In April 1805, they struck out again. In June they arrived at the Great Falls of the Missouri, but soon thereafter the Missouri became too shallow for easy navigation. After weeks of traveling through a "wild and mountainous country," the explorers located the source of the Missouri. Beyond the adjacent ridge they envisioned an expansive plain falling gently away to the western shores.

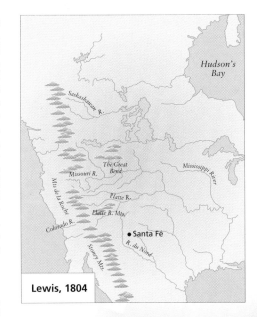

Lewis, 1804

But upon attaining the summit, they found instead only a succession of "immense ranges of high mountains." In October, when they finally arrived at the "River of the West"—the raging Columbia River—it had become obvious that the northwest passage of geographical lore did not exist.

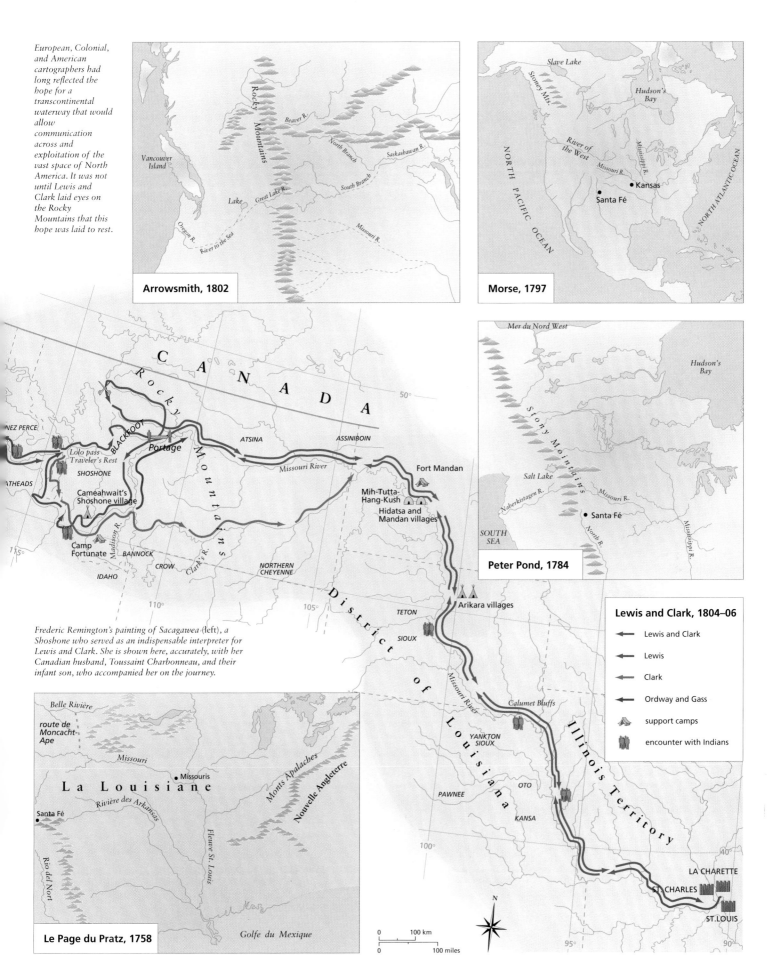

European, Colonial, and American cartographers had long reflected the hope for a transcontinental waterway that would allow communication across and exploitation of the vast space of North America. It was not until Lewis and Clark laid eyes on the Rocky Mountains that this hope was laid to rest.

Arrowsmith, 1802

Vancouver Island

Rocky Mountains

Beaver R.

North Branch

Saskashawan R.

South Branch

Lake

Great Lake R.

Oregon R.

River to the Sea

Missouri R.

Morse, 1797

Slave Lake

Stoney Mts.

Hudson's Bay

NORTH PACIFIC OCEAN

River of the West

Missouri R.

Mississippi R.

• Kansas

Santa Fé

NORTH ATLANTIC OCEAN

Peter Pond, 1784

Mer du Nord West

Hudson's Bay

Stony Mountains

Salt Lake

Naberkistagen R.

Missouri R.

SOUTH SEA

• Santa Fé

North R.

Mississippi R.

CANADA

Rocky Mountains

NEZ PERCE

Lolo pass
Traveler's Rest

BLACKFOOT

Portage

ATSINA

ASSINIBOIN

SHOSHONE

FLATHEADS

Caméahwait's Shoshone village

Missouri River

Fort Mandan

Mih-Tutta-Hang-Kush

Hidatsa and Mandan villages

Camp Fortunate

Madison R.

BANNOCK

CROW

Clark's R.

NORTHERN CHEYENNE

IDAHO

50°

115°

110°

105°

District of Louisiana

Arikara villages

TETON

SIOUX

Frederic Remington's painting of Sacagawea (left), a Shoshone who served as an indispensable interpreter for Lewis and Clark. She is shown here, accurately, with her Canadian husband, Toussaint Charbonneau, and their infant son, who accompanied her on the journey.

Lewis and Clark, 1804–06

← Lewis and Clark
← Lewis
← Clark
← Ordway and Gass
⛺ support camps
🚶 encounter with Indians

Missouri River

Calumet Bluffs

YANKTON SIOUX

PAWNEE

OTO

KANSA

100°

Illinois Territory

LA CHARETTE

ST. CHARLES

ST. LOUIS

40°

95°

90°

Le Page du Pratz, 1758

Belle Rivière

route de Moncacht-Ape

Missouri

La Louisiane

• Missouris

Rivière des Arkansas

Santa Fé

Rio del Nort

Fleuve St. Louis

Monts Apalaches

Nouvelle Angleterre

Golfe du Mexique

N

0   100 km

0   100 miles

THE WAR OF 1812
NEW WORLD REFLECTIONS OF EUROPEAN CONFLICT

The War of 1812 was a by-product of the centuries-long conflict between Great Britain and France that came to a climax in the wars of the French Revolution and Napoleon. The United States became involved chiefly because it sought to trade with both sides, each of which, while eager to obtain American products, did everything in its power to prevent Americans from trading with its enemy. In the end, the United States declared war on Great Britain rather than France because the powerful British navy did more damage to American shipping. Anglophobia dating back to the Revolution (and the expectation that sparely-populated Canada would be an easy target) also tipped the balance.

Congress declared war on Great Britain in June 1812. That summer and fall, American frigates won three brilliant single-ship engagements against British vessels at scattered points in the Atlantic. But the British fleet soon concentrated against them, and thereafter the frigates were pinned to their moorings while British squadrons ranged unopposed along the coast.

On land, the war passed through three phases, distinct both in place and time. The longest phase, lasting from July 1812 to the fall of 1814, took place along the Canadian border all the way from Detroit to Lake Champlain, and was almost universally disastrous for American arms. General William Hull, governor of the Michigan Territory, attempting a foray into Canadian territory, was sent scurrying back to Detroit, where he surrendered to Canadian pursuers without firing a shot. British units also seized forts Mackinac and Dearborn at the northern and southern ends of Lake Michigan. In October, another American force attempted to invade Canada from Fort Niagara, only to be driven back. A third, designed to capture Montreal from a base at Plattsburg, New York, had to be abandoned when New York militiamen refused to advance across the border.

In September 1813, an American squadron on Lake Erie commanded by Captain Oliver Hazard Perry destroyed a British fleet at Put-in-Bay, thus gaining control of the lake. This compelled the British to evacuate Fort Detroit. General William Henry Harrison pursued them and in October won a solid victory in the Battle of the Thames. However, another British force captured Fort Niagara and burned the town of Buffalo. Later on, in 1814, fighting taking place in the Lake Champlain area proved equally indecisive.

The second phase of the war involved a British amphibious attack on Washington and Baltimore. In mid-August 1814 a force of 4,000 veteran Redcoats landed at the mouth of the Pautuxent River southwest of the capital and routed a much larger American army at Bladensburg. With President Madison and the members of Congress in ignominious flight, the British troops swept into undefended

Washington and burned the White House and other government buildings to the ground. They then re-embarked and sailed up Chesapeake Bay to attack Baltimore. Their combined land-sea attack (immortalized in "The Star Spangled Banner") began on September 12, but American militiamen had constructed solid fortifications. When a night-long naval bombardment of Fort McHenry failed to cause the defenders to surrender, the British withdrew to their ships and sailed off to Jamaica in the Caribbean, where the British prepared for what became the last phase of the war, an attack on New Orleans.

On Jamaica, the British had gathered an army of 11,000 men commanded by Sir Edward Pakenham and a fleet of 60 ships to transport it to the mouth of the Mississippi. New Orleans was defended by General Andrew Jackson, fresh from victories over British-backed Indians in Alabama and Florida. Pakenham landed his troops at Lake Borne east of New Orleans and marched them through swampy land toward New Orleans.

Jackson placed his men and cannons behind a palisade along a dry canal five miles south of the city. To attack this formidable position, the British had to cross an open field between the

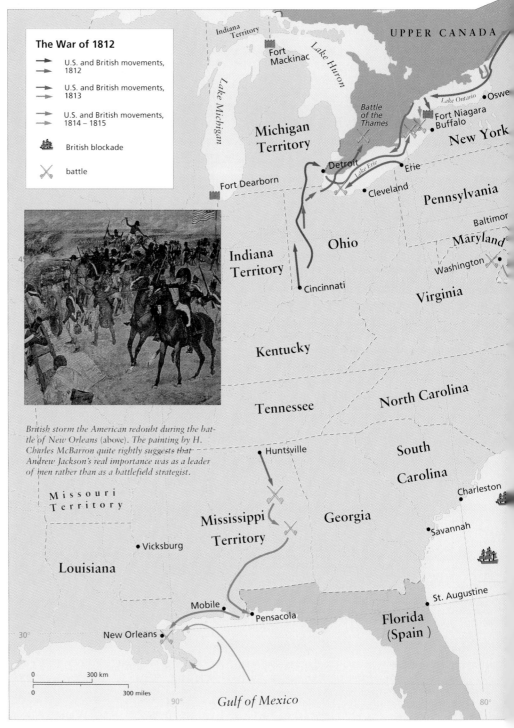

British storm the American redoubt during the battle of New Orleans (above). The painting by H. Charles McBarron quite rightly suggests that Andrew Jackson's real importance was as a leader of men rather than as a battlefield strategist.

The War of 1812

→→ U.S. and British movements, 1812

→→ U.S. and British movements, 1813

→→ U.S. and British movements, 1814 – 1815

British blockade

✕ battle

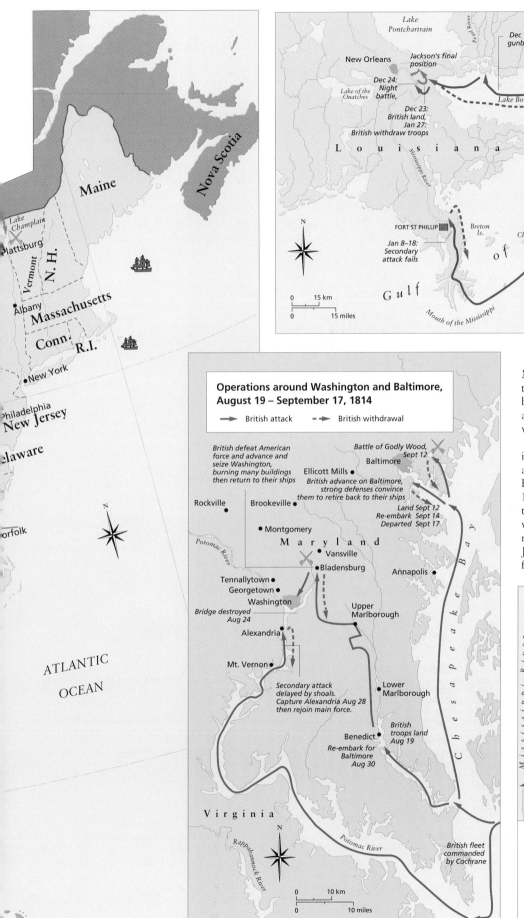

British New Orleans campaign, November 22, 1814 – February 11, 1815

- → British advance
- → Jackson's night attack
- ⇢ British withdrawal
- ▦ fort
- 〰 fortification

Lake Pontchartrain

New Orleans

Jackson's final position

Dec 24: Night battle,

Dec 23: British land, Jan 27: British withdraw troops

Lake of the Ouatches

Lake Borgne

Pearl River

Dec 14: American gunboats destroyed

Dec 13: British fleet arrives, troops sent to sieze outlying islands and forts

Nov 11: Jackson returns from Pensacola operation, leaving for New Orleans Nov 22, almost all of his troops are left in Mobile under Winchester's command

Mobile

Mobile Bay

L o u i s i a n a

Mississippi River

North Chandeleur Is.

of

Mexico

FORT ST PHILLIP

Breton Is.

South Chandeleur Is.

Jan 8–18: Secondary attack fails

G u l f

Mouth of the Mississippi

0 — 15 km
0 — 15 miles

N

Operations around Washington and Baltimore, August 19 – September 17, 1814

- → British attack
- ⇢ British withdrawal

British defeat American force and advance and seize Washington, burning many buildings then return to their ships

Battle of Godly Wood, Sept 12

Baltimore

Ellicott Mills

British advance on Baltimore, strong defenses convince them to retire back to their ships

Land Sept 12
Re-embark Sept 14
Departed Sept 17

Rockville

Brookeville

Montgomery

Potomac River

M a r y l a n d

Vansville

Bladensburg

Annapolis

Tennallytown
Georgetown

Washington

Bridge destroyed Aug 24

Alexandria

Mt. Vernon

Upper Marlborough

Secondary attack delayed by shoals. Capture Alexandria Aug 28 then rejoin main force.

Lower Marlborough

Benedict

Re-embark for Baltimore Aug 30

British troops land Aug 19

Chesapeake Bay

V i r g i n i a

Rappahannock River

Potomac River

British fleet commanded by Cochrane

N

0 — 10 km
0 — 10 miles

ATLANTIC
OCEAN

Mississippi and an impenetrable swamp. This they did on January 8, 1815, bayonets fixed, bravely and repeatedly, but unsuccessfully and at terrible cost. General Pakenham himself was among the dead.

The loss of life was especially tragic because it was unnecessary. Representatives of the antagonists had been meeting at Ghent in Belgium since summer, and on December 24, 1814, they signed a treaty ending the war on the basis of *status quo ante bellum*. But the victory gave a powerful boost to American morale and to the political career of Andrew Jackson, and it reconciled the British to having failed again to defeat their former colonies.

Battle of New Orleans, January 8, 1815

- → British advance
- → U.S reinforcement
- ⇢ British withdrawal
- ▪ U.S. forces
- ▪ British forces
- 〰 U.S. fortification

JACKSON
(5,700, 3,200 engaged)

formal gardens

Cypress swamps

canal

ditch

ditch

ditch

Mississippi River

Cypress swamps

LAMBERT
(reserve)

PACKENHAM
(8,000)

0 — 400 m
0 — 400 yds

N

CAPITALISM

THE MAKING OF THE WORKING CLASS

In the early 1800s, most manufactured goods were produced by skilled artisans in small workshops located in river-towns or coastal ports. As population growth and improvements in transportation swelled the market for goods of all kinds, men of means or dreams expanded production. The most prominent entrepreneurs were the Boston capitalists who built huge water-powered cotton mills along the rivers that sliced through the hills of New England. But most manufacturers, depending on workmanship more than motive power, set up shop in the mercantile towns and cities where skilled labor was plentiful. The increasing size of these workshops during the 1830s and 1840s profoundly transformed the nature of work and the relationship between employer and employee.

During the 18th century, skilled workers learned their skill during their teens while serving as apprentices to master workmen. After five to seven years of training, they became journeymen and began to earn wages. Eventually, if they were reasonably talented, frugal, and industrious, they opened a shop of their own, usually on the first floor of their home, and took on apprentices. Because apprentices often lived and worked under the same roof as their master and his family, it was natural for the master to treat them much like his children. Often apprentices married the master's daughter, helping to keep the trade in the family.

Historical geographer Alan Pred found that in New York City this traditional relationship among artisans persisted into the 1800s. As late as 1840 all but a few master bakers lived in or near the buildings that housed their ovens—along with their apprentices and journeymen. For these men the "journey to work" was but a skip down the stairs or a stroll down the street.

Antebellum economic growth eroded this artisanal pattern. Historian Paul Johnson examined this process in Rochester, New York. In 1823, the Erie Canal was completed as far as Rochester, enabling grain from the Genesee Valley to reach international markets in New York City.

During the next ten years, Rochester became the fastest growing city in the nation. During this boom, master workers enlarged their shops, took in new apprentices, and focused increasingly on profits rather than their traditional obligations to workers. One aspect of this shift is depicted in the two maps *top right*, which indicate the residences of journeymen shoemakers and their masters in 1827 and in 1834. In the earlier years, many journeymen shoemakers lived with or near their masters. After experiencing seven extraordinarily prosperous years, however, few masters continued to reside with their journeymen, evidence that the journeymen were becoming estranged—physically and psychically—from those who paid their wages.

Unlike 20th-century American cities, where the poor generally reside in the congested downtown, the mid-19th-century city inverted this phenomenon, as historian Sam Bass Warner showed in his study of Philadelphia. In 1850 affluent Philadelphians and the incipient middle classes resided in the core of the city while factory workers lived in the shanties and boarding houses that had been thrown up along the periphery. This conclusion (and the map *bottom right*) are based on census data indicating that fewer male factory workers lived in downtown Philadelphia than were employed by the factories located there. The opposite was true in the region just beyond the core. The lower classes—not the well-to-do—commuted to work.

The emergence of middle class residential suburbs awaited the development of streetcars and intra-city subways and railroads after the Civil War.

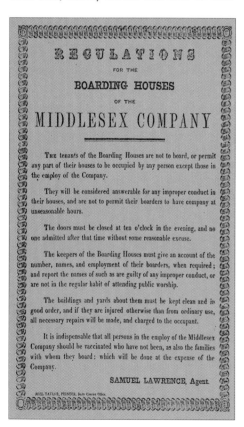

Boarding-house regulations, circa 1850. The transformation of apprentices and journeymen into factory employees meant that they would now have to find housing of their own. Most young men boarded with private families; but sometimes factories helped recruit a labor force by maintaing their own boarding houses. These regulations extended the discipline of the factory to the residence.

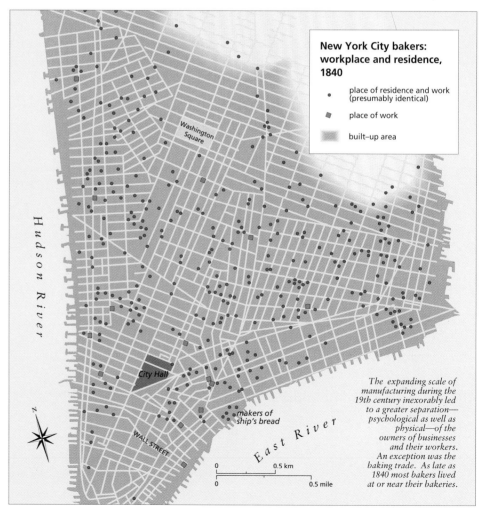

New York City bakers: workplace and residence, 1840

- place of residence and work (presumably identical)
- place of work
- built–up area

The expanding scale of manufacturing during the 19th century inexorably led to a greater separation—psychological as well as physical—of the owners of businesses and their workers. An exception was the baking trade. As late as 1840 most bakers lived at or near their bakeries.

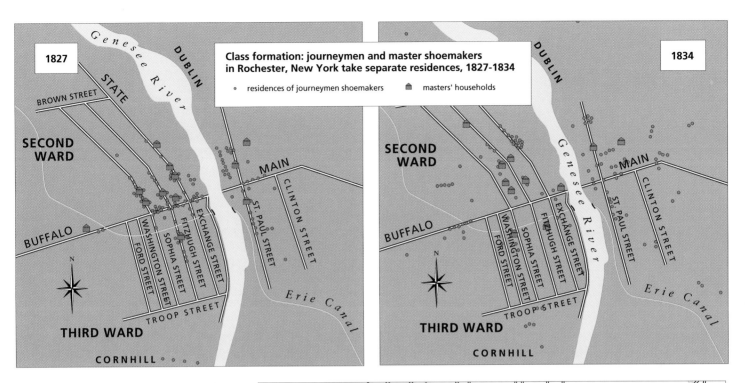

1827

1834

Class formation: journeymen and master shoemakers in Rochester, New York take separate residences, 1827-1834

• residences of journeymen shoemakers ⌂ masters' households

Elevated railway in New York City, circa 1880. As the downtown business districts of New York, Philadelphia, Boston, and other cities grew larger, the journey to work extended as well. Workers weary from ten-hour-days in the factory or store or business office demanded transportation. Horse-drawn streetcars were replaced by steam-powered railways that vaulted over congested urban areas on elevated tracks. The "el"—as it was called—was then replaced by underground subways. Advances in transportation pushed the suburbs deeper into the countryside.

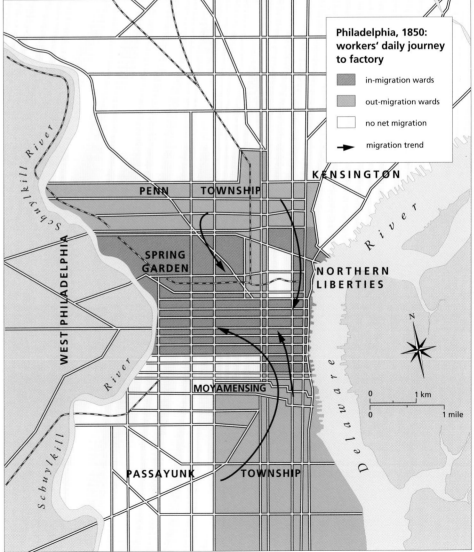

Philadelphia, 1850: workers' daily journey to factory

▨ in-migration wards

▨ out-migration wards

☐ no net migration

➜ migration trend

POLITICS IN THE JACKSONIAN ERA
BANKS AND TRADE TARIFFS

Two economic issues vexed politics during the Jacksonian Era: the character of the nation's banking system and the question of protecting American producers against foreign competition by placing high tariffs on foreign goods.

Throughout colonial and early national history Americans were mostly producers of raw materials; nearly all manufactured products consumed had to be imported. Therefore, encouraging foreign trade was not a controversial issue; after independence, imports were taxed only to raise revenue, not in order to keep foreign products out of the country. However, the distruption of trade with Europe during the Napoleonic Wars stimulated local manufacturing, and when the war ended, new

"infant industries" sought and received "protection" from foreign competition in the form of high import tariffs. Hard times following the Panic of 1819 further strengthened protectionist forces.

Tariff of 1828
A protective tariff was enacted in 1816 without serious controversy, but with experience, sharp sectional divisions developed. Manufacturers in New York, Pennsylvania, and the other middle states and people in the Ohio Valley wanted still higher tariffs. The latter because many of their products such as hemp, flax, and wool were used in manufacturing and because they were convinced that their prosperity depended on the "home market" for their grain and other farm produce developing in the growing eastern industrial cities. Henry Clay's "American

System" policy of protecting industry and building roads and canals in order to lower the cost of moving goods between east and west was the political cement that held these two groups together.

Southerners, however, were increasingly opposed to protection because their cotton, tobacco, and other staple crops were largely sold abroad. They preferred to buy European manufactures and felt threatened by high duties of any kind, which increased the prices of the things they bought. New Englanders were divided. Merchants and shipbuilders objected to anything that restricted trade, and cotton textile manufacturers could compete successfully with Europeans without protective duties. Woolens manufacturers, however, demanded protection against foreign woolens, but were opposed to duties on foreign raw

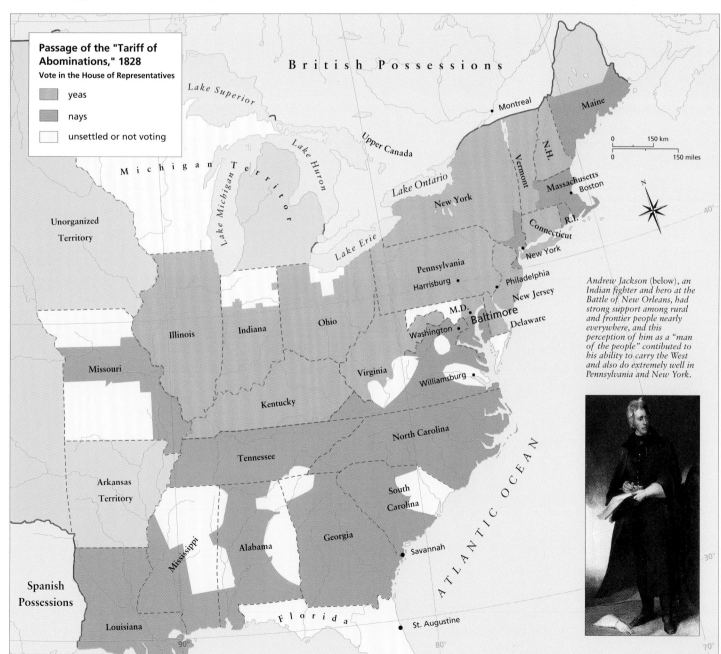

Passage of the "Tariff of Abominations," 1828
Vote in the House of Representatives

- yeas
- nays
- unsettled or not voting

Andrew Jackson (below), an Indian fighter and hero at the Battle of New Orleans, had strong support among rural and frontier people nearly everywhere, and this perception of him as a "man of the people" contributed to his ability to carry the West and also do extremely well in Pennsylvania and New York.

wool. As the caustic Congressman John Randolph of Virginia remarked during the debate on the 1824 tariff, "the merchants and manufacturers of Massachusetts and New Hampshire repel this bill, while men in hunting shirts, with deerskin leggings, want protection for home manufactures."

In 1827, a bill designed to help the woolens-manufacturers failed by the narrowest of margins. That summer a convention of manufacturers meeting at Harrisburg, Pennsylvania, called for higher duties on woolens and many other products. The result was a tariff law, the so-called "Tariff of Abominations."

If Randolph's quixotic comment was appropriate in 1824, it would have been even more to the point four years later. In 1828 the presidential campaign was getting under way, the candidates being President John Quincy Adams and Andrew Jackson. Jackson was burning for revenge; he believed he had been cheated of the office four years earlier when a four-cornered contest had been thrown into the House of Representatives because no candidate had a majority of the Electoral College vote. Jackson had more votes than any of the others, but Adams was elected when Clay swung his supporters to him. When Adams wasthen appointed Clay Secretary of State (an office held by the previous three presidents immediately before their election), Jackson denounced this "corrupt bargain" and set out to right this wrong in the election of 1828.

Jackson had backing in every section, but for that reason he did not want to take a stand on a divisive issue like the tariff. A tariff bill that his backers in each section could vote their separate interests on, but which would not actually pass, would service his candidacy best. However, all but his most dedicated backers in Congress were more concerned with what the voters in their districts wanted than with electing Jackson president, which is another way of saying that politics was still primarily state-centered rather than national. This meant first of all that a solid majority favored protection, but also that agricultural interests were predominant. The House Committee on Manufactures held hearings at which the representatives of 28 manufacturers, more than half of them from the woolens industry, made their case. But when the committee got down to drafting the bill, members from agricultural districts took command. They put duties on wool cloth designed to "furnish full protection" but "not go beyond that point." Then they voted "to extend every protection which the nature of the case will admit to the grower of American wool," and they placed similar high duties on hemp, flax, lead, and other raw materials.

The bill caused consternation among the New England congressmen and they introduced amendments raising the duties on woolen cloth and lowering those on raw wool. Southerners were also furious. Almost to a man they voted against every effort to raise the rates on cloth. But they also voted against the amendments reducing the tariff on raw wool.

Their only hope was that by making the final bill unpalatable to New England, that section would vote with them to defeat it.

This desperate strategy failed. Enough New England congressmen, mostly from rural districts, joined with a heavy majority of those from the middle states and the west to carry the day in the House, 105 to 94. In the Senate, where the high tariff forces were stronger, a few concessions had to be made to the New England opposition, but the bill, substantially unchanged, was approved 26 to 21.

Election of 1828

The failure of the Jacksonians' strategy and of the South's hopes of forcing what today might be called a "poison pill" down the throats of the New England manufacturers did not prevent Jackson from winning the presidential election, 178 Electoral votes to Adams's 83. Besides sweeping New England, Adams carried most of the Atlantic seaboard from Maryland north, but not a single southern state and nothing west of the Appalachians. The sectional character of the vote was ominous.

Particularly galling to southern leaders was the way the Jacksonians had written the new tariff bill and maneuvered it through Congress. John C. Calhoun of South Carolina had been Adams's vice president, but he had agreed to seek office again as Jackson's running mate. He was especially bitter about the new tariff and his re-election did not mollify him in the slightest. After the election he told Jackson that if the tariff was not reduced promptly, serious trouble would result. He then returned to South Carolina and wrote the *South Carolina Exposition and Protest*, which argued that the Constitution only gave the federal government the power to tax the people in order to raise revenue. The 1828 tariff was not merely "abominable," it was also "unconstututional, unequal, and oppressive." More important, Calhoun claimed that an individual state could "interpose" its authority to protect itself against unconstitutional acts. In other words it could nullify a federal law.

Jackson was, of course, a southerner. But he was not much interested in the tariff question and he was much too patriotic to countenance the idea of nullification. He urged Congress to reduce the tariff but he never pressed the issue and when Congress got around to writing a new tariff law in 1832 it lowered duties only slightly. This caused Calhoun to resign as Vice-President. When he entered the Senate in the hope that other southern states would cooperate; it came to nothing.

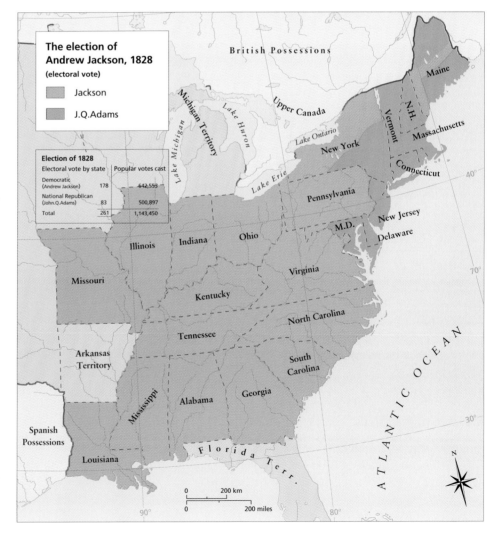

The election of
Andrew Jackson, 1828
(electoral vote)

Jackson

J.Q.Adams

Election of 1828		
Electoral vote by state		Popular votes cast
Democratic (Andrew Jackson)	178	642,553
National Republican (John.Q.Adams)	83	500,897
Total	261	1,143,450

REMOVAL OF THE INDIANS
THE "TRAIL OF TEARS"

By the third decade of the 19th century, tens of thousands of white settlers, lured by the promise of cheap virgin land west of the Appalachians, were flooding through the Cumberland Gap into Kentucky, Tennessee, and the upper Mississippi. Meanwhile, planters in Charleston and Savannah, craving the rich bottom lands of the Mississippi and Alabama rivers, were crowding onto ships sailing for New Orleans or Mobile. One consequence of these land and sea migrations was the encirclement of the major Indian tribes of the southeast, whose right

The Cherokees suffered terribly on their long journey from the Appalachians to the plains west of the Mississippi (left). The long trek across Missouri and Arkansas became known as the "Trail of Tears," shown here in a painting by Robert L. Lindneux.

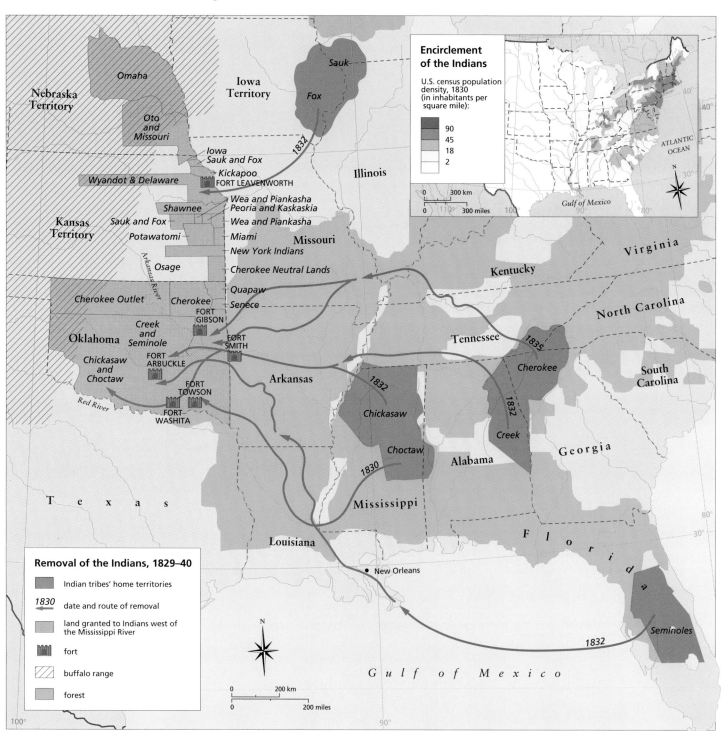

Encirclement of the Indians

U.S. census population density, 1830 (in inhabitants per square mile):

- 90
- 45
- 18
- 2

Removal of the Indians, 1829–40

- Indian tribes' home territories
- *1830* date and route of removal
- land granted to Indians west of the Mississippi River
- fort
- buffalo range
- forest

to remain where they were had been guaranteed by treaty. But would the United States keep to its word?

Some southern Indians had already fled before the advance of the whites, or followed the receding trail of the buffalo westward. As early as 1816, the federal government had negotiated treaties with restless bands of Cherokees and Choctaws. They agreed to exchange millions of acres in the Southeast for holdings of equal size in the Arkansas Territory. The United States further promised to exclude white settlers from these lands. By the late 1820s, however, squatters had staked out farms on Indian land all along the Arkansas and White rivers. The government now proposed that the Indians move to more remote holdings in the Ozarks and Ouachitas, or, beyond that, to the unorganized territory north of the Red River.

In 1823, Secretary of War John Calhoun declared that the Indians could not remain upon lands destined for whites. A permanent solution to the Indian "problem" lay in their resettlement to the "Great American Desert," land he deemed unfit for habitation by white men and women. By 1830, the Indian tribes of the Southeast had been nearly surrounded by white farming settlements. White farmers practiced sedentary agriculture, reflected in the relatively high density of population; the Indians, however, preferred a pastoral life sustained by hunting, gathering, and non-intensive farming. Five years later presidential candidate Andrew Jackson cemented his support in the deep south by calling for the removal and relocation of the Indians. Jackson defended the plan as a means to protect the Indians from the "degradation and destruction to which they were rapidly hastening."

In 1830, he pushed the Indian Removal Act through Congress. His Indian administrators negotiated 94 removal treaties; by 1835 Jackson proudly announced that only a handful of Indians would remain east of the Mississippi.

Many tribes resigned themselves to removal. Between 1831 and 1833, some 15,000 Choctaws migrated from central Mississippi to the region west of Arkansas Territory. In *Democracy in America,* Alexis de Tocqueville described the plight of Indian families, including infants and the elderly, many of them near death from hunger, disease, or exposure, attempting to cross the ice-choked Mississippi at Memphis: "They possessed neither tents nor wagons, but only their arms and some provisions. I saw them embark to pass the mighty river, and never will that solemn spectacle fade from my remembrance. No cry, no sob, was heard among the assembled crowd; all were silent."

But the miseries of the Choctaws and the Chickasaws, who traveled part of the way on flatboats, could scarcely compare to the ordeals of the Cherokees and the Creeks, who had to cover nearly twice the distance on foot. The Cherokees journeyed across Tennessee to Nashville, and then across western Kentucky to Golconda on the Ohio. The interminable

overland passage across the state of Missouri and Arkansas territory became simply known as the "Trail of Tears."

A few tribes—the Sauk (Wisconsin Territory), the Fox (Iowa Territory), and the Seminoles (Florida)—chose to resist. In 1832, Chief Black Hawk, whose band of Sauk and Fox Indians had collided with hostile Sioux west of the Mississippi, attempted to plant corn in lands that they had formerly occupied east of the river. The Illinois militia sprang into action to drive the Indians into Wisconsin Territory. They inflicted a terrible slaughter

upon the Indian women and children but the Black Hawk War is remembered less for the atrocities against the Indians than for the fact that future adversaries, Captain Arbaham Lincoln and Lieutenant Jefferson Davis, took part in the campaign.

In 1835, Seminoles attacked white settlements, ambushed relief garrisons, and then melted back into the Everglades. Their resistance crumbled after the capture two years later of Osceola, their leader. By 1842, all but several hundred Seminoles had been removed west to Oklahoma.

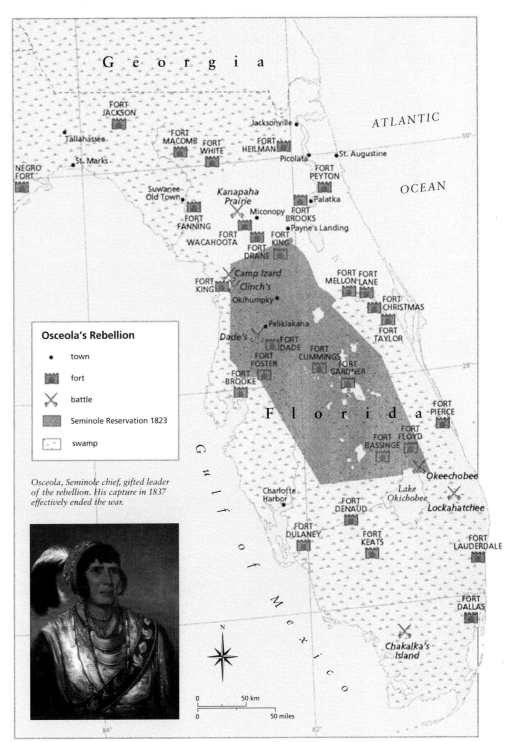

Osceola, Seminole chief, gifted leader of the rebellion. His capture in 1837 effectively ended the war.

POLITICS AFTER JACKSON
THE RISE OF THE WHIGS: CLASS OR ETHNIC POLITICS?

Andrew Jackson dominated American politics long after his death in 1845. Small western and southern farmers and city artisans and laborers tended to be Democrats because they identified that party with "Jacksonian" democracy and equal opportunity. The Whig party was founded and supported by people who disliked Jackson: merchants and other upper-class people who objected to Jackson's glorification of the common man; bankers who considered his attack on the Bank of the United States a threat to a stable currency and economic expansion; believers in states' rights who saw in Jackson's denunciation of nullification and his aggressive use of presidential power a threat to their liberty.

The very name, Whig, a symbol of patriotic resistance to British tyranny during the Revolution, was a reference to the supposed tyranny of "King Andrew," who had threatened to hang Calhoun when the latter insisted that he, rather than the Supreme Court, was the arbiter of what was and what was not constitutional, and who vetoed bills with no other reason than that he did not like them. Nevertheless, social and economic issues and interests did affect how people voted, whatever their emotional ties to Jackson or any other colorful leader. These tended to reflect sectional voting patterns, the most divisive issue being, of course, slavery. Other important ones were tariff and banking policies, and "internal improvements," the name given to government-sponsored means of transportation: roads, canals, and eventually railroads.

Internal improvements were especially vital to the growth and prosperity of the states west of the Appalachian Mountains. A farmer in Kentucky, Tennessee, Ohio, Indiana, or Illinois could not get his tobacco or his wheat, corn, or other grain to market without such means of transport, and no matter how rich his soil, how large his harvest, he was doomed to a crude and uncomfortable existence if he had to depend entirely on what he could produce on his own land. Farmers needed hard-surfaced roads even to reach nearby towns where artisans worked and items such as salt, gunpowder, and tools were sold. To reach the East Coast and obtain access to hungry European consumers, water transportation was essential. In the days spent getting over the mountains, a horse pulling a wagonload of oats from Ohio to Philadelphia would have consumed far more oats than the wagon could hold long before reaching the city.

In the years after Jackson's retirement, the Whig party consistently championed government support of internal improvement projects. The outstanding Whig leader, Henry Clay, had, in his American System, long urged such a policy. His argument was that if easterners would help to pay for roads and canals, westerners would support high tariffs protecting eastern manufactured products against foreign competition. Tariffs would make manufacturers' goods more expensive, Clay admitted, but the manufacturers and the laborers they employed would be a market for western produce. In any case, without cheap transportation, western farmers would have no money to buy manufactured products at any price. Clay had also opposed Jackson's veto of the Bank of the United States, arguing that the Bank was a guarantee of economic stability and an essential source of the capital needed for the development of transportation and other business enterprises.

The case of Ohio demonstrates the political impact of internal improvements clearly. The completion of New York State's Erie Canal in 1825 opened the first direct water route between the Great Lakes and New York City. Thereafter Ohio farmers (whose only earlier water route to the east coast was down the Mississippi River to New Orleans by barge and then by ocean-going vessel around Florida) needed only to get their crops to a port on Lake Erie to take advantage of the direct route. The opening of the Ohio and Erie Canal between Portsmouth, on the Ohio River, and Cleveland in 1833 and of the Miami and Erie River Canal between Cincinnati and Toledo in 1845 brought prosperity to the counties along these waterways. The completion of the National Road through Columbus and on to Springfield, Ohio, by 1838 made the water routes easily available to yet other areas of the state. Most of these counties produced from then on Whig majorities, while counties remote from the canals tended to vote for the Democrats.

Voting in Mississippi also reflected the commercial orientation of the Whig party and the appeal of the Democrats to ordinary people. The fertile districts along the Mississippi where cotton was grown on large plantations voted Whig, while poorer up-country regions were usually Democrat. Every county along the river from Wilkinson on the Louisiana border to almost the Tennessee line gave Whig presidential candidates majorities, most of them substantial in 1836, 1840, and 1844.

A similar socio-economic division characterized voting in New York City in this period. Historians disagree as to whether the basic issue was economic or cultural.

Probably it was both since the wards that were predominantly Whig were the wealthiest and those that voted for the Democrats had a high proportion of immigrants.

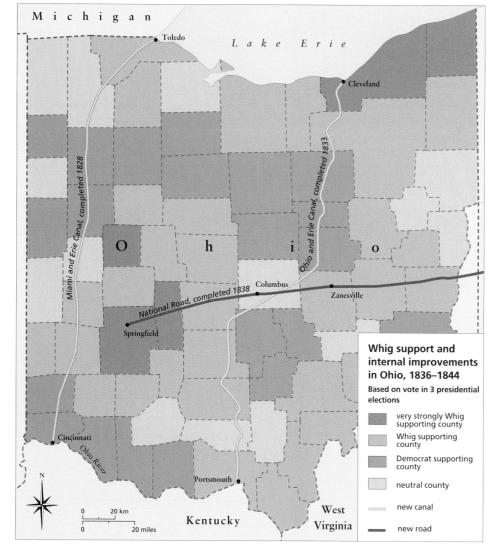

Whig support and internal improvements in Ohio, 1836–1844

Based on vote in 3 presidential elections

- very strongly Whig supporting county
- Whig supporting county
- Democrat supporting county
- neutral county
- new canal
- new road

Class and ethnicity in New York City, 1834–1840

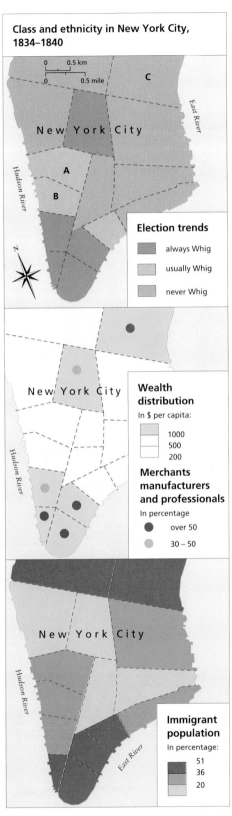

Election trends

- always Whig
- usually Whig
- never Whig

Wealth distribution

In $ per capita:
- 1000
- 500
- 200

Merchants manufacturers and professionals

In percentage
- over 50
- 30 – 50

Immigrant population

In percentage:
- 51
- 36
- 20

The top two maps, which juxtapose political patterns in mayoral and gubernatorial races from 1834–1840, support the traditional thesis that the Whigs were the party of the well-to-do, and the Democrats, of the workers. Historians such as Lee Benson have more recently suggested that ethnic divisions were more important than class. He noted that in New York City some less-than-prosperous wards (A, B) usually voted Whig, and one wealthy ward (C) never produced a majority for the Whig candidate. He explained seeming anomalies such as these by the importance of ethnicity in New York politics .

Class and presidential voting in Mississippi, 1836–1844

- very strongly Whig supporting county
- Whig supporting county
- Democrat supporting county
- evenly divided
- best cotton land, largely plantation

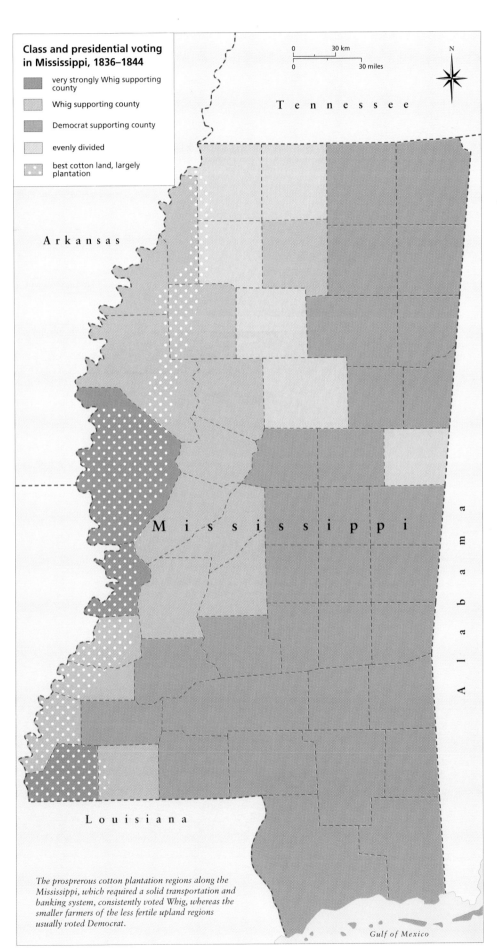

The prosprerous cotton plantation regions along the Mississippi, which required a solid transportation and banking system, consistently voted Whig, whereas the smaller farmers of the less fertile upland regions usually voted Democrat.

89

THE BURNED-OVER DISTRICT
RELIGIOUS FERVOR AS SETTLERS MOVE WEST

In 1824, Charles Grandison Finney, having just received "a mighty baptism of the Holy Ghost," set out for the upper Mohawk Valley, a "burnt district," where the smoldering stumps of the recently cleared forests evoked the religious volatility of the settlers themselves. From 1825 through 1831, Finney held revivals throughout the area, but his success at inflaming passions in the "burned-over district" was replicated by many other charismatic leaders. The Mormon prophet Joseph Smith found a ready audience for his new religion there. Similarly, the Antimasonic Crusade, which viewed Freemasonry as the work of Satan, originated in western New York, established a political base there, and eventually left a deep imprint upon national politics. Religious enthusiasms also sustained the millennial and communitarian sects that cropped up among the westward-moving Yankees.

Historian Whitney R. Cross maintained that the "Burned-Over District" provided a case study in the westward transit of New England culture. Entire communities of young New Englanders, drawn chiefly from the scrub-covered hill-country of western sections of Connecticut, Massachusetts, and Vermont, emigrated to the area of New York west of the Adirondack and Catskill mountains. They brought with them a religious intensity unguided by a firmly established orthodoxy. Having arrived in western New York, often by means of the Erie Canal (completed in 1825), they occupied the marginal farms of the pioneers, who had already moved on to cheaper and more fertile lands further west. As their prospects of quick riches evaporated, the restless settlers of the "Burnt-Over District" readily sought release in millennial and communitarian religion.

Finney's Revivals

Finney sought to avoid the emotional excesses of earlier evangelists, but his terrifying evocation of hell and his insistence that people could overcome sin appealed to the Yankee emigrants. Young men and women flocked to Finney's religious meetings at Utica in 1825. The following year he ignited a revival in Rome, New York, which, according to one observer, "scattered the fire over all this region of country." Soon afterwards, ministers throughout New York begged Finney to inspire (and enlarge) their congregations. After successful campaigns throughout southern and western New York State and central Pennsylvania, Finney toured the major cities of the eastern seaboard, culminating in a spectacular revival at Rochester in 1831.

Mormons

According to Mormon tradition, 18-year-old Joseph Smith, whose family had left Vermont to settle in Palmyra, New York, was visited by the angel Moroni in 1823. The angel announced that God had selected Smith to restore Christ's church. It later told him of the existence of certain "plates" of gold, written in the mysterious language of a "reformed Egyptian." They recounted the history of the lost tribe of Israel in North America. Aided by magical spectacles, Smith "translated" the plates into English and published them as *The Book of Mormon* (1830). Almost immediately, people flocked to his sect. When the Mormons' success caused conflict with their "Gentile" neighbors, Smith led his beleaguered converts into Kirtland, Ohio in 1831, then onto Independence, Missouri in 1838, and Commerce (renamed Nauvoo), Illinois in 1839. His church, which now had about 18,000 members, encountered further hostility after Smith endorsed polygamy. Smith was jailed and killed by anti-Mormons. His church, now under the leadership of Brigham Young, again trekked westward, and was eventually to settle in Utah.

Antimasonry

In 1826, William Morgan, a disgruntled ex-Freemason from Batavia, New York, announced his intention to publish the secret Masonic rituals. Shortly thereafter several Masons abducted Morgan on a charge of petty theft and imprisoned him in Canandaigua (just south of Palmyra). Morgan then disappeared, never to be seen again. Only six of his abductors came to trial; four were convicted of conspiracy and sentenced to short jail terms. When it became known that many of the jurors, prosecutors, and even Governor DeWitt Clinton, belonged to the order, critics claimed that justice had been miscarried.

In scores of villages throughout western New York, ministers thundered against the order. In 1827, 15 "Antimasons" were elected to the New York Assembly. This attracted the

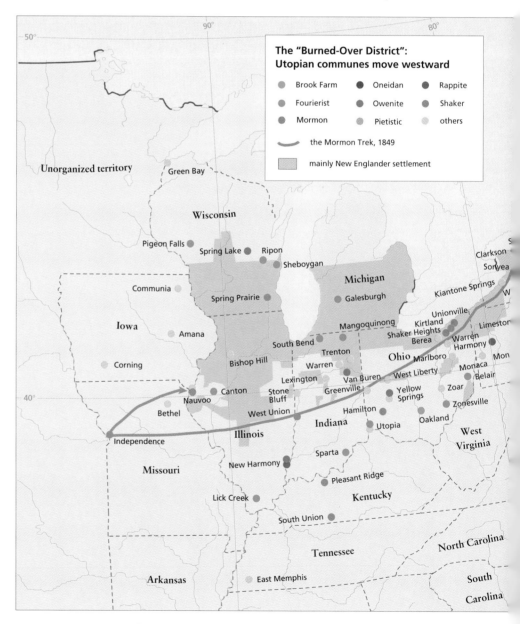

The "Burned-Over District":
Utopian communes move westward

- Brook Farm
- Fourierist
- Mormon
- Oneidan
- Owenite
- Pietistic
- Rappite
- Shaker
- others

— the Mormon Trek, 1849

mainly New Englander settlement

attention of politicians throughout the Northeast. William H. Seward and Thurlow Weed formed the Antimasonic Party, the first significant "third" party in the nation's history. In the presidential election of 1832, the Antimasonic candidate, William Wirt, carried Vermont, much of the "Burned-Over District," and some Yankee regions further west. He drew enough Whig support from Henry Clay to elect Andrew Jackson, a Democrat and, ironically, a Freemason.

Utopian Communities

The Shakers, a millennial group that originated in 18th-century England, came to America in 1774 and founded a utopian community at Lebanon, New York (1787). Although not native to the "Burned-Over District," the Shakers quickly gained a foothold in Yankee communities throughout the Northeast. After the turn of the century, the Shakers, who practiced celibacy and gained membership almost

The Shakers, a millennialist sect that regarded sexual intercourse as sinful, transformed lust into religious ecstasy. In the above rite, the circles of men danced in one direction, and the women, the other; they were never to touch. The dancing was frenzied.

entirely by attracting new converts, established their utopian communities throughout the Ohio Valley. Other religious sects, such as the Perfectionists, who established the Oneida Community in central New York State in 1848, the Rappites (or Rappists), and the Pietists also established important communitarian settlements, mostly in areas already settled by Yankee emigrants. Even the secular communitarian settlements, such as the Fourierist "phalanxes" and the socialist utopias of Robert Owen, fed off the ferment characteristic of Yankee settlement patterns.

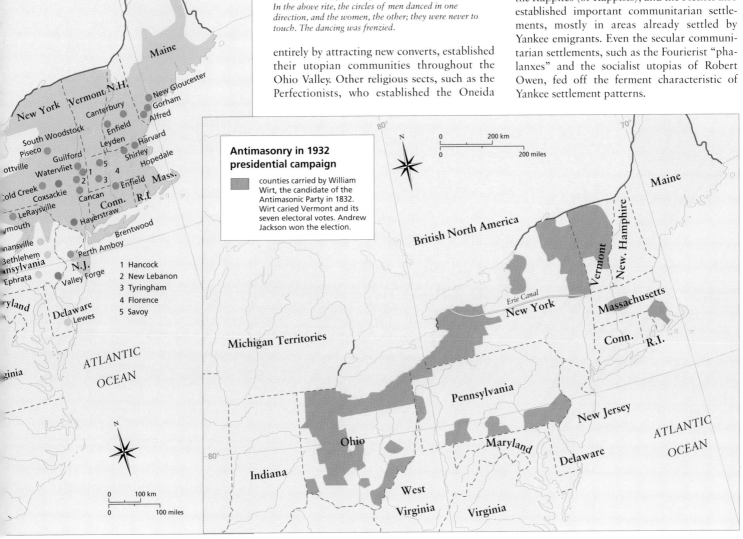

Antimasonry in 1932 presidential campaign

counties carried by William Wirt, the candidate of the Antimasonic Party in 1832. Wirt caried Vermont and its seven electoral votes. Andrew Jackson won the election.

UTOPIAN COMMUNITIES
SEXUALITY AND ARCHITECTURE

If deviance helps define "normal" standards of behavior, the utopian communities that proliferated from 1820 to 1850 provided a sharp contrast to the prevailing values and structures of bourgeois society. The best-known utopias featured novel conceptions of marriage and sexuality. The Shakers, who identified sexual desire as the "very seat and fountain head of all sin," minimized contact between men and women, while the Oneidians, followers of John Humphrey Noyes, enshrined sexual intercourse as a "medium of fellowship with the body of Christ." The Mormons sought to replicate the "celestial marriage" of the polygamous patriarchs of the Old Testament. As a framework for their beliefs and social relations, each of these societies adopted a different approach to community organization and the design of buildings.

The Shakers and Celibacy

Although the Shakers denounced "architecture" as an "absurd and abnormal" diversion of resources properly destined for the Kingdom of Heaven, they painstakingly worked to ensure that all aspects of the built environment reflected their solemn belief in an austere God and their abhorrence for the commingling of the sexes. The characteristic high-backed chairs, which Charles Dickens thought "partook of the general grimness" of the sect, discouraged slothful or disrespectful posture. A human body accustomed to deprivations was thought to be less susceptible to more powerful enticements such as that which had befallen Adam. The Millennial Laws adopted by the founders even required members to "cut square" their bread and meat and to "lie straight" while sleeping. Lest members slip into Edenic reveries, the Shakers avoided siting communities in picturesque settings. Conversation between men and women outdoors was prohibited, and to lessen the opportunities for dalliances, driveways and pathways were laid out according to an orthogonal grid. The Round Barn is notable insofar as it defied the Shaker penchant for right angles. In this case practicality transcended theology: a single worker, driving a wagon in a circular pattern on the second floor, could drop enough hay to feed scores of cattle.

The Shaker community was divided into groups of "families," each comprised of approximately 100 members living in the main dwelling. The Church Family Dwelling (1830) at Hancock, Massachusetts, illustrated the Shakers' separation of the sexes. Men and women ate in the first-floor dining room, but sat at separate tables. The bedrooms were located on the second and third floors. Separate stairways were provided for men, who resided on the west side of each floor, and women, who lived on the opposite side of the corridor. Men worked in the nearby fields, barns or workshops; women, in the Sisters' Shop and the dairy and wash houses.

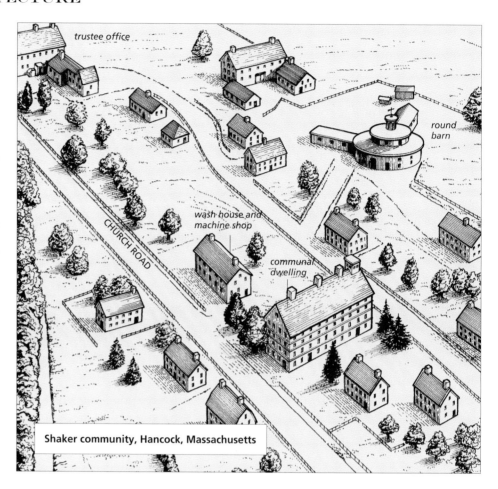

Shaker community, Hancock, Massachusetts

trustee office

round barn

wash house and machine shop

communal dwelling

CHURCH ROAD

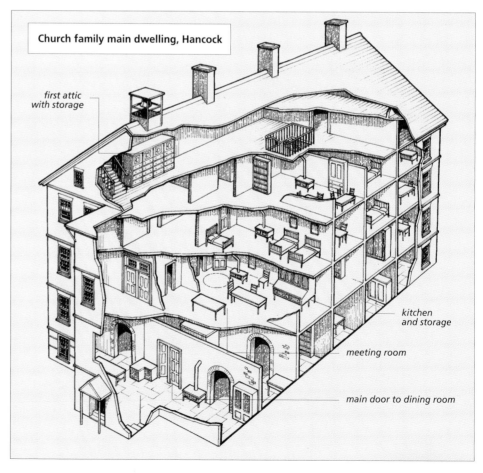

Church family main dwelling, Hancock

first attic with storage

kitchen and storage

meeting room

main door to dining room

The Oneidans and "Complex Marriage"

If the Shakers viewed sexuality as sinful, John Humphrey Noyes, founder of the Oneida Community, believed that sexual intercourse evoked the hermaphroditic union of God the Father, who manifested male attributes, and Christ, the Son, who manifested female attributes. When "purified" of the possessiveness of romantic love, the ecstasy of orgasm signified communion with God. From this principle evolved the concept of "complex marriage," involving the frequent—and often obligatory—change of sexual partners. To avoid unwanted pregnancies, men practiced *coitus interruptus*. Young males and "leakers"—men who had not mastered the technique—were only allowed to have relations with menopausal women.

The "law of fellowship" declared as false "all love which is at work in a private corner, away from the general circulation." The institutionalization of this principle occurred first by accident. As the winter of 1848 approached, the third floor of the Oneidan's first "mansion" remained uncompleted. Noyes decided to leave half of the floor as a single apartment for men and women. At the center was a sitting "room." The beds were located around the perimeter, seperated from each other and from the sitting room by seven foot high strips of cloth. Members praised the "increased sociality" of this "Tent Room" and the concept became institutionalized in the second mansion house (1861-1878). The sitting room, greatly enlarged, now opened up to a second floor balcony. Bedrooms were located off the sitting room and the balcony. This helped control interaction and supervision of members.

The Mormons and Polygamy

From 1841 through 1843, Joseph Smith experienced the revelations that formed the ideological foundations of the Mormon church. Some revelations led to the establishment of special endowment and sealing ceremonies that extended earthly marriage into the hereafter. This "higher" relation was called "celestial marriage," a ceremony performed by the Mormon Priesthood. Smith's Revelation on the Eternity of the Marriage Convenant, which by Mormon tradition occurred on July 12, 1843, authorized the practice of polygamy.

Practices like these, Smith realized, required the authority of the church and the solemnity of ritual. Several months after the first revelation, he began construction of the Temple at Nauvoo, Illinois. The basement featured a font used in a special ceremony that enabled Mormons to baptize deceased relatives and friends by proxy. The Main Assembly Hall was unexceptional. Located on the top floor of the Temple were rooms for "female preparation," "wardrobe," and "male preparation," in which candidates were made ready for initiation ceremonies, whose forms were largely derived from Masonic ritual. The extraordinary powers that these rites conferred upon the men of the Priesthood underscored the patriarchal authority implicit in polygamous marriages.

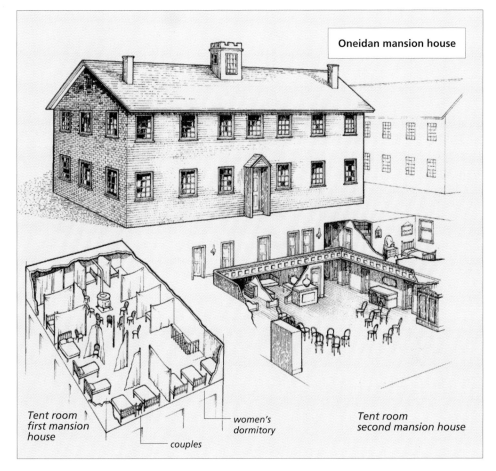

Oneidan mansion house

Tent room
first mansion
house

women's
dormitory

couples

Tent room
second mansion house

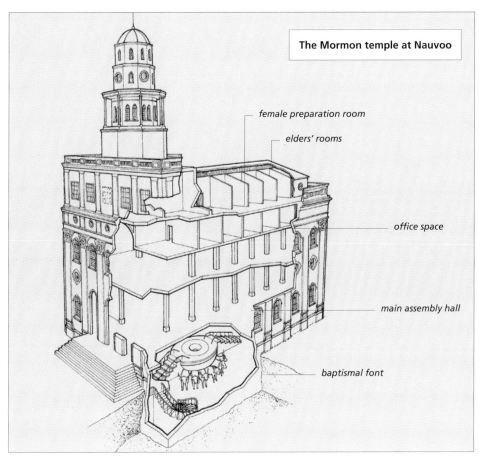

The Mormon temple at Nauvoo

female preparation room

elders' rooms

office space

main assembly hall

baptismal font

FERTILITY AND THE FRONTIER
LIMITATIONS ON FAMILY SIZE IN THE EMERGING MIDDLE CLASS

In his Essay on the Principle of Population, English philosopher Thomas Malthus shattered the Enlightenment's optimism about the limitless potential of the mind. Malthus reasoned that because human beings were driven by irrepressible sexual urges, population growth would eventually outstrip the supply of food. Famine, disease and misery were inevitable. Writing in 1798, Malthus found the extraordinary population increase of the United States "probably without parallel in history." This he attributed mostly to the "extreme cheapness of good land." But contrary to Malthus' predictions, American fertility began to decline early in the 19th century. The trend has continued to the present, interrupted only briefly by the "baby boom" following the Second World War. As the frontier receded, did settlers respond to diminished farming prospects by restraining their sexual impulses?

Traditionally, a young man did not propose marriage, nor a woman accept it, until he was sufficiently well-established to support a family. Some historians have argued that as land became scarcer—and thus more expensive—young people married later in life, reducing the wife's childbearing years. Once married, moreover, young farming couples, confronted with higher land costs, sought to limit their families by abstaining from intercourse, by practicing *coitus interruptus* or by having abortions, which were legal in most states until the mid-19th century.

But this view of the relationship between population density and fertility has been challenged by demographers such as John Modell, who studied fertility in Indiana in 1820. He found that women in the most densely populated counties, located north of the Ohio River near Cincinnati, often had relatively large families. Similiarly, many of the least densely populated counties had low fertility. A causal relationship between cheap land on the frontier and large families is unproven.

Furthermore, the lowest levels of fertility were found not among farm women in settled (and presumably overcrowded) rural areas but among city dwellers, who seldom pondered the availability of arable land. The graph (*far right*) shows that although the fertility of women declined both in New England and the east north central states (Ohio, Indiana, Illinois, Michigan, and Wisconsin), within each region women in cities had fewer children than women in rural areas, where children could readily be put to work. A comparison of the 1810 and 1850 maps, viewed in this way, suggests that the decline in fertility east of the Mississippi was mostly caused by the spread of urbanization.

But the decline in fertility was so general a phenomenon, and lasting for such a long period, that no explanation based solely on the availability of land or patterns of urbanization will suffice. Normative factors rather than geographical ones may best explain the decline in fertility.

Women's historians have observed that in the late 18th and early 19th centuries an ideology of domesticity confined women to the home even as it enshrined their role as custodians of the young. Mothers intent on guiding each child's moral development, and fathers, intent on saving enough money to establish a foothold in the emerging middle class, together decided to limit their families.

In 1810 (map below), Massachusetts and Rhode Island, the most densely populated states in the nation, also had the lowest level of fertility, defined here as the number of children under 10 years of age per 1,000 women aged 16 to 44. Women in Rhode Island had the fewest number of children: 1,405 children for every 1,000 women; Massachusetts came next, with 1,421 children. Population density declined—and fertility increased— from south to west. The highest fertility rates were on the frontier: especially in the Louisiana Territory (2,375), Indiana (2,307), Ohio (2,303), and Tennessee (2,302).

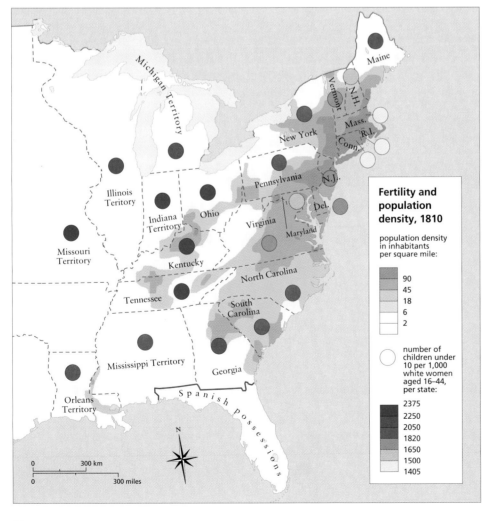

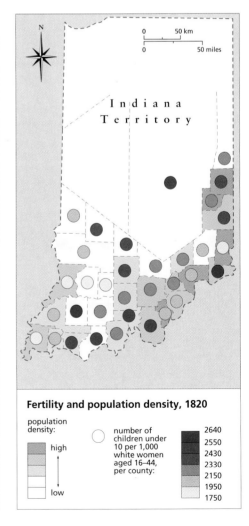

Fertility and population density, 1850

population density in inhabitants per square mile:

	90
	45
	18
	6
	2

number of children under 10 per 1,000 white women aged 16–44, per state:

	2005
	1650
	1550
	1350
	1150
	1000
	857

In 1850 (map above and graph right), population density increased nearly everywhere, and fertility declined almost proportionately. Massachusetts and Rhode Island still had the lowest fertility rates (857 and 910, respectively). In 1850, the "old frontier" of Ohio, Indiana, Kentucky, and Tennessee no longer had the highest fertility rates, which were found in the Oregon Territory (2,005), Arkansas (1,843), Mississippi (1,776), and Texas (1,745). In 1850, Ohio was about as densely populated as Massachusetts in

1810; and the 1850 Ohio fertility rate nearly matched that of Massachusetts 40 years earlier (1,421).

Homesteading family on the Nebraska plain (below). A posed shot, surely of the entire family, yet there are only two children, widely separated in age. This differs from the usual frontier family with many children who could help exploit the vast open spaces. Did the parents, imitating middle-class city dwellers, intentionally limit the number of offspring?

Fertility decrease, 1800–1970

—— United States

New England (Maine, New Hampshire, Vermont, Massachusetts, Rhode Island, Connecticut):
—— urban   ---- rural

East North Central (Ohio, Indiana, Illinois, Michigan, Wisconsin):
—— urban   ---- rural

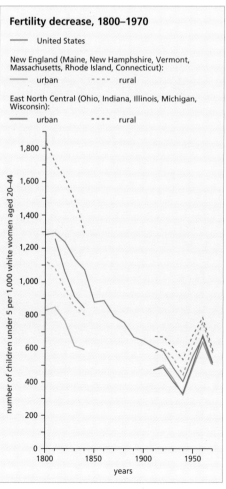

IRISH AND GERMAN IMMIGRATION
EUROPEANS FLOCK TO THE UNITED STATES

In The Uprooted, Oscar Handlin explained that he had set out to write a history of immigrants in America; then he came to the realization that immigrants are American history. Handlin's truism applied especially to the decades after 1820. During the preceding three decades, only about 8,000 immigrants had trickled into the United States each year. Many Europeans doubted the viability of the new republic in the North American wilderness; others found their emigration plans disrupted by the Napoleonic wars. But from 1820 through 1860, Europe annually sent more than 120,000 emigrants to the United States; and by 1860, one in eight of the nation's 32 million people had been born in Europe.

Emigration from Ireland

By far the largest number of immigrants came from Ireland. Napoleon's defeat in 1815 brought peace and an end to war-inflated grain prices. In Ireland, disgruntled landlords plowed grain crops under, planted grass for animal fodder, and evicted tenants. Some of the dispossessed sought work in Dublin, Belfast, or other Irish cities; others emigrated to Canada or the United States. But most remained in rural Ireland, hoping to eke out a living by growing potatoes on small, scrubby plots of land. Thus the population of Ireland, despite the diminishing acreage devoted to cropland, rose from 6.8 million in 1821 to more than 8 million in 1841.

In the autumn of 1845, disaster struck when disease ravaged the potato crop. Thousands starved or, weakened from hunger, succumbed to one of the epidemics that swept across Ireland. Thousands braved a winter crossing of the Atlantic, willing to endure, as one said, any misery "save that of remaining in Ireland." During the next six years, the blight continued almost unabated.

During this time the population of Ireland fell by almost 25 percent, but the demographic consequences of the Great Famine varied by region. Dublin gained thousands of famine refugees. Adjacent counties on the fertile east coast experienced modest population decrease. Prosperous (and Protestant) northern Ireland also witnessed only a modest drop in population. On the other hand, south and central Ireland lost nearly one-third of their pre-famine population. On the west coast, land was poor, the farms were small and primitive, and the people wretchedly destitute. During at least one of the years of the Great Famine, more than half the residents of Mayo, Galway, Kerry, Clare, and Limerick counties received public relief as paupers. Unable to pay for passage to the United States, many of them died.

In central Ireland, however, depopulation resulted chiefly from emigration. The inhabitants of Cavan, Monaghan, Roscommon, and neighboring areas, though poor, were not so desperate as their west country brethren. Many had accumulated just enough sheep, cows, cooking implements, and furniture to pay transatlantic fares. In all, nearly a million Irish died; another million emigrated to America.

German Emigration

German emigration to the United States in some respects paralleled the Irish experience. Until 1860, most German immigrants came from rural areas that had suffered from over-population, particularly along the Rhine. German emigration increased sharply with the onset of the potato blight during the mid-1840s, and peaked in 1854 as 215,000 Germans emigrated to the United States.

Settlement in the United States

The Irish and Germans usually settled—at least initially—in the port cities of the Northeast. The Irish concentrated in urban areas along the northeastern seaboard and the Erie Canal. In 1870, more than a quarter of a million inhabitants of New York City (including Brooklyn) had been born in Ireland. Boston and Philadelphia also had large Irish communities. Irish peasants who had sold all their goods to buy passage to America often lacked the money—and perhaps the desire—to become farmers in the United States. While Handlin believed that these uprooted Irish lost their emotional bearings in the big American cities, other historians have been struck by the Irish peasants' adaptability to urban life.

Hundreds of thousands of German immigrants went to the western frontier. Many bought farms in Michigan, Wisconsin, and Minnesota. They also flocked to midwestern cities. In St. Louis, Cincinnati, and in Louisville in 1870, German-born immigrants outnumbered Irish-born immigrants by about two to one.

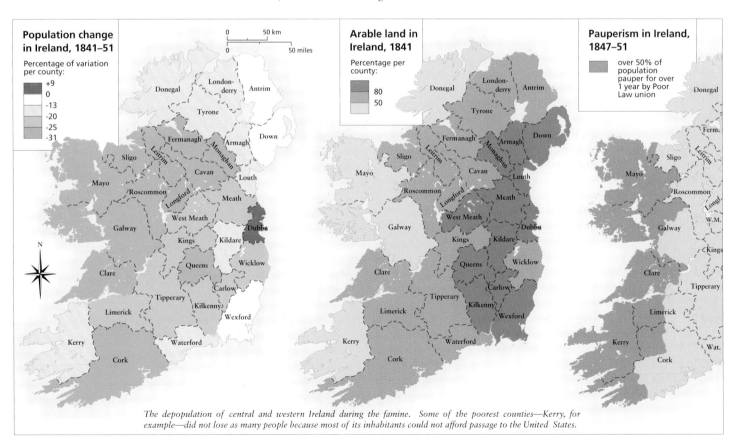

The depopulation of central and western Ireland during the famine. Some of the poorest counties—Kerry, for example—did not lose as many people because most of its inhabitants could not afford passage to the United States.

Uncle Sam beckons the adventurous, poor, and desperate of Europe to the 'land of promise.'

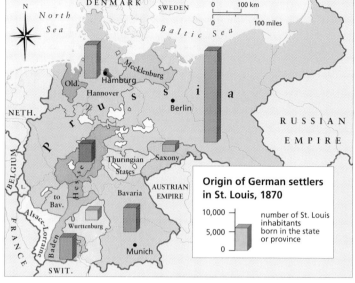

Origin of German settlers in St. Louis, 1870

number of St. Louis inhabitants born in the state or province

10,000
5,000
0

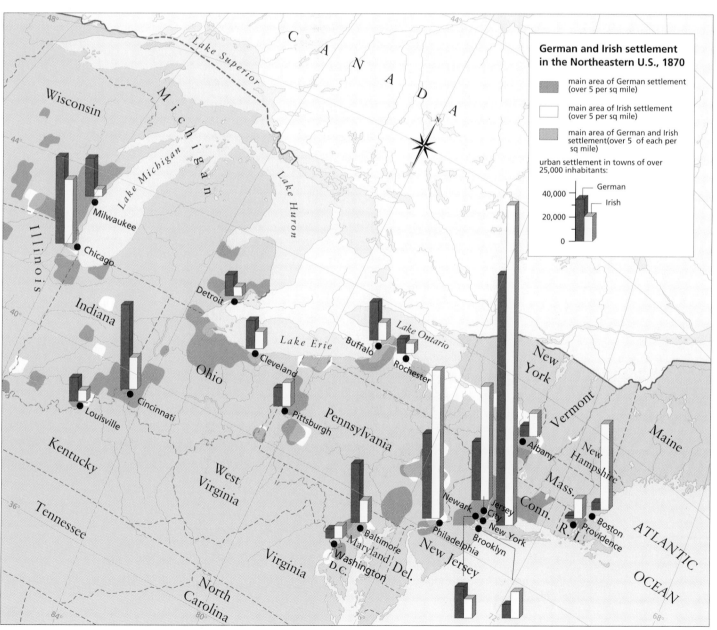

German and Irish settlement in the Northeastern U.S., 1870

- main area of German settlement (over 5 per sq mile)
- main area of Irish settlement (over 5 per sq mile)
- main area of German and Irish settlement (over 5 of each per sq mile)

urban settlement in towns of over 25,000 inhabitants:

German
Irish

40,000
20,000
0

THE WAR WITH MEXICO

AMERICA CONQUERS THE SOUTHWEST

In 1836, settlers from the United States who had moved to the Mexican province of Texas rebelled, declared their independence, and after a series of battles, drove the Mexican troops sent to suppress the uprising south of the Rio Grande. The Texans then elected Sam Houston president of the new republic and voted overwhelmingly to seek annexation by the United States. Chiefly because Texas would become a slave state, Congress was unable to agree to accept it. But in 1844 James K. Polk was elected president on a platform calling for annexation. As a result, in December 1845, Texas was admitted to the Union.

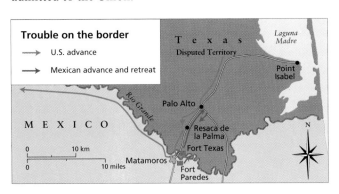

Trouble on the border

→ U.S. advance

→ Mexican advance and retreat

Texas
Disputed Territory

Laguna Madre

Point Isabel

MEXICO

Rio Grande

Palo Alto

Resaca de la Palma

Fort Texas

Matamoros

Fort Paredes

N

0   10 km
0   10 miles

Although the Texans had established an independent government in 1836, the Mexicans had not recognized it. In addition, the border between Mexico and the Republic was in dispute, Texas claiming it was the Rio Grande, Mexico the Nueces River, 150 miles to the north. Polk first offered to buy Texas (and also California) from Mexico, but the Mexicans refused even to discuss the matter. Polk then ordered troops commanded by General Zachary Taylor to advance to the Rio Grande.

By late April 1846, the Mexicans had established Fort Paredes, named after the general who had just appointed himself president of Mexico, at Matamoros, on the south bank of

the Rio Grande, and American troops had built Fort Texas on the north bank. The Mexicans then sent about 6,000 troops across the river. They besieged Fort Texas and advanced north to Palo Alto. Taylor responded by attacking. On May 8, at the head of a force of 2,300 men, he defeated the Mexicans at Palo Alto, and the next day, after another clash at Resaca de la Palma, raised the siege of Fort Texas and drove the Mexican army back across the Rio Grande. On May 13, after Polk had announced that "war exists," Congress formally declared war.

By the end of June, Taylor had almost 15,000 soldiers ready to invade Mexico. He established a base at Camargo, up river from Matamoros, and launched an attack on Monterey. After a five-day battle (September 20–24), the city surrendered. Next, after a two-month armistice, he advanced to Saltillo, where he was reinforced by troops under General John E. Wool, who marched across difficult terrain from San Antonio. At the Battle of Buena Vista (February 1847) the Americans defeated a Mexican force three times their size commanded by General Antonio Santa Anna.

Meanwhile, all of California and the rest of northwestern Mexico was falling into American hands. With the help of Captain John C. Frémont, who was heading a surveying expedition in California when the war broke out, Americans in the San Francisco area staged a revolt and established the Republic of California. In a rapid series of events that August, United States naval forces in Pacific waters seized Monterey, San Francisco, Sonoma, and then Santa Barbara and Los Angeles. Commodore Robert F. Stockton promptly declared California part of the

United States and appointed himself governor.

Far to the east, as soon as war had been declared, Colonel Stephen Watts Kearney had set out from Fort Leavenworth at the head of 1,700 men, their destination Sante Fe, capital of the province of New Mexico. Kearney occupied Santa Fe without a fight on August 18. He then sent part of his force, led by Colonel Alexander Doniphan, southward to support the army commanded by Zachary Taylor and pushed on to California with a small contingent of dragoons. He occupied San Diego on December 12, then joined with Commodore Stockton to subdue the last Mexican resistance in southern California.

Doniphan's troops occupied El Paso in late December, crossed the Rio Grande, defeated a Mexican force in the Battle of the Sacramento River, occupied Chihuahua, and reached Buena Vista in time to participate in Taylor's attack.

Meanwhile, President Polk, who feared with good reason that Taylor, a Whig, would turn his military success to political advantage, authorized Winfield Scott, general-in-chief of the army, to organize an expedition to attack Mexico City. Scott gathered supplies and an army of 10,000 men at Camargo, then proceeded by sea to Tampico, where he established a base. Next his army sailed to Vera Cruz, a fortified city on the Gulf of Mexico directly east of Mexico City. After a brief siege, the Mexican garrison surrendered late in March. From Vera Cruz the Americans marched swiftly inland along the road to Mexico City. In mid April, at Cerro Gordo, they defeated a much larger Mexican army under Santa Anna, who was now president of Mexico, in a struggle marked by bloody hand-to-hand fighting. Then they pressed on through mountainous country to Puebla, where Scott paused to await supplies and fresh troops.

Finally, in September, after two more hard battles, the Americans captured Molina del Rey and the fortress of Chapultepec on the outskirts of Mexico City. On September 14, they occupied the capital.

United States troops in bloody hand-to-hand fighting (below) at Cerro Gordo defeat a much larger Mexican army lead by Santa Anna, who was also president of Mexico.

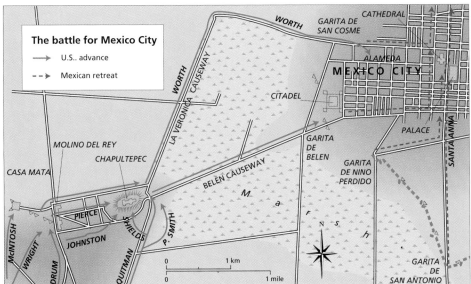

The battle for Mexico City

→ U.S.. advance

--→ Mexican retreat

WORTH   GARITA DE SAN COSME   CATHEDRAL

ALAMEDA

MEXICO CITY

WORTH

LA VERONICA CAUSEWAY

CITADEL

MOLINO DEL REY

CHAPULTEPEC

CASA MATA

GARITA DE BELEN

PALACE

GARITA DE NINO PERDIDO

SANTA ANNA

BELÉN CAUSEWAY

M   a   r   s   h

PIERCE

McINTOSH

WRIGHT

JOHNSTON

SHIELDS

P. SMITH

QUITMAN

DRUM

N

0   1 km
0   1 mile

GARITA DE SAN ANTONIO

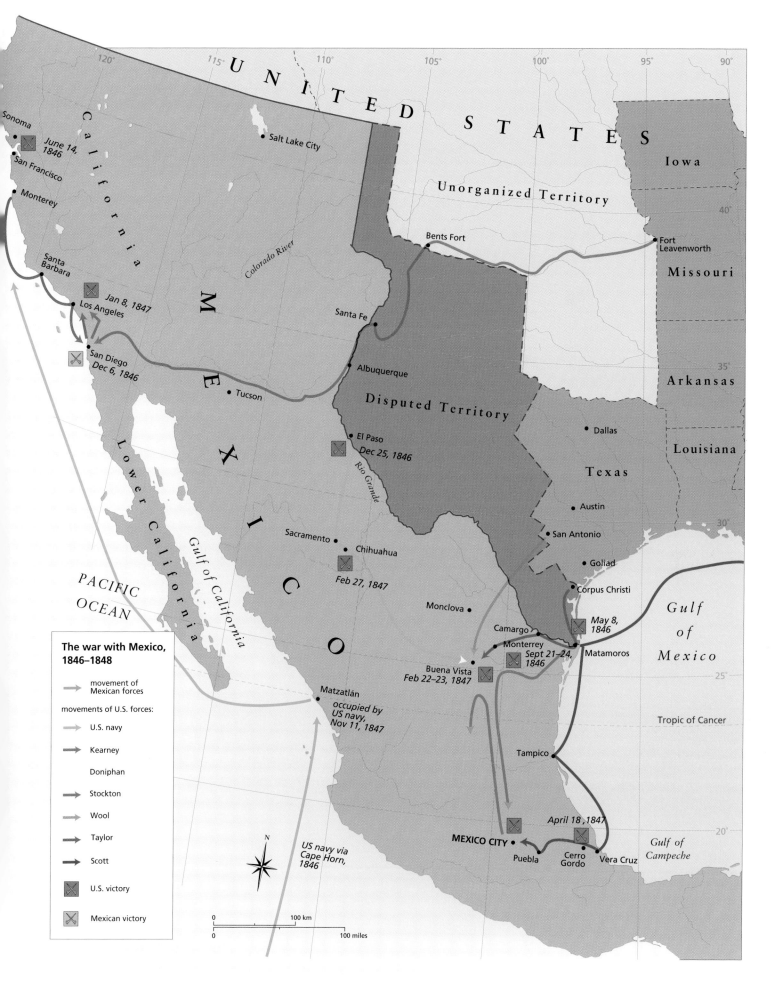

Sonoma
June 14, 1846
San Francisco
Monterey
Santa Barbara
Los Angeles
Jan 8, 1847
San Diego
Dec 6, 1846
Tucson

Salt Lake City

UNITED STATES

Iowa

Unorganized Territory

Bents Fort

Fort Leavenworth

Missouri

Santa Fe

Albuquerque

Arkansas

El Paso
Dec 25, 1846

Disputed Territory

Dallas

Louisiana

Colorado River

M E X I C O

Rio Grande

Texas

Austin

San Antonio

Lower California

Gulf of California

Sacramento

Chihuahua
Feb 27, 1847

Goliad

Corpus Christi

Monclova

PACIFIC OCEAN

Camargo

Monterrey
Sept 21–24, 1846

Matamoros

Buena Vista
Feb 22–23, 1847

May 8, 1846

Gulf of Mexico

Matzatlán
occupied by
US navy,
Nov 11, 1847

Tropic of Cancer

Tampico

The war with Mexico, 1846–1848

→ movement of Mexican forces

movements of U.S. forces:
→ U.S. navy
→ Kearney
　 Doniphan
→ Stockton
→ Wool
→ Taylor
→ Scott
◻ U.S. victory
◻ Mexican victory

N

US navy via
Cape Horn,
1846

April 18, 1847

MEXICO CITY

Puebla
Cerro Gordo
Vera Cruz

Gulf of Campeche

0 — 100 km
0 — 100 miles

PART 4: SLAVERY AND THE CIVIL WAR

Though known as the South's "peculiar institution," slavery was no mere regional eccentricity but a fundamental constituent of the life of a frontier nation. Forms of forced labor had spread through much of the western hemisphere as it was being colonized—for while there were abundant lands suitable for the cultivation of commercially desirable crops, compliant workers were not locally available in any number. Slavery helped America carve out its place in the world economy, cotton becoming not simply a major export but a raw material of the industrial revolution. By the mid-19th century, as the nation fulfilled its "manifest destiny to overspread the continent," the growth of the nation intertwined with slavery in still another fashion. The availability of western land was seen as a necessary ingredient of the social mobility northerners treasured, and many worried lest free state settlers be crowded out of frontier territories by slaves and their masters. Equally adamently, white southerners believed slavery's banishment from the west spelled their political—and, some contended, economic— doom and insulted their honor.

THE SLAVE SYSTEM
A SIMPLE INVENTION CHANGES THE COURSE OF HISTORY

Slavery existed in North America from early in the 17th century and was the dominant labor system in some parts of the South from the early 18th, but by the time of the Revolution the growth of the "peculiar institution" appeared to have been checked. Sea Island cotton was being grown along the Georgia and South Carolina coasts at the time of the Revolution, but was extremely sensitive to frost and its cultivation was not expanding. But in 1793, Eli Whitney, a young graduate of Yale University, invented the cotton gin, a simple, hand-operated machine that revitalized both slavery and cotton cultivation and changed the course of American history.

The cotton gin was used to separate the seeds of cotton plants from the fluffy white fiber. It was important because it made it commercially profitable to grow "upland" cotton, a hardy variety that flourished over wide areas of the South, but which unlike Sea Island cotton was extremely difficult to de-seed by hand. A single slave operating a cotton gin could remove the seeds from 50 times as much cotton in a day as he could with his fingers. In 1793, only 3,000 bales of cotton were produced in the United States. In 1800 output reached 100,000 bales, roughly 500 million pounds, and by the early

1820s annual production was averaging more than 400,000 bales. This was only the beginning. Output exceeded 1 million bales in the mid-1830s, 2 million in the 1840s, 3 million in the 1850s, and was approaching 4 million on the eve of the Civil War.

This growth required a huge expansion of the area where cotton was grown. First, cotton took over the fertile Appalachian Piedmont in a band running from southern Virginia into Georgia. Then it spread westward across central Alabama and Mississippi and into the rich alluvial soil of the banks of the Mississippi River, in a broad band from Tennessee and Arkansas to southern Louisiana. Finally, in the 1840s and 1850s, the crop spread into the eastern sections of Texas.

Parallel to this expansion went an expansion of slavery, both numerically and geographically. In 1800, there were fewer than a million slaves in the United States, the vast majority concentrated in the states south of Pennsylvania and the Ohio River. In 1808 Congress prohibited the importation of more slaves, but by 1830 there were well over 2 million slaves in the United States and by 1860 there were 4 million.

The growth of the slave population of the United States by natural increase was unique in the Western hemisphere, and testifies to the relatively healthy climate of the cotton belt and to

the price of slaves, which tripled in 30 years, reaching nearly $2,000 for what was known as "a prime field hand" and still more for a skilled carpenter or cook. Although slavery was a vicious exploitation of human labor, the value of slaves encouraged most slaveholders to provide adequately for their physical needs.

However, the westward expansion of cotton cultivation served to worsen what was an inherently bad institution. When a planter moved west with his slaves and worldly goods, it might mean more hard work for the slaves, clearing land and constructing houses and outbuildings, but it did not in most cases separate the slaves from their families and closest friends. But land in the Mississippi delta, the Alabama black belt, and East Texas was especially fertile. Production and profits soared and with them the need for labor. The price of a slave tended to be several hundred dollars higher there than in eastern sections.

This situation encouraged planters in the Upper South to sell their "surplus" slaves. Slave trading became a big business; one large firm, Franklin and Armfield, bought thousands of slaves yearly and shipped them by sea to New Orleans or "down the river" to Natchez, where they were sold at auction. In the 1850s, about 200 men were engaged in selling slaves in New Orleans alone. At both the selling and buying ends of this noxious commerce, husbands were

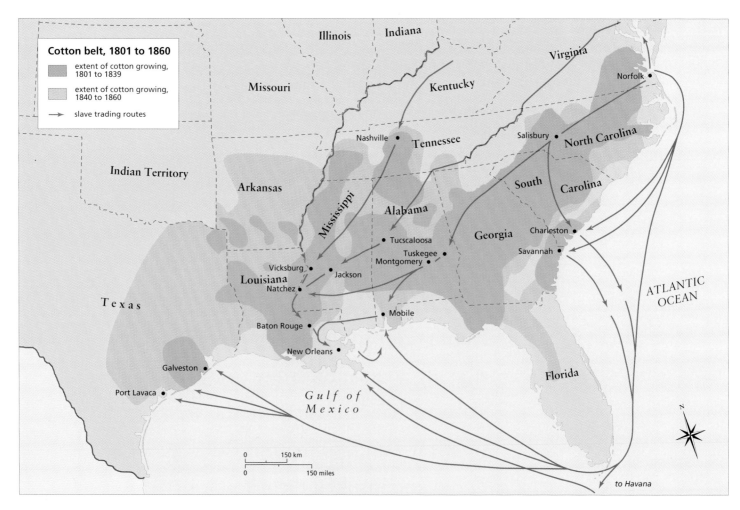

Cotton belt, 1801 to 1860

■ extent of cotton growing, 1801 to 1839
■ extent of cotton growing, 1840 to 1860
→ slave trading routes

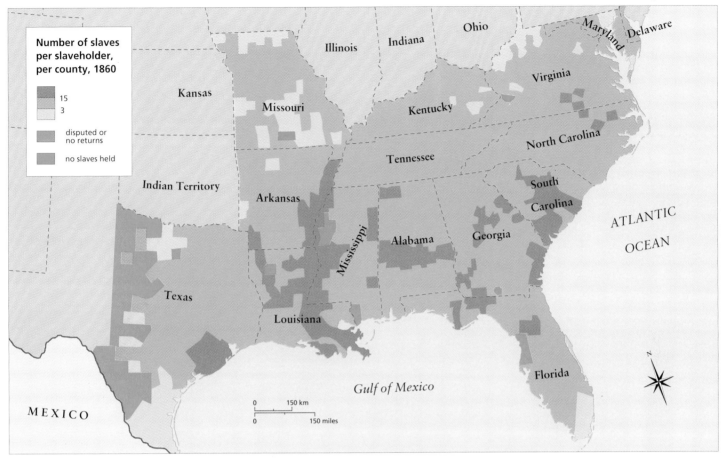

Number of slaves per slaveholder, per county, 1860

15
3

disputed or no returns

no slaves held

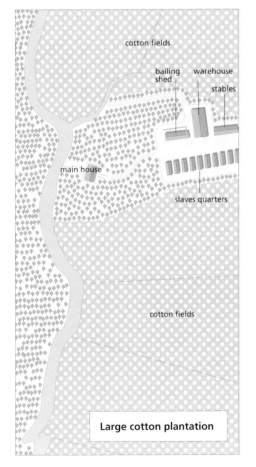

cotton fields

bailing shed

warehouse

stables

main house

slaves quarters

cotton fields

Large cotton plantation

In this poster (below), the slave dealers Hewlett and Bright of New Orleans, Louisiana, advertise the sale, on behalf of the departing owner (who was due to sail to Europe), of ten slaves. They ranged in age from Sarah, an experienced cook of 45 year, to Emma, a ten year old orphan child. Their fate was decided on May 13, 1835.

often separated from wives, and children from their parents. Such separations were more often than not as permanent as death; even if they knew where a relative or friend had been sent, slaves had no way to communicate, since nearly all were illiterate. Teaching slaves to read or write was against the law in most southern states.

Growing cotton was a profitable business, and the largest profits went to those with the largest and most fertile farms. These plantations required more slave labor, and the price of slaves was rising. Inevitably, the ownership of slaves became concentrated in fewer hands. In 1860, only one white family in four in the south owned any slaves at all. About 46,000 southerners out of a white population of 8 million owned 20 or more slaves in that year, but only a couple of hundred of these owned 200. Being a slaveholder was expensive, or, to be a slaveholder of any size, you had to be rich. Since the *average* slave cost at least $1,000 in the late ante bellum period, buying that many, and enough land to employ them efficiently, required what amounted to a small fortune at a time when an ordinary laborer, North or South, was earning no more than five dollars a week.

Thus it was that slavery and plantation agriculture went hand in hand, the better suited the land for cotton, the larger the agricultural unit, and the more dense the black population. This had profound effects on southern society and politics, as well as upon southern agriculture.

SLAVERY IN THE TERRITORIES
WESTWARD EXPANSION AND SECTIONALISM

In 1776, when the Second Continental Congress formally declared that "all men are created equal" and possessed of the God-given right to "liberty," every one of the 13 colonies that were about to become sovereign states contained substantial numbers of people of African birth or descent who were being held in bondage. The Revolution that this Declaration of Independence began did result in the ending of slavery in large sections of the new nation, but the process by which the institution was eventually eradicated was long and extremely complex, even in the so-called "free" states. According to the census, there were still 18 slaves in the northeastern states in 1860.

By 1784, Pennsylvania and the New England states had acted to end slavery. This was followed around the turn of the century by New York and New Jersey. Except for Massachusetts alone no state emancipated existing slaves.

The other states provided that the children of slaves born thereafter were to be freed upon reaching maturity. None of the other original 13 states did away with the institution of slavery voluntarily.

In the Northwest Ordinance of 1787, Congress barred slavery from the territory between the Ohio and Mississippi rivers and the Great Lakes, what later became the states

of Ohio, Indiana, Illinois, Michigan, and Wisconsin. The admission of new southern states kept the number of free and slave states in balance. In 1820, as part of the compromise that admitted Missouri to the Union as a slave state and Maine as a free state, slavery was barred from the rest of Louisiana territory west of Missouri and north up to the border with British North America (Canada).

The acquisition of California and the rest of the Southwest after the Mexican War, 1846 – 48, raised the question of slavery in the territories again. A further compromise was worked out in Congress. California was admitted to the Union as a free state and the fate of slavery elsewhere in the Southwest was left in the hands of its settlers. This was known as "popular sovereignty."

With slavery already barred from the Oregon Territory, this apparently ended the need for congressional action. But only four years later, the subject of slavery in the territories was revived by the passage of Senator Stephen A. Douglas's Kansas-Nebraska Act, which repealed the Missouri Compromise ban on slavery in the region west of Iowa and Missouri and substituted popular sovereignty.

Douglas conceived of the law as a way to give southerners a chance to maintain the sectional balance, which would be tilted toward the North if both Kansas and Nebraska became free states. But it caused consternation in the North, and bloodshed in the Kansas

Territory, where pro- and anti-slavery settlers battled to control the territorial government.

Three years later, the Supreme Court tried to settle the question in the case *Dred Scott* v. *Sanford*. Scott was a slave who had been taken by his master into Illinois and then into territory free under the Missouri Compromise before returning to slave territory.

With the help of a white lawyer, Scott sued for his freedom, arguing that his residence in places where slavery was illegal had made him and his wife, whom he had married in free territory, free. In an extremely complicated decision, the Court rejected this argument and in addition declared that the already-repealed Missouri Compromise had been unconstitutional. Slaves were property, and since under the Fifth Amendment the federal government could not deprive anyone of life, liberty, or property, slaveowners could not be prevented from bringing their slaves into any territory. Minnesota Territory, the unorganized regions of the Louisiana Purchase, and even Oregon and Washington Territories in the Northwest, were thereby opened to slavery.

The Dred Scott case only heightened existing tensions and, "no foot of soil became slave because of it."

Oregon and Kansas became free states in 1859 and 1861, and Nevada during the Civil War in 1864, The ratification of the Thirteenth Amendment in 1865 put the question of slavery in the territories permanently to rest.

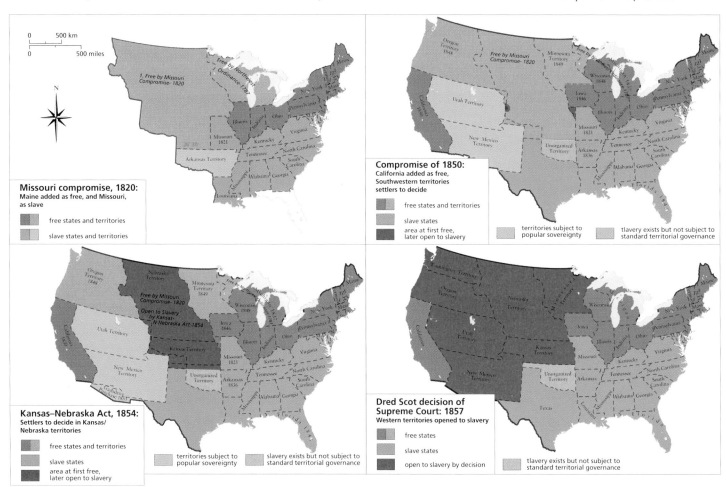

Missouri compromise, 1820:
Maine added as free, and Missouri, as slave

- free states and territories
- slave states and territories

Compromise of 1850:
California added as free, Southwestern territories settlers to decide

- free states and territories
- slave states
- area at first free, later open to slavery
- territories subject to popular sovereignty
- tlavery exists but not subject to standard territorial governance

Kansas–Nebraska Act, 1854:
Settlers to decide in Kansas/Nebraska territories

- free states and territories
- slave states
- area at first free, later open to slavery
- territories subject to popular sovereignty
- slavery exists but not subject to standard territorial governance

Dred Scot decision of Supreme Court: 1857
Western territories opened to slavery

- free states
- slave states
- open to slavery by decision
- tlavery exists but not subject to standard territorial governance

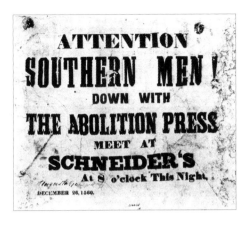

Hastily produced hand bill (above) invites Southerners to a pro-slavery meeting. Reaction in the south to northern agitation became so violent that local people who opposed slavery moved north.
A group of escaped slaves (right) with their liberator Harriet Tubman: this self effacing secret agent of the underground railroad is said to have led north as many as 300 people.

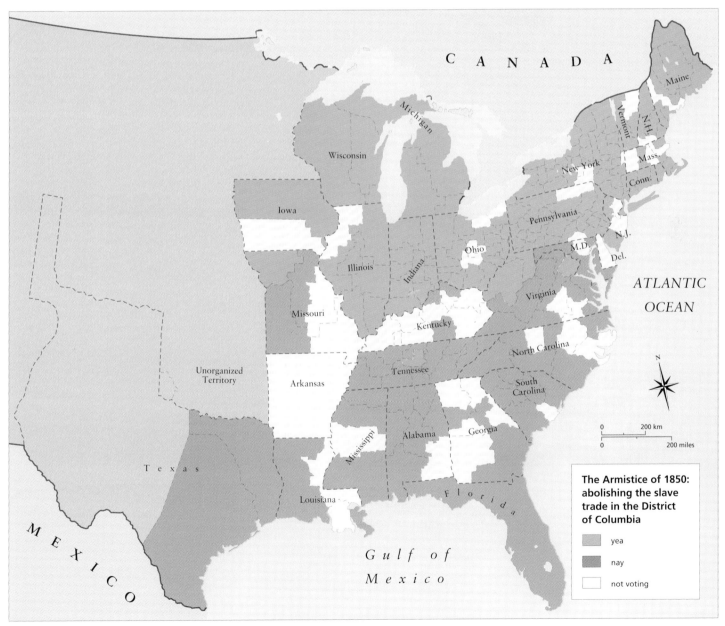

The Armistice of 1850: abolishing the slave trade in the District of Columbia

yea

nay

not voting

ABOLITIONISTS AND RUNAWAYS
THE FAILURE OF THE UNDERGROUND RAILROAD

That slaves resented their bondage goes without saying. That many sought to escape is easily demonstrated. How many runaways made their way to freedom, however, is another question. In the 17th century, and later in frontier districts, numbers of slaves and white indentured servants escaped by melting into the forest. Many joined up with the Indians, and some fashioned small, self-sufficient communities in the wilderness. Later, as the country became more settled, escape became difficult. In 1855, a southern judge estimated the total at 60,000. Spread over 200 years this seems inconsequential. But many more ran off only to be captured or to return voluntarily, exhausted, starving, or disheartened.

American slaveowners pursued runaways vigorously and punished those they caught brutally. But until the rise of the abolitionist movement in the North, southerners treated the problem as inherent to the system and dealt with it accordingly. When they failed to capture runaways they published their descriptions in newspapers, offering rewards for their capture. Abolitionism changed this. Slaveowners detested abolitionists both because of their efforts to deprive them of property and because of their insistence that the ownership of human beings was immoral. Abolitionists sought to distribute anti-slavery tracts in the South, but this was ineffective (since few slaves could read) and was easily blocked by banning such literature from the mails. More infuriating to southerners was the so-called Underground Railroad, a clandestine network of supporters who were said to give refuge to fugitives and to pass them on from one "station" to another on the line to freedom in Canada.

The underground railroad was neither as organized nor as extensive as legend suggests. More important, it did not exist in any of the slave states; most runaways had a long way to go before they could count on the help of any free person. Nevertheless, abolitionism made the runaway problem a sectional conflict in a way that it had never been before, and the problem was intensified by the passage of a strong Fugitive Slave Act as part of the Compromise of 1850.

Slaveowners resented northern help to runaways out of proportion to its extent and effectiveness. During the 1850s only about a thousand slaves escaped a year, roughly one quarter of one percent of the 4 million slaves in the country. Furthermore, those from the southwestern states escaped to Mexico, where nothing could be done to recover them. And almost all of those who fled northward came from the border states, where slavery was relatively unimportant and in decline. The number of slaves who managed to get from the cotton belt to any free state was tiny, and was confined to blacks with special skills or circumstances.

The experiences of some of the slaves who did escape makes this clear. One of the most famous runaways was Frederick Bailey, who grew up in Maryland, an important advantage. When he was eight a white woman taught him the rudiments of reading, a skill he assiduously developed. His owner hired him out to a succession of masters in and around Baltimore, where he greatly broadened his knowledge of the world. In 1834, while working as a field hand, he ran off, but returned when he could not discover a way to escape. Later, back in Baltimore, he became a ship's caulker. In 1838, after another abortive attempt to escape, he borrowed the papers of a free black sailor and boarded a train to Wilmington, Delaware. There he took a steamer to Philadelphia, followed by another train to New York. In New York, a black abolitionist took him under his wing and sent him to Newport, Rhode Island, and thence to New Bedford, Massachusetts, where he changed his name to Douglass to lessen the danger of being traced and forced back into slavery. As Frederick Douglass he went on to become a major figure in the abolitionist movement, and after the Civil War, an important black leader. Douglass was determined to be free, intelligent and otherwise endowed, but he was also extremely lucky.

The experience of William and Ellen Craft, slaves in Georgia, is illuminating. Ellen, light-skinned enough to pass as white, dressed in men's clothes and posed as an ailing planter. Her husband accompanied her as the "planter's" slave servant. In 1848 they boarded a train in Macon, proceeded to Savannah, then on in stages that were unlikely to attract attention: by ship to Charleston and Wilmington, North Carolina; to Petersburg, Richmond, and the Potomac by train; by river to Washington, and finally by train to Philadelphia, New York, and Boston. Their escape required knowledge and money that no ordinary slave possessed.

Other famous runaways include: Josiah Henson, a Kentucky plantation slave who in 1830 escaped with his wife and children (this was most unusual) into Indiana; the Hensons went on on foot to Sandusky, Ohio, by lake steamer to Buffalo, New York, and finally found refuge in Canada. William Wells Brown, of Missouri, who escaped while in Cincinnati, having accompanied his master there by river boat in 1834, and Anthony Burns, a Virginian who stowed away on a ship bound for Boston in 1854. Burns was captured and forcibly returned to his master, but outraged Bostonians purchased his freedom.

Born Isabella, a slave, in or around 1797 (no one recorded her birth), Sojourner Truth (below) was sold from one family to another in the Hudson Valley. In 1826, a kindly farmer bought her freedom. She got caught up in the religious excitements of the era, for a time fell under the spell of a religious zealot named Robert Matthias, and, in 1843, became an ardent and powerful exponent of abolitionism.

The myth of the 'underground railway'

- free states
- slave states
- slaves over 70 percent of total population, 1860
- mythic representation of runaway exodus

Henry Highland Garnet escaped with his family from a plantation in Kent County, Maryland, on the eastern shore of Chesapeake Bay, in 1824. Henry, age nine, proceeded overland to Wilmington, Delaware, then to New Hope in Bucks County, Pennsylvania. The family settled in New York City, later residing in Troy, New York; Jamaica; Washington, D.C.; and New York City. He was appointed minister to Liberia in 1881, where he died in 1882.

James W. C. Pennington escaped from a farm near Hagerstown, Maryland, in 1827. He traveled on foot in the direction of Baltimore where he was captured near Reisterstown, Maryland, but escaped. He then headed northwest into Adams County, Pennsylvania, where he stayed for several months. He then traveled northeast through Lancaster County to East Nautmeal in Chester County, Pennsylvania. Finally, he settled near New York.

Josiah Henson escaped on foot with his wife and children from Davies County, Kentucky, in 1830. They crossed the Ohio River and headed into southern Indiana. They walked northeast to Cincinnati, and then across Ohio to Sandusky, on to Lake Erie. from there took a boat to Buffalo, New York, and crossed the Niagara River to Canada. They later resided in Dawn, Ontario. He died in Ontario in 1884.

Frederick Douglass escaped from Baltimore, Maryland in 1838, disguised as a sailor, and with borrowed seaman's papers. He traveled by train to Wilmington, Delaware, there he took a boat to Philadelphia, from there he took a train to New York City. After a short time, he traveled to Newport, Rhode Island, by sea, and then by stage, to New Bedford, Massachusetts, where he settled. He later resided in Rochester, New York, and Washington, D. C. After diplomat services in Haiti, he died in Washington in 1895.

William and Ellen Craft escaped from the Deep South in 1848. They traveled by rail from Macon to Savannah, Georgia, boarded a ship to Charleston, South Carolina, then took another ship to Wilmington, North Carolina. From there, they traveled by train via Petersburg and Richmond, Virginia, to a point near Fredericksburg, Virginia, where they took another ship up the Potomac River to Washington, D.C. and, again by rail, to Philadelphia, stopping in Baltimore. Eventually, they settled in Boston. Later they resided in Great Britain and then back in Bryan County, Georgia. They both died in Charleston, South Carolina; William in 1890, and Ellen in 1897.

Harriet Tubman left Dorchester County, Maryland, on the eastern shore of Chesapeake Bay, in 1849. What little is known about her escape is that she made her way to Philadelphia. Later returning south to help other slaves escape, it is said she helped as many as 300 to their freedom. She later resided in Cape May, New Jersey; St. Catharines, Ontario; and Auburn, New York. She died in 1913.

Anthony Burns escaped in 1854 from Richmond, Virginia, stowing away on a ship to Boston, Massachusetts. He was apprehended in Boston and, under the terms of the Fugitive Slave law, was returned, to Richmond causing tumult among the residents of Boston, who purchased his freedom in 1855, later resided in Oberlin, Ohio; Indianapolis; and St. Catharines, Ontario, where he died in 1862.

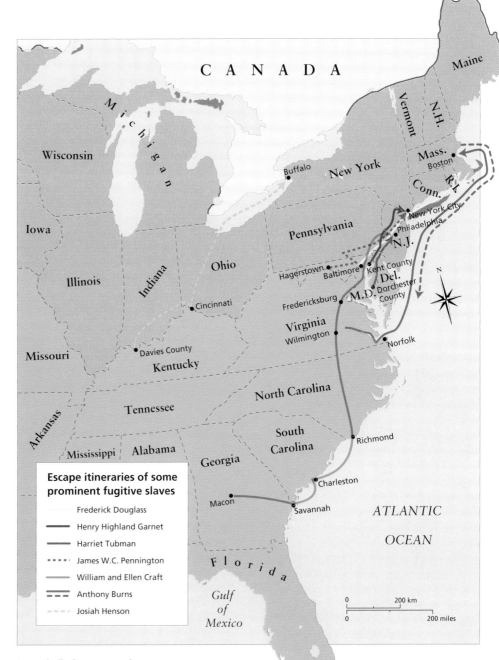

Escape itineraries of some prominent fugitive slaves

— Frederick Douglass
— Henry Highland Garnet
— Harriet Tubman
--- James W.C. Pennington
— William and Ellen Craft
--- Anthony Burns
--- Josiah Henson

A reward offer for a runaway slave (below) issued in Bardstown, Kentucky on September 3, 1838.

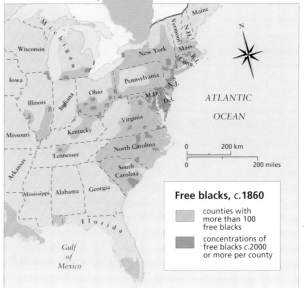

$150 REWARD

RANAWAY from the subscriber, on the night of the 2d instant, a negro man, who calls himself *Henry May*, about **22** years old, **5** feet **6** or **8** inches high, ordinary color, rather chunky built, bushy head, and has it divided mostly on one side, and keeps it very nicely combed; has been raised in the house, and is a first rate dining-room servant, and was in a tavern in Louisville for **18** months. I expect he is now in Louisville trying to make his escape to a free state, (in all probability to Cincinnati, Ohio.) Perhaps he may try to get employment on a steamboat. He is a good cook, and is handy in any capacity as a house servant. Had on when he left, a dark cassinett contee, and dark striped cassinett pantaloons, new—he had other clothing. I will give **$50** reward if taken in Louisville; **100** dollars if taken one hundred miles from Louisville in this State, and **150** dollars if taken out of this State, and delivered to me, or secured in any jail so that I can get him again. WILLIAM BURKE

Bardstown, Ky., September 3d, 1838.

Free blacks, c.1860

▢ counties with more than 100 free blacks

▣ concentrations of free blacks c.2000 or more per county

THE COMING OF THE CIVIL WAR

"FREE SOIL, FREE MEN, FRÉMONT!"

The successful negotiations that resulted in the Compromise of 1850 appeared to settle, once and for all, the vexing question of slavery in the western territories, and since no more than a relative handful of abolitionists talked of federal action to end slavery in states where it already existed, the danger of slavery causing the break-up of the Union appeared to be over. Senator Stephen A. Douglas of Illinois, who had maneuvered the complex Compromise through Congress, predicted that a "final settlement" had been achieved. It was time, he said, to "stop the debate and drop the subject." Few predictions have been more inaccurate, few suggestions more ignored.

The nation's road to disunion and civil war can be followed graphically in the presidential elections of 1852, 1856, and 1860. The Democratic candidate in 1852 was Franklin Pierce of New Hampshire. Pierce had served in both houses of Congress, but had retired in 1842 because of a drinking problem. He continued actively in local politics, however, and apparently overcame his alcoholism. He won the nomination after a long convention deadlock. The Whig candidate was General Winfield Scott, a distinguished military adminstrator and battlefield commander, but a vain, querulous, and politically inexperienced person. A third candidate, John P. Hale, was a former Democrat who had been read out of that party because be opposed the annexation of Texas. He ran on the Free Soil ticket.

After a relatively uneventful campaign, Pierce won an overwhelming victory in the Electoral College: 254 to 42, losing only Vermont, New Hampshire, Kentucky, and Tennessee. His popular majority was less impressive: 1.6 million to Scott's 1.3 million. Hale got 150,000, which is half of what Martin Van Buren had received as a Free Soiler four years earlier. Most significantly, both major parties remained strong in all sections. Despite the furor roused by Harriet Beecher Stowe's *Uncle Tom's Cabin*, which had been published in March, 1852 the Compromise of 1850 seemed to be holding.

The opposite was true four years later. The revival of the question of slavery in the territories by the Kansas-Nebraska Act of 1854 and the violence that followed its passage in "Bleeding Kansas" resulted in the collapse of the Whigs and the formation of the Republican party and the American, or Know-Nothing, party. The Republicans nominated John C. Frémont, a famous western explorer who was without political experience but strongly opposed to the extension of slavery. The Republicans believed that slavery must be kept out of all remaining territories: "Free soil, free men, Frémont! " The Know-Nothings ran expresident Millard Fillmore, a bland, compromising politician, who was also nominated by the remnants of the Whig party.

The Democratic choice was James Buchanan of Pennsylvania, who had held one or another political office almost continuously since 1815. Having been minister to Great Britain under Pierce, he had not been involved in the conflict over Kansas. More important, it was clear that the Republicans would sweep the Northeast and much of the Middle West.

The Democrats had a solid grip on the South. This made the tier of states running from Pennsylvania west crucial, and of these, Pennsylvania was the largest. Buchanan's long prominence seemed a valuable asset in his home state. And indeed it was, he carried Pennsylvania, and also Indiana and Illinois,

Published in 1852, two years after the Fugitive Slave Law, Uncle Tom's Cabin *sold more than 300,000 copies in a single year. Harriet Beecher Stowe was an accomplished writer, but her real genius lay in her ability to elicit the sympathies of her readers. For middle-class Northerners, women especially, the selling of the sainted Uncle Tom away from his family was a shocking violation of the Victorian "cult of domesticity".*

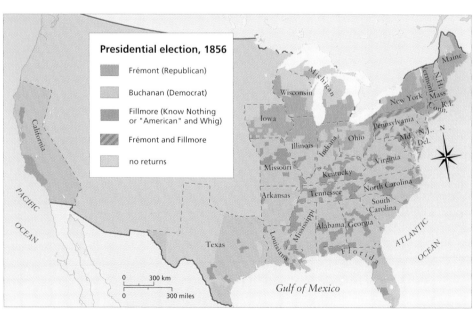

gaining a total of 174 electoral votes to Frémont's 114. Fillmore won only Maryland's 8 electoral votes. The popular vote was Buchanan 1.84 million, Frémont 1.34 million, Fillmore 876,000.

Once in office Buchanan tried to force a pro-slavery government on Kansas, bringing down on him the wrath of most northerners. The Supreme Court, in the Dred Scott case, tried to settle the issue by declaring that slave holders had a constitutional right to take their property into all the territories.

This roused still more opposition. By 1860 the Democratic Party had split in two. Senator Douglas, who argued that the residents of each territory should decide whether or not to legal-ize slavery, was nominated by the northern Democrats. Buchanan's vice president John C. Breckinridge was the choice of the southern wing of the party.

The Republicans settled on Abraham Lincoln of Illinois, who had won national attention in a series of debates with Douglas during their battle for Douglas' Senate seat in 1858. A fourth candidate, John C. Bell of Tennessee, was nominated by a new Constit-utional Union party.

With this line up, the result was a foregone conclusion. Lincoln carried California, Oregon, and all of the northern states, obtain-ing 180 electoral and 1.86 million popular votes. Douglas got 1.28 million popular votes, mostly in the North, but he only received 12 electoral votes, those of Missouri and part of New Jersey.

Breckinridge however won the South's 72 electoral votes, six times as many as Douglas, but he only received 848,000 popular votes. Bell carried the states of Virginia, Tennessee, and Kentucky, with 39 electoral votes and 593,000 popular votes.

Lincoln was the clear winner, although he got less than 40 percent of the popular vote.

Lincoln (left) as depicted in 1860 campaign literature. With the Democratic party split between north and south, Lincoln's election was assured. He did not campaign or give political speeches. In the election, he carried every Northern free state except New Jersey. But in ten Southern states, he did not receive a single popular vote.

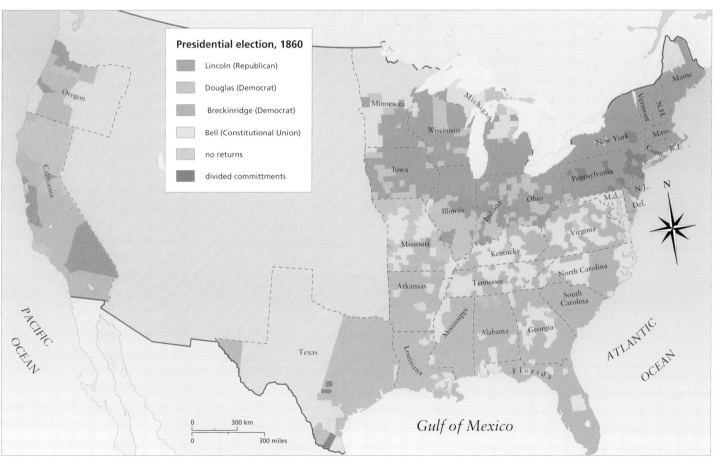

Presidential election, 1860

- Lincoln (Republican)
- Douglas (Democrat)
- Breckinridge (Democrat)
- Bell (Constitutional Union)
- no returns
- divided committments

SECESSION OF THE SOUTH
AND WEST VIRGINIA BECOMES A STATE OF THE UNION

A large majority of the white people of the North, including Abraham Lincoln, took up arms in the Civil War to prevent the southern states from seceding, not to free the slaves. This may seem absurd on the face of it: the states that seceded were all slave states; the controversy over slavery in the territories had long been a source of conflict between North and South; and the war certainly resulted in the abolition of the institution. But the statement is technically correct. The North fought because of slavery and destroyed slavery in order to win the struggle, but the purpose of the Lincoln administration and those who backed it was to save the Union.

On the surface the white people of most of the slave states seemed overwhelmingly in favor of secession. As soon as Lincoln's victory became clear, the legislature of South Carolina ordered the election of a special convention to consider leaving the Union. On December 20, the delegates voted unanimously to do so. Mississippi, Florida, and Alabama followed swiftly, and by February 1, Georgia, Louisiana, and Texas had also seceded, in each case by margins of better than four to one. Within a week, delegates of the seceded states met in Montgomery, Alabama, drafted a constitution, and established a provisional government, the Confederate States of America.

Then, after the attack on Fort Sumter and Lincoln's call for volunteers to resist secession, Virginia, Arkansas, Tennessee, and North Carolina, which had refused to secede merely because the Republicans had won the presidency, also left the Union. In Virginia the convention voted 103 to 46 to secede and in a referendum voters supported the decision by 96,750 to 32,134.

The speed and decisiveness of the secession movement conceals the fact that large numbers of southerners strongly disapproved of the decision to leave the Union. Some, like Robert E. Lee, put loyalty to the United States above everything except loyalty to their native state. Lee resigned his army commission only after Virginia seceded, doing so, he said, because he felt honor bound to "share the misery" of his fellow Virginians. "I cannot raise my hand against my birthplace, my home, my children," he explained simply. Others opposed secession because they were afraid the South would be defeated if war resulted. Most nevertheless accepted the decision once it had been made and supported the Confederate cause.

There were, however, important sections of the South where a majority of the people were strongly opposed to secession. These were

Charleston, (above) looking over the center of the town toward the harbor, and Fort Sumter, photographed in 1860.

mostly areas that were unsuited to plantation agriculture and where there were few slaves. Most of these were in mountainous regions: Western Virginia and North Carolina, northern Georgia and Alabama, and eastern Tennessee. These were areas generally unsuited to the cultivation of cotton and where the soil was relatively poor. The people were not sympathetic to blacks, but they apparently did not think preserving slavery against a still-hypothetical threat grounds for leaving the Union. Eastern Tennessee counties opposed secession by two to one; those where 30 percent or more of the people were slaves (slaves, of course, were not consulted) favored secession by seven to one. In Virginia, the northwestern counties where there were few slaves voted three to one against leaving the Union; those with many slaves supported secession by ten to one. The northwestern counties then, in effect, seceded from Virginia and established a pro-Union government that in June 1863 became the state of West Virginia.

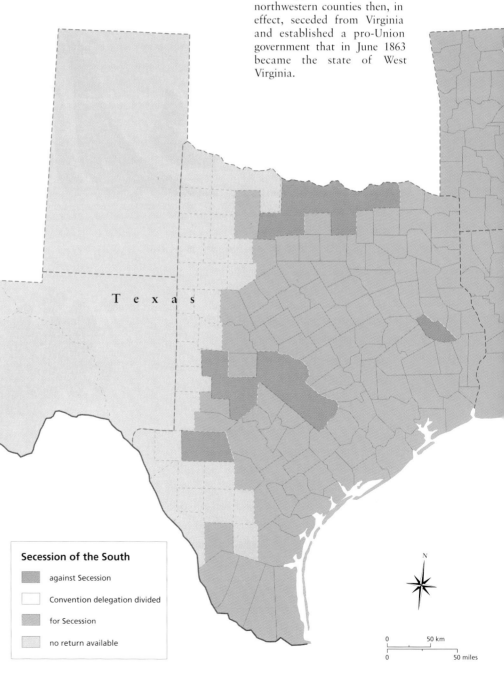

T e x a s

Secession of the South

- against Secession
- Convention delegation divided
- for Secession
- no return available

0   50 km

0   50 miles

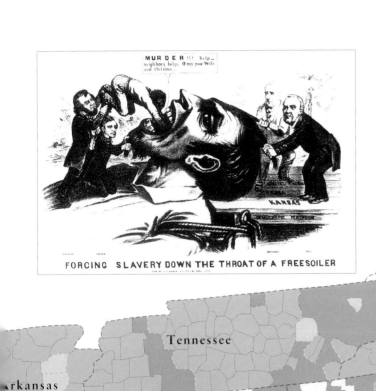

FORCING SLAVERY DOWN THE THROAT OF A FREESOILER

A pro-Republican cartoon (left) attacks the Democrats for forcing slavery on Kansas freesoilers.

Virginia

North Carolina

Tennessee

Arkansas

South Carolina

Georgia

Alabama

Louisiana

Florida

CHARLESTON
MERCURY
EXTRA:

Passed unanimously at 1.15 o'clock, P. M. December 20th, 1860.

AN ORDINANCE

To dissolve the Union between the State of South Carolina and other States united with her under the compact entitled "The Constitution of the United States of America."

We, the People of the State of South Carolina, in Convention assembled, do declare and ordain, and it is hereby declared and ordained,

That the Ordinance adopted by us in Convention, on the twenty-third day of May, in the year of our Lord one thousand seven hundred and eighty-eight, whereby the Constitution of the United States of America was ratified, and also, all Acts and parts of Acts of the General Assembly of this State, ratifying amendments of the said Constitution, are hereby repealed; and that the union now subsisting between South Carolina and other States, under the name of "The United States of America," is hereby dissolved.

THE
UNION
IS
DISSOLVED!

A special edition (above) of the Charleston Mercury hit the streets only fifteen minutes after the approval of the Ordinance of Secession on December 20, 1860.

The plantation master (left) shows a white lady, plantation slavery as it was meant to be: prosperous, industrious and self-sustaining. One slave, presumably contented, reclines atop the wagon. Encumbered with such illusions, the South went to war.

111

THE CIVIL WAR
RESOURCES AND WAR AIMS

In 1861, the nation went to war with itself. Yet in many respects, two societies came to blows as well. Unlike civil wars in some other lands, the antagonists were identified with strictly defined, geographically distinct and cohesive territories. Both free labor North and slave South brought a distinct array of resources to the fight. The North possessed obvious advantages in the manpower and material available for warmaking. But even though it limited its war aims to the preservation of the Union, it would have to fight a war of conquest and occupation. The Confederacy, on the other hand, needed only to fight a defensive war. Yet the very things for which independence had been declared—slavery and states rights—would make that independence all the more difficult to defend.

The Union enjoyed an immediately apparent superiority in men and resources. Even if the divided border states are excluded, almost 20 million Yankees faced only 9 million Southerners. Since the Confederacy would not arm its 3.5 million slaves, the Union advantage in available military manpower was even greater. Union armies through the war would maintain about a 2.5 to 1 numerical superiority. American industry had been nurtured in the North, and the raw materials, skilled labor, and manufacturing facilities necessary to outfit large armies were concentrated there. Northern states accounted for over 90 percent of the pig iron, firearms, cloth, and footwear the United States produced in 1860.

The North had more immediately available financial resources, too, Southern capital being bound up in land and slaves. Finally, the Union proved better able to transport men and material to far-flung fronts. Neither side had a terribly well integrated network. But the North had much more mileage—per capita and per square mile—and more rolling stock, and its industry produced nearly all of American locomotives.

The North extended its advantage early in the war by securing four slaveholding states—Kentucky, Missouri, Maryland, and Delaware—for the Union. The Lincoln administration employed arrests and military force to cow pro-secessionist officials and legislators in Missouri and Maryland. In Kentucky, it behaved more subtly, tolerating the state's pretensions to neutrality until Unionists could muster their strength. Union control would remain far from absolute in the border states—Marylanders and Kentuckians wore the gray as well as the blue, while Missourians fought one another both in the regular armies and in bitter guerrilla warfare. Yet the Confederacy had been deprived of rich territory. Had Maryland, Kentucky, and Missouri seceded, the Confederacy's potential military manpower would have increased by 45 percent, its manufacturing capacity by 80 percent, and its supply of horses and mules by almost 40 percent. The Confederacy would have surrounded

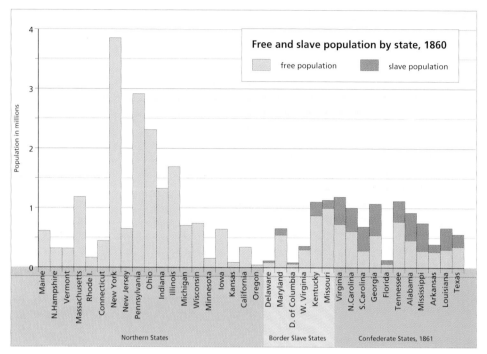

Free and slave population by state, 1860

Industry and raw materials, 1860

copper

silver and gold

anthracite

bituminous coal

iron ore

textiles

Principle manufacturing cities:

value of product over $100,000,000

value of product over $10,000,000

Union states, 1861

Confederate states, 1861

West Virginia, state 1863

Washington and strengthened its hold on the Mississippi, while the Ohio River might have served as a line of defense.

As a number of great powers have learned, however, a general superiority of resources hardly guarantees victory. The South held its own aces. Textiles had powered the industrial revolution, and the South provided some three-quarters of the world's cotton. It virtually monopolized American production of this most important export. The Confederacy hoped that dependence on "King Cotton" would undermine Northern determination to wage war and influence Europe to support Southern independence.

Ultimately, the Union made more of its respective advantages. Almost from scratch, both sides quickly assembled the largest armies that America had ever seen. By July 1861, hundreds of thousands were in uniform. The Union expanded its considerable industrial and agricultural capacity during the war, managing simultaneously to meet military and civilian needs. But the Confederate government also cultivated its war industry. Southern firms, most significantly Richmond's Tredegar Iron Works, succeeded in limiting shortages of arms and ammunition. Yet Confederate failures more than balanced successes. It could not exploit the world's dependence on cotton as much as it hoped, being hindered by the Union blockade and its own muddled policies. While Europe found alternate sources of cotton in Egypt and India, crop failures at home increased its need for Northern wheat, corn, beef, and pork. The Confederacy also increased its food production but could not ensure that food reached areas of greatest need. Neither did the Confederacy establish its financial independence. While the Union met the emergency with bond sales, greenbacks, tariffs, and national banks, the South's reliance on printing paper money condemned it to 9,000 percent inflation during the war, as compared to the North's 80 percent.

More than inadequate infrastructure and a flawed policy hobbled Southern mobilization. The Confederacy, deficient in manpower and material, had to manage its resources carefully. But being dedicated to states rights and local autonomy, it proved less ideologically equipped to do so. The military draft that the Confederacy introduced nearly a year before the Union, Richmond's attempts more rigidly to control military supply, its impressment of slave labor, its tax in kind on agriculture—all caused conflicts with state authorities and seemed to many citizens betrayals of the Confederacy.

If slavery was the cornerstone of the Confederacy, as its vice president said, such was a shaky foundation for a nation at war. Nothing in the North presented a problem comparable to Southern society's dependence on its slaves, for the Confederacy's wellbeing rested, in part, on a population whose best interests seemed to demand the victory of its masters' enemies.

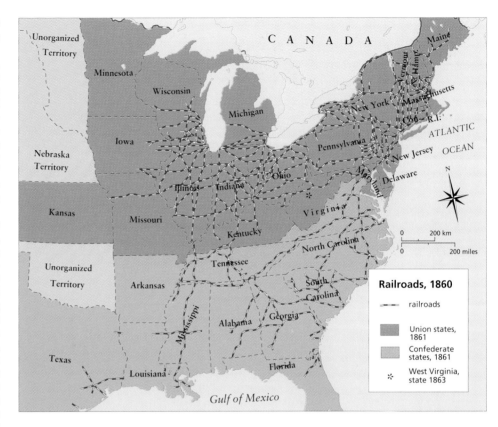

Railroads, 1860

- railroads
- Union states, 1861
- Confederate states, 1861
- West Virginia, state 1863

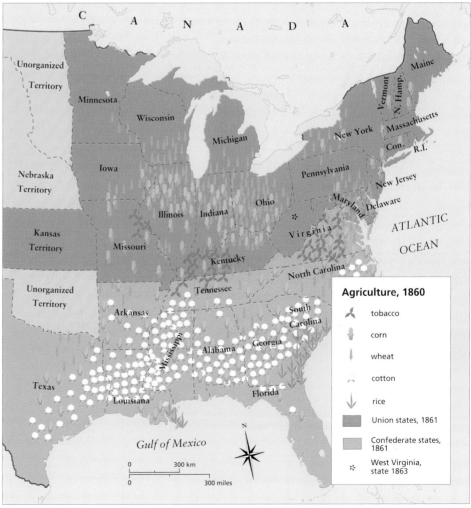

Agriculture, 1860

- tobacco
- corn
- wheat
- cotton
- rice
- Union states, 1861
- Confederate states, 1861
- West Virginia, state 1863

THE CIVIL WAR

1861 - 1862

In 1865, Lincoln reflected back on the beginning of the conflict: "Neither party expected for the war the magnitude or the duration which it has already attained... Each looked for an easier triumph, and a result less fundamental and astounding." The first one and a half years of fighting offered both sides a harsh education. Confederate forces, especially Robert E. Lee's Army of Northern Virginia, won memorable victories but discovered that their independence could be secured only by cruel and lonely struggle. The Union, suffering a number of ignominious defeats, began to learn that progress would come not in fighting Southern armies alone, but also waring upon Southern resources and institutions. With the Union advance in the West and Emancipation Proclamation, the means and meaning of Union victory began to emerge.

Throughout the war, the attention of the public and of military and political leaders often focused on that portion of Virginia which lay between Richmond and Washington. The British burning of Washington in 1814 demonstrated that the capture of a capital did not necessarily mean the end of a war, yet both Union and Confederacy devoted much energy to defending their own seat of government and menacing their enemy's. Cries of "Forward to Richmond" prodded an ill-prepared North to strike late in July 1861 at Confederate forces at Manassas. The Confederates, demonstrating the tactical value of railroads by reinforcing themselves from the Shenandoah Valley, sent the Yankees fleeing. Too disorganized to press the advantage, though, South as well as North learned that this war would hardly be won in a single stroke.

Eight months later, the Union again campaigned against the Confederate capital. General George McClellan's army sailed down the Chesapeake to advance upon Richmond via the peninsula formed by the James and York rivers. McClellan's habit of overestimating enemy strength and his solicitude for his new army led him to hesitate, however, before Confederate defenses at Yorktown and outside Richmond. Robert E. Lee took advantage of McClellan's caution. Thomas "Stonewall" Jackson's men rampaged up the Shenandoah in May and June, preventing additional Union forces from threatening Richmond. At the end of June, Lee himself attacked. The "Seven Days" battles forced McClellan back into a defensive position on the James River.

Elsewhere, the Union pursued a less showy but ultimately more profitable strategy—the use of its superior resources to damage the South's ability to make war. Having the manpower to defend only the most strategic points on its seaboard, the Confederacy was forced very early to yield important stretches of coastline. Reducing the ports available to the South, the Union was better able to effect the blockade which ultimately reduced Southern seaborne

trade to one-third of its antebellum volume.

West of the Appalachians, as on the coast, the Union attacked Confederate resources and communications. In contrast to Virginia, where major rivers acted as defensive barriers, in the West they afforded the Union opportunities to bisect the Confederacy, as in the case of the Mississippi, or to advance into its heartland, as in the case of the Tennessee and Cumberland. General Ulysses S. Grant and Flag Officer Andre Foote seized the latter opportunity in February 1862, moving against Forts Henry and Donelson. Their victories gave the Union control of an important agricultural and industrial area and forced the surrender of Nashville, Tennessee's capital. As Grant moved further down the Tennessee, the Confederates struck back. The unprecedented carnage at Shiloh (April 6–7) did not dislodge the Yankees from the Tennessee interior but broke their momentum there. Elsewhere in the West, though, Union troops strengthened their hold on Missouri and northern Arkansas and forced the Confederates to yield vital

points on the Mississippi. Union ships fought their way into New Orleans—the South's largest city—and Memphis. Within a year of Manassas, the Union held vital portions of the Southern interior as well as the Mississippi north of Vicksburg and south of Port Hudson.

This western string of successes ended at about the same time as McClellan's Peninsular campaign. Not content simply to stall Union efforts, Confederate armies on both sides of the Appalachians marched north, hoping to rally Kentucky and Maryland to the cause, win European recognition of their government, and strike at Northern morale before the November elections. The western offensive began in late August. Generals Braxton Bragg and Edmund Kirby Smith covered much ground in the next month, butreceived little more than cheers from

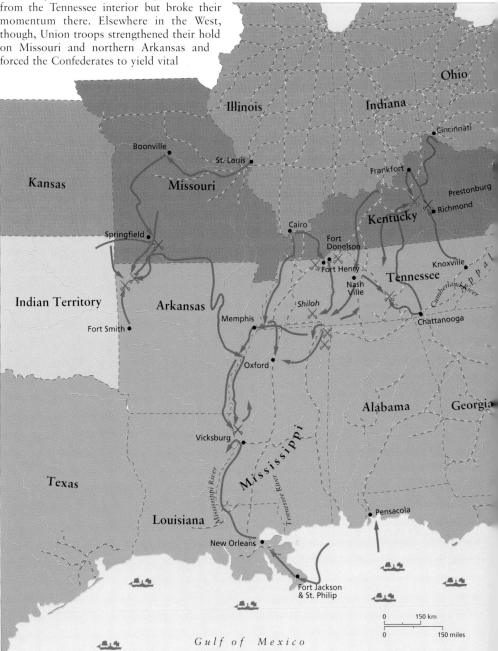

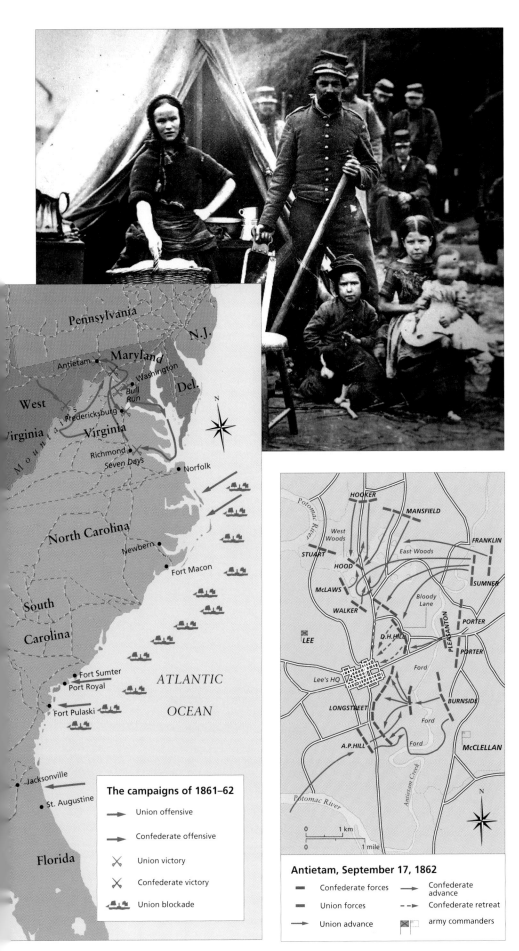

sympathetic Kentuckians. Outnumbered and inadequately provisioned, the Confederates withdrew after the inconclusive Battle of Perryville (October 8). In the East, the sequence of advance and withdrawal was more rapid. As the Union departed from the James, Lee maneuvered north, thrashing a Yankee force near the 1861 Manassas battlefield. His tired army then pushed into western Maryland, but a copy of Lee's orders fell into Union hands. Predictably, McClellan did not take advantage of this windfall as rapidly as he might have, but by mid-September Lee's army was backed against the Potomac. The fighting along Antietam Creek (September 17) made for the deadliest single day of the war. Almost 6,000 perished—twice the number of American combat deaths in the War of 1812, the Mexican War, and the Spanish-American War combined. The Confederate army stretched thin but never snapped for McClellan failed to commit fresh reserves during the battle or attack Lee afterwards as he hobbled back into Virginia. For this, Lincoln exiled "the young Napoleon" to private life.

Antietam stands as an examplar of the human cost of this conflict. At Bloody Lane, as at so many similarly name Civil War sites, familiar tactics—like close-order infantry assaults—and murderous innovations—like rifled muskets—mixed to grisly effect. But Antietam stands, too, as a pivotal moment. The repulse of Lee effectively ended Southern hopes for European aid. And Antietam gave Lincoln the victory he felt he needed to issue the Emancipation Proclamation.

At the end of 1862, Northern morale touched bottom. A third attempt on Richmond had ended disastrously at Fredericksburg. Still, the war had by then defined itself in ways which in the long-term favored the Union. For the Confederacy, it would be a solitary fight, without formal support from abroad. For the North, success would not come through brilliant victories or the quick capture of Richmond. But its greater resources would allow it to cut Southern arteries, bleed Confederate armies, and cripple the Confederacy's ability to provide for itself. The newly declared war on slavery aimed directly at the South's Achilles heel. It remained to be seen if the North had the spirit or stamina to see such a war through to victory.

The vicious battle between Antietam Creek and Sharpsburg launched at dawn on September 17. Line after line of Union infantry smashed into Confederate positions eventually driving the Confederates towards Sharpsburg. Late in the day Confederate reinforcements arrived and blunted the Union push, thus ending the fighting.

The campaigns of 1861–62

→ Union offensive

→ Confederate offensive

✕ Union victory

✕ Confederate victory

⛴ Union blockade

Antietam, September 17, 1862

▬ Confederate forces

▬ Union forces

→ Union advance

→ Confederate advance

--→ Confederate retreat

🚩 army commanders

EMANCIPATION AND BLACK MILITARY SERVICE
THE SECOND AMERICAN REVOLUTION

Not Lincoln's Emancipation Proclamation alone, but the ambitions of countless slaves, the pressure of Radicals and abolitionists, and the progress of the war itself transformed a struggle to preserve the Union into the promise of a "new birth of freedom." With emancipation and black enlistment, as well as the growing disaffection of whites on both sides, the war between North and South became one which also pitted Southerner against Southerner and, far less cataclysmically, Northerner against Northerner. Indeed, it is in the destruction of slavery—in part by slaves themselves—that the Civil War truly earned the title that the historians Charles and Mary Beard bestowed upon it, "the Second American Revolution." This war toppled the New World's largest slaveholding class.

less solicitous of slaveholders, either on principle or because they did not want to waste army time on non-military matters. Benjamin Butler, commanding troops in southeast Virginia, pioneered a policy of declaring fugitives from rebel masters "contraband" of war and put them to work for the army.

Lincoln hated slavery, but he doubted the federal government's constitutional power to interfere with it where it already existed, and was eager, too, to reassure those slaveowners and Democrats who supported the Union but would not countenance emancipation. Those determined that slavery be destroyed dealt with Lincoln's objections, and with Northern apathy, by citing military necessity. Slaves constituted a vital portion of the Southern labor force. Their numbers, abolitionists reasoned, should be brought to bear against, rather than in support of, the Confederate war effort. Increasingly, radicals in Congress persuaded

Blacks, eager that the war become one for freedom, proved eager to insure that it was won. The argument for the enlistment of black troops, like that for emancipation, involved an appeal to necessity. The army had learned the value of freed people's labor. Surely, given declining enlistments among whites, it could profit by augmenting its combat strength with black troops. Further, many believed, now that emancipation was a war aim, the population most directly to benefit should shoulder arms. As black troops began to be raised, haphazardly in 1862 and more systematically in 1863, both escaped Southern slaves and Northern free blacks enlisted. Despite discrimination in pay and promotion, black soldiers and sailors fought with distinction on all fronts—from Louisiana to the South Carolina coast. Over 180,000 served by war's end, comprising almost 10 percent of Union armed forces. In the South, emancipation and enlistment

The storming of Fort Wagner by the 54th Massachusetts on the evening of July 18, 1863 (left). Composed of black volunteers but led by Robert Gould Shaw, a white abolitionist, the 54th Massachusetts breached the ramparts but was eventually thrown back, sustaining heavy losses. Although the focal point of this lithograph is the death of Shaw, the broader significance of the battle appears in the foreground, where two black soldiers are bayoneting their Confederate foes.

Although the Confederacy fought to preserve slavery and although the Union denied any intention of destroying it, the war undermined the peculiar institution from early on. As white men left for the army, discipline and daily routines on Southern plantations and farms inevitably changed. The Confederate government itself disrupted master–slave relationships by requiring slaveowners to yield up bondsmen for defense-related labor. Masters who, seeking to escape Confederate impressment or Yankee encroachment, transported their slaves to less vulnerable locations, protected their investment at the expense of further unsettling the system. But it was the slaves' own actions that most weakened slavery, for many blacks took the war to be the occasion of their freedom—whatever the rival governments declared. From the beginning, slaves in the upper South and border states flocked to Union lines in large numbers. Even more came as the army moved forward.

The Northern army was avowedly an instrument for preserving the Union and not destroying slavery, and many commanders initially turned fugitives away or aided loyal masters in recovering their property. Other soldiers were

more conservative Republicans that slavery's disruption could be justified as a war measure and that victory without emancipation would spell further sectional conflict. In 1861 and 1862 Congressional Republicans passed a series of measures prohibiting slavery in Washington, D. C. and the territories and eroding rebels' rights to slave property. This progress climaxed in the Second Confiscation Act of July 1862, declaring "forever free" rebel masters' slaves who had come under Union control. At this point, Lincoln, adopting the military necessity argument, acted. His Emancipation Proclamation, announced September 22, only freed slaves in states, or parts of states, that were in rebellion. Yet it acknowledged Union armies to be agents of liberation, and lent the Northern cause a luster, both at home and abroad, that it had hitherto lacked. By war's end, Missouri, Maryland, West Virginia, as well as occupied Louisiana, Arkansas, and Tennessee also embraced emancipation. In early 1865, the Lincoln Administration won Congress's approval of the Thirteenth Amendment. Its eventual ratification guaranteed slavery's demise both in the South and in recalcitrant border states.

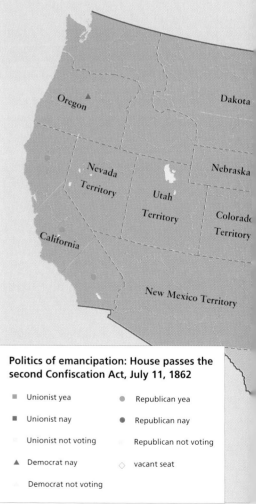

Politics of emancipation: House passes the second Confiscation Act, July 11, 1862

▪ Unionist yea	● Republican yea
▪ Unionist nay	● Republican nay
Unionist not voting	Republican not voting
▲ Democrat nay	◇ vacant seat
Democrat not voting	

advanced unevenly. Typically, slaves could join the war only when Federal armies marched into their midst. Thus, the parts of Tennessee and Louisiana captured early in the war contributed over 20,000 black soldiers each, while less than 50 black Texans are recorded as having served the Union. In the North, over two-thirds of black males aged 18 to 45 apparently enlisted. And the tens of thousands of enlistments in the border states effectively expanded the terms of Lincoln's Proclamation. The army did not actively exclude escaped slaves.

If Republicans often justified emancipation as an expedient, it proved politically inexpedient in many ways. Democrats railed against black freedom and Republican war policy. Conscription, they argued, burdened ordinary folk for the benefit of blacks and the affluent whites who could afford substitutes. Representing urban, working class, often Irish Catholic, constituencies, as well as Midwestern regions with economic and social ties

Black soldiers in the Union Army

Union territory

border slave state

Confederate territory

extent of Union control, spring 1864

numbers of black soldiers serving in the Union Army, by state

20,133
10,000
1,000
47

to the South, Democrats lined up with conservative Unionists against measures like the Second Confiscation Act. Anti-war sentiment emerged, too, especially in the Midwest. But the most violent outbreak of opposition occurred in New York City in July 1863. The four-day Draft Riot was a class, a political, and a racial confrontation. Of the more than 100 persons killed, at least 11 were blacks murdered by white mobs.

Just as all Northerners would not support a war for emancipation, not all white Southerners would support the Confederacy. Resistance stirred among those who had opposed secession in non-plantation areas in the Appalachians and Texas. But hostility to the Confederacy grew, too, among Southerners who had initially supported what they saw as a fight for self-determination. Confederate taxation, impressment, and conscription policies that appeared to favor large slave-owners seemed to trample on rights secession was intended to defend while forcing the yeomanry to bear disproportionate burdens. Desertion mounted as food and labor shortages wreaked havoc in their home states. Some soldiers returned to their families, some joined bands of resisters, some marauded.

As the war continued, then, the Confederacy had not simply to contend with a better-equipped North, but growing numbers of black and white Southerners who had determined that its cause was not their own.

DAY OF DECISION

JULY 3, 1863

If ever a great war turned on the events of a single day, it was in the Civil War, and the day was July 3, 1863. The historian Allan Nevins called his history of the Civil War The War to Save the Union, and it was on that day more than any other that the Union was saved. Until then, the tide of battle had fluctuated, but in general the Confederates had won most of the important engagements. In the Eastern Theater, Robert E. Lee had outmaneuvered a succession of Union commanders and riddled the cream of the northern army, driving it repeatedly from the field. In his latest campaign, after his overwhelming victories at Fredericksburg and Chancellorsville in Virginia, he had marched north, clear across Maryland and into Pennsylvania. To the west, the fighting had been less one-sided, but Union casualties had been enormous and the chief northern objective, to gain control of the Mississippi River in order to cut off Texas, Arkansas, and Louisiana from the rest of the Confederacy, had not been achieved.

Campaigns around Vicksburg, 1862–63

→ Grant's advance, April–May 1863
→ Confederate raids
---- unsuccessful attempts to flank Vicksburg
◣ Confederate forces

The Siege of Vicksburg, ended a carefully planned and brilliantly executed Union campaign, Ulysees S. Grant's masterpiece. Grant approached Vicksburg from his base in Memphis in mid-April with a force of 100,000 men. They realized that the defenses of the city made an attack from that direction or an approach from the west impracticable. He therefore kept his troops on the Louisiana side of the Mississippi River, marched past Vicksburg's defenses, and crossed back far to the south at Bruinsburg.

Next, abandoning his communications, he struck, not north towards Vicksburg, but east. There were two Confederate armies in the area:

one, based in Vicksburg, under John C. Pemberton, the other in Jackson, the capital of Mississippi, under Joseph E. Johnston. Grant got between them and won a series of engagements against his divided enemies. On May 14 be captured Jackson, routing Johnson's troops.

Grant then turned west against Pemberton, driving his forces behind Vicksburg's fortifications. After a fruitless (and relatively costly) attempt to take the city by storm, he placed it under seige and began to pound it methodically with artillery. Through the heat of June, the Confederates held out despite incessant Union shelling and dwindling supplies of food and other essentials. Finally, on July 3, Pemberton proposed an armistice to arrange "terms for the capitulation of Vicksburg." Grant responded with his famous demand for "unconditional surrender" and Pemberton had to agree. On July 4 Grant's men entered Vicksburg in triumph. Thereafter, Union gunboats controlled the entire length of the Mississippi, cutting the Confederacy in two.

General Lee's main objective in invading Pennsylvania was more psychological than military. He had no expectation that he could capture a major northern city or force the surrender of the Union army. But by demonstrating that 75,000 Confederate soldiers could march about and sustain themselves deep in enemy

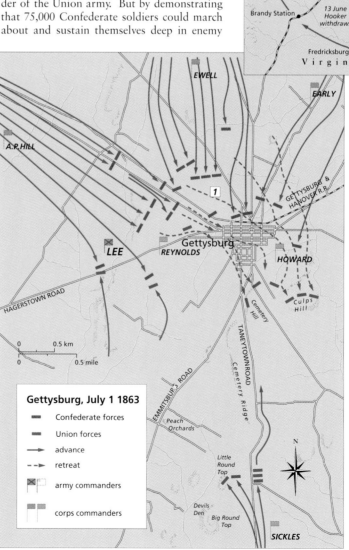

Invasion of the North, 1863

→ Union movements
→ Confederate movements
● Union forces
● Confederate forces

Gettysburg, July 1 1863

— Confederate forces
— Union forces
→ advance
--→ retreat
⚑ army commanders
⚑ corps commanders

July 1

1 Opening shots of the battle fired July 1 5.30 a.m. Confederate and Union forces converge on Gettysburg.
Union forces fall back on Cemetery Hill.

July 2

2 4 p.m. to dusk: Confederates attack lightly defended Union left. They take Devils Den but Union secures Little Round Top.

3 5.30 p.m. to dusk: Confederates attack the Peach Orchard, Union driven back to Cemetery Ridge.

4 6.30 p.m. to dark: Confederates attack Culps Hill and Cemetery ridge but gain little ground.

July 3

5 5.30 a.m.: attacks continue on Culps Hill, ultimately unsuccessful.

6 3 p.m.: Pickett, Pettigrew and Trimble's infantry advance. Confederate attack fails with huge losses, some 5,600 men.

territory, he hoped once and for all to destroy the northern public's will to resist secession and southern independence.

In pursuit of this goal, the Confederates fanned out across the Pennsylvania countryside. By July 1 some units were within ten miles of the state capital at Harrisburg. Lee was not looking for a decisive battle; indeed he was uneasy because he had lost contact with the eyes of the army, the cavalry under General Jeb Stuart, who was supposed to keep him informed about Union movements. But on that day, a Confederate troop had entered Gettysburg looking for shoes only to encounter Union soldiers in the street. Taken totally by surprise, each side fell back and called for reinforcements, and by the next day two powerful armies were lined up on parallel high ground outside the town. From their positions on Seminary Ridge, the Confederates bombarded the Union forces dug in on aptly named Cemetery Ridge and then, in repeated waves, they charged into the teeth of Union fire. On 3 July troops under General George Pickett actually broke into the Union lines only to be driven back by Union counterattacks. On July 4, the two armies, having suffered between them 50,000 casualties, rested on their arms, incapable of making further effort. Then the Confederates left the battlefield and marched wearily back into Virginia.

Pickett's charge at the Battle of Gettysburg, as imagined in a painting by Thure de Thulstrup. Born Bror Thure Thulstrup in Sweden, the son of the secretary of naval defense in Sweden, Thulstrup in 1868 graduated from the National Military Academy in Stockholm, joined the French Foreign Legion and served in France during the war *with Germany in 1871. His attention turned to art and he settled in New York later in the decade.*
This painting was one of his earliest of the Civil War. Like most of the others, it was taken from the Union perspective—the one that was generally shared by his New York and Boston patrons.

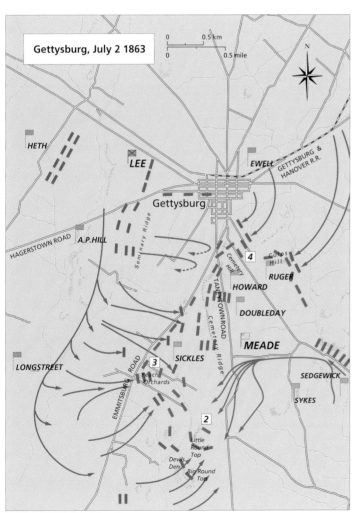

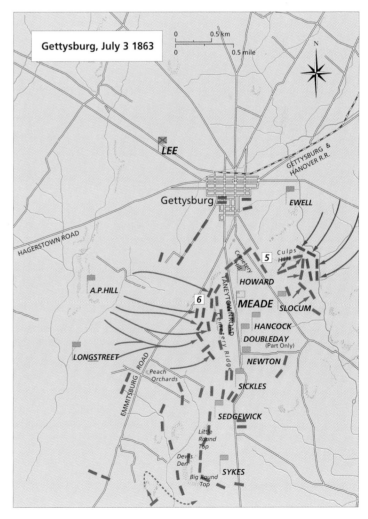

TOTAL WAR

1864-1865

"We are not only fighting hostile armies but a hostile people,"declared William T. Sherman. "and must make old and young, rich and poor, feel the hard hand of war." In many respects, North and South had been fighting a "total" war from the beginning. Both had mobilized their resources and their citizenry to a degree unprecedented in American history. Many commanders understood they had not simply to parry and thrust but to war upon the enemy's sustenance and spirit. By 1863, the Union crusaded against slavery, Southern society's very foundation. But in 1864, Union leaders increased the intensity and extended the scope of this total war, and their campaigns anticipated the warfare of the 20th century as much as they recalled that of 1861. Devastating the Confederacy, they also very nearly exhausted Union morale.

The Union had won crucial victories at Gettysburg and Vicksburg, but the outcome of the war remained far from certain. In Tennessee, Union troops had advanced slowly after the Battle of Murfreesboro at the beginning of 1863. Finally taking Chattanooga, a vital rail junction, in September, the Yankees found themselves trapped there after the fiasco at Chickamauga on September 19-20. Only the arrival of General Grant, and a virtually spontaneous overrunning of a Confederate stronghold, relieved the situation. The Confederacy had reason to hope, though, that the Northern public's patience might run out, given any more of the snail-paced progress and near disasters evident in the Chattanooga campaign. If they could hold on until November 1864, the Confederates might ensure the defeat of Lincoln at the hands of a doubtlessly more conciliatory Democrat. What the rebels perhaps did not count on was that in 1864 the Union would find terrible new ways to test the weary South's material and spiritual reserves.

In contrast to Union generals like McClellan and Don Carlos Buell, whose campaigns had targetted the enemy's armed forces almost exclusively, Grant and Sherman had, during the Vicksburg campaign, carried war to noncombatants, seizing supplies from the countryside and wrecking railroads, warehouses, and factories that supported the war effort. In 1864, the Union would practice this sort of warfare on a mass scale. Grant and Sherman, each in his own way, anticipated 20th century conflict, Grant by bleeding the enemy without respite, Sherman by making the resources and morale of civilians the target of military action.

Grant, named commander of all Union armies after his victory at Chattanooga, moved east in early 1864, determined to run down Lee's army whatever the cost. The campaign that ensued was marked initially by relentless bloodletting, then by a protracted siege and trench warfare. In early May, Grant engaged Lee in northern Virginia, near the Chancellorsville battle site. Despite suffering

heavy losses in the "Wilderness," Grant, unlike his predecessors, refused to pull the battered Union troops back. Instead, in the following weeks, he repeatedly marched them to Lee's right. Tens of thousands were killed or wounded charging entrenched Confederate positions at Spotsylvania and Cold Harbor. Grant hoped to draw Lee out for a decisive conflict—he did not intend simply to wage a war of attrition against a smaller army that could not as easily replace its losses. But, while moving considerably closer to Richmond, Grant's army suffered nearly 60,000 casualties in somewhat over a month. Fewer Conferates were killed or wounded (some 40,000), but their army lost a similar proportion of its initial numbers.

In mid-June, Grant moved across the James, hoping to surprise the Confederates at Petersbrug, an important rail center. The Yankees, however, failed to move quickly and over nine months of seige followed. Elaborate trench systems were constructed, as Grant slowly edged his lines south and west. The legendarily nimble Army of Northern Virginia was tied down, and Lee knew his outnumbered, ill-equipped army could not hold on indefinitely. But neither could the Yankees. The appalling casualties of the campaign and the apparent stalemate in front of Petersburg threatened to exhaust the Northern will to fight. For a time the Democrats seemed poised to take the presidency and, though divided between "war" and "peace" factions, they were expected to treat the Confederacy more gently. A series of victories in late summer and autumn—on the part not of Grant at Petersburg but of Admiral Farragut at Mobile Bay, Sheridan in the Shenandoah Valley, and, especially, Sherman at Atlanta—saved the day. Lincoln won a 55% majority over opponent and erstwhile subordinate, George McClellan.

Constant battle, entrenched positions, and high casualties were less characteristic of the total war waged in Georgia and the Carolinas. Sherman had maneuvered his way south to the outskirts of Atlanta by July, threatening to cut the already bisected Confederacy into thirds. Taking Atlanta in early September, he determined that rather than pursue Confederate forces, he would "make Georgia howl." He intended to ravage an important supply area and demonstrate that Southern civilians could not expect to be insulated from war. In November, Sherman's men burned everything of possible military use and marched out of Atlanta, abandoning their supply line north. Headed toward Savannah, the army, with the help of escaped slaves and Southern stragglers, cut a gash in the countryside dozens of miles wide, destroying railraods, seizing property, burning and plundering. That same autumn, Virginia's rich Shenandoah Valley was similarly swept bare by a general, Philip Sheridan, determined to leave the rebel populace "nothing but their eyes to weep with over the war."

At Savannah, Sherman's army turned north. Fire-eating South Carolina suffered even more than Georgia. The burning of the state capital,

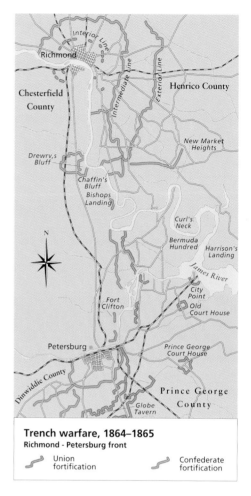

Trench warfare, 1864–1865
Richmond - Petersburg front

Union fortification   Confederate fortification

Columbia, in February 1865 came to symbolize for many the cruelty of Sherman's warfare. In fact, the burning was not a deliberate military act—unlike the wrecking in subsequent days of various of Columbia's militarily significant facilities. Instead, Confederate attempts to torch stockpiled cotton, a strong wind, and the rioting of drunken Yankees, liberated slaves, and local ne'er-do-wells combined to destroy over 450 buildings. Still, Columbia unmistakably revealed to Americans a new face of war, one in which the distinction between military and civilian would be increasingly blurred.

Though the war had become frighteningly innovative, it ended in a conventional way—with the formal surrender of armies. Confederate forces had marched north from Georgia, only to be bled very nearly to death at the battles of Franklin and Nashville in late 1864. Lee held on at Petersburg, but losses in the Carolinas reduced food, supplies, and hope. Desertion increased. In early April, Lee's men abandoned Petersburg and Richmond, attempting to rendezvous with what remained of the Army of Tennessee. Quick-moving Yankees cut them off. The shrunken, hungry army surrendered at Appomattox on April 9. In subsequent weeks, Confederate forces in the Carolinas and west of the Mississippi followed suit. Though President Jefferson Davis called for guerrilla warfare, Confederate citizens would sacrifice no more.

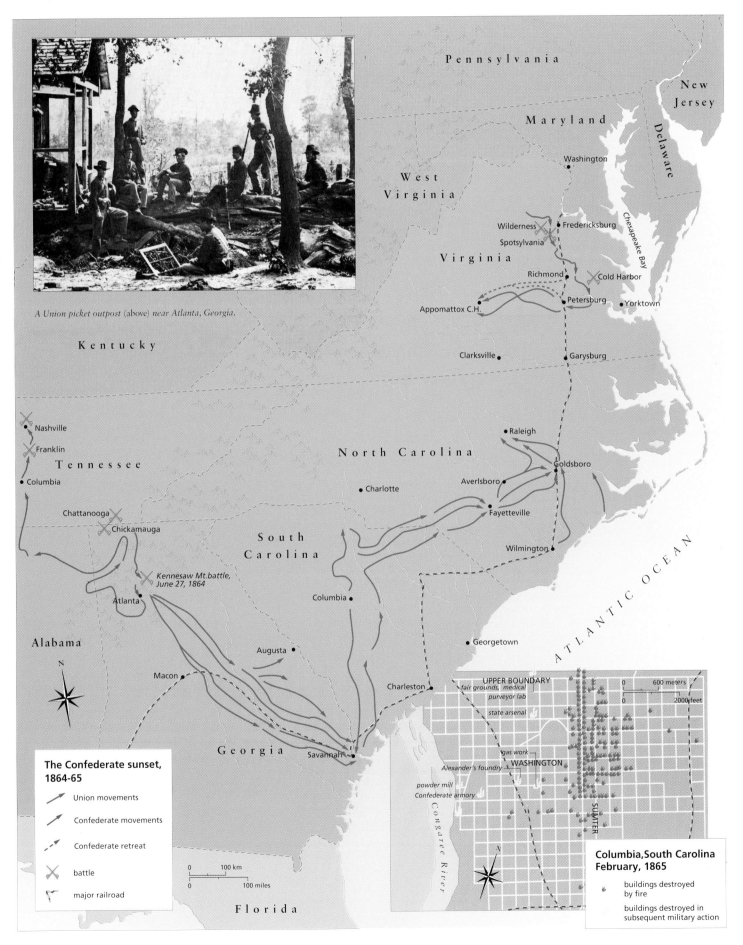

A Union picket outpost (above) near Atlanta, Georgia.

Pennsylvania

New Jersey

Maryland

West Virginia

Delaware

Chesapeake Bay

Washington

Wilderness ✕ Fredericksburg
Spotsylvania

Virginia

Richmond ✕ Cold Harbor
Petersburg Yorktown
Appomattox C.H.

Clarksville Garysburg

Kentucky

Nashville ✕

Franklin ✕

Tennessee

Columbia

Raleigh

North Carolina

Charlotte

Goldsboro
Averlsboro
Chattanooga ✕

Chickamauga ✕

Fayetteville

South Carolina

Wilmington

Kennesaw Mt.battle,
June 27, 1864 ✕

Atlanta

Columbia

Alabama

Augusta

Macon

Georgetown

ATLANTIC OCEAN

Georgia

Savannah

Charleston

**The Confederate sunset,
1864-65**

↗ Union movements

↗ Confederate movements

⇢ Confederate retreat

✕ battle

major railroad

0   100 km
0   100 miles

Florida

**Columbia, South Carolina
February, 1865**

buildings destroyed
by fire

buildings destroyed in
subsequent military action

UPPER BOUNDARY
fair grounds, medical
purveyor lab

state arsenal

gas work

Alexander's foundry   WASHINGTON

powder mill
Confederate armory

Congaree River

SUMTER

0   600 meters
0   2000 feet

N

THE POLITICS OF RECONSTRUCTION
REINVENTING SOUTHERN GOVERNMENT

The South lost a quarter of its white men of military age to the Civil War. Its farms and plantations had been ravaged, and two-fifths of its livestock and half of its farm machinery had been destroyed. Much of its nascent industrial base and railroad network lay in ruins. Yet reconstruction would involve far more than coping with such losses. At war's end, the nation had yet to determine on what terms the South would resume its place in American political life. Nor had it defined the status of former slaves and former Confederates or the roles they would play in civil affairs. Black and white Southerners of various classes, Congress, the Executive—all pressed their own agendas. Out of the contention emerged a dramatic, though in many ways shortlived, reconfiguring of Southern politics and public life.

Through 1864 and early 1865, Lincoln and Radical Republicans had differed over reconstruction issues. How quickly and thoroughly would citizenship rights be extended to former slaves and restored to former rebels? How radically would the political life of the reconstructed South differ from that of antebellum times? Who would control the readmission of states to Congress? Should the nation attempt to rapidly reconcile Southern whites to the Union and emancipation or more carefully craft a new order in the South?

As war's end made these issues all the more pressing, Lincoln's murder left the nation with a far less flexible and savvy President.

Radicals quickly learned that Tennessee Unionist Andrew Johnson did not share their commitment to black political equality and the use of federal power to reshape the South. Moderate Republicans, who initially had little enthusiasm for either black suffrage or a quarrel with Johnson, grew increasingly restive, too. Johnson exercised his pardoning powers liberally, restoring property and political status to the antebellum elite he had once excoriated. State governments established under his auspices seemed grudging in their acceptance of defeat.

Southerners generally elected leaders who, though initially opposing secession, had served the Confederacy. "Black Codes" severely circumscribed freedpeople's civil rights while binding them to agricultural labor. Reports of widespread violence against blacks, Unionists, and Yankees convinced Republicans that greater federal authority had to be exercised. After Johnson vetoed bills extending the life of the Freedmen's Bureau and providing federal guarantees of certain civil rights, Congress drafted the Fourteenth Amendment, which stated that all Americans enjoyed rights that states were bound to respect, restricted office-holding among antebellum public servants who aided the Confederacy, and promised a reduction in a state's Congressional representation in proportion to the number of adult males denied suffrage. Johnson and the Southern legislatures spurned the amendment. This, and continued violence, persuaded Republicans that the Southern governments ought to be replaced, the military given greater authority, and black suffrage explicitly mandated.

The Reconstruction Acts of 1867 divided the former Confederacy (except Tennessee) into five military districts and allowed commanders to remove office-holders. Constitutional conventions were to be elected by blacks and those whites not barred from office-holding. States would be readmitted to Congress after voters approved constitutions guaranteeing black suffrage and the Fourteenth Amendment had been ratified. Though Congress and Johnson continued to battle, even to the point of impeachment, these acts marked a climax. They reshaped a former slave society's politics in unprecedented ways.

Aided by the temporary disfranchisement or abstention of many conservative whites, Republican governments assumed command in the South. Southern Republican parties were tenuous, contentious coalitions, the largest and most striking element of which was the freed population. Barely a decade after the Dred Scott decision, blacks composed a majority of the citizenry of South Carolina, Mississippi, and Louisiana, and a sizeable minority elsewhere. Though blacks had been organizing politically since wartime, they initially found themselves voting chiefly for white candidates. Black office-holding at the state and local level expanded over time, though rarely to proportions commensurate with their share of the electorate. These politicians differed greatly in background and philosophy, but found common ground on issues like civil rights and educational policy.

A second element of the Republican coalition was also concentrated in the black belt and Southern cities—Northerners who, for a variety of motives, had migrated South after the war. Whether inspired by philanthropy, self-interest, or both, "carpetbaggers" often tended to be more supportive of economic modernization and civil rights initiatives than the white Southerners among the coalition. These "scalawags" were a far larger and more disparate group, including loyal yeomen from the white upcountry, formerly Whig planters, and entrepreneurs. Though sometimes representing plantation districts, scalawag officeholders were more likely than carpetbaggers to hail from white majority areas, often centers of wartime Unionism like East Tennessee.

The policies of the reconstructed states varied as much as their relative mix of blacks, scalawags, and carpetbaggers. They expanded social services and founded public school systems. This multiplication of governmental responsibilities led to pronounced increases in taxation, angering the small landowners that many Republicans had hoped to woo. Reconstruction regimes went farther than most Northern states in establishing black rights. Some state parties, though, in the absence of black majorities, downplayed black participation and demands, wishing not to alienate potential white converts. The desire to avoid a racially polarized politics also prompted attention to economic development policy, particularly state aid to railroads. Such promotion accorded, too, with Republican desires to fashion a more entrepreneurial South. These policies ultimately proved divisive, however, because some felt that constituents would be better served by debt relief or land reform and because state activism invited corruption and debt, which undermined Republican legitimacy.

Ultimately, Republicans neither expanded their white constituency nor kept peace among themselves. By the early 1870s, their regimes had fallen or were tottering in Tennessee, Virginia, Georgia, Texas, North Carolina, and Alabama. Taxation and corruption allowed Democrats to take the high road in public debate, while terrorist bands like the Ku Klux Klan warred upon Republicans and blacks. Although Congress passed laws in 1871 authorizing federal prosecution of such violence, Northern willingness to intervene in Southern affairs was waning.

Many felt that the nation had fulfilled its obligations to the freed population and the Southern governments. The Grant Administration's scandals quickened a reform impulse that was devoted to "good government" and laissez-faire economics. These Liberal Republicans had little patience for the Reconstruction regimes—Horace Greeley's 1872 presidential campaign endorsed Southern "home rule." The Panic of 1873 and the subsequent depression strengthened Southern Democrats' arguments for "retrenchment and reform," and drew Northern attention to economic issues. As labor and agrarian protest intensified, many Republicans' egalitarianism dissipated.

In Congress, Republican fortunes plunged with the economy. They lost control of the House in 1874, initiating a long period of divided rule.

Conservatives, correctly sensing that the federal government had little stomach for further interference, launched violent campaigns against Republicanism in Mississippi, Alabama, Louisiana, and South Carolina. The Compromise of 1877 merely confirmed Northern Republicans' abandonment of Reconstruction. Democrats acquiesced in the counting of disputed electoral votes for Rutherford Hayes, who accepted the demise of the remaining Reconstruction regimes.

"Redeemer" Democrats quickly cut down on government responsibilities and expense, and steadily narrowed blacks' rights as citizens and workers.

Yet if conservative whites had been restored to power at home, the commanding presence that Southerners had established in all three branches of the federal government between 1789 and 1860 had all but vanished.

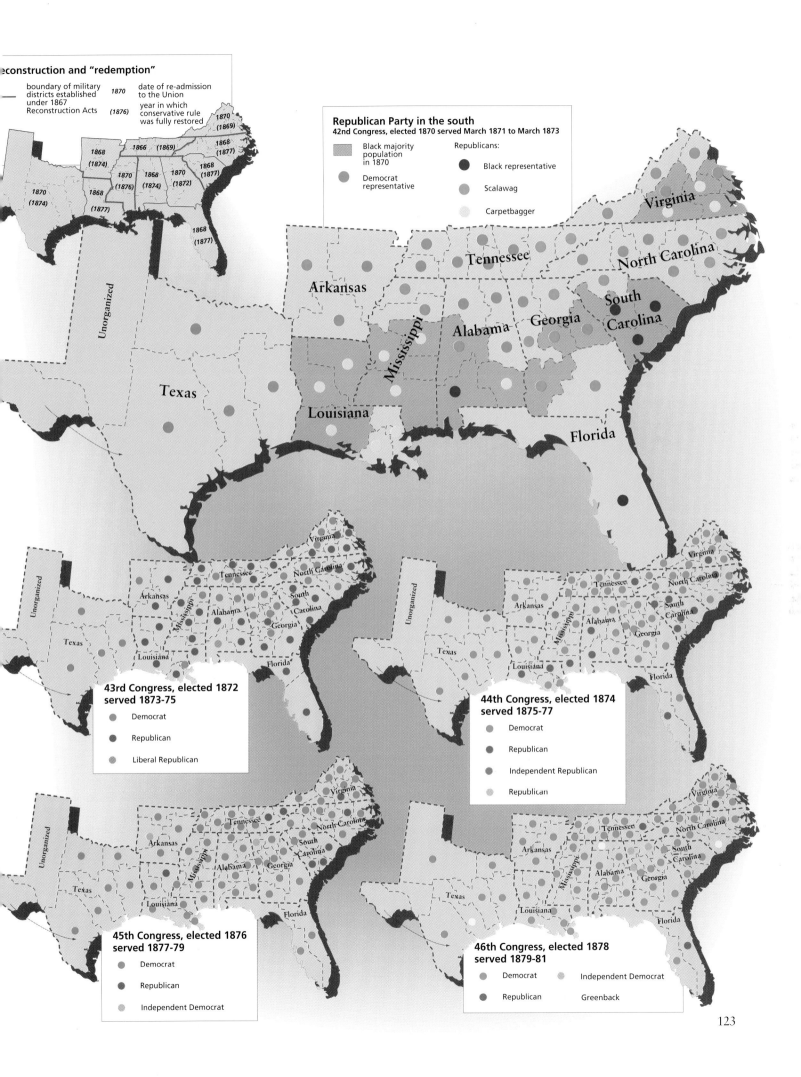

Reconstruction and "redemption"

boundary of military districts established under 1867 Reconstruction Acts

1870 date of re-admission to the Union

(1876) year in which conservative rule was fully restored

Republican Party in the south
42nd Congress, elected 1870 served March 1871 to March 1873

Black majority population in 1870

Democrat representative

Republicans:

Black representative

Scalawag

Carpetbagger

Unorganized

Texas

Arkansas

Tennessee

North Carolina

Virginia

Mississippi

Alabama

Georgia

South Carolina

Louisiana

Florida

43rd Congress, elected 1872 served 1873-75

Democrat

Republican

Liberal Republican

44th Congress, elected 1874 served 1875-77

Democrat

Republican

Independent Republican

Republican

45th Congress, elected 1876 served 1877-79

Democrat

Republican

Independent Democrat

46th Congress, elected 1878 served 1879-81

Democrat

Republican

Independent Democrat

Greenback

RECONSTRUCTION
LAND AND LABOR

"Society has been completely changed by the war," wrote a Louisiana planter in late 1865. "The [French] revolution … did not produce a greater change in the 'Ancien Regime' than this had in our social life." Emancipation represented not only the confiscation of billions of dollars worth of private property, but the destruction of a labor system and a social and legal institution. Fundamental questions had to be answered. How would work be organized and compensated? Who would hold title to land formerly cultivated by slaves—erstwhile masters or erstwhile bondsmen? Would the South continue as a great producer and exporter of staple crops? Would blacks' freedom mean more than—as future President James Garfield put it—"the bare privilege of not being chained?"

During the war, a great deal of slave-cultivated land fell into Union hands. Free labor was established in conquered parts of the Confederacy, but on varying terms. In coastal South Carolina, where many masters fled upon the approach of Yankee troops and blacks comprised a large majority, freedpeople seemed determined to grow food crops on their own plots of land. General Sherman, eager to rid his army of its trail of refugees, apparently extended the promise of proprietorship by his Special Field Order No. 15 of January 1865. A sizeable strip of coast south of Charleston was set aside for black settlement, where each family was to be allotted 40 acres. In Louisiana and through the Mississippi Valley, where there were larger numbers of resident planters, however, many more blacks were compelled by the army to work for wages on the plantations of loyal owners or Northern leaseholders.

The differing arrangements which emerged during wartime bespoke fundamentally different visions of freedom and of the future of the South. Blacks clearly understood freedom as more than an end to whipping, the separation of families, and immobility; it also involved the autonomy that came with establishing their own churches and schools, organizing themselves politically, and acquiring land on which they could support their families independent of former masters' authority. Some Radicals supported their quest for proprietorship—if necessary, through the confiscation of rebel planters' lands. Many Northerners, however, defined freedom as the simple ability to dispose of one's labor as one saw fit and accept the consequences. Individual blacks would be free to achieve whatever their talent and diligence allowed, but most would presumably begin as wage-earning agricultural laborers. Like many Northerners holding such views, former slave-owners hoped, too, for a quick revival of Southern staple production.

The aspirations of neither former slave nor former master would be entirely realized. The abrogation of the South's postwar "Black Codes" ensured that planters' control over their labor force would not be as formal or extensive as many wished. Far more momentous, however, was the failure of land reform. President Johnson quickly guaranteed most former Confederates' title to their abandoned or confiscated land, including much within the area covered by Sherman's order. Late 1865 and early 1866 saw the displacement of many black families settled on such land. Congress, too, refused to concede former slaves' arguments that they had earned title to plantation land through decades of working it. Relatively few Republicans believed that the federal government was entitled to intervene in Southern property relations in this manner. Instead they believed that equality before the law would breed equality of opportunity, not recognizing that intractable poverty and racism would hinder upward mobility even among the most determined and capable freedmen. The Freedmen's Bureau, whose mandate had included settlement of the freed on abandoned land, devoted itself to insuring—or, in many cases compelling—"fair" contracts between white landowners and their black labor force.

Widespread landlessness left blacks vulnerable but not entirely powerless, for theirs was the only labor immediately available for plantation cultivation. Their near-monopoly on labor, the near-monopoly of whites on landownership, and the wartime ruin of the South's credit and capital fundamentally shaped subsequent arrangements. Freedpeople resisted routines and requirements reminiscent of slavery—by removing women and children from the fields, working shorter hours, avoiding gang labor, and moving about to seek the best terms. Out of blacks' desire for greater autonomy and less supervision, and landowners' desire to guarantee their labor supply through the harvest and to share their risk in event of crop failure, emerged the sharecropping and share tenancy system—especially in cotton areas where less stringent capital and labor requirements allowed production to be more easily decentralized than in sugar and rice regions. Families cultivated individual pieces of land, dividing its produce with their landlord, the size of their share depending upon the extent to which the landlord supplied them with stock, tools, and provisions. While in many cases large landholdings, such as the Barrow plantation in Oglethorpe country, Georgia, remained in the hands of their antebellum owners, they were no longer worked by centrally organized gangs of laborers. Instead, the plantation workforce was scattered about on tenant plots.

The full implications of the spread of sharecropping became clear only with the collapse of Southern Republicanism and a long-term decline in agricultural prices. Republican state governments' lien laws guaranteeing laborers their due, limitations on the eviction of the tenants, and the like initially encouraged croppers to regard themselves as part-owners of their crops. The presence of Republican, even black, public officials limited planters' efforts to secure greater control over their workforce—though extralegal coercion persisted. With redemption, however, Democratic legislatures and courts defined sharecroppers not as partners in the crops but as wage laborers paid in kind, and gave landlords sole authority over crops their tenants grew. Fencing and game laws, and increased penalties for vagrancy and petty theft, prevented the landless from otherwise providing for themselves. Low cotton prices and exorbitant credit prices meant that sharecroppers could not prosper or, in many cases, even make good on their debts to either landlords or the merchants to whom they mortgaged their share of the crop for supplies.

Poverty and exploitation would not be black

Sherman Reservation, 1865

Black settlement area set aside by General Sherman's Special Field Order No. 15

South Carolina · Santee River · Savannah River · Charleston · James Island · Wadmalaw Island · Beaufort · Edisto Island · Port Royal · St Helena Island · Savannah · Hilton Head · Georgia · St Catherine Island · Sapelo Island · Cumberland Island · Florida

0   60 km
0   60 miles

Texas

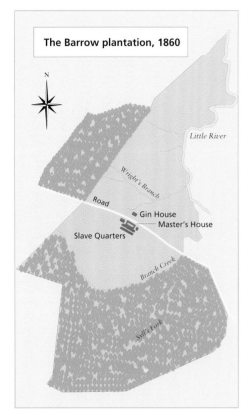

The Barrow plantation, 1860

N

Little River

Wright's Branch

Road

■ Gin House

Master's House

Slave Quarters

Branch Creek

Syll's Fork

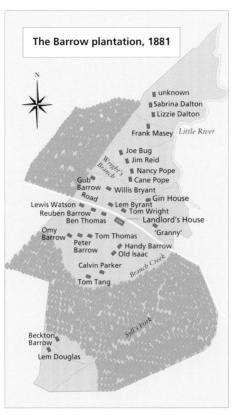

The Barrow plantation, 1881

N

■ unknown

■ Sabrina Dalton

■ Lizzie Dalton

■ Frank Masey   *Little River*

■ Joe Bug

■ Jim Reid

Wright's Branch   ■ Nancy Pope

■ Cane Pope

Gub   ■ Willis Bryant

Barrow

Road   ■ Gin House

Lewis Watson   ■ Lem Byrant

Reuben Barrow   ■ Tom Wright

Ben Thomas   ■ Landlord's House

Omy   'Granny'

Barrow   ■ Tom Thomas

Peter   ◆ Handy Barrow

Barrow   ◆ Old Isaac

Calvin Parker   *Branch Creek*

■ Tom Tang

Beckton

Barrow

■ Lem Douglas   *Syll's Fork*

Southerners' lot alone. The emergence of sharecropping in plantation areas coincided with the intensification of commercial cotton cultivation in the Southern backcountry. Falling agricultural prices, rising taxes, and the high costs of credit led formerly self-sufficient white farmers into one-crop agriculture, debt, and sometimes, landlessness.

In the South's role in the national and international economy, the dependence of black and white tenants would be writ large. Lacking adequate capital, the South's economic development was dominated by Northern and European investors and focused in low-wage extractive and basic processing industries. Far poorer than most of the nation, an underdeveloped South exported crops, raw material, and crudely processed goods.

Planters and their descendants might still be found amongst local elites, but their influence at the regional level was diluted by the rise of other powerful interest groups and by the South's subordinate position in the nation's economy and politics. Freedpeople and their descendants saw their own subordination extended and formalized as the 19th century ended. With the passage of Jim Crow segregation and disfranchisement measures, not only the promise of independence, but also that of equality before the law, had been betrayed.

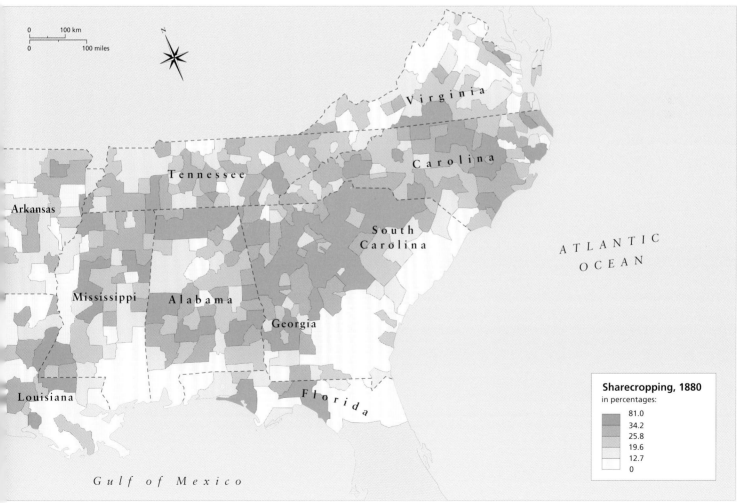

0   100 km

0   100 miles

N

Virginia

Carolina

Tennessee

Arkansas

South
Carolina

ATLANTIC
OCEAN

Mississippi   *Alabama*

Georgia

Louisiana

Florida

Sharecropping, 1880

in percentages:

■ 81.0
■ 34.2
■ 25.8
□ 19.6
□ 12.7
□ 0

Gulf of Mexico

PART 5: THE GILDED AGE

Mark Twain fastened the adjective to the age, and it has stuck: Gilt but not golden—a glittering veneer of probity, piety, and substance barely concealing the rot of corruption, greed, and superficiality. Impressive churches towered as monuments to Christian purpose, yet the nation's boardrooms and statehouses were awash in fraud. Womanhood was everywhere wreathed in flowery verse, yet prostitution pervaded the cities. Business generated more wealth than ever before, yet workers toiled in oppressive factories and lived in squalid tenements. Statesmen proclaimed the moral obligation to carry the torch of civilization to "backward" lands, yet dispossessed the Native Americans and, after freeing the Filipinos from the tyranny of the Spanish Empire, forced them at gunpoint into the American. This and more speak of the hypocrisy of the age. But goodness is as endemic to our species as hypocrisy, and the Gilded Age also witnessed the establishment of humanitarian institutions—hospitals, schools, colleges, libraries, museums, public health facilities—that a wealthier and ostensibly less hypocritical age struggles merely to maintain.

TOWARD A NATIONAL RAILWAY NETWORK
FRAGMENTATION AND STANDARDIZATION

Some maps suggest that on the eve of the Civil War the nation possessed an integrated rail network. But hsitorians George R. Taylor and Irene D. Neu have cautioned that such maps "confuse rather than clarify" the relationships among the railroads. The main map more accurately depicts a system fragmented by incompatible trackage. Freight originating in Sedalia, Missouri traveled to St. Louis along the 5 foot 6 inch track of the Pacific Railroad; to Cincinnati along the 6 foot Ohio and Mississippi; to Pittsburgh along the 4 foot 10 inch Pittsburgh, Columbus and Cincinnati; and to Philadelphia along the 4 foot 6¹/₂ inch Pennsylvania Railroad. At each stop the cargo would be reloaded, or the cars hoisted onto new axles.

New England
Most antebellum railways were financed by local merchants seeking to protect or expand trade with farmers in the hinterland. After Providence, Rhode Island had constructed the Blackstone Canal to Worcester, Massachusetts, Boston promoters recaptured their trade with that region by building the Boston and Worcester Railroad, one of the first in New England. Its tracks were 4 feet 81/2 inches wide. They then underwrote a web of railways radiating from Boston, each consistent with the "standard gauge" tracks of the Boston and Worcester Railroad. New York City merchants, hoping to encroach on the Boston trade, insisted that their railroads in western New England and the Hudson River Valley be compatible with the Boston lines. Meanwhile, Portland merchants, fearful that their trade with the Maine hinterland and the St. Lawrence region would be diverted to piers and wharves in Boston, financed a network of 5 foot 6 inch gauge railroads terminating in their city. They also persuaded Canadian businessmen to adopt the larger gauge track for the Grand Trunk Railroad.

The Mid Atlantic
The tracks of the three major railroads connecting New York City with the West differed in gauge. The New York Central adopted standard, the Erie Railroad chose an unusually wide 6 foot track, and most New Jersey lines conformed to 4 feet 10 inches, which became known as the "New Jersey" gauge. Philadelphia merchants imposed standard gauge on nearly all of the Pennsylvania railways. On learning that the Baltimore and Ohio Railroad, also standard-gauged, planned to compete for trade in southern Pennsylvania, they pressured the state legislature to block the Baltimore and Ohio, which finally settled upon an Ohio River terminus located at Wheeling, West Virginia.

The South and Midwest
Most Southern railroads adopted the 5 foot gauge recommended by the chief engineer of the Charleston and Hamburg railroad in 1829.

A major exception was North Carolina, where merchants in the eastern parts of the state, seeking to impede the flow of produce from interior counties south to Charleston and north to Richmond, built standard 4 foot 8¹/₂ gauge lines.

The railways in the Midwest were predominantly standard gauge. However, in 1848 Ohio passed a law requiring that all lines within the state must adhere to the 4 foot 10 inch gauge, the "Ohio gauge." Various eastern railways, underscoring the need to facilitiate through traffic, eventually forced the state to grant some exceptions. Meanwhile, merchants in St. Louis, alarmed by the web of standard gauge railroads radiating from Chicago, financed the wide-gauged Ohio and Mississippi Railroad to Cincinnati, and a 5 foot 6 inch railroad into the Missouri hinterland.

Adoption of Standard
By the 1880s profit-seeking financiers and investors had wrested control of the railroads from the local merchants. Because profits were dependent on the volume of through traffic, the owners of non-standard railroads quickly shifted to the more common standard gauge. In 1886 the Southern roads also adopted standard, substantially completing the nationwide rail network.

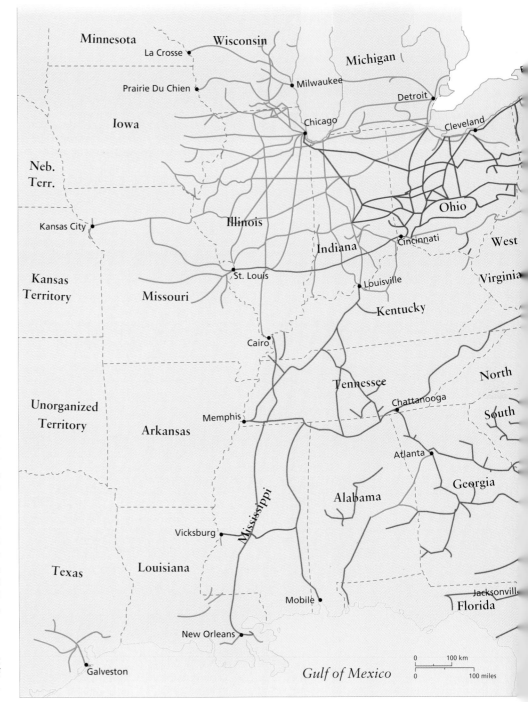

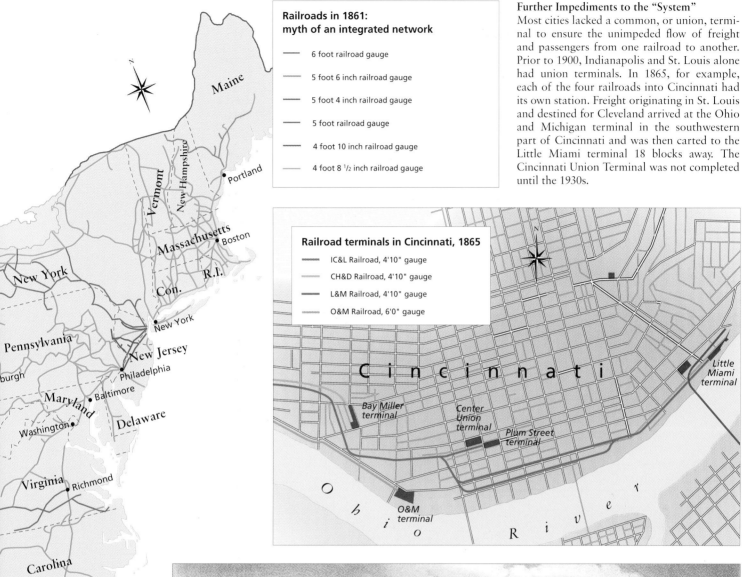

**Railroads in 1861:
myth of an integrated network**

—— 6 foot railroad gauge

—— 5 foot 6 inch railroad gauge

—— 5 foot 4 inch railroad gauge

—— 5 foot railroad gauge

—— 4 foot 10 inch railroad gauge

—— 4 foot 8 ½ inch railroad gauge

Further Impediments to the "System"

Most cities lacked a common, or union, terminal to ensure the unimpeded flow of freight and passengers from one railroad to another. Prior to 1900, Indianapolis and St. Louis alone had union terminals. In 1865, for example, each of the four railroads into Cincinnati had its own station. Freight originating in St. Louis and destined for Cleveland arrived at the Ohio and Michigan terminal in the southwestern part of Cincinnati and was then carted to the Little Miami terminal 18 blocks away. The Cincinnati Union Terminal was not completed until the 1930s.

Railroad terminals in Cincinnati, 1865

—— IC&L Railroad, 4'10" gauge

—— CH&D Railroad, 4'10" gauge

—— L&M Railroad, 4'10" gauge

—— O&M Railroad, 6'0" gauge

Across the continent, westward the course of Empire takes its way, by painter Fanny Palmer, reproduced by Currier and Ives in 1868. Following in the wake of the distant wagon trains is the railroad, and with it a church, school, and farmers. In the lower right foreground, nearly pushed out of the picture and obscured by the smoke of the train, are two Indians. It is unclear whether Palmer's depiction of them was triumphant or ironic.

RAILROADS, CANALS, AND ECONOMIC GROWTH
WERE THE RAILROADS INDISPENSABLE?

In 1891, financier Sidney Dillon credited the railroads for the stupendous economic growth of the previous half century. Without them, he claimed, most of the nation's natural resources would have remained untouched. Civilization would have "crept slowly on" and the immense spaces from the Appalachians to the Pacific would have remained "an unknown and unproductive wilderness." That the railroads were indispensable to economic growth had been a commonplace of historical writing; but in 1964 it was challenged by Robert Fogel. While conceding that the railroads opened the Great Plains to agriculture and stimulated investment, he insisted that comparable benefits could have been achieved by

improving and extending the nation's canals and waterways.

Throughout the last half of the 19th century, the primary function of the railways was to bring Midwestern grain to the large cities of the East. The major railroads linked the major wheat markets of the upper Great Plains (principally Minneapolis, Chicago, and Duluth) and the corn markets of the central Midwest (Chicago, St. Louis, and Kansas City) to the cities dotted along the Atlantic Coast from Boston to Baltimore.

The existence of many competing rail lines tended to keep freight charges fairly low, as attempts to "pool" the available traffic and fix high rates usually collapsed. Generally low freight rates encouraged farmers to develop the

vast food-growing potential of the Great Plains and reduced the cost of daily bread to urban workers—savings to the nation that contributed to economic growth.

But Fogel maintained that navigable waterways, extended through new canal construction, could have proven nearly as successful at joining the food-producing and food-consuming sections of the country.

The map to the right shows the navigable rivers and canals as of 1890 along with proposed canals that were never built. The map also delineates the parts of the nation where commercial farming was feasible if transportation were available to take crops to markets. By juxtaposing this data, the map suggests that the best farmland would have been satisfactorily serviced by boats that could have carried

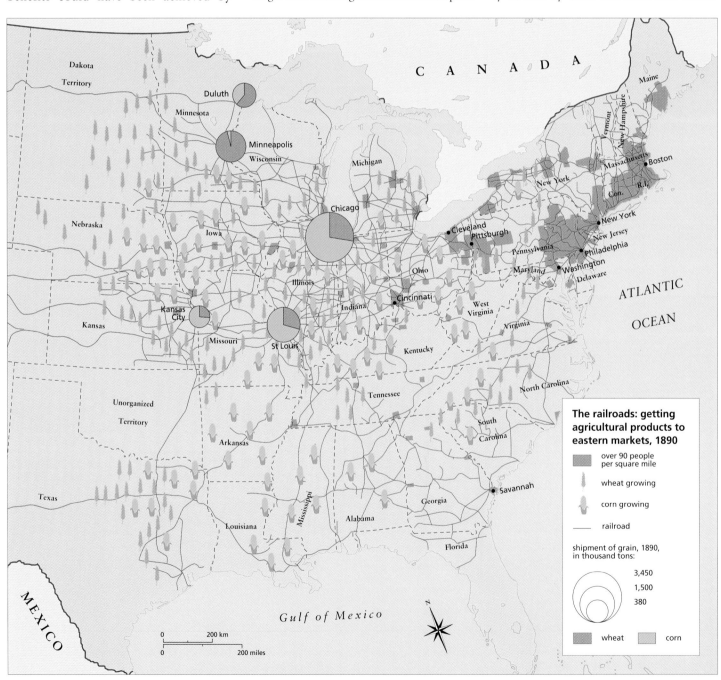

The railroads: getting agricultural products to eastern markets, 1890

- over 90 people per square mile
- wheat growing
- corn growing
- railroad

shipment of grain, 1890, in thousand tons:
- 3,450
- 1,500
- 380

wheat   corn

grain to the port cities of the East. This hypothetical map further suggests that a water-based transportation system would have greatly altered the relationship among regions. In the absence of the railroads, the dry upper Great Plains would have remained nearly undeveloped, while commercial agriculture would have been concentrated in the Mississippi, Ohio, and Missouri River valleys, and along the rivers that emptied into the Gulf of Mexico and the Atlantic. The major centers of grain shipment would have been New Orleans, St. Louis, Cincinnati, Memphis, and Charleston.

A water-based transportation system had several serious limitations. Boats were much slower than trains and many canals and rivers were impassable during winter. Most business-es would therefore have been forced to maintain larger—and more costly—inventories. But Fogel believed that higher inventory costs would almost have been compensated by savings in long distance freight rates. The cost of shipping wheat from Chicago to New York in 1890 for example was 5.2 cents per ton-mile by rails, but only 1.4 cents by water. By his estimate, a water-based transportation system would have generated freight rate savings of about $38 million, and additional costs in inventory, wagon haulage, and spoilage of $111 million. The railways thus "saved" only $73 million, about three-fifths of one percent of the national income. In his view, the railroads promoted growth, but were not indispensable to it.

But the railroads also stimulated economic development in more subtle ways. The demand for rails was a mainstay of the iron and steel industry. In the 1860s, for example, about 40 percent of the nation's iron was made into rails; by 1890, after steel had been substituted for iron, the railways consumed about 44 percent of the steel output. Moreover, the railways gave rise to advances in steam and machine technology. Whether comparable investments in boats and canals would have generated similar economic benefits is, ultimately, incalculable. More problematic still is the question of whether the North would have won the Civil War if it had been deprived of the rail network that enabled it to quickly shift men and supplies. If so, would the persistence of slavery in the South have retarded economic growth?

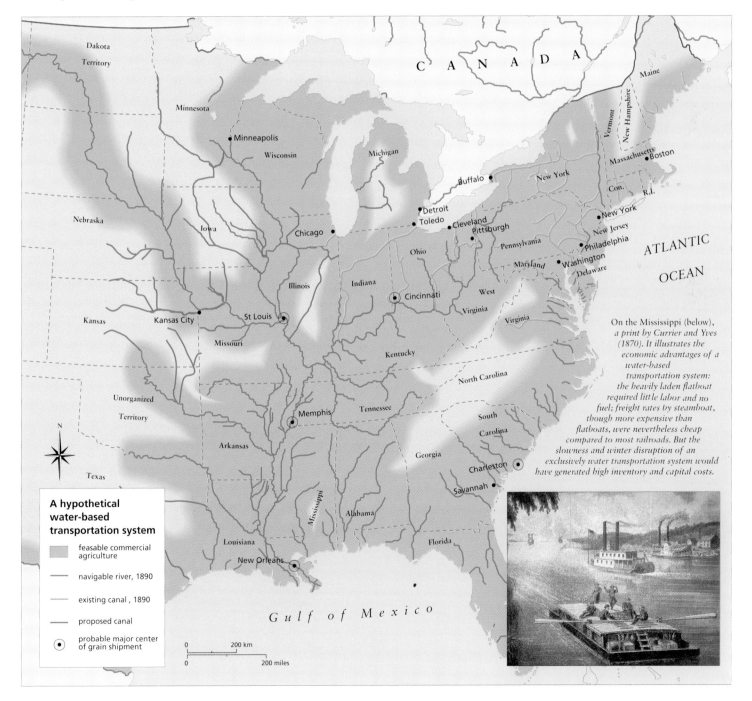

On the Mississippi (below), a print by Currier and Yves (1870). It illustrates the economic advantages of a water-based transportation system: the heavily laden flatboat required little labor and no fuel; freight rates by steamboat, though more expensive than flatboats, were nevertheless cheap compared to most railroads. But the slowness and winter disruption of an exclusively water transportation system would have generated high inventory and capital costs.

A hypothetical water-based transportation system

- feasable commercial agriculture
- navigable river, 1890
- existing canal , 1890
- proposed canal
- probable major center of grain shipment

THE INDIANS CRUSHED
CUSTER'S LAST STAND

For 250 years the Indians had been driven back steadily, yet on the eve of the Civil War they still inhabited nearly half the United States. The survivors of most of the eastern tribes were living peacefully in what is now Oklahoma. In California, the forty-niners had made short work of the local tribes. Elsewhere in the West—in the deserts of the Great Basin between the Sierra and the Rockies, in the mountains themselves, and on the semi-arid, grass-covered plains between the Rockies and the edge of white civilization in eastern Kansas and Nebraska—almost a quarter of a million Indians dominated the land.

But their tenure was precarious, depending on the good faith of a U.S. government that had disregarded treaties whenever they had proven disadvantageous. While white settlers, cowboys, and adventurers continued to encroach upon their land, the Indians seethed.

The first to rise in rebellion were the Sioux of the northern plains. In August 1862, after federal troops had been withdrawn from frontier forts to fight the Confederacy, the Sioux took to the warpath, slaughtered dozens of isolated white families, ambushed small parties, and besieged Fort Ridgely in Minnesota. Within a month local militia and volunteers crushed the rebellion. Thirty-eight of the Indians were subsequently hanged—the largest mass execution in U.S. history.

Violence then flared throughout the West: among the Sioux and Cheyenne in the Dakotas; the Kiowas in northern Texas; the Modoc in California; the Apache in Arizona and New Mexico; and the Arapahos in Wyoming and Montana. The Indian Wars had commenced. Though expert at guerrilla warfare, the Indians proved no match for large contingents of a battle-hardened U.S. army. (Even the Sioux victory at Little Big Horn attested to Custer's conviction that a tiny cavalry force could defeat ten times their number of Indians.) Indeed, the term "Indian Wars" is a misnomer, for the one-sided clashes often devolved into simple butchery. Armed resistance ended, perhaps characteristically, with the slaughter of 150 Sioux at Wounded Knee in 1890.

Defeat in battle was symptomatic of an even more profound disruption of tribal life. Some fifteen million buffalo had provided the plains Indians with food, clothing, and shelter. But the Union Pacific Railroad, completed in 1869, divided the herd, disrupted its migratory patterns, and rendered it vulnerable to professional buffalo hunters. By 1890, buffalo were all but extinct, leaving Indians hungry and homeless.

Custer's Debacle to Little Big Horn

In 1874 gold was discovered in the Black Hills, wherein dwelt the gods of the Sioux and the Cheyenne. The following year thousands of miners descended upon the area, most of which had been ceded to the Sioux. Incensed

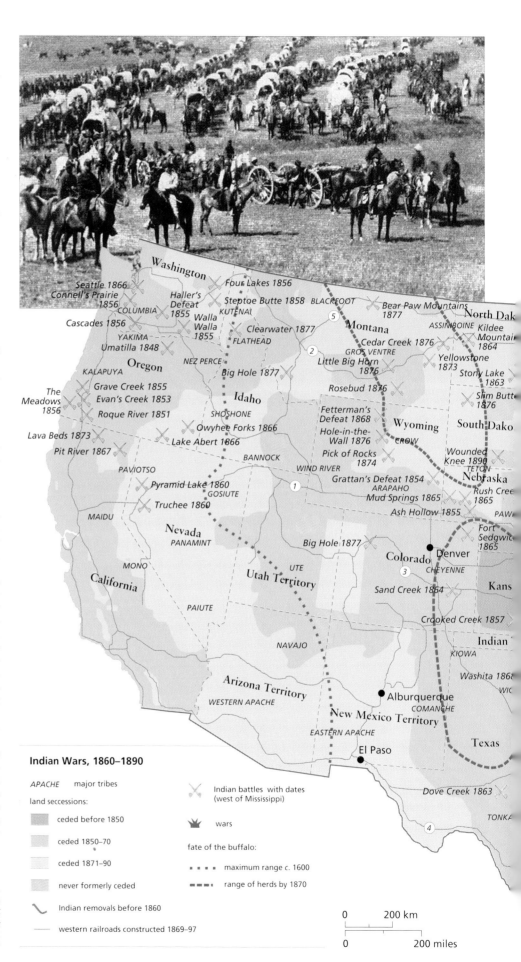

Indian Wars, 1860–1890

APACHE   major tribes

land seccessions:

⬛ ceded before 1850

⬛ ceded 1850–70

⬛ ceded 1871–90

⬛ never formerly ceded

⤸ Indian removals before 1860

— western railroads constructed 1869–97

⚔ Indian battles with dates (west of Mississippi)

♛ wars

fate of the buffalo:

• • • • maximum range c. 1600

▪ ▪ ▪ ▪ range of herds by 1870

0   200 km

0   200 miles

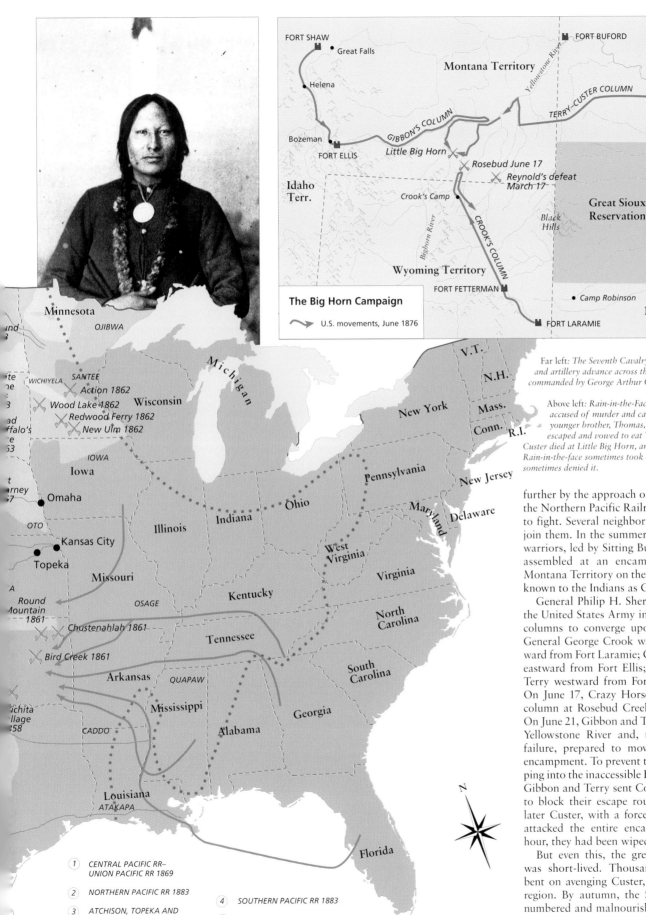

The Big Horn Campaign

⟿ U.S. movements, June 1876

FORT SHAW • Great Falls

FORT BUFORD

Montana Territory

Helena

Bismarck
FORT ABRAHAM LINCOLN

Bozeman

GIBBON'S COLUMN

TERRY–CUSTER COLUMN

Little Big Horn

FORT ELLIS

Rosebud June 17

Reynold's defeat March 17

Dakota Territory

Idaho Terr.

Crook's Camp

Great Sioux Reservation

Black Hills

CROOK'S COLUMN

Bighorn River

Wyoming Territory

FORT FETTERMAN

Camp Robinson

Nebraska

FORT LARAMIE

Minnesota

OJIBWA

WICHIYELA

SANTEE

Action 1862

Wood Lake 1862

Redwood Ferry 1862

New Ulm 1862

Wisconsin

Michigan

V.T.

N.H.

New York

Mass.

Conn. R.I.

IOWA

Iowa

Omaha

OTO

Kansas City

Topeka

Missouri

Illinois

Indiana

Ohio

Pennsylvania

New Jersey

Maryland

Delaware

West Virginia

Round Mountain 1861

OSAGE

Kentucky

Virginia

North Carolina

Chustenahlah 1861

Bird Creek 1861

Tennessee

Arkansas

QUAPAW

South Carolina

Mississippi

Georgia

CADDO

Alabama

Louisiana

ATAKAPA

Florida

N

① CENTRAL PACIFIC RR–UNION PACIFIC RR 1869

② NORTHERN PACIFIC RR 1883

③ ATCHISON, TOPEKA AND SANTA FE RR 1883

④ SOUTHERN PACIFIC RR 1883

⑤ GREAT NORTHERN RR 1893

Far left: The Seventh Cavalry's columns of wagons and artillery advance across the North Dakota Plains, commanded by George Arthur Custer, mid-June 1836.

Above left: Rain-in-the-Face, a Sioux warrior, was accused of murder and captured by Custer's younger brother, Thomas, in 1874. Rain-in-the-face escaped and vowed to eat Tom Custer's heart. Tom Custer died at Little Big Horn, and his heart was missing. Rain-in-the-face sometimes took credit for the deed, and sometimes denied it.

further by the approach of surveying crews for the Northern Pacific Railroad, the Sioux chose to fight. Several neighboring tribes decided to join them. In the summer of 1876 some 3,000 warriors, led by Sitting Bull and Crazy Horse, assembled at an encampment in southern Montana Territory on the Little Bighorn River, known to the Indians as Greasy Grass.

General Philip H. Sheridan, commander of the United States Army in the West, sent three columns to converge upon the encampment. General George Crook was to advance northward from Fort Laramie; Colonal John Gibbon eastward from Fort Ellis; and General Alfred Terry westward from Fort Abraham Lincoln. On June 17, Crazy Horse ambushed Crook's column at Rosebud Creek and drove it back. On June 21, Gibbon and Terry converged at the Yellowstone River and, unaware of Crook's failure, prepared to move south toward the encampment. To prevent the Indians from slipping into the inaccessible Big Horn Mountains, Gibbon and Terry sent Colonel George Custer to block their escape route south. Four days later Custer, with a force of 264 men, rashly attacked the entire encampment. Within an hour, they had been wiped out.

But even this, the greatest Indian victory, was short-lived. Thousands of U.S. cavalry, bent on avenging Custer, converged upon the region. By autumn, the Sioux warriors, outnumbered and malnourished, surrendered and returned to the reservation.

133

STRANGERS AT THE CITY GATES
IMMIGRATION 1850–1880

That the major sources of immigration to the United States shifted from northwestern to southeastern Europe in the late 19th century and from Europe to Asia and Latin America more recently—is illustrated elsewhere in this volume. But equally significant are several continuities in the immigration experience. **Most immigrants have been poor, and their poverty has placed constraints upon their choice of residence. Lacking money for transportation, they have often remained in the cities in which they first arrived, and lacking skills and education, they have been forced to live where housing was cheap and unskilled jobs were plentiful.**

The great port cities of the early 19th century—New York, Boston, and Philadelphia—served as the primary channels through which the first waves of northwestern European immigrants passed. Although many of the more prosperous immigrants, especially the Germans, made their way to the cities and farms of the Midwest and the North Central states, most immigrants, especially the Irish, remained in the port at which they had originally disembarked, or they moved to smaller

sities within its economic orbit. In 1850, more than half of the nation's 2.2 million foreign-born were found in New York, Pennsylvania, Massachusetts or New Jersey.

The commercial ascendancy of antebellum New York City, Philadelphia, and Boston conferred advantages of size that contributed to their industrial transformation later in the century. In a nation chronically short of workers, these cities offered a large and diverse pool of laborers whose wages could be kept low because their tenement lodgings were so cheap. Moreover, antebellum commercial cities provided access to a wide range of industrial suppliers, insurance, banking services, and consumer markets.

At the turn of the 20th century, millions of Italians and eastern Europeans passed through these ports and nearby cities, found work in labor-intensive factories, and took up residence in neighborhoods that had once housed Irish, British or German immigrants. In 1910, when the nation's foreign-born had swelled to over 13 million, almost half—5.6 million—still resided in the four major states of the Northeast.

By then, a dense constellation of industrial cities, benefiting from their proximity to raw materials and to the enormous agricultural

hinterland of the Midwest, had formed along the shores of Lake Erie.

Further west, Chicago had emerged as the nation's industrial colossus. Hundreds of thousands of German, Russian, Italian, Hungarian, and Swedish immigrants were drawn to Illinois, Ohio, and Michigan to work in the huge steel mills and agricultural processing factories.

California also attracted large numbers of immigrants, mostly from Germany and Italy. Not reflected on the map of 1910 were 34,000 inhabitants of that state born in Japan. *(See Japanese Immigrants, Japanese Internees, p 200–201)* The steady stream of foreigners to California in the early 20th century became swollen by an influx of Mexicans, Filipinos, and Vietnamese a half-century later.

By 1980 more than one quarter of the nation's foreign-born lived in California. Texas and Florida had also received hundreds of thousands of immigrants, many of them from Mexico and the West Indies.

Nevertheless, the declining cities of the Northeast remained important centers of immigration. Indeed, New York, New Jersey, Massachusetts, and Pennsylvania together attracted more immigrants than California.

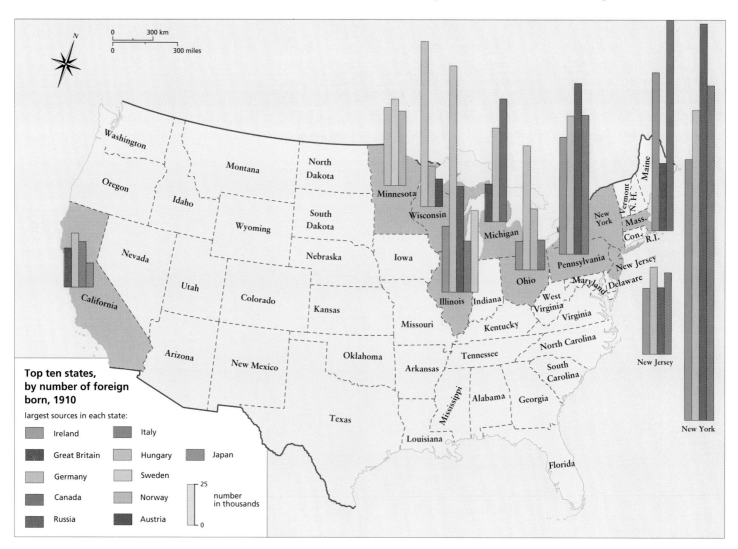

Top ten states, by number of foreign born, 1910

largest sources in each state:

- Ireland
- Great Britain
- Germany
- Canada
- Russia
- Italy
- Hungary
- Sweden
- Norway
- Austria
- Japan

25 — number in thousands — 0

The first glimpse of New York harbor and the Statue of Liberty for some of the "huddled masses" from the period of great European migrations, 1880–1920. They would disembark and face a medical examination at Ellis Island, the point of entry for almost all of these emigrants, where they could be refused entry on medical grounds.

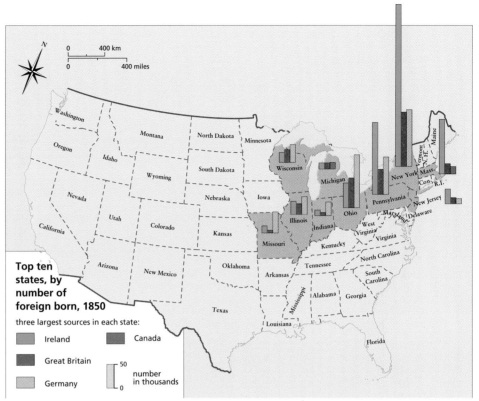

Top ten states, by number of foreign born, 1850

three largest sources in each state:

- Ireland
- Canada
- Great Britain
- Germany

number in thousands

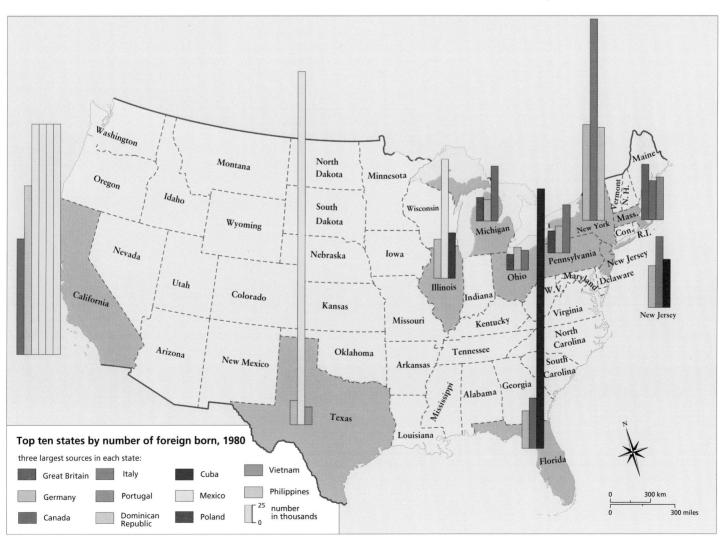

Top ten states by number of foreign born, 1980

three largest sources in each state:

- Great Britain
- Italy
- Cuba
- Vietnam
- Germany
- Portugal
- Mexico
- Philippines
- Canada
- Dominican Republic
- Poland

number in thousands

FROM SHTETL TO STOOP
JEWISH IMMIGRATION

In 1880 the Jewish population throughout the world was about seven and a half million. More than half lived in an enclave of western Russia known as the Pale of Settlement; another 2 million lived in adjacent sections of Austria-Hungary or Germany. The United States, by contrast, was the home of fewer than 250,000 Jews, most of German descent. The next 35 years brought an inundation of 2 million Jews from eastern Europe to industrial cities throughout the United States. By 1920, nearly four times as many Jews lived in New York City as in Warsaw, and Chicago was the home to more Jews than Budapest and Vienna combined.

Why Jews left

The "Pale of Settlement" was a section of Russia beyond which Jews were prohibited from settling. Established in 1791 by Catherine the Great, it encompassed western Russia and Russian-held territory in Poland. Subsequent edicts imposed additional restrictions on Jewish life within the Pale. In 1835, Jews were expelled from a 35-mile wide strip of land along the western border of the Pale, and from the cities of Kiev, Nikolaev, and Svestopol. Within a 150-mile wide region east of the Dnieper River, Jews were forced to leave rural villages and settle in nearby country towns, called shtetls.

The plight of the Jews was further exacerbated by economic factors. In 1800, most of Russia's 2 million Jews lived in Byelorussia (White Russia) and Lithuania. During the next 80 years, as the Jews were increasingly confined to shtetls in the Pale of Settlement, the Jewish population increased fourfold. The main streets and marketplaces of thousands of shtetls became choked with unemployed and underemployed tradesmen and laborers.

Millions drifted southward into Ukraine, where Jews were increasingly drawn into competition with local townspeople. Anti-semitic flare-ups, though commonplace, were to some extent kept in control by Czar Alexander II. But in March 1881 he was assassinated. His successor, Alexander III, loosed a torrent of anti-semitic violence. By summer, gangs in hundreds of towns in Ukraine had plundered Jewish homes and shops. These anti-Jewish attacks, or pogroms, continued intermittently from then on until the Russian Revolution of 1917.

Gorzd: Portrait of a Lithuanian Shtetl

Gorzd was a rural town, or shtetl, 100 miles northwest of Kovno, much like thousands of others within the Pale of Settlement. By the end of the 19th century it numbered some 3,000 people, half of whom were Jewish. The center of economic activity within the shtetl was the marketplace, where peasants from neighboring villages would gather on Thursdays to sell produce and buy necessities from dairymen, peddlers, shoemakers, tailors, tan-

ners, and blacksmiths. Many of the artisans and tradesmen were Jewish, as were the laborers who moved goods to and from warehouses.

Gorzd's main thoroughfare—Tamozhne Street—led to Germany. The wealthier residents lived along this street near the center of town; the impressive facades of their houses reminded Gorzders of Kovno, Lithuania's largest and most prosperous city. Toward the edge of town, Tamozhne Street dipped into a valley known as the "alley" neighborhood, where many of the town's Jewish artisans and tradesmen resided. Behind their homes, they kept goats or chickens, maintained barns, cultivated vegetables in garden patches, and otherwise retained ties of the agricultural life from which they had earlier been barred.

Although Jews and non-Jews came together in the marketplace, they usually socialized separately. Jewish life centered on the synagogue and ancillary organizations such as the *besmedresh*, a place where adult men studied the Talmud. During most of the 19th and early 20th centuries, relations between Jewish and non-Jewish Gorzders were congenial. This changed during the 1930s with the rise of Hitler in Germany, and with the emergence of a Nazi-inspired party in Lithuania.

On June 22, 1941, the first day of Operation Barbarossa, the Nazi invasion of Soviet Russia, German troops entered Gorzd, set it on fire, and herded the Jews into the marketplace. Two days later, German soldiers marched the Jewish men to a field at the end of Tamozhne Street, forced them to dig trenches and undress, and

then cut them down with machine-gun fire. Two days later the Germans trucked the Jewish women and children to a nearby village. They, too, were taken into the woods and shot. One of those who escaped provided the drawing on which this reconstruction is based.

Jews in New York City

In 1870, New York City was home to 80,000 Jews. By 1915, New York's Jewish population had swelled to 1.4 million. Almost a half a million Jews crowded into a 120-block section of the Lower East Side of Manhattan. Though packed into the most densely populated section of the city, the Jews maintained distinct ethnic communities based on Old World linguistic and cultural associations. Emigrants from the Russian Pale congregated south of Grand Street. Jews from the Austro-Hungarian Empire, where conditions had been nearly as bad as those in the Russian Pale, replicated in their residential patterns the ethnic divisions of the polyglot empire from which they had fled: the Hungarians lived north of Houston, and the Galicians lived in the region immediately to its south. Rumanian and Middle Eastern Jews crowded into tenements east of Broadway and north of Grand.

Jewish immigrants in other ways implanted Old World traditions into the concrete and stone of the Lower East Side. Peddlers, tradesmen, and artisans who had sold their wares in the marketplace of shtetls commonly resumed such activities, plying pushcarts laden with fish, fruits, buttons, clothing. After several

Jewish population in Eastern Europe and Russia, c.1900

■ over 15% of population Jewish

■ over 10% of population Jewish

— Pale of Settlement in Russian Empire

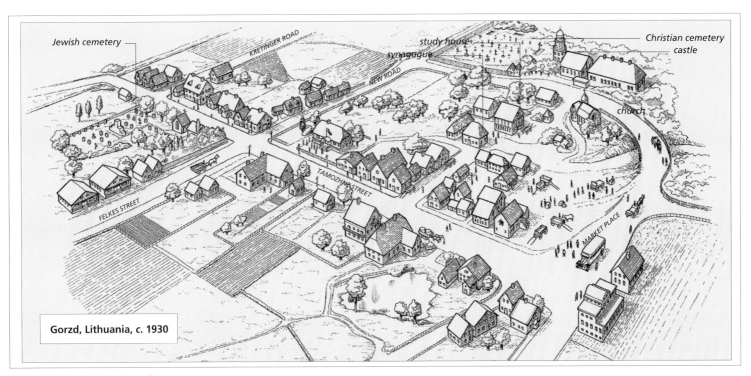

Gorzd, Lithuania, c. 1930

years peddlers often saved up enough money to establish butcher shops, bakeries, grocery stores, candy stands, delicatessens, or cigar stores. Other Jews—women and children as well as men—worked in the garment factories and cigar and tobacco shops that crowded the district on the northern edges of the Lower East Side.

This famous photograph of Hester Street in New York City (below) shows both the powerful influences of the city on Jewish life, and also the persistence of many of the features of the European shtetl.

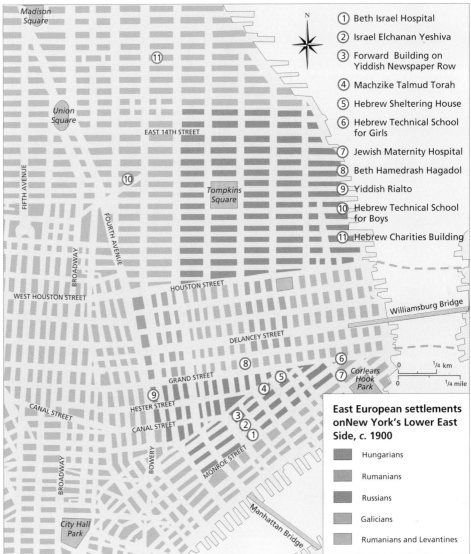

1. Beth Israel Hospital
2. Israel Elchanan Yeshiva
3. Forward Building on Yiddish Newspaper Row
4. Machzike Talmud Torah
5. Hebrew Sheltering House
6. Hebrew Technical School for Girls
7. Jewish Maternity Hospital
8. Beth Hamedrash Hagadol
9. Yiddish Rialto
10. Hebrew Technical School for Boys
11. Hebrew Charities Building

East European settlements on New York's Lower East Side, c. 1900

Hungarians
Rumanians
Russians
Galicians
Rumanians and Levantines

THE CONQUEST OF CHOLERA
CLEAN WATER AND PUBLIC HEALTH

Cholera was not the most lethal disease to afflict 19th-century Americans. Malaria and tuberculosis claimed far more lives. But cholera was unusually awful in that it struck with so little warning and such terrible symptoms: crippling abdominal spasms, unremitting diarrhea, and sudden dehydration. On learning of an outbreak of cholera in Montreal on June 6, 1832, most well-to-do New Yorkers abandoned the city. On June 18, the disease crossed the Canadian border and, moving along waterways, hit Whitehall, New York, on June 18, and New York City on June 26. By the end of August, it had spread throughout the land. Several outbreaks struck the following two years, and in 1849, 1854, 1866, and 1873.

Snow's Hypothesis
Most physicians in the mid-19th century thought that cholera was caused by some sort of atmospheric malaise that descended upon urban slums and targeted unwashed and ignorant immigrants. John Snow, a prominent London anesthetist, believed otherwise.

In 1849, after a cholera epidemic had killed more than 14,000 Londoners, Snow published a pamphlet in which he maintained that the disease was a "poison" that spread from the feces of infected persons through sewers into the Thames River, contaminating some sections of the City's water supply. He maintained that a disproportionate number of cholera

fatalities occurred in areas of London served by the Southwark and Vauxhall Water Works and the Lambeth Water Company, companies that drew water from the Thames. Companies that served the remainder of the City obtained water from other rivers or springs, or from sites on the Thames upriver, before it had been polluted by London sewage. Fewer of their customers came down with the disease, or so Snow contended.

At the time, little was made of Snow's hypothesis, but a cholera epidemic that ravaged London in 1853 gave him the opportunity to prove it. The previous year, the Lambeth Water Company had built a new waterworks upriver at Thames Ditton; it no longer pumped water from its works nearly opposite the Parliament buildings. The Southwark and Vauxhall Water Works continued to draw water from the lower Thames. In one large section of south London, the two companies ran lines down the same streets and competed for customers. Snow determined that of the 334 persons who had lived in this area and died of cholera, 286 were served by the Southwark and Vauxhall Company, and only 14 from the Lambeth Company. The remainder drew their water directly from the Thames or from public pumps. In 1883, Robert Koch identified Snow's "poison" as a specific bacterium.

Consequences in America
In the spring of 1866, physicians in New York City braced for another worldwide outbreak of

cholera. Confronted by Snow's evidence, they concluded that the city must do everything possible to prevent sewage from infecting the city's water supply. Not trusting the Tammany politicians with the task of cleaning up the city, the people of New York created a powerful Metropolitan Board of Health and gave it wide powers to ensure the health of the city. Historian Charles Rosenberg claims that the creation of the New York Board of Health was one of the most significant dates in the history of public health. The Metropolitan Board of Health spearheaded an ambitious campaign to build an extensive network of aqueducts connecting the city with distant reservoirs and watersheds, ensuring a superb water supply for centuries to come.

Other cities lagged behind New York. When a cholera outbreak struck New Orleans in February 1873, it spread up the Mississippi River valley, ravaging low-lying urban areas where drinking water had been contaminated by sewage.

Nashville, Tennessee, was one example. The city's pumping station on the Cumberland River was originally located upriver; but as the city spread eastward, sewage from the new residential areas flowed into Brown's Creek and then into the Cumberland above the pumping station. Sewage from the rest of the city seeped into several streams, from which many residents drew their drinking water. The Capitol Hill district, on the high ground, had relatively few fatalities from the disease. That summer, 647 people from Nashville died of cholera.

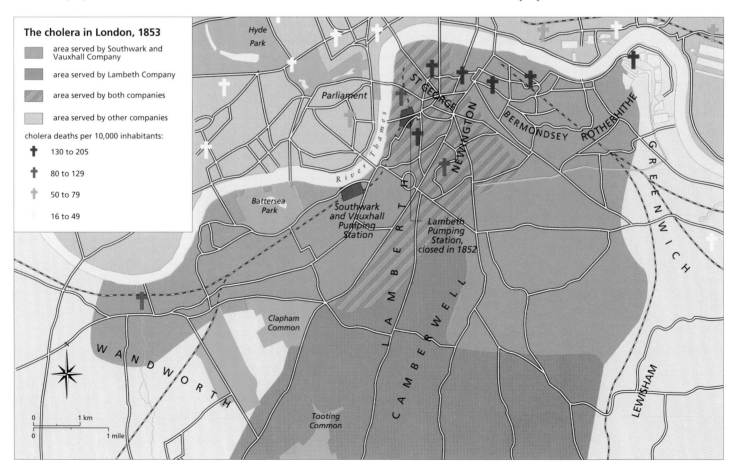

The cholera in London, 1853

- area served by Southwark and Vauxhall Company
- area served by Lambeth Company
- area served by both companies
- area served by other companies

cholera deaths per 10,000 inhabitants:

- † 130 to 205
- † 80 to 129
- † 50 to 79
- † 16 to 49

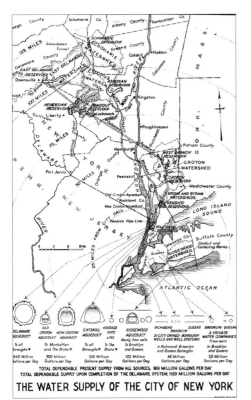

THE WATER SUPPLY OF THE CITY OF NEW YORK

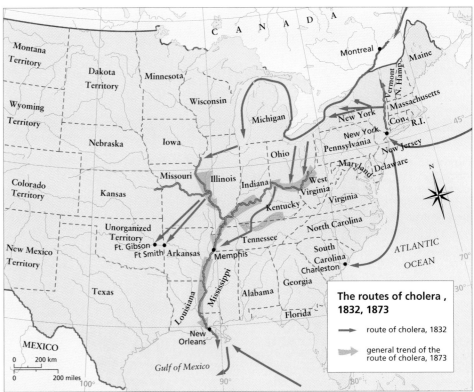

The routes of cholera, 1832, 1873

→ route of cholera, 1832

⇨ general trend of the route of cholera, 1873

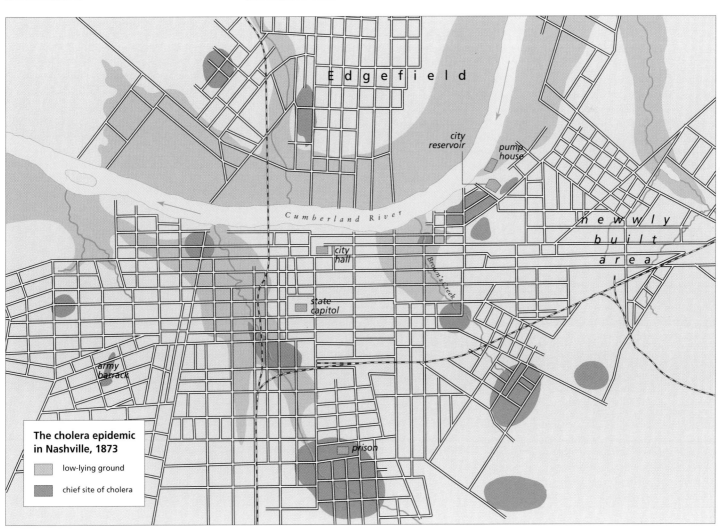

The cholera epidemic in Nashville, 1873

low-lying ground

chief site of cholera

PROSTITUTION IN 19TH-CENTURY NEW YORK
VICTORIAN GENDER IDEOLOGY

In 1858 Walt Whitman commented that 19 out of 20 of the nation's city-dwelling young men were "more or less familiar" with houses of prostitution. Although prostitution was common in all 19th-century American cities, the problem was nowhere more acute than in New York City. By the time of the Civil War, Gotham housed over 600 brothels. As many as 13,000 women—roughly 10 percent of the city's female population—worked as prostitutes at some point in their lives. Many doctors, sanitary reformers and politicians lobbied to legalize and regulate the practice. The ensuing controversy over prostitution highlights the most glaring inconsistency of Victorian gender ideology: men's enshrinement of "true womanhood," and their reliance on prostitutes.

Prior to 1820, illicit sex was mostly confined to three neighborhoods in New York City. The best-known location for prostitutes on the west side was the two block area directly behind St. Paul's Chapel and just south of Columbia College. This district, aptly called "the Holy Ground," was situated on property owned by the Episcopal Church of New York. Farther east, on the other side of the City Common (later City Hall Park), prostitutes congregated in the taverns along George (later Spruce) Street, only two short blocks from the Park Theater and four blocks from the East River wharves. A third sex district, accommodating men who worked in the shipping, dock and marine industries, was located on the outer, northeast edge of the city on East George (later Market) Street.

As the city spread northward up the length of Manhattan, new prostitution districts emerged. From 1820 to 1910, prostitutes openly solicited in nearly every neighborhood. The most ambitious entrepreneurs gravitated to the theater and entertainment districts. From 1820 to 1850, there were four major theater districts. Five Points, at the center of the fast-developing metropolis, was the most infamous slum of its day. There, as one visitor remarked, "nearly every house and cellar is a groggery below and a brothel above." "African Grove," on the west side along Church and Chapel Streets, where resided most of the city's Afro-Americans; and two districts adjacent to the East River that served the carnal needs of mariners, sailors, and laborers who worked nearby. Water and Cherry Streets were to the south, and Corlear's Hook to the north.

The construction of new factories and warehouses along the west side and in Five Points after 1850 forced many prostitutes uptown. The area near Broadway and north of Canal Street functioned as the main center of prostitution. The fine, recently-built row houses served as brothels, and the "monster" hotels that dominated Broadway, along with a plethora of theaters, saloons, and restaurants all attracted the leading madams and prostitutes. Absent were the slum conditions and low-income immigrants and racial groups that typified the earlier districts. For over a decade, this neighborhood, with its numerous nightlife establishments, catered to a middle-class and elite clientele.

After the Civil War, the geography of prostitution underwent further change. The "Tenderloin" located north of 23rd Street between Fifth and Eighth Avenues, became the most famous sex district in New York. The Tenderloin stretched to 34th Street by 1880, to 42nd Street by 1890, and to 57th Street by the turn of the century. Numerous restaurants and theaters (including, after 1883, the Metropolitan Opera House) filled Broadway, but Sixth Avenue became a haven for concert saloons with prostitutes. The adjoining side streets were crammed with brothels.

"The Rialto," near Union Square along 14th Street, served as a second major sex district. Close to the elite mansions along Fifth Avenue and Gramercy Park, this neighborhood also featured theaters and restaurants. Farther south, a third district appeared along Allen Street in the immigrant and tenement neighborhood of the Lower East Side, a few blocks east of the Bowery. Finally, a scattering of smaller districts was found in lower Manhattan, notably in Little Italy, Chinatown, Water Street, and the neighborhoods south of Washington Square Park.

Timothy Gilfoyle

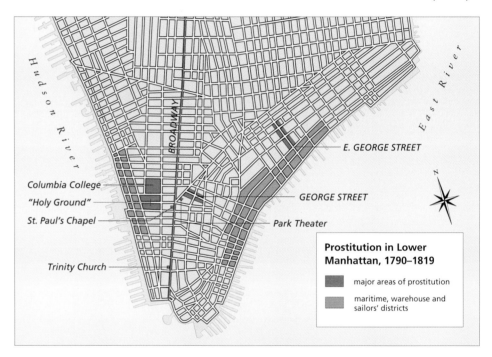

Columbia College
"Holy Ground"
St. Paul's Chapel
Trinity Church
E. GEORGE STREET
GEORGE STREET
Park Theater

Prostitution in Lower Manhattan, 1790–1819

■ major areas of prostitution

■ maritime, warehouse and sailors' districts

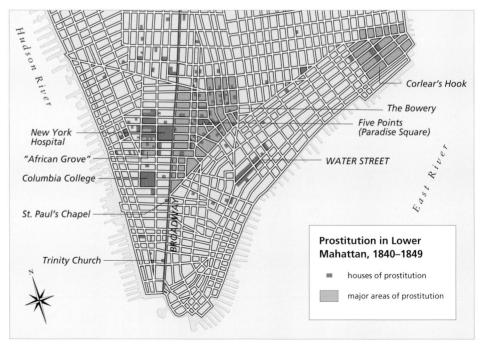

New York Hospital
"African Grove"
Columbia College
St. Paul's Chapel
Trinity Church
Corlear's Hook
The Bowery
Five Points (Paradise Square)
WATER STREET

Prostitution in Lower Mahattan, 1840–1849

■ houses of prostitution

■ major areas of prostitution

Above: "Butt Ender's" Prostitution Exposed, *published in 1839, was one of the early guidebooks that directed interested parties to New York's leading brothels. The publication also satirized leading "purity" reform groups such as the Female Moral Reform Society, which sought to eradicate prostitution.*

Longacre Square, New York, 1901

- churches
- hotels
- manufacturers, warehouses, other commercial
- police, fire, national guards
- houses of prostitution
- schools
- single family
- theaters, music halls

1 Knickerbocker Theater   2 The Casino
3 Empire Theater   4 Metropolitan Opera House
5 Broadway Theater   6 American Theater
7 Hammerstein's Victoria Music Hall   8 Lyric Theater

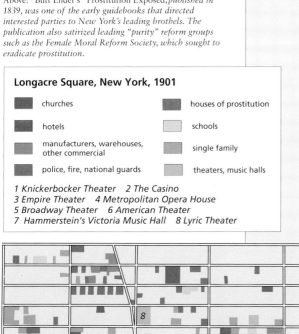

Prostitution moves uptown: areas of prostitution, 1880–1884

- houses of prostitution
- tenement area
- entertainment area

PATERNALISM AND WORKER'S COMMUNITIES
HOUSING AND INDUSTRIAL LABOR

Although the United States emerged as an industrial power after the Civil War, its factory owners were not an omnipotent ruling class, nor its workers a miserable proletariat. Industrialists who struggled to survive intense competition, technological change, and downturns in the business cycle watched with mounting desperation as skilled workers, many of them union members, clung ever tighter to shop rules that allowed them to determine who could work and how. During the 1880s and 1890s, many industrialists, in addition to relieving competitive pressure by forming monopolies (see The Creation of U.S. Steel, p 144–145), attempted to wrest control of the workplace from the workers. This precipitated an outbreak of strikes, lockouts, and bloody clashes.

Homestead: A Company Town
Some industrialists sought to gain leverage over workers by controlling their housing, compounding the threat of eviction to that of dismissal. But company housing was often so poor that it only exacerbated worker resentments. One example was Homestead, Pennsylvania, built in 1872, part of the Carnegie steel empire. Although the furnaces of the Carnegie Steel Company straddled the Monongahela River, most workers lived on its south bank, just up the hill from the steel works in Munhall, a district crammed with boarding houses and tenements, most of them owned by the Carnegie Land Company. Munhall lacked paved streets and sewers. When the wind shifted to the north, the towering smokestacks of the open-hearth furnaces belched soot and fumes into the workers' homes.

Journalist Hamlin Garland wrote that the streets were "horrible" and the houses deplorable. "Everywhere the yellow mud of the streets lay kneaded into sticky masses, through which groups of pale, lean men slouched in faded garments, grimy with soot and dirt of the mills," he explained.

Planned Company Communities: Pullman
Some observers warned that employees who lived in such squalid conditions would inevitably fall prey to the enervating solicitude of brothel or bottle or to the radical nostrums of labor agitators. By providing decent housing in a well-planned community, owners would gain the loyalty of their workers and instill in them habits of regularity and sobriety.

Many of the early experiments in industrial paternalism were found in Europe, most notably the workers' colonies of Alfred Krupp, the German steelmaker. The most famous of this workers' communities was Schederhof, built in 1872.

Like Homestead, Schederhof was sited near the steelworks and railways, but where the forbidding hulks of the Homestead furnaces dominated the skyline as unremittingly as did the workers' lives, the Schederhof colony looked upon an English-style park. And where the houses in Homestead grew in a chaotic tangle, workers' appartments in Schederhof were laid out in a symmetrical grid. Single family houses, reserved for especially valued employees, were placed in neat rows opposite the park.

Whether George Pullman, the manufacturer of the railroad sleeper cars bearing his name, derived his plan for a model company town from Krupp is still debated. In any case, he built Pullman, Illinois, in 1881 according to plans exhibiting a similar preoccupation with order and a fascination for parks.

Homestead: a company town

- Carnegie Steel Co.
- Carnegie Land Co. Holdings
- ○ saloon
- † church
- ◆ amusements
- ■ school

Monongahela River

CARNEGIE STEEL COMPANY

Whitaker Creek

Park · Library · Munhall · Park

West Homestead

N

0   200 m
0   900 feet

Economist Richard Ely, though impressed by the appearance and amenities of Pullman, found that residents resented the company's domination. Subject to authority of others during the day, workers at Pullman—and elsewhere—longed to spend their scant free time in a home, however simple, of their own. They snatched up cottages such as those built by Chicago developer Samuel Gross. (The bedroom in the advertisement measured 5 feet 5 inches by 7 feet 6 inches .) From 1880 to 1892 Gross sold over 7,000 houses, many costing as little as $800.

WHERE ALL WAS DARKNESS, NOW IS LIGHT.

A HOME AT $10 A MONTH

S.E.GROSS' ASHLAND AVE AND 47TH STREET SUBDIVISION

BRANCH OFFICE COR. ASHLAND AVE & 47TH ST.

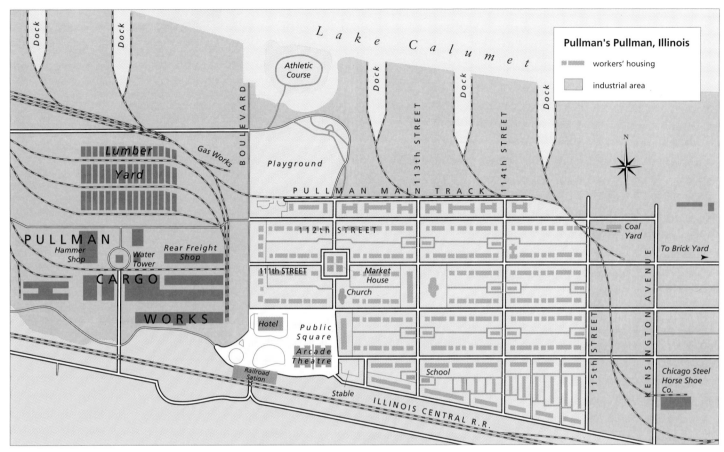

If the economic function of Homestead was all too apparent, Pullman's buildings were designed to disguise the community's industrial purposes. Visitors, arriving at the Illinois Central station, walked on curving paths around a man-made lake to the elegant administration buildings.

Further south, the visual center of town was a public square featuring another park and a two-level shopping arcade. A Romanesque church, owned by Pullman, stood just off the square. Pullman also owned all of the housing, which consisted of mostly two- and three-roomed tenements.

But few company towns, even those reflecting the enlightened paternalism of a Pullman, were successful. Homestead (1892) and Pullman (1894) provided the setting for two of the nation's most significant—and violent—labor confrontations.

A contemporary depiction of the 1894 Pullman strike during which the National Guard was deployed to drive away from company property an angry mob of striking workers. The National Guard used Pullman built railcars as a barricade and fired into the advancing strikers.

THE CREATION OF U.S. STEEL
THE FIRST BILLION-DOLLAR CORPORATION

At the turn of the 20th century, the American economic system approached a crossroads: would cut-throat competition continue to slash prices and wreak havoc among rival firms, or would the major financiers and their allies build a more stable and less competitive economic order? In 1900, the future of American capitalism depended, or so it seemed, on the outcome of the impending war between Andrew Carnegie, the steelmaker who believed that the maxim "survival of the fittest" should apply to business, and J.P. Morgan, the king of American finance who sought to ensure high prices and economic order by establishing a "community of interest" among the giant corporations.

Aside from their antithetical economic philosophies, Carnegie and Morgan were moving toward a confrontation over steel. During the 1870s and 1880s, Carnegie had pioneered the Bessemer process for producing steel, first introduced at the Edgar Thomson Steel Works ; gained control of huge deposits of iron ore in the Menominee Range of hills in Wisconsin; forced the Pennsylvania and B & O railroads to give him preferential rates; suppressed unionism and, 1892, defeated strikers at the Homestead plant. By 1890, having crushed most of his competitors in western Pennsylvania, Carnegie had become the nation's foremost steelmaker. In 1900 he determined to extend his industrial empire to the manufacture of finished steel products such as wire and tubing and to entice new railroads to lay track to his mines and furnaces.

These plans alarmed Morgan. Carnegie's new rail lines would precipitate a new round of freight wars and undermine the underpinnings of the entire rail industry, which Morgan had painstakingly reorganized and refinanced. Furthermore, Carnegie's new finished steel plants would destroy Morgan's National Tube Company. Rather than fight Carnegie, however, Morgan decided to buy him out. When Carnegie proposed a price of $480 million, Morgan accepted on the spot.

Two months later, Morgan organized United States Steel, a giant amalgamation of coal and ore mines, steel furnaces, rolling mills, wire and tubing plants, railroads, and steamers. Capitalized at $1.1 billion, it brought under one management 180 previously independent businesses. To Carnegie's 19 blast furnaces in western Pennsylvania, Morgan added the furnaces of Federal Steel (20), mostly in the Chicago and Cleveland areas, National Steel (18), in Ohio and western Pennsylvania, and those of many smaller steelmakers. To his holdings in National Tube, he joined several other producers of finished steel products. The most important were American Steel and Wire, American Bridge, American Steel Hoop, and American Tin Plate. By 1906, U.S. Steel owned or controlled 65 iron ore mines in the Lake Superior region, 93 blast furnaces, 1,100 miles of railroad, and over 700 iron and steel works.

It produced nearly 90 percent of the nation's steel output.

The creation of U.S. Steel had a huge impact on Pittsburgh. Though it closed 60 Pittsburgh plants, it remained by far the largest employer. Steelworkers who fell from favor with the U.S. Steel management had few alternatives nearby, and local politicians gave the city's major employer almost unlimited license to pollute the air and water and allowed housing and public sanitation to deteriorate below the already low standards that prevailed in most cities.

In 1911, President Taft initiated antitrust action against the behemoth. In a landmark decision, the Court ruled that although U.S. Steel dominated the market, it had not employed "unfair means" in its struggles with competitors.

The government appealed the case and the Court again affirmed that "the law does not make mere size an offense." U.S. Steel would not be broken up. Morgan's hopes for an economy dominated by the big corporations had, at least for a time, prevailed.

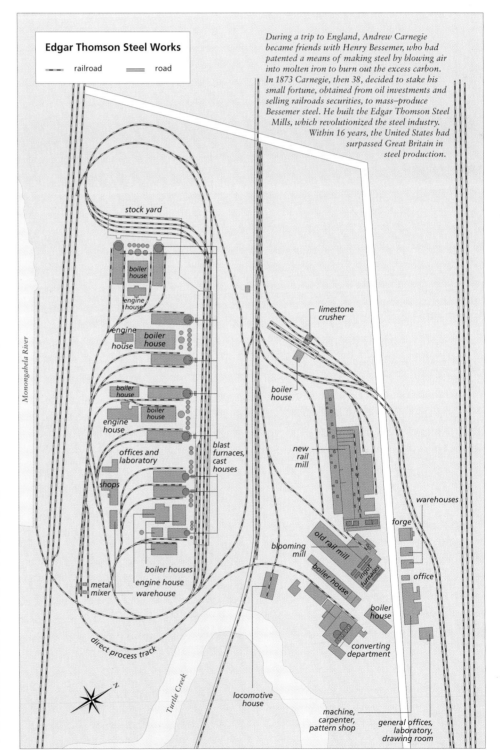

Edgar Thomson Steel Works

railroad   road

During a trip to England, Andrew Carnegie became friends with Henry Bessemer, who had patented a means of making steel by blowing air into molten iron to burn out the excess carbon. In 1873 Carnegie, then 38, decided to stake his small fortune, obtained from oil investments and selling railroads securities, to mass–produce Bessemer steel. He built the Edgar Thomson Steel Mills, which revolutionized the steel industry. Within 16 years, the United States had surpassed Great Britain in steel production.

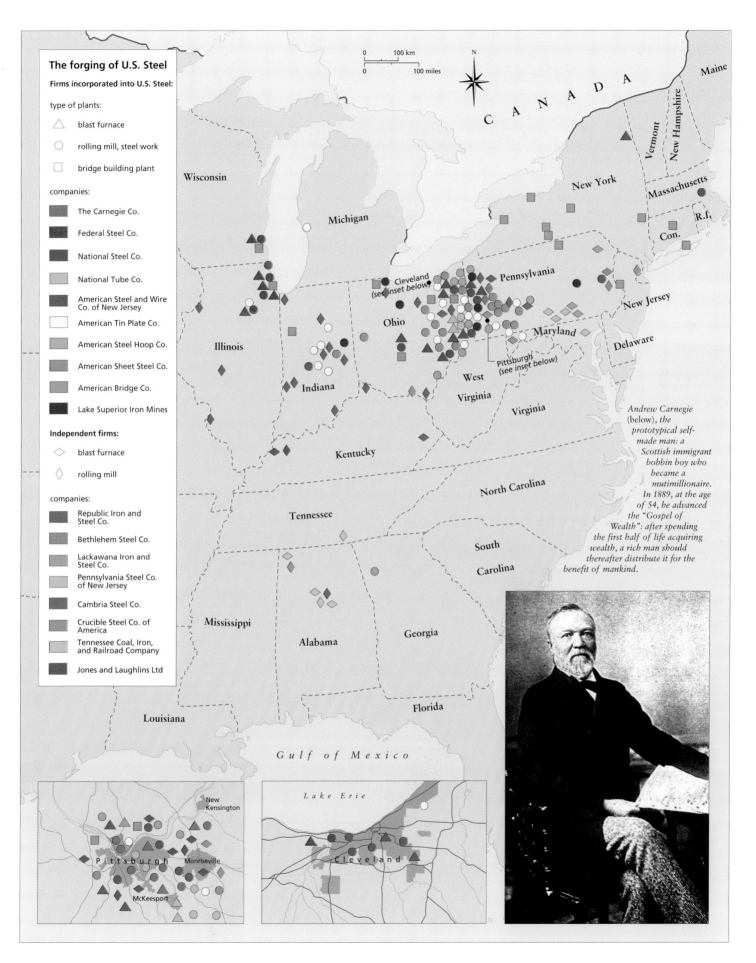

The forging of U.S. Steel

Firms incorporated into U.S. Steel:

type of plants:

△ blast furnace

○ rolling mill, steel work

□ bridge building plant

companies:

- The Carnegie Co.
- Federal Steel Co.
- National Steel Co.
- National Tube Co.
- American Steel and Wire Co. of New Jersey
- American Tin Plate Co.
- American Steel Hoop Co.
- American Sheet Steel Co.
- American Bridge Co.
- Lake Superior Iron Mines

Independent firms:

◇ blast furnace

◇ rolling mill

companies:

- Republic Iron and Steel Co.
- Bethlehem Steel Co.
- Lackawana Iron and Steel Co.
- Pennsylvania Steel Co. of New Jersey
- Cambria Steel Co.
- Crucible Steel Co. of America
- Tennessee Coal, Iron, and Railroad Company
- Jones and Laughlins Ltd

Andrew Carnegie (below), the prototypical self-made man: a Scottish immigrant bobbin boy who became a mutimillionaire. In 1889, at the age of 54, he advanced the "Gospel of Wealth": after spending the first half of life acquiring wealth, a rich man should thereafter distribute it for the benefit of mankind.

145

THE RISE OF POPULISM
AGRARIAN DISCONTENT IN THE SOUTH AND WEST

"We meet in the midst of a nation brought to the verge of moral, political, and material ruin," thundered the People's Party in 1892, as it began its first national campaign. Many businessmen and workers would indeed be ruined by the financial panic of the following year. The downward spiral for the farmers who provided the bulk of the new party's support, however, had begun years before, starting more slowly but seeming all the more inexorable. Believing that the credit system and middlemen robbed them and that the Democrats and Republicans had failed them, discontented agrarians organized at the local, state, and national levels. Particularly in the South, on the Plains, and in the Rockies, the "Populists" presented the most thoroughgoing challenge to the two-party system since the 1850s.

The quarter-century following Appomattox saw a vast expansion of commercial agriculture. Settlers and railroads pressed further onto the Great Plains, while areas of the upland South previously given chiefly to self-sufficient farming began to grow cotton for market. Such expansion did not necessarily herald "good times" for all farmers, however. Prices for many agricultural products fell—in part because of increased domestic production, but also because of similar expansion on other continents and the American government's own financial policies. Seeking to return to the hard money system abandoned during the Civil War, the government refused in the 1870s and 1880s to let the volume of currency expand at the same rate as population or business activity. Tight money increased interest rates while depressing prices, making the debts farmers contracted to buy land and raise crops more difficult to repay. Western and Southern cultivators also complained that their burdens were multiplied by the high charges of the railroads and other intermediaries that linked them to distant markets. In bad years, the price received at harvest time for a bale of cotton or bushel of wheat did not always exceed the costs of producing and marketing it.

The crop lien system made the circumstances of Southern farmers especially bleak. With credit scarce and land values low, Southerners had, in effect, to mortgage a crop in advance to the local merchant for the supplies necessary to grow it. Paying high credit prices while receiving less and less for the cotton that their creditors demanded they grow, many fell into perpetual debt. White yeomen lost their land and joined emancipated blacks in the swelling ranks of sharecroppers and ten-

ants. Outside Dixie, the proportions of non-landowing farmers grew, too. Settlement of the Plains created a speculative bubble that burst with the droughts of the late 1880s. Many with large mortgages were foreclosed upon.

Farmers did not suffer silently, however. The Grange and Greenback efforts of the 1870s were followed in the Midwest and South by the more expansive farmer's alliance movement. Local groups coalesced into state organizations, eventually yielding two great regional bodies with hundreds of thousands of members, known as the Northwestern and Southern Alliances, and a separate Colored Farmers' Alliance. The alliances demanded effective federal control of railroads and government intervention to expand the money supply. They also oversaw numerous cooperative projects that hoped to provision farmers at low interest rates and control marketing directly. The refusal of

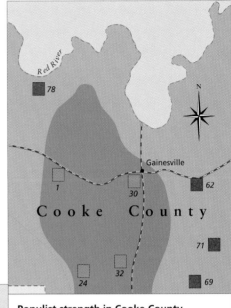

Populist strength in Cooke County, Texas, gubernatorial elections 1894

- voting box, with percentage 69 of populist vote
- good quality farmland
- poorer quality farmland
- railroad

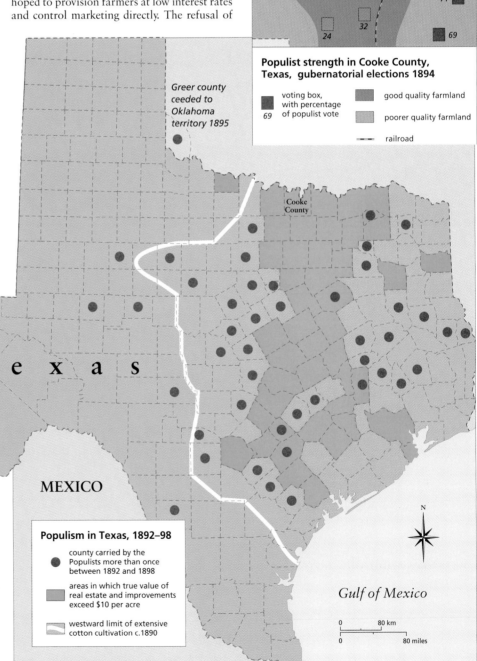

Greer county ceeded to Oklahoma territory 1895

Populism in Texas, 1892–98

- county carried by the Populists more than once between 1892 and 1898
- areas in which true value of real estate and improvements exceed $10 per acre
- westward limit of extensive cotton cultivation c.1890

MEXICO

Gulf of Mexico

0   80 km

0   80 miles

banks and wholesalers to deal with the Southern Alliance's ambitious but cash-starved state exchanges helped to draw the formally non-partisan organizations into politics. When Southern Democrats spurned demands that the federal government provide low interest paper money loans to farmers as well as run the nation's railroads and telegraphs, many Southern Alliancemen joined their Western brethren in forming an independent third party.

The People's Party aspired to be a national organization, uniting farmers and laborers. Only in the Rocky Mountain states, however, did the 1892 ticket, headed by James Weaver, score well among non-agrarians. There, Populists' support for an expansion of the money supply through the unlimited coinage of silver and their sympathy for labor won them the support of mining interests and workers both. Elsewhere, their inability to win significant percentages of the vote east of the Mississippi or north of the Ohio indicated they had failed to rally urban, industrial areas and, more troubling still, many farmers.

Populists generally did best where the agricultural economy was most fragile and livelihoods less secure. Although Populist farmers were not invariably poorer than their non-Populist counterparts, they typically lived in more isolated places where the soil was less productive and more vulnerable to drought or other natural disasters and where the extensive cultivation of cash crops was a relatively recent phenomenon. In Texas, the birthplace of the Southern Alliance, Populists concentrated in the more marginal areas of the state's cotton-growing regions (they were less strong in the thinly populated ranch lands of west and south Texas). The dry and broken land of the farming frontier and the pine woods of east Texas yielded far richer harvests for the People's Party than the more valuable farmland of the black and Grand prairies and the coastal plain. Even within a single north Texas county, precinct boxes in the rough and sandy soils of "Cross Timbers" areas showed far higher Populist percentages than those in richer prairie lands or in the county seat. In Texas and elsewhere through the South, Populists faltered in former plantation areas with large black populations. The Texas party typically won black counties near the Gulf Coast only when it made common cause with Republicans. Blacks' loyalty to that party—as well as the mutual suspicion of white and black, sharecropper and landowner—proved difficult to overcome. Throughout the South, white Democrats in black counties also won elections through coercion and fraud.

Nationally, the Populist vote climbed through the 1894 elections, but the party could not capitalize on its gains. Even in places like Kansas, Nebraska, Colorado, North Dakota, and Minnesota, where it had won governorships or significant power in the legislature, Populists could never capture complete control of state governments or the courts or escape dependence on fusion arrangements with other parties. In the South, Populists, allied with

Republicans, ran the closest races since Reconstruction, but only in North Carolina did they loosen the Democrats' grip on power. And, in the aftermath of the Panic of 1893, urban workers turned not to populism but to the G.O.P. Many Populists came to feel that the party should streamline its appeal, focusing on the free silver issue which was dividing the major parties. When the Democrats in 1896 nominated silverite William Jennings Bryan, the People's Party followed suit, despite the objection of many who felt fusion to be a surrender of key Populist principles. The submergence of the party's identity in the failed Bryan crusade decimated the movement. So, too, did a subsequent rise in agricultural prices and the expansion of the money supply with the increased mining and refining of gold.

Farmer in Texas at his plow. Cotton was the most important cash crop for most Texas farmers into the 20th century. But low and declining cotton prices from 1870–90 contributed to political discontent and the rise of the Populists. Southern farmers were forced into a position of morgaging their crop in advance for food and supplies necessary to grow it.

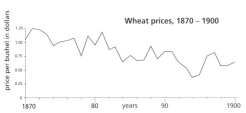

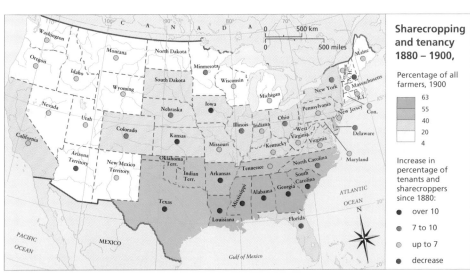

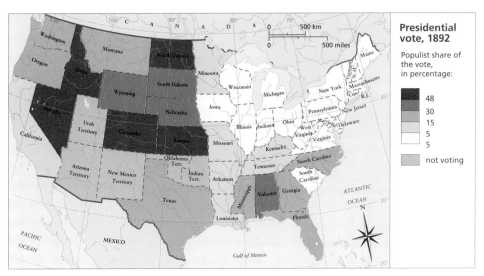

MONEY AND POWER

THE ELECTION OF 1896

Like the elections of 1861, 1932, and 1968, the 1896 contest between William McKinley and William Jennings Bryan seemed to contemporaries to involve more than simply choosing a President. Coming amidst national crisis, the election was treated by many as a referendum on America's destiny. Clarence Darrow believed in 1892 that Bryan—his courtroom antagonist at the Scopes Trial thirty years hence—was leading "the greatest battle of modern times between the plutocrats and the producers." Republican Henry Cabot Lodge, on the other hand, insisted Bryan's opponents were "fighting to save the country from a disaster which would be second only to 1861."

With the Panic of 1893, hard times and political turmoil spread beyond the agrarian West and South . Farm prices fell even further, banks and businesses failed in great number, and unemployment reached unprecedented levels. The issue of money became the means by which many Americans debated the depression—its meaning, causes, and cures. Many Republicans, Democrats, and Populists in mining, cotton and wheat states had long favored returning the country to its pre-1873 policy of allowing unlimited coinage of silver as well as gold. The depression quickened the agitation for "free silver," viewed by many not as a narrow fiscal adjustment but as a multifaceted reform measure. Increasing the amount of money in circulation would not only restore prosperity by raising crop prices, but expand credit, breaking the stranglehold Eastern interests held on the nation's finances. Defenders of the gold standard also invested free silver with enormous potential. It would ruin America's good name in the international financial community at the same time inflation robbed wage-earners and creditors.

Democratic President Grover Cleveland led the fight against free silver. But his heavy-handed efforts to shore up the gold standard embittered Southern and Western Democrats and their many pro-silver constituents. Party divisions and the failure of Cleveland's policies to ease hardship doomed the Democracy in the off-year congressional elections of 1894. Labor, immigrant groups, Americans of all sorts, abandoned the party. Its recent gains in the Northeast and Midwest evaporated. The Populist vote increased by over 40 percent, but Republicans profited the most, seizing control of Congress and increasing their House delegation by over 100 seats.

Though the depression continued, Republicans found they could not assume 1896 would be a replay of the 1894 landslide. Silver was changing the shape of politics. Free silver factions worked from within and without, threatening to divide and reconstitute the parties. They had their most telling effect among the Democrats. Cleveland's unpopularity and the defeat of Eastern Democrats in 1894 lent more power within the party to the West and

Nebraskan Presidential Candidate, William Jennings Bryan

South, where a strong silver stance was essential in challenging local Populists and silver Republicans. Free silver Democrats prevailed at the party convention, writing a platform repudiating Cleveland's policies and nominating Nebraskan William Jennings Bryan. Bryan's appeal reached beyond Democratic ranks, such that Populists, who had once hoped to rally defecting silver Democrats, found themselves reduced to seconding his nomination. The GOP was left to take up the gold standard—though its nominee, Ohio's William McKinley, like many Republicans, preferred to straddle the money question and promote a protective tariff. The party proved willing to alienate its own silverites to secure the loyalty of Republican and Democrat "goldbugs" alike.

There were striking contrasts between the Bryan and McKinley campaigns. In many respects, the Republicans' Campaign seems glaringly modern, and not simply because they sought to identify display of the American flag with support of their candidate and positions. Orchestrated by industrialist Marcus A.

Hanna, a coordinated national effort raised millions of dollars from wealthy individuals and large corporations. Pamphlets and speakers targeted every sort of constituency. Ill-organized and ill-financed, the Democratic campaign made innovations of its own. While McKinley's "front porch" campaign consisted of heavily scripted encounters with visiting delegations, Bryan barnstormed across the nation, delivering hundreds of speeches. Though Democrats wooed labor, calling for an end to the use of injunctions against strikes and stricter control over corporate trusts, silver dominated their appeals. Higher farm prices would underwrite prosperity for all Americans, but perhaps more importantly, free silver would guarantee government and finance served the people, not powerful business interests. The Republicans' discussion of silver was equally charged. Newspapers and clergymen joined in denouncing free silver as an attack on property, allowing debtors to pay their obligations in devalued currency. They portrayed Bryan as an unstable demagogue, an ally of socialists and anarchists. McKinley also appealed to workers and farmers, arguing that their interests would be served not by inflation but by a protective tariff to create jobs, raise wages, and cultivate domestic demand.

As expected, McKinley won the Northeast while Bryan took the South, the Plains, and the Rocky Mountain silver mining states. Though Bryan won more votes than Cleveland had in 1892, Republicans triumphed by sweeping the hotly contested Midwestern states between Ohio and Iowa. There and elsewhere, Republicans had expanded their support in urban and industrial areas. This indicated not only business backing but that the GOP had secured its 1894 gains amongst labor.

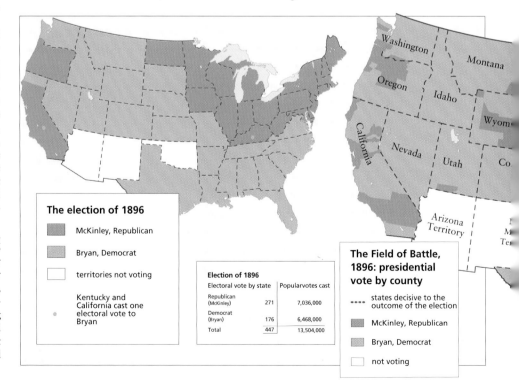

The election of 1896

- McKinley, Republican
- Bryan, Democrat
- territories not voting

Kentucky and California cast one electoral vote to Bryan

Election of 1896		
Electoral vote by state		Popularvotes cast
Republican (McKinley)	271	7,036,000
Democrat (Bryan)	176	6,468,000
Total	447	13,504,000

The Field of Battle, 1896: presidential vote by county

- - - - states decisive to the outcome of the election
- McKinley, Republican
- Bryan, Democrat
- not voting

McKinley's promise of prosperity attracted many workers, though others were coerced by employers and creditors into supporting him. The party seems, too, to have attracted increasing numbers of German-Americans and Catholics, seemingly uninterested in free silver and put off by Bryan's agrarian evangelism. The farm vote was likewise important to McKinley, for while 1896 has sometimes been caricatured as a city-country contest, Bryan faltered in rural areas east of the Missouri River, scoring better, in fact, in a number of Northeastern cities than in the surrounding countryside. Rural Americans, differing in interest, political tradition, class and ethnic backgrounds, rarely vote as a unit, and in 1896 there were clear differences in the situations of farmers north of the Ohio and east of the Missouri Rivers, engaged in a more diversified and prosperous agriculture and thus less saddled with debt and tenancy, and their Western and Southern counterparts. Bryan did better where the connection between tight money and agrarian distress was obvious—in poorer states more devoted to cotton or wheat.

After two decades of divided government at the national level, GOP victories in 1894 and 1896 ushered in a period of Republican domination which, with one major interruption, continued through the 1920s. Though the South became solidly Democratic with black disfranchisement and Populism's demise, Republican gains in the Northeast and Midwest were more decisive. Democratic inroads among Repuplican silverites and farmers in the West proved transitory. 1896 clearly marked a further maturation of the political power of the urban, industrial, and business sectors and a further strengthening of their attachment to the GOP. With the defeat of Bryan and the disintegration of Populism a strain of agrarian dissent that had focused America's attention on questions of money and power dissipated.

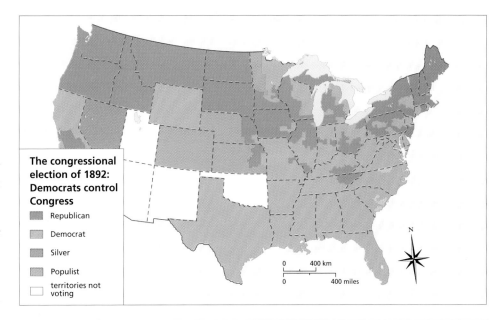

The congressional election of 1892: Democrats control Congress

- Republican
- Democrat
- Silver
- Populist
- territories not voting

0   400 km
0   400 miles

N

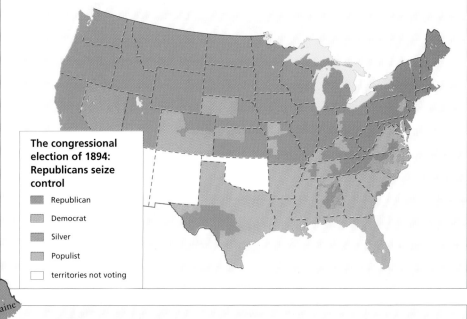

The congressional election of 1894: Republicans seize control

- Republican
- Democrat
- Silver
- Populist
- territories not voting

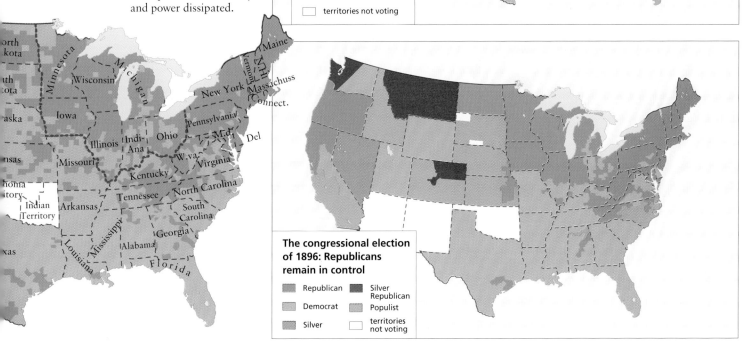

The congressional election of 1896: Republicans remain in control

- Republican
- Democrat
- Silver
- Silver Republican
- Populist
- territories not voting

THE BOUNDARY DISPUTES OF THE 1890s

THE END OF ANGLO- AMERICAN HOSTILITY

In the brief period between 1895 and 1903 a profound change occurred in the relationship between the United States and Great Britain, a change highlighted by two boundary disputes in remote parts of the Western Hemisphere. The first involved the boundary between Venezuela and British Guiana. The second involved the line separating Yukon Territory in Canada from the United States Territory of Alaska. The Venezuela boundary dispute brought the United States and Great Britain to the edge of war. The Alaskan controversy, where far more was at stake, was resolved in prefect amity by urbane diplomats meeting quite casually in London and at various English country houses.

The boundary between Venezuela and British Guiana ran through a tangled jungle that might or might not contain gold. The claims of both sides were exaggerated, but what made the dispute dangerous was the fact that the president of the United States, Grover Cleveland, insisted that his government would treat any expansion of British territory as a violation of the Monroe Doctrine. After first refusing even to respond to this American proclamation, Lord Salisbury, the British Prime Minister, flatly rejected the argument that the Monroe Doctrine applied to the dispute, whereupon Cleveland announced that he would appoint a commission to determine the boundary unilaterally, and that if the British attempted to occupy any part of Venezuela beyond that line, the United States would employ "every means in its power" to prevent them from doing so. This threat caused the British to have second thoughts. War with the United States would be "an absurdity," the colonial secretary quickly announced. The British agreed to arbitration, and the war scare evaporated. The result was anticlimactic: when the arbitrators heard the case, they awarded most of the land in dispute to Great Britain.

The Alaskan Controversy

The roots of the Alaskan controversy ran back to the American purchase of that vast region from Russia in 1867. A Russo-British treaty of 1825 had set the boundary between Alaska and British Canada in a straight line south from the Arctic to Mt. St. Elias on the Gulf of Alaska, but it dealt vaguely with the boundary of the convoluted coastal panhandle, saying only that it ran 30 miles inland from the ocean. The exact line seemed to be of no importance in 1825 or in 1867.

However, the discovery of gold in the Klondike in 1898 raised the possibility that there might be more in the panhandle region. If any was found, Canadian and American prospectors would rush there and trouble might easily result. Because the area was a trackless wilderness, to reach the gold fields miners would have to come by ship from Vancouver or Seattle to Skagway or Dyea on a deep estuary known as the Lynn Canal. If the boundary of Alaska ran directly across country 30 miles from the Gulf of Alaska, those towns, currently controlled by the United States, would be in British Canada and open to unrestricted access by Canadian prospectors. If the line followed the sinuosities of the coastline, the towns would be on American soil and Canada would have no outlet to the sea along the panhandle.

To settle the dispute, the United States and Great Britain appointed in 1903 a tribunal of "impartial jurists of repute" consisting of three Americans (Secretary of War Elihu Root, Senator Henry Cabot Lodge of Massachusetts, and George Turner, a former Senator from Washington), two Canadians, and one Englishman, Lord Alverstone, the British Lord Chief Justice. All the members were of some "repute," but only Alverstone was a jurist and none was in any sense impartial. In his instructions to the Americans, President Theodore Roosevelt ordered them to insist on the American version of the boundary. He warned an English newspaperman that if no agreement was reached "I shall send up engineers to run our line as we assert it and I shall send troops to guard and hold it."

With the Canadians equally adamant, the decision depended on Lord Alverstone, which in effect meant that the British government had

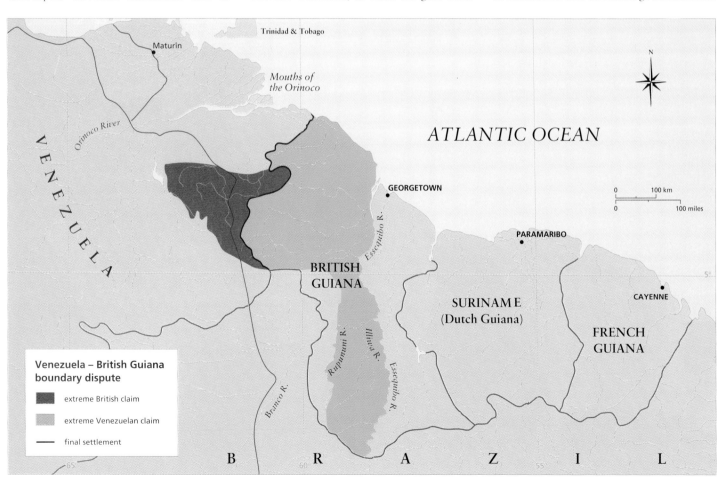

Venezuela – British Guiana boundary dispute

- extreme British claim
- extreme Venezuelan claim
- —— final settlement

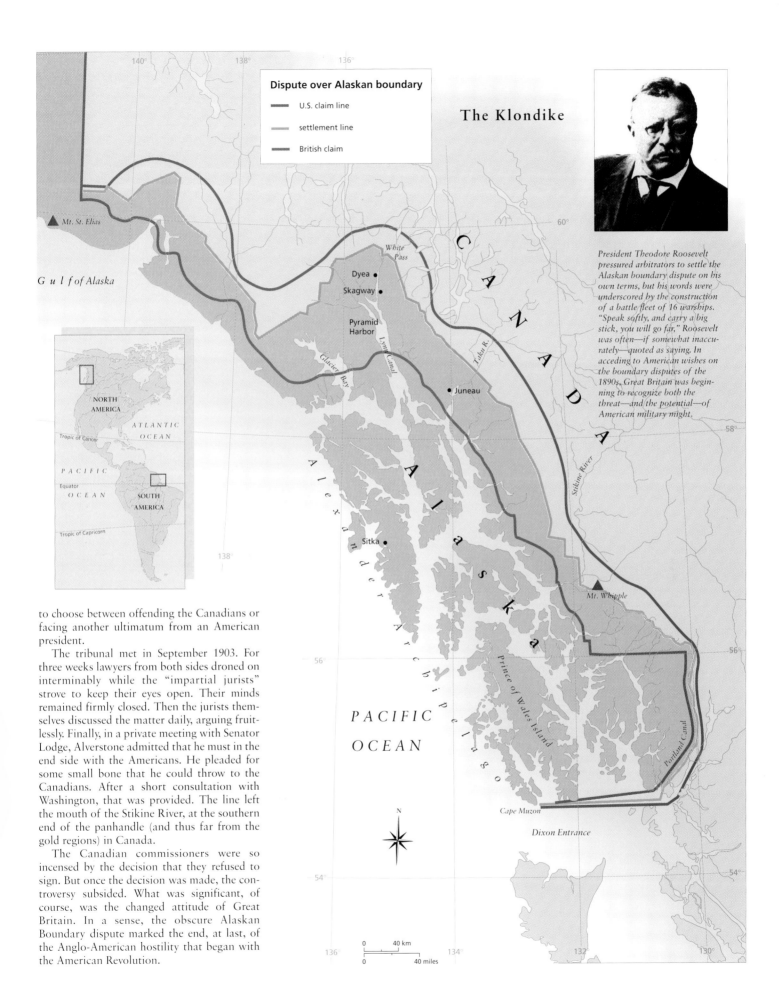

Dispute over Alaskan boundary

— U.S. claim line

— settlement line

— British claim

The Klondike

President Theodore Roosevelt pressured arbitrators to settle the Alaskan boundary dispute on his own terms, but his words were underscored by the construction of a battle fleet of 16 warships. "Speak softly, and carry a big stick, you will go far," Roosevelt was often—if somewhat inaccurately—quoted as saying. In acceding to American wishes on the boundary disputes of the 1890s, Great Britain was beginning to recognize both the threat—and the potential—of American military might.

to choose between offending the Canadians or facing another ultimatum from an American president.

The tribunal met in September 1903. For three weeks lawyers from both sides droned on interminably while the "impartial jurists" strove to keep their eyes open. Their minds remained firmly closed. Then the jurists themselves discussed the matter daily, arguing fruitlessly. Finally, in a private meeting with Senator Lodge, Alverstone admitted that he must in the end side with the Americans. He pleaded for some small bone that he could throw to the Canadians. After a short consultation with Washington, that was provided. The line left the mouth of the Stikine River, at the southern end of the panhandle (and thus far from the gold regions) in Canada.

The Canadian commissioners were so incensed by the decision that they refused to sign. But once the decision was made, the controversy subsided. What was significant, of course, was the changed attitude of Great Britain. In a sense, the obscure Alaskan Boundary dispute marked the end, at last, of the Anglo-American hostility that began with the American Revolution.

THE COURSE OF EMPIRE

AMERICA IN THE PACIFIC

Secretary of State William Seward (1865–1869) dreamed of an American empire, with Mexico City as its capital, stretching from the Arctic to Panama and from Iceland to Hawaii. Although in 1867 he succeeded in buying Alaska and annexing the Midway Islands, his grandiose plans for a far-flung American empire were continually rebuffed by Congress. Americans, he complained, were so absorbed in domestic affairs that they failed even to entertain "the higher, but more remote, questions of national extension." Thirty years later, President William McKinley annexed Hawaii and Guam and seized the Philippines. What had caused the shift in policy—and in public sentiment?

Missionary Zeal

One factor was the proliferation of Protestant missions throughout the world. From 1870 to 1900, the number of Protestant missions founded by Americans increased five-fold. China alone attracted thousands of American missionaries eager to spread their version of God's message to its 400 million unconverted inhabitants. Japan and the Philippines were other important centers of missionary work. By introducing American goods and customs to the "natives," the missionaries stimulated trade and promoted cultural exchanges. Many churchgoers back home, continually reminded of their obligation to support foreign missions, came to appreciate the need to uplift "primitive" peoples and extend to them the Kingdom of Christ.

But the wellsprings of Christian charity could become tainted by condescension and racism, as when President McKinley told Methodist churchmen that he had sought God's "light and guidance" on whether to annex the Philippines after the defeat of Spain. "And one night late it came to me," he explained. Rather than grant independence to the Filipinos, whom he believed "unfit for self-government," he concluded that the United States must take the islands, "educate the Filipinos, and uplife and Christianize them, and by God's grace do the very best we could by them, as our fellow-men for whom Christ also died."

Access to the China Market

Revisionist historians contend that pious rhetoric concealed a desperate craving among some industrialists and businessmen for foreign markets. Increasingly large and well-capitalized factories churned out more and more goods, saturating the American market. Prices, profits, and wages fell in a deflationary cycle. Severe depressions in the 1870s and 1890s, followed by unprecedented labor violence, offered a grim portent of impending economic collapse.

Some industrialists and their allies in government hoped to reverse the trend by tapping into the huge potential markets of the Far East, especially China. This required the establishment of an "informal empire" of coaling stations and naval bases to protect lines of trade. According to the revisionists, the United States seized the Philippines, a land of dubious trading prospects, to gain a foothold for trade with China, which European powers had already carved into preferential trading spheres.

During the 1890s, U.S. exports to China rose from $3 milion to $15 million, proof of the region's growing economic importance to the United States. American exports to the Far East in 1900 were relatively insignificant. Of nearly $1.4 billion in total foreign exports of that year, only $15 million, most of it agricultural products, went to China, and $29 million to Japan. Europe ($1.04 billion) and Canada ($95 million) remained America's most important trading partners. The great China market was an illusion although then, as now, its mistiness has rendered it no less appealing to some American politicians and businessmen.

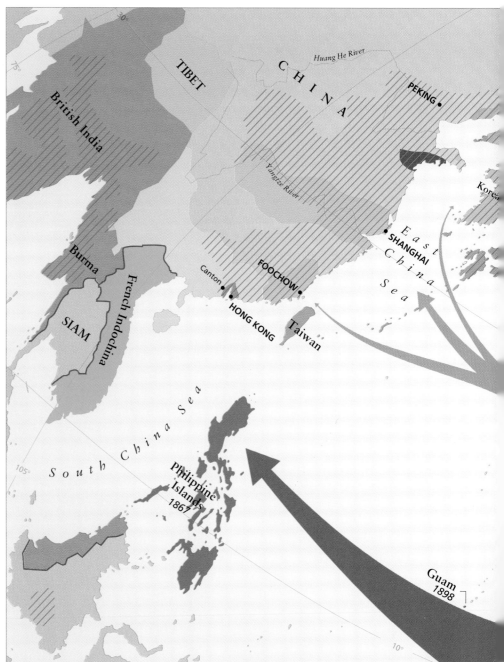

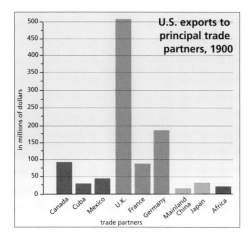

U.S. exports to principal trade partners, 1900

in millions of dollars

trade partners

Left: *The emergence of the United States as a world power was most obviously accomplished by the creation of a "Great White Fleet" of modern battleships, whose voyage around the world in 1907–1909 was celebrated in Heery Reterdahl's painting. Reuterdahl, a Swede who was commissioned to do illustrations of the Chicago World's Fair in 1893, decided to make America his home. He served as a newspaper correspondent during the Spanish-American war, did a series of pictures on "Navies of the World," and observed the Vera Cruz campaign of 1914. Reuterdahl was an unbridled enthusiast of the navy, as is suggested by his romanticized depiction of the "Great White Fleet" passing through the Straits of Magellan.*

Below: *A recruiting poster for the "Great White Fleet," circa 1910. As is customary in this genre, the appeal is both to the young man's wallet ($17–77 per month in pay) and to his vanity ("first outfit of uniform free").*

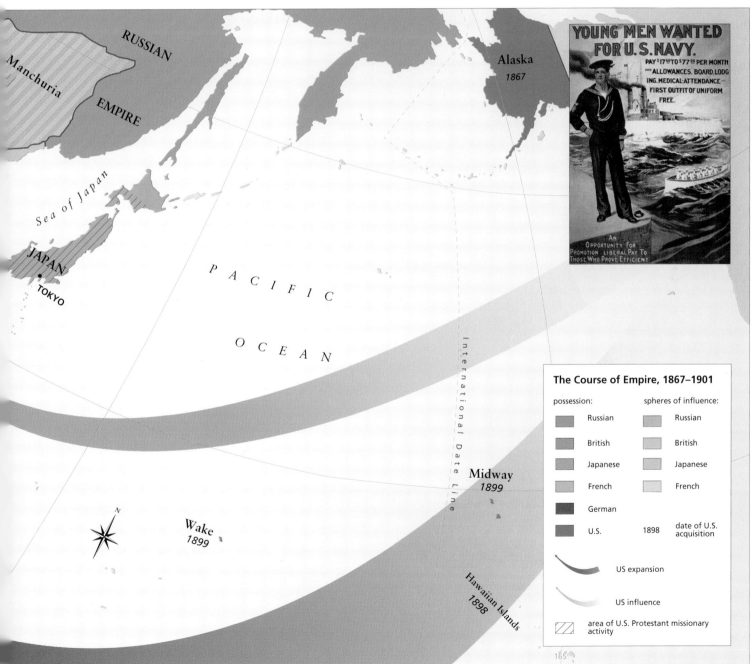

The Course of Empire, 1867–1901

153

THE SPANISH-AMERICAN WAR
DECISIVE U.S. VICTORIES AT MANILA BAY AND SANTIAGO

Cuban nationalists first revolted against Spain in 1868, prompting some Americans to call upon the United States to aid the insurgents. Spain managed to pacify the rebels and allay American critics by promising reforms, which arrived more slowly than the reinforcements for its army of occupation. By the mid 1890s, when revolution again swept the island of Cuba, Spanish forces numbered about 70,000. Tensions between the United States and Spain simmered until February 15, 1898, when the U.S. battleship Maine mysteriously exploded and sank in Havana harbor, 260 of her crew perishing. Many Americans assumed—no doubt wrongly—that the Spanish government was behind the disaster. On April 11, President McKinley acceded to their demands for war, which Congress ratified on April 19th.

Gunnery Practice at Manila

Although the U.S. entered the war to drive Spain from Cuba, the first action took place on the other side of the globe, in the Philippine Islands. Weeks earlier, Assistant Secretary of the Navy Theodore Roosevelt had alerted Commodore George Dewey, who was in command of the United States Asiatic Squadron located in Hong Kong, to move against the Spanish base at Manila if war came. When word of the declaration of war reached the Squadron on April 30, Dewey steamed from Hong Kong across the South China Sea. On the night of April 30 he entered Manila Bay, expecting to find the Spanish fleet in an anchorage protected by shore batteries in the city. At daybreak, with none of the enemy in sight, he steamed south toward Canacao Bay, where he spotted the enemy fleet at anchor off Sangley Point. At 2 miles the Americans turned starboard and opened fire, moving parallel to the Spanish squadron but beyond range of its antiquated guns. Dewey reversed direction and closed to within one mile of the Spaniards. Shortly after noon, all nine of the Spanish ships had been destroyed. The Spanish garrison at Manila was trapped. Not a single American was killed in the engagement.

The Fall of Santiago

The Spanish hold on Cuba was equally tenuous. Because Cuban insurgents controlled much of the countryside, the Spanish forces had to be supplied by sea. Yet one week before Dewey's stunning victory at Canacao Bay, Admiral William Sampson of the Atlantic Squadron got underway from Key West, blockaded the north coast of Cuba, and began to stretch his patrols to complete the encirclement of the island.

Meanwhile, Spanish Admiral Pascual Cervera, who in March had warned that his fleet would meet "a certain and frightful disaster" if it went against the U.S. Navy, pleaded with his superiors not to send his squadron to the Caribbean. But preferring a military disaster to an ignoble acquiescence in the dismantling of its empire, the Spanish government ordered Cervera to block the expected American invasion of Puerto Rico or Cuba. Failing in that, he was to release pressure on the Caribbean by attacking Charleston or some other American city.

On May 19, Cervera and his flotilla slipped into Santiago harbor. Ten days later they were sighted and bottled up by Sampson's squadron. No longer threatened by Cervera, the 17,000-man American expeditionary force commanded by General William Shafter departed from Tampa, Florida, and landed 15 miles east of Santiago. His soldiers immediately pushed into a malarial jungle, following a wagon trail leading to the city.

The situation of the Spanish forces was desperate. With Sampson's fleet standing watch over the harbor, and Cuban rebels harassing the approaches to the interior, the Spanish garrison in Santiago would inevitably run out of food and supplies. But General Arsenio Linares clung to the hope that if the American advance could be stopped and its fleet kept at bay, the Americans would succumb to malarial fevers before his own men died of starvation.

However, Linares almost ensured an American victory by ranging his 10,400 men in a semi-circle around the harbor. About one third of his troops were positioned along the west side of the harbor, an additional 400 at Morro Castle, and a reserve of 1,900 in Santiago City. On July 1, when 8,000

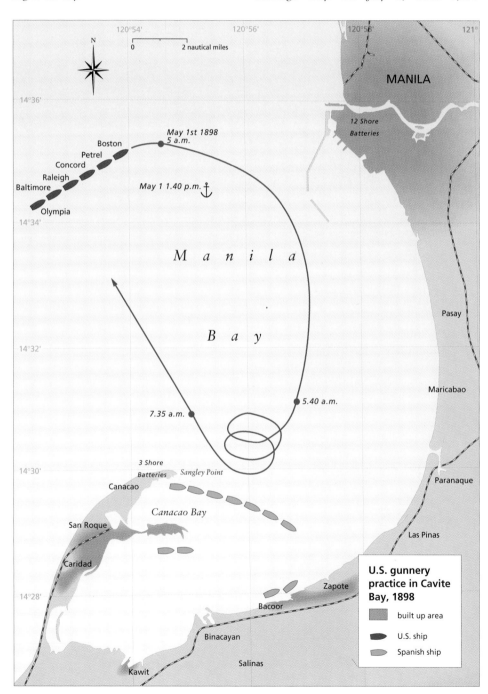

U.S. gunnery practice in Cavite Bay, 1898

built up area

U.S. ship

Spanish ship

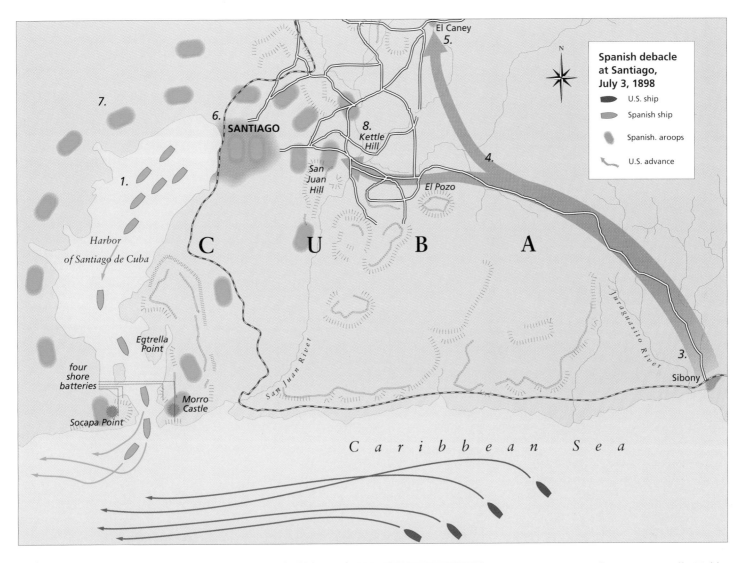

Spanish debacle at Santiago, July 3, 1898

- U.S. ship
- Spanish ship
- Spanish. aroops
- U.S. advance

El Caney
5.

6. SANTIAGO

7.

8. Kettle Hill

San Juan Hill

El Pozo

4.

1.

Harbor of Santiago de Cuba

C U B A

Jaraguasito River

3.

Sibony

San Juan River

Egtrella Point

four shore batteries

Morro Castle

Socapa Point

Caribbean Sea

Americans stormed San Juan Hill, Teddy Roosevelt in the van, they were opposed by only 500 Spaniards. A secondary attack at El Caney, in which the Spaniards were outnumbered by ten to one, was also an overwhelming American victory.

With Santiago harbor in range of American artillery on San Juan Hill, Admiral Cervera had to run the blockade. On July 3, his six black-hulled ships, flags proudly flying, steamed forth from the harbor and fled westward along the coast. Like hounds after rabbits, Sampson's fleet took up the chase. In less than two hours all but one of the Spanish ships had been destroyed; the last, initially faster than its pursuers, ran out of good coal and was caught 50 miles west of Santiago. Only one American lost his life.

Santiago surrendered on July 17. On August 12, one day before the garrison in Manila surrendered, Spain agreed to leave Cuba.

The U.S.S. Maine mysteriously exploded while at anchor in Havana harbor at 9.40 p.m. on February 15 (left). The Americans immediately blamed the Spanish authorities for this outrage, crowds gathered in Washington to mourn the loss of 266 American lives, and President McKinley cautioned patience. Meanwhile a popular saying proclaimed "Remember the Maine and to Hell with Spain!"

THE FRUITS OF EMPIRE
THE U.S. ANNEXES HAWAII AND COLONIZES THE PHILIPPINES

During the Senate debate over President McKinley's request to intervene in Cuba, Henry M. Teller of Colorado proposed an amendment disclaiming any intention of adding Cuban territory to the United States. "When we go out to make battle for the liberty and freedom of Cuban patriots," he declared, the world should know that "we are not doing it for the purpose of aggrandizement of ourselves or the increasing of our territorial holdings." The Teller Amendment passed without opposition. Despite this assurance, however, war fever led to the annexation of Hawaii and, following the U.S. victory over Spain, the acquisition of a colonial empire in the Pacific.

The annexation of Hawaii

In January 1893, a cabal of wealthy resident sugar planters, virtually all of whom were Americans or of American descent, connived with John L. Stevens, the United States Minister, to depose the xenophobic ruler of the Hawaiian islands, Queen Liliuokalani. The rebel junta hoisted the Stars and Stripes above government buildings and proclaimed Hawaii a U.S. protectorate. But few in Washington were eager to annex Hawaii. A poll of the House of Representatives revealed that only 83 members favored annexation, far short of the margin necessary. The proposal languished until war broke out with Spain.

On May 4, 1898—just three days after Dewey's stunning victory at Cavite—a joint resolution calling for the annexation of Hawaii was introduced into the House. (Supporters of annexation, doubting that a two-thirds majority could be attained in the Senate, had settled upon a joint resolution because it required a simple majority vote.) On June 15, the House approved it by a vote of 209 to 91; a month later the Senate passed it by a similar margin. Representative Hugh Dinsmore of Arkansas, a foe of annexation, explained that scores of normally sensible Congressmen had been infected, like their constituents, with "war fever."

A map of the vote suggests that susceptibility to this imperialistic ailment varied by region. While the Republican Northeast staunchly favored annexation, much of the rest of the country remained divided on the issue. Representatives from sugar cane producing regions of the South voted solidly against annexing Hawaii, which produced nearly as much sugar cane as the entire continental United States. Opposition was also strong in parts of the South and the border states where racial concerns transcended traditional political and economic matters. Dinsmore doubted whether the dark-skinned Hawaiians were fit for citizenship. Champ Clark of Missouri, noting the high percentage of Chinese and Japanese living in the islands, decried the prospect of a Chinese member of Congress, "with his pigtail hanging down his back," discoursing "in pidgin English" with

the likes of Henry Cabot Lodge. Race also figured in the thinking of John F. Fitzgerald (President John Fitzgerald Kennedy's grandfather), representing a predominantly Irish constituency, and the sole New Englander to vote against annexation. "Are we to have a Mongolian State in this Union?" Fitzgerald thundered. Still other Congressmen predicted that the acquisition of Hawaii would lead to even more dubious imperial adventures—such as conquest of the Philippines.

War against the Filipinos

Dewey's destruction of the Spanish squadron at Cavite stranded the garrison within the walls of Manila. As Dewey awaited arrival of an American army Filipino nationalists led by Emilio Aguinaldo rose up against the Spanish throughout Luzon. A force numbering 30,000 Filipinos took positions outside Manila and ringed the city with 14 miles of trenches. Late in June the first contingents of the American army splashed ashore at Cavite and moved on Manila, where they found their path blocked by the entrenched Filipinos. The American general then tricked Aguinaldo into allowing his men to take positions inside the Filipino lines. The Spanish garrison surrendered in August to the Americans, who occupied Manila, much to the dismay of Aguinaldo and his supporters. Relations between the Filipinos and the Americans deteriorated further. When McKinley in late December announced his decision to annex the entire archipelago, war with the Filipino nationalists seemed inevitable.

On the evening of February 4, 1899, when General Elwell Otis, commander of the American army, had moved several regiments from within the Filipino perimeter at Manila to a position at Santa Mesa threatening the

Filipino flanks, an overzealous American picket in the area fired upon several Filipino loiterers. Within minutes the entire American line erupted in gunfire. By dawn the Americans had overrun the Filipinos, and several thousand defenders were dead in the trenches. Aguinaldo's army fled northward in chaos, pursued by Americans marching northward along the country's only railway line. At Caloocan the Americans blundered into an ambush and put the town to the torch. Within several weeks they seized Malolos, the seat of Aguinaldo's government. Meanwhile, another American army, supported by gunboats, moved southeast along the Pasig River, blasting Filipino soldiers and civilians and burning the rice crops of the fertile Laguna de Bay region. Aguinaldo, whose main forces had been

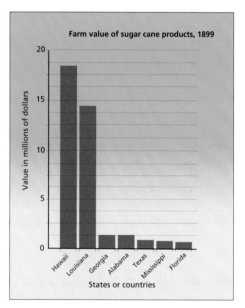

Farm value of sugar cane products, 1899

House vote on annexation of Hawaii, June 15, 1898

- pro-annexation
- anti-annexation
- sugar beet
- sugar cane

not voting members are not indicated

destroyed in the battles, adopted guerrilla warfare tactics. Goaded by sneak attacks and instances of cruelty to captives, American soldiers, most of whom had little respect for Filipinos to begin with, responded in kind.

In November, Otis resolved to catch Aguinaldo's forces in a pincer, one column moving north toward Tarlac and another, after landing at Dagupan, moving south along the same railway. Aguinaldo fled just ahead of the Americans and began a long trek into the jungles and across the mountains of Luzon. Meanwhile, the war dragged on for several years, consisting of a succession of senseless atrocities rather than a sequence of battles. Fittingly, the decisive action of the war, on March 23, 1901, was the devious capture of Aguinaldo at Palanan by Brigadier General Frederick Funston, who, posing with a group of commandos as prisoners of war, pulled out concealed weapons and seized their bewildered captor.

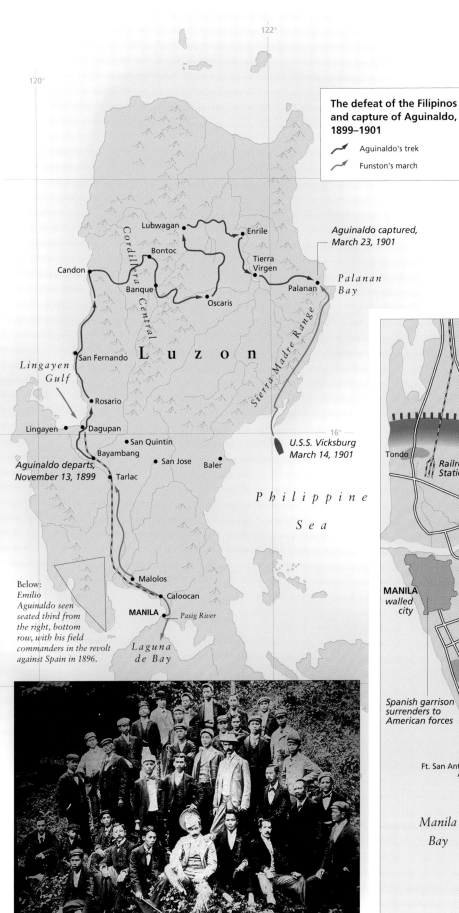

The defeat of the Filipinos and capture of Aguinaldo, 1899–1901

⌁ Aguinaldo's trek

⌁ Funston's march

Aguinaldo captured, March 23, 1901

U.S.S. Vicksburg March 14, 1901

Aguinaldo departs, November 13, 1899

Below: *Emilio Aguinaldo seen seated third from the right, bottom row, with his field commanders in the revolt against Spain in 1896.*

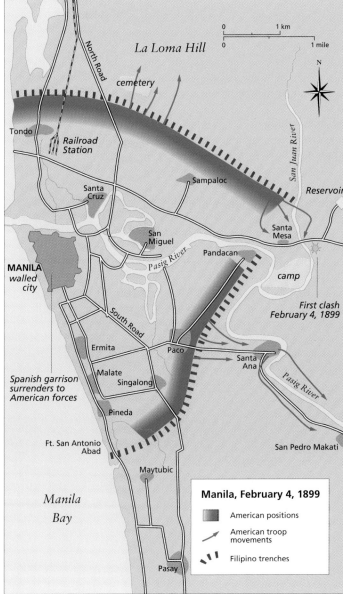

Manila, February 4, 1899

▬ American positions

↗ American troop movements

▰▰▰ Filipino trenches

First clash February 4, 1899

Spanish garrison surrenders to American forces

PART 6: AMERICA IN THE EARLY 20TH CENTURY

How one views an era depends on the vantage point. During the prosperous first two decades of the 20th century, a bracing spirit of reform was in the air and many Americans marched off on crusades: uplifting "inferior" races; reforming municipal government; busting the trusts; prohibiting the sale of booze; gaining rights for women; and putting an end to the onslaught of the Huns in Europe. These reforming impulses lost much of their appeal during the Great Depression, when many Americans were mired in poverty; when big business and industry had collapsed and seemed beyond recovery; when prohibition had given rise to organized crime; when women's rights had been sacrificed to economic necessity; and when Europe lay smoldering in ruins, about to blaze forth in another conflagration. Then came the long presidency of Franklin D. Roosevelt and his "New Deal." Did it constitute a more effective and politically astute extension of progressive reform? Or did it, while cloaked in the rhetoric of change, merely preserve corporate capitalism from revolutionary discontents at home and totalitarian foes abroad?

PANAMA

A PATH BETWEEN SEAS

That the Atlantic and Pacific Oceans would eventually be joined by a canal through Central America had long appeared inevitable. Spanish officials laid out the first route across the isthmus of Panama in 1534, but the King of Castile rejected the plan when court theologians warned that if God wanted the oceans to be connected, He would have done so Himself. Little came of subsequent Spanish, British, French and American proposals, but the discovery of gold in California in the late 1840s sent thousands of prospectors scrambling westward and rekindled interest in a canal. In 1850 the United States and Britain agreed to the joint construction and operation of an isthmian canal.

The question of where it should be built remained unresolved. In 1866, Admiral Charles H. Davis, after conceding to Congress that astonishingly little was known about the interior of Central America, surmised that a canal could be constructed along any of 19 routes through Mexico, Honduras, Nicaragua or the Colombian provinces of Panama and Darien. In his view, the three most promising went through Nicaragua, by way of the San Juan River to Lake Managua, and through Panama, between Colon and Panama City or across the wilderness of Darien. Davis recommended the latter route.

In 1879, while American explorers and surveyors were gathering information on all possible routes, Ferdinand de Lesseps, the builder of the Suez Canal, announced plans to build a passageway between Colón and

Panama City. Promising to complete the canal within 12 years for $132 million dollars, he formed a syndicate to raise the requisite funds and took command of the French enterprise.

A Sea-Level Canal

De Lesseps tried to repeat his success at Suez by building a sea-level canal at Panama. This was a fatal mistake. Unlike the dry, flat expanses of Suez, Panama was drenched by tropical rains that surged down mountain rivers and streams. The raging Chagres River, which criss-crossed the route of the canal, would have to be diverted, or its floodwaters would inundate the ships below and fill the canal with mountains of mud. French engineers considered and then rejected a plan to carry the Chagres *over* the canal on a viaduct at Matachin; instead they planned to erect one of the largest dams ever built, a 150-foot-high earthen structure stretching across the valley at Gamboa. They further proposed to divert the tremendous volume of water from the upper Chagres *across* the continental divide into the Pacific.

By 1885, excavation work, impeded by frequent mud slides and the mountain of rock at the Culebra Cut, had fallen far behind schedule. Yellow fever and malaria had killed probably more than 20,000 workers, a statistic that the canal company thought imprudent to make public. Most important, no one had come up with a satisfactory design for the Chagres Dam. De Lesseps, now 80, informed shareholders that the canal would cost twice as much as he had estimated.

By 1887, having lost the confidence of investors, De Lesseps finally abandoned his goal of a sea-level passageway. He proposed—as a temporary expedient—to dam the Chagres at Bohia and create an artificial lake about 160 feet above sea level. Ships would be lifted to Lake Bohia by locks at La Boca and Paraiso on the Pacific side, and Bohio Soldado on the Atlantic side. But this concession to geographical reality came too late. In 1889,

MEXICO

BELIZE

HONDURAS

TEGUCIGALPA

GUATEMALA

Sierra Madre

GUATEMALA

SALVADOR

SAN SALVADOR

Lake Managua

PACIFIC OCEAN

Davis' alternatives for an interoceanic canal, 1866

■ ■ ■ proposed routes

0   100 km

0   100 miles

3300
650
0 ft

de Lesseps declared his firm bankrupt; French courts later tried and convicted him of having misled shareholders.

As French locomotives, dredging equipment, and steam shovels rusted in the jungles of Panama, the United States was emerging as a world power. In 1898, its navy shattered Spanish fleets in both the Pacific and Atlantic oceans. But proponents of naval power, such as Theodore Roosevelt, Assistant Secretary of the Navy, had agonized over the two-month voyage of the U.S.S. *Oregon* from Californian waters, around South America, to join the American fleet's attack on Cuba. A U.S.-controlled canal, they reasoned, would effectively double the strength of the navy.

In 1901, President McKinley was assassinated and Roosevelt, the new president, redoubled efforts to build a canal under United State auspices. He initially favored a route through Nicaragua, several hundred miles closer to American ports than Panama. But when the French offered to unload their holdings in Panama for the bargain-basement price of $40 million, Roosevelt accepted immediately.

The Colombian government, however, refused to so cheaply relinquish their rights to Panama. When the Panamanians, egged on by the French company, staged a revolution against Colombia in 1903, Roosevelt sent a cruiser to intervene on their behalf. The new Panamanian Republic, with an official of the French company serving as Secretary of State, signed a treaty granting the United States a zone 10 miles wide in perpetuity.

All that remained was to build the canal. American engineers, confronted with the problem of the raging Chagres, decided to enlist the river as their chief asset. They proposed to erect a dam downriver at Gatun, within five miles of the Atlantic Ocean. Fed by the Chagres, Gatun Lake, covering 164 square miles of jungle, would serve as the main avenue across the isthmus. Thus ships entering the canal on the Pacific side at Panama City would be raised 85 feet by locks at Miraflores, then pass through the cut at Culebra and enter the waters of Gatun Lake. At the Gatun Locks,

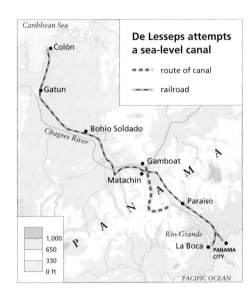

De Lesseps attempts a sea-level canal
- - - route of canal
—•—•— railroad

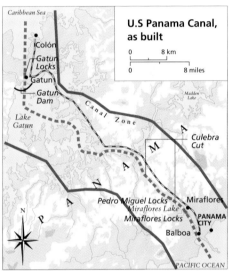

U.S Panama Canal, as built

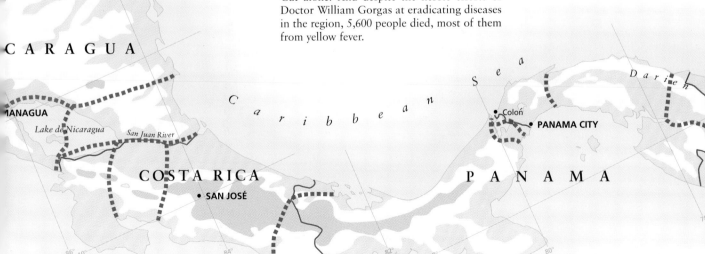

they would be lowered to the Atlantic.

Work started in 1904 and was completed in 1914. During that time, more than 230 million cubic yards of earth were excavated, nearly eight times the French total. Almost 100 million cubic yards were taken from the Culebra Cut alone. And despite the heroic efforts of Doctor William Gorgas at eradicating diseases in the region, 5,600 people died, most of them from yellow fever.

A view of the Panama Canal (above left) showing how George W. Goethals created Gatun Lake by daming the Chagres River. While this ingenious plan greatly reduced the excavation and simultaneously controlled the turbulent Chagres, it required the construction of cumbersome locks to raise and lower ships.

WOMEN'S SUFFRAGE
A CENTURY OF STRUGGLE

"We hold these truths to be self-evident: that all men and women are created equal." This feminist paraphrase of the Declaration of Independence was propounded by Elizabeth Cady Stanton, Lucretia Mott, and others at the first women's rights convention, held in Seneca Falls, New York, in 1848. But the Nineteenth Amendment, which gave women the most basic of "inalienable" rights—the right to express their "consent" to be governed through exercise of the ballot—was not ratified until 1920. The long delay was caused by dissension within the movement, by urban bosses fearful of reform, by white southerners seeking to perpetuate the disenfranchisement of blacks, and mostly by Victorian assumptions that women belonged at home rather than in politics.

After Seneca Falls, the crusade for women's suffrage was overshadowed by the movement to abolish slavery and by the Civil War itself. In early 1869, the Radical Republicans, seeking to build a power base in the South, proposed in Congress a 15th Amendment guaranteeing blacks the right to vote. It included no reference to women. An outraged Susan B. Anthony vowed: "I will cut off this right arm of mine before I will ever work for or demand the ballot for the Negro and not the woman." Believing they had been betrayed by male politicians, Stanton and Anthony immediately founded the militant National Woman Suffrage Association, from which men were excluded. Shortly thereafter, another group, calling itself the Woman Suffrage Association, proposed a more cautious strategy of winning the ballot through initiatives at the state level.

The wisdom of this approach appeared to be confirmed later in 1869 when six of the nine members of the Senate of Wyoming Territory elected to give women the vote. Several of the Senators happened to be married to "strong" suffragists; others may have endorsed the measure simply to embarrass the governor. In nearby Utah, meanwhile, Mormon leader Brigham Young sought to deflect proposed Congressional legislation illegalizing polygamy, a practice endorsed by the Mormon Church *(see Utopian Communities, p 92–93)*. Intent on demonstrating that the Mormons accorded the "weaker" sex special rights and privileges, Young persuaded Utah Territory to give women the vote in 1870.

From 1870 to 1910 suffragists conducted 480 campaigns in 33 states to let voters decide whether women should vote in Presidential elections. This resulted in 17 referenda, mostly in Western states, two of which enfranchised women: Colorado in 1893, and Idaho in 1896.

Suffrage leaders, most of whom had by now put aside their differences, were concerned that none of their victories had occurred in a politically significant state. In 1896 they raised $19,000 for a tremendous campaign in California. Anthony and Anna Howard Shaw gave hundreds of speeches throughout the state and lined up endorsements from both the Republican and Populist parties and even from the rabidly anti-Catholic, anti-immigrant American Protective Association.

When the nearly 250,000 votes had been counted, however, women's suffrage lost by a margin of 26,744. Southern California, which had been settled mostly by Midwestern Protestants, supported the measure, as did Protestant-dominated Modoc and Humboldt counties in the north. Anthony noted that the margin of defeat had come from San Francisco, which opposed women's suffrage by 3 to 1, and from the "slum" districts of Oakland. She cited a leaflet from the Liquor Dealers' League urging saloonkeepers to do "all you can" to defeat the measure. The Irish Catholic working-class area south of the Market District, which contained some 440 saloons, rolled up the highest totals against the measure.

The failure in California disheartened leaders of the movement. From 1896 through 1909—a period suffragists termed "the doldrums"—no new major initiatives succeeded. In 1911 they again looked to California, where a second referendum was to be held. The San Francisco wardheelers and saloonkeepers again worked against women's suffrage, but this time it passed by 3,587 votes. By 1914 most other Western states had followed suit.

During World War I the women's suffrage movement gained momentum in the East. While bosses at Tammanay Hall had engineered the defeat of the referendum in New York in 1915, by 1917 they concluded that passage was inevitable and instructed supporters to refrain from opposing the measure lest women, once empowered by the franchise, vote them out of office. On election night in 1917, upstate New York was evenly divided on women's suffrage, while Tammany-dominated New York City provided a 100,000 margin in its favor.

In January 1918, President Woodrow Wilson endorsed the proposed Woman Suffrage (Nineteenth) Amendment to the Constitution. On May 21, 1919, the House of Representatives passed a resolution in its favor. Most of the opposing votes came from Southern Congressmen who believed that a campaign to bring women to vote would inevitably lead to a reexamination of the Jim Crow laws that had disenfranchised Blacks. Of the ten states that failed to ratify the 19th Amendment, only one—Delaware—was north of the Mason-Dixon line.

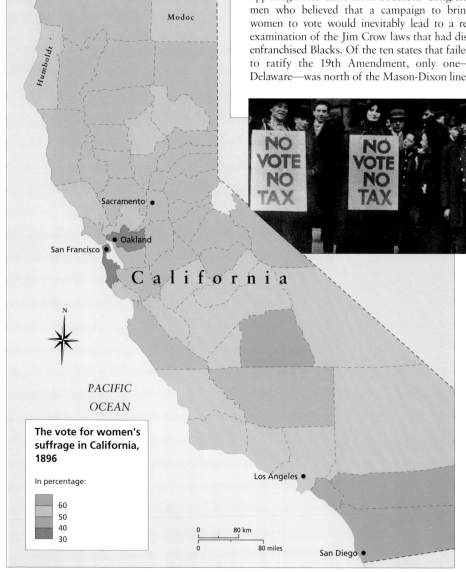

The vote for women's suffrage in California, 1896

In percentage:

	60
	50
	40
	30

Women's suffrage, 1896–1914

- states that first adopted full women's suffrage from 1869 through 1896
- states that first adopted full women's suffrage from 1910–1914
- states that had not adopted full women's suffrage by 1914

0 ___ 250 km
0 ___ 250 miles

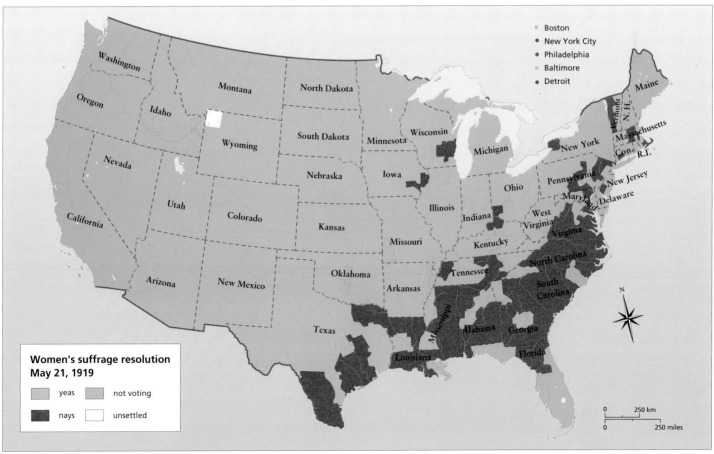

- Boston
- New York City
- Philadelphia
- Baltimore
- Detroit

Women's suffrage resolution May 21, 1919

- yeas
- nays
- not voting
- unsettled

0 ___ 250 km
0 ___ 250 miles

THE UNITED STATES IN WORLD WAR I
DECISIVE INTERVENTION IN A WAR OF ATTRITION

In early 1917, nearly three years after Europe had plunged into war, Germany resumed its campaign against neutral shipping, hoping to starve the British into submission and to deprive Allied armies of American supplies. On April 2, after several American ships had been sunk by U-boats, President Woodrow Wilson pronounced Germany guilty of "throwing to the wind all scruples of humanity" and called on Congress to declare war. The decision was timely: the Allies were running out of supplies; their troops, decimated by nearly three years in the trenches, were disheartened and rebellious; and czarist Russia, which had engaged millions of German troops in the east, had just been toppled by Bolshevik revolutionaries.

During the first three years of the Great War, both sides had absorbed millions of casualties in futile attempts to break through the other's formidable defenses. America's intervention in this war of attrition proved decisive. This was largely because the Germans were forced to attempt an all-out offensive before America could bring to bear its vast economic and military resources. The United States, though woefully ill-prepared for war, nevertheless success-

fully convoyed the first units of the American Expeditionary Force (AEF) to French ports at Brest, St. Nazaire, and Bordeaux during the summer of 1917. They reached Paris on Independence Day and took up positions on the front near Verdun in October.

In March 1918, the Germans launched their great spring offensive. The French center buckled and German troops advanced to within 37 miles of Paris. Early in June the AEF fought its first major engagements, driving the Germans back from Chateau-Thierry and Belleau Wood. In July, 270,000 Americans and a larger French force counterattacked north of Chateau-Thierry. They shattered the German offensive. In September, the American First Army, comprising 500,000 men, again combined with the French and wiped out the German salient at St. Mihiel, south of Verdun.

Late in September, no less than 1.2 million doughboys threw themselves into the Argonne Forest against German positions west of Verdun. During October, while the French and British advanced in the north, the Americans inched through the southernmost defenses of the Hindenburg Line. In this one offensive, the AEF suffered 120,000 casualties. On November 11, with Allied armies advancing on all fronts, the Germans signed the Armistice.

A 1917 U.S. recruiting poster (below) *alludes to the German submarine campaign. The sinking of the British liner* Lusithania *in 1915 had resulted in the loss of nearly 1,200 persons, including 128 Americans.*

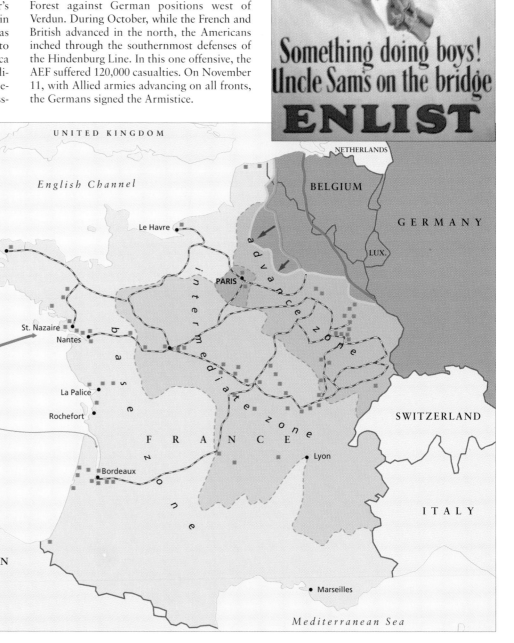

Something doing boys!
Uncle Sams on the bridge
ENLIST

To the front, 1917–1918

- occupied by Germany, March 31, 1918
- U.S. troop shipping route, with number involved
- main railroad used
- storage depot
- U.S. zones
- front line, March 31, 1918
- German spring offensive, 1918
- front line, July 18, 1918
- front line, November 18, 1918

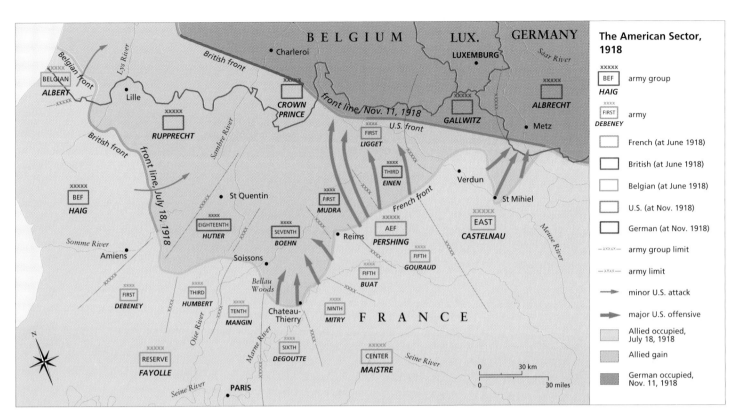

The American Sector, 1918

XXXXX [BEF] *HAIG*	army group
[FIRST] *DEBENEY*	army
[ ]	French (at June 1918)
[ ]	British (at June 1918)
[ ]	Belgian (at June 1918)
[ ]	U.S. (at Nov. 1918)
[ ]	German (at Nov. 1918)
–·×·×·×·–	army group limit
–×·×·×·×–	army limit
→	minor U.S. attack
⟶	major U.S. offensive
░	Allied occupied, July 18, 1918
▒	Allied gain
▓	German occupied, Nov. 11, 1918

U.S. participation in the war

Total armed forces, including Army, Navy, Marine Corps:	4,800,000
Total men in the Army:	4,000,000
Men who went overseas:	2,086,000
Men who fought in France:	1,390,000
Greatest number sent in one month:	306,000
Greatest number returning in one month:	333,000
Total registered in draft:	24,234,021
Total draft inductions:	2,810,296
Greatest number inducted in one month:	400,000
Graduates of Line Officers' Training schools:	80,468
Tons of supplies shipped from U.S. to France:	7,500,000
Cost of war to April 30, 1919:	$ 21,850,000,000
Cost of Army to April 30, 1919:	$ 13,930,000,000
Battles fought by U.S. troops:	13
Months of U.S. participation in the war:	19
Days of battle:	200
Days of duration of Meuse-Argonne battle:	47
U.S. in Meuse-Argonne battle:	1,200,000
U.S. casualties in Meuse-Argonne battle:	120,000
U.S. battle deaths in war:	50,000
U.S. wounded in war:	236,000
U.S. deaths from disease:	56,991
Total deaths in the Army:	112,422

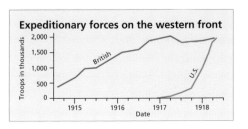

Expeditionary forces on the western front

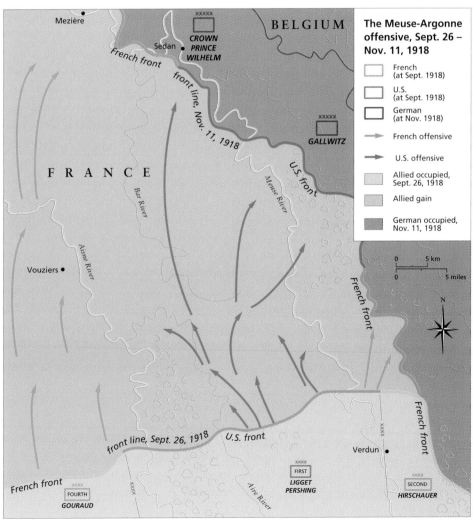

The Meuse-Argonne offensive, Sept. 26 – Nov. 11, 1918

[ ]	French (at Sept. 1918)
[ ]	U.S. (at Sept. 1918)
[ ]	German (at Nov. 1918)
→	French offensive
⟶	U.S. offensive
░	Allied occupied, Sept. 26, 1918
▒	Allied gain
▓	German occupied, Nov. 11, 1918

THE GEOGRAPHY OF "STUPIDITY"

"INTELLIGENCE," RACE, AND ILLITERACY

In April 1917, several weeks after the United States declared war on Germany, Robert M. Yerkes, president of the American Psychological Association, called upon his profession to promote the "increased efficiency" of the army and navy by selecting officers and assigning ranks from among recruits according to their intelligence. Psychologists would devise and administer the requisite tests. The army, which preferred to determine rank by seniority, initially resisted Yerkes' proposals, claiming that he was primarily interested in conducting a nationwide psychology experiment. But in December the War Department endorsed intelligence testing for all recruits. "Psychology," Yerkes proclaimed, had achieved "a position which will enable it to substantially help to win the war."

lished a massive study based on a sample of 100,000 tests. It compared the states "with respect to intelligence." Because of what he believed to be the "striking differences in intelligence" of the races, Yerkes kept data on blacks and whites separate. The study indicated that the average white recruit from the South was considerably less "intelligent" than the average white living elsewhere. The highest scores came from Oregon, Washington, and the Rocky Mountain states. The South—and New Jersey—had the lowest scores.

A similar pattern prevailed among blacks, although there were insufficient numbers of black recruits from the Far West to provide a complete set of data. Blacks in Ohio, Illinois, and New York scored better than blacks from most states in the South. Interestingly, the average scores of blacks from Ohio, Illinois, and New York were higher than the average scores

of whites from Mississippi, Kentucky, Arkansas, and Georgia. Carl C. Brigham of Princeton, a psychologist involved with the testing, reasoned that the high proportion of blacks in the South had lowered the intelligence of whites there, and the Northern blacks, having had the wits to leave the South, tended to be smarter than those of their race who remained in Dixie. He refused to concede either that the tests failed to measure intelligence or that blacks were inherently as intelligent as whites.

Intelligence testing was abandoned by the army in 1919, never to be resumed. Such tests instead became institutionalized in American higher education, when Brigham and other wartime psychologists persuaded the College Entrance Examination Board to offer what later became known as the Scholastic Aptitude Tests.

Yerkes and his staff tested some 1,750,000 men at 24 army camps. The test, which took less than an hour to complete, was administered by pschologists, who assigned grades ranging from A to E. A special test consisting mostly of figures and drawings was given to recruits who could not read. Soldiers who received a C minus—"low average intelligence"—were thought fit only for "ordinary private." Those who received D or below were judged "rarely suited" for tasks requiring "forethought, resourcefulness or sustained alertness."

In 1921 Yerkes, who had instructed examiners to note the hometown of each recruit, pub-

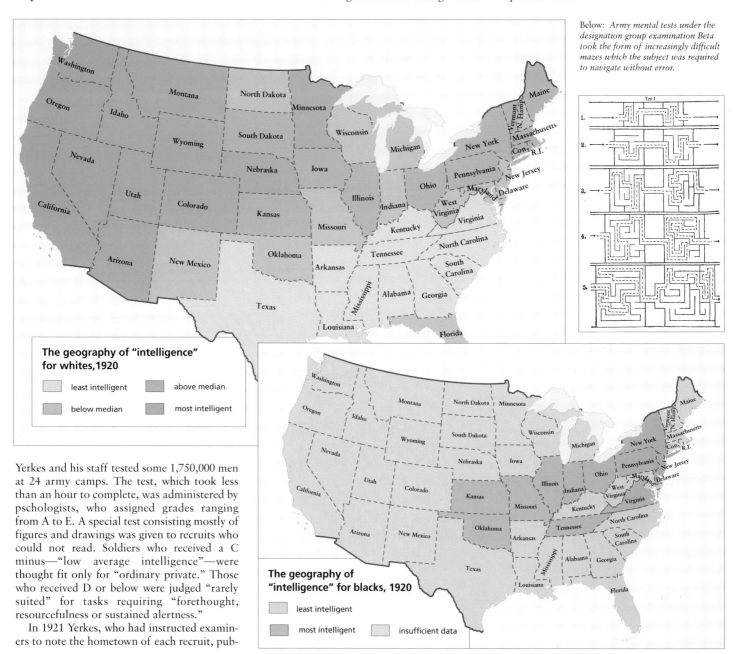

Below: *Army mental tests under the designation group examination Beta took the form of increasingly difficult mazes which the subject was required to navigate without error.*

The geography of "intelligence" for whites, 1920

- least intelligent
- below median
- above median
- most intelligent

The geography of "intelligence" for blacks, 1920

- least intelligent
- most intelligent
- insufficient data

The Geography of Illiteracy

Although Yerkes believed that his tests measured inherent faculties of thinking and reasoning, many of his questions required familiarity with white, middle-class American society and culture. Test 8, for example, included the following questions:

> 7) Bud Fisher is famous as (a) an actor (b) an author (c) a baseball player (d) a comic artist
> 18) Velvet Joe appears in advertisements for (a) tooth powder (b) dry goods (c) tobacco (d) soap
> 10) "Hasn't scratched yet" is used in advertising a (a) duster (b) flour (c) brush (d) cleanser
> 30) The Knight engine is used in the (a) Packard (b) Lozier (c) Stearns (d) Pierce Arrow

Mastery of information such as this depended more on educational background and access to information than reasoning skills. Yerkes' state-by-state analysis of "intelligence" in fact provided a means for assessing statewide educational systems and the state levels of literacy.

That the geography of "intelligence" corresponded to that of illiteracy can be seen in the map on the right. As late as 1910, half the black voters and a quarter of the whites were illiterate in many parts of Kentucky, North Carolina, and the deep South. High rates of illiteracy were due to the South's weak economy, the difficulties of educating children in a farming environment, the hostility of white Southerners to schools established during Reconstruction, and the cost of building and maintaining separate schools for black and white children. Southerners voted far less money for educating their children than people elsewhere in the nation. Furthermore, the low expenditures per pupil throughout the South failed to reflect the white school boards' tendency to allocate less funds to the black schools.

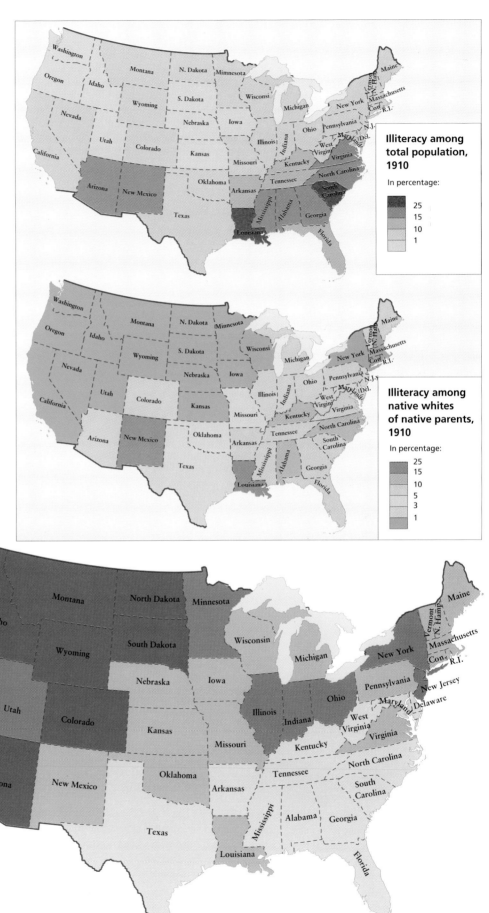

Illiteracy among total population, 1910
In percentage:
25
15
10
1

Illiteracy among native whites of native parents, 1910
In percentage:
25
15
10
5
3
1

Daily expenditure per pupil on public schools, 1909–1910
In dollars:
24
19
14

THE SPANISH INFLUENZA PANDEMIC
A PLAGUE RAVAGES MODERN AMERICA

In the spring of 1918, a mild outbreak of respiratory flu went virtually unnoticed. The American people, having gone to war a year before, were preoccupied with news of a German offensive. Through the summer and fall, despite a sudden onslaught of a new and deadly strain of the flu, public attention remained fixed on the war. Yet more American soldiers would die from the Spanish influenza than would fall in battle. In all, the disease would take the lives of more than the combined total of American battle fatalities during World War I, World War II, and the Korean and Vietnam wars, and claimed 25 million lives worldwide.

The Origins of the Great Pandemic

Influenza outbreaks were also reported in China, Japan, and France during the spring of 1918, but the precursor to the virulent disease that struck six months later probably originated in the midwestern United States. This conjecture is based on a peculiarity of the Spanish influenza. Nearly all flu epidemics take a toll on people in a weakened condition, especially infants and the elderly. From 1900 through 1916 the great majority of flu victims were over 60 or under 10.

But the Spanish influenza struck hardest at men and women in their twenties or thirties, generating a "W"-shaped age-morbidity curve. Why this flu should be so lethal among the most vigorous age groups has never been fully explained. In any case, the telltale "W"-shaped curve was also found during the flu that broke out that spring in the Midwest, mostly in army training centers.

Worldwide Dispersion

From these camps, the flu virus was probably carried with the American Expeditionary Force on troop ships to Europe. On April 15, the disease flared up at army camps at Bordeaux, a chief disembarkation port for American troops, and soon appeared on the Western front (see The United States in World War I, p 164–165). Because the governments of belligerent nations censored news about the flu, most people were unaware of its seriousness. Spain, a neutral power, fully reported the dimensions of the impending calamity, prompting many to assume that it had originated there.

In June, British soldiers on an expedition to Murmansk came down with the flu and probably transmitted it to Russia. As the disease abated in the United States that summer, it swept through western Europe, North Africa, India, China, the Philippines, Japan, and New Zealand. Almost simultaneously it erupted in Cuba, Puerto Rico, and the Panama Canal.

As the virus encountered a multitude of hosts and conditions, it mutated into an unprecedentedly lethal strain. In August this "second wave" inundated almost simultaneously Persia, West Africa, and Brest, France, a port through which most of the 2 million men of the American Expeditionary Force would pass.

The Epidemic in the United States

On August 27, three American sailors, recently arrived in Boston from France, were stricken with the flu. Within two weeks, 2,000 soldiers and sailors had contracted the disease and 35 died of respiratory failure. Several days later the disease exploded among the civilian population. Within a few days, Boston's death rate had skyrocketed; within five weeks the disease had raced across the nation.

The rapidity with which the disease proliferated has long puzzled scholars. Some believe that a dormant form of the disease must have been widely diffused prior to the September outbreak; how else could it have almost simultaneously broken out in such far-flung communities as Boston, Charleston, Chicago, Richmond, San Francisco, San Antonio, and Indianapolis? Others claim that the disease originated in Boston and then spread to a handful of secondary centers, most of them near military bases, from which the disease then diffused into the nearby countryside.

Influenza in Chicago

Unlike tuberculosis or cholera, diseases that preyed upon the poor and the ill-housed (see The Conquest of Cholera, p 138–169), the Spanish influenza virus, transmitted by air according to the vagaries of the winds, showed little preference for the lower classes. Influenza-related deaths roughly corresponded to population density rather than socioeconomic residential patterns. Chicagoans living in the middle class areas north of 12th Street were almost as likely to contract the disease as the immigrants and blacks who lived in the tenements to the south.

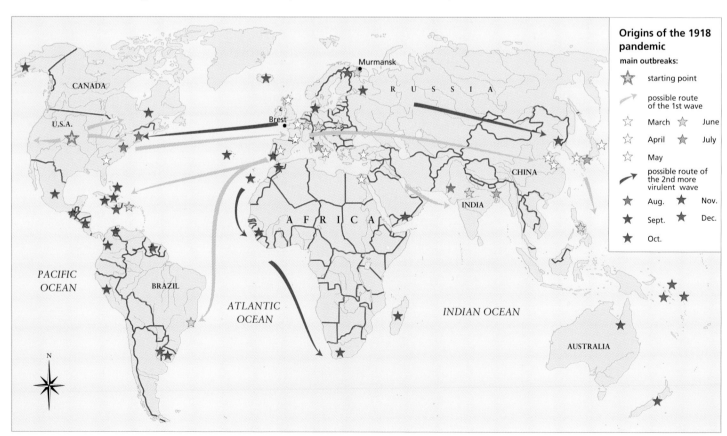

Age profiles of influenza victims

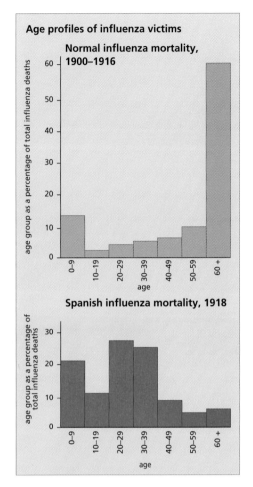

Normal influenza mortality, 1900–1916

age group as a percentage of total influenza deaths

age

Spanish influenza mortality, 1918

age group as a percentage of total influenza deaths

age

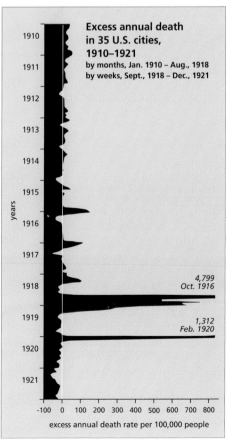

Excess annual death in 35 U.S. cities, 1910–1921

by months, Jan. 1910 – Aug., 1918
by weeks, Sept., 1918 – Dec., 1921

years

4,799
Oct. 1916

1,312
Feb. 1920

excess annual death rate per 100,000 people

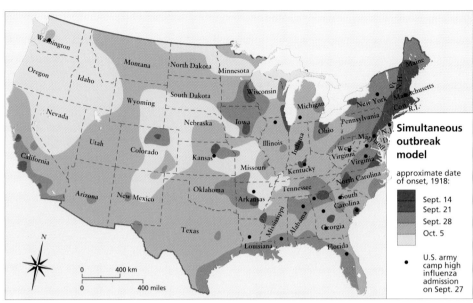

Simultaneous outbreak model

approximate date of onset, 1918:

- Sept. 14
- Sept. 21
- Sept. 28
- Oct. 5

● U.S. army camp high influenza admission on Sept. 27

0   400 km
0   400 miles

N

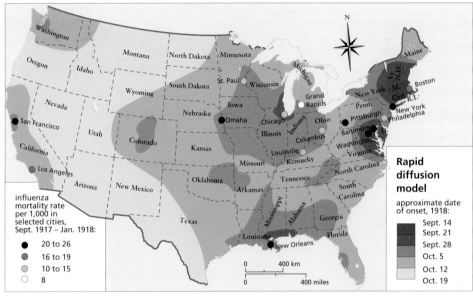

influenza mortality rate per 1,000 in selected cities, Sept. 1917 – Jan. 1918:

- ● 20 to 26
- ● 16 to 19
- ● 10 to 15
- ○ 8

Rapid diffusion model

approximate date of onset, 1918:

- Sept. 14
- Sept. 21
- Sept. 28
- Oct. 5
- Oct. 12
- Oct. 19

N

0   400 km
0   400 miles

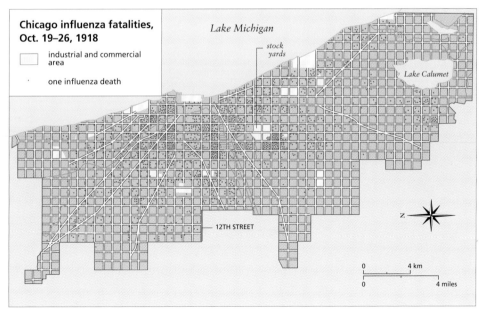

Chicago influenza fatalities, Oct. 19–26, 1918

☐ industrial and commercial area

· one influenza death

Lake Michigan

stock yards

Lake Calumet

12TH STREET

0   4 km
0   4 miles

THE CRUSADE FOR PROHIBITION
WET VERSUS DRY

Prohibition of the manufacture or sale of alcoholic beverages, which became part of the Constitution with the ratification of the 18th Amendment in 1919, was one of the nation's most peculiar crusades. It proved nearly impossible to enforce and was repealed in 1933. Why the nation chose to adopt the measure has been the source of much scholarly debate. Historian Richard Hofstadter called the movement a "pinched, parochial substitute for reform" that drew its support from rural Protestants who despised urban life and the immigrant culture that flourished there. Other historians, noting that many cities supported prohibition and many rural areas opposed it, have linked the movement to the ascendancy of middle-class culture.

During the 1850s, most Northeastern states enacted prohibition statutes. The rise of the immigrant political machines after the Civil War led to the repeal of most statewide "dry" laws. By 1905 only Maine, Kansas, and North Dakota were dry. But during the 10 years after 1904, as more than 1 million immigrants entered the United States annually, the prohibition campaign found new life. By 1915 11 more states and hundreds of municipalities had gone dry. By the time the 18th Amendment took effect in 1920, the great majority of states had already adopted prohibition.

Opposition to prohibition was strongest in the urban Northeast; in Chicago-dominated Illinois; in states with large German populations such as Wisconsin and Minnesota; and in Missouri and California, where the breweries and liquor industry wielded political influence (*see Women's Suffrage, p 162–163*). However, a fuller understanding of the dynamics of prohibition requires an examination of voting patterns at the state and municipal level.

The Dry Campaign in Washington and Michigan

Although the struggle over prohibition was everywhere complicated by local issues and factions, the general voting pattern in the states of Washington and Michigan were characteristic of trends throughout the nation. In 1914, when the turnout exceeded that of the presidential election two years earlier, Washington approved a prohibition initiative by a 52 percent margin. The rural counties in the central and eastern parts of the state provided the greatest dry pluralities, while the three largest cities—Seattle, Spokane, and Tacoma—opposed the measure by substantial margins. But Everett and Bellingham, the next largest cities, voted for prohibition. The margin of victory was provided by the millworkers, many of whom went to church, owned homes, and aspired to middle class status.

Despite their success in the South and West, the prohibition forces had by 1916 failed to win any of the industrial states in the Northeast or Midwest. The crushing blow to

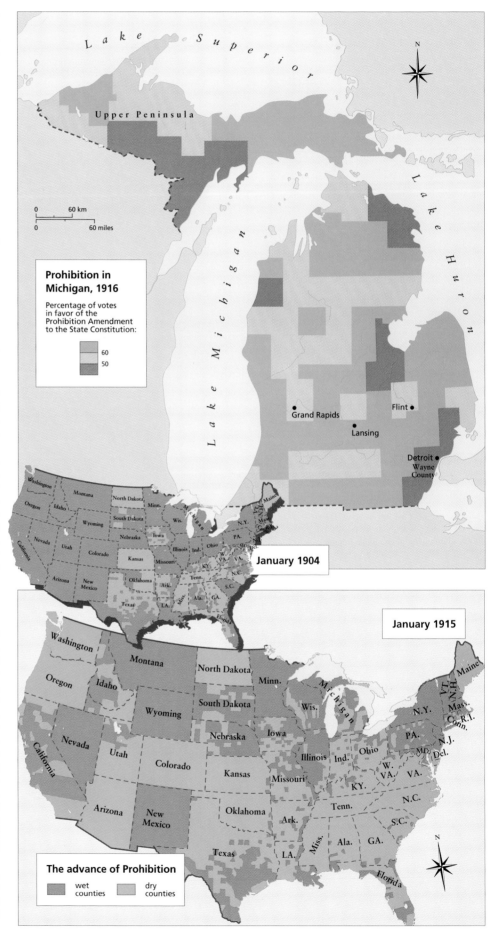

Prohibition in Michigan, 1916

Percentage of votes in favor of the Prohibition Amendment to the State Constitution:

60
50

January 1904

January 1915

The advance of Prohibition

wet counties   dry counties

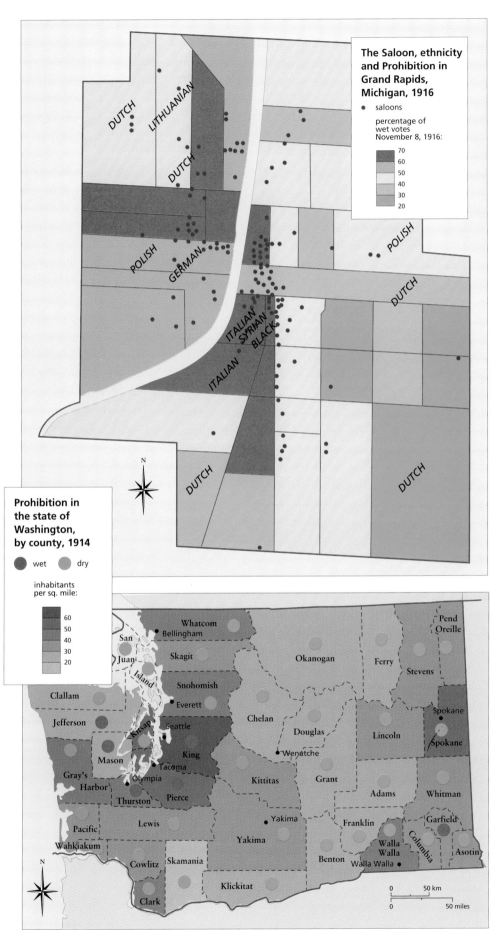

The Saloon, ethnicity and Prohibition in Grand Rapids, Michigan, 1916

• saloons

percentage of wet votes November 8, 1916:

70
60
50
40
30
20

DUTCH · LITHUANIAN · DUTCH · POLISH · GERMAN · ITALIAN · SYRIAN · BLACK · ITALIAN · POLISH · DUTCH · DUTCH · DUTCH

Prohibition in the state of Washington, by county, 1914

● wet ● dry

inhabitants per sq. mile:

60
50
40
30
20

Whatcom · Bellingham · San Juan · Skagit · Okanogan · Ferry · Pend Oreille · Stevens · Island · Snohomish · Everett · Chelan · Spokane · Clallam · Jefferson · Kitsap · Seattle · Douglas · Lincoln · Spokane · Mason · King · Tacoma · Wenatche · Grant · Adams · Whitman · Gray's Harbor · Olympia · Kittitas · Thurston · Pierce · Lewis · Yakima · Franklin · Garfield · Pacific · Yakima · Walla Walla · Columbia · Asotin · Wahkiakum · Benton · Walla Walla · Cowlitz · Skamania · Klickitat · Clark

0   50 km
0   50 miles

Carry Nation, arrested some 30 times for her vehement attacks on "demon alcohol," was the most visible, if not the most effective, of the prohibition advocates. By 1920, when the Prohibition amendment was added to the Constitution, she had been largely forgotten.

the wets came in November of that year, when Michigan approved prohibition by a vote of 353,000 to 285,000. The dry vote generally came from the rural counties, and the wet vote came from Detroit and its environs, and from the Upper Peninsula, which had many foreign-born laborers. But as in Washington, many cities in Michigan voted for prohibition. And while Wayne County (Detroit) voted against the measure, the margin—1,400 votes—was far short of the 25,000 that the wets had predicted. The strength of prohibition in these cities foreshadowed the campaign's successes in the urban Northeast.

Why Grand Rapids Voted for Prohibition

Grand Rapids, a center of furniture manufacturing with a population of over 110,000, was one the largest cities in Michigan. Nearly 40 percent of the voting-age males were foreign-born. A local prohibition initiative in 1910 failed by 7,000 votes (39 percent), but the dry forces regrouped in time for the 1916 initiative. The day before the vote, Billy Sunday, a professional baseball player turned evangelist, came to town and denounced the saloon as the "incarnate fiend of hell." The following day the city supported prohibition by a margin of 57 percent.

The map at left shows the location of all 160 of the saloons and indicates how each precinct voted. Most saloons were located in or adjacent to the working-class, immigrant neighborhoods near the factories situated along or to the west of the Grand River. These areas generally voted wet, with the Polish precincts providing the greatest pluralities. The Dutch, heirs of an abstemious Calvinist tradition, for the most part voted dry. But these ethnic tensions may have been less significant than class distinctions, for the middle class neighborhoods in the eastern and southern sections of town, which included many second-generation immigrants, supported prohibition.

AMERICAN SOCIALISM IN ITS HEYDAY

1901–1920

Founded in 1901, the Socialist Party of America would be a center of radicalism in a reform-minded age. Both more and less than a political party, it lacked impressive numbers and, in some places, even the semblance of an effective electoral organization. But with its newspapers, encampments, parades, and debates, it became an integral and invigorating part of its members' lives. Like the major parties, the S.P. gained power as it built within its ranks a broad coalition—doctrinaire Marxists and the legatees of more homegrown radical traditions, immigrant New York City sweatshop workers and tenant farmers in southern Oklahoma. If this diversity ultimately helped to splinter the S.P., it would also be what distinguished the party from its narrower and less influential successors.

The most obvious feature of American socialism is, perhaps, the modesty of its achievement, as compared with the social democratic parties of Western Europe. In its peak year, 1912, the Socialist Party of America averaged 120,000 members, and its perennial standard-bearer, Eugene Debs, garnered 6 percent of the presidential vote. Its counterparts in Britain, Germany, and France captured a signficantly larger portion of the electorate in these years and eventually headed national governments.

In debating the reasons for this comparative weakness, observers have long cited higher standards of living in America, social and geographical mobility, an egalitarian ethos, an ethnically heterogeneous—and, presumably divided—working class, engrained habits of two-party voting, and the major parties' skill at assimilating reform impulses. However, such phenomena apparently did not "immunize" all Americans against socialism—nor, incidentally, did they prevent bitter labor strife in the late 19th and early 20th centuries.

If the Socialist Party remained relatively small, it was not, between 1901 and 1920, merely a sect of like-minded devotees. Instead, it was the organizational expression of a range of radical tendencies—from labor militance to neo-Populism to simon-pure Marxism. While sharing an ultimate goal of public ownership of the means of production, members frequently, sometimes violently, disagreed over the S.P.'s priorities, strategies, organizational structure, and most appropriate constituency. Some insisted that Socialists militantly press for revolutionary transformation. Others endorsed more conventional political and educational efforts to convert the citizenry and win power. Socialists divided, too, over the party's relationships to workers' organizations such as the powerful American Federation of Labor (AFL) to its right and the less respectable but more inclusive Industrial Workers of the World (IWW) to its left.

Factionalism over such issues sprang from a more basic diversity. In spite of the wishes of some Socialists, the party was not primarily an organization of the factory proletariat. It established itself throughout the nation, often winning its largest proportion of votes west of the Mississippi (it remained generally weak in the Southeast, where the laboring classes were divided by race and, in the case of blacks, even disenfranchised). In different regions, this decentralized party organized different sorts of people, made different demands, even spoke a different language.

In parts of the urban, industrial Northeast and Midwest for example, particularly New York, Pennsylvania, and Wisconsin, the S.P. included many immigrants, old and new, and was devoted to electoral efforts, often linked to established unions, and attuned to the social democratic Marxism of Western Europe. In the Great Plains and Southwestern states, the party represented a far more agrarian constituency, indulging a radicalism steeped in the language of evangelical Protestantism. The Socialists of the Rocky Mountain states and the Pacific Northwest worked among a more marginalized industrial population of miners and timberworkers. Living under harsh and isolated conditions, often allied with the IWW, they had little use for the half-way measures, electoral politics, or middle-class niceties favored by eastern comrades. In addition to the state organizations, the party included relatively autonomous foreign language federations that conducted business in the native tongues of various immigrant groups.

Two of the S.P.'s strongest regional organizations—those of Milwaukee, Wisconsin, and of Oklahoma—best illustrate Socialism's diversity in this era. Both organized precinct-by-precinct and crafted platforms responsive to the immediate needs and desires of their constituencies. Yet these constituencies could not have been more different. Milwaukees's Social Democratic Party worked amidst a large foreign-born population. Closely tied to local AFL affiliates, it found its most reliable support in the well-organized German-American community of skilled workers and shopkeepers, but also made inroads among Poles, Milwaukee's second largest ethnic population. In addition to labor and ethnic support, it cultivated middle-class progressives by promising honest government, modernized city services, and municipal control of various utilities and franchises. Milwaukee sent Socialist leader Victor Berger to Congress for several terms and had a socialist mayor for all but four years between 1910 and 1940.

Few urban workers, first or second generation ethnic Americans, or middle-class progressives could be found among the thousands of Oklahomans who made their state organization the largest in the S.P. in 1910. Instead, Socialism was an overwhelmingly rural phenomenon, centered in counties with the lowest valuations per farm and high rates of farm tenancy and mortgaged property. As tenancy skyrocketed, the S.P. became a fully competitive third party in the impoverished cotton country in the south of the state and also among the

Agrarian Socialism, Oklahoma, 1912

Percentage of presidential Socialist vote:

- 30
- 15

heavily indebted wheat-growers to the west. Attuned to Populist traditions, Oklahoma Socialists called not for collectivized agriculture but demanded that tenants be allowed to occupy individual plots of state-owned land and that the government sponsor cooperative storage, processing, and marketing facilities.

Milwaukee and Oklahoma were not the only places where the party entrenched itself. By 1912, Socialists held 1,200 offices in 340 municipalities across the nation. Between 1910 and 1920, they ran cities as different as Schenectady, Butte, Berkeley, and Minneapolis, and served in 18 state legislatures. New York City sent Socialist Meyer Landon to Congress. Of course, party power was always localized and never unchallenged. Socialist change was not to be enacted on such a small and tentative scale. But Socialists did push cities and towns towards expanded services, municipal ownership, and towards greater sympathy for labor.

Many localities that did not boast Socialist

Sources of Socialist strength

⬛ cities and towns where Socialist periodicals were published 1912–1918

● cities and towns where Socialist mayors or municipal officers were elected, 1911–1920

Below: The anti-radical fervor whipped up by America's entrance into the First World War in 1917 only intensified after the Bolshevik revolution in Russia later that year. A wartime and postwar "red scare" tarred not only Americans who embraced the Soviet experiment, but those who indulged a more homegrown radicalism, and contributed to new restrictions being imposed on immigration in the 1920s.

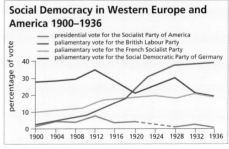

Milwaukee embraces Socialism, 1916

▨ wards giving Socialist candidate, Daniel Hoan, 50% or more of votes in mayoral election

▨ German predominant

▨ Polish predominant

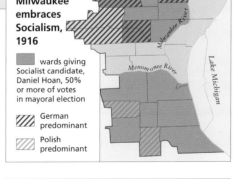

Social Democracy in Western Europe and America 1900–1936

—— presidential vote for the Socialist Party of America
—— paliamentary vote for the British Labour Party
—— paliamentary vote for the French Socialist Party
—— paliamentary vote for the Social Democratic Party of Germany

administrations were homes to Socialist newspapers or periodicals. Socialist publications ranged from nationally-distributed weeklies and monthlies like the *Appeal of Reason* (Girard, KS)—the largest circulating Socialist organ—and the *International Socialist Review* (Chicago) to daily newspapers such as the *Milwaukee Leader*, to trade union journals and shortlived small town sheets.

That many of these publications disappeared during the World War I was symptomatic of a larger disruption of American Socialism. Unlike its Western European counterparts, the Socialist Party of America refused to sanction its country's participation in the conflict. Socialists thus became the target of official harassment and vigilante persecution. Federal espionage and sedition statutes allowed authorities to bar Socialist material from the mails and to indict party members—including Debs and Berger—for obstructing the war effort. Intimidation, jailings, and the

repression of its press decimated the organization outside the urban Northeast and Midwest. At the same time, the Russian Revolution deepened divisions among Socialists in less vulnerable areas. Almost all initially supported the revolution, but many on the party's left, especially in the rapidly growing language federations, insisted that the party re-shape its doctrine and organization to fit the Bolshevik model. Factional warfare splintered the crippled party. By September 1919, two avowedly Communist organizations had seceded. While Debs ran a respectable presidential campaign from behind bars, by the end of 1920 the S.P. had lost the bulk of its membership.

Party fortunes would slightly improve with the onset of the Depression, and Communist and farmer-labor parties thrived in certain places, but never again would radicalism enjoy that combination of widespread local influence and organizational unity experienced during the heyday of the Socialist Party.

THE MAKING OF BLACK HARLEM
BOOM, BUST, AND MIGRATION FROM THE SOUTH

In 1890 Harlem, a fashionable middle and upper class community eight miles north of City Hall, was New York's first suburb. But within four decades it had become the largest black community in the nation, a cultural crossroads where blacks from the rural South first experienced urban life and acquired a distinctive and vibrant sense of racial identity. Harlem, LeRoi Jones wrote, "erased" the provincial traits and associations of black migrants and taught them the "essential uniformity" of all members of their race. Harlem's rapid transformation from white suburb to black cultural capital was the result of a convergence of local, national and international economic and demographic forces.

Nineteenth-century Harlem: Boom and Bust

As thousands of foreign immigrants poured into lower Manhattan during the last third of the 19th century, many well-to-do New Yorkers built spacious brownstones in Harlem, which promoters touted as "a suburban colony" possessing "all the advantages of city life." The extension of subway lines into Harlem in 1898 initiated a frenzy of apartment construction and real estate speculation. Harlem soon became glutted with housing. When the market collapsed in 1904, many of the buildings were left vacant. A black realtor persuaded the owner of several empty apartments on 134th

Street east of Lenox Avenue to fill the buildings with black tenants. Within several years thousands of blacks had moved into the area.

White property owners attempted to halt the spread of blacks west of Lenox Avenue by buying up black properties and evicting the tenants. Black realtors countered by buying white properties in the area. This racial struggle was decided during the 1920s, when 119,000 whites left Harlem and 87,000 blacks moved in. By 1930 165,000 blacks—nearly three-quarters of the entire Manhattan black population—resided in Harlem.

Migration from the South

According to the census of 1930, well over half of the blacks who migrated to New York City had come from Virginia and the Carolinas, and about a quarter from the West Indies. The migration of blacks from the South predated the Civil War, when small numbers of slaves from the border states fled northward (*see Abolitionists and Runaways, p 106–107*). After the Civil War most ex-slaves remained in the rural South where they worked as sharecroppers or hired hands. Their children, however, grew restive over the ascendancy of harsh segregational regimes; often they refused to follow in the weary footsteps of their impoverished parents. In 1907 W.E.B. DuBois observed that many young blacks, finding the "narrow repression and provincialism" of the rural South "simply unbearable," made their way to cities in the North and Midwest. Harlem, in particular, served as a magnet, "the symbol of

liberty and the Promised Land to Negroes everywhere," the Reverend Adam Clayton Powell, Sr. wrote.

This demographic shift is indicated in the table on the opposite page. During the 1920s about three-quarters of a million blacks left the South. Racism alone fails to explain this trend, for almost 400,000 whites also migrated from the South. For example, about 200,000 more blacks migrated out of South Carolina than into it during the 1920s, but so did 52,000 whites. The county map of population migration for South Carolina, North Carolina and Virginia during the 1920s suggests that the discontent of the migrants—black and white—was fueled by a more general dissatisfaction with farm life and Southern agriculture. Most rural counties experienced a net out-migration, while many cities gained population, such as Richmond, Virginia; Greensboro and Raleigh-Durham, North Carolina; and Columbia and Greenville, South Carolina.

The black migration northward peaked during the Great War, which had cut off the influx of cheap labor from southern and southeastern Europe. Many industrialists sent agents to recruit Southern blacks to work in factories in the North. Relatively high wages during the 1920s accelerated the northward movement of blacks to the industrial cities of the North and Midwest. There they were crowded into tenements, or into the large brownstone buildings that had been built for single famlies but were now rapidly subdivided into multi-family apartments.

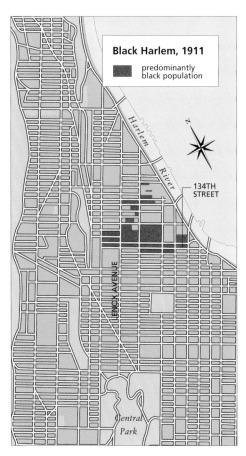

Black Harlem, 1911
predominantly black population
134TH STREET
Harlem River
LENOX AVENUE
Central Park

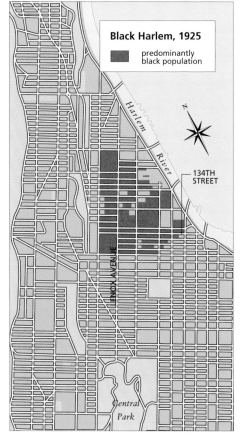

Black Harlem, 1925
predominantly black population
134TH STREET
Harlem River
LENOX AVENUE
Central Park

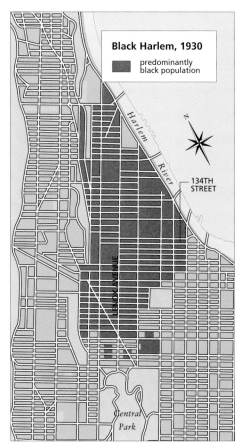

Black Harlem, 1930
predominantly black population
134TH STREET
Harlem River
LENOX AVENUE
Central Park

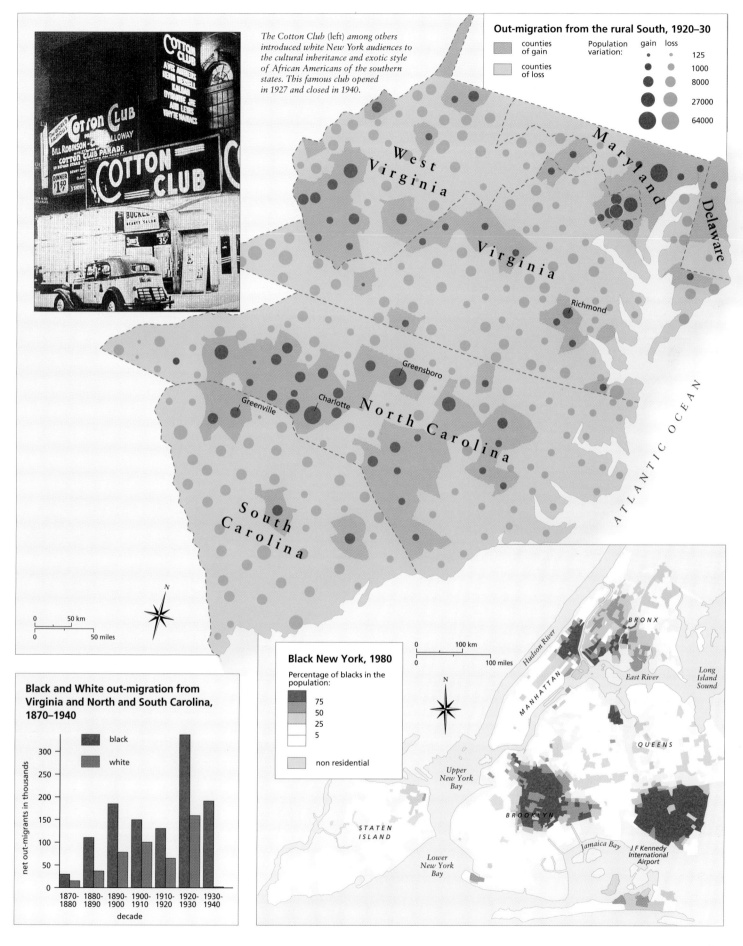

The Cotton Club (left) among others introduced white New York audiences to the cultural inheritance and exotic style of African Americans of the southern states. This famous club opened in 1927 and closed in 1940.

Out-migration from the rural South, 1920–30

counties of gain

counties of loss

Population variation: gain loss

125
1000
8000
27000
64000

West Virginia

Maryland

Virginia

Delaware

Richmond

Greensboro

Greenville

Charlotte

North Carolina

South Carolina

ATLANTIC OCEAN

0   50 km

0   50 miles

N

Black and White out-migration from Virginia and North and South Carolina, 1870–1940

black

white

net out-migrants in thousands

300

250

200

150

100

50

0

1870-1880 1880-1890 1890-1900 1900-1910 1910-1920 1920-1930 1930-1940

decade

Black New York, 1980

Percentage of blacks in the population:

75
50
25
5

non residential

0   100 km

0   100 miles

N

Hudson River

BRONX

East River

Long Island Sound

MANHATTAN

QUEENS

Upper New York Bay

STATEN ISLAND

BROOKLYN

Jamaica Bay

J F Kennedy International Airport

Lower New York Bay

CRIME AND CAPITAL PUNISHMENT
THE PRESERVATION OF ORDER DURING THE DEPRESSION

Societies in the midst of social and political upheaval have often imposed the death penalty as a means of preserving order. In 1641, the beleaguered leaders of Massachusetts Bay Colony passed laws calling for the death of those who worshipped "any other God but the Lord God." The execution of 19 "witches" at Salem a half century later can be understood partly as an attempt to maintain religious faith in an increasingly secularized community. During the 18th century, the English upper classes, fearful of rural vagrants and the industrial poor, elevated pickpocketing and similar crimes against property to capital offenses. And during the Great Depression, more people were executed in America than in any other decade for which reliable records are available.

The effect of capital punishment on would-be murderers has been debated for centuries. Most studies based on statistical evidence raise doubts over the effectiveness of civil executions in deterring murder. The main map, for instance, shows that the states with the most executions from 1930 to 1934 often had the highest murder rates in succeeding years, while states that had abolished the death penalty or imposed it infrequently usually had much lower murder rates. Georgia, North Carolina, and Texas—three of the five states with the most executions in the early 1930s—ranked first, fifth, and ninth respectively in murder rates five years later. And all of the states that had abolished capital punishment prior to the 1930s—Michigan, Rhode Island, North Dakota, Wisconsin, Minnesota, and Maine—had very low homicide rates later in the decade. Together New York and California—both of which were populous—executed 131 individuals in the early 1930s, but had relatively low murder rates.

Means of Capital Punishment, 1930
By the time of the American Revolution, condemned prisoners were executed in public, usually by hanging. Proponents of public executions insisted that such spectacles served as a striking reminder of the consequences of violent crime. Critics argued that public executions degraded victim and viewer alike. In 1835, New York became the first state to prohibit public executions, and the last public executions in the United States were held in the 1930s. In August 1936, some 20,000 spectators witnessed the hanging of a black, Rainey Bethea, convicted of rape in Owensboro, Kentucky. The following May, several hundred spectators paid to watch the hanging of Roscoe Jackson in Galena, Missouri.

For nearly a century after the adoption of the Eighth Amendment, which forbade "cruel and unusual punishments," hanging was the approved method of execution in nearly all states. This changed in the 1880s, when the Edison Company, which promoted direct current for electrification systems, staged public demonstrations of the lethal effects on animals of alternating current, which was being marketed by Westinghouse. Some observers reasoned that alternating current would also kill humans, and in 1888 the New York State legislature chose electrocution, presumably seeing it as a more humane mode of execution than hanging. On August 6, 1890, William Kemmler, a convicted murderer, was the first person to be electrocuted in the United States. Although his execution was botched and by all accounts Kemmler suffered horribly, most states soon shifted from hanging convicts to electrocuting them.

In 1921 the Nevada legislature passed the "Humane Death Bill," which provided that condemned prisoners would be executed in their cells, suddenly and without prior notice, with a lethal dose of gas. Governor Emmet Boyle, who opposed capital punishment, signed the bill into law, assuming that the courts would overturn this punishment as "cruel and unusual." But to his dismay, the Nevada Supreme Court upheld the law. Prison officials, recognizing that the poison gas could not be administered in the condemned man's cell, then constructed the first gas chamber. On February 8, 1924, Gee Jon, a convicted murderer, was executed with cyanide gas. Arizona, Colorado, North Carolina, California, Wyoming, Missouri, and Oregon shifted from hanging or electrocution to lethal gas shortly thereafter.

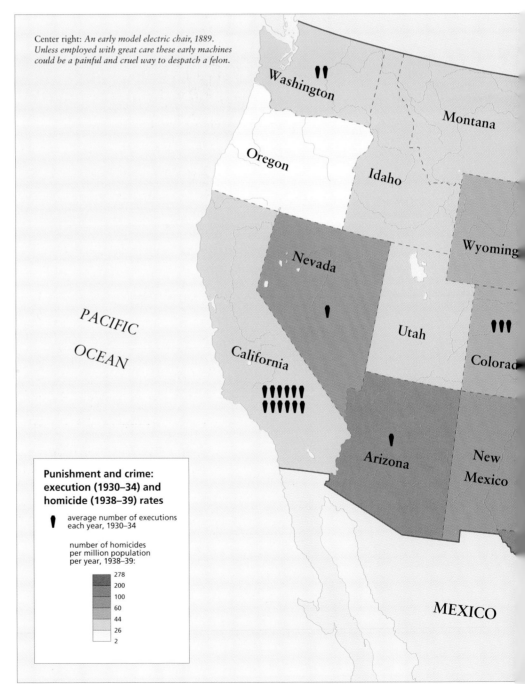

Center right: *An early model electric chair, 1889. Unless employed with great care these early machines could be a painful and cruel way to despatch a felon.*

Punishment and crime: execution (1930–34) and homicide (1938–39) rates

average number of executions each year, 1930–34

number of homicides per million population per year, 1938–39:

278
200
100
60
44
26
2

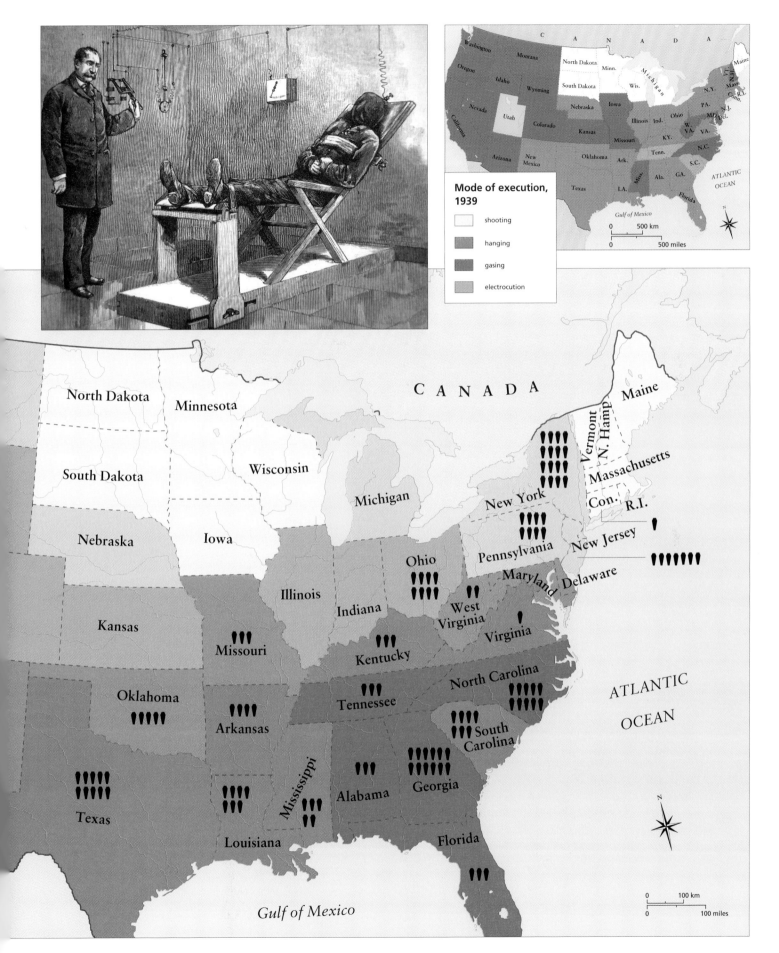

Mode of execution, 1939

shooting

hanging

gasing

electrocution

THE DUST BOWL
DROUGHT AND DESPAIR ON THE GREAT PLAINS

The drought of the mid-1930s raised havoc on the Great Plains. Terrible dust storms denuded the region of huge amounts of topsoil and forced thousands of families to abandon the land and head west to California in a migration immortalized in John Steinbeck's novel The Grapes of Wrath. But it was not the first prolonged dry spell to strike the area. A generation earlier a similar drought drove settlers from Kansas and Nebraska, their wagons bearing slogans like: "In God we trusted; in Kansas we busted." But the drought of the 1930s, coming in the midst of the Great Depression, was particularly severe and almost impossible to bear.

The United States government has established Climatological Benchmark Stations at strategic points throughout the country, and careful track is kept of how much rain falls. In general, the amount of rain in the central section of the United States decreases west and north of the lower Mississippi Valley towards the Rocky Mountains. The station in Louisiana averages over 50 inches of rain a year, the one in Montana 17.6 inches, the one in New Mexico only 8.5 inches. In and beyond the western sections of the Dakotas and the states to the south, annual precipitation is often inadequate for raising most crops, but the amount of rain can vary greatly. There is often plenty in western sections of the plains for several years, but

a dry cycle may follow. Crop yields rise and fall with these changes, but in extremely dry years there is no harvest at all in hard-hit areas. This has been known for more than a century.

Comparison of data collected during the 1930s at the benchmark stations in and around the great central breadbasket of the United States with the production of wheat and corn in that area reveals how the drought affected the region. The leading wheat states in the late 1920s and early 1930s were Kansas, North Dakota, and South Dakota; the leading corn producers were Iowa, Illinois, and Nebraska. In 1934 and 1936 rainfall was below average throughout the region, but its effect on the production of grain depended on the absolute

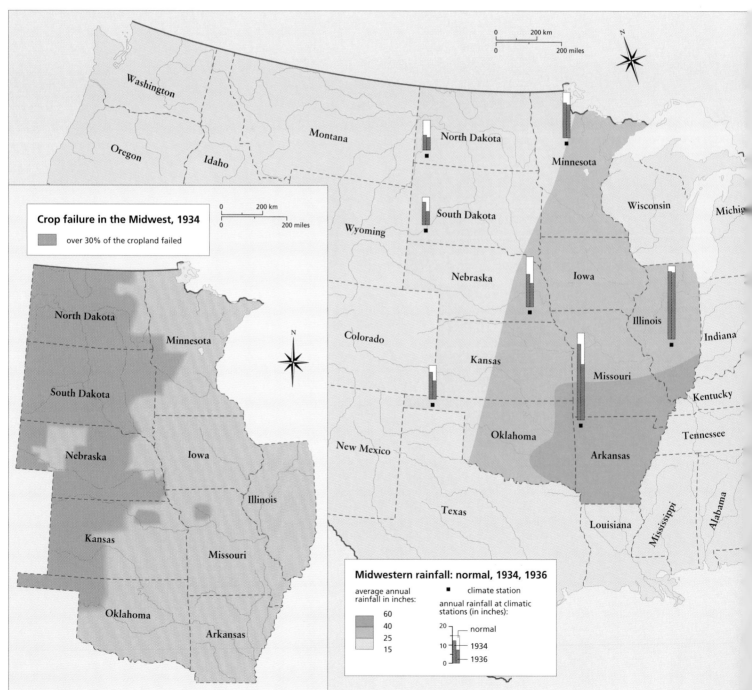

Crop failure in the Midwest, 1934

over 30% of the cropland failed

Midwestern rainfall: normal, 1934, 1936

average annual rainfall in inches:

- 60
- 40
- 25
- 15

■ climate station

annual rainfall at climatic stations (in inches):

- 20 — normal
- 10 — 1934
- 0 — 1936

amount. Rainfall was only 3.5 inches below normal in western Oklahoma in 1934. Two years later, rainfall in Louisiana was more than 15 inches below normal. But the result was drought in Oklahoma in 1934, whereas output in Louisiana actually increased in 1936.

In impact of the decline on the fortunes of farmers was also affected by the price per bushel that their reduced output could command. Wheat sold for about 94¢ a bushel in South Dakota in 1934, well over the national average. But the wheat crop was only 598,000 bushels, a mere 2 percent of the state's normal output. Nebraska produced about 21.3 million bushels of corn in 1934 and 105.5 million bushels in 1935. But the price fell from 87¢ a bushel to 55¢; as a result corn growers received less than twice as much as they had in 1934. In 1936, the drought returned to Nebraska and output fell to 26.8 million bushels, only about 5 percent more than it had been in 1934. Corn brought $1.16 a bushel in 1936, however, so Nebraskans thus got 60 percent more for their crop in 1936 than they had in 1934.

Cimarron County, Oklahoma, photographed in 1936 by Arthur Rothstein, emphasized the desperate plight of thousands of small farmers whose holdings on the Great Plains were subject to the vagaries of nature. Unable to sustain their families, hundreds of thousands fled west.

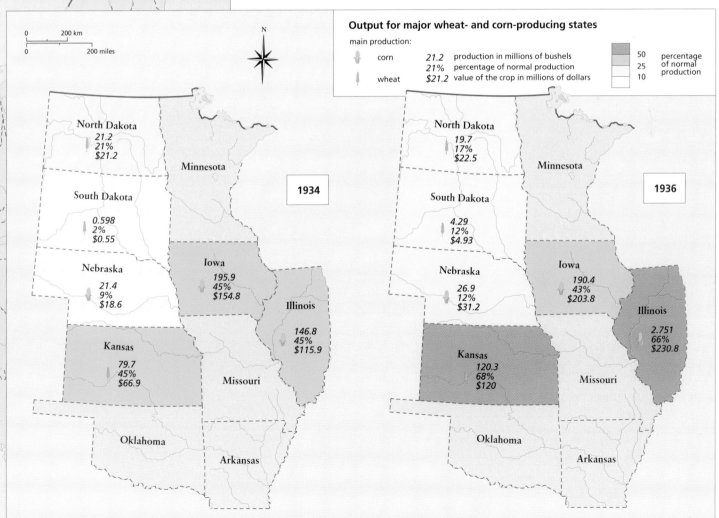

Output for major wheat- and corn-producing states

main production:

corn	21.2	production in millions of bushels
wheat	21%	percentage of normal production
	$21.2	value of the crop in millions of dollars

percentage of normal production: 50 / 25 / 10

1934

North Dakota
21.2
21%
$21.2

South Dakota
0.598
2%
$0.55

Nebraska
21.4
9%
$18.6

Kansas
79.7
45%
$66.9

Iowa
195.9
45%
$154.8

Illinois
146.8
45%
$115.9

Minnesota

Missouri

Oklahoma

Arkansas

1936

North Dakota
19.7
17%
$22.5

South Dakota
4.29
12%
$4.93

Nebraska
26.9
12%
$31.2

Kansas
120.3
68%
$120

Iowa
190.4
43%
$203.8

Illinois
2.751
66%
$230.8

Minnesota

Missouri

Oklahoma

Arkansas

FROM NEW ERA TO NEW DEAL
POLITICAL UPHEAVAL IN THE GREAT DEPRESSION

Between 1928 and 1936, a monumental political shift took place in the United States. During the 1920s, the Republican presidential candidates, Warren Harding, Calvin Coolidge, and Herbert Hoover, had won overwhelming victories. In 1928, Hoover received more than 21 million votes, while his opponent Alfred E. Smith received only 15 million. Hoover's Electoral College margin was 444 to 87, the largest ever up to that time. Four years later, however, the count was almost exactly reversed; Franklin D. Roosevelt received 22.8 million votes to Hoover's 15.7 million. In 1936, the shift was completed. Roosevelt defeated Republican Alfred M. Landon, 27.7 million popular votes to 16.6 million. Landon won only Maine and Vermont.

This political upheaval was a reaction to the economic upheaval known as the Great Depression that began after Herbert Hoover's inauguration, became obvious when the stock market crashed in October 1929, and did not end until 1940, after the outbreak of World War II. In 1928, the Democrats carried only two counties in Ohio, a populous state with a mixed agricultural and industrial economy that was usually closely contested. Four years later, the Democrats won Ohio by 1.3 million votes to 1.2 million and in 1936 they swept the state by 1.7 million votes to 1.1 million.

Montana, where the economy was based on mining and agriculture, was solidly Republican in the 1920s. It went for Hoover by a vote of 113,000 to 79,000 in 1928, the Democrats carrying only three counties in the state. But in 1932, Roosevelt swept Montana by 127,000 votes to 78,000. Only the sparsely populated Sweet Grass county voted for President Hoover, by a narrow margin of 784 to 761. Four years later Roosevelt carried Sweet Grass by 783 to 664 and won every other county in the state, many by huge margins. The disparate elements of Roosevelt's New Deal coalition—unemployed industrial workers, dispossessed farmers, disillusioned intellectuals—were fused by the despair of the time to form a mighty political force that shattered the political order that had prevailed since the Civil War. The New Deal coalition itself endured, albeit in attenuated form, into recent decades.

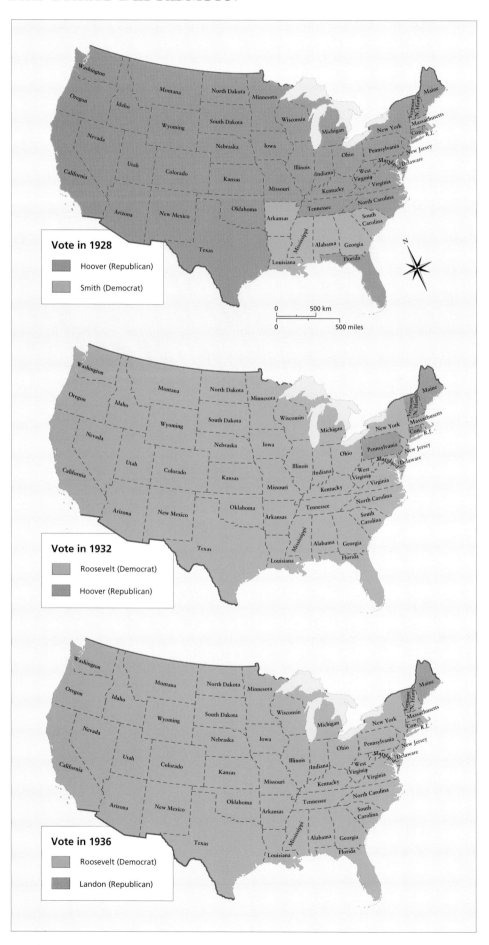

Vote in 1928
- Hoover (Republican)
- Smith (Democrat)

Vote in 1932
- Roosevelt (Democrat)
- Hoover (Republican)

Vote in 1936
- Roosevelt (Democrat)
- Landon (Republican)

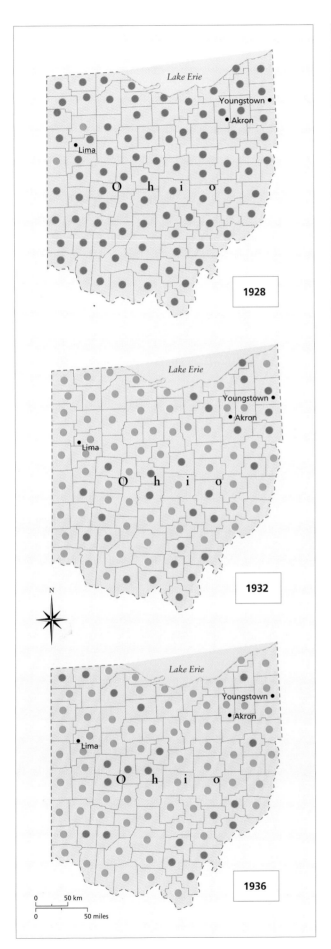

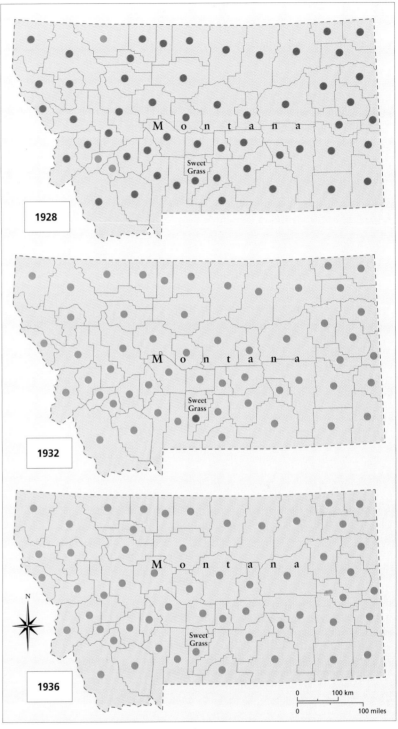

Political upheaval in Ohio and Montana: 1928–1936

- county with Democrat majority in presidential election

- county with Republican majority in presidential election

Far left: Franklin D. Roosevelt on a whistle-stop train journey across the U.S. during his Presidential election campaign of 1932.

Right: Franklin D. Roosevelt's huge victories in 1932 marked an epochal transformation in the political ladscape at the local as well as national level. In 1932, F.D.R. carried Ohio, which had voted Republican in all but two presidential elections since the birth of the party in the 1850s (Woodrow Wilson took the state in 1916 and 1920). Montana had also usually voted Republican. F.D.R. not only carried both states in 1932, and by huge margins in 1936, he also carried divergent sections and constituencies within the states, from the farming regions of around Lima, Ohio, to the industrial centers of Akron and Youngstown. In Montana, F.D.R. won the cattle grazing counties in the south and east, as well as the mining regions in the west and south and the timber country in the northwest.

THE GREAT DEPRESSION
UNEMPLOYMENT AND RELIEF

The most striking characteristic of the Great Depression was the severity and duration of unemployment. At least 13 million people (one worker in four) were unemployed in early 1933, and as late as 1940, when the economy was reviving rapidly, more than 10 percent of the labor force was still idle. President Herbert Hoover had insisted that federal relief of the jobless was inappropriate; he expected state and local agencies to deal with the problem as they had in past depressions. Franklin Roosevelt, however, accepted federal responsibility from the start and the aid dispensed by New Deal agencies was the most important factor in Roosevelt's extraordinary popularity.

Among the earliest New Deal agencies to deal with unemployment, the Federal Emergency Relief Administration (FERA), headed by Harry Hopkins, quickly dispensed $500 million in the form of grants to the state relief organizations. Hopkins believed that what the jobless needed was work, however, not merely handouts. Roosevelt responded in November 1933 by creating the Civil Works Administration which soon put four million people to work repairing roads and public buildings and performing many skilled tasks. The cost to the government was enormous and the CWA program was soon ended. However, relief under FERA continued, and in May 1935 Roosevelt put Hopkins in charge of a new agency, the Works Progress Administration, which became the "permanent" New Deal relief agency.

When WPA finally ended during World War II, it had dispensed $11 billion to 8.5 million people. Much of what was done was make-work (described by critics as "boondoggles"), but WPA also employed artists to decorate public buildings, writers to turn out guide-books and do research, as well as actors and other theater people. There was also a more long-range Public Works Administration (PWA), run by Secretary of the Interior Harold L. Ickes, which constructed dams, public housing and highways, as well as military airports and warships, including the aircraft carriers *Yorktown* and *Enterprise*.

WPA was by far the most politically important of these programs. It is safe to say that no city of any size in the country does not bear the mark WPA in its post offices, schools, parks, and other utilities. In the New York City area, for example, LaGuardia Airport, Jones Beach, and the parkways leading to it, dozens of parks, bridges, and municipal swimming pools, originated as WPA projects.

The agency spared no effort in making its achievements known to the public. It published posters, schematic diagrams, city maps, and maps of the country showing where schools, streets, parks, sewers, and airports constructed by WPA were located. The WPA also issued semiannual statistics showing the number of people on the WPA payroll in each state. These correlate inversely with trends in the economy.

This trend is demonstrated by a comparison of changes in WPA employment and steel production. The recession of 1937–38 was in large part caused by Roosevelt's decision to cut back on WPA in 1937, and recovery came swiftly when he reversed course in 1938.

Below: The WPA is best known for its large construction projects in the cities, but hundreds of thousands of unemployed farmers were put to work in highway, irrigation, and anti-erosion projects as well. Though conceived as a humanitarian measure that would also jump-start the economy, the WPA also functioned as a huge patronage machine for the Democratic Party—one reason the program was so bitterly criticized.

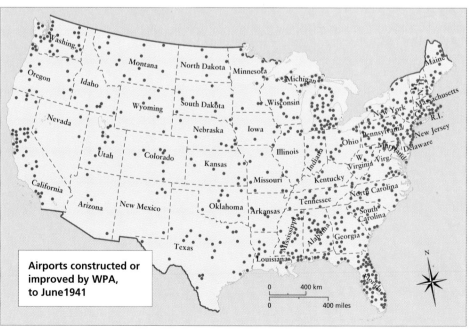

Airports constructed or improved by WPA, to June 1941

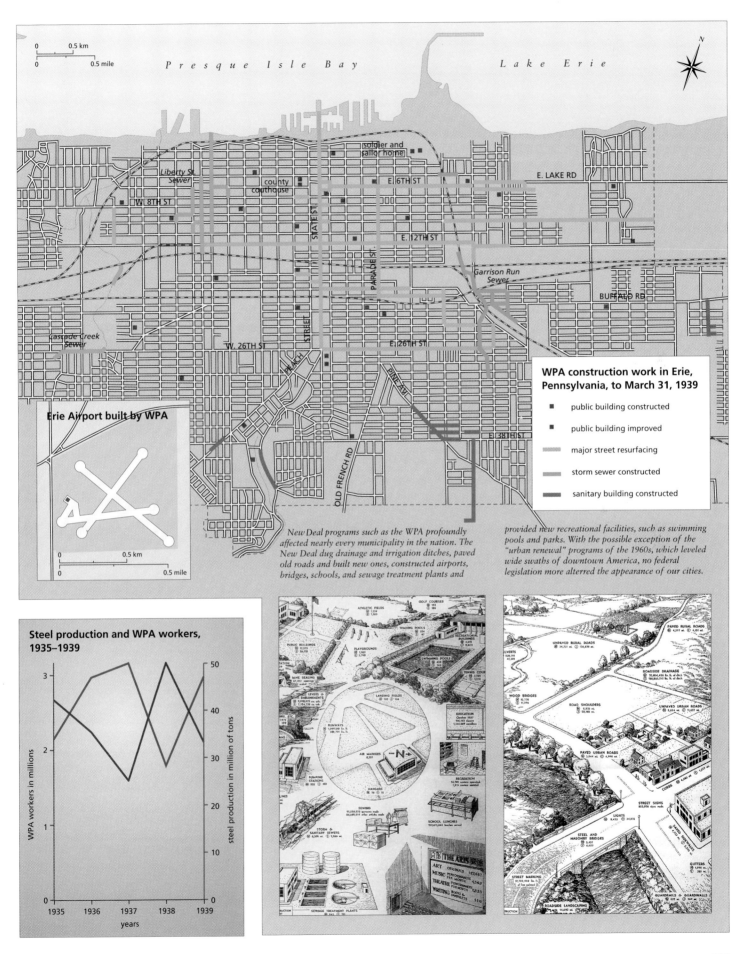

0 0.5 km
0 0.5 mile

Presque Isle Bay   *Lake Erie*

N

soldier and
sailor home

*Liberty St.
Sewer*

county
courthouse

E. 6TH ST

E. LAKE RD

W. 8TH ST

STATE ST

E. 12TH ST

PARADE ST

*Garrison Run
Sewer*

BUFFALO RD

*Cascade Creek
Sewer*

W. 26TH ST

STREET

E. 26TH ST

PEACH

PINE AV.

E. 38TH ST

OLD FRENCH RD

Erie Airport built by WPA

0 0.5 km
0 0.5 mile

WPA construction work in Erie, Pennsylvania, to March 31, 1939

- ■ public building constructed
- ■ public building improved
- ▬ major street resurfacing
- ▬ storm sewer constructed
- ▬ sanitary building constructed

New Deal programs such as the WPA profoundly affected nearly every municipality in the nation. The New Deal dug drainage and irrigation ditches, paved old roads and built new ones, constructed airports, bridges, schools, and sewage treatment plants and provided new recreational facilities, such as swimming pools and parks. With the possible exception of the "urban renewal" programs of the 1960s, which leveled wide swaths of downtown America, no federal legislation more alterred the appearance of our cities.

Steel production and WPA workers, 1935–1939

WPA workers in millions

3

2

1

0

1935 1936 1937 1938 1939
years

steel production in million of tons

50

40

30

20

10

0

FORGING THE DEMOCRATIC COALITION

SHIFTS IN VOTING PATTERNS

The Great Depression was not the only reason for the political revolution of the 1930s. Indeed, throughout the previous decade important social and demographic changes caused a shift in voting patterns that was favorable to the Democrats. Thousands of the "new" immigrants, most of them Catholic or Jewish, were concentrated in large eastern and middle western cities. In 1920, Harding carried the 12 largest cities in the nation by large margins, but in 1928 a small majority of the voters in these cities voted for the Democratic "Al" Smith, an Irish Catholic born and brought up on "the sidewalks of New York."

Smith lost support in rural areas and cities where the native-born Protestant population predominated, however. Voters in southern cities in particular, although traditionally Democratic, deserted the party in droves in 1928. Dallas, for example, which had elected the Democrats by nearly three to one in 1920, voted for the Republican candidate, Herbert Hoover, by almost two to one in 1928. In Ohio, Hoover carried Cincinnati, Akron, Columbus, and Toledo by large margins. But Cleveland, which had a large immigrant population, and had been won by Harding in 1920, went Democratic in 1928.

One northern urban group that resisted the trend toward the Democrats in 1928 was the blacks. Thousands of southern blacks had migrated to northern cities during World War I, attracted by jobs in the booming shops and factories. Life was not easy for them; most lived crowded together in ramshackle ghettoes and they were discriminated against in many ways. But in addition to improving their standard of living, they could vote in the northern states, something few had been able to do in the South at that time.

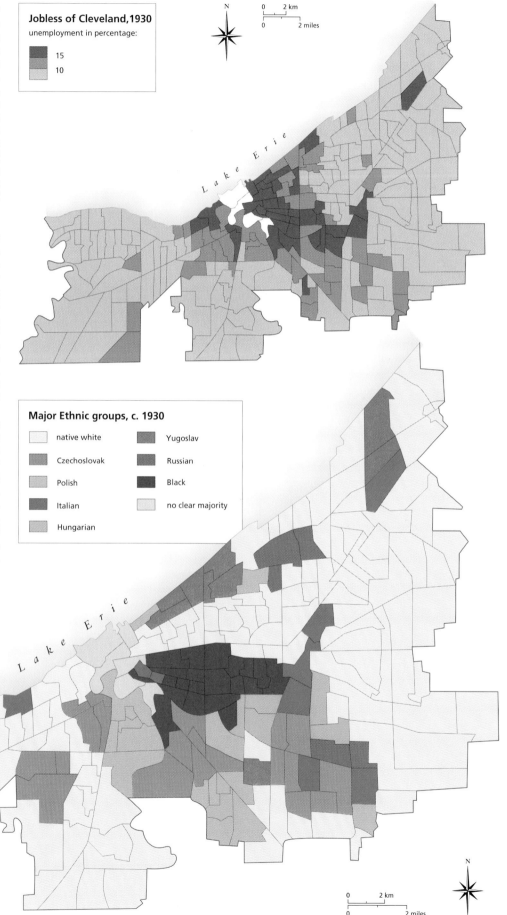

Jobless of Cleveland, 1930

unemployment in percentage:

- 15
- 10

Major Ethnic groups, c. 1930

- native white
- Czechoslovak
- Polish
- Italian
- Hungarian
- Yugoslav
- Russian
- Black
- no clear majority

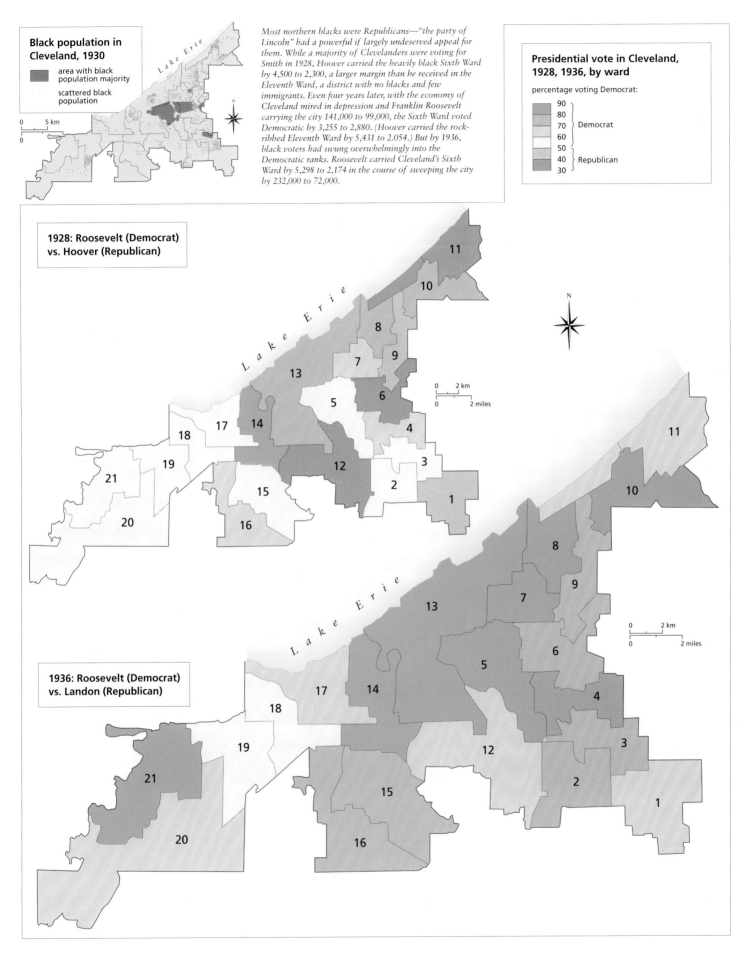

Black population in Cleveland, 1930

- ▓ area with black population majority
- · scattered black population

0   5 km

0

Most northern blacks were Republicans—"the party of Lincoln" had a powerful if largely undeserved appeal for them. While a majority of Clevelanders were voting for Smith in 1928, Hoover carried the heavily black Sixth Ward by 4,500 to 2,300, a larger margin than he received in the Eleventh Ward, a district with no blacks and few immigrants. Even four years later, with the economy of Cleveland mired in depression and Franklin Roosevelt carrying the city 141,000 to 99,000, the Sixth Ward voted Democratic by 3,255 to 2,880. (Hoover carried the rock-ribbed Eleventh Ward by 5,431 to 2.054.) But by 1936, black voters had swung overwhelmingly into the Democratic ranks. Roosevelt carried Cleveland's Sixth Ward by 5,298 to 2,174 in the course of sweeping the city by 232,000 to 72,000.

Presidential vote in Cleveland, 1928, 1936, by ward

percentage voting Democrat:

90	
80	
70	Democrat
60	
50	
40	Republican
30	

1928: Roosevelt (Democrat) vs. Hoover (Republican)

0   2 km

0   2 miles

1936: Roosevelt (Democrat) vs. Landon (Republican)

0   2 km

0   2 miles

ISOLATIONISM IN THE 1930s
ETHNIC POLITICS AND FOREIGN RELATIONS

In his Farewell Address of September 1796, President Washington warned Americans about "the insidious wiles of foreign influence." He urged them to have "as little political connection as possible" with foreign countries. Insulated from the political turmoil of the Old World by the vast expanses of two oceans, for over 100 years American statesmen participated only sporadically in foreign affairs and with little evident coherence. This changed in 1917, when President Woodrow Wilson led the nation on a crusade to make the world "safe for democracy." Subsequent revulsion for the Great War, its human sacrifice and its outcome contributed to the rise of isolationist sentiment in the 1920s and 1930s.

Dictators on the Loose
On the night of September 18, 1931, Japanese officers at the industrial center of Mukden ordered their men aboard the Japanese-owned South Manchurian railroad and sent them to attack Chinese positions throughout Manchuria, which accounted for 40 percent of Japan's foreign investment and trade. The Japanese quickly overran the Nationalist Chinese, most of whose forces were engaged against Mao Tse-tung's Communists further south.

In February 1932, Tokyo installed a puppet regime in Manchuria, which it renamed Manchukuo. As the Nationalists concentrated on eliminating their Communist rivals, Japan prepared to conquer the remainder of China.

In July 1937, Japanese forces in Manchuria struck across the border and occupied Peking and Tientsin. In August they landed at Shanghai and drove up the Yangtze River, capturing Nanking in December. By early January they had taken the coastal cities of Tsingtao and Hangchow and much of the lower Yellow River. Nearly everywhere, the Japanese inflicted frightful losses on civilians. President Roosevelt de-

nounced the Japanese as aggressors and called for "positive endeavors" against them. America was inching toward war with Japan.

Meanwhile, after the Nazis had seized power in Germany in 1936, Hitler sent troops into the Rhineland, which the Treaty of Versailles had declared permanently demilitarized, and in 1938, he annexed Austria (the Anschluss). He then demanded that Czechoslovakia cede the Sudetenland, a region inhabited by some 3 million Germans. As Czechoslovakia mobilized for war, the British prime minister Neville Chamberlain and French premier Edouard Daladier conferred with Hitler at Munich. After extracting from Hitler the promise that the Sudetenland was "the last territorial claim which I have to make in Europe," Allied leaders pressured the Czechoslovaks to accede to his demands. Within six months, contrary to his agreement with the British and French premiers, Hitler gobbled up the remainder of Czechoslovakia. Roosevelt protested the action.

The Ludlow Amendment
Many Americans well recalled the Great War's seemingly pointless bloodshed, and they sought to prevent Roosevelt from dragging the United States into the impending war in Asia and Europe. In 1935, Democratic Congressman Louis Ludlow of Indiana proposed a new constitutional amendment "to keep Americans out of slaughter pens in foreign countries." The Ludlow Amendment prohibited Congress from declaring war

German and Irish foreign-born c. 1940

1000 and above per county

San Francisco area

Los Angeles area

Japanese expansion

empire 1920–30

expansion 1931

expansion 1933

expansion 1941

German expansion, 1938–39

1 Rhineland occupation, March 1936

2 union with Germany, March 1938

3 Sudetenland to Germany, October 1938

4 state annihilated 1939

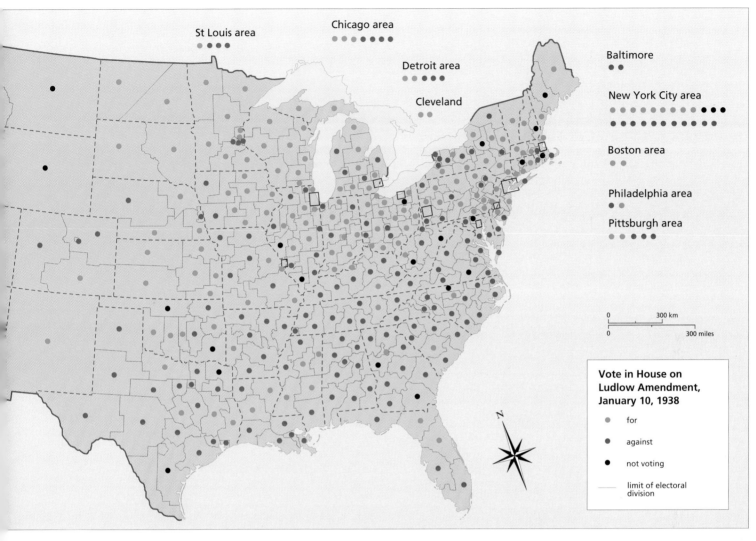

St Louis area

Chicago area

Detroit area

Cleveland

Baltimore

New York City area

Boston area

Philadelphia area

Pittsburgh area

0   300 km

0   300 miles

Vote in House on Ludlow Amendment, January 10, 1938

●   for

●   against

●   not voting

—   limit of electoral division

N

without the prior approval of a majority of the nation's voters, except in the event of attack. For several years congressional leaders kept the measure bottled up in committee, but when Japan resumed its conquest of China in 1937, more and more congressmen signed Ludlow's petition for discharge. In early December, after Japan set off a war-scare by sinking the United States gunboat, *Panay*, enough additional congressmen signed the petition to bring the Ludlow Amendment before the entire House. The session was scheduled for January 10, 1938.

President Roosevelt, who wanted a free hand in foreign policy, threw his administration against the amendment. He ordered James A. Farley, postmaster general and chairman of the Democratic National Committee, to pressure Democrats to vote against the resolution. Just minutes prior to the vote, Speaker of the House William Bankhead attacked the Ludlow Amendment as a "radical" and "revolutionary" assault upon democracy. He then read aloud a letter from Roosevelt, who argued that the amendment would "cripple" his ability to conduct foreign affairs.

The Ludlow Amendment resolution was defeated by a shockingly narrow margin of 209 to 188. Delegations from Kansas, South

Dakota, North Dakota, and Wisconsin unanimously supported the isolationist measure, and only a handful of congressmen from Minnesota, Nebraska, Indiana, Michigan, and Ohio voted against it. The Far West and New England divided evenly on the question. Opposition to the isolationism came chiefly from large northeastern cities and from the South, where more than four-fifths of the congressmen voted against the resolution.

Historians have long debated the geography of isolationism. Some contend that isolationist sentiment was particularly strong among Midwestern farmers, who had traditionally resented eastern industrialists and bankers. Progressive senators such as Gerald P. Nye of North Dakota, who had earlier investigated Wall Street's arms trade during the Great War, readily opposed policies that might again draw the nation into a war that chiefly served eastern and internationalist bankers and industrialists. Other scholars have concluded that the most important strongholds of American isolationism were found among German-Americans, and to a lesser degree, Irish-Americans—ethnic groups that opposed war against Germany and supported Great Britain. The maps above show a correlation between the presence of large German con-

stituencies and support for isolationism in Wisconsin, Minnesota, and Michigan.

On the other hand, most congressmen from cities with large Irish and German populations, such as Boston, Philadelphia, Pittsburgh, Chicago, and New York, voted against the resolution. Still other historians assert that isolationism arose out of ignorance; historian Thomas A. Bailey found that people who had never attended high school were more likely to support isolationism than more educated citizens. However, the South, which was the most interventionist region, was plagued with the nation's worst educational system *(see The Geography of "Stupidity", p 166–167).*

Enduring regional partisanship constituted an important and neglected aspect of the politics of isolationism. Despite Roosevelt's landslide victories, the Midwest voted against isolationism. Similarly, the congressional delegations from the South were dominated by Democrats, two-thirds of whom voted for isolationism. Although the narrowness of the defeat of the resolution unnerved some of the President's advisers, the vote revealed that his congressional coalition of southern and big-city Democrats would be sufficient to endorse his increasingly interventionist foreign policies.

AMERICA ENTERS WORLD WAR II
SURPRISE ATTACK ON PEARL HARBOR

The Japanese bombing of Pearl Harbor came as a surprise, but by December 1941 some Japanese attack was both inevitable and expected by American military and naval planners. In 1937, Japan had resumed its war on China in open violation of the Open Door policy. President Roosevelt responded first by urging American manufacturers not to sell any more airplanes to the Japanese. In 1940, Congress placed strict limits on the sale of aviation gasoline to Japan and put a total stop to the export of scrap iron and machine tools. These measures did not cause the Japanese to change their course, and a clash was bound to occur.

In an effort to avoid war and find some mutually satisfactory solution to the crisis, the Japanese ambassador and secretary of state Cordell Hull held a series of meetings in Washington in early 1941. Hull insisted that Japan should cease its aggression in Southeast Asia and pull all its troops out of China. This the Japanese were unwilling to do; instead they

invaded Indochina, causing President Roosevelt to ban all export of petroleum products to Japan. Without oil the Japanese could neither fight a war nor maintain their domestic economy. The embargo seemed to be a way to force them to end their aggression. The trouble with this approach, of course, was that Japan had an alternative. There was plenty of oil in Southeast Asia and the Japanese resolved to take it by force.

By the night of December 6, Admiral Chuichji Nagumo's fleet of six carriers and a host of other warships had reached a point about 250 miles north of Hawaii, close enough for torpedo and dive bombers to reach Pearl Harbor and return to their carriers without refueling. Early the next morning, they struck in two waves.

The attack came as a total surprise to the Americans. As the map shows, the battleships, cruisers, and lesser vessels of the Pacific fleet lay at anchor in neat rows. They and the hundreds of planes at Hickam Field and other airstrips were devastated. 3,600 American servicemen were killed or wounded in the attack,

more than 1,000 of the dead were sailors on USS *Arizona*, which was destroyed when its forward magazine was hit in the first moments of the attack. Of the battleships, only USS *Nevada* managed to get under way, and it was so battered by bombs and torpedoes that it remained out of service until 1943. Only USS *Pennsylvania*, the flagship of the fleet, escaped major damage, chiefly because it was in drydock at the time and was not hit by torpedoes.

Only chance prevented the defeat from being still worse. The aircraft carriers of the Pacific fleet were at sea, and were thus not damaged by the raid. Both the *Lexington* and the *Enterprise* had left Pearl Harbor only days earlier. Had they been there, they would almost certainly have been sunk and the entire course of the Pacific war would have been different.

Top left: *picture from a Japanese bomber of American battleships at anchor in Pearl Harbor, December 7, 1941. The battleships were easy targets, but the attack failed to neutralize the U.S. Pacific fleet because its most potent weapons—three aircraft carriers—were not in port.*
Bottom left: *rescue team in action.*

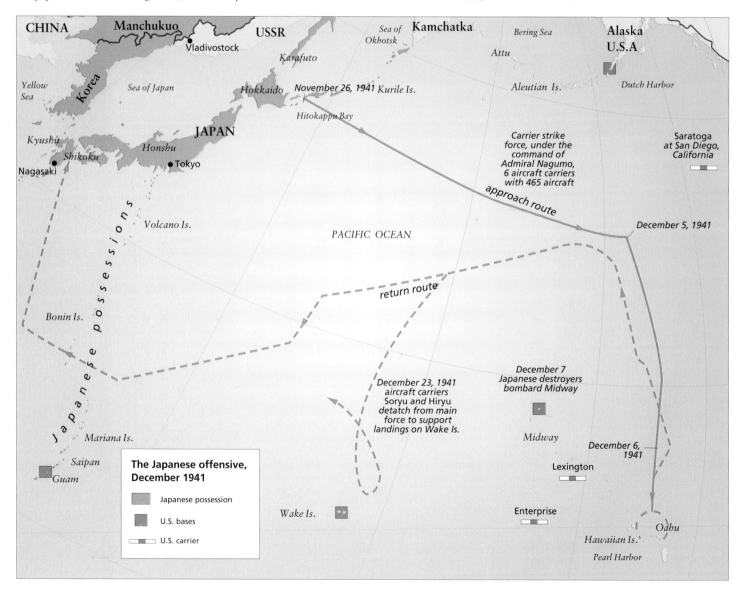

188

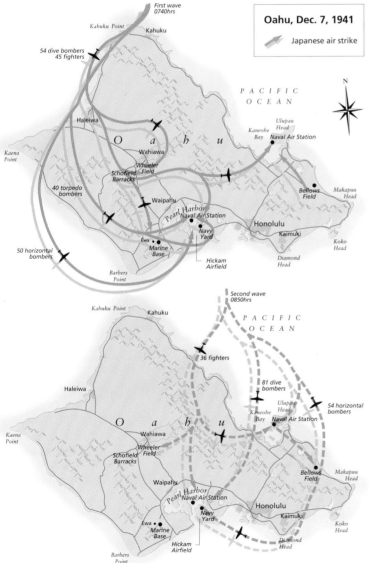

Oahu, Dec. 7, 1941

Japanese air strike

First wave
0740hrs

Kahuku Point
Kahuku

54 dive bombers
45 fighters

Kaena
Point

Haleiwa

O a h u

Wahiawa

Wheeler
Field

Schofield
Barracks

40 torpedo
bombers

Waipahu

Pearl Harbor
Naval Air Station

Ewa
Marine
Base

Navy
Yard

Hickam
Airfield

50 horizontal
bombers

Barbers
Point

PACIFIC
OCEAN

Kaneohe
Bay

Ulupau
Head

Naval Air Station

N

Bellows
Field

Makapuu
Head

Honolulu

Kaimuki

Diamond
Head

Koko
Head

Second wave
0850hrs

Kahuku Point
Kahuku

PACIFIC
OCEAN

36 fighters

81 dive
bombers

Kaena
Point

Haleiwa

O a h u

Wahiawa

Wheeler
Field

Schofield
Barracks

Waipahu

Pearl Harbor
Naval Air Station

Ewa
Marine
Base

Navy
Yard

Hickam
Airfield

Barbers
Point

Kaneohe
Bay

Ulupau
Head

Naval Air Station

54 horizontal
bombers

Bellows
Field

Makapuu
Head

Honolulu

Kaimuki

Diamond
Head

Koko
Head

battleship
cruiser
destroyer
submarine
other

Detroit

Raleigh

Curtiss

Utah

East Loch

Ford Island

U.S. Naval
Air Station

Pearl
Harbor

signal
tower

Nevada

Arizona

Tennessee

Maryland

Vestal

W. Virginia

Oklahoma

California

Oglala

New Orleans
San Francisco

oil tanks

submarine
base

Pennsylvania

Shaw

Cassin

St Louis

Helena

Downes

Honolulu

Pearl Harbor, December 7, 1941

sunk

damaged

undamaged

THE BATTLE OF MIDWAY
THE BEGINNING OF A JAPANESE RETREAT IN THE PACIFIC

With the Pacific Fleet paralyzed by the Pearl Harbor disaster, the Japanese juggernaut rolled ahead almost unopposed. The American islands of Guam and Wake were swallowed by Japan in December 1941. Japanese armies swept through Burma, Thailand, Malaya, and most of the Dutch East Indies between January and March. By early April, the Philippine Islands were in their hands too. A month later, in the Battle of the Coral Sea northeast of Australia, planes from the American carriers Lexington and Yorktown attacked an enormous Japanese convoy headed for New Guinea, forcing the troop ships to turn back, but the Lexington was lost in the fight and the Yorktown was damaged.

To engage the rest of the American carriers in battle, Japanese fleet Admiral Isokoru Yamamoto decided to attack Midway, the last American base west of battered Pearl Harbor. To seize this tiny atoll, he marshalled a fleet of 16 submarines, 8 carriers, 9 battleships, 6 heavy cruisers and a host of destroyers, transports, and supply vessels; when an auxiliary fleet designed to strike the Aleutian Islands is counted, the armada consisted of 162 vessels, commanded by Admiral Nagumo.

On June 4, many of Nagumo's ships and planes that had participated in the attack on Pearl Harbor bombed Midway in preparation for the planned invasion. But by the time they reached the island, its defending planes were already airborne and its harbor was empty of warships. While their own planes were in the air, the Japanese carriers had to hold a fixed course in order to retrieve them. This enabled the three American carriers Yorktown, Enterprise, and Hornet, commanded by admirals

Frank Fletcher and Raymond Spruance, and positioned north of Midway, to time attacks on the Japanese carriers so as to hit them with torpedo and dive bombers while their aircraft were being refueled. Japanese gunners took a heavy toll, especially on the low-flying torpedo bombers, 50 of which were downed, but the dive bombers struck with devastating effectiveness. Before the day was over, Nagumo's four carriers, Kaga, Soryu, Akagi, and Hiryu had been damaged beyond repair. All went to the bottom within hours.

Japanese dive bombers managed to hit the Yorktown, which had to be abandoned. Since his air power had been wiped out, there was nothing for Admiral Yamomoto to do but call off the invasion of Midway. When the Americans refused to engage the Japanese battleships and cruisers in a conventional sea battle, he had to return to Japan.

The only part of the Japanese plan that succeeded was the attack by Admiral Kakuji Kakuta's strike force on the Dutch Harbor naval base in the Aleutian Islands on June 3. Yamamoto had designed this attack as a ruse; he expected the American Pacific Fleet

to steam north, thus opening the way to Midway for his main force. Japanese planes bombed Dutch Harbor and Japanese troops occupied Attu and Kiska islands in the remote western Aleutians, but damage to the base was easily repaired and the islands were of small importance.

The dramatic American victory in the Battle of Midway was one of the most important of the entire war. It boosted Allied morale and marked the beginning of a slow but inexorable Japanese retreat in the Pacific theater. It also demonstrated the vital importance of air power in naval warfare, a lesson that the Japanese had failed to learn in the Battle of the Coral Sea. Not one of the dozens of battleships and cruisers on either side ever fired a shot or even came in sight of an enemy vessel.

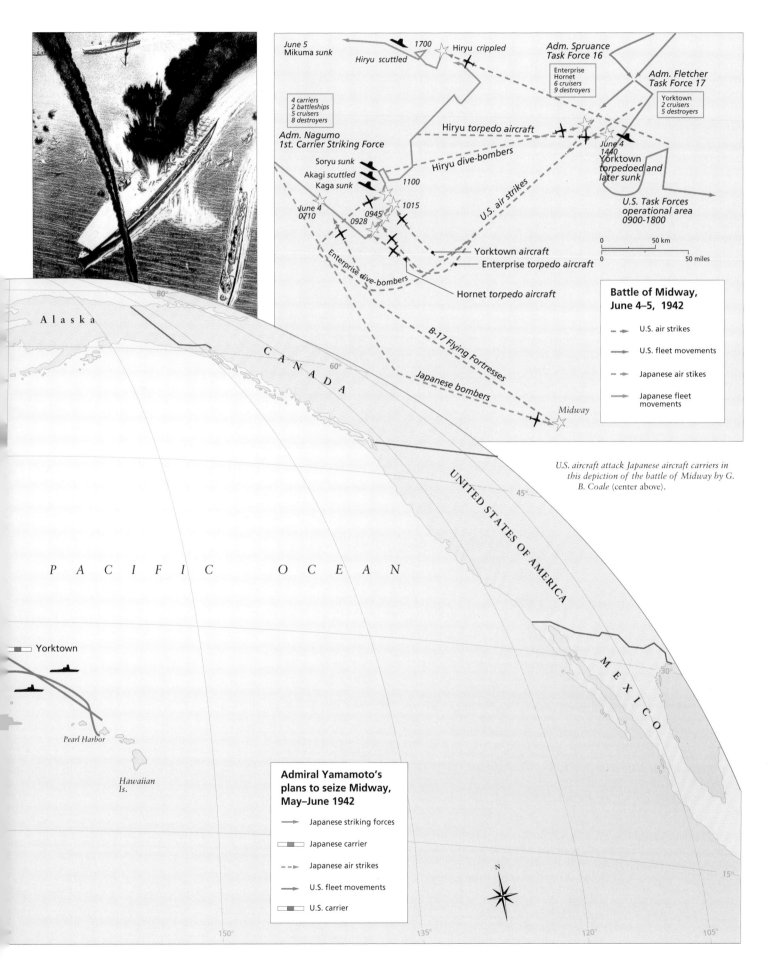

**Battle of Midway,
June 4–5, 1942**

- - → U.S. air strikes

─── U.S. fleet movements

- - → Japanese air stikes

─── Japanese fleet movements

June 5
Mikuma sunk

1700

Hiryu *crippled*

Hiryu *scuttled*

Adm. Spruance
Task Force 16

Enterprise
Hornet
6 cruisers
9 destroyers

Adm. Fletcher
Task Force 17

Yorktown
2 cruisers
5 destroyers

4 carriers
2 battleships
5 cruisers
8 destroyers

Adm. Nagumo
1st. Carrier Striking Force

Hiryu *torpedo aircraft*

Hiryu *dive-bombers*

June 4
1440
Yorktown
torpedoed and
later sunk

Soryu *sunk*

Akagi *scuttled*

Kaga *sunk*

1100

U.S. Task Forces
operational area
0900–1800

June 4
0710

1015

0945
0928

U.S. air strikes

Enterprise dive-bombers

0   50 km

0   50 miles

Yorktown *aircraft*

Enterprise *torpedo aircraft*

Hornet *torpedo aircraft*

B-17 Flying Fortresses

Japanese bombers

Midway

*U.S. aircraft attack Japanese aircraft carriers in
this depiction of the battle of Midway by G.
B. Coale (center above).*

Alaska

CANADA

UNITED STATES OF AMERICA

MEXICO

PACIFIC   OCEAN

Yorktown

Pearl Harbor

Hawaiian
Is.

**Admiral Yamamoto's
plans to seize Midway,
May–June 1942**

──→ Japanese striking forces

▭ Japanese carrier

- - → Japanese air strikes

──→ U.S. fleet movements

▭ U.S. carrier

N

THE UNITED STATES IN THE EUROPEAN THEATER
THE DESTRUCTION OF GERMAN ARMIES IN THE WEST

In the Pacific theater, the war was primarily an American operation, although British, Australian and other Allied forces contributed to the defeat of Japan. In Europe, while the American role was enormous, the struggle was far more complicated, involving as it did the armies of Great Britain, the Soviet Union, Free France, Canada, Australia, and the other British dominions, as well as units made up of emigrés from nations overrun by Germany. To make the part played by the American armies clear, this map isolates them from the activities of all other forces, friends and enemies alike, as well as from the naval aspects of the conflict.

Although the United States was engaged in fighting in the Pacific from the day that the Japanese bombed Pearl Harbor, President Roosevelt and other Allied leaders decided that Germany and Italy provided a more immediate threat and therefore adopted a "Europe First" strategy. In December 1941, the Axis powers controlled all of continental Europe except neutral Spain, Portugal, Switzerland, and Sweden. In Russia, their armies stood at the gates of Moscow and Leningrad, and they controlled most of North Africa west of Egypt. America's first task, aside from providing material support for British and Soviet forces, was to build up a large army in preparation for an eventual invasion of the continent from bases in Great Britain, and to undertake systematic air strikes with the British against Axis cities and communications.

In November 1942, while these activities were in progress, an army commanded by Dwight D. Eisenhower invaded North Africa. In collaboration with a British army driving west from Egypt, the Americans overwhelmed General Erwin Rommel's *Afrika Korps* and occupied Tunis in May. In July, again with the British, they invaded Sicily, and in September they swept into southern Italy.

The Italian dictator Benito Mussolini was overthrown just as the Italian invasion began, and his successors took Italy out of the war, but the Germans defended the country as determinedly as if it were their own soil. Subduing them on the rugged Italian peninsula was tedious and extremely costly work. Beginning in January 1944, Monte Cassino, a stronghold on the so-called Gustav Line south of Rome, was repeatedly attacked by United States and New Zealand troops. It was not overrun until late May. American units entered the undefended city of Rome on June 4. By August they had advanced as far as the German's Gothic Line south of Bologna and Genoa, but could not break through the German positions and complete the conquest of Italy until the spring of 1945.

Meanwhile, on June 6, 1944, two days after the fall of Rome, the great Allied invasion began; American, Canadian, and British troops, supported by 6,500 ships and 12,000 planes and under the overall command of General Eisenhower, stormed ashore at five beaches in French Normandy. By the end of the day, 155,000 men had landed, but casualties were heavy. Thereafter, more slowly than had been hoped but steadily, the beachhead was consolidated and expanded. In early August, American armored divisions broke through the German defenses and swept south and east into the French heartland. Paris fell to French and American units on August 25, and by the end of September most of France and Belgium had been liberated.

In mid-December 1944, with the Allied armies holding a broad front near the German border from the Netherlands to Switzerland, the Germans suddenly counterattacked. They drove a deep wedge into southern Belgium in the direction of the important port of Antwerp, but their thrust was contained, halted, and then driven back. This "Battle of the Bulge" was the Germans' last offensive, but they continued what was by then a hopeless struggle. In March 1945, American units crossed the Rhine River at Remagen and by mid-April Allied forces were installed along the Elbe River, about 60 miles west of Berlin, where by prearrangement with the Soviets, Eisenhower had decided to stop. Berlin fell to Soviet troops on May 2; and on May 8, Germany surrendered.

Above: *American troops move inland from the Normandy beachhead. By the end of June, 1944, after 24 days of fighting, American forces had suffered over 37,000 casualties. It would take another 11 months of hard fighting to destroy the German army in northwest Europe. Of the eight Allied armies deployed in northwest Europe, five were American.*

Operation Cobra
July 1944

ATLANTIC OCEAN

Bay of Biscay

SPAIN

The liberation of Europe

→ main movements of U.S. armed forces in North African and European campaigns, 1942–45

→ movements of Western Allies

→ movements of Eastern Allies

strategic air attacks of U.S. air forces based in Great Britain (1942–45), North Africa (1943) and Italy (1943–45)

territory still held by the armed forces of the 3rd Reich, May 9, 1945

neutral countries

Operation Shingle
January 1944

major operations involving U.S. forces in the European theater

Tangier •

Operation Torch
November 8, 1942

Ora

Spanish Morocco

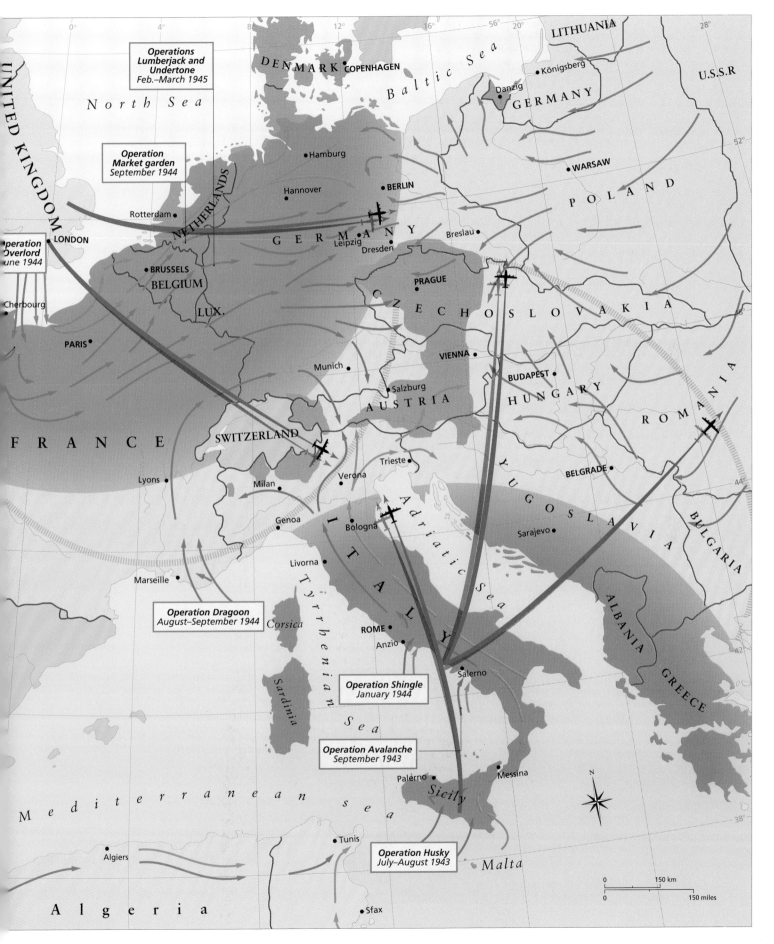

THE ALLIED INVASION OF NORTHERN EUROPE
THE END OF THE WAR COMES INTO SIGHT

The decision to mount a cross-Channel invasion of France was made by Roosevelt and Churchill at the Casablanca Conference in January 1943, but who would lead the attack and when it would take place was determined only gradually. There were only two areas on the French coast within the range of British-based fighter planes where the terrain was suitable for the massive operation planned: one in the Calais area, the other in Normandy. In July, the Normandy site was selected. In December, General Eisenhower was named Supreme Commander, and British General Montgomery was put in charge of the actual attack, which was launched on June 6, 1944.

Five army corps, two American, two British, and one Canadian, supported by a flotilla of 6,000-odd vessels struck at beaches codenamed Utah, Omaha, Gold, Juno, and Sword at dawn. During the night, paratroopers had been dropped behind both ends of the beach to protect the invaders' flanks. The Germans were confused at first, but resisted fiercely. However, only at Omaha Beach, which was guarded by steep cliffs, did the invaders suffer heavy casualties during the actual landings. By the end of the day, 155,000 Allied soldiers had landed.

To supply these troops and the tens of thousands more who soon followed, floating docks and breakwaters had to be set up along the unprotected beaches. An underwater oil pipe line was also laid across the Channel. Total domination of the air—the Allies concentrated 12,000 planes in the area, whereas the Germans had only a few hundred—greatly aided the attackers. Nevertheless, consolidating the position was both time consuming and extremely costly; it took four days merely to close the gaps between the five beachheads. Caen, which according to the plan was to have been occupied on D-Day, was not captured for more than a month.

Progress came in the smallest of increments. American units made the first substantial breakthrough at the west end of the beachhead when they cut off Cherbourg by capturing Barneville on the Gulf of St. Malo on June 17. Cherbourg was occupied 10 days later, but only after the Germans had wrecked the harbor installations so important for supplying the invading armies. Thereafter, despite continuing hard fighting and almost incessant aerial bombing, the front remained relatively stable well into July.

Finally, with the British attacking in force east of Caen in the hope of easing German resistance further west, General Omar Bradley's First Army captured St. Lô on July 18 and then advanced south and west as far as Avranches, on the Gulf of St. Malo, which fell on July 31. Then, at last, came the real breakthrough. Within a week the Americans had placed Brest, at the extreme western tip of France, under siege. By August 10, the armored divisions of General George Patton had reached Le Mans, and other units had captured St. Nazaire and Nantes on the lower Loire. Instead of sweeping south along the Atlantic coast, the Americans then wheeled eastward in a broad arc north from the Loire as the Germans fell back from Normandy swiftly to escape being trapped. Chartres and Orleans fell on August 17 and two days later troops crossed the Seine both north and south of Paris. Heavy fighting broke out within the capital between German forces and the populace. Eisenhower delegated the honor of officially liberating Paris to General Philippe Leclerc, commander of a Free French armored division, who formally occupied the city on August 25.

By December 1944, France had been substantially cleared of enemy troops and the Allied armies stood in force along a front that ran from the North Sea to Switzerland. German resistance continued and formidable border defenses remained to be breached, but victory seemed assured. At this point, however, at the direct order of Hitler, the Germans launched an all-out attack along the border between Belgium and Luxembourg. This was aimed at breaking through to the sea at Antwerp and splitting the Allied armies in two.

The plan was foolhardy and thus unexpected. On December 16, spearheaded by waves of tanks, the Germans burst through a weakly defended point in an American-held sector. Confusion reigned, partly caused by the surprise and partly engineered by German troops dressed in American uniforms.

The Germans advanced about 50 miles toward Antwerp, but by Christmas it was clear that they would never reach that objective. The surrounded American stronghold at Bastogne held out. Superior Allied forces closed in from both flanks and by mid-January everything that the Germans had taken had been regained. Both sides suffered enormous losses of men and equipment in this "Battle of the Bulge," but the losses were more easily borne by the Allies. The end of the war in Europe was now in sight.

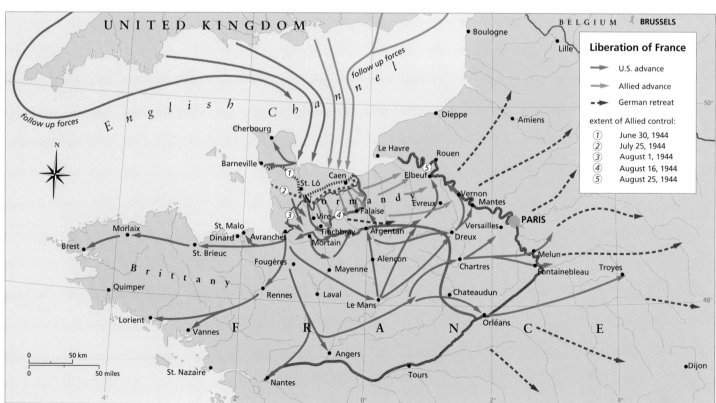

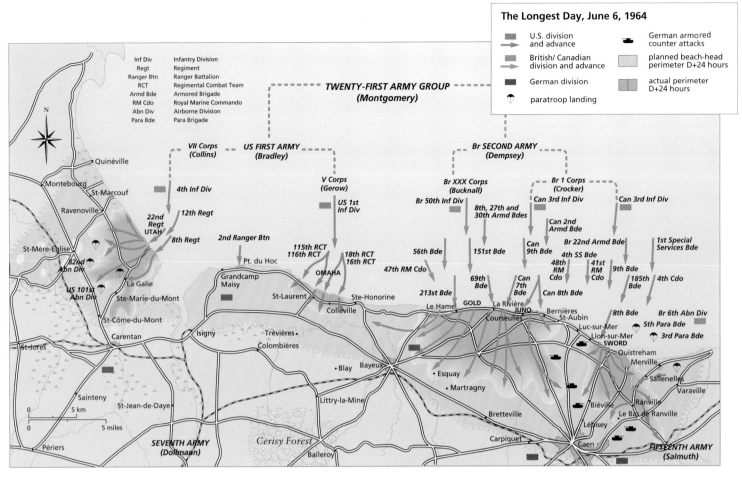

The Longest Day, June 6, 1964

▮→	U.S. division and advance	▬	German armored counter attacks
▮→	British/Canadian division and advance	▮	planned beach-head perimeter D+24 hours
▮	German division	▮	actual perimeter D+24 hours
☗	paratroop landing		

Inf Div	Infantry Division
Regt	Regiment
Ranger Btn	Ranger Battalion
RCT	Regimental Combat Team
Armd Bde	Armored Brigade
RM Cdo	Royal Marine Commando
Abn Div	Airborne Division
Para Bde	Para Brigade

TWENTY-FIRST ARMY GROUP
(Montgomery)

VII Corps (Collins) US FIRST ARMY (Bradley)

Br SECOND ARMY (Dempsey)

4th Inf Div

V Corps (Gerow)

Br XXX Corps (Bucknall) Br 1 Corps (Crocker)

Br 50th Inf Div Can 3rd Inf Div Can 3rd Inf Div

22nd Regt UTAH 12th Regt US 1st Inf Div 8th, 27th and 30th Armd Bdes Can 2nd Armd Bde

8th Regt 2nd Ranger Btn Can 9th Bde Br 22nd Armd Bde 1st Special Services Bde

115th RCT 116th RCT 18th RCT 16th RCT 56th Bde 151st Bde 4th SS Bde

82nd Abn Div Pt. du Hoc 47th RM Cdo 48th RM Cdo 41st RM Cdo 9th Bde

La Galie Grandcamp Maisy OMAHA 213st Bde 69th Bde Can 7th Bde Can 8th Bde 185th Bde 4th Cdo

US 101st Abn Div Ste-Marie-du-Mont St-Laurent Le Hamel GOLD La Rivière JUNO 8th Bde Br 6th Abn Div

St-Côme-du-Mont Colleville Ste-Honorine Courseulles St-Aubin 5th Para Bde

Carentan Isigny Trévières Luc-sur-Mer 3rd Para Bde

St-Jores Colombières Blay Bayeux Esquay Bernières Lion-sur-Mer SWORD

Sainteny Littry-la-Mine Martragny Ouistreham Merville

St-Jean-de-Daye Bretteville Biéville Ranville Sallenelles

SEVENTH ARMY (Dollmann) Cerisy Forest Carpiquet Le Bas de Ranville Varaville

Périers Balleroy Caen FIFTEENTH ARMY (Salmuth)

Quinéville · Montebourg · St-Marcouf · Ravenoville · St-Mère-Eglise

N

0 5 km
0 5 miles

The Allies to the rescue in Western Europe, 1944. Two and a half years after the United States entered the war, American soldiers (such as those pictured below) finally stormed into occupied France with their British and Canadian allies. The GIs encountered stiff resistance from the Nazis in Normandy and, later, at the Battle of the Bulge, but by the end of 1944 they had fought their way to Germany's frontiers. In the meantime, the Soviet Red Army closed in on the Reich from the east.

Battle of the Bulge, December 1944

➤	German attacks December 16–20
➤	German attacks December 21–24
⌒	U.S. front on the night of December 15
⋯	U.S. front on the night of December 20
⋯	Allied front on the night of December 24
☗	German airborne drop on the night of December 15

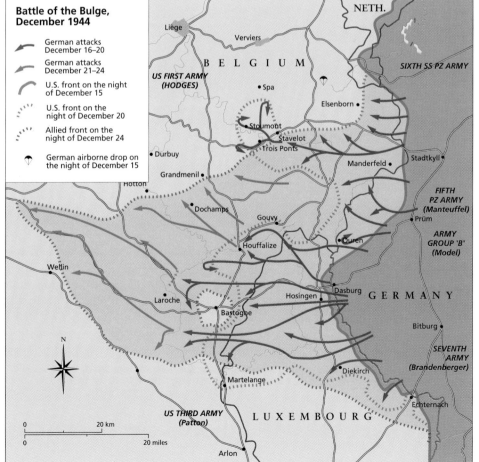

NETH.

Liège Verviers

BELGIUM

US FIRST ARMY (HODGES)

SIXTH SS PZ ARMY

· Spa

Elsenborn

· Stoumont

Stavelot

· Durbuy Trois Ponts Manderfeld Stadtkyll

Grandmenil

· Hotton

FIFTH PZ ARMY (Manteuffel)

· Dochamps Gouvy Prüm

· Houffalize Ouren ARMY GROUP 'B' (Model)

· Wellin

Laroche Hosingen Dasburg GERMANY

Bastogne Bitburg ·

SEVENTH ARMY (Brandenberger)

· Martelange Diekirch

US THIRD ARMY (Patton) LUXEMBOURG Echternach

Arlon

N

0 20 km
0 20 miles

195

PACIFIC COUNTERATTACK
THE JAPANESE ARE BROUGHT TO BRINK OF DEFEAT

Japanese expansion in the southwest Pacific was brought to a halt by the battles of the Coral Sea and Midway, but driving the Japanese back took a long and bloody struggle. Two separate forces, one largely a navy and Marine operation commanded by Admiral Chester Nimitz, the other a land operation commanded by General Douglas MacArthur, were involved.

The counterattack began with the American invasion of Guadalcanal, the largest of the Solomon Islands, a campaign that lasted from August 1942 until the following February. There were several titanic naval battles in which battleships were involved, but the capture of what became Henderson Field, which brought land-based planes into the fight, was probably decisive in winning the island.

Next the Americans swept through the Gilbert and Marshall islands, capturing Tarawa in November 1943, Kwajalein in late January 1944, and Eniwetok two weeks later. By the end of the summer Guam and Saipan in the Marianas were in American hands. Another major Japanese

base, Truk in the Caroline Islands, was destroyed by air strikes without the large loss of life that would have been involved in trying to invade it. From the Marianas, land-based bombers were within range of Japan itself.

Now the forces of Nimitz and MacArthur combined to strike the Philippines and then advance on Japan. General MacArthur's troops had already retaken New Guinea and parts of the Dutch East Indies. In June, an all-out attempt by the Japanese navy to prevent the landing of troops in the Philippines resulted in overwhelming sea-air victories for the United States in the Philippine Sea, namely the "Turkey Shoot," in which American planes downed 219 planes while losing only 29, and the sinking of three Japanese carriers and the damaging of four more by submarines and planes. After the Americans landed on

Leyte Island, south of Luzon, on October 20, the Japanese threw their remaining ships and planes into the Battle of Leyte Gulf, but they were overwhelmed by immensely superior forces and lost four carriers, three battleships and many smaller vessels. Thereafter Japan was incapable of mounting any kind of sustained air or sea attack.

The reconquest of the Philippine archipelago took many months. The Japanese soldiers fought bitterly and fell back slowly; as elsewhere, they tended to fight to the last man, and few were taken prisoner. By the end of January 1945, the fate of the islands had been decided.

On February 19, while fighting in the Philippines continued, Marine units stormed ashore on the tiny island of Iwo Jima, important because fighter escorts based on its two airstrips would be able to provide protection

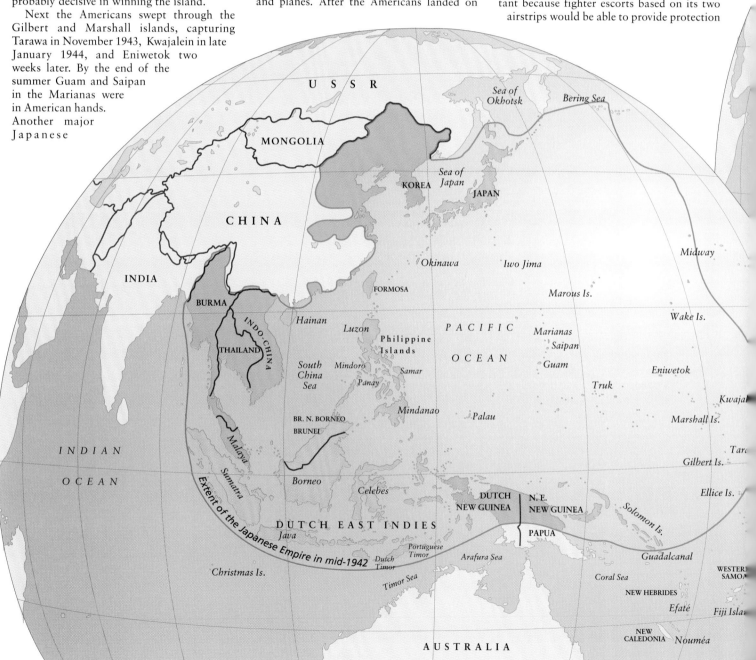

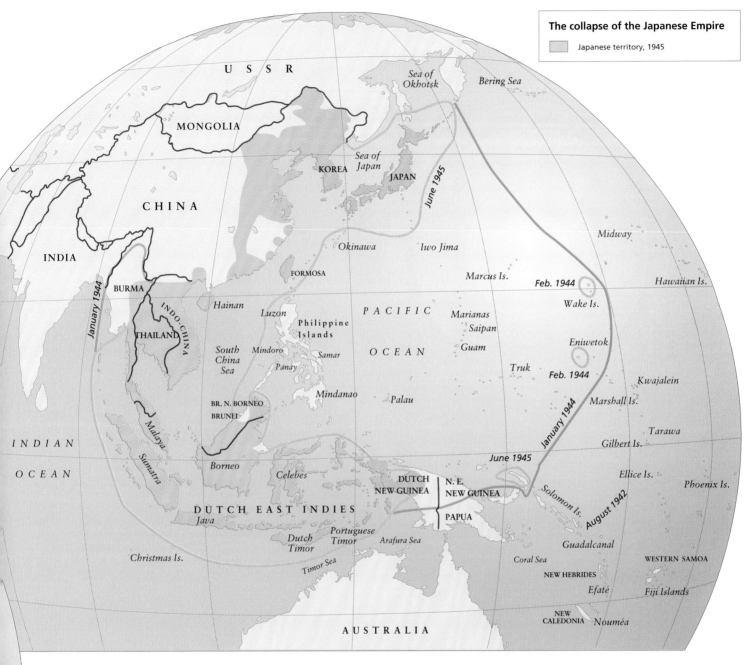

The collapse of the Japanese Empire

Japanese territory, 1945

U S S R

MONGOLIA

Sea of Okhotsk

Bering Sea

KOREA

Sea of Japan

JAPAN

June 1945

CHINA

Midway

Okinawa

Iwo Jima

FORMOSA

Marcus Is.

Hawaiian Is.

INDIA

Feb. 1944

Wake Is.

BURMA

January 1944

Hainan

Luzon

Philippine Islands

P A C I F I C

Marianas

Saipan

THAILAND

INDO-CHINA

South China Sea

Mindoro

Samar

O C E A N

Guam

Eniwetok

Truk

Feb. 1944

Kwajalein

Panay

Marshall Is.

Mindanao

Palau

January 1944

BR. N. BORNEO

BRUNEI

Tarawa

Malaya

Gilbert Is.

I N D I A N

Borneo

June 1945

Ellice Is.

Phoenix Is.

Sumatra

O C E A N

Celebes

DUTCH NEW GUINEA

N. E. NEW GUINEA

Solomon Is.

August 1942

DUTCH EAST INDIES

PAPUA

Java

Dutch Timor

Portuguese Timor

Arafura Sea

Guadalcanal

WESTERN SAMOA

Christmas Is.

Coral Sea

NEW HEBRIDES

Efaté

Fiji Islands

Timor Sea

NEW CALEDONIA

Nouméa

AUSTRALIA

On June 15, 1944, 700 amphibious vehicles carrying men of the second and fourth Marine divisions landed on Saipan and met with heavy resistance from the 32,000 men commanded by Lieutenant General Yoshitsugu Saito. Little by little, in determined groups, the marines forced their way inland and by nightfall had established a bridgehead, though suffering the loss of some 2,000 men. By this time the U.S. Navy and Marine Corps had almost perfected the amphibious assault, but the Japanese themselves nearly perfected multi-layered defenses to such assaults.

for the heavy bombers that were striking Japan from bases in the Marianas, which was beyond the fighters' range. After a month of heavy fighting, Iwo Jima was secured. Then, on April 1, army units struck at the last Japanese outpost, Okinawa, which was even closer to the main Japanese islands. There was much hard fighting, by the end of April most of Okinawa was in American hands and by June the battle was over. United States forces suffered about 75,000 casualties in subduing these two islands.

The end was now certain, but it seemed likely that an invasion of Japan proper would be even more costly. This helps to explain why the atom bombs were dropped on Hiroshima, August 6, and Nagasaki, August 9. On September 2, formal surrender took place in Tokyo Bay aboard USS *Missouri*.

THE MANHATTAN PROJECT AND ITS AFTERMATH
THE DAWN OF A NEW AGE

At 2:45 a.m. on August 6, 1945, Colonel Paul Tibbets took off in his B-29 from Tinian air base and flew to Iwo Jima, then toward the southern top of Honshu Island. At 8:50 a.m. he achieved landfall over Shikoku, Japan, and proceeded west across the Inland Sea. Several minutes later he spotted Hiroshima harbor. After locating the target—the T-shaped Aioi Bridge just above a fork in the Ota River—he released a 4-ton bomb. Forty-three seconds later, a blinding light flashed through the cockpit and shock waves jolted the plane upward. When Tibbets turned the plane back toward the city, he saw a mushroom-shaped cloud ascend from a blackened mass that had been Hiroshima.

The uranium bomb that initiated the atomic age was the culmination of the Manhattan Project, a secret U.S. enterprise that in three years transformed a speculative notion by theoretical physicists into a mechanism of unimaginable destruction.

The $2-billion project entailed the collaboration of university scientists, private industry, and the U.S. army. It had two main components: production of the explosive raw material—either uranium 235 or plutonium, an element made from uranium—and the design and construction of the bomb itself. Theoretical research on uranium 235 was centered at Berkeley; research on plutonium was carried out at the University of Chicago. The uranium 235 was produced at Oak Ridge, Tennessee; the plutonium was produced at Hanford, Washington. Early in the project, the chief bomb design facility, headed by J. Robert Oppenheimer, was removed to Los Alamos, a tiny community in the desert north of Albuquerque, New Mexico.

Project physicists, certain that the U235 bomb would go off as planned, saw no reason to waste its precious fissionable material in a test. A bomb made of the more unstable plutonium was successfully detonated on July 16, 1945, at Alamagordo, New Mexico. On July 24, President Harry Truman authorized use of these weapons to force Japan into submission.

Incendiary Bombing at Dresden
Secretary of War Stimson abhorred the bombing of cities, but the precedent for such atrocities had been set by German attacks on London. The Allies retaliated with the fire-bombing of Dresden on February 13, 1945, resulting in the almost complete destruction of the city and the death of 130,000 people, and with the firebombing of Tokyo, killing 100,000 people and injuring nearly 1 million, most of them civilians. The atomic bomb represented the logical—albeit horrendous—extension of this indiscriminate lethality.

Hirsohima
By the spring of 1945, most Japanese cities, having already been reduced to rubble by incendiary or conventional bombs, were regarded as unsuited to demonstrate the destructiveness of the atomic bomb. Hiroshima, "the largest untouched target," was the preferred target of the War Department, which ordered that it be spared further conventional bombing attacks. The choice of Hiroshima was further justified by the fact that the Imperial Army Fifth Division was headquartered in an ancient castle there. Kokura, Nagasaki, and Niigata were included in the final list of potential targets.

Tibbets' bomb fell within 800 feet of its target on the Ota River. The area within a mile and a half radius of the point of explosion was ruined instantaneously. Of 76,000 buildings in Hiroshima, 48,000 were shattered by the blast or completely destroyed by fire. Almost everyone within a half-mile of the explosion perished immediately. Total fatalities approached 140,000. A further 60,000 would die from radiation poisoning or other injuries sustained in the attack.

Nagasaki
Because Japan did not surrender immediately, U.S. army officials ordered a second atomic bomb to be dropped. The target city was Kokura, on the north coast of Kyushu. But on August 9, Kokura was obscured by clouds and the pilot of the B-29 flew to the secondary target, Nagasaki, home of the Mitsubishi factories that had manufactured the torpedoes used at Pearl Harbor. Clouds hung over the harbor, so the bombardier aimed for a stadium several miles upriver. The bomb exploded just above the Nagasaki Medical College and Hospital, the Chinzoo High School, and the Yamazato Elementary School. The explosion, though twice as powerful as that which obliterated Hiroshima, was confined by the steep hills on both sides of the river. Moreover, civil defense authorities, having anticipated an incendiary attack, had demolished swaths of buildings to serve as firebreaks. Seven thousand school children, assigned to clear debris in the firebreaks, were among the first of the 75,000 to die. Japan surrendered on August 15.

Radiation Leaks at Hanford
The plutonium for the Nagasaki bomb had been produced by nuclear reactors at Hanford, Washington. Driven by the exigencies of war, plant operators had repeatedly released radioactive by-products into the atmosphere, extensively contaminating portions of the Pacific Northwest. But the most serious contamination occurred four years after the war. In December 1949, the Atomic Energy Commission, seeking to determine whether or not its instruments could detect plutonium plants in the Soviet Union, arranged for 5,500 curies of radioactive iodine to be released at Hanford. The people of southeastern Washington were never notified of the release, which was 11,000 times greater than the AEC's official "tolerance threshold." By contrast, the release of 15 to 24 curies of radioactive iodine during the Three Mile Island accident in 1979 prompted the evacuation of the area around Harrisburg, Pennsylvania.

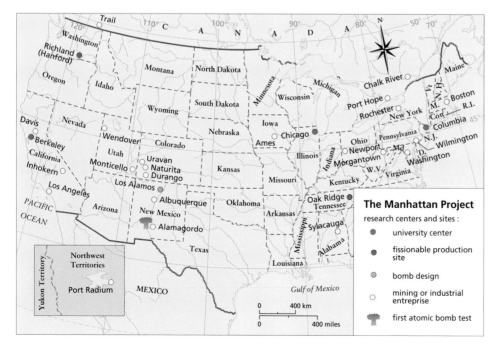

The Manhattan Project

research centers and sites :

- university center
- fissionable production site
- bomb design
- mining or industrial entreprise
- first atomic bomb test

0   400 km

0   400 miles

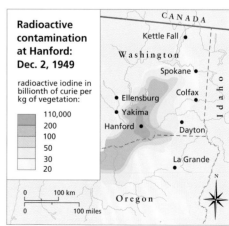

Radioactive contamination at Hanford: Dec. 2, 1949

radioactive iodine in billionth of curie per kg of vegetation:

- 110,000
- 200
- 100
- 50
- 30
- 20

0   100 km

0   100 miles

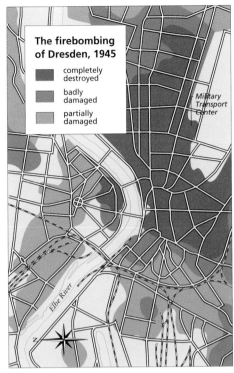

The firebombing of Dresden, 1945

- completely destroyed
- badly damaged
- partially damaged

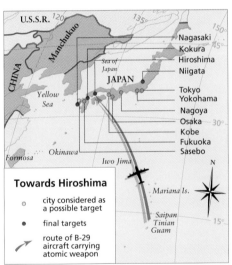

Towards Hiroshima

- ○ city considered as a possible target
- ● final targets
- ⤳ route of B-29 aircraft carrying atomic weapon

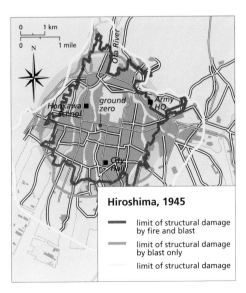

Hiroshima, 1945

- limit of structural damage by fire and blast
- limit of structural damage by blast only
- limit of structural damage

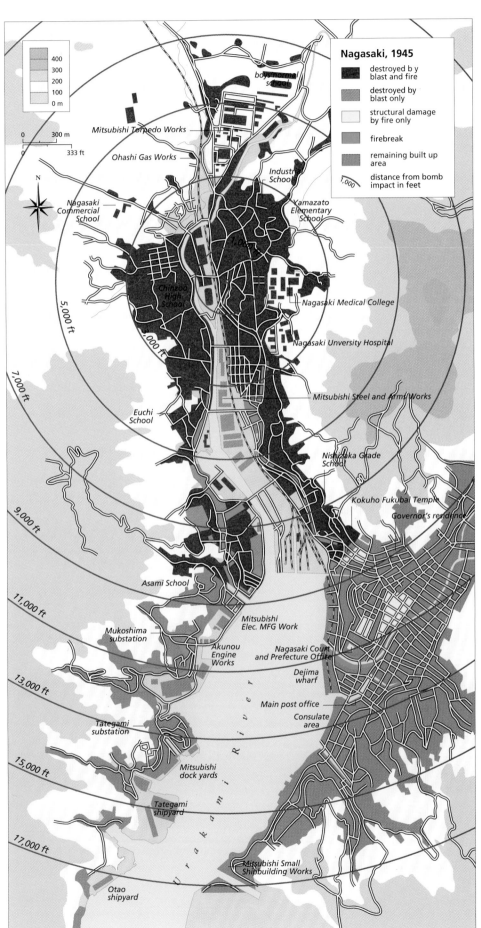

Nagasaki, 1945

- destroyed by blast and fire
- destroyed by blast only
- structural damage by fire only
- firebreak
- remaining built up area
- 1,000 distance from bomb impact in feet

JAPANESE IMMIGRANTS, JAPANESE INTERNEES
DETENTION AND EVACUATION IN THE WAKE OF PEARL HARBOR

Japanese emigration to Hawaii began in 1868, when the isolationist Tokugawa clan that had ruled Japan for centuries was overthrown by Matsuhito, the self-proclaimed Meiji Emperor. Matsuhito sought to weaken opposing traditional warlords by abolishing feudalism and encouraging trade with the West. Later that year, Hawaiian planters arrived in Tokyo and Yokohama, seeking to recruit unemployed young men to work on sugar plantations. Several hundred laborers signed contracts and left for Hawaii. But these Japanese city dwellers, many of them vagrants, proved ill-suited to agricultural labor in a foreign culture. Most returned to Japan, often at the expense of the planter, within one or two years of their departure.

Subsequent Hawaiian labor contractors searched among the landless or impoverished farmers of southwestern Honshu or Kyushu, particularly the coastal districts that traditionally sent sons to sea or to serve as warriors. After 1882, this region was ravaged by a succession of storms, floods, and droughts. During the next 13 years, 30,000 Japanese emigrated to Hawaii as contract laborers; three-quarters came from Hiroshima or Yamaguchi, and most of the remainder from nearby Kumamoto or Fukuoka.

After 1890, when Japanese emigration increased sharply, most of the emigrants came from the same regions that had sent contract laborers to Hawaii. Based on the data compiled from 1899 through 1903, 85,000 Japanese were issued passports for destinations other than Korea or China; four-fifths of this number booked passage on ships for Hawaii or the mainland United States. Half of these passports had been issued for residents of Hiroshima, Kumamoto, Yamaguchi, or Fukuoka. All but one of the remaining districts with over 2,000 emigrants were from southwestern Honshu or Kyushu. (The exception was Niigata.)

Emigration to California

From 1890 to 1924, 295,820 Japanese came to the mainland United States, especially California. Most of the early Japanese immigrants to California worked as hired hands on farms in the San Francisco Bay region, but by 1910 they had moved down the Salinas River Valley to Los Angeles and east into the Central Valley formed by the Sacramento and San Joaquin rivers. Other Japanese escaped the rigors of rural life to work as domestic servants or to run small shops and restaurants in San Francisco, Los Angeles, Sacramento, Fresno, or other California towns and cities.

Wartime Evacuation and Internment

After Japan's attack on Pearl Harbor on December 7, 1941 (see America enters World War II, p 188–189), panicky West Coast politicians called for the detention and evacuation of all persons of Japanese extraction. General John L. DeWitt, commander of West Coast defenses, claimed that the 112,000 Japanese and Japanese-Americans in his region were "potential enemies" preparing for "concerted action" against his command. On February 19, 1942, President Franklyn D. Roosevelt signed Executive Order 9066 empowering DeWitt and other military officials to evacuate and intern the Japanese, most of them American citizens, who had been forced to sell their property and to report to regional assembly centers. From there they were transported to relocation centers and internment camps in remote sections of eastern California, the Rocky Mountain states, Arizona, New Mexico, North Dakota, and Arkansas.

After the war, most Japanese made their way back to the communities that they had been forced to leave. In 1950, it is probable that more Japanese lived in Los Angeles, San Francisco, and Fresno than before the war. Interned Japanese were less likely to return to the farms of the Sacramento, San Joaquin, Salinas, and Imperial valleys. The extreme example is Imperial County, which reported only 200 Japanese in 1950—1,400 fewer than had lived there in 1940.

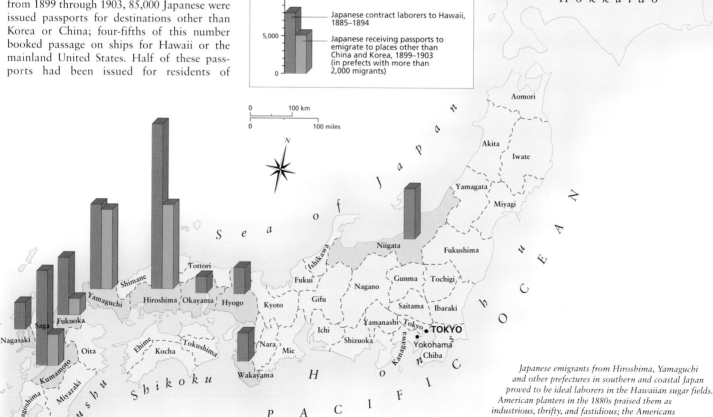

Sources of Japanese emigrants, 1880–1903

number of migrants per prefect:

Japanese contract laborers to Hawaii, 1885–1894

Japanese receiving passports to emigrate to places other than China and Korea, 1899–1903 (in prefects with more than 2,000 migrants)

Japanese emigrants from Hiroshima, Yamaguchi and other prefectures in southern and coastal Japan proved to be ideal laborers in the Hawaiian sugar fields. American planters in the 1880s praised them as industrious, thrifty, and fastidious; the Americans complained that workers from Tokyo, Yokohama and other urban areas tended to be "lazy and self-indulgent" and prone to "gambling."

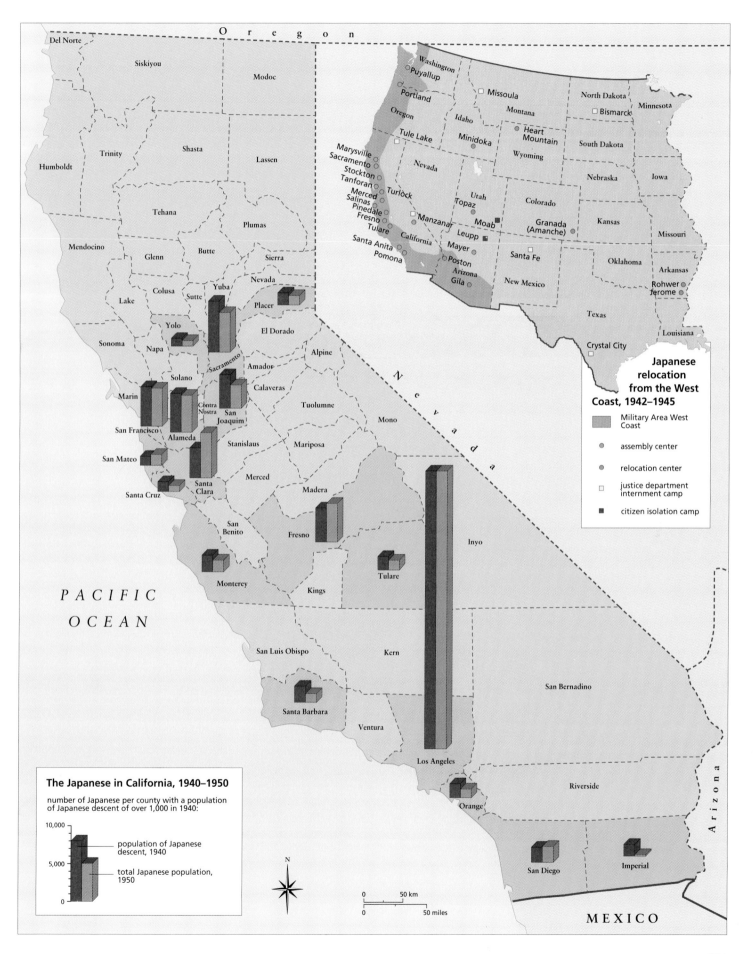

Del Norte

O r e g o n

Siskiyou

Modoc

Humboldt

Trinity

Shasta

Lassen

Mendocino

Tehana

Plumas

Glenn

Butte

Sierra

Lake

Colusa

Sutte

Yuba

Nevada

Placer

Yolo

El Dorado

Sonoma

Napa

Alpine

Amador

Sacramento

Solano

Calaveras

Marin

Contra
Nostra

San
Joaquim

Tuolumne

San Francisco

Alameda

Stanislaus

Mariposa

San Mateo

Santa
Clara

Mono

Santa Cruz

Merced

Madera

San
Benito

Fresno

PACIFIC

Monterey

Kings

OCEAN

Tulare

Inyo

San Luis Obispo

Kern

San Bernadino

Santa Barbara

Ventura

Los Angeles

Riverside

Orange

San Diego

Imperial

A r i z o n a

N e v a d a

N

MEXICO

Washington
Puyallup

Portland

Oregon

Missoula

North Dakota

Minnesota

Bismarck

Montana

Tule Lake

Idaho

Minidoka

Heart
Mountain

Wyoming

South Dakota

Marysville
Sacramento
Stockton
Tanforan
Merced
Salinas
Pinedale
Fresno
Tulare

Turlock

Nevada

Utah
Topaz

Moab

Colorado

Nebraska

Iowa

Manzanar

Leupp

Granada
(Amanche)

Kansas

Missouri

Santa Anita
Pomona

California

Mayer

Poston

Santa Fe

Oklahoma

Arkansas

Arizona

New Mexico

Rohwer
Jerome

Gila

Texas

Louisiana

Crystal City

**Japanese
relocation
from the West
Coast, 1942–1945**

Military Area West
Coast

⦿ assembly center

● relocation center

▫ justice department
internment camp

■ citizen isolation camp

The Japanese in California, 1940–1950

number of Japanese per county with a population
of Japanese descent of over 1,000 in 1940:

10,000

5,000

0

population of Japanese
descent, 1940

total Japanese population,
1950

0   50 km

0   50 miles

PART 7: POST-WAR AMERICA

Having barely cleaned up from the victory celebrations, many Americans looked uneasily to the future. Would rapid demobilization and the cancellation of war contracts push the nation back into the Great Depression? Would the discontents of the poor catch fire this time and explode in revolution? The answer came quickly, and it was emphatic. Paced by the auto and housing industries, the postwar economy surged forward; and politics were mostly placid, despite the usual froth of scandal and personal enmity, for the Democratic and Republican parties rested upon similar ideological foundations. Even the intellectuals, many of whom had embraced radical nostrums in the 1930s, now exalted America's polity for having transcended the social and ideological antagonisms of Europe. By the mid-1960s, however, the social fabric of the nation began to fray. The affluence and confidence of some Americans appeared to intensify the poverty and despair of others, a contrast all the more unsettling for being so often etched in white and black.

WHITE FLIGHT
TO THE SUN AND THE SUBURBS

The Great Depression of the 1930s shook millions of landless farmers and unemployed workers loose from their roots. When war came in 1941, many people gravitated to the defense plants that sprang up in the Far West, especially California. After the war, more young people streamed westward for high-paying jobs in the booming aircraft and electronics industries. Their numbers were swollen by retired persons who, despairing of northern winters, longed to relax in the "sunbelt." From 1940 through 1960, more than 6 million Americans relocated to California alone. By 1963, it had passed New York to become the most populous state in the Union. Arizona, Nevada, and Florida grew even more rapidly.

More than 90 percent of the people migrating to the Far West and mountain states were white; most came from states of the Great Plains or the South. An even higher proportion of whites moved to Florida. At the same time, blacks were leaving the South in droves and relocating to the industrial Northeast and Midwest. Of the more than 3 million blacks who quit Southern states, 2 million were from Mississippi, Alabama, Georgia, or South Carolina.

To the Suburbs

In addition to these shifts between regions, another demographic transformation was altering the appearance of cities and the nature of race relations. Middle-class whites were flooding into the suburbs (see The suburban dream, p 206–207), and their places were being taken by a steady stream of blacks from Southern states.

Federal housing officials contributed to this pattern of racial segregation by providing mortgages to the new suburbs and denying them to city dwellers. The FHA "Residential Security Map" for St. Louis for 1937, for example, gave the highest ratings to the white suburbs of University City, Ladue, Clayton, and Webster Groves. The predominantly black neighborhoods around the business-district were given the lowest ratings. Federal

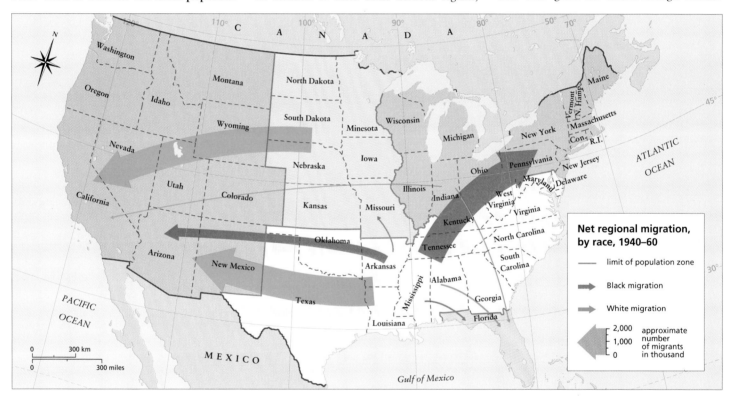

Net regional migration, by race, 1940–60

— limit of population zone

→ Black migration

→ White migration

2,000 / 1,000 / 0 approximate number of migrants in thousand

An End to Annexation

The rift between poor urban blacks and middle-class suburban whites was intensified by the failure of annexation campaigns in the 20th century. Cities have always grown outward as well as upward. During the 19th century, as population spilled beyond the city limits, suburban residents seeking municipal water, sewer, police, and fire services commonly petitioned to be annexed. In 1854, Philadelphia, sited on two square miles of land, annexed 128 square miles. In 1889, Chicago added the South Side, covering 133 square miles. In 1898, the nation's most populous city, New York, annexed Brooklyn, the fourth largest city, along with Queens, Staten Island, and the Bronx.

But as historian Kenneth T. Jackson has observed, 20th-century suburbanites, having fled the city, have fiercely opposed annexation proposals. St. Louis, which almost quadrupled its total area in 1876, has not succeeded in any subsequent annexations. Thus the increasingly black—and poor—inner cities have been forced to rely on their own diminishing resources to solve staggering problems of poverty, crime, and housing.

In the past four decades, annexation has taken place almost entirely in the new cities of the "sunbelt" and Far West, where the disparity in income or racial composition between the city and the suburbs is not great. From 1930 to 1980, Dallas achieved a ten-fold increase in area; during the same period, Phoenix grew from 10 square miles to 325 square miles.

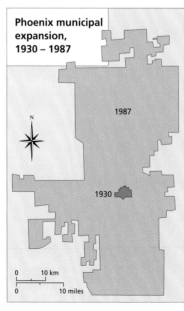

Phoenix municipal expansion, 1930 – 1987

1987

1930

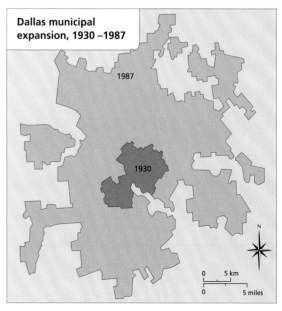

Dallas municipal expansion, 1930 –1987

1987

1930

lending agencies expanded upon their blue-chip rating for Ladue, noting that the community featured expensive homes and wooded estates and was inhabited by "capitalists and other wealthy families" without even a single "foreigner or black." Conversely, federal appraisers intentionally downgraded neighborhoods with a "rapidly increasing Negro population." From 1934 through 1960, the FHA underwrote 75,000 mortgages for over $650 million in St. Louis and its suburbs. But only 12,000 of these mortgages, for a total of $94 million, were issued for properties within the St. Louis city limits.

Denied federally-insured loans, the decrepit, congested housing stock of downtown St. Louis deteriorated rapidly. The market for houses and apartments in the area collapsed. Panicky whites accepted whatever they could get for their homes and fled the city. Their places were often taken by blacks recently arrived from the rural South. During the 1950s, the white population of the city of St. Louis declined by more than 200,000, while the black population increased by 100,000. Much of the city's declining central core was now almost entirely black. Meanwhile, the suburban townships in St. Louis County west of the city gained nearly 300,000 people, an astounding increase of 73 percent. More than 99 percent of the suburban residents were white.

With mortgages underwritten by the FHA, whites left the city for the leafy, sunlit, and safe gardens of suburbia.

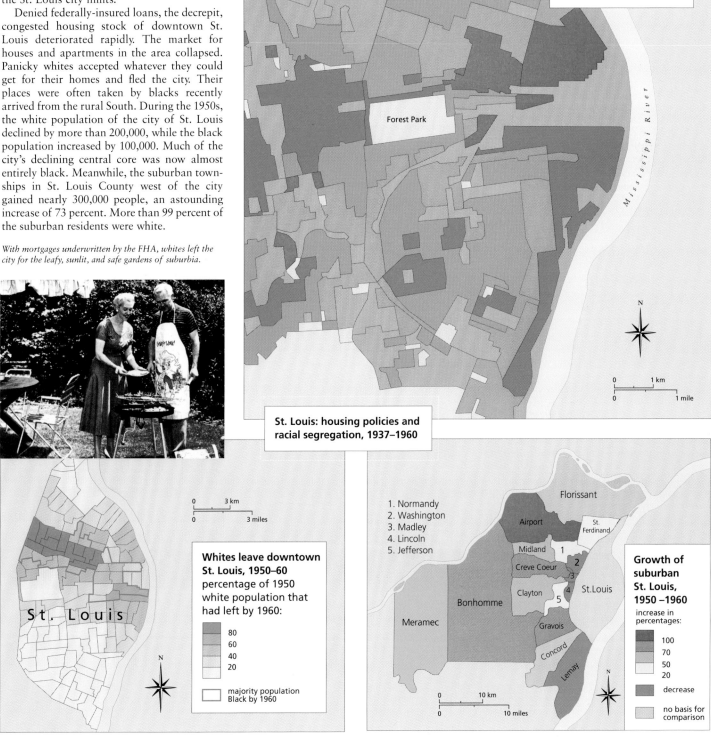

Federal Housing Authority real estate "security" rating, 1937
- highest
- second highest
- second lowest
- lowest
- industrial or commercial, or not assessed

Forest Park

Mississippi River

St. Louis: housing policies and racial segregation, 1937–1960

Whites leave downtown St. Louis, 1950–60
percentage of 1950 white population that had left by 1960:
- 80
- 60
- 40
- 20
- majority population Black by 1960

St. Louis

1. Normandy
2. Washington
3. Madley
4. Lincoln
5. Jefferson

Florissant
Airport
St. Ferdinand
Midland
Creve Coeur
Clayton
Bonhomme
Meramec
Gravois
Concord
Lemay
St. Louis

Growth of suburban St. Louis, 1950–1960
increase in percentages:
- 100
- 70
- 50
- 20
- decrease
- no basis for comparison

THE SUBURBAN DREAM

CENTRAL PARK AND LEVITTOWN

Nineteenth-century Americans, though exhilarated by their nation's burgeoning cities and industries, often expressed misgivings over the cultural ramifications of urban life. Even as Ralph Waldo Emerson extolled the virtues of civilization and the benefits of science, he assailed the city as artificial, unnatural and bereft of solitude. And Walt Whitman, who in 1868 confessed to having been taken in by the enchantments of Broadway, four years later placed Manhattan under a "moral microscope" and found it "crowded with petty grotesques, malformations, phantoms, playing meaningless antics." From the mid-19th century to the present, Americans have dreamt of reconciling the economic benefits of the city with the bucolic pleasures of the country.

The solution was to be found in the creation of self-consciously picturesque commuter communities just beyond the city limits. The first such suburb was Llewellyn Park, built in 1856 in West Orange, New Jersey, by Llewellyn S. Haskell, a wealthy New York merchant and member of the Perfectionist sect. Haskell hired Alexander Jackson Davis, author of *Rural Residences* (1837), to plan the community. Llewellyn Park was designed for New York City businessmen who desired "accessible, retired, and healthful homes in the country." Davis accordingly improved upon nature by clearing expansive vistas and framing them with rocks and trees; by constructing seven miles of gracefully winding roads and giving them names such as Tulip, Mountain, and Passive; and by adding a fifty-acre pedestrian "Ramble" through the adjacent woods.

But middle class New Yorkers could hardly afford the time and cost of the thirteen-mile train commute from Llewellyn Park to Manhattan, much less the price tag of the large homes on their three-acre lots. Most 19th-century planners consequently preferred to bring the psychic and cultural advantages of the countryside into the city. While Davis was laying out the serpentine roads of their suburban retreat, Frederick Law Olmsted and Calvert Vaux were designing curvilinear paths and roadways for New York City's Central Park. They rejected as models the broad boulevards and symmetrical designs of European parks; in their opinion, the purpose of the urban park was not to serve as adornment for the city itself, nor to reiterate the logic that underlay its greatness, but to provide a picturesque respite from those functional exigencies. This they accomplished by interrupting the grim succession of rectangular blocks that had marched northward up the island with graceful footpaths that meandered through the natural hills and rocky outcroppings.

The dream of a detached suburban home persisted through the late 19th and early 20th centuries. That this dream became a reality for hundreds of thousands of middle and lower middle class white Americans was the achievement of Abraham Levitt and his sons, William and Alfred. Anticipating the acute shortage of housing following World War II, the Levitts in 1946 bought 4,000 acres of potato farm on Long Island, bulldozed the entire tract, and plopped down thousands of 30' by 25' slabs of concrete upon which they assembled essentially pre-fabricated homes at a rate of nearly thirty a day. The homes sold for the bargain price of $6,990. By the end of the 1950s, Levittown was nearly complete, consisting of 17,400 houses. Thousands of builders around the nation copied the Levitts' techniques and pirated their designs.

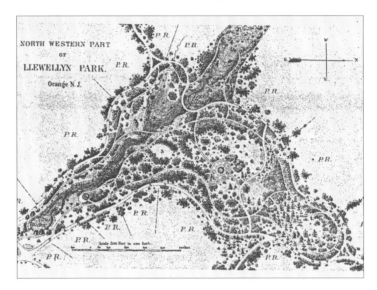

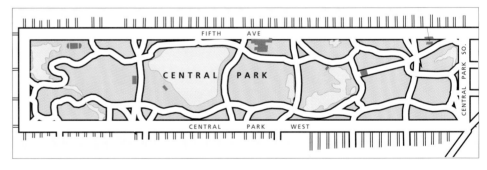

(Left) *The original plan of Llewellyn Park, New Jersey, the nation's first planned suburban community (1856). The developers improved upon nature by making it tidy and picturesque, with planned asymmetry and curvilinear roads.*

The original "Greensward" plan (bottom) *for Central Park (1858) sought to impose a similar conception of nature upon the functional, rectangular grids of Manhattan. Central Park as built* (below) *added more pathways and roads.*

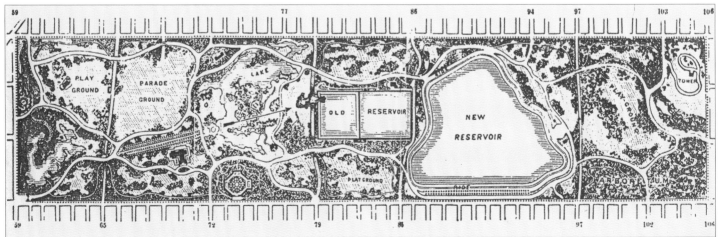

Mass-production economies required that Levitts' houses be essentially identical in form and construction. The layout of the ground floor almost never varied: the living room and kitchen looked out upon the front lawn; two bedrooms were at the back. The total living space was 750 square feet, although many families finished off the attic. The exteriors varied little. By 1950 the Levitts' offered four superficially different models. The sameness of the homes was matched by the demographic profile of the inhabitants. Most couples were in their thirties; virtually none were black.

(Right) In addition to Levittown, Long Island, the Levitts constructed "Levittowns" outside Philadelphia and in Willingboro, New Jersey. Although these Levittowns were more densely populated than some cities, the Levitts evoked an anti-urban imagery by using carvilinear streets instead of rectangular urban blocks, and by naming those streets after foliage and flowers (Sweetbriar, Daffodil, Farmbrook) or, more obviously, after contented and restful emotional states (Friendly, Freedom, Graceful, Good).

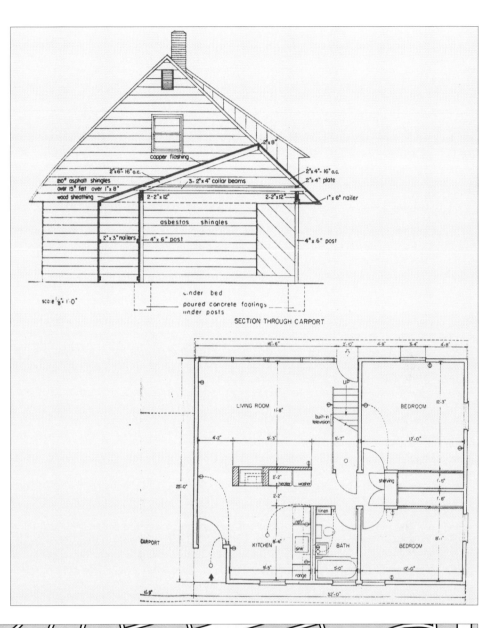

SECTION THROUGH CARPORT

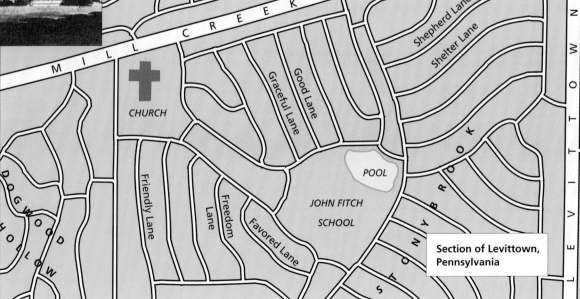

Section of Levittown, Pennsylvania

207

THE AGE OF THE AUTOMOBILE
MOTOR CARS FOR THE MULTITUDE

"I will build a motor car for the great multitude," proclaimed Henry Ford in 1909, shortly after he had begun mass-producing his Model T—the "Tin Lizzie"—an automobile "so low in price that no man making a good salary will be unable to own one." In that year Americans owned 300,000 automobiles; by 1925 more than 20 million motorcars—many of them Model Ts—were bouncing along the cobblestone streets of the nation's cities, or plowing through its deeply rutted country roads. Ford's inexpensive cars captured the public's imagination from the start, but the final triumph of the automobile over other forms of transportation depended on the construction of thousands of miles of low-friction asphalt and concrete roadways.

Rise of the Freeways
In most communities, road construction was accomplished by a coalition of automobile owners and retailers, oil company dealers, road builders, and land developers who demanded that federal, state and local governments build high-speed expressways for the exclusive use of automobiles. One of the first such roadways was the Long Island Motor Parkway, completed in 1911. During the 1930s, California, a state whose growth coincided with and largely depended on the ascendancy of the automobile, planned a vast network of expressways. The first section of the system, the Arroyo Seco Parkway (now the Pasadena Freeway), was financed by Los Angeles businessmen seeking to channel traffic into downtown Los Angeles. It was completed in 1940. To the businessmen's consternation, however, the new freeway choked the downtown streets with cars, encouraged the flight of city dwellers to Pasadena and sent real estate prices there soaring. Suburban developers and builders elsewhere demanded that their communities be hooked up to freeways. Similar if somewhat less extensive systems developed in most other states.

The Interstate Highway System
Planning for a national network of roadways began during World War II. In the 1940s and early 1950s, a powerful lobby consisting of General Motors and the other car makers, the oil, rubber, asphalt, and construction industries, the trucking and bus companies, and the labor unions, pressured Congress to place gasoline taxes into a Highway Trust Fund, whose revenues could not be diverted to other uses. The Interstate Highway act, which created a 41,000-mile system, was enacted into law in 1956. The required funding was 90 percent provided by the federal government.

The automobile is responsible for much that is distinctive in American culture. Courtship, which once proceeded on the front porch of the girl's parents, shifted during the 1920s, as historian Beth Bailey put it, to the "back seat"

of the boy's automobile. The characteristic nuclear family acquired a breezy informality by taking nourishment together (of a sort) in "drive-in" and "fast food" restaurants, by watching "drive-in" movies, and by traveling to "See the U.S.A. in a Chevrolet." Even iconoclasts—like the beat writer Jack Kerouac—sought their adventures On the Road.

The superhighways helped to knit the nation together, efface the distinctions between country and city, and relieve local roads of unwanted through-traffic. These benefits are suggested by the maps of Rhode Island (below), which show how the construction of Interstate I-95 reduced travel time to Providence from Washington County by about 15 to 20 minutes. Moreover, the volume of traffic on local roads adjacent to the interstate fell about 10 percent.

But all too often the construction of high-speed highways resulted in a tremendous increase in the overall volume of traffic. The case of Los Angeles in instructive. In the early 1950s the downtown streets of the city were already clogged with traffic . Much of this traffic was to be diverted by the completion of the

Hollywood, Harbor, and Santa Monica Freeways. By the late 1950s and early 1960s the plan appeared to be working. South Figueroa Street, Sunset Boulevard, and Washington Boulevard, streets that had carried between 25,000 and 40,000 cars a day in 1954, now carried between 10,000 and 20,000. On the other hand, adjacent expressways—the Harbor Freeway, the Hollywood Freeway, and the Santa Monica Freeway, had almost attained their capacity of 126,000 cars each. The city, satisfied that the freeways had solved its transportation problems, allowed its modest surface rail public transportation system to be dismantled.

But by the late 1980s, traffic in central Los Angeles had reached staggering levels. The three major freeways together carried nearly a million cars each day; and South Figueroa, Sunset Boulevard, and Washington Boulevard—like many other local streets—were almost as congested with traffic as they had been in the 1950s. Nearly two-thirds of the downtown area now consists of highways, parking lots, and interchanges. In 1984, belatedly recognizing the error of its ways, Los Angeles broke ground for an 18-mile subway.

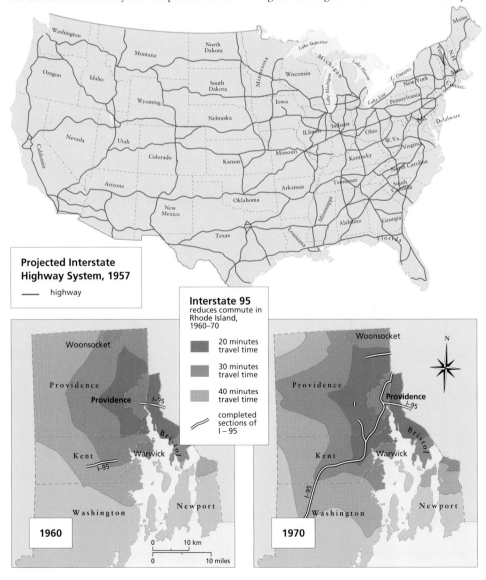

Projected Interstate Highway System, 1957
—— highway

Interstate 95
reduces commute in Rhode Island, 1960–70

- 20 minutes travel time
- 30 minutes travel time
- 40 minutes travel time
- completed sections of I–95

1960

1970

0   10 km
0   10 miles

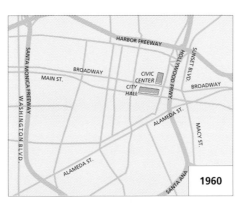

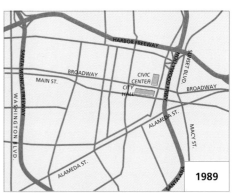

Traffic in Downtown Los Angeles, 1954–89
Freeways relieve congestion, and then make it worse

	local street	freeway
normal flow		
over-capacity		

1954

1960

1989

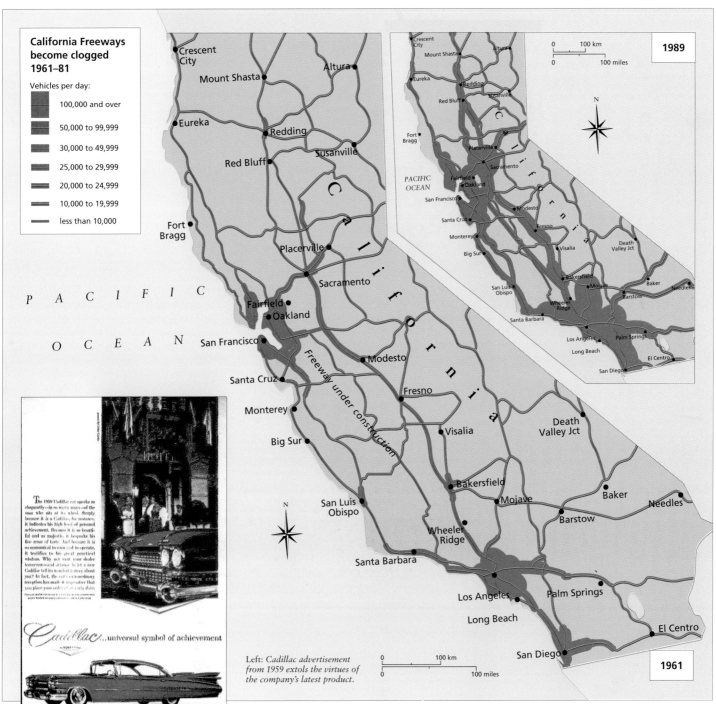

California Freeways become clogged 1961–81

Vehicles per day:

- 100,000 and over
- 50,000 to 99,999
- 30,000 to 49,999
- 25,000 to 29,999
- 20,000 to 24,999
- 10,000 to 19,999
- less than 10,000

1989

1961

PACIFIC OCEAN

PACIFIC OCEAN

California

Freeway under construction

Crescent City
Mount Shasta
Altura
Eureka
Redding
Red Bluff
Susanville
Fort Bragg
Placerville
Sacramento
Fairfield
Oakland
San Francisco
Modesto
Santa Cruz
Fresno
Monterey
Big Sur
Visalia
Death Valley Jct
San Luis Obispo
Bakersfield
Mojave
Baker
Needles
Wheeler Ridge
Barstow
Santa Barbara
Los Angeles
Palm Springs
Long Beach
San Diego
El Centro

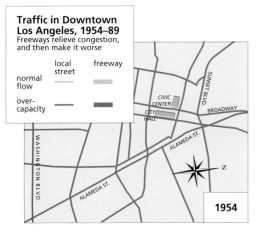

Cadillac... universal symbol of achievement

Left: Cadillac advertisement from 1959 extols the virtues of the company's latest product.

THE BROWN DECISION
SEGREGATION IN THE SOUTH

In 1954, when the Supreme Court in Brown v. Board of Education struck down segregation in public education, only three of the 4,355 school districts in the South were integrated. In 8 Southern states no black children attended school with whites. The Brown decision thus held the promise of dismantling the elaborate system of racial segregation that Southern officials had painstakingly erected since Reconstruction. Many doubted that such momentous reforms could be accomplished through federal edict. One of the skeptics was the man charged with enforcing the order: President Dwight D. Eisenhower. "The fellow who tries to tell me you can do these things by force is just plain nuts," he told an aide.

The Crisis in Little Rock

Mindful of Eisenhower's irresolution, almost all Southern governors and school officials ignored the federal district courts that had ordered them to comply with Brown. In 1957, all schools in Alabama, Florida, Georgia, Louisiana, Mississippi, North Carolina, South Carolina, and Virginia remained completely segregated.

In the fall of that year a moderate school board in Little Rock, Arkansas—a city that viewed itself as a symbol of the "New South"—admitted nine black students to all-white Central High. Governor Orval Faubus, anticipating a stiff challenge from staunch segregationists in the 1958 Democratic primary, called up the National Guard and ordered them to prevent the black students

As white onlookers taunt, Elizabeth Eckford attempts to register at Little Rock's Central High School in 1957.
Eckford was one of nine black students who had been admitted to the formerly all-white high school when the Little Rock School board agreed to comply with the Federal Court orders following the Brown decision.

from attending Central High. "Forcible integration," he said, "endangered public order."

Each morning for three weeks the black students and their parents walked past a jeering mob of white adults to Central High, only to be turned back by the Guardsmen. This spectacular defiance of the Supreme Court, captured by a corps of reporters and a battery of television cameras, forced Eisenhower to dispatch the 101st Airborne Division to escort the black students to classes. Faubus retaliated by closing Little Rock's high schools in 1958.

If Faubus's electoral gambit had thrust the nation into one of its most serious constitutional crises since the Civil War, it also generated local landslides and catapulted him to national attention. As indicated in the maps, prior to the Little Rock episode, Faubus's support came mostly from the Ozark and Ouachita mountains. Few blacks lived in these areas and issues of race were relatively insignificant. But after the Little Rock crisis, the "mountain candidate" of 1954 and 1956 became known as the "Delta favorite." His electoral base broadened and shifted to the cotton-growing lowlands of the Arkansas and the Mississippi rivers, where plantations had once predominated and blacks now often outnumbered whites, who attempted to keep blacks "in their place" by force of law.

The Political Lessons of Little Rock

Politicians throughout the Deep South recognized the applicability of Faubus's strategy to

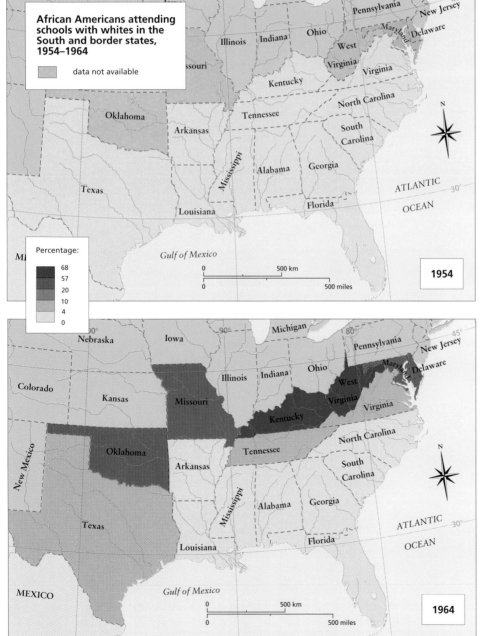

African Americans attending schools with whites in the South and border states, 1954–1964

data not available

Percentage:
68
57
20
10
4
0

1954

1964

their own states. In 1962, when a federal court had ordered the all-white University of Mississippi to enroll James Meredith, a black man, Governor Ross Barnett seized control of the university and promised: "No school will be integrated in Mississippi while I am your Governor." President John Kennedy finally sent federal troops to escort James Meredith to classes.

That same year George Wallace followed the Faubus script in his campaign for the governorship of Alabama, vowing to stand "in the schoolhouse door," if necessary, to block integration. When federal courts ordered the admission of black students to the University of Alabama in 1963, Wallace proved true to his word. As federal officials walked up the steps of the registration build-ing, Wallace stood at attention and blocked their way. As they edged around him, he ceremoniously bumped into them four times. Then he delivered a speech and withdrew. His segregationist credentials established, Wallace won re-election by a huge margin and ran for the presidency in 1968. He carried five Southern states.

Acting under the orders of Governor Orval Faubus, Arkansas troops prevented black students from attending Central High. President Eisenhower, though dismayed by the Brown decision, eventually sent Federal troops to Little Rock and forced Faubus to give way. Faubus closed all of Little Rock's schools in 1958.

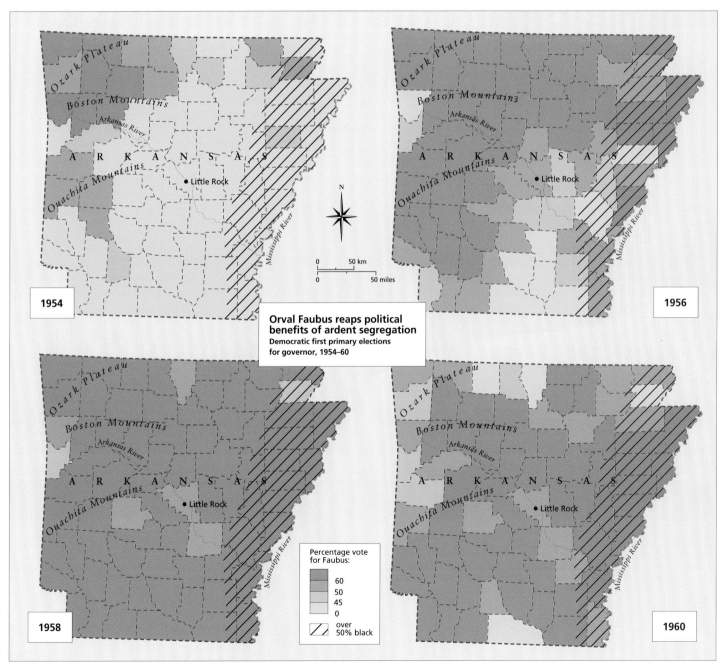

Orval Faubus reaps political benefits of ardent segregation
Democratic first primary elections for governor, 1954–60

1954

1956

1958

1960

Percentage vote for Faubus:

60
50
45
0

over 50% black

CIVIL RIGHTS

KING, KENNEDY, AND JOHNSON

"I have a dream today," boomed Martin Luther King, Jr. to the sea of faces engulfing the Lincoln Memorial and spilling back to the Washington Monument. "Tell us, tell us," someone shouted. "I have a dream today," King continued, "that my four little children will one day live in a nation where they will not be judged by the color of their skin but by the content of their character." President John F. Kennedy, watching on television, remarked to an aide: "He's damn good." At the White House minutes later, King and a delegation of black leaders asked Kennedy to beef up the president's civil rights bill. Kennedy declined. Instead he lectured them on the political geography of the 88th Congress.

King and Kennedy

Kennedy explained that although the Democrats in the House of Representatives held nearly 260 seats, 40 more than a majority, Southern Democrats would surely oppose any civil rights bill. Kennedy, studying a list, totted up the probable Democratic votes in each state delegation: "Alabama, of course, none," he began. "Alaska, one. Arizona, you've got one sure and one doubtful. Arkansas, nothing." When he had finished, the tally of probable Democrats for the existing bill reached only 158 to 160. The remaining 60 votes necessary for passage would have to come from the Republicans, whose support, Kennedy dryly observed, would be "hard to get."

The black leaders implored the President to appeal directly to the voters. Kennedy, who had no intention of leading a civil rights crusade, changed the subject. While King and his supporters wanted to dramatize the injustice of racism by staging well-publicized confrontations with Southern rednecks, Kennedy sought to defuse the issue of civil rights lest it drive a wedge between black and Southern Democratic voters—whose support had been essential to his victory over Richard M. Nixon three years earlier.

During the 1960 campaign, when King had been jailed for leading a demonstration in Atlanta, Kennedy telephoned King's wife, Coretta, offering his sympathy and assistance. Several days later Robert Kennedy, John's brother and campaign manager, persuaded the judge in the case, a Democrat, to release King on bail. Kennedy's staff, nervous that white Southerners would bolt the Democratic Party if they learned of the phone calls, downplayed their significance; some denied that they had ever occurred. But on the Sunday before election day, they distributed to black ministers 2 million copies of a statement in which the King family expressed their gratitude to John Kennedy. Whether the leaflet, known as the "blue bomb," decisively influenced black voters will never be known. In any case, Kennedy won nearly 70 percent of the black vote—enough to provide the margin of victory in four states with a total of 95 electoral votes: Illinois (27), Michigan (20), New Jersey (16), and Pennsylvania (32). Kennedy won the presidency by 94 votes.

If black voters were indispensable to Kennedy's victory, white Southern Democrats had proven equally so: Kennedy also carried eight Southern states with 94 electoral votes: Alabama (5), Arkansas (8), Georgia (12), Louisiana (10), Missouri (13), North Carolina (14), South Carolina (8), and Texas (24). Kennedy had won most of these states by appealing to white Democrats who had traditionally opposed the party of Lincoln. (Blacks, having long been disenfranchised, were not yet a significant factor in Southern elections.) After the election Kennedy recognized that if Southerners came to view him as an enthusiastic proponent of civil rights, he might in 1964 become the first Democratic candidate for president since Reconstruction to lose the South. As president, therefore, Kennedy kept Martin Luther King at arms length and placed civil rights low on his list of legislative priorities.

But events overtook Kennedy's complacency: The "Freedom Riders," dramatic attempts to integrate interstate bus routes in the South in 1961; King's crusade to fill the jails of Birmingham, Alabama, with thousands of school children in 1963; the murder of Medgar E. Evers, an NAACP official, in Jackson, Mississippi (1963). In the spring of 1963 Kennedy drafted legislation to empower the federal government to prohibit discrimination in public accommodations and in federal programs. In June he took his civil rights bill (H.R. 7152) to the House. In November, when Kennedy was cut down by an assassin's bullet, the bill was mired in the Rules Committee. The task of pushing it through Congress fell to the new president, Lyndon Baines Johnson, a Southerner.

Lyndon Johnson and the Civil Rights Act

Unlike Kennedy, who feared the loss of the Democratic South, LBJ, a quintessential Texan who knew that northern liberals regarded him with suspicion, seized upon the Civil Rights bill as a way to win their support for the Democratic nomination in 1964. He squeezed the bill out of the Rules Committee, steered it onto the floor of the House, and assembled a bipartisan coalition to manage its

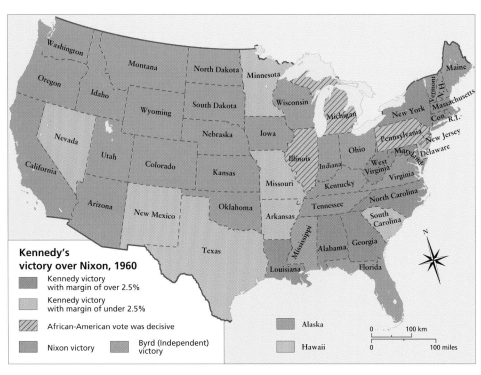

Kennedy's victory over Nixon, 1960

- Kennedy victory with margin of over 2.5%
- Kennedy victory with margin of under 2.5%
- African-American vote was decisive
- Nixon victory
- Byrd (Independent) victory
- Alaska
- Hawaii

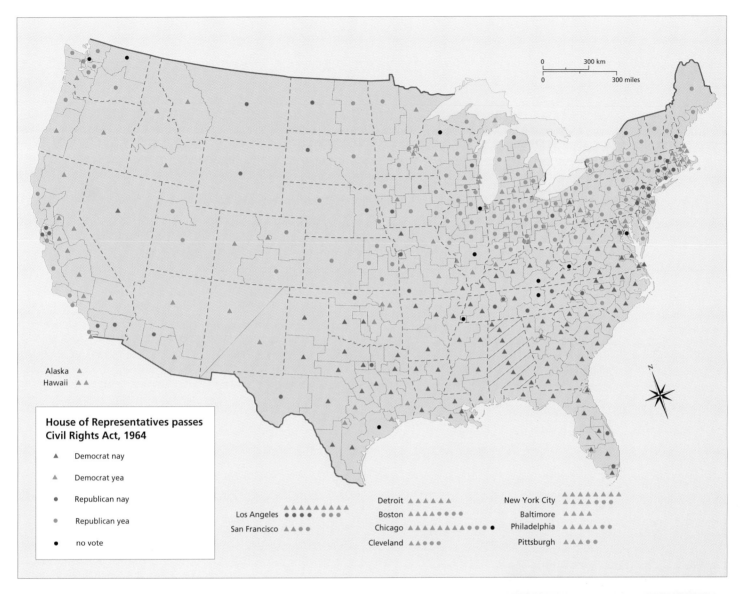

House of Representatives passes Civil Rights Act, 1964

▲ Democrat nay

▲ Democrat yea

● Republican nay

● Republican yea

● no vote

Alaska ▲
Hawaii ▲▲

Los Angeles ▲▲▲▲▲▲▲▲
● ● ● ● ● ●

San Francisco ▲▲ ● ●

Detroit ▲▲▲▲▲▲

Boston ▲▲▲▲ ● ● ●

Chicago ▲▲▲▲▲▲▲▲ ● ● ●

Cleveland ▲▲ ● ● ●

New York City ▲▲▲▲▲▲▲
▲▲▲▲▲▲▲

Baltimore ▲▲▲▲

Philadelphia ▲▲▲▲ ● ●

Pittsburgh ▲▲▲ ● ●

passage on the floor of the House.

Howard W. Smith, a Virginia Democrat, led the opposition. When it became evident that the bill would pass, he slyly proposed an amendment that, in addition to barring discrimination in employment on account of race or religious beliefs, would also prohibit it on account of gender. Smith hoped that the amendment, which threatened to transform almost every workplace in the nation, would cause moderate and conservative Republicans to vote against the entire bill. As the bill's managers scrambled to squash the Smith amendment, a bipartisan group of women representatives declared their support for what they called "this little crumb of equality." The bill's supporters, after hastily rethinking the political consequences of opposing women's rights, meekly endorsed the amendment.

Left: JFK's political task was formidable: to hold together Southern and Northern wings of the Democratic party at a time when racial issues were taking center stage. He sensibly chose to emphasize his indisputable personal charm and youthful initiative-and his opponent's lack of the same.

To Smith's chagrin, the Civil Rights bill—including his women's rights plank—passed by a vote of 290 to 138. As the map shows, Kennedy's predictions on the votes of the Democrats had proven accurate: 152 Democrats voted for the bill, only a handful of them from the South. But almost as many Republicans (138) supported the bill as Democrats. Large Republican delegations from Illinois and Pennsylvania voted unanimously in favor of the bill. Only one Republican in each of the delegations from New York and Ohio opposed it. The bill also received strong bipartisan support in the Senate, which for the first time ever terminated a filibuster on civil rights legislation. On July 2 1964, Johnson signed it into law.

Martin Luther King (right), Jr., like JFK, was weakened by dissent within his constituency. King's attempt to promote integration by non-violent means ran afoul of Black Muslims such as Elijah Muhammad, who insisted on the seperation of blacks and whites, and also of radicals such as H. Rap Brown and Stokely Carmichael, who advocated that non-violence be replaced by "black power".

THE STRUGGLE FOR VOTING RIGHTS
FREEDOM SUMMER AND SELMA

On August 15, 1961, Bob Moses, a black teacher from New York, led two blacks to register at the courthouse in Liberty, Mississippi, a town where no blacks had voted in decades. As they approached the courthouse steps, white toughs attacked and beat them. Bleeding from a gash in his head, Moses staggered into the courthouse and requested the necessary forms. He was refused. He came back the next day, and, though repeatedly beaten and jailed, he returned again and again. The local black man who drove him around town was shot through the head. The man who fired the gun—Liberty's representative in the state legislature—was never charged with a crime.

The Fifteenth Amendment, adopted during Reconstruction guaranteed the rights of all male citizens–including former slaves–to vote. But after Reconstruction's end, the federal government grew less inclined to enforce such rights in the South, allowing white conservatives to circumvent the Fifteenth Amendment by imposing poll taxes poor blacks (and whites) could not pay and by allowing white registrars to reject individual black applicants on the all-too-subjective grounds of illiteracy or unfamiliarity with the state constitution.

Thus, in 1960, only one in 20 voting-age blacks in Mississippi was registered to vote; in Alabama and South Carolina the ratio was only one in six. Most blacks could not vote in any Southern state save Tennessee.

In the early 1960s, Moses, director of the Mississippi voter registration program of the Student Non-Violent Co-ordinating Committee (SNCC), demonstrated the inequities of state laws that made registration all but impossible. Equally important, he provided detailed but dispassionate accounts of the violence to which blacks were subjected when they attempted to vote. Donations poured into the offices of SNCC, which launched a campaign in the fall of 1963 to register Mississippi blacks for a mock gubernatorial election. Some 80,000 disenfranchised blacks took part in this "election"—proof that historically low registration levels were not the result of black apathy.

That winter, SNCC recruited and trained 700 college students, most of whom were white, to take part in Freedom Summer, its most ambitious voter registration project. On June 8, 1964, the students arrived in rural Mississippi. Within two weeks, three of the volunteers had been killed: James Chaney, a black Mississippian; Michael Schwerner, a white civil rights worker; and Andrew Goodman, a white college student from New

York. Scores more were beaten or arrested.

In early 1965, Martin Luther King, Jr. built upon the momentum of Freedom Summer to initiate a voter registration drive in Selma, Alabama, where only 333 out of the 15,000 eligible blacks could vote. Some 3,400 demonstrators, including King, were arrested, but the campaign foundered until a protester was shot to death in nearby Perry County. On March 7, 1965—"Black Sunday"—nearly 1,000 blacks and a few whites marched through Selma and onto the Edmund Pettus Bridge. There, while the television cameras rolled, a phalanx of state troopers armed with clubs and tear gas waded into the demonstrators.

By spotlighting the white reign of terror that prevailed in parts of the South, Freedom Summer and Selma shocked moderates and pressured the president and Congress to address voting rights. On March 15, President Lyndon Johnson proposed a Voting Rights Act that would send federal registrars into the South. It was swiftly enacted into law.

The pressure of federal examiners, combined with a heightened awareness of the importance of the vote among blacks, transformed politics throughout the South. Black registration increased sharply after 1965. By 1968, a majority of voting-age blacks were registered in every state of the South. Within

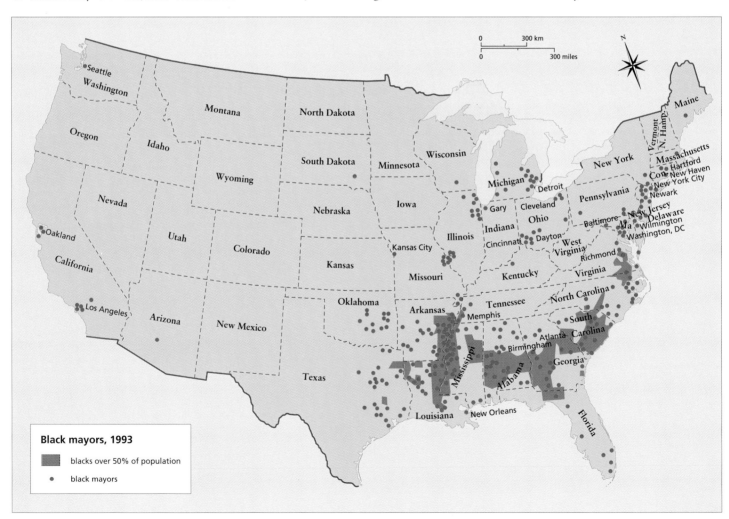

Black mayors, 1993

blacks over 50% of population

• black mayors

twenty years the percentage of registered blacks in the South was within ten points of the level for whites. By 1992 proportionately more blacks were registered than whites in Louisiana and Tennessee.

The political consequences of this trend are indicated by the maps *(below)* of the Mississippi House of Representatives in 1967 and 1987. In 1967, a single black served in the legislature; in 1987 there were 18. The seat in remote Liberty, Mississippi, formerly held by the white who had murdered Bob Moses's driver, was now occupied by a black man.

The number of elected black mayors also increased significantly. In 1968 blacks served as mayors in only 16 towns or cities throughout the nation; nearly half of these officials had been appointed. By 1993, over 350 blacks held that office. (Within a year, however, African-American mayors no longer presided over the nation's two largest cities.) Not surprisingly, blacks were most likely to win election in the black majority communities of the Deep South, in the large cities to which blacks had gravitated after World War II and in certain suburbs of those cities.

Martin Luther King, Jr. and supporters on a protest march in the rain, Montgomery, Alabama, 1965 (Right).

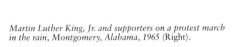

Black voter registration in the South, 1960 and 1992

1960   1992

Alabama

Arkansas

Florida

Georgia

Louisiana

Mississippi

North Carolina

South Carolina

Tennessee

Texas

Virginia

0   20   40   60   80

percentage of voting-age black population

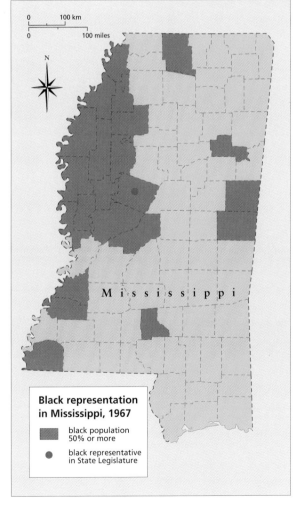

0   100 km
0   100 miles

N

Black representation in Mississippi, 1967

black population 50% or more

black representative in State Legislature

Mississippi

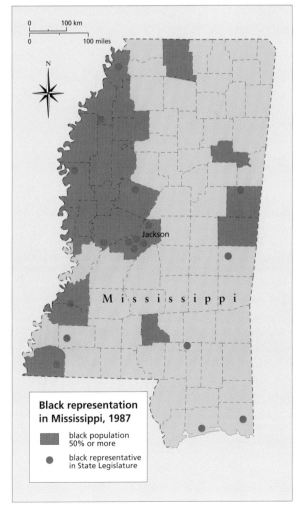

0   100 km
0   100 miles

N

Jackson

Black representation in Mississippi, 1987

black population 50% or more

black representative in State Legislature

Mississippi

THE RACE RIOTS OF THE 1960s
THE FIRE NEXT TIME

In 1963, novelist James Baldwin wrote that although blacks could not possibly take power in America, they were "well placed indeed" to "precipitate chaos" and "bring down the curtain on the American dream." Young blacks, he noted, were losing patience with the tactics of civil rights leader Martin Luther King, Jr. In their eyes, non-violent demonstrations all too often yielded dead protesters rather than social justice. "If we do not dare everything," Baldwin warned, "the fulfillment of that prophecy, recreated from the Bible in song by a slave, is upon us: 'God gave Noah the rainbow sign, no more water, the fire next time.'" Seldom has prophecy been more accurate—or more ignored.

On August 11 1965, as the sun dropped behind the one- and two-story bungalows of the mostly black community of Watts in south Los Angeles, many people gathered on their porches and front lawns seeking relief from the heat. They watched as a white motorcycle officer pulled over a young black man and arrested him for drunken driving. The man's mother arrived and a scuffle broke out. The crowd, now numbering in the hundreds, pressed closer to get a better look. The arresting officer radioed for help and drew his revolver. Reinforcements arrived, sirens screaming, and more onlookers were drawn to the scene. Some began to throw rocks and bottles. Others wandered along adjacent streets, overturning cars and hurling objects at stores and passing motorists. During the next five days, Watts was swept by fire, looting, and bloody fighting between local residents and 15,000 National Guardsmen. Thirty-four people were killed, nearly 1,000 wounded, and 4,000 arrested. Much of Watts was in ashes.

Why was Los Angeles the first modern American city to be rocked by such extensive racial violence? Poverty certainly inflamed the fury of the adult black men in Watts, 30 percent of whom were unemployed. The map *(above)* shows that most of the violence occurred in the poorest sections of south Los Angeles. But blacks who took part in the rioting were almost as likely to live in the best sections of Watts as in the worst. And as slums go, Watts, with wide avenues and tidy single family houses, compared favorably in many respects with the ghettoes of the older cities of the North and Midwest, where grimy streets and hulking tenements bred crime and despair. The Urban League even rated Los Angeles first among 68 cities in quality of life for blacks. If poverty alone fueled black resentment, other ghettoes would have exploded long before Watts.

Perhaps as significant as their poverty was the blacks' isolation. Of the almost 1,000 buildings that were destroyed or looted, most were located in the almost all-black district south of the Civic Center. After World War II, whites throughout the nation had begun to flee the inner cities, but in Los Angeles this trend took on staggering proportions. Massive free-

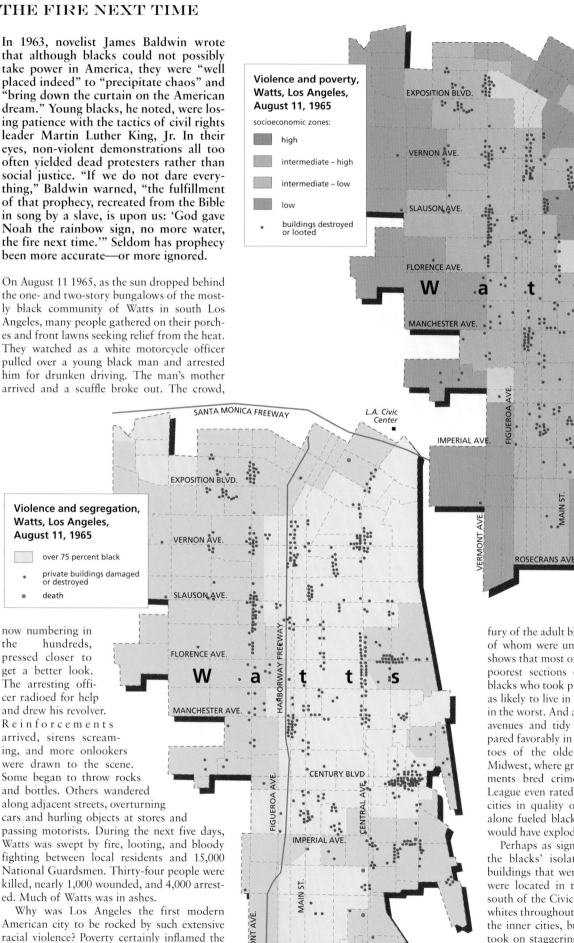

Violence and poverty, Watts, Los Angeles, August 11, 1965

socioeconomic zones:
high
intermediate – high
intermediate – low
low
· buildings destroyed or looted

Violence and segregation, Watts, Los Angeles, August 11, 1965

over 75 percent black
· private buildings damaged or destroyed
· death

way construction enabled the city to sprawl over thousands of square miles. Blacks who lacked cars depended on an increasingly inadequate public transport system (see the Age of the Automobile, p 208–209). Those who could afford to move to the suburbs encountered realtors unwilling to show them houses. Many blacks consequently came to regard their all-black enclave as a prison, and the police who patrolled it as jailers. As their community went up in flames, they chanted "Burn, Baby Burn!"—words that seemed to promise instantaneous liberation.

The Conflagration Spreads

The ashes of Watts had not yet cooled when riots broke out in Chicago after a black woman was struck and killed by a firetruck. During the summer of 1966, violence erupted in Chicago, New York, Cleveland, Detroit, Atlanta, San Francisco, Oakland, and many smaller cities. That fall, black and white leaders expressed forebodings over the future. But virtually no one was prepared for what happened in 1967. During the spring and early summer, thousands of people were arrested during disturbances in Louisville, Houston, Tampa, Cincinnati, and other cities, mostly in the South and Midwest. In July, riots broke out in Newark, New Jersey, after police arrested and beat a black cab driver. The National Guard was called in to restore order but the Guardsmen, unnerved by snipers, often fired indiscriminately. When they were withdrawn five days later, 25 people lay dead.

Extremists of both races exulted in the violence. White segregationists claimed that it proved the incompatibility of the races. Black radical H. Rap Brown pronounced the Newark riots a "consciousness raising" experience. "Violence is as American as apple pie," he gloated. Less than a week later, a 14-square mile section of Detroit was engulfed by the nation's worst riot in more than a century. Where looters in Newark had generally spared stores with signs reading "Negro-owned" or "Blood," rioters in Detroit destroyed the businesses and homes of blacks as well as whites. Forty-three people were killed, 1,300 buildings were reduced to brick and ashes, and thou-

In a scene eerily reminiscent of the nearly simultaneous Pentagon briefings on the escalation of the war in Vietnam, a U.S. Army official reports on the build-up of some 15,000 National Guardsmen and federal troops in Detroit. Of the paratroopers sent to restore order just north of Tiger Stadium, more than 40 percent had served in Vietnam.

sands were left homeless, most of them black. A grim Mayor Jerome Cavanagh remarked: "It looks like Berlin in 1945."

Racial disturbances followed in scores of cities, from New York, Philadelphia, and Chicago to small towns such as Cambridge, Maryland; Poughkeepsie, New York; and Wilberforce, Ohio; from cities with large black populations such as Birmingham, Alabama (40 percent); Nashville, Tennessee (38 percent); and East St. Louis (45 percent), to cities where blacks were a tiny minority, as in New Britain, Connecticut (three percent), Long Beach, California (three percent), and Providence, Rhode Island (three percent). No one has explained why some cities erupted in violence while others were spared.

In February 1968, the Kerner Commission, which had been appointed by President Johnson to investigate the riots, echoed Balwain's prophecy: American was "moving toward two separate societies, one black, one white—separate and unequal." Johnson, preoccupied with the Viet Cong's Tet Offensive in Vietnam and domestic political crisis, paid little attention. Meanwhile, on March 28, Martin Luther King, Jr. led a protest in Memphis, Tennessee, over the city's treatment of black sanitation workers. To his dismay, the march turned violent. King fled Memphis that evening but returned one week later, intent on proving that non-violence remained feasible. There he was murdered by a white man, James Earl Ray. Blacks in more than 100 cities unleashed their anger in paroxysms of burning and looting.

Four years of violence, 1965–1968

riot that resulted in injuries or deaths:

- 1965
- 1966
- 1967
- 1968

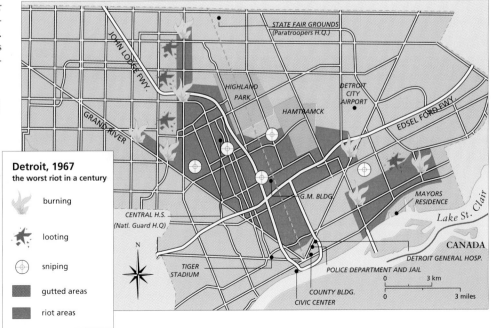

Detroit, 1967
the worst riot in a century

- burning
- looting
- sniping
- gutted areas
- riot areas

INTEGRATING THE SCHOOLS

A TALE OF THREE CITIES

In 1968, 14 years after the Supreme Court had ruled that segregated schools deprived blacks of an equal education, almost two-thirds of all black students nationwide went to schools where minority enrollment exceeded 90 percent. The highest proportion of predominantly black schools was still found in the Deep South and border states, but even outside the South, about half of all black children attended schools where less than one in ten students was white. Unlike the South, where segregated schools had been mandated by statute, racially imbalanced schools in Northern and Midwestern cities were caused by the clustering of blacks downtown and whites in the suburbs (see White Flight, p 204–205).

Little Rock after Faubus

As the 1964 map of Little Rock indicates, all of its schools remained segregated seven years after Faubus's celebrated defiance of the Supreme Court and President Eisenhower *(see The Brown Decision, p 210–211)*. Central High was still entirely white, as were nearly all of the schools in white areas of northern and western Little Rock. Most blacks lived in the eastern section of town or in housing projects in the Granite Mountain district to the southwest, and attended all-black schools in those areas.

In the late 1960s the Little Rock school district began to bus black students to the white schools. The program gained momentum during the 1970s. By 1980, as the second map suggests, no more all-white or predominantly white public schools remained in Little Rock. With the exception of one small, nearly all-black elementary school in Granite Mountain, the racial composition of Little Rock's schools varied by no more than 15 percent. The map also reveals that many whites abandoned Little Rock for the suburbs. Thus, although Little Rock school officials had virtually eradicated segregation, the entire district was becoming racially imbalanced. Central High was almost two-thirds black. In an effort to reverse this trend, in 1983 Little Rock school officials successfully sued Pulaski County, which had its own mostly white school district, to rejoin the Little Rock school district. Whether they will succeed in their larger goal of providing black and white children with an equal education remains in doubt.

Boston

The most bitter struggle over school desegregation occurred not in the Deep South, but in Boston, the "cradle of liberty." In 1973, over half of the black children attended schools where black enrollments exceeded 90 percent. On June 21, 1974, federal district judge W. Arthur Garrity ruled that the Boston School Committee had "knowingly carried out a systematic program of segregation." Referring specifically to the area where the black ghetto of Roxbury abutted the white, working-class community of Dorchester, he found that the

nearly all-black elementary schools were located within a few blocks of nearly all-white schools; in every instance the Boston School Committee had drawn school boundaries so as to maximize segregation.

Garrity ordered that thousands of black children from Roxbury and Mattapan be bused to the white high schools in the Irish community of South Boston, as well as to Charlestown and Hyde Park. He did not attempt to bus students across the bridges and tunnels that separated the Italian enclave of East Boston from the rest of the city. Garrity vowed to cross-bus elementary school students the following year.

Racial tensions flared as soon as the high schools opened that fall. White mobs stoned buses carrying black students to Charlestown High and South Boston High. After a racial disturbance at Hyde Park High, Governor Francis Sargent sent hundreds of National Guardsmen to restore order. When a white student was stabbed at South Boston High, a mob of angry whites surrounded the building and taunted the black students trapped inside, who were eventually sneaked out of a back door by police.

Firebrands such as Louise Day Hicks, who

denounced Garrity's plan as "the product of a callous, despotic mind," voiced the rage of many working-class white ethnics. Like Faubus nearly 20 years earlier, Hicks became a local celebrity; and also like Faubus, her futile efforts to stop integration only ensured that it would be accomplished with considerable anguish. Many whites pulled their children out of public schools, or moved to the suburbs. But by the early 1980s, Garrity's plan had substantially integrated the Boston schools.

Newburgh, New York

Although Little Rock and Boston commanded the spotlight, hundreds of American communities also wrestled with the problem of school

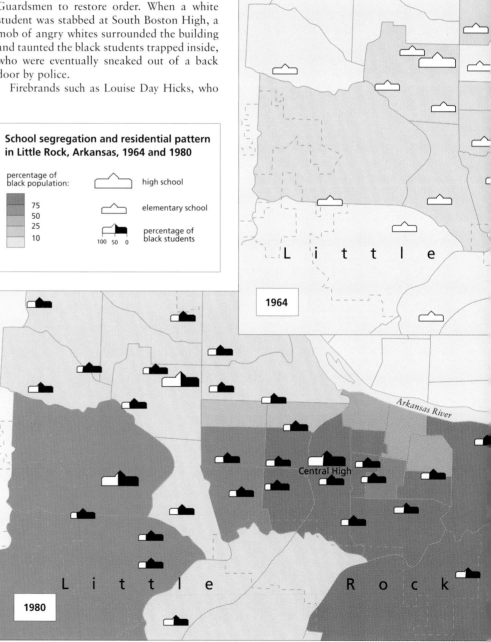

School segregation and residential pattern in Little Rock, Arkansas, 1964 and 1980

percentage of black population:

75
50
25
10

high school

elementary school

percentage of black students
100 50 0

1964

1980

Arkansas River

Central High

L i t t l e   R o c k

integration. One of these less celebrated cities was Newburgh, New York. Located on the west bank of the Hudson River 60 miles north of New York City, Newburgh was one of many cities to which southern blacks had migrated after World War II. They settled in the decaying downtown section near the river and their children attended the mostly black neighborhood schools. The whites lived further from downtown in the newer section of the city and nearby suburbs.

Intent on opposing plans to attenuate its racially imbalanced elementary schools, the school board during the late 1960s hired as superintendant Edwin Klotz, a right winger who had defended the fascist dic-

tator, Francisco Franco, had drafted an anti-busing ordinance for California, and had won the plaudits of its conservative governor, Ronald Reagan. Under Klotz's leadership, the Newburgh schools remained racially imbalanced.

But cooler heads eventually won control of the board and dismissed Klotz. Working with New York State officials, they agreed to a program that sought to persuade white parents to send their children to "magnet" elementary schools, each of which had once been predominantly black but now featured a distinctive pedagogy or curriculum. In Newburgh (and in many other communities as well), the magnet schools proved more successful than anyone had imagined. Competition among whites to send their children to "magnet" schools is now so keen that officials must select them by lottery. The needs of children had at last transcended the politics of fear.

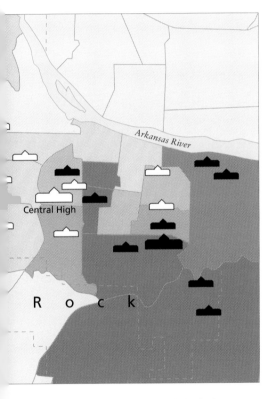

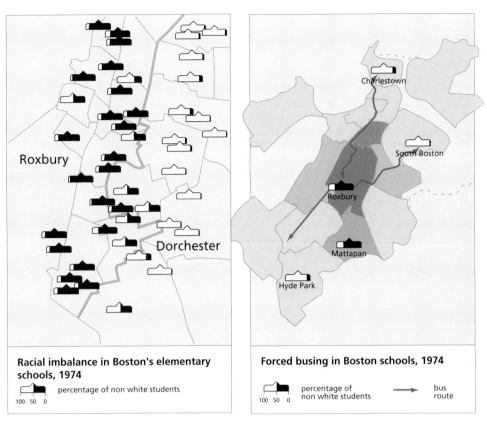

Racial imbalance in Boston's elementary schools, 1974

percentage of non white students
100 50 0

Forced busing in Boston schools, 1974

percentage of non white students

bus route
100 50 0

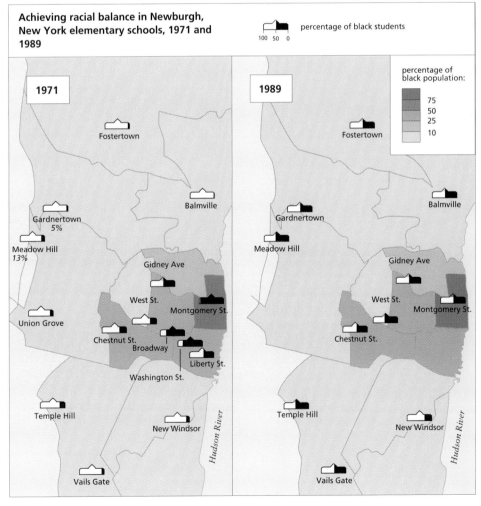

Achieving racial balance in Newburgh, New York elementary schools, 1971 and 1989

percentage of black students
100 50 0

1971

1989

percentage of black population:

75
50
25
10

RESTORATION OF DEATH
THE FALL AND RISE OF CAPITAL PUNISHMENT

In 1971 the NAACP Legal Defense Fund appealed the State of Georgia's sentence of death against William Furman, a black man convicted of murder. The LDF produced evidence showing that African Americans were more likely to be executed than whites convicted of similar crimes and also argued that evolving standards of human decency had rendered the death penalty a "cruel and unusual punishment" in violation of the Eighth Amendment. On June 29, 1972, the Supreme Court granted the appeal and overturned the death penalties of 35 states including Georgia. The decision seemed consistent with a broader international trend toward abolition of capital punishment, but by the end of that decade the United States had resumed executions and by the 1990s was carrying them to such an extent that, in many cases, they garnered very little public notice.

In the *Furman* decision, Justice William O. Douglas maintained that statutes that left sentencing to the discretion of juries or judges were "pregnant with discrimination" against poor defendants or members of an "unpopular minority." That the penal system had discriminated against African Americans in particular could not be denied. Almost 60 percent of all executions had occurred in the South, where more than two-thirds of those put to death for murder were non-whites. All but a handful of the executions for rape took place there. For much of the 20th century nine out of ten of those executed for this crime were black, a ratio that had declined only slightly during the 1950s and 1960s.

Other justices noted in the 1972 decision that because of the declining number of executions since the 1950s, the death penalty had become a "freakish" punishment whose imposition "smacked of little more than a lottery system." The overall number of executions had

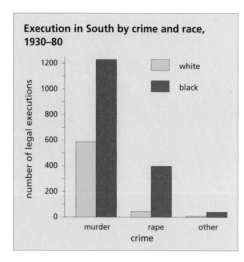

Execution in South by crime and race, 1930–80

y-axis: number of legal executions
x-axis: crime (murder, rape, other)
legend: white, black

peaked in the 1930s, when 1,670 persons were executed by state and local authoriries, but during the 1960s, fewer than 200 persons were put to death. Indeed, at the time of the *Furman* decision, no execution had been carried out in the U.S. since 1967. This apparent reluctance to execute, the justices reasoned, underscored a shift in "contemporary values" against capital punishment. Though the framers of the Constitution had not regarded the death penalty as "cruel and unusual" (they had mandated due process before an individual could be deprived of "life, liberty or property"), many people throughout the world had come to view capital punishment as reprehensible. Movements to abolish or limit the death penalty had emerged in Europe, in fact, as early as the 18th century and scored a number of successes there in the following years. In the United States, too, there had been several waves of legislation repealing the death penalty in various states, inspired by evangelical or, later, Progressive reformism. Both in Europe and the United States the efforts had often been reversed—in America particularly during the Depression when a crime wave inspired a num-

ber of states to restore the death penalty. The revulsion against Nazi genocide, however, strengthened the abolition movement after World War II. Important American allies, most notably West Germany and England, ended capital punishment. A number of American states followed their example during the 1960s, Oregon voters rejecting the death penalty by a wide margin and New York, Vermont, and Iowa abolishing it for all but extraordinary circumstances, such as the murder of policemen.

It might have been expected, then, that *Furman* would simply formalize a de facto end of capital punishment. But in the wake of a soaring crime rate and the widespread perception that vicious criminals had been too gently dealt with by the American legal process, 37 states revised their death penalty statutes so as to address the Supreme Court's procedural objections. In 1976 the Court upheld the amended Georgia statute, arguing that it provided sufficient safeguards against discriminatory and capricious sentencing. Initially, however, states were slow to resume executions. Gary Gilmore willingly placed himself before a Utah firing squad the following year, but a death sentence was not carried out against a prisoner's wishes until 1979 when the state of Florida electrocuted John Spinkelink. The momentum increased distinctly during the 1980s, as conservatism reigned supreme. After 1983 at least a dozen people were put to death in the typical year (1988 being the only execption), sometimes several times that number. By the beginning of 1994, 225 persons had been executed since Gilmore's death. Again the South led the way, particularly Texas but also Florida, Louisiana, and Georgia. By the 1990s, however, the death penalty was also being carried out in such decidedly non-Southern states as Washington and California. In the wake of the 1994 Republican electoral sweep, even the state of New York reintroduced capital punishment.

Despite the more scrupulous post-*Furman*

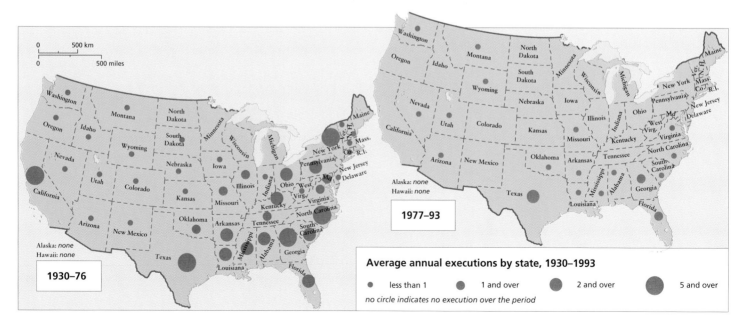

1930–76

1977–93

Alaska: *none*
Hawaii: *none*

Average annual executions by state, 1930–1993

● less than 1   ● 1 and over   ● 2 and over   ● 5 and over

no circle indicates no execution over the period

Execution by decade, including lynchings, 1890–1993

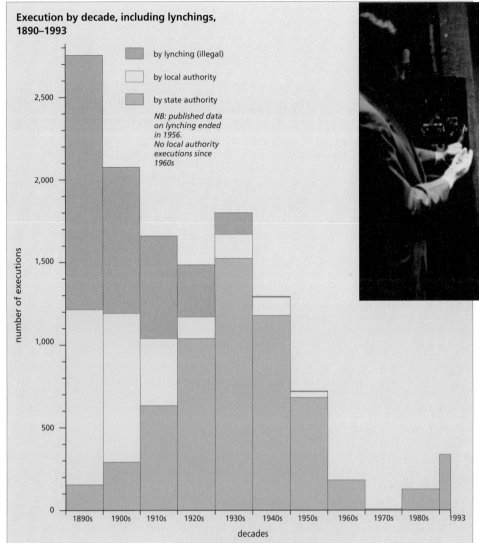

- by lynching (illegal)
- by local authority
- by state authority

NB: published data on lynching ended in 1956. No local authority executions since 1960s

number of executions

decades: 1890s 1900s 1910s 1920s 1930s 1940s 1950s 1960s 1970s 1980s 1993

Final Scene in Lepke (1975), *with Tony Curtis playing Louis "Lepke" Buthalter, New York gang boss executed in the electric chair at Sing Sing (1944). Most executions were not of New York mobsters, but of poor blacks in the South. Films such as* To Kill a Mockingbird (1962), *in which Gregory Peck defends a black man falsely accused of rape, contributed to public sentiment against capital punishment.*

guidelines, a distinct racial differential remained. Black people were sentenced to death and executed out of all proportion to their percentage of total population (death penalty proponents could point, however, to higher rates of criminal convictions amongst African Americans). This was not simply a Southern phenomenon. In 1995, there were more blacks on death row than whites in Pennsylvania, New Jersey, Ohio and Illinois.

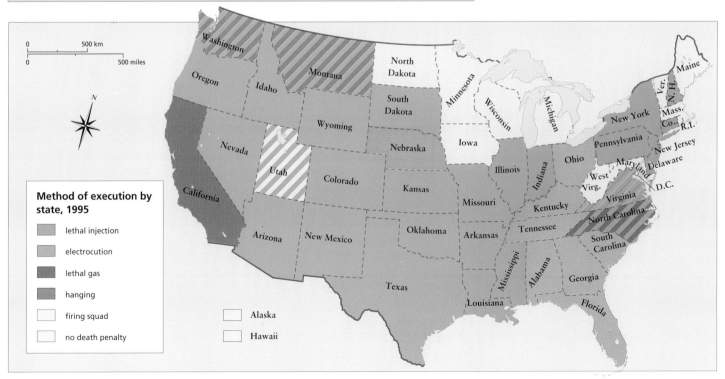

Method of execution by state, 1995
- lethal injection
- electrocution
- lethal gas
- hanging
- firing squad
- no death penalty

Alaska
Hawaii

DEFEAT OF THE EQUAL RIGHTS AMENDMENT
SUBURBAN AND RURAL BACKLASH

On March 22, 1972, the U.S. Senate voted 84 to 8 for a Constitutional amendment ensuring the "equality of rights under the law shall not be denied or abridged ... on account of sex." The Equal Rights Amendment (ERA), which had already been approved by the House of Representatives by a vote of 354 to 23, appeared headed for prompt ratification. The platforms of both the Republican and Democratic Parties supported ERA, as did the American Bar Association, Common Cause and nearly every major women's organization. It seemed a foregone conclusion that the requisite thirty-eight states would ratify ERA by March 22, 1979—the deadline imposed by Congress.

Many legislators raced to go on record in support of equal rights for women. Only hours after the Senate vote, the state legislature of Hawaii unanimously ratified ERA. Delaware, Nebraska, New Hampshire, Idaho, Iowa, and Kansas, followed within a week. On March 30, after a brief debate, all but nine of the 142 members of the Texas House of Representatives voted for ratification. By the end of the year, 22 states had approved ERA.

In the spring of 1973, however, Phyllis Schlafley, a former vice-president of the National Federation of Republican Women and publisher of a conservative newsletter, initiated a "Stop ERA" campaign. She argued that the proposed amendment would force women to use the same bathrooms as men, subject young women to the draft, deprive divorced women of alimony and child custody, and make married women legally responsible for providing 50 percent of household income. "Women want and need protection," she insisted. Although most polls indicated that a large majority of voters supported ERA, Schlafley's words struck a responsive chord in many men and women who had become unnerved by the gender revolution of the 1960s.

Schlafley's attack caused many state legislators to reconsider their position. By the end of the year only eight additional states endorsed the amendment. Three states ratified in 1974, and only two more during the next three and a half years. By the fall of 1978 only 35 states had ratified, three short of the three-quarters ERA needed to become part of the Constitution. Furthermore, four of the states that had earlier ratified subsequently rescinded their support, an action of uncertain legality. In the fall of 1978, Congress voted to extend the deadline for ratification to June 30, 1982. Opponents denounced this as unconstitutional.

ERA supporters held little hope that the Deep South—Mississippi, Alabama, Georgia, South Carolina or North Carolina—could be won over. Utah and Nevada, states with significant Mormon populations, were also given up as lost because the Church of Jesus Christ of Latter-Day Saints officially opposed ERA on the grounds that men and women were meant to perform different roles. Pro-ERA forces therefore targeted Illinois, the only Northern industrial state still remaining in the "anti-ERA" column. They reasoned that victory there might pressure two additional states—perhaps Oklahoma, Florida, or North Carolina—to support the ERA.

ERA Fails in Illinois

Unfortunately for ERA supporters, Illinois law required that both houses of the legislature endorse Constitutional amendments by a three-fifths majority. In 1972 the Illinois Senate had provided exactly the requisite margin, but the House fell short by 14 votes. In the wake of this defeat two different groups emerged to champion ERA in Illinois: the aggressively feminist National Organization for Women, founded by Betty Friedan, author of *The Feminine Mystique* (1963); and a more moderate, politically bipartisan group called Illinois ERA. Schlafley, an Illinois resident, spearheaded the "Stop ERA" campaign, staffed largely by fundamentalist churchwomen.

Nearly a dozen times during the mid to late 1970s one or the other house of the Illinois leg-

Ratification of Equal Rights Amendment, 1972–1978

- states ratifying 1972
- states ratifying 1973
- states ratifying 1974–77
- states unratified
- states later rescinding ERA

Alaska

Hawaii

islature voted on ERA; usually a majority favored the measure, but the margin of support invariably fell just short of a three-fifths majority. In the spring of 1982, with the Congressional deadline of June 22 looming large, NOW approved more desperate tactics. In mid-May, six pro-ERA women began a hunger strike. "Certainly justice for women is as worth dying for as justice for men has ever been," one of the protestors, Sonia Johnson, said from a hospital bed. On June 3, seventeen women chained themselves to the Illinois Sentate chamber and vowed not to leave until legislators passed ERA. Four days later state police cut the women loose and dragged them away.

The protests attracted nationwide media attention and millions of dollars poured into NOW coffers. But the militant strategy probably did more harm than good. Governor James Thompson, a Republican and sometime ERA supporter, declared that the "chains haven't helped." The Republican House Speaker dismissed the protesters as "idiots." In 1978 pollsters found that registered voters in Illinois favored ERA by a 58 to 29 percent margin; but when polled again in June, 1982, the percentages had nearly reversed: 38 percent for and 45 percent against.

When the Illinois House put the amendment to a vote on June 22, it was 103–72 in favor, four yes votes short of passage. On June 24 the Illinois Senate fell one vote short of approving a last ditch measure to force the House to reconsider. The "Equal Rights Amendment" was dead.

Many people identified NOW workers as "cosmopolitan." And NOW's message of women's inherent equality appealed especially to young men and women living in cities. But it unsettled men and woman accustomed to more traditional roles. Judy Topinka, a Democratic member of the House and an ERA supporter, recalled the calamitous performance of a NOW speaker who told an ethnic audience that because women were smaller than men, they were well-suited to fight in tanks.

The vote on June 24 illustrated the convergence of cultural and political factors that defeated ERA. Of the 29 Senators supporting ERA, sixteen—all of them Democrats—were from Chicago. Opposition to ERA came largely from suburban Republican legislators and from rural legislators of both parties.

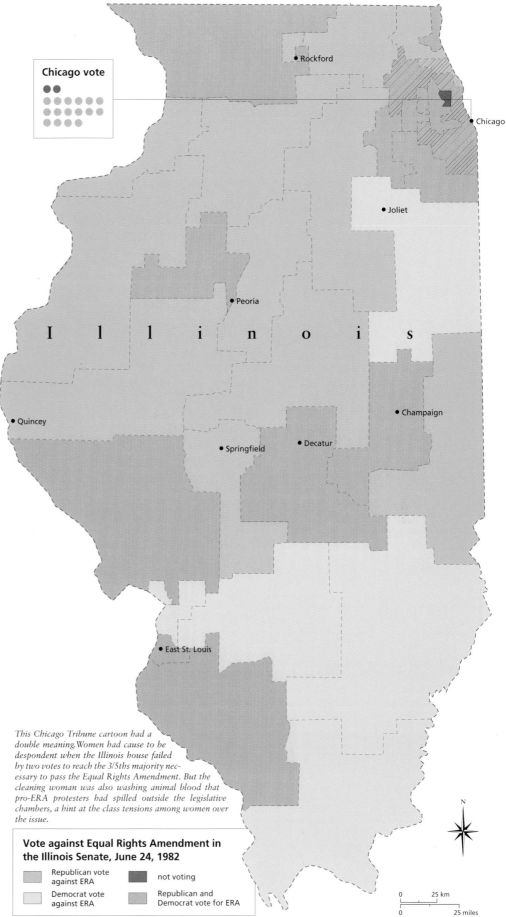

This Chicago Tribune cartoon had a double meaning. Women had cause to be despondent when the Illinois house failed by two votes to reach the 3/5ths majority necessary to pass the Equal Rights Amendment. But the cleaning woman was also washing animal blood that pro-ERA protesters had spilled outside the legislative chambers, a hint at the class tensions among women over the issue.

Vote against Equal Rights Amendment in the Illinois Senate, June 24, 1982

Republican vote against ERA

Democrat vote against ERA

not voting

Republican and Democrat vote for ERA

Chicago vote

0   25 km

0   25 miles

REPUBLICANS ASCENDANT
PRESIDENTIAL ELECTIONS 1968–1988

Several weeks after Richard M. Nixon, a Republican, had defeated Hubert H. Humphrey for the presidency in 1968, Kevin M. Phillips, a key Nixon strategist, completed a book that he brashly entitled *An Emerging Republican Majority.* Nixon's victory, Phillips contended, represented an "epochal shifting of national gears." FDR's Democratic coalition of Catholics, northern blacks, organized labor, and Southerners was coming undone, Phillips claimed, and it was being supplanted by a dominant Republican Party based in the Heartland, South and California. Phillip's predictions, coming just four years after Democrat Lyndon B. Johnson had won the presidency by the greatest margin in the nation's history, struck many as preposterous.

But Phillips was proven right: Republicans proceeded to win four of the next five presidential elections, always by a wide margin. His prediction that eighteen states—mostly in the Midwest or along the border of the Deep South—would become Republican bastions were confirmed. Republicans carried fourteen of these states in every election from 1964 through 1988. Of the remainder, three—Tennessee, North Carolina and Florida—went to the Republican presidential candidate in every election save 1976, when the Democrat was a southerner, Jimmy Carter. The Republicans also carried Texas four times during the period.

That the Heartland would sustain the Republicans came as little surprise; even during the FDR triumphs of 1940 and 1944, the Dakotas, Nebraska, Kansas, Iowa, and Colorado went to the GOP.

The "Southern Strategy"
But the defection of the South, a bulwark of the Democratic party since Reconstruction, signalled a major transformation of American politics. The Deep South first broke with the Democrats in 1964 when Barry Goldwater, a conservative Republican, denounced the civil rights and social welfare programs of Lyndon Baines Johnson. Goldwater, though trounced by LBJ nearly everywhere else, swept the Deep South and in the process broke the Democratic Party's grip upon white Southerners.

In 1968 Phillips persuaded Nixon to drive a wedge further between Southern white and Northern black Democrats by backtracking on an earlier endorsement of civil rights. Alabama Governor George Wallace, a segregationist who ran for the presidency on a third party ticket, took most of the Deep South, but Nixon carried the border states. Republicans then won the region in every subsequent election through 1988 except 1976. Southern Democrats found their pockets of support largely among Mexican-Americans in south and southwestern Texas, and among the newly enfranchised blacks who constituted a majority in lowland Mississippi, Louisiana, Arkansas, and in the "Black Belt" west of Montgomery,

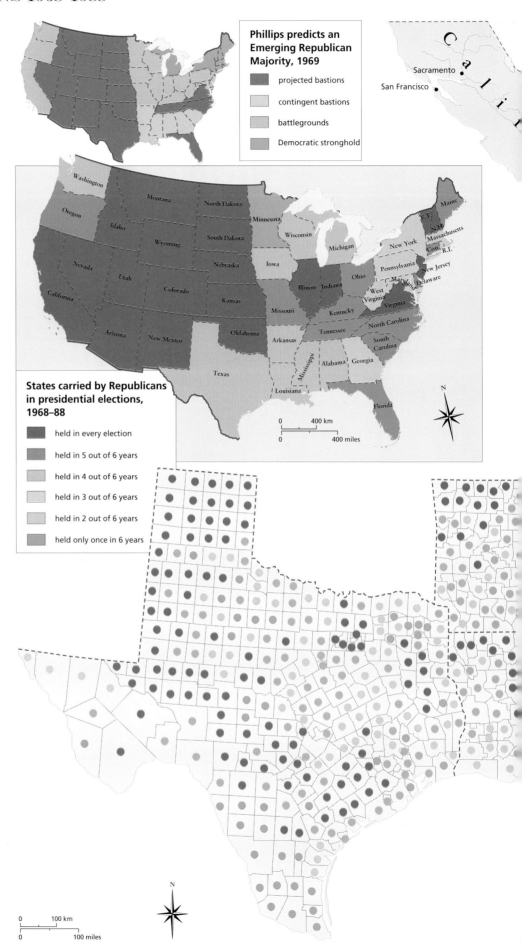

Phillips predicts an Emerging Republican Majority, 1969

- projected bastions
- contingent bastions
- battlegrounds
- Democratic stronghold

States carried by Republicans in presidential elections, 1968–88

- held in every election
- held in 5 out of 6 years
- held in 4 out of 6 years
- held in 3 out of 6 years
- held in 2 out of 6 years
- held only once in 6 years

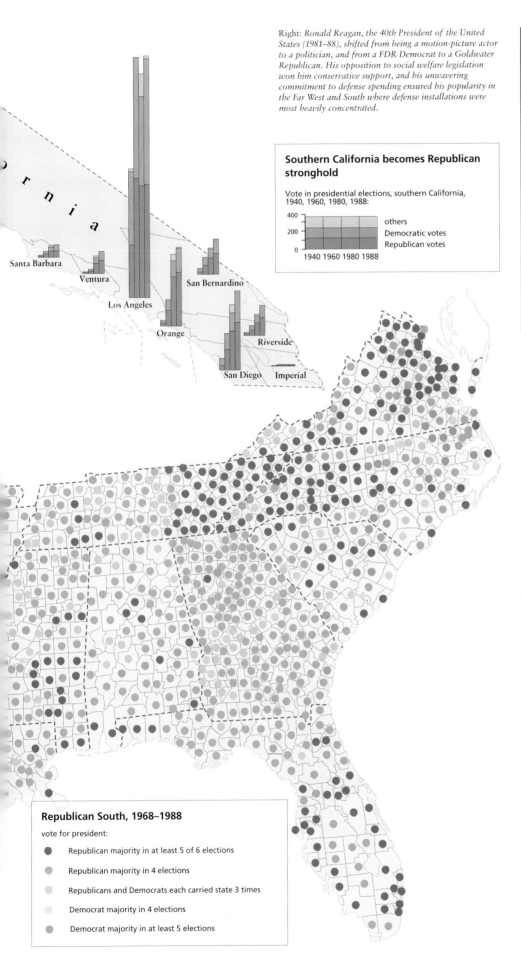

Right: Ronald Reagan, the 40th President of the United States (1981–88), shifted from being a motion-picture actor to a politician, and from a FDR Democrat to a Goldwater Republican. His opposition to social welfare legislation won him conservative support, and his unwavering commitment to defense spending ensured his popularity in the Far West and South where defense installations were most heavily concentrated.

Southern California becomes Republican stronghold

Vote in presidential elections, southern California, 1940, 1960, 1980, 1988:

others
Democratic votes
Republican votes

1940 1960 1980 1988

Santa Barbara
Ventura
Los Angeles
Orange
San Bernardino
Riverside
San Diego   Imperial

Republican South, 1968–1988

vote for president:

● Republican majority in at least 5 of 6 elections

● Republican majority in 4 elections

○ Republicans and Democrats each carried state 3 times

○ Democrat majority in 4 elections

● Democrat majority in at least 5 elections

Alabama.

Republican Gains in the Sun Belt

Phillips recognized that Republican domination of the sparsely populated Midwestern Heartland and the South would not overcome Democratic strength in the big cities of the industrial North. Victory would go to the party that carried several "battleground" states, of which California was the most important. Republican ascendancy was inevitable, Phillips maintained, because the Sun Belt and especially southern California were experiencing a tremendous influx of middle class, conservative voters. Many of these people regarded their flight from the Northeast as a conscious repudiation of Democratic liberalism. Moreover, southern California's postwar economic boom had been fueled by the construction of a vast complex of military facilities and defense plants. The region's conservatism regarding social welfare programs was matched by its hawkishness in foreign affairs.

That the chief occupant of the White House has come from southern California during four of the six elections between 1968 and 1988 is proof of the region's national political significance. In 1968, the eight counties of southern California gave Nixon, a resident of San Clemente, a 400,000-vote plurality, enough to overcome a 200,000-vote deficit in northern California. Ronald Reagan, a Hollywood actor-turned-governor, built his national career upon a solid foundation of electoral support in southern California. He carried the region by more than a million votes in 1984. Four years later it generated a 600,000-vote plurality for Republican George Bush, enough to offset Democrat Michael Dukakis's 200,000-vote majority in the remainder of the state.

However, Bush did not win Los Angeles. This suggests that even in southern California the Democrats had managed to retain many of their traditional supporters.

PART 8: AMERICA AND THE WORLD AFTER WWII

The central issue of the postwar decades was whether Communism would fill the void formed by the crushing defeat of Germany and Japan. By war's end in 1945, Stalin's Red Army, having driven Hitler's war-machine back to Berlin, already occupied much of eastern Europe; moreover, Soviet-backed insurgents were on the move in China, Korea, and Indochina. American policymakers, having learned from the fatal irresolution of French and British diplomats to Hitler's ultimata, determined to contain Communism before it gained irresistible momentum. They granted billions of dollars of economic aid to allied nations, initially through the Marshall Plan, and they ringed the Soviet Union with anti-communist bases and military alliances. But America's "winning weapon," ever since Hiroshima, remained its awesome and ever-expanding nuclear arsenal. The Soviets went all-out to acquire their own atomic weaponry, and soon mutual fear prevented the superpowers from allowing heated disputes to erupt in nuclear conflagration. But the Cold War occasionally boiled over, in Korea in 1950 and, more than a decade later, in Vietnam.

THE MARSHALL PLAN AND THE COLD WAR
HUMANITARIAN AID AND ECONOMIC CONTAINMENT

In February 1945, as Nazi Germany was being ground down by the Soviet Union's Red Army in the east and by the forces of the United States and Great Britain in the west, Allied leaders met at Yalta to chart Europe's future. Stalin's intent was to dominate eastern Europe, which he deemed essential to Soviet security. Roosevelt and Churchill proposed that Poland and other nations formerly under Nazi rule be granted the appearance of self-determination and democracy. Stalin finally signed a document in which he vaguely promised to "assist" liberated peoples in forming "broadly representative" governments and to "facilitate where necessary" free elections.

In fact, Stalin almost immediately installed Communist governments in Poland, Rumania, and Bulgaria; there were no free elections. Critics fumed that FDR had betrayed the people of eastern Europe as well as the principles for which America had gone to war. Some claimed that FDR, who died two months after Yalta, had been too ill to attend to the Soviet threat. In fact, though, FDR had little choice but to accede to Soviet control of eastern Europe. The Red Army had invaded German soil in August, 1944; by December it had occupied much of German Prussia, Poland, Rumania, Bulgaria and Hungary. The joint U.S.-British advance, delayed that same month by the German counteroffensive in the Ardennes, would not cross the Rhine until after Yalta. FDR, recognizing that no words could persuade Stalin to relinquish territory won in battle, was forced to settle for the Soviet leader's improbable reassurances.

On May 7, five days after the German garrison in Berlin had surrendered, U.S. and Soviet armies converged at the River Elbe. From 1945 until very recently, Soviet and American soldiers have trained their gunsights upon each other across the border to East and West Germany. An attempt by either side to dislodge the other would almost surely have precipitated a nuclear war. It was an era, as Raymond Aron trenchantly put it, where peace was impossible, and war improbable. The "cold war" has more commonly been applied to the protracted U.S.-Soviet confrontation.

Adopting the Marshall Plan

Following the defeat of Germany, economic collapse and social revolution posed more of a menace to Western Europe than the Red Army. During the summer of 1947, Secretary of State George Marshall announced plans for a massive infusion of American goods and money to rebuild Europe. President Truman asked Congress to allocate $17 billion over the next five years for the European Recovery Program, or Marshall Plan. The proposal was opposed by extremists in both parties. On the left, Henry Wallace denounced the ERP as economic imperialism and claimed that would exacerbate tensions with the Soviet Union. A coalition of Republican conservatives, most of them from the West and Midwest, complained that the ERP would waste taxpayers' money and contribute to the rise of socialism in Europe.

But when the vote was held in March 1948, the ERP passed by huge majorities. The overwhelming margin of victory in the House of Representatives—329 to 74—indicates the extent to which isolationism had been discredited by Hitler and the Second World War.

This is further indicated through a comparison of the House vote on the isolationist Ludlow Amendment, which had fallen just short of passage in 1938, and the vote on the Marshall Plan. In each case, isolationism drew most of its strength from the Midwest. But where isolationism during the 1930s had also received substantial support from New England and from the far West (see Isolationism in the 1930s, p 186–187), no representative from New England voted against the Marshall Plan. Of the large congressional delegations from New York, Pennsylvania, and New Jersey, only six representatives voted against this extreme interventionism. This number included the pro-Communist representative from New York City, Vito Marcantonio, and the maverick Democrat from Harlem, Adam Clayton Powell, Jr.

The changing mood of the country was indicated by the number of pro-isolationist congressmen who 10 years later voted for the Marshall Plan: 112 congressmen voted on each measure. Of the 45 congressmen who had supported the Ludlow Amendment in 1938, two-thirds voted for the Marshall Plan. Those who had switched included such conservative stalwarts as Everett Dirksen (Illinois), Charles Hallack (Indiana), Fred Hartley (New Jersey), and even Louis Ludlow (Indiana), author of the Ludlow Amendment.

The Marshall Plan in Action

The United States's major ally—the United Kingdom—received the largest Marshall Plan allocation ($3.2 billion). Another ally—France—received the next largest share ($2.7 billion). But two former enemies also benefited from substantial allocations: Italy ($1.5 billion) and West Germany ($1.4 billion).

That the Marshall Plan helped recast the economic infrastructure of Europe is suggested by the dramatic increase in industrial production and agricultural output from 1948 to 1951 among ERP recipient countries.

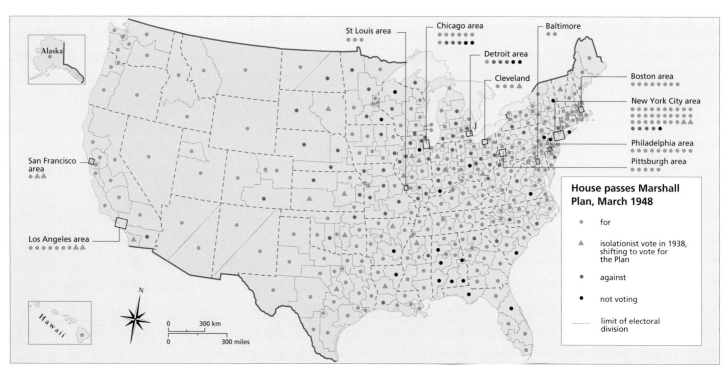

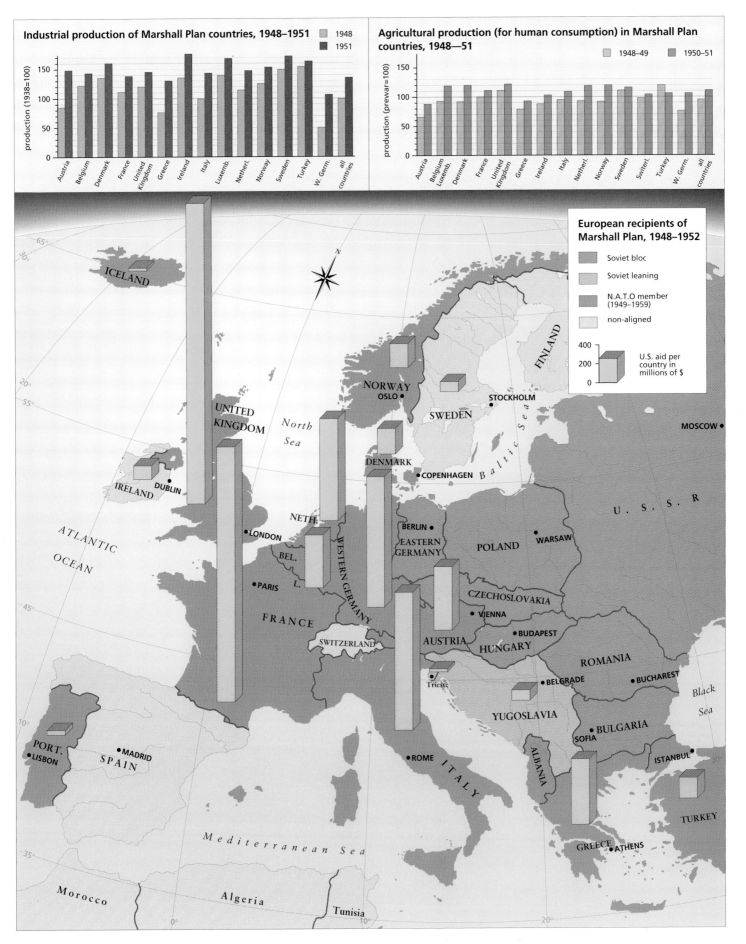

Industrial production of Marshall Plan countries, 1948–1951

production (1938=100)

Legend: 1948, 1951

Countries: Austria, Belgium, Denmark, France, United Kingdom, Greece, Ireland, Italy, Luxemb., Netherl., Norway, Sweden, Turkey, W. Germ., all countries

Agricultural production (for human consumption) in Marshall Plan countries, 1948—51

production (prewar=100)

Legend: 1948–49, 1950–51

Countries: Austria, Belgium, Luxemb., Denmark, France, United Kingdom, Greece, Ireland, Italy, Netherl., Norway, Sweden, Switzel., Turkey, W. Germ., all countries

European recipients of Marshall Plan, 1948–1952

- Soviet bloc
- Soviet leaning
- N.A.T.O member (1949–1959)
- non-aligned

U.S. aid per country in millions of $ (400, 200, 0)

ICELAND

NORWAY — OSLO

SWEDEN — STOCKHOLM

FINLAND

MOSCOW

UNITED KINGDOM

North Sea

DENMARK — COPENHAGEN

Baltic Sea

U.S.S.R

IRELAND — DUBLIN

ATLANTIC OCEAN

NETH.

BERLIN

EASTERN GERMANY

POLAND — WARSAW

LONDON

BEL.

WESTERN GERMANY

L.

PARIS

CZECHOSLOVAKIA

FRANCE

SWITZERLAND

VIENNA

AUSTRIA — HUNGARY — BUDAPEST

ROMANIA — BUCHAREST

Trieste

BELGRADE

Black Sea

PORT. — LISBON

MADRID

SPAIN

YUGOSLAVIA

BULGARIA — SOFIA

ROME

ITALY

ALBANIA

ISTANBUL

TURKEY

Mediterranean Sea

GREECE — ATHENS

Morocco

Algeria

Tunisia

DROPSHOT

WAR WITH THE USSR IN 1957

The adage that generals often conceive of the next war as a replay of the one they had just fought is amply illustrated by Dropshot, the contingency plan developed in 1949 by the Joint Chiefs of Staff for war with the Soviet Union. Dropshot was based on the assumption that "on or about" January 1, 1957, the Soviet Red Army, like the Nazi Wehrmacht before it, would attack the West without warning, slash across the northern plains of Europe, lay siege to Britain, and, within six months, overrun most of Europe and Asia. But World War III would differ from its predecessor in one crucial respect: from the start, the United States would have plenty of atomic bombs.

The Soviet Advance

Dropshot reflected the Pentagon's doubts about the sufficiency and preparedness of American conventional forces in Europe, and the uncertain economic and military prospects of France, Britain, and Italy in the postwar years. Germany, divided into zones of occupation and devastated by war, appeared an even more dubious military asset.

The Joint Chiefs decided that West Germany, lacking a natural line of defense, would have to be abandoned. After the initial Soviet thrust, the forces of the "Western Union" would fall back to an arc extending from the Rhine to the Alps and along the Piave River to the Adriatic. But this position could probably be held only "temporarily" against the larger forces of the Red Army. The Joint

Chiefs predicted that within one month the Red Army would break through the Rhine-Alps-Piave line, and within three months reach the Pyrenees and Sicily .

By this time, secondary Soviet offensives in the north would have pushed through Denmark and invaded Scandinavia, while in the south one Soviet army corps would have pushed past the Dardanelles, taken western Turkey, and advanced toward Cairo and the Suez; another would seize the oilfields of Saudi Arabia and the Persian Gulf. The Soviets would also prevail in the Far East, taking Korea, China, and even several islands of Japan. Within three months of their initial assault, most of Eurasia would be under Soviet control, an accomplishment that had eluded Hitler.

The Atomic Counterattack

The United States, possessing an atomic arsenal ten times larger than the Soviets', would retaliate by unleashing an atomic-bombing campaign "of such staggering effectiveness" that the Soviet Union would be forced to surrender. Nearly all of the Soviet Union west of Moscow was within range of American heavy bombers based in the northeastern United States (flying over the Arctic Ocean) and in Britain, while all of the Soviet Union except the Urals could be hit by medium bombers from Alaska, the eastern Mediterranean, Britain, and Okinawa.

During the first three months of the war, American planes would drop 300 atomic bombs and thousands of tons of conventional bombs upon Soviet targets. The Soviet Union

would immediately capitulate, or its industrial and military infrastructure would be so shattered that the Red Army would succumb to a two-pronged U.S. counteroffensive, beginning with a cross-channel invasion of the Netherlands and an attack upon the Bosporus and then up the Black Sea basin.

The Threat to the United States

The Joint Chiefs assumed that the Soviets would try to preempt the air offensive by bombing American bases in Europe, the Mediterranean and the Far East. However, Soviet bombers, laden with atomic bombs, could not reach most mainland American targets and return home. The JCS concluded that Soviet war planners would either send their bomber pilots on one-way suicide missions against American targets, or they would conceal atomic bombs in freighters destined for American ports. Map *(below right)* shows the location of military and civilian installations the Pentagon regarded as essential.

Lacking a far-flung network of bomber bases, the Soviet Union commenced a crash-program to develop intercontinental missiles. In 1957, the Soviets stunned Americans—and the Pentagon—by sending into space the first man-made satellite, "Sputnik," propelled by a rocket capable of delivering atomic bombs to the United States. Launched in the year Dropshot had projected for a Soviet attack, Sputnick rendered the plan obsolete (it was declassified in 1977.) By the early 1960s, the war planners were studying a new type of nuclear confrontation *(see Planning Armageddon, p 252–253).*

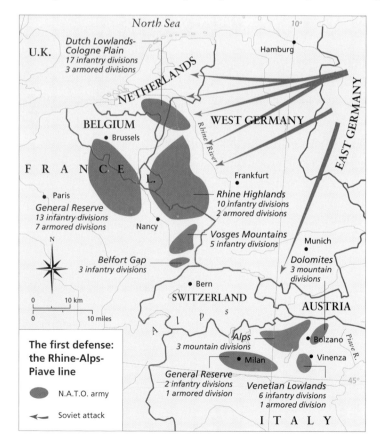

The first defense: the Rhine-Alps-Piave line

- N.A.T.O. army
- Soviet attack

Dutch Lowlands-Cologne Plain
17 infantry divisions
3 armored divisions

General Reserve
13 infantry divisions
7 armored divisions

Rhine Highlands
10 infantry divisions
2 armored divisions

Vosges Mountains
5 infantry divisions

Belfort Gap
3 infantry divisions

Dolomites
3 mountain divisions

Alps
3 mountain divisions

General Reserve
2 infantry divisions
1 armored division

Venetian Lowlands
6 infantry divisions
1 armored division

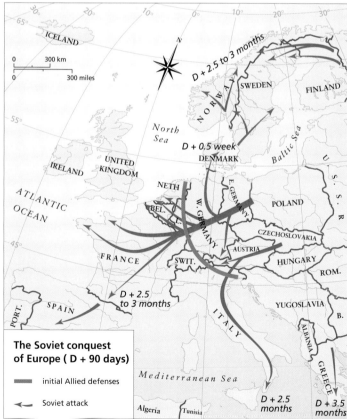

The Soviet conquest of Europe (D + 90 days)

- initial Allied defenses
- Soviet attack

D + 2.5 to 3 months
D + 0.5 week
D + 2.5 to 3 months
D + 2.5 months
D + 3.5 months

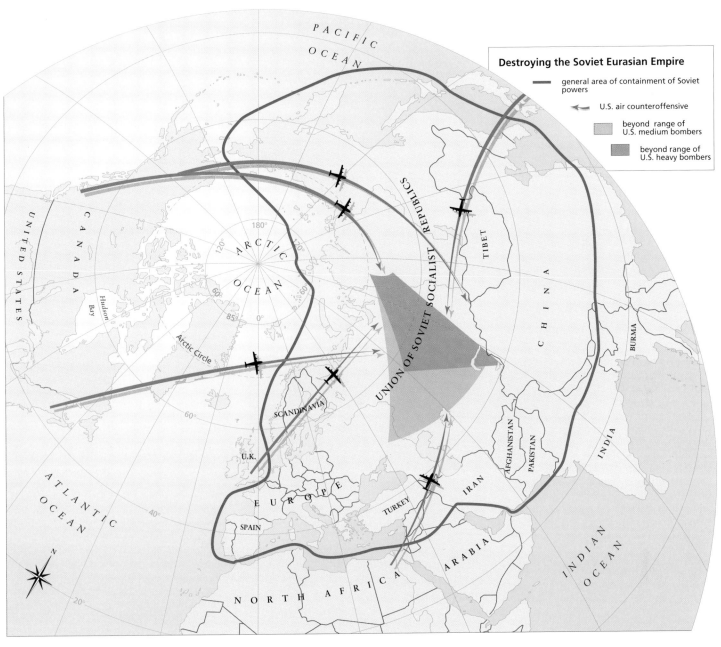

Destroying the Soviet Eurasian Empire

— general area of containment of Soviet powers

← U.S. air counteroffensive

beyond range of U.S. medium bombers

beyond range of U.S. heavy bombers

Dropshot relied on strategic bombers such as the one below to deliver the crushing nuclear blow to the Soviet Union. But in 1957 the Soviet launched Sputnik, the first artificial satellite, and its powerful rockets would soon be tipped with nuclear weapons. Dropshot quickly became obsolete and was scrapped, to be replaced by a far more terrifying scenario (see Planning Armageddon, p 252–253)

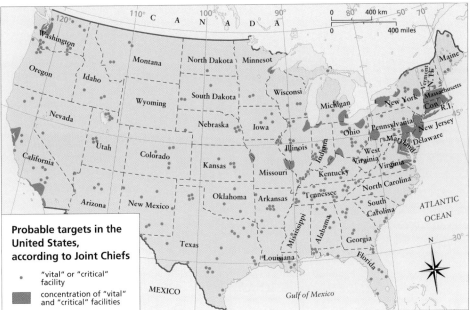

Probable targets in the United States, according to Joint Chiefs

• "vital" or "critical" facility

concentration of "vital" and "critical" facilities

AMERICA'S FRONTLINE
BERLIN AND THE DEFENSE OF WEST GERMANY

During the closing months of World War II, as Nazi Germany crumbled before the Soviet armies in the east and American and British armies in the west, Allied leaders resolved to divide and occupy Germany, ensuring that it could never again plunge the world into war. American policymakers were slow to realize that in the absence of a strong Germany, postwar Europe would be dominated by the mighty Red Army of the Soviet Union. The United States, having fought to achieve Germany's unconditional surrender, soon after the war endorsed its reunification, reconstruction, and remilitarization, policies the Soviets vehemently opposed. The fate of Germany became the most intractable problem in the confrontation that became the Cold War.

After the surrender of Nazi Germany, the Soviet Union seized the northern half of East Prussia. The remainder of East Prussia as well as Pomerania and Silesia were assigned to Poland, partly as compensation for Polish territory annexed by the Soviet Union. The Soviets also occupied what was to become East Germany, while American, French, and British troops set up zones of occupation in western Germany. Berlin, deep inside the Soviet-held sector, was also divided into four zones, each to be occupied by an Allied power.

After the war the United States, Britain, and France increasingly regarded their zones as a unified administrative entity, but the Soviets refused to acknowledge the legitimacy of "West Germany," or to loosen their grip upon the eastern sector. In June, 1948, when West Berlin adopted a single, unified currency, the

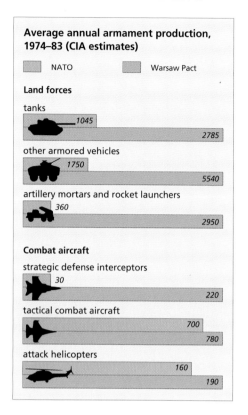

Average annual armament production, 1974–83 (CIA estimates)

NATO — Warsaw Pact

Land forces

tanks
NATO 1045
Warsaw Pact 2785

other armored vehicles
NATO 1750
Warsaw Pact 5540

artillery mortars and rocket launchers
NATO 360
Warsaw Pact 2950

Combat aircraft

strategic defense interceptors
NATO 30
Warsaw Pact 220

tactical combat aircraft
NATO 700
Warsaw Pact 780

attack helicopters
NATO 160
Warsaw Pact 190

Soviets, who viewed this as an intolerable act of German nation-building, halted all surface traffic into the city, depriving its two and a half million residents of food and supplies.

Berlin Airlift
Unwilling to abandon West Berlin or to risk war by forcing armed truck convoys through the Soviet blockade, President Truman chose to

shuttle food, clothing, raw materials and medicine into West Berlin by air. In July flights began landing at Tempelhof, Gatow, and Tegel airports. They continued for nearly a year. By the spring of 1949 the Allies daily sent nearly 1,000 airplanes with almost 8,000 tons of supplies. The Soviets lifted the blockade in May.

The success of the airlift helped unify the American, French, and British zones and draw them into closer alliance with the West. In 1949 they were combined to form the German Federal Republic (West Germany). It was admitted to the North Atlantic Treaty Organization (NATO), the mutual defense alliance of the Western powers. East Germany, formally constituted as the German Democratic Republic, joined the Warsaw Pact, the Soviet-aligned military alliance.

A Nuclear Defense
Pentagon officials initially doubted that West Germany could be successfully defended against a Soviet attack. Berlin, surrounded on all sides by Soviet and Warsaw Pact forces, was vulnerable. In the event of a full-scale Soviet attack, the original plans called for Western armies to withdraw to the Rhine, abandoning almost all of Germany (see *Dropshot*, p 230–231.)

But West Berlin's growing political significance and West Germany's industrial and military resurgence necessitated a change in strategy. By the mid-1960s NATO resolved to hold the eastern frontier against a Soviet invasion. NATO strategists soon concluded that the larger Warsaw Pact forces (see graph,) could be stopped only by using nuclear weapons.

They imagined a war in which Soviet infantry seize the garrison in Berlin while tank

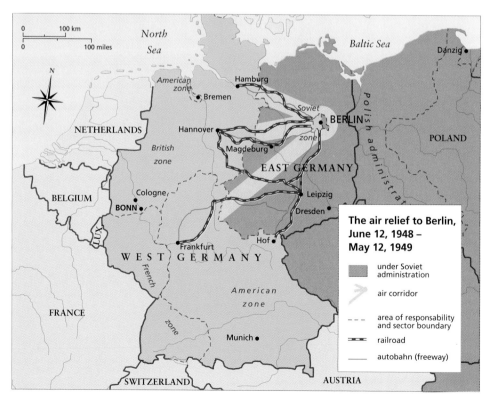

The air relief to Berlin, June 12, 1948 – May 12, 1949

- under Soviet administration
- air corridor
- area of responsability and sector boundary
- railroad
- autobahn (freeway)

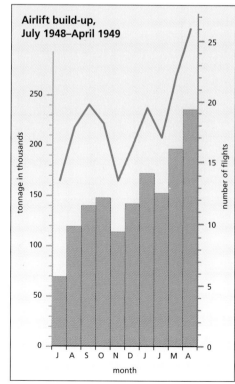

Airlift build-up, July 1948–April 1949

tonnage in thousands / number of flights

month: J A S O N D J F M A

divisions charge across the border in an offensive across the north German plain toward Bremen; through the Fulda Gap toward Frankfurt, and through the Hof corridor toward Nurnberg.

Although NATO assumed that many of its advanced defenses would be overrun, including some special units with atomic devices, most of its approximately 2,000 tactical nuclear weapons would be secure. This nuclear firepower would almost surely halt the Soviets, but it would also devastate West Germany. Even assuming the cities were spared from direct hits, much of the country would be covered by deadly fallout, borne eastward by the prevailing winds.

In 1971 the Association of German Scientists concluded that a limited attack such as that depicted here would result in the destruction of the Federal Republic of Germany "as a viable 20th-century nation."

The Berlin Wall: In 1961 Soviet Premier Nikita Khrushchev declared that West German control over Berlin was "intolerable" and demanded that it be turned over to East Germany, a Warsaw Pact power. American President John F. Kennedy, who had just taken office, proclaimed Berlin "essential" to "the entire Free World" and promised to defend it. Khrushchev retaliated by building a heavily-defended wall to stop the exodus of skilled workers to West Bserlin. The Berlin Wall, an all-too tangible symbol of Communist domination, was dismantled after the collapse of the Soviet Union.

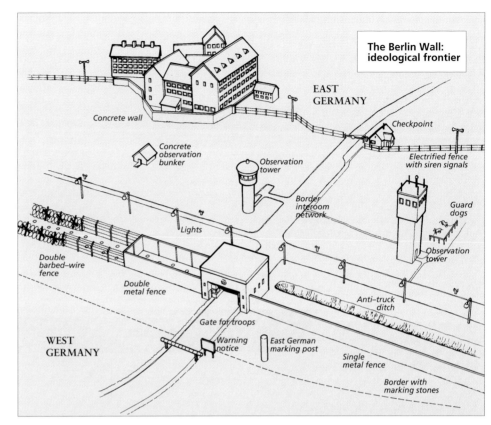

The Berlin Wall: ideological frontier

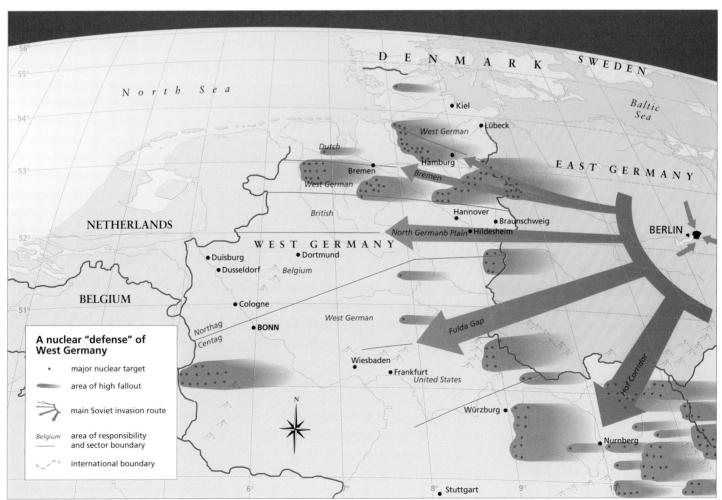

A nuclear "defense" of West Germany

- major nuclear target
- area of high fallout
- main Soviet invasion route
- *Belgium* area of responsibility and sector boundary
- international boundary

KOREA

DEFENDING THE PERIPHERY

To Americans who had watched in silence as Hitler picked off Austria, Czechoslovakia, and Poland (see Isolationism in the 1930s, p 186–187), the victory of Mao Tse-tung's Communist armies over Chiang Kai-shek's Chinese nationalists in late 1949 seemed to portend a new era of totalitarian aggression. Mao's victory also raised the possibility of a Communist strike against American allies in Asia and Europe simultaneously. Lest American forces be stretched too thin, risking vital positions in Berlin, the Mediterranean, or Japan, Secretary of State Dean Acheson announced in January, 1950 that the nation's Pacific defensive perimeter extended from the Aleutians along the Ryukyus to the Philippines. It did not include Taiwan, to which the remnants of Chiang's army had fled in 1949, nor Korea.

After World War II the province of Korea was taken from Japan and divided along the 38th parallel, the Russians controlling the northern half of the country, the Americans the southern. By September, 1948 there were two "independent" governments in Korea, the Democratic Peoples's Republic, backed by the Soviet Union, and the Republic of Korea, backed by the United States. On June 25, 1950, six months after Acheson had placed South Korea beyond

the protective umbrella of the United States, North Korean armored divisions struck across the 38th parallel. Seoul, the South Korean capital, fell within three days. Panicky South Korean officers blew up the bridges over the Han River before all their troops had crossed. The South Korean army was now in shambles.

Meanwhile, President Harry Truman, disregarding Acheson's earlier, circumscribed boundaries of the nation's defensive perimeter, chose to intervene. (His entire cabinet, Acheson included, endorsed the decision.) With the backing of the UN Security Council, Truman ordered American soliders into battle. In all, 16 UN member nations contributed troops to what remained a predominantly American venture.

The first UN divisions arrived in mid-July and took up positions just north of Taejon. The North Koreans overran these quickly and forced the outnumbered UN and South Korean armies southward. By late August, the UN forces had been confined to a

toehold in the southeast which was called the Pusan Perimeter.

MacArthur's Gamble at Inchon

While the North Koreans tightened the noose at Pusan, MacArthur planned a daring amphibious invasion at Inchon, near Seoul, deep in enemy-held territory. At first the Joint Chiefs of Staff rejected the operation as too risky. If the landing, which had to occur at high tide, encountered delays, the landing craft and support ships would be grounded on the two-mile wide mud flats. Moreover, the North Koreans could be expected to amply garrison Seoul, crucial to their supply lines south. MacArthur countered that because the invasion was perilous, the enemy would be unprepared for it; and the military significance of Seoul made it that much more important to take.

MacArthur was proven right on both points. On September 15, after an

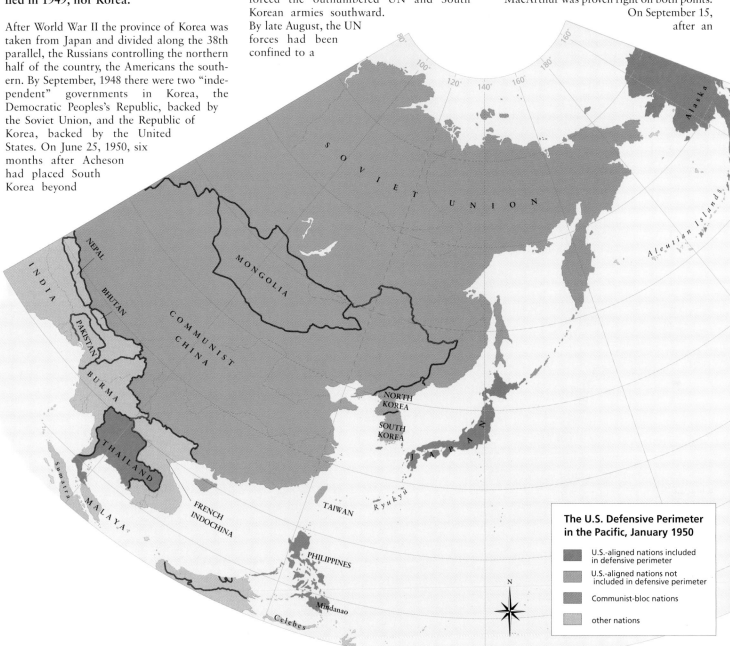

The U.S. Defensive Perimeter in the Pacific, January 1950

- U.S.-aligned nations included in defensive perimeter
- U.S.-aligned nations not included in defensive perimeter
- Communist-bloc nations
- other nations

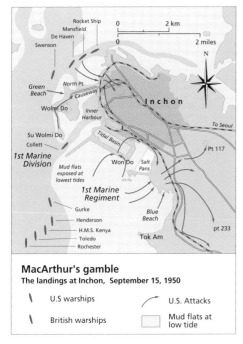

MacArthur's gamble
The landings at Inchon, September 15, 1950

\ U.S warships

\ British warships

↗ U.S. Attacks

▭ Mud flats at low tide

On June 25, eight North Korean divisions, equipped with Russian-built T-34 tanks, poured across the 38th parallel and captured Seoul, the capital of South Korea, within three days, and nearly the entire nation within eight weeks. By late August, only a small enclave north of Pusan, reinforced by American infantry, remained beyond North Korean control.

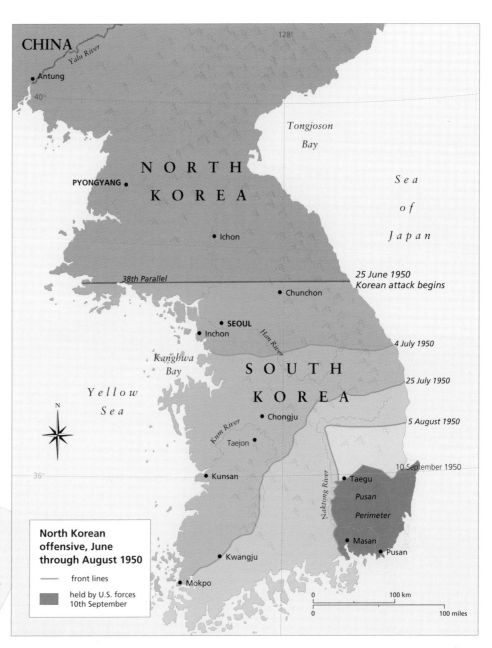

North Korean offensive, June through August 1950

— front lines

▨ held by U.S. forces 10th September

intense bombardment of North Korean positions on the island of Wolmi Do, the Marines crashed their landing craft into the seawalls and charged up the code-named Green, Red and Blue Beaches. By nightfall, they had captured Inchon. Only 20 attackers were killed in the operation. MacArthur took Seoul within the week, severing the North Korean supply lines. The outflanked North Korean main force fled northward. By early October, Truman permitted MacArthur to pursue them across the 38th parallel, On October 20 he captured Pyongyang, the North Korean capital and by late November had advanced to within one hundred miles of the Yalu River, the boundary between North Korea and China.

U.S. Marines landing in LST's at Inchon (left), whose treacherous mud-flats (in distance) were thought to be impregnable to amphibious assault. That, MacArthur told doubters, was why the North Koreans would be surprised.

KOREAN STALEMATE

MacARTHUR'S GAMBLE

South Korea had been saved by MacArthur's daring gamble at Inchon. His stunning victory, moreover, presented an opportunity to demolish the North Korean army, to expel the Communists from the North, and to unify Korea under the South Korean regime. This, too, was risky, for the Soviet Union, Communist China or both might enter the war to prevent the destruction of an ally and the installation of an anti-Communist government on their borders. But MacArthur, having won the great gamble at Inchon, was poised to throw the dice once again. On September 27, 1950, Truman signed the directive authorizing MacArthur to cross the 38th parallel: "Your military objective is the destruction of the North Korean Armed Forces."

MacArthur proposed a reprise of his Inchon strategy. As one army pursued the 25,000 North Koreans that had straggled back across the 38th parallel, another army would make an amphibious landing at Wonsan on the northeastern coast of North Korea, again trapping the North Koreans. On October 9, American and British armored divisions and the revitalized South Korean army roared across the 38th parallel. The next day the Chinese Ministry of Foreign Affairs issued a warning: "The American war of invasion in Korea has been a serious menace to the security of China from its very start."

On October 15, Truman flew to Wake Island to confer with MacArthur, who outlined his strategy of again trapping the North Koreans by means of an amphibious invasion deep in their territory. Organized resistance in North Korea would end by Thanksgiving, MacArthur reported, and much of the American army would return to Japan by Christmas, and could be redeployed to strategically sensitive areas in Europe by January. But Truman asked, what were the odds that the Soviets or Chinese would intervene? "Very little," MacArthur responded. And if they were foolish enough to try, his army would crush them.

This time MacArthur's strategy failed. The port at Inchon became clogged, reducing supplies for the offensive operations and delaying the amphibious assault. On October 26, when landing craft hit the beaches at Wonsan, they were met by South Korean soldiers who, traveling by land routes, had entered the city two weeks earlier. Towards the west coast, Pyongyang, the North Korean capital, had fallen on October 20. In November the major UN armies, skirting the mountains in the center, were racing toward the Yalu River, the boundary between North Korea and China. By late November some units had advanced to within 100 miles of China.

The Chinese Intervene

On November 26, 33 Chinese divisions, 300,000 men, having crossed the Yalu at night and hidden in the mountains, smashed MacArthur's forces. Those UN forces that had ventured into the mountains were entirely cut off: some, taking huge losses, fought heroically through the Chinese to safety. Neither of the major UN armies, operating on opposite sides of the peninsula, could come to the aid of the other. In their haste to advance, moreover, the UN armies had left behind some of their heavy weapons and were consequently vulnerable to attack. In the west, the Eighth Army retraced its steps back through Pyongyang and across the 38th parallel; the UN armies in the east fled to the coast and were evacuated by sea.

By spring, the front had stabilized near the 38th parallel. There it remained, with minor shifts and great loss of life, during the next two bitter years.

MacArthur blamed Truman for the debacle. Had the bridges over the Yalu been bombed, as MacArthur had requested, the Chinese would have been unable to intervene, or so MacArthur contended. Truman, incensed, complained that MacArthur's advance had been reckless, the product of an all-consuming ego. Truman eventually sacked MacArthur; and the general's sharp criticisms contributed to Truman's decision not to seek re-election in 1952. A decisive end to the war in Korea would be achieved by the new president, Dwight D. Eisenhower.

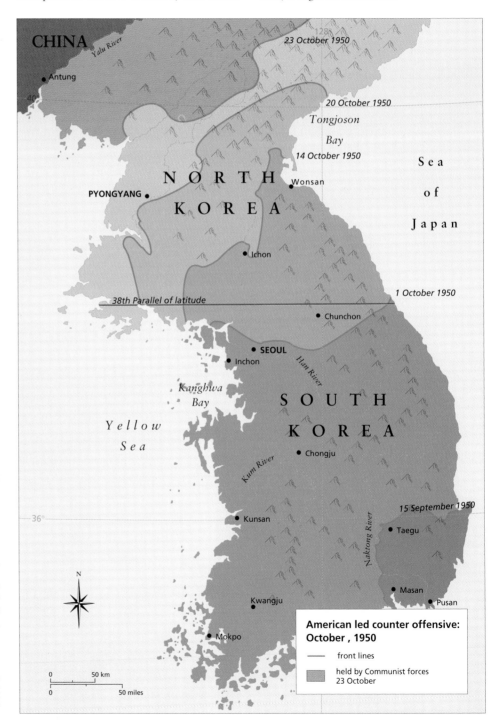

American led counter offensive: October, 1950

— front lines

held by Communist forces 23 October

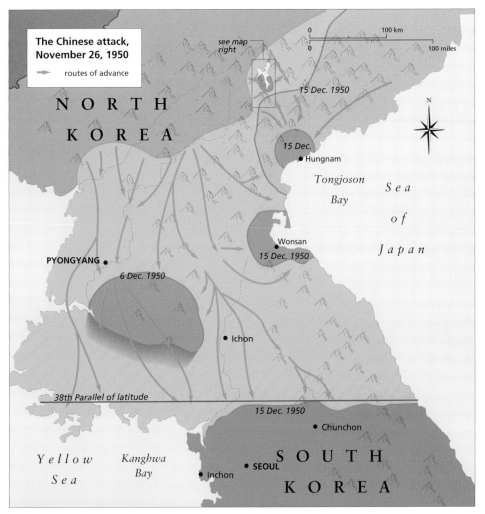

**The Chinese attack,
November 26, 1950**

→ routes of advance

N O R T H
K O R E A

see map
right

0   100 km
0   100 miles

15 Dec. 1950

15 Dec.
● Hungnam

*Tongjoson
Bay*

S e a

of

J a p a n

● Wonsan
15 Dec. 1950

PYONGYANG ●

6 Dec. 1950

● Ichon

38th Parallel of latitude

15 Dec. 1950

● Chunchon

*Y e l l o w
S e a*

*Kanghwa
Bay*

S O U T H

● Inchon   ● **SEOUL**

K O R E A

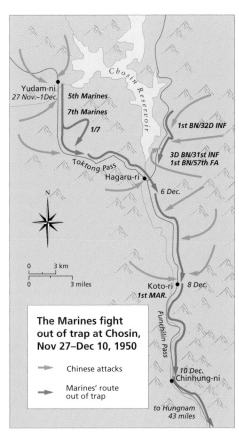

Chosin Reservoir

Yudam-ni
27 Nov.–1 Dec.   **5th Marines**

7th Marines

1/7

1st BN/32D INF

**3D BN/31st INF
1st BN/57th FA**

Toktong Pass

Hagaru-ri

6 Dec.

N

0   3 km
0   3 miles

Koto-ri   8 Dec.
1st MAR.

Funchilin Pass

**The Marines fight
out of trap at Chosin,
Nov 27–Dec 10, 1950**

→ Chinese attacks

→ Marines' route
out of trap

10 Dec.
● Chinhung-ni

*to Hungnam
43 miles*

Below: *An American soldier in Korea. The picture was
similar to many taken during World War II; but the rout of
the American army in late November had no precedent.*

THE FRENCH IN VIETNAM
AN ENTANGLEMENT WITHOUT END

In May, 1961 French president Charles de Gaulle advised the new American president, John F. Kennedy, against sending forces to Vietnam. "For you," he warned, "intervention will be an entanglement without end." Citing the experience of the French, who had lost 70,000 men in a protracted war with Vietnamese nationalists, he added: "I predict that you will, step by step, be sucked into a bottomless military and political quagmire." Kennedy, who had promised in his famous inaugural that his administration was prepared to "pay any price" and "oppose any foe" in the defense of liberty, disregarded de Gaulle's warning. Within six months, Kennedy sent several thousand military "advisers" to help South Vietnamese forces resist what he defined as the spread of Communism. America's longest war had now commenced, and by the end of the decade de Gaulle's prophecy would come true.

The French Experience in Indochina
During the mid-19th century the French hoped to tap the fabled wealth of southern China via the Mekong River, which empties into the South China Sea. In 1863 they seized Cochin China, the southernmost region of the Empire of Vietnam, and established rice plantations in the Mekong delta. That same year they persuaded King Norodom of Cambodia to accept French protection. Subsequently finding the upper Mekong unnavigable, they lost interest in Cambodia and the even more remote jungle kingdom of Laos. Instead they pushed up the Red River, which connects the Gulf of Tonkin with Yunnan province in China, and occupied Tonkin, in northern Vietnam. Deprived of rice revenues of Cochin China and the Red River delta, the Vietnamese empire soon crumbled. In 1883 the French stormed Hanoi, the capital of Tonkin, and Hue, the capital of Annam and the country as a whole. The imperial court at Hue simultaneously announced the capitulation of the nation and the loss of their emperor, who had just died, as they put it, of sorrow. "Keep him in your hearts and avenge his memory," they proclaimed.

From then on the country was plagued by revolts and insurrections. The most important revolutionary was Ho Chi Minh, who organized the Indochinese Communist Party in 1930 and an army, which became known as the Vietminh.

After Pearl Harbor, Japan overran all of Southeast Asia. Japanese military authorities ruled Indochina through a puppet regime composed of French officials. After the Allied liberation of France, Japan deposed the French and ruled Indochina directly. The surrender of Japan in August, 1945 created a political vacuum, soon filled by the Vietminh.

The French, however, were not about to allow their most important colony to slip away and sent an army to re-claim their former possession. Riots against the French broke out throughout Vietnam. After one such episode in November 1946, a French cruiser shelled Haiphong. Dismissing Vietnamese claims that more than 20,000 perished, the French admiral insisted that the bombardment had caused "no more than" 6,000 civilian deaths. The French immediately drove the Vietminh from the large villages and cities of the deltas and coastal areas to the mountainous interior. Ho's stronghold was a rugged jungle area near the Chinese border known as the Viet Bac.

In September 1947, French general Jean Etienne Valluy dispatched a force into the Viet Bac, boasting that he would "eliminate all organized resistance in three months." His heavily-armed troops repeatedly blundered into ambushes, and then fell back to a defensive perimeter in the Red River delta, leaving a string of outposts and forts along the Chinese border.

In 1950, Ho overran most of these border posts. French relief columns bogged down and sustained huge losses, and in 1951 the last of the forts was evacuated. Of the original 10,000 soldiers at the border posts, 6,000 were dead. A new French commander, Jean de Lattre, erected fortifications around the perimeter of the delta.

During 1951 the Vietminh, intent on gaining rice and recruits from the Red River region, repeatedly attacked the de Lattre line. They lost some 20,000 men without breaking through de Lattre's defenses. In 1953, having learned the perils of frontal assaults against co-ordinated and well-supported defenses, Ho attacked isolated French positions in western Vietnam and Laos.

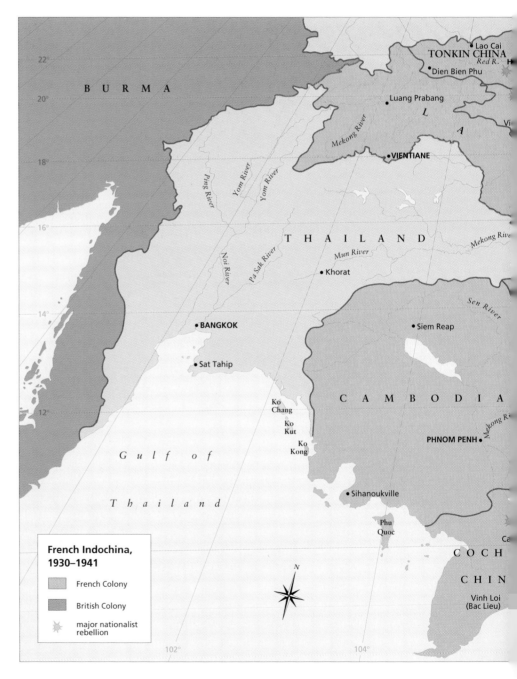

French Indochina, 1930–1941

French Colony

British Colony

major nationalist rebellion

The newest French commander, General Henri Navarre, sought a defensible outpost from which he could impede the movement of men and supplies from the Viet Bac into Laos. He imagined that the Vietminh, when frustrated by this obstacle, would launch a suicidal frontal assault against it. The place he chose was a broad plateau, surrounded by hills, called Dien Bien Phu.

The United States and the Navarre Plan

France asked the United States, which was already underwriting almost half of the cost of the war, for an additional $400 million for the Navarre operation. The Joint Chiefs of Staff, long frustrated by de Lattre's passivity, urged agreement and in September, 1953 the Eisenhower administration committed $385 million to the enterprise. Secretary of State John Foster Dulles publicly proclaimed that Navarre would "break the organized body of Communist aggression" by the end of 1955.

In November 1953, 12,000 French soldiers were air-dropped into Dien Bien Phu. General Vo Nguyen Giap, the Vietminh commander, immediately threw every available unit against Dien Bien Phu. By March, 1954 nearly 50,000 Vietminh soldiers had been amassed there. Navarre had assumed that such a large force could not be supplied in such a remote area, but an equal number of porters brought in rice from Than Hoi and heavy artillery from the Viet Bac to the battlefield. From the hills above Dien Bien Phu, the Vietminh knocked out the airfield, shot down supply planes, and reduced the garrison's defenses to rubble.

The French pleaded for a massive American air strike to save Dien Bien Phu. Arthur Radford, Chairman of the Joint Chiefs of Staff, devised Operation Vulture, which would use atomic bombs to "save" Dien Bien Phu. Eisenhower rejected the plan, and the garrison surrendered on May 7.

At the peace negotiations in Geneva that summer, the French agreed to abandon all of Vietnam north of the 17th parallel, and to allow an election in 1956 to determine who would rule the entire country. As France prepared to evacuate the area even below the parallel, Eisenhower made plans to transform it into a new nation: South Vietnam, he anticipated, would serve as a bulwark against Communism. He was supported in this by the young Democratic Senator John F. Kennedy, who called Vietnam "the cornerstone of the Free World."

French parachutists descend on a Vietminh supply base near Lang Son. Despite successes such as this, French efforts in Indochina ended in tragedy.

Vietminh resistance in French Indochina

Vietminh dominated zones, 1949

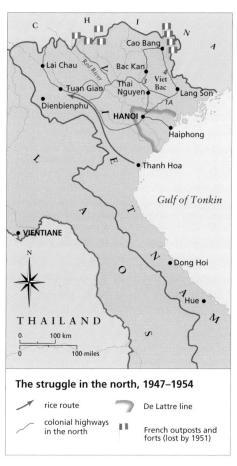

The struggle in the north, 1947–1954

↗ rice route   De Lattre line

colonial highways in the north   French outposts and forts (lost by 1951)

THE BATTLE OF AP BAC
THE KEY TO FURTHER AMERICAN COMMITMENT

The task of building a democratic nation south of the 17th parallel fell to Ngo Dinh Diem. A devout Catholic in a predominantly Buddhist nation, a reactionary who emulated a 19th-century Confucian emperor, Diem was an unlikely choice to conduct this experiment in democracy. In 1955, to demonstate his enthusiasm for democracy to Americans, he ran for premier of South Vietnam in a "national" election. He took 98.2 percent of the vote, including 605,000 of the 450,000 registered voters in Saigon. President Eisenhower, who had no illusions about Diem's popularity, flatly predicted that Ho Chi Minh would win the reunification election required by the Geneva accords the following year. With Eisenhower's support, Diem blocked that election.

From 1956 through 1961, while Ho tightened his hold on the north, the United States poured more than a billion dollars into South Vietnam, most of it for ARVN, the South Vietnamese army. In early 1961 Ho ordered thousands of guerrillas into the south. (Americans referred to them as Vietnamese Communists, or, in Vietnamese, Viet Cong, an epithet the guerrillas themselves adopted.) For several years the Viet Cong confined their attacks to hit and run raids on isolated ARVN units. This changed, as journalist Neil Sheehan noted, with the Battle of Ap Bac.

The Battle of Ap Bac

During the last week of 1962, U.S. intelligence officers intercepted a radio message indicating that some 120 Viet Cong were headquartered in the adjacent hamlets of Tan Thoi and Ap Bac. John Paul Vann, the American adviser to the ARVN division west of Saigon, planned to attack them. On January 2, 1963, several battalions of South Vietnamese regional militia and three companies of ARVN infantry would converge on the hamlets. Trapped in a pincer, the Viet Cong would have to flee across the rice paddies to the west, where they could be cut down by the .50 caliber machineguns of thirteen armored personnel carriers.

The Viet Cong commander intended to prove that a well-disciplined guerrilla force could resist American firepower. Having learned of the assault in advance, he hid his men in foxholes and irrigation ditches along the dykes and treelines and ordered them to concentrate their fire on incoming helicopters. Under no circumstances should they expose themselves by running toward the rice paddies.

When the first battalion of the South Vietnamese regional militia came to within thirty yards of the southern treeline of Ap Bac, the Viet Cong opened fire. The company commander fell dead immediately and the guardsmen, who could not see the enemy, retreated in confusion back toward an irrigation ditch, where they were raked by a Viet Cong platoon hidden in a coconut grove to the right. Improperly-directed artillery repeatedly over-

shot the Viet Cong positions.

Vann, watching from a spotter plane, ordered American helicopters to land ARVN reinforcements west of the battlefield. As the helicopters approached, bullets from the western treeline ripped through their aluminum skins. Within five minutes, four helicopters had crashed. A helicopter that came to rescue the pilots was also shot down. The ARVN scrambled for cover, few bothering to fire at the unseen enemy. The American advisers called for a flanking maneuver toward the southern treeline, but ARVN officers rejected this as too dangerous.

Next, two AD-6 Skyraider fighter-bombers launched a napalm attack, but the canisters fell on the villages instead of the soldiers. The Viet Cong kept firing, although the suffocating heat from the jellied gasoline could be felt even from the ARVN positions. When the Americans proposed a napalm strike on the adjacent treeline, the ARVN lieutenant shook his head. "Napalm too close," he said.

To rescue the downed American pilots, Vann, seething overhead, ordered in the ARVN armored personnel carriers, but the Vietnamese commander refused to move: "I don't take orders from Americans," he explained to his American adviser. Vann obtained the necessary order from ARVN headquarters, but the armored carriers had difficulty crossing several canals, one of which the Vietnamese commander pronounced unpassable. Vann cursed the officer and ordered the American to take command of the company. "Shoot that rotten, cowardly son of a bitch right now and move out," Vann screamed over the open radio. The Vietnamese officer grudgingly ordered the carriers forward.

Shortly before 1:00 p.m. the Viet Cong spotted the personnel carriers, which were thought to be invulnerable to small arms fire. As each came within range, the Viet Cong picked off the machinegunner, who was exposed atop the vehicle. A carrier armed with a flamethrower managed to approach the treeline, but the fuel had been improperly mixed and it failed to ignite. Several Viet Cong then raced forward and drove the last of the carriers back with hand grenades.

The offensive had failed, but Vann was determined to make the Viet Cong pay for their victory. He pleaded with the Vietnamese division commander to parachute several ARVN battalions to a blocking position east of the hamlets, thereby trapping the Viet Cong. The ARVN commander, who had previously been reprimanded by Diem for losing too many men, instead ordered the paratroopers to land near the armored carriers. "You want them to get away," Vann shouted. "You're afraid to fight. You know they'll sneak out this way and that's exactly what you want."

Even the pointless parachute landing was a fiasco, for the paratroopers missed the drop zone and landed in front of enemy positions north of Tan Thoi. When night came, the Viet Cong slipped out to the northeast.

The Battle of Ap Bac demonstrated the ineptitude of the South Vietnamese as well as the skill and determination of the Viet Cong. Attacked by a force four times their size and pounded by tons of napalm, 600 artillery shells, 100 rockets, and over 5,000 rounds of rifle and machinegun fire, the guerrillas lost only eighteen dead and thirty-four wounded. They killed 80 South Vietnamese and wounded

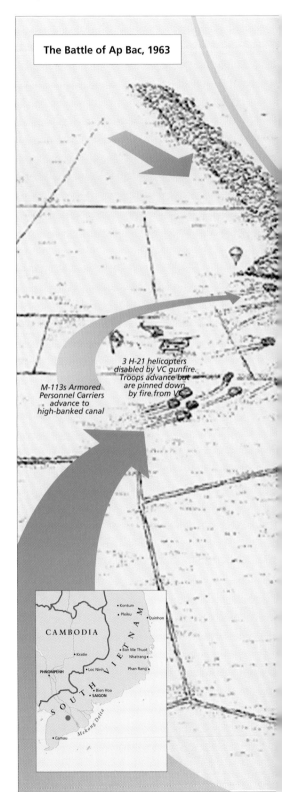

The Battle of Ap Bac, 1963

3 H-21 helicopters disabled by VC gunfire. Troops advance but are pinned down by fire from VC

M-113s Armored Personnel Carriers advance to high-banked canal

CAMBODIA

Kontum
Pleiku
Quinhon
Ban Me Thuot
Kratie
Nhatrang
PHNOMPENH
Loc Ninh
Phan Rang
Bien Hoa
SAIGON
SOUTH VIETNAM
Camau
Mekong Delta

100 more. Three American advisers died and eight were wounded.

American generals concluded from this and subsequent battles that the war could only be won if Americans took over the fighting. When Vann, who knew otherwise, was scheduled to appear before the Joint Chiefs of Staff, the meeting was cancelled by General Maxwell Taylor, President Kennedy's protegé.

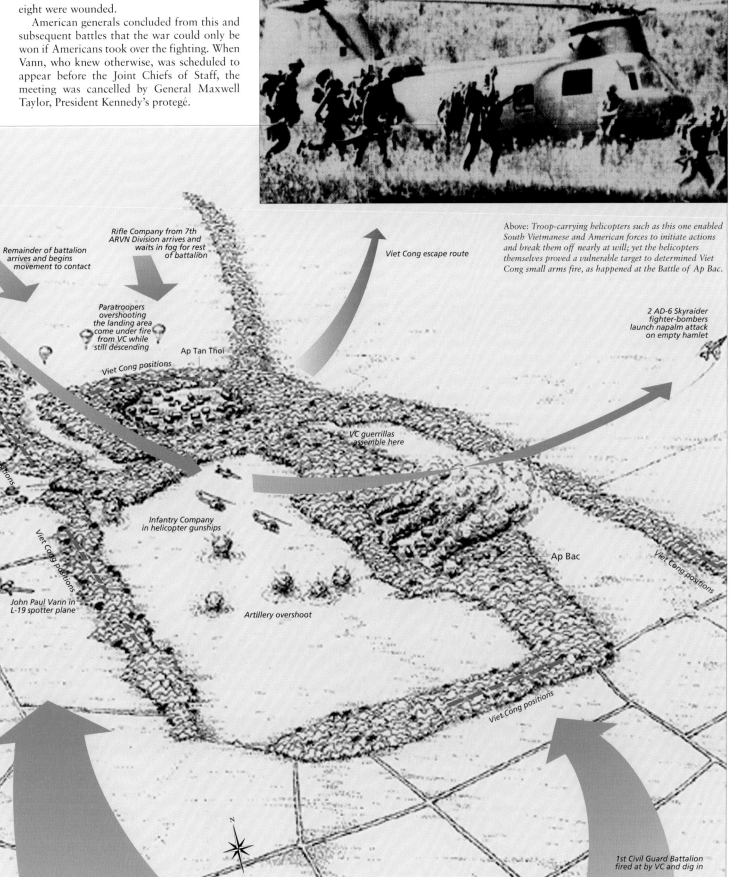

Above: Troop-carrying helicopters such as this one enabled South Vietmanese and American forces to initiate actions and break them off nearly at will; yet the helicopters themselves proved a vulnerable target to determined Viet Cong small arms fire, as happened at the Battle of Ap Bac.

Remainder of battalion arrives and begins movement to contact

Rifle Company from 7th ARVN Division arrives and waits in fog for rest of battalion

Viet Cong escape route

Paratroopers overshooting the landing area come under fire from VC while still descending

2 AD-6 Skyraider fighter-bombers launch napalm attack on empty hamlet

Ap Tan Thoi

Viet Cong positions

Cong positions

VC guerrillas assemble here

Infantry Company in helicopter gunships

Ap Bac

Viet Cong positions

Viet Cong positions

John Paul Vann in L-19 spotter plane

Artillery overshoot

Viet Cong positions

N

1st Civil Guard Battalion fired at by VC and dig in

THE "HEARTS AND MINDS" OF THE VIETNAMESE

PACIFICATION SUBORDINATED TO MILITARY SUCCESS

Having defined victory in terms of "body counts," the United States won nearly every shooting battle of the Vietnam war, but it lost the only contest that in the end mattered: the struggle for the "hearts and minds" of the Vietnamese people. Whether English-speaking Americans in South Vietnam, most of them white, could have prevailed over a Vietnamese nationalist such as Ho Chi Minh seems doubtful. But efforts to win over the Vietnamese failed primarily because American and South Vietnamese officials subordinated "pacification" to military success. In 1968 the United States spent $14 billion on bombing and search and destroy operations, but only $350 million on pacification and economic aid to the villages. Although President Johnson periodically spoke of the need to "exhibit more compassion" for the people of Vietnam, he insisted that the countryside would be pacified only after the Viet Cong had been destroyed. Policies designed to yield high "body counts" created a deep reservoir of hatred from which the Viet Cong continuously drew sustenance. Moreover, much of the American humanitarian aid was either squandered on ill-conceived projects or stolen by South Vietnamese officials and contractors.

The Failure of Pacification in Duc Lap

The battle for the "hearts and minds" of the Vietnamese was fought in the 2,000 villages where more than 70 percent of the people lived. The village of Duc Lap, which encompassed a loose aggregation of hamlets, some of them nameless, was like other rice-growing villages in the Mekong delta. In 1945 it consisted of some 25 far-flung hamlets, each housing six to ten families.

The village had been untouched by World War II, but after Ho Chi Minh declared Vietnam's independence in August, 1945, some residents declared themselves to be Viet Minh and ruled in his name. In May, 1947, six months after war had erupted between France and the Viet Minh, French soldiers came to Duc Lap, killed twelve of the Viet Minh in a battle at the schoolhouse in Chanh, and drove the rest away, many of them going north to join Ho. After the Geneva agreements, the French departed from the village. The people who remained in Duc Lap supported Diem, but hated the cruel and corrupt officials he sent to govern them. In 1960 armed "revolutionaries" from the north infiltrated Duc Lap and called for the villagers to overthrow Diem and his officials.

In May, 1963, ARVN soldiers and their American advisers arrived at Duc Lap with plans to transform the village into a "strategic hamlet." They erected barbed-wire fences around the area that included Duc Hanh A and Duc Hanh B and built nearly 200 houses for almost 1,000 peasants. Those who lived in the strategic hamlet were promised govern-

ment protection, while anyone who chose to remain outside the fences at night was presumed to be Viet Cong and subjected to ARVN mortar barrages.

From the outset, however, the government failed to protect the inhabitants. Some Viet Cong obtained identification cards and, working from within the strategic hamlets, tore holes in the fences and terrorized government supporters. During the fall of 1963 some villagers chose to remain in their old homes at night, preferring to take their chances with the Viet Cong to life under government supervision. After Diem's downfall in November, the peasants left the strategic hamlets in droves.

In April, 1964, the United States and South Vietnam initiated a more comprehensive pacification plan. An entire battalion of South Vietnamese soldiers was sent to protect Duc Lap while engineers under American supervision built barbed-wire fortifications around six hamlets along the major roads in the area.

But after six months, the plan began to come undone. Several rounds from the ARVN mortars fell short, killing the battalion commander and the American adviser. The new commander frequently sent the battalion out to search for the Viet Cong, leaving the village nearly defenseless. During one such mission, the Viet Cong entered Duc Hanh A and B, blew up the fences and government dispensaries, and ripped down the South Vietnamese flag. On another occasion, they sneaked into Chanh and killed several ARVN. When the battalion was rushed to Saigon to participate in a coup, the Viet Cong immediately entered Duc Hanh A and B, again destroyed the fortifications, and killed one of the hamlet chiefs. The other chief resigned several days later, thereby ending even

nominal government supervision of the hamlet. The areas beyond the strategic hamlets were completely controlled by the Viet Cong, who had mined or dug gaping holes in most of the roads.

Provincial officials in Bao Trai sought to reopen the road to Cu Chi by building a fortified outpost at Duc Hanh C. Just after midnight on April 9, 1965, the Viet Cong slipped through the maze of gates, blew up the blockhouse, and killed or captured the entire ARVN detachment. The battalion stationed at nearby Chanh refused to come to the aid of the outpost. In June the Viet Cong erected earthen roadblocks *within* several of the strategic hamlets and taunted the ARVN by planting a banana tree and flowers in one of the barricades. Fifty Viet Cong brazenly marched into Go Cao and demanded that the peasants give them rice. Now the ARVN battalion rarely strayed from Chanh.

Three times that fall the Viet Cong overran the ARVN compound. Early in 1966 American officials announced that pacification had failed in Duc Lap and that the village was being abandoned.

Dislocating the Peasants

Westmoreland originally conceived of "search and destroy" as a means of killing Viet Cong, but the failure of pacification provided further justification for his strategy: these enormously destructive missions would drive peasants into

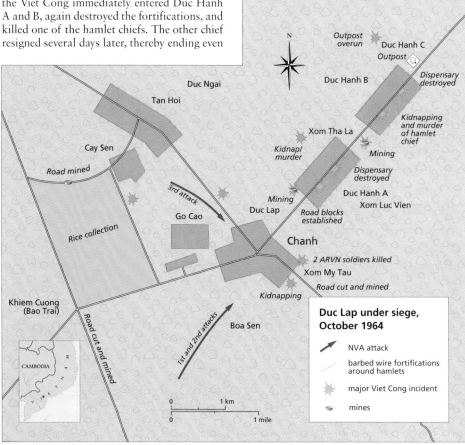

Duc Lap under siege, October 1964

↗ NVA attack

barbed wire fortifications around hamlets

✴ major Viet Cong incident

mines

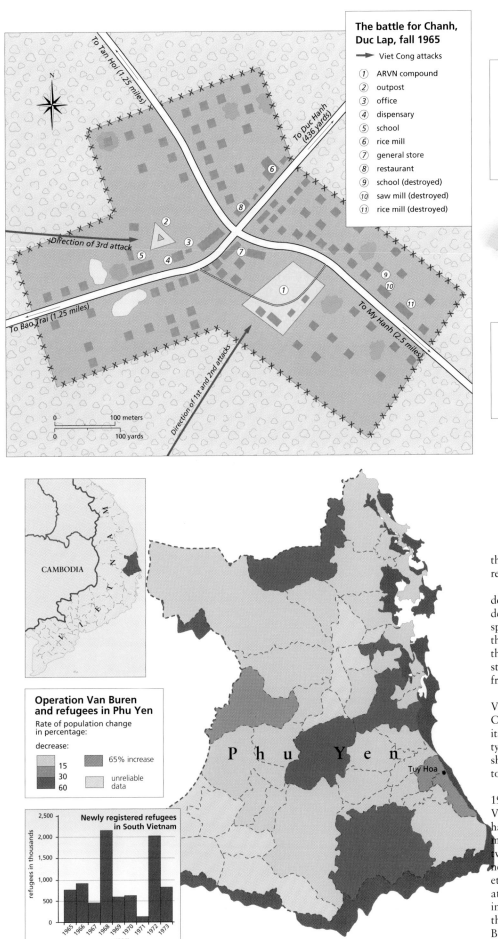

The battle for Chanh, Duc Lap, fall 1965

→ Viet Cong attacks

1. ARVN compound
2. outpost
3. office
4. dispensary
5. school
6. rice mill
7. general store
8. restaurant
9. school (destroyed)
10. saw mill (destroyed)
11. rice mill (destroyed)

To Tan Hoi (1.25 miles)
To Duc Hanh (436 yards)
Direction of 3rd attack
To Bao Trai (1.25 miles)
Direction of 1st and 2nd attacks
To My Hanh (2.5 miles)

0 100 meters
0 100 yards

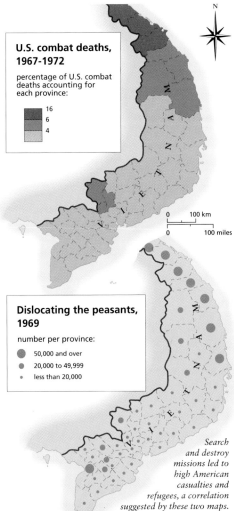

U.S. combat deaths, 1967-1972

percentage of U.S. combat deaths accounting for each province:

- 16
- 6
- 4

0 100 km
0 100 miles

Dislocating the peasants, 1969

number per province:

- 50,000 and over
- 20,000 to 49,999
- less than 20,000

Search and destroy missions led to high American casualties and refugees, a correlation suggested by these two maps.

Operation Van Buren and refugees in Phu Yen

Rate of population change in percentage:

decrease:
- 15
- 30
- 60
- 65% increase
- unreliable data

CAMBODIA

Phu Yen

Tuy Hoa

Newly registered refugees in South Vietnam
refugees in thousands
2,500 / 2,000 / 1,500 / 1,000 / 500 / 0
years 1965 1966 1967 1968 1969 1970 1971 1972 1973

the cities, thereby depriving the Viet Cong of recruits and rice.

That "search and destroy" operations would depopulate the countryside had been amply demonstrated by Operation Van Buren in the spring of 1964. As American marines slashed through the hills of Phu Yen province, more than 70,000 peasants fled their villages. Many streamed into Tuy Hoa, swelling its population from 50,000 to 82,500 almost overnight.

The refugees imposed a burden the South Vietnamese government could not meet. Conditions in Tuy Hoa were squalid, and sanitary facilities almost non-existent. Often thirty families lived in a single structure built of tin sheeting. And the peasants, who had nothing to do, seethed.

At one time or another between 1964 and 1969, nearly three and a half million South Vietnamese became refugees. Saigon, which had a population of less than one and a half million in 1962, was swollen by the arrival of two and a half million newcomers during the next six years. The fabric of Vietnamese society quickly came undone. Westmoreland's attempt to save South Vietnam by transforming it into an enormous refugee camp rivaled the French decision to build a fortress at Dien Bien Phu.

AMERICANIZATION OF THE WAR
SEARCH AND DESTROY

On the morning of June 11, 1963 American reporters, having been summoned by Buddhist monks to a busy intersection in downtown Saigon, watched horror-stricken as a 73-year-old monk, Thich Quang Duc, walked to the middle of the street, sat down and assumed the lotus position. After other monks had poured gasoline over his shaved head, he lit a match. As his charred body toppled to the pavement, a young monk with a microphone chanted in English and Vietnamese: "A Buddhist priest becomes a martyr." The Buddhists' rebellion, precipitated by Diem's bloody persecution, reverberated throughout Vietnam. On November 1, a South Vietnamese general, acting with President Kennedy's silent acquiescence, sent his troops into the Presidential Palace and toppled the Diem regime. Diem was assassinated.

Search and Destroy

After the fall of Diem a succession of coups paralyzed the government of South Vietnam and a string of defeats demoralized its army. How Kennedy would have reacted to this no one can know. Lyndon Johnson, who became president after Kennedy was assassinated on November 22, planned to sustain South Vietnam at all costs. During the 1964 presidential campaign he called himself the "peace candidate" and promised not to send American boys to fight "a war that ought to be fought by the boys of Asia," but after crushing his "hawkish" Republican opponent, Barry Goldwater, he intensified the bombing of North Vietnam and gradually committed hundreds of thousands of American ground forces to the war.

Initially the American soldiers were to secure "enclaves" around American air bases and ports at Da Nang, Nha Trang, Qui Nhon, Phu Bai and Chu Lai. On March 8, 1965, several battalions of Marines waded ashore at Da Nang. However, William C. Westmoreland, commander of American troops in Vietnam, chafed at this defensive strategy. He favored a war of attrition. American soldiers, supported by thousands of helicopter gunships, fighter-bombers, and howitzers, would wear down the Viet Cong. These aggressive tactics would require an additional 200,000 American soldiers—the first of many requests for more troops.

On June 27, 1965, while Johnson pondered the Westmoreland proposal, the general launched his first "search and destroy" operation. Fighter-bombers, artillery, and helicopter gunships blasted a Viet Cong stronghold in a tropical rain forest north of Saigon. However, alerted by the bombardment, the Viet Cong had hidden in tunnels and thickets. When the American infantry pushed into the jungle, they found few of the enemy. Nevertheless, Johnson agreed to Westmoreland's plan and dispatched the

additional troops. But Ho Chi Minh, who also endorsed a war of attrition, had sent thousands of North Vietnamese regulars down the Ho Chi Minh trail into the central highlands of South Vietnam with orders not to break off battles until they had inflicted losses on the Americans. In September these North Vietnamese divisions threatened American airbases at Pleiku and Kontum. On October 19 they attacked Plei Me and ambushed the ARVN relief column from Pleiku. Westmoreland called in the 1st Cavalry Division (Airmobile) and ordered it to "do more than merely contain the enemy; he must be sought out aggressively and destroyed."

The commander of the Air Cavalry, who assumed that the North Vietnamese had withdrawn to an area west of Plei Me and south of Highway 19, sent several battalions of soldiers in Huey helicopters to flush them out. The Americans encountered only stragglers. Further to the south an advance squad of air cavalrymen stumbled upon a North Vietnamese field hospital and captured it. They found there documents indicating that the North Vietnamese division headquarters was located in the Ia Drang Valley near the Chu Pong Mountains. Cavalrymen were immediately helicoptered to a patch of elephant grass which they called Landing Zone Mary. They hid in the woods and ambushed a North Vietnamese regiment.

However, other cavalrymen at Landing Zone X-Ray were surrounded by North Vietnamese the moment they touched down. The American commander called in airstrikes and artillery nearly upon his own position and drove off the attackers. The next day the North Vietnamese attacked a battalion at Landing Zone Albany. After desperate hand-to-hand fighting, the North Vietnamese fell back.

Several days later the Americans pulled out of Ia Drang. In four days of fighting 230 Americans and well over a thousand North

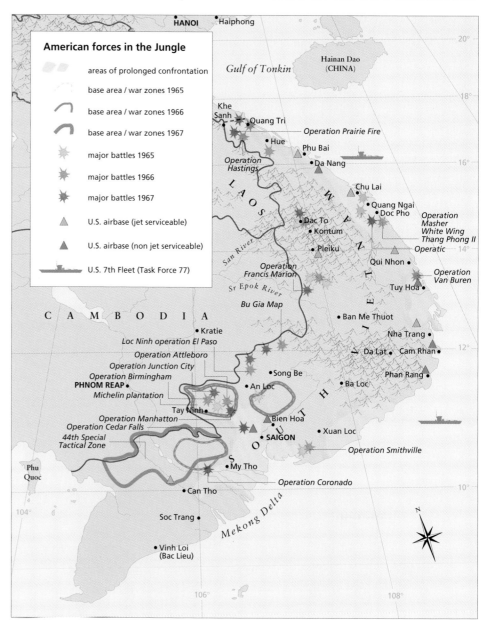

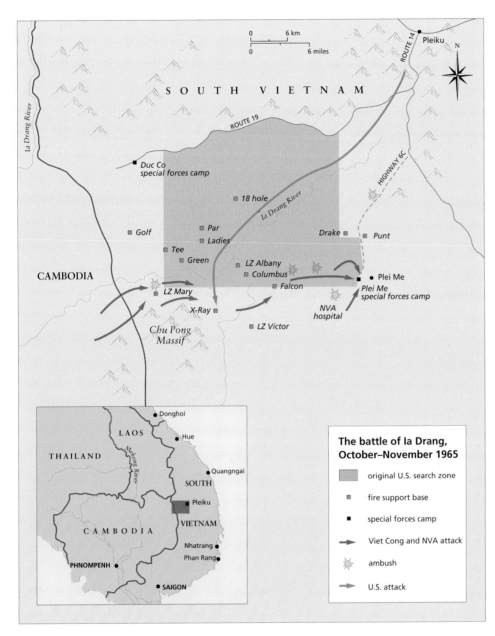

The battle of Ia Drang, October–November 1965

▨	original U.S. search zone
◻	fire support base
◼	special forces camp
→	Viet Cong and NVA attack
✳	ambush
→	U.S. attack

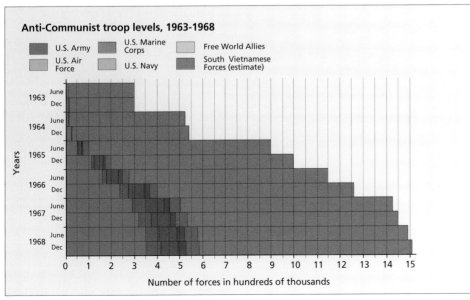

Anti-Communist troop levels, 1963-1968

▨ U.S. Army	▨ U.S. Marine Corps	▨ Free World Allies
▨ U.S. Air Force	▨ U.S. Navy	▨ South Vietnamese Forces (estimate)

Number of forces in hundreds of thousands

President Johnston (above), *who campaigned as the "peace candidate" in 1964, escalated the war in the summer of 1965.*

Vietnamese had been killed. To the generals, at least, "search and destroy" had proven its worth. During the next two years Westmoreland launched scores of such operations throughout South Vietnam. By the end of 1967, he had more than a half million American soldiers under his command. He was convinced that the United States was on the verge of winning the war.

The Bombing of North Vietnam

In August 1964, two American warships in the Gulf of Tonkin off the coast of North Vietnam radioed confused reports of being attacked by North Vietnamese gunboats. Johnson promptly ordered a retaliatory strike. Sixty-four jets from nearby aircraft carriers hit coastal facilities and patrol boats at Vinh. In February, 1965, after Viet Cong commandos had raided the American airbase at Pleiku, the President ordered strikes at military installations across the 17th parallel. Within a week these strikes were transformed into "Operation Rolling Thunder," the sustained and gradually intensifying bombing of North Vietnam. In April, 3,600 bombing raids were launched against North Vietnamese positions, almost all of them in the southern panhandle. In June, Johnson approved the use of giant B-52 bombers. The number of sorties rose to 4,800.

Johnson initially allowed no strikes north of the 20th parallel, fearing that the Chinese and Russians might be drawn into the war if he attacked Hanoi or Haiphong. As the war intensified, however, Johnson increased the number of missions and allowed them to hit targets deeper in North Vietnam. In 1967, 226,000 tons of bombs were dropped on North Vietnam, including targets on the outskirts of Hanoi and Haiphong and close to the Chinese border.

The bombing had little effect on the war in the South and it failed to force North Vietnam to negotiate. But it proved increasingly costly to the United States. As American bombers approached Hanoi and Haiphong, they increasingly encountered Soviet-made fighters and surface-to-air missiles. From 1965 the United States lost more than 950 American aircraft costing roughly $6 billion. Hundreds of airmen languished in North Vietnamese prison camps.

THE TET OFFENSIVE
A SHOCKWAVE THROUGH AMERICAN POLITICS

During 1967, the lengthening lists in newspapers of local boys killed or wounded in Vietnam fueled criticism that the war had degenerated into a bloody stalemate. A mood of deepening skepticism coalesced into a visible movement on October 21, when nearly 100,000 protesters, most of them students, gathered in Washington. In November, President Johnson summoned Westmoreland home to reassure the nation. The general dutifully informed Congress that while the United States had been losing the war in 1964, it was now winning. He produced graphs indicating that two-thirds of the South Vietnamese lived in "relatively secure" government areas, a percentage that had climbed steadily since 1965. He added that almost half the enemy battalions had ceased to be "combat-effective." He told the National Press Club that the United States had reached the point "where the end begins to come into view" and hinted that a "phaseout" of American troops might

begin within two years. Westmoreland's calm professionalism impressed nearly everyone, but he succeeded all too well. He left the public unprepared for momentous events in Vietnam that soon shattered public confidence in the war.

The Attack on the Embassy

At 2:45 a.m. on January 31, 1968, as firecrackers went off throughout Saigon in celebration of Tet—the lunar new year—a Peugeot truck and a taxicab drove slowly past the side gate of the American Embassy. Suddenly their occupants, Viet Cong commandos, opened fire on the two MPs stationed outside. The sentries fired back, then dashed inside the gate and locked it. A moment later an explosion tore through the high wall surrounding the embassy. More commandos poured into the compound. "They're coming in! Help me!" the sentry yelled into his radio, which then went silent. Two MPs on patrol in a jeep nearby sped down Thong Nhut

Boulevard; as they approached the intersection they were shot down by more commandos. The Viet Cong inside the courtyard fired anti-tank rockets at the embassy, shattering the great teakwood front doors and littering the lobby with debris. Within, a handful of Marines, armed only with pistols and small arms, exchanged fire with Viet Cong who were now crouching behind concrete flower pots. American reinforcements, unaware of the hole in the wall, could not get past the locked gates into the compound, and a relief helicopter was driven off by fire from the ground. Nearby, Colonel George D. Jacobson, adviser to the US ambassador, killed a commando who had sneaked to the second floor of his villa. At dawn, MPs finally crashed a jeep through the front gate of the embassy and finished off the commandos. Several hours later, Westmoreland and a group of ashen-faced reporters entered the battered compound. After noting that all 19 of the Viet Cong commandos were dead, the general concluded: "The enemy's well-laid plans went afoul."

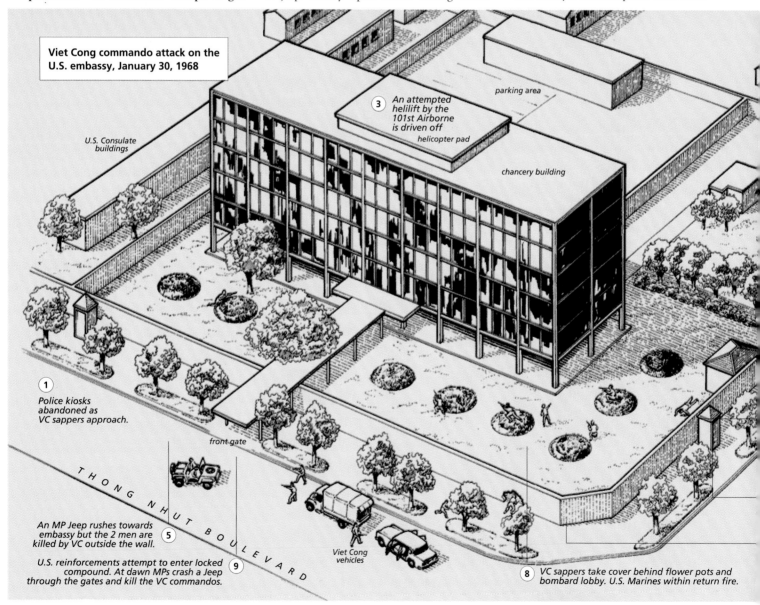

Viet Cong commando attack on the U.S. embassy, January 30, 1968

③ An attempted helilift by the 101st Airborne is driven off

parking area

helicopter pad

U.S. Consulate buildings

chancery building

① Police kiosks abandoned as VC sappers approach.

front gate

THONG NHUT BOULEVARD

⑤ An MP Jeep rushes towards embassy but the 2 men are killed by VC outside the wall.

Viet Cong vehicles

⑨ U.S. reinforcements attempt to enter locked compound. At dawn MPs crash a Jeep through the gates and kill the VC commandos.

⑧ VC sappers take cover behind flower pots and bombard lobby. U.S. Marines within return fire.

The Tet Offensive

The attack on the embassy was one of many assaults launched that day throughout South Vietnam. During the first 24 hours of the Tet Offensive the Viet Cong sent 84,000 men—nearly all of their combat-ready battalions—into action. They struck five or six major cities, 34 of 44 provincial capitals, 64 district capitals, scores of hamlets, the Presidential Palace, the South Vietnamese military headquarters, and the two busiest airports in the world—Tan Son Nhut Airport at Saigon and the giant American airbase at Bien Hoa. Nearly 7,500 Viet Cong and North Vietnamese regulars stormed Hue, the ancient capital of Vietnam, and held the city for nearly three weeks.

Westmoreland, after spending more than two years searching for the enemy in the jungles of Vietnam, claimed that the presence of thousands of Viet Cong on the outskirts of the cities provided the United States with a "great opportunity" to land a fatal blow. Johnson added that the Tet Offensive had been "a complete failure." Such assurances, however, were belied by the nightly news, which showed a determined enemy holding out against tanks and fighter-bombers, and by the Joint Chiefs of Staff, which advised the President to call up the reserves and send an additional 206,000 men to Vietnam. In the first two weeks of Tet, 1,100 American soldiers were killed.

"What the hell is going on?" anchorman Walter Cronkite muttered as the first reports on Tet came in. "I thought we were winning the war!" During the six weeks after the attack on the embassy, opinion polls indicated that nearly one person in five switched from being a "hawk" to a "dove." President Johnson's rating nose-dived; only one in four respondents approved of his handling of the war. On March 12, Senator Eugene McCarthy, an avowed "dove" virtually unknown outside Minnesota, nearly defeated Johnson in the Democratic presidential primary in New Hampshire. Several days later Senator Robert F. Kennedy announced his candidacy for the presidency. The leading Republican candidate, Governor George Romney of Michigan, withdrew his support for the war, saying he had been "brainwashed" by the army during a fact-finding trip to Vietnam. On March 31, Johnson stunned the world by announcing that he would not run for reelection; he instead promised to devote his remaining months to negotiating an end to the war.

Although the Tet Offensive sent a shock wave through American politics, it was a military failure. Apparently Ho Chi Minh had expected that a coordinated strike upon the population centers of South Vietnam would precipitate a general uprising of the refugees and bring about the collapse of the Saigon government. But the refugees, inured to hope as well as to tragedy, did not join the revolution, and with their backs to the wall the South Vietnamese soldiers fought well. American troops, deftly shuttled by helicopter to one hot spot after another, inflicted huge losses on the Viet Cong, killing by some estimates nearly half the original assault force. Johnson left office having failed to bring the war to a conclusion, but by then the North Vietnamese regulars had been forced to bear the brunt of the war. The Viet Cong was nearly finished as a fighting force.

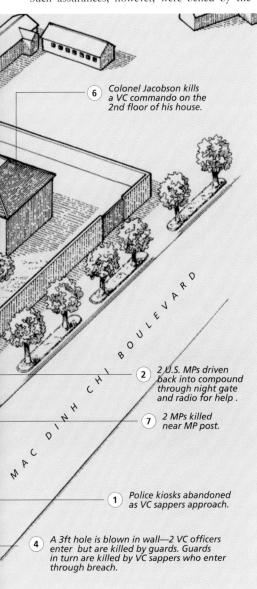

6 Colonel Jacobson kills a VC commando on the 2nd floor of his house.

2 2 U.S. MPs driven back into compound through night gate and radio for help.

7 2 MPs killed near MP post.

1 Police kiosks abandoned as VC sappers approach.

4 A 3ft hole is blown in wall—2 VC officers enter but are killed by guards. Guards in turn are killed by VC sappers who enter through breach.

MAC DINH CHI BOULEVARD

A Viet Cong commando (left) is taken into custody after the attack on the U.S. embassy buildings in Saigon.

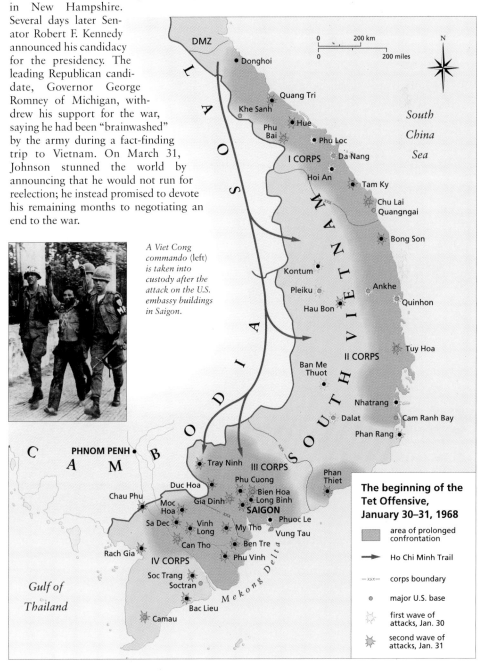

The beginning of the Tet Offensive, January 30–31, 1968

- area of prolonged confrontation
- Ho Chi Minh Trail
- corps boundary
- major U.S. base
- first wave of attacks, Jan. 30
- second wave of attacks, Jan. 31

ENDING THE VIETNAM WAR
PEACE WITH HONOR?

"I'm not going to end up like LBJ, holed up in the White House," Richard M. Nixon remarked during his campaign for the presidency in 1968. "I'm going to end that war. Fast." He announced that he had a plan to achieve "peace with honor" but refused to disclose it until after the election. Nixon narrowly defeated Hubert H. Humphrey, whose support of the war as Johnson's Vice President had alienated antiwar Democrats.

As president, Nixon failed to bring the war to a quick or honorable conclusion. His strategy for ending it had two parts. He sought to build a consensus at home by gradually withdrawing American troops, and to intimidate North Vietnam into negotiating a settlement by intensifying the bombing and threatening further escalation. Hanoi, recognizing the inconsistency in this position, refused to make concessions and patiently awaited the departure of the Americans.

Nixon's strategy, called "Vietnamization," rested on the unlikely premise that South Vietnam could defend itself after the departure of American troops. To buy time for his vulnerable ally and to pressure North Vietnam, Nixon unleashed the most devastating nonnuclear bombing assaults the world had ever seen, many of them upon suspected Communist positions in neutral Cambodia and Laos.

The first of these assaults occurred in March, 1969 when Nixon ordered American B-52s to hit suspected Communist strongholds in Cambodia and Laos. Over the next 15 months, more than 100,000 tons of bombs were dropped on Cambodia during the oddly-named Operation Menu, directed against targets dubbed Breakfast, Lunch, Supper, Dinner, Snack and Dessert. By falsifying bombing records to suggest that the targets were located in South Vietnam, Nixon's administration kept the bombing secret even from much of the government.

Hanoi still refused to negotiate. In April, 1970 Nixon sent some 32,000 American and 48,000 South Vietnamese troops into Cambodia to clear out the Communist sanctuaries. He called the action an "incursion" and defended it as necessary to "guarantee the continued success of our withdrawal and Vietnamization programs." In fact, the operation had little lasting military effect; the Communist positions were "quickly restored to almost normal efficiency," the CIA concluded.

The invasion had more significant repercussions. Pushed further west, the North Vietnamese increasingly supported the Khmer Rouge, a fanatical band of insurgents fighting the Pro-U.S. Cambodian government. In the United States, student protestors shut down college campuses throughout the nation. During confrontations at Kent State University and Jackson State College, National

Guardsmen and police killed six students. The Senate, outraged over the escalation of the war, voted overwhelmingly to terminate the Tonkin Gulf Resolution of 1964.

Nixon, seeking to quiet domestic opposition, accelerated the withdrawal of American soldiers from South Vietnam. Yet he intensified the bombing of North Vietnam and sent South Vietnamese soldiers, supported by American air power, into Laos. North Vietnam threw 36,000 regulars against the South Vietnamese and, after six weeks of heavy fighting, drove them back into South Vietnam.

In March 1972 when only 6,000 American combat soldiers remained in South Vietnam, North Vietnamese troops, spear-headed by tanks, struck across the 17th parallel. Nixon ordered retaliatory air strikes against North Vietnam. "The bastards have never been bombed like they're going to be bombed this time," he promised.

The North Vietnamese offensive stalled, Nixon won reelection against George McGovern, an antiwar Democrat. On January 8, 1973, after further bombing assaults, a settlement was reached: the Americans would leave, the prisoners would be returned, and North Vietnamese and South Vietnamese troops would adhere to a ceasefire.

Congress Opposes the President
In fact, the fighting continued much as before. North Vietnamese and South Vietnamese

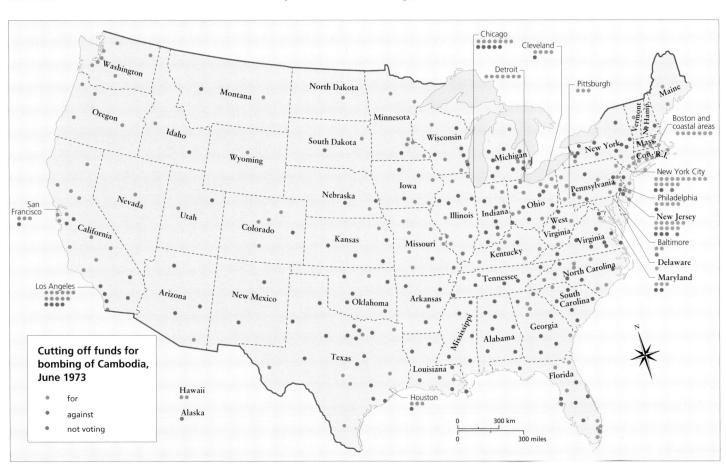

Cutting off funds for bombing of Cambodia, June 1973
- for
- against
- not voting

forces pressed for additional territory. Although the last American troops left Vietnam by the end of March, the United States continued to provide substantial military support to South Vietnam. Moreover, in Cambodia, largely ignored in the peace settlement, Nixon intensified the bombing of Khmer Rouge forces.

During the summer of 1973, as the Nixon presidency reeled before revelation of his complicity in the Watergate coverup, antiwar leaders in Congress proposed to restrict the bombing of Cambodia. "Cambodia is not worth one American life," House majority leader Thomas P. "Tip" O'Neill explained. On June 25 the House voted 235 to 172 to cut off funds for the bombing of Cambodia.

Antiwar sentiment was strongest in urban and suburban areas and in the Far West. A majority of representatives in the South and Midwest voted against the resolution. The exceptions were North Carolina and Missouri, where the Congressional delegations were headed respectively by Senator Sam Ervin, chairman of the Watergate committee, and Senator Thomas Eagleton, author of the bill ending the bombing.

On June 17, Nixon vetoed the bill, claiming it would "cripple or destroy" prospects of peace in Southeast Asia, and the House fell just short of the two-thirds majority needed to override. Mike Mansfield, the majority leader of the Senate, warned Nixon that the amendment

would be attached to other bills "again and again, until the will of the people prevails." The President reluctantly agreed to terminate the bombing on August 15.

The Fall of South Vietnam

In September 1974, after Nixon's resignation, Congress slashed military aid to South Vietnam. That fall North Vietnam determined that the "opportune moment" had come. In January, 1975 it initiated a two-year plan to conquer South Vietnam with an attack on Phuoc Long province. The ARVN crumbled with a rapidity that surprised even the attackers.

In March, North Vietnamese forces advanced on Hue and Danang. ARVN abandoned the cities and fell back toward Saigon. During the trek south, the South Vietnamese army, on paper the fourth largest fighting force in the world, evaporated. On May 1 the Viet Cong entered Saigon and renamed it Ho Chi Minh City. Two weeks earlier, the Khmer Rouge had captured Phnom Penh. The war in Indochina was over.

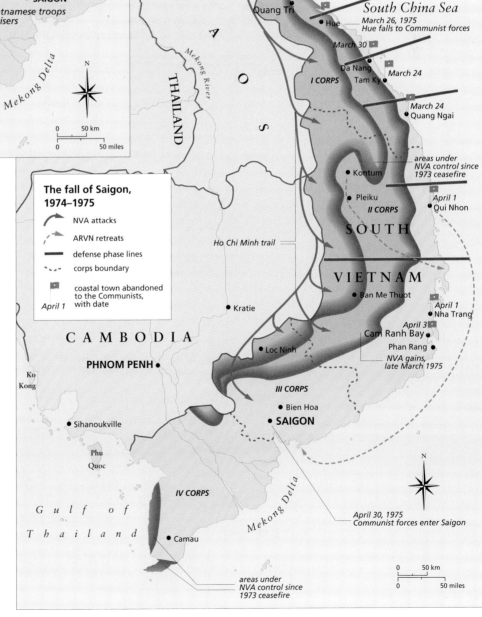

ONE GIANT LEAP FOR AMERICA
TO THE MOON

By the late 1950s the Cold War pitted Soviet and American scientists in a grim but nearly equal struggle to devise atomic weapons of unimaginable destructiveness. This technological equilibrium was shattered in October, 1957, when the Soviets launched Sputnik, the first artificial earth satellite. If Soviet rockets could send satellites streaking into orbit, they could also be tipped with nuclear weapons and obliterate American cities in a matter of minutes. President Eisenhower discounted the Soviet threat; and Air Force general Curtis LeMay dismissed Sputnik as "just a hunk of iron." Nevertheless, Eisenhower stepped up the U.S. Mercury program which, after some spectacular failures, shot a small satellite into space in early 1958.

Democrats, divided over racial issues, joined in censuring the Republican administration for allowing the Soviets to attain supremacy in space. During the presidential campaign of 1960, John F. Kennedy, the Democratic candidate, hammered away at his Republican opponent, Richard M. Nixon, for widening the "space gap" while Vice President; Nixon rebuked Kennedy for trying to "hitch his political wagon to the Soviet sputnik." But widespread fears that the United States had relinquished its lead in technology contributed to the appeal of the youthful and vigorous Democrat. Kennedy won the election, though by a paper-thin margin.

On April 12, 1961, just months into the Kennedy presidency, the Soviet Union put the first manned satellite into orbit and brought it safely back to earth. American prestige plummeted further the next week when U.S.-backed commandoes botched an invasion of Communist Cuba. Kennedy was buoyed by the successful suborbital flight on May 5 of astronaut Alan Shepard Jr. Later that month Kennedy shocked nearly everyone when he announced his goal of landing an American on the moon before the end of the decade. "If we can get to the moon before the Russians, then we should," he declared.

Congress, though initially staggered by the projected cost of this manned mission to the moon, called Project Apollo, endorsed the first of many multi-billion dollar appropriations for the enterprise. By the end of 1961, ground was broken for a huge new space complex in Houston, Texas, in the home state of Lyndon Johnson, Vice President and a space enthusiast.

Less than a year after the Soviet orbital flight, an Atlas rocket—similar to those that carried long-range nuclear warheads—lifted astronaut John Glenn into orbit. After five hours in space and three circuits of the earth, Glenn brought his craft down in the Atlantic 800 miles southeast of Bermuda. Three more flights, the last occurring in May 1963, marked the successful completion of Project Mercury.

The next phase was called Project Gemini, an allusion to the two-man payload of the capsules. The 12 Gemini missions from 1965 through 1966 featured extended flights, rendezvous and docking maneuvers, and space walks. Meanwhile, NASA was building the gigantic three-stage Saturn boosters that would lift seven million pounds from the ground and power Apollo's forty-four ton command and lunar landing modules into space. Gemini, like so much of the space program, had proceeded nearly on schedule.

But the first manned Apollo flight, scheduled for Feburary 1967, never took place. During a test an electrical arc ignited the spacecraft's pure oxygen, killing three astronauts. The tragedy delayed the space program, but its lead over the Societs was by now secure. (In April, a manned Soviet spacecraft lost control during re-entry, slammed into the ground, and was destroyed.)

Subsequent Apollo missions exceeded expectations. Apollo 8 (1968) attained lunar orbit; Apollo 9 (March, 1969) tested the lunar module; Apollo 10 (May) surveyed possible landing sites on the moon and practiced docking with the lunar module. On July 16, 1969, astronauts Neil Armstrong, Mike Collins and Buzz Aldrin were blasted into orbit 620,000 feet above the earth aboard Apollo 11. During the second orbit, another rocket pushed the spaceship beyond earth's gravity and set it on course for the moon. The lunar and command modules separated and docked, nose to nose. Three days later the spacecraft arrived in lunar orbit about 75 miles above the surface of the moon.

Armstrong and Aldrin crawled into Eagle, the landing craft, which then separated from the command module. A few minutes later, on July 20, 1969, Eagle gently touched down on the Sea of Tranquillity. While millions throughout the world stared at their grainy television pictures, Aldrin aimed his camera at Neil Armstrong, who descended a ladder on the exterior of Eagle, hopped onto the surface of the moon, and offered a dedication which, though garbled in transmission, was later deciphered: "That's one small step for man. One giant leap for mankind."

With the safe return of the crew of Apollo 11, the race to the moon had been won—before the close of the decade.

To the Moon

1   launch, July 16, 2:32 p.m. BST

2   second stage ignition, 2:34 p.m.

3   third stage ignition, earth orbit, 2:41 p.m.

4   thruster burn for moon trajectory, 5:22 p.m.

5   journey toward moon, nearly three days

6   transposition and docking of command and lunar modules

7   thruster burn for lunar orbit, July 20, 6:22 p.m.

8   lunar module separation, command module waits in orbit, 7:12 p.m.

9   lunar module approaches surface of moon moon, command module waits in orbit, 9:18 p.m.

10   lunar module ascends for rendezvous with command module, July 21, 6:53 p.m.

11   LM–CM docking, 8.27 p.m.

12   lunar module jettisoned, July 22, 2:24 a.m.

13   thruster burn for earth course, 5:57 a.m.

14   mid-course correction, slow for earth re-entry, thruster burn for earth re-entry, 9:02 p.m.

15   atmospheric re-entry, July 24, 5:35 p.m.

16   splashdown, 5:50 p.m.

Aldrin's descent, as photographed by Armstrong (right). While Aldrin and Armstrong were cavorting as the first men on the moon, Mike Collins continued his lonely circuits of the moon in the command module. Armstrong and Aldrin remained on the moon for nearly one full earth day.

Astronaut Edwin Aldrin on the moon, July 1969 (above). Reflected in his helmet visor are flight commander Neil Armstrong, who took this picture, and their spacecraft. Some 600 million people witnessed this historic event on television.

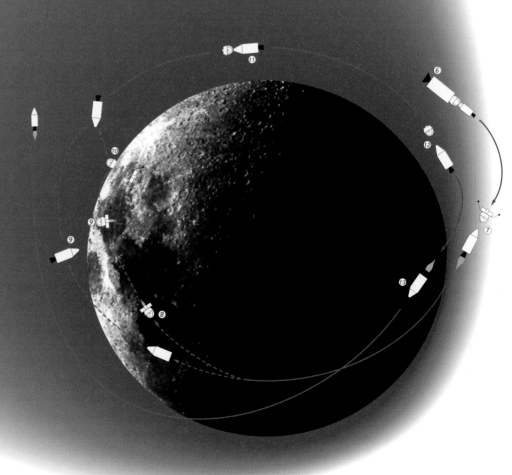

Left: *Launch of Apollo 11 on July 16, 1969 from Pad 39A, Cape Kennedy at 2:32 in the afternoon. Within 12 minutes, the 3,000-ton Saturn V boosters had lifted the spacecraft to an orbit 117 miles above the earth. The three pilots, pictured here, were Mike Collins, Neil Armstrong and Edwin Aldrin.*

PLANNING ARMAGEDDON
PREPARING FOR NUCLEAR WAR

By the mid-1980s American and Soviet arsenals each possessed over 20,000 nuclear weapons, many of them hydrogen bombs, each capable of obliterating 300 to 400 square miles. Everyone in the world could be killed many times over. Critics believed the enormous stockpiles of nuclear weaponry proof that Soviet and American military planners had gone mad. In fact, the nuclear arms race had evolved during the previous three decades according to the dictates of a highly intellectualized "game theory," which called for strategists on each side to anticipate—and then influence—the other's behavior. They insisted that only by planning for armageddon could it be avoided.

The Evolution of Counterforce
During the 1950s the American nuclear war plan called for its bombers and missiles to hit nearly ever Soviet military base and major city simultaneously. But strategists in the RAND Corporation, which advised the Air Force on target selection, observed that neither side could win such a war, nor afford, therefore, to begin one. If the Soviets sent their tank divisions against the smaller American and NATO garrisons in West Berlin, the American President, unwilling to initiate all-out nuclear war, would have to back down. The excesses of the American plan rendered it ineffective.

The strategists called for a more limited war plan, which became known as counterforce. It presumed a two-stage nuclear war: in the above example, the American President would have the capacity to retaliate against an attack on Berlin by firing a large percentage—but not all—of the nation's nuclear weapons at Soviet military and nuclear facilities. Russian cities would be spared. Soviet generals, on perceiving that their nuclear forces had been shattered but that their cities were still intact, would presumably refrain from a nuclear strike on American cities, opting instead to launch what remained of their missile forces against the American reserves. This counterattack would surely fail, enabling the President to use his remaining nuclear weapons to force a Soviet surrender.

In an American counterforce strike on Soviet nuclear facilities on the Black Sea, medium-range ballistic missiles, fired from U.S. submarines in the Mediterranean Sea or Indian Ocean, or from land-based launchers in Western Europe, would wipe out Soviet missile sites, submarine pens, and air bases. The major regional population centers—Odessa, Sevastopol, and Kerch—would be left alone—at least until after the first exchange.

In 1962, acting on the recommendation of Secretary of Defense Robert McNamara, President John F. Kennedy announced that he had replaced the all-out war plan with a counterforce strategy. The Soviets followed suit. In a possible variant of a counterforce strike on the Midwest, Soviet ICBMs, fired over the Arctic from Siberia, would target Minuteman missile silos in North Dakota and Missouri and the

Strategic Air Command near Omaha. Downtown Omaha and other major cities would be avoided. Because the survival of any enemy nuclear installation would almost ensure a calamitous retaliation, generals on each side endeavored to ensure that all possible targets would be swamped with bombs and missiles. The nuclear arms race was on.

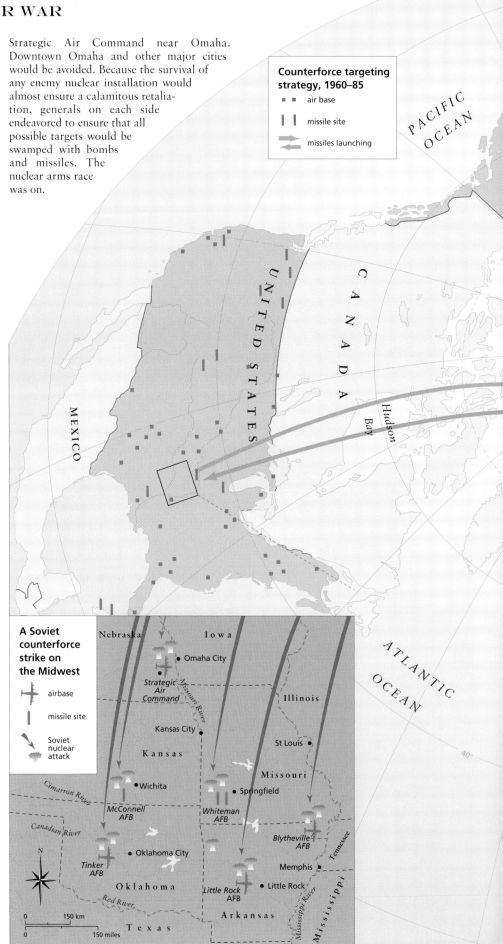

Counterforce targeting strategy, 1960–85
- air base
- missile site
- missiles launching

A Soviet counterforce strike on the Midwest
- airbase
- missile site
- Soviet nuclear attack

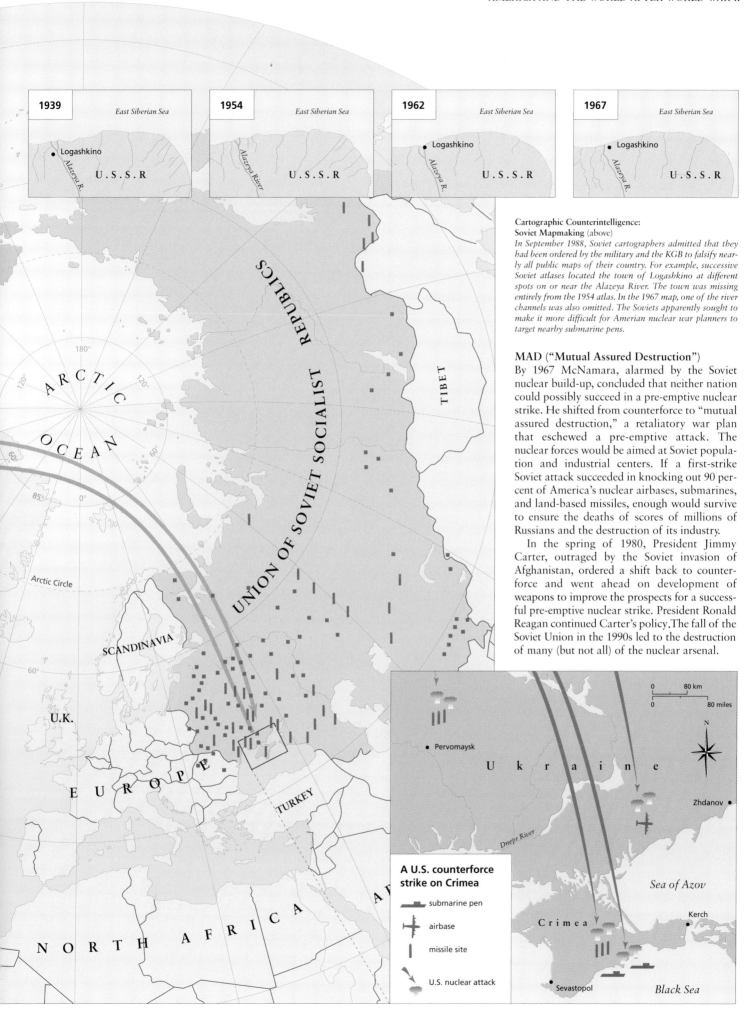

1939 East Siberian Sea

Logashkino

U.S.S.R

Alazeya R.

1954 East Siberian Sea

Alazeya River

U.S.S.R

1962 East Siberian Sea

Logashkino

U.S.S.R

Alazeya R.

1967 East Siberian Sea

Logashkino

U.S.S.R

Alazeya R.

Cartographic Counterintelligence:
Soviet Mapmaking (above)
In September 1988, Soviet cartographers admitted that they had been ordered by the military and the KGB to falsify nearly all public maps of their country. For example, successive Soviet atlases located the town of Logashkino at different spots on or near the Alazeya River. The town was missing entirely from the 1954 atlas. In the 1967 map, one of the river channels was also omitted. The Soviets apparently sought to make it more difficult for American nuclear war planners to target nearby submarine pens.

MAD ("Mutual Assured Destruction")

By 1967 McNamara, alarmed by the Soviet nuclear build-up, concluded that neither nation could possibly succeed in a pre-emptive nuclear strike. He shifted from counterforce to "mutual assured destruction," a retaliatory war plan that eschewed a pre-emptive attack. The nuclear forces would be aimed at Soviet population and industrial centers. If a first-strike Soviet attack succeeded in knocking out 90 percent of America's nuclear airbases, submarines, and land-based missiles, enough would survive to ensure the deaths of scores of millions of Russians and the destruction of its industry.

In the spring of 1980, President Jimmy Carter, outraged by the Soviet invasion of Afghanistan, ordered a shift back to counterforce and went ahead on development of weapons to improve the prospects for a successful pre-emptive nuclear strike. President Ronald Reagan continued Carter's policy. The fall of the Soviet Union in the 1990s led to the destruction of many (but not all) of the nuclear arsenal.

ARCTIC

OCEAN

180°

120°

120°

60°

0°

60°

90°

85°

60°

Arctic Circle

SCANDINAVIA

UNION OF SOVIET SOCIALIST

REPUBLICS

TIBET

U.K.

EUROPE

TURKEY

NORTH AFRICA

A U.S. counterforce strike on Crimea

⬛ submarine pen

✈ airbase

▌ missile site

↘ U.S. nuclear attack

Pervomaysk

U k r a i n e

Dnepr River

Zhdanov

Sea of Azov

Kerch

C r i m e a

Sevastopol

Black Sea

0   80 km

0   80 miles

N

PART 9: AMERICA, AN EVOLVING SUPERPOWER

The collapse of the Soviet Union in the early 1990s confirmed the judgment of the architects of containment nearly a half century earlier. Military expansion and especially a high-tech arms race, they believed, would exhaust the inefficient economy of the Soviet Union. By the 1990s the peoples of the Soviet Union, denied the goods and services most modern nations took for granted, demanded change. The Soviet state flinched before this challenge and, to nearly everyone's amazement, it withered away. The United States had won the Cold War. But as Americans surveyed their crumbling inner cities, rusting factories, and outmoded public transportation, few took much satisfaction in the victory. New problems appeared and old ones persisted. AIDS cut a wide swath through several generations. Abortion remained a source of bitter and divisive debate. And despite the fact that the United States stood as the sole superpower, foreign leaders often challenged its leadership and mocked its attempts at imposing order upon the world.

THE FIRST INFORMATION REVOLUTION

PUBLISHING, 1767–1980

The American book business grew up with the country. Yet its development was keyed not simply to the expansion of the population, the emergence of a distinctly American intellectual life, or the rise and decline of various cities as cultural meccas. Though publishing has often prided itself on being other than the average profit—seeking business, it has been as profoundly shaped by industrialization, the creation of a national market, and corporate growth as any facet of American economic life. The rise of publishing companies in the 19th century, the concentration of the trade in New York City, the role of corporate conglomerates in the production and sale of literature in the late 20th century—all illustrate the complex relations of culture and commerce, intellect and industry.

British North America's first great city, Boston, was also its premier publishing center. The colonies' first press was established in neighboring Cambridge in 1638, and from that time until the revolution, the Boston area nearly always led America in number of titles published. By 1700, of the British Empire's cities, only London surpassed it in number of imprints. Boston's pre-eminence, however, was not simply the product of Puritan New England's lively intellectual tradition, though religious works were the most frequently published titles both in the city and the colonies as a whole. Boston had more people, more commerce, and much political activity, and, thus, more of a market and a need for the printed word. As other towns grew, they, too, became publishing centers. And as Philadelphia, with its rich hinterland, overtook Boston in population, commerce, and political importance, so, too, did it overtake Boston in the production of books. While the dislocations of war may have been the immediate cause of Boston's publishing decline in the 1770s, Philadelphia did not, for several decades afterward, surrender its lead.

In the 19th century, American book publishing spread west with the population. But it also experienced the kinds of transformation evident in other arenas of economic life in an era of industrial revolution. As in so many industries, a greater specialization of function developed as business expanded. In 17th- and 18th-century America, publishing had been very much a household industry. Single individuals or establishments tended to be printers, publishers, and sellers of books (as well as of newspapers). In the more dynamic 19th-century economy, the manufacture of books, their promotion, financing and distribution, and their retailing became more distinct fields, pursued by different firms or by different groups within the emerging large concerns. At the same time, the development of steamboat navigation, canals, and railroads made regional and interregional trade easier and cheaper. This expansion of markets and more pro-

nounced division of labor both underwrote and presupposed a series of technological advances. Mechanization and related improvements in presses, papermaking, bookbinding, typesetting, and type founding allowed many more books to be published at less expense. In the meantime, population growth, the spread of public education, and the concentration of more Americans in urban areas created additional demand for literature.

These developments concentrated rather than diffused the industry, especially after the Civil War. Large firms clustered in a few cities where manufacturing and commercial facilities were abundant. Their ability to publish inexpensive literature and distribute it nationwide discouraged the printing of books elsewhere. In 1880, as in 1767, Boston, Philadelphia, and New York were the top three publishing centers. But whereas they had accounted for 63 percent of 1767 titles, they accounted for 86 percent of 1880 titles. The three cities' ranking had shifted, however. New York City, with the completion of the Erie Canal in the 1820s and the growth of railroads west, became America's leader in population, inter-regional trade, and finance. Not only its attractiveness

to writers, but its ability to finance and distribute their work, made New York the hub of American publishing.

New York retained its dominance through the 20th century. Yet its share of an enormously expanded industry had appeared to drop by 1980. Economic and demographic growth in the West and Southwest, and the vigor of university and small presses and textbook publishers accounted for some of this diffusion. But publishing facilities also sprang up in suburbs of traditional publishing sites, reflecting the flight of industry from city centers. Still, the most significant trends in 20th-century book publishing were not geographic. The industry grew rapidly after World War II with the explosion of paperback reprints, distributed not only through traditional trade channels, but through magazine wholesalers. With the G.I. Bill, the baby boom, and the advent of the space age, demand for text, technical, and reference books—long staples of the industry—multiplied. As in the 19th century, growth was accompanied by transformation. Old family firms went public; mergers abounded. The 1970s and 80s saw many well-established publishers acquired by large "communications"

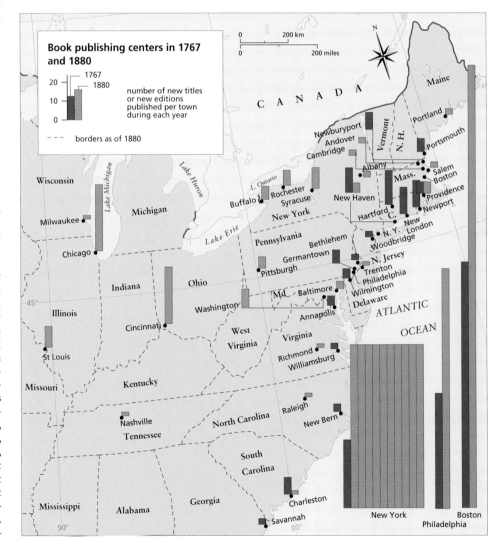

Book publishing centers in 1767 and 1880

number of new titles or new editions published per town during each year

borders as of 1880

Book publishing centers, 1980

number of titles published per town accounting for at least 0.25% of the total U.S. publication

conglomerates and multinational companies whose interests extended far beyond books. Such developments certainly had their parallels in other industries. Some observers worried, however, that a new breed of bottom line management, might be particularly dangerous in publishing, perhaps limiting the risk-taking involved in producing often unprofitable works of art and intellect.

Bookselling, too, has experienced both growth and a certain consolidation. Books had always been sold not only by bookstores, but by other retailers and through the mail. Independent booksellers had long complained of being undersold by discount stores, or even publishers. Such complaints increased in the 1970s and 80s, with the rapid growth of a handful of national and regional chains. Until the 1990s often "low inventory, low service" operations, these chain stores concentrated on marketing popular items to a broad audience. With resources to secure good locations and generous terms from publishers, chains' share of the book trade quadrupled between 1972 and 1987. Between 1981 and '87 the number of chain outlets grew at fifteen times the rate of independents. In Austin, Texas, with the nation's highest book sales per household in 1986, such trends were evident. In the late 1960s, the city's book trade was parceled out among downtown and university area independent booksellers, text and religious bookstores, and department stores. As a result of Austin's growth, by the late 1980s, the number of bookstores had climbed. But a good deal of the increased trade had been garnered by the chain stores which proliferated on the city's more recently developed peripheries—in malls and along suburban thoroughfares.

The rise of the chain store: bookselling in Austin, Texas, 1969 and 1988

- independent bookstore
- college textbook store
- religious book store
- department store with book department
- national or regional chain store

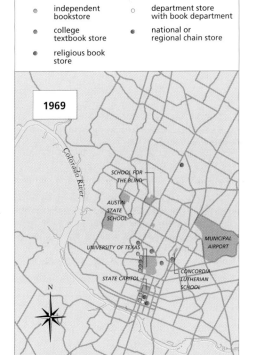

As American cities grew in the 1970s and 1980s, bookselling followed the population. In the newer suburbs—such as Austin's booming northern and western peripheries—books were often sold by national and regional chain retailers. The chains frequently proved more than a match for traditional independently-owned bookstores.

AMERICA'S HISPANICS

A NEW DIVERSITY

Until the 1960's, Europe and Africa had been the chief sources of those immigrant populations which, willingly or unwillingly, transformed America. Since then, Latin America and Asia have taken the lead in supplying the raw material of national diversity, the top five sources of legal immigrants by 1994 being Mexico, China, the Philippines, the Dominican Republic and Vietnam. Most Latino newcomers, joining a Spanish heritage population whose residence in the United States preceded that of many other ethnic groups, shared a common language and a common faith. Yet to term Hispanics a rapidly expanding "minority group" would be misleading. For just as the new Asian immigrants also include Koreans, Indians and Arabs, America's Latino population contains within itself a kaleidoscope of distinctive histories and cultures.

in government spending had become widespread. Citizens complained that newcomers were taking "Americans'" jobs or that taxpayers were being burdened by the expense of social services provided to recent—and in many cases illegal—arrivals.

The presence of an undocumented population, estimated at from 3 to 4 million persons in 1994—the majority of whom were believed to be from Latin American nations and only a portion of whom were counted by the Census—makes any statistical conclusions about Hispanics inexact. It is clear, however, that Latinos, on average, have received less education, are more urbanized , are poorer, and are more likely to work in low-paying blue collar and service jobs than non-Hispanic whites.

Yet such generalizations obscured crucial differences, for Latinos vary widely in cultural, ethnic and class background. In some respects, such as the prevalence of female-headed households, Puerto Ricans have had as much in common with African-Americans than

Southwest's expanding railroads, mines, and agriculture. Since then, the volume and destination of Mexican immigrants have responded to changes in America's economy. During the Depression, the U.S. deported Mexican workers, while in the following decade it sanctioned their import. As agriculture mechanized and manufacture expanded in the Southwest and Midwest, Mexican-Americans became an increasingly urban population. Mexico has become the nation's largest single source of immigrants, but in 1990 some two-thirds of Latinos of Mexican heritage were American-born (as opposed to somewhat less than 30 percent of those of Cuban or Dominican origin).

Like Mexicans, Puerto Ricans—who, as American citizens, move freely between the island and the mainland—have tended to be drawn into a low wage, regional job market. Migration boomed after World War Two as the accelerated industrialization of Puerto Rico's plantation economy displaced countless workers. After the 1950s, net migration fell off, and in some years was even reversed, as the exodus eased conditions on the island and as many of the New York industries which employed Puerto Ricans declined.

The thousands leaving Cuba by the beginning of the 1960s were not seeking work as much as refuge. Opponents of Fidel Castro's regime, many of them well off, created an "enclave economy" in Miami, complete with Cuban-run businesses and banks. The number of Cuban emigres varied with shifts in Cuban and U.S. policy, the most dramatic of which allowed 125,000 to depart during 1980's "boatlift." The influx of Central Americans in the late 1970s and 1980s also included many refugees. Yet upheaval, repression, and widespread poverty were often intertwined in countries like El Salvador. Many fled in the interest of both life and livelihood.

The rapid growth of Hispanic immigration in the 20th century, its changing composition, and its sensitivity to American economic fluctuations were well illustrated in Houston, Texas. Unlike San Antonio or Los Angeles, Houston had not been settled by Latinos, and its Mexican-American population remained small before 1900. The town's increasing importance as a rail, shipping, cotton and oil industry center drew Mexican laborers who settled in *barrios* near the ship channel, east of downtown. Migration to Houston slowed during the Depression, but between 1950 and 1990, the Hispanic population increased by over 1000 percent, reaching an estimated 450,000 (27.6 percent of the total). Increasingly, Central Americans, particularly undocumented Salvadorans, joined the city's resident Mexican-Americans, their proportion of total Hispanic population more than doubling in the 1980s, to over 20 percent. This growth in size and diversity, but also the fortunes of Houston itself, reshaped the

Residents of Hispanic origins, 1990

- 1,000,000 and over
- 500,000 to 999,999
- 100,000 to 499,999
- under 100,000

components of the Hispanic population, top 8 states:

- Mexican
- Puerto Rican
- Cuban
- other

The number of Latinos in the United States increased by over 250 percent between 1950 and 1980, and by over 50 percent in the following decade. They accounted for nine percent of the nation's residents by 1990. Of the 22 million Hispanics counted that year, some 60 percent were of Mexican origin, 12 percent were of Puerto Rican descent, 5 percent were Cuban-American, and almost 23 percent were categorized by the Census as "other Hispanics". This growth in part stemmed from high fertility rates, Latinos tending to have more children than either non-Hispanic whites or blacks. Complementing this, though, was a vast expansion of Hispanic immigration since World War II, fueled by changes in U.S. laws and involving both legal and "undocumented" entrants. These immigrants were not always made to feel welcome, especially where local economies were faltering or calls for reductions

with other Hispanics. Even generalizations about Latino fertility were deceptive, Cuban-Americans having fewer children than the American population as a whole. Moreover, distinct histories have yielded distinct regional concentrations. In 1990, over four-fifths of Mexican-Americans lived in four Southwestern states. The mainland Puerto Rican population, on the other hand, is centered in New York City and environs and Cuban-Americans increasingly concentrated in Florida. The Census' "other Hispanics" were more far-flung—they ranged from Central American refugees living in Eastern cities to Coloradans and New Mexicans claiming descent from early Spanish settlers (there were approximately 80,000 Mexicans in the South-west at the time of American annexation).

Mexican citizens first migrated to the United States in large number at the end of the 19th century and provided cheap labor for the

Hispanic community. Rents collapsed with the oil slump of the 1980s, such that the growing Latino population could not only expand the boundaries of traditional Mexican-American neighborhoods east and north of downtown, but create predominantly Central American enclaves in apartment complexes in southwest Houston. But by the same token, the sort of industrial jobs which had drawn Mexicans to Houston began to disappear, to be replaced by lower paying and less secure service employment.

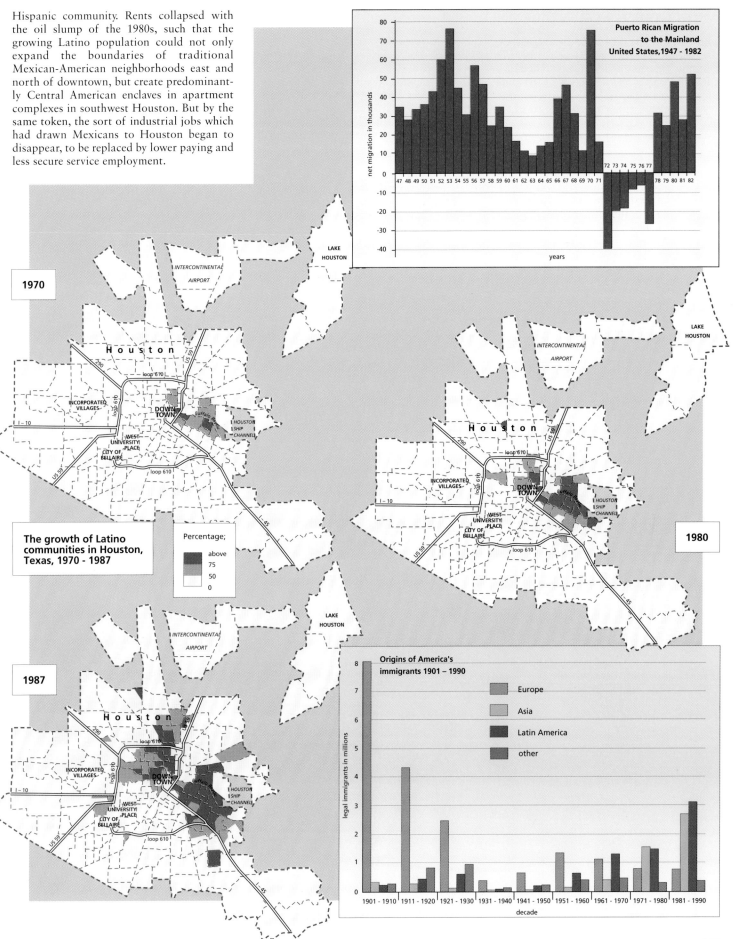

Puerto Rican Migration to the Mainland United States, 1947 - 1982

The growth of Latino communities in Houston, Texas, 1970 - 1987

Percentage;
- above
- 75
- 50
- 0

1970

1980

1987

Origins of America's immigrants 1901 – 1990
- Europe
- Asia
- Latin America
- other

ENERGY VERSUS THE ENVIRONMENT
THE GREAT DILEMMA

The U.S., once blessed with vast forests and seemingly inexhaustible deposits of coal and oil, has seldom been plagued by the fuel shortages common to many other nations. But after World War II America's voracious appetite for energy finally outstripped available resources. The United States was still importing one-third of its oil by 1973, when the principal oil-producing nations cut off exports to the West. Petroleum prices skyrocketed, triggering an inflation that crippled the economy. President Jimmy Carter sought to reduce oil imports by increasing the output of nuclear and coal-fired power plants, proposals that enraged environmentalists. How to provide the cheap energy essential to economic growth while preserving the environment has yet to be resolved.

Oil and the Environment

All fossil fuels produce carbon compounds that pollute the air and trap the solar heat that reflects off the earth's surface (see *Global Warming p 16–17*). Oil poses a further environmental threat arising from the huge distances supertankers must travel from the regions that produce the oil to the industrial nations that consume it. Middle Eastern oil is shipped thousands of miles through the Indian Ocean and the Straits of Singapore to Japan, Taiwan, and Korea; around Africa to Great Britain and western Europe; across the Mediterranean to southern Europe and eventually the United States. Oil from Venezuela and Mexico is transported to American refineries on the Atlantic Coast. Each year, supertankers discharge into the oceans a million metric tons of oil as ballast; another half million tons are spilled in tanker accidents. The most serious occurred in 1989 when the Exxon Valdez ran aground off Alaska and spilled more than 10 million gallons of crude oil (*see map right*).

Coal and Acid Rain

The world's supply of coal, presently the most plentiful source of cheap energy, will last into the 23rd century at current rates of use. But coal when burned emits high levels of carbon dioxide, a major factor in global warming. Furthermore, the towering smokestacks of coal-fired factories and power plants spare nearby localities but spew thick clouds of sulfur dioxide high into the atmosphere, where it is borne great distances by the wind, becomes dissolved in water droplets and returns to earth as acid rain, a dilute form of sulfuric acid. Acid rain destroys plants and animals, disrupts ecological systems, contaminates fisheries and drinking water, and erodes buildings and statues.

Most sulfur dioxide is emitted from coal-burning factories and power plants in the industrial Midwest, especially Ohio, Indiana, and Illinois. The regions most seriously affected by acid rain include the central Atlantic coastal plain, the highlands of Florida, and the southwestern Adirondacks, areas where about half of the lakes and streams have become acidic. Acid rain has extensively damaged conifer forests in the Appalachians.

The Nuclear Alternative

On March 28, 1979, the nuclear reactor at Three Mile Island (TMI) in Pennsylvania went out of control, forcing the evacuation of nearly 150,000 people. Six years later the new Soviet leader, Mikhail Gorbachev, endeavored to save his country's faltering economy by embarking on a crash program to develop nuclear energy. On April 26, 1986, after night operators of the nuclear plant at Chernobyl had short-circuited safety systems during a test, the reactor began fissioning wildly and then blew up, pumping tons of radioactive material into the atmosphere. The radioactive cloud lingered perversely over Europe, contaminating crops and subjecting an estimated 30,000 persons to radiation doses that may eventually prove fatal. The nuclear power industry, which had long touted reactors as a safe and clean alternative to fossil fuels, was at least for a time crippled by political fallout from these accidents. Concerns about storage of atomic wastes, some of which remain radioactive for centuries, have further called into question the viability of nuclear energy.

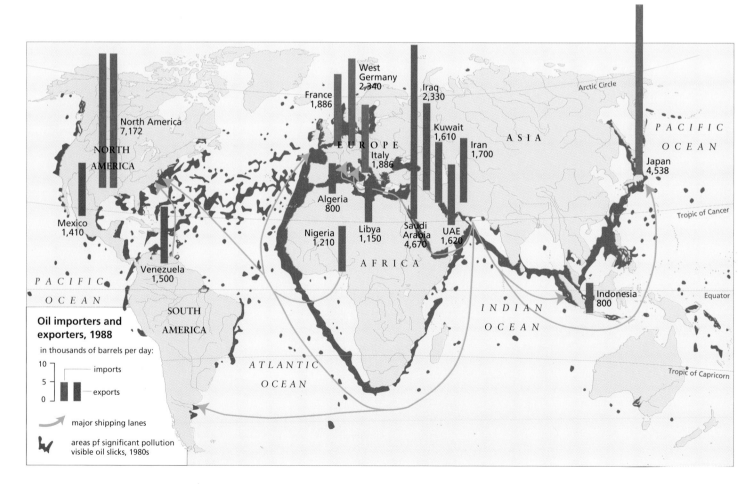

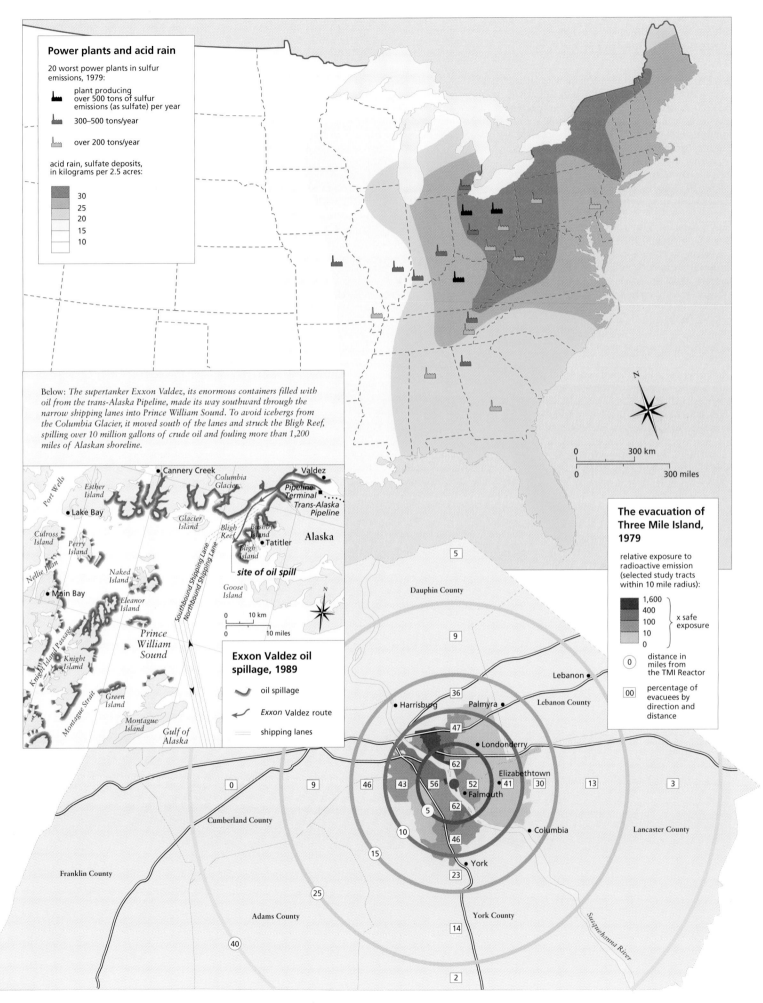

Power plants and acid rain

20 worst power plants in sulfur emissions, 1979:

plant producing over 500 tons of sulfur emissions (as sulfate) per year

300–500 tons/year

over 200 tons/year

acid rain, sulfate deposits, in kilograms per 2.5 acres:

30
25
20
15
10

Below: *The supertanker Exxon Valdez, its enormous containers filled with oil from the trans-Alaska Pipeline, made its way southward through the narrow shipping lanes into Prince William Sound. To avoid icebergs from the Columbia Glacier, it moved south of the lanes and struck the Bligh Reef, spilling over 10 million gallons of crude oil and fouling more than 1,200 miles of Alaskan shoreline.*

Port Wells

Cannery Creek

Esther Island

Valdez

Columbia Glacier

Pipeline Terminal

Trans-Alaska Pipeline

Lake Bay

Glacier Island

Bligh Reef

Bushby Island

Alaska

Culross Island

Perry Island

Bligh Island

Tatitler

Nellie Juan

Naked Island

site of oil spill

Goose Island

Main Bay

Eleanor Island

Prince William Sound

0   10 km

0   10 miles

Knight Island Passage

Knight Island

N

Exxon Valdez oil spillage, 1989

oil spillage

Exxon Valdez route

shipping lanes

Southbound Shipping Lane

Northbound Shipping Lane

Green Island

Montague Strait

Montague Island

Gulf of Alaska

N

0   300 km

0   300 miles

The evacuation of Three Mile Island, 1979

relative exposure to radioactive emission (selected study tracts within 10 mile radius):

1,600
400   x safe
100   exposure
10
0

⓪ distance in miles from the TMI Reactor

⬜00⬜ percentage of evacuees by direction and distance

Dauphin County

5

9

36

Lebanon

Harrisburg

Palmyra

Lebanon County

47

Londonderry

62

Elizabethtown

0   9   46   43   56   52   41   30   13   3

Falmouth

5

62

10

46   Columbia

Cumberland County

Lancaster County

15

York

Franklin County

23

25

Adams County

York County

14

40

Susquehanna River

2

261

AIDS

THE NEW PLAGUE

In December, 1980 Dr. Michael Gottlieb was baffled by the case of a young patient at UCLA who suffered from a rare bacterial infection called pneumocystis carinii pneumonia (PCP). PCP usually attacked infants or adults with impaired immune systems, but this young man had been strong and fit. The following March two more PCP patients were admitted to the UCLA hospital. When Gottlieb learned of another two local PCP cases, he notified the Center of Disease Control in Atlanta, which on June 5, 1981, issued a nationwide alert on the "unusual" outbreak of PCP among five healthy men in Los Angeles. It added that the men were homosexuals. Within months, they would be dead.

The CDC report set off alarms in San Francisco and New York, where several physicians had also treated gay men suffering from PCP or from a rare cancer called Kaposi's sarcoma, which also afflicted people with defective immune systems. By September the CDC had learned of nearly 100 cases of PCP and Kaposi's, nearly all in New York City, San Francisco or Los Angeles. All but a handful of the patients were white, male—and gay.

By early 1982, health officials proposed to call the syndrome "gay related immunodeficiency" (GRID), but it soon became evident that PCP and Kaposi's sarcoma were also appearing in non-gays. That fall the doctors decided on a more neutral name for the disease: "acquired immune-deficiency syndrome" (AIDS). By the end of the year about 1,000 persons had come down with AIDS. They included 727 gays, 155 intravenous drug users, 50 Haitians, 7 hemophiliacs and some others.

The CDC concluded that AIDS was caused by a lethal virus known as HIV, spread chiefly through anal intercourse between men, or through contaminated needles shared by intravenous drug abusers. That AIDS was contagious was suggested by the fact that nearly two-thirds of the initial 1,000 AIDS patients were from New York City, San Francisco and Los Angeles, cities that were closely identified with a free-wheeling gay culture.

By the mid-1980s, AIDS had spilled out of the major cities of the East and West coasts and swept through gay populations throughout the nation. Similarly high rates of HIV infection were found among homosexual populations in various major cities in 1987, ranging from 52 percent in San Francisco, 50 percent in Philadelphia-Pittsburgh, 49 percent in Boston, 48 percent in Los Angeles, 44 percent in Atlanta, and 41 percent in Chicago. Unlike gays, many of whom are affluent and mobile, intravenous drug users less frequently spread the disease to cities outside New York City.

This is reflected in the fact that HIV infection among intravenous drug users approached 50 percent only in New York City and its environs. In Seattle-Tacoma, Los Angeles, Madison-Milwaukee, and Atlanta, less than 10 percent of the intravenous drug users showed evidence of HIV infection.

However, the spread in the latter years of the 1980s of "safe sex" practices among the gay population to some extent changed the profile of America's AIDS victims in the 1990s. A declining proportion of new AIDS cases were attributed to homosexual sex and an increasing percentage to i.v. drug use and heterosexual contact. No longer was AIDS a disease predominantly of white men. In 1986 about 26 percent of new AIDS cases had occurred among African-Americans; in 1994, 40 percent did. The figure for women was 8 percent in 1986 and 18 percent in 1994. Nor was AIDS any more a scourge of large cities alone but reached small towns and into the countryside. An increasingly less selective killer, AIDS in 1992 was second only to accidents as the leading cause of death among Americans between 25 and 44. By 1995, as the United States celebrated the 50th anniversary of the end of the Second World War, it had lost nearly 300,000 of its people to the plague—almost as many Americans as had died in the combat half a century before.

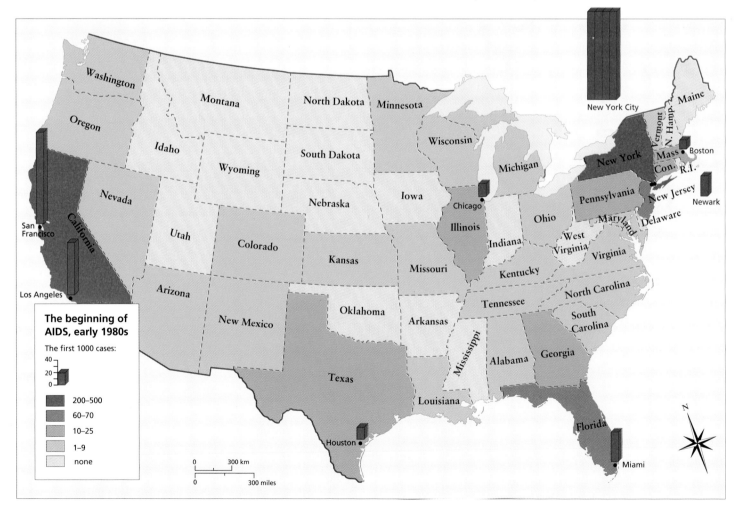

The beginning of AIDS, early 1980s

The first 1000 cases:

- 200–500
- 60–70
- 10–25
- 1–9
- none

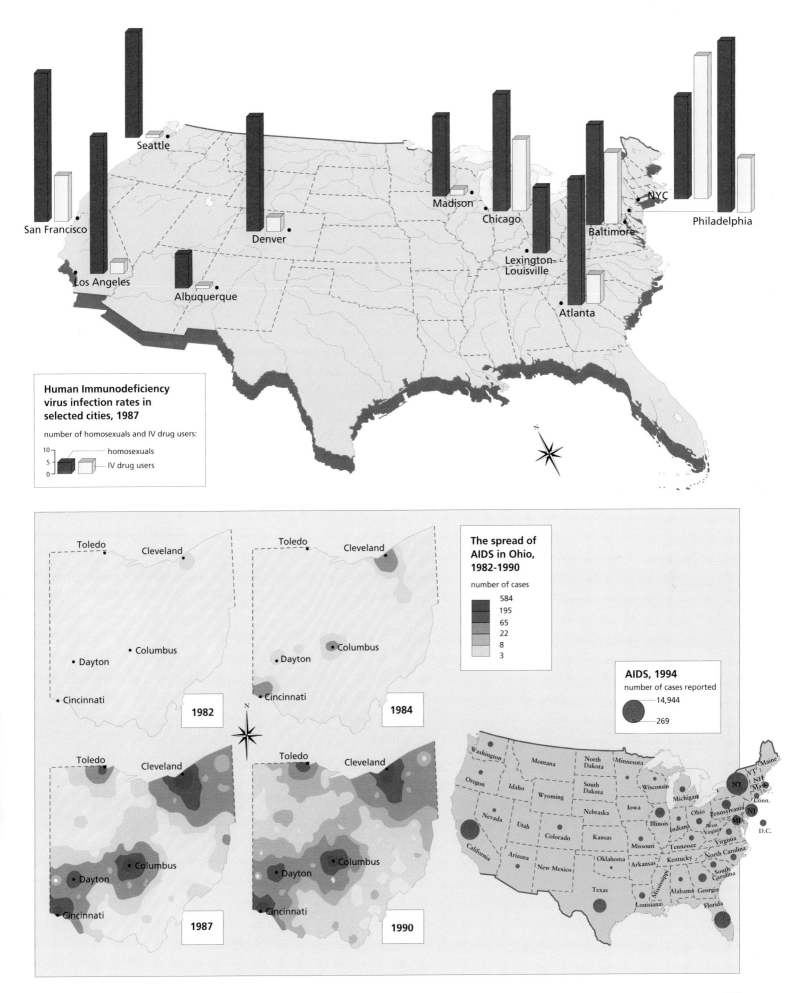

Human Immunodeficiency virus infection rates in selected cities, 1987

number of homosexuals and IV drug users:

10
5
0
homosexuals
IV drug users

The spread of AIDS in Ohio, 1982-1990

number of cases

584
195
65
22
8
3

AIDS, 1994

number of cases reported

14,944

269

THE ABORTION CONTROVERSY
TO ROE VERSUS WADE AND AFTER

In 1969, 25-year-old Norma McCorvey was unmarried, unemployed—and pregnant. She made up a story that she had been raped and asked a doctor to perform an abortion. He explained that in Texas, as in almost every other state, abortion was illegal except when necessary to perserve the woman's life. McCorvey contacted a lawyer who persuaded her to challenge the Texas anti-abortion law. Using the pseudonym, "Jane Roe," she filed suit against the Dallas County prosecutor, Henry Wade. In 1973 the U.S. Supreme Court, in Roe v. Wade, struck down all statutes that interfered with a woman's right to abortion. Outraged conservatives voted to overturn the decision. The ensuing debate has raged into the 1990s.

The U.S. Constitution did not refer to abortion, and no state restricted that practice until 1821, when Connecticut prohibited the use of "deadly poisons" in the procedure. During the next 20 years, nine more states and the territory of Iowa imposed similar restrictions on abortions. In 1859 the American Medical Association, alarmed that surgical abortions resulted in the deaths of far more women than would die in childbirth, called for the "general suppression" of the practice. By 1900, every state except Kentucky had enacted anti-abortion statutes. With minor modifications, these laws remained on the books throughout the first half of the 20th century.

During the early 1950s the widespread use among pregnant women of the tranquilizer thalidomide resulted in horrendous birth defects among thousands of babies; during the early 1960s an epidemic of German measles swept the nation, also causing irreversible harm to many fetuses. The spectacle of these babies, many of whom languished in vegetative states, and the agony of their families contributed to the demand for legal abortions. By 1967, when the AMA endorsed abortion rights, more than a million American women were undergoing illegal—and often needlessly unsafe—abortions every year.

In 1970, Hawaii became the first state to repeal its criminal abortion statute. The battle over abortion in New York became especially vociferous, pitting liberals, feminists, and the medical establishment against conservatives and the Roman Catholic Church. The State Senate narrowly voted in favor of repeal, but on April 9, 1970, the New York Assembly became deadlocked at 75 votes on each side of the question. Then Assemblyman George Michaels, who represented a largely Catholic constituency in the Finger Lakes, stepped to the podium and declared that he could not stand in the way of abortion reform. He switched his vote to yes, conceding that his support of abortion rights would mean an end to his political career. (Michaels, a Republican, failed to win renomination the following year.) Support for abortion was strongest in urban areas, especially Manhattan and the Bronx, and in the suburbs of New York and Rochester; opposition to legalized abortion was concentrated in rural districts and in ethnic Catholic districts such as Queens (in New York City) and along the Mohawk Valley.

During the next three years, Alaska and Washington repealed their anti-abortion laws, and many other states modified existing statutes to permit abortion to save the woman's life, or when she had been impregnated through rape or incest. Louisiana, Pennsylvania, and New Hampshire prohibited abortion for any reason. Roe v. Wade overturned all existing state laws restricting abortion.

The Era of Legalized Abortion

The years immediately following Roe v. Wade witnessed a rapid expansion of abortion facilities throughout the nation. From 1973 to 1980, the number of abortions performed annually in the United States rose from 745,000 to over 1, 500,000. At that point, however, this growth leveled off, the annual number of abortions hovering at about that figure through the 1980s and early 1990s. The abortion rates per 1,000 women 15 to 44 years old had, by 1992, in fact, fallen below the levels of the early 80s.

During this period, anti-abortion forces had become increasingly well-organized, making their presence felt most particularly in the Republican party but also mounting increasingly militant street demonstrations. Reconfigured by right-to-life presidents Reagan and Bush, the Supreme Court, in such cases as Webster v. Reproductive Health Services (1989) and Planned Parenthood of Southeastern Pennsylvania v. Casey (1992), by narrow majorities declined to reverse Roe, but it did allow states to impose certain conditions, such as waiting periods, before abortions could be performed and upheld prohibitions on the use of public funds for them. Many doctors refused to involve themselves in abortions, most medical students were not trained in the procedure, and in many areas no clinics existed to meet local demand for the service. This was especially the case in more rural communities.

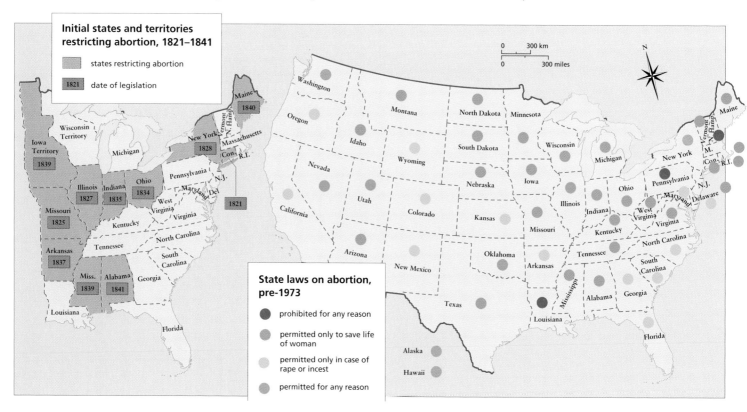

Initial states and territories restricting abortion, 1821–1841

- states restricting abortion
- 1821 date of legislation

State laws on abortion, pre-1973

- prohibited for any reason
- permitted only to save life of woman
- permitted only in case of rape or incest
- permitted for any reason

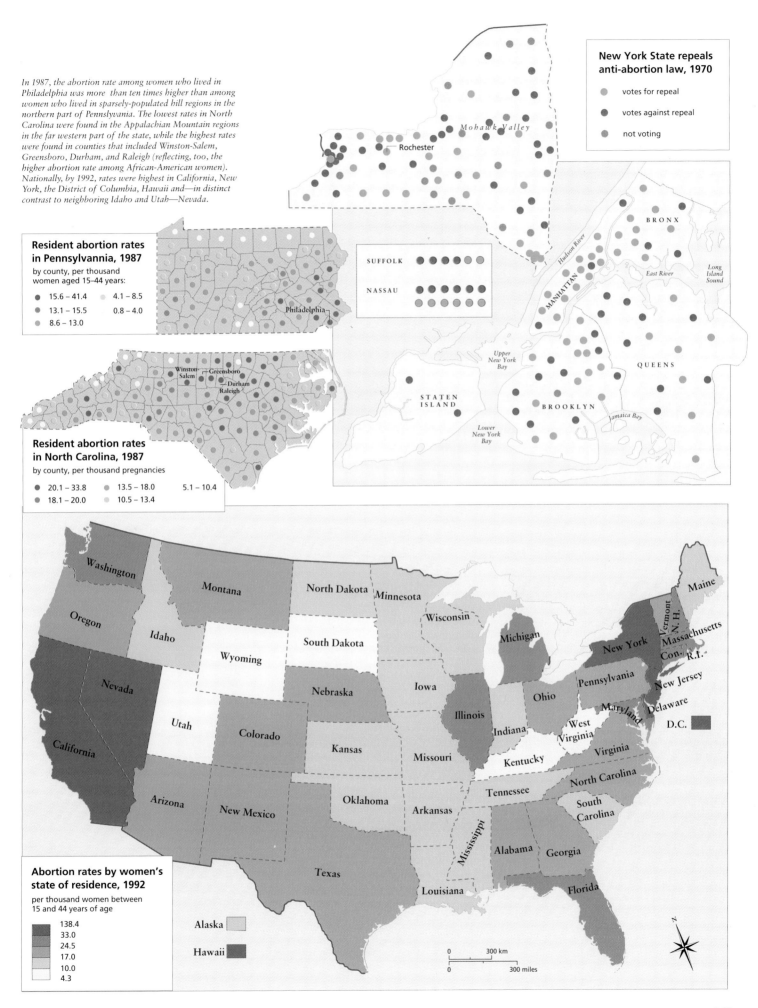

In 1987, the abortion rate among women who lived in Philadelphia was more than ten times higher than among women who lived in sparsely-populated hill regions in the northern part of Pennsylvania. The lowest rates in North Carolina were found in the Appalachian Mountain regions in the far western part of the state, while the highest rates were found in counties that included Winston-Salem, Greensboro, Durham, and Raleigh (reflecting, too, the higher abortion rate among African-American women). Nationally, by 1992, rates were highest in California, New York, the District of Columbia, Hawaii and—in distinct contrast to neighboring Idaho and Utah—Nevada.

New York State repeals anti-abortion law, 1970

- votes for repeal
- votes against repeal
- not voting

Resident abortion rates in Pennsylvannia, 1987

by county, per thousand women aged 15–44 years:

- 15.6 – 41.4
- 13.1 – 15.5
- 8.6 – 13.0
- 4.1 – 8.5
- 0.8 – 4.0

Resident abortion rates in North Carolina, 1987

by county, per thousand pregnancies

- 20.1 – 33.8
- 18.1 – 20.0
- 13.5 – 18.0
- 10.5 – 13.4
- 5.1 – 10.4

Abortion rates by women's state of residence, 1992

per thousand women between 15 and 44 years of age

- 138.4
- 33.0
- 24.5
- 17.0
- 10.0
- 4.3

Alaska

Hawaii

265

A NEW WORLD ORDER

A NEW ERA OF PEACE?

By 1990, Mikhail Gorbachev's efforts at reforming the Soviet Union appeared to have culminated in its economic and military collapse. The Red Army was withdrawing from eastern European nations and non-Communists were replacing them. After decades of "Cold War," Americans eagerly awaited a new era of peace. Theses hopes were clouded in August when Iraq invaded Kuwait and remained so even with the Allied victory early in 1991 and the break-up of the Soviet Union later that year. Ethnic nationalism and, sometimes, mere gangsterism sparked potentially contagious conflicts both in formerly Communist and third world nations. Presidents felt compelled to continue to send American soldiers abroad, often in the company of United Nations forces. While the international deployment of U.S. military personnel retained certain of its Cold War configurations—with large numbers stationed in western Europe and Japan—the pattern of actual intervention lacked the coherence that anti-Communism had once imposed on U.S. foreign policy.

Despite the United States' subsequent involvements in Somalia, Haiti, Bosnia, and elsewhere, the Gulf War represented the signal military event of the early post-Cold War years. Anxious to secure huge oil fields, the United States, Britain, and Egypt had dispatched troops to Saudi Arabia immediately upon Saddam Hussein's invasion of neighboring Kuwait. The United Nations Security Council, with Gorbachev's support, hastily imposed an embargo on trade with Iraq. In late November the Security Council voted overwhelmingly to authorize the use of force to drive Iraqi troops from Kuwait if they had not withdrawn by January 15, 1991.

Meanwhile, nearly a half million soldiers, the great majority of them American, poured into Saudi Arabia. They were accompanied by tens of thousands of tanks, armored vehicles, and supplies that where shipped into Dhahran and other bases near the Kuwait-Saudi Arabia border. By January 1, 1991, 38 nations, including many Arab states, had joined the coalition against Iraq.

Saddam, curiously unmoved by this display of world opinion and military might, ordered his half-million men to hold their positions in the desert. There they remained on Tuesday, January 15.

That morning President Bush signed a directive authorizing General H. Norman Schwartzkopf, commander of the coalition forces, to commence a bombing campaign against Iraq. On January 17, shortly after midnight, more than 1,000 fighters, bombers and other aircraft took off from air bases in Saudi Arabia and other Gulf states and from carriers in the Mediterranean, the Red Sea, and the Persian Gulf. Their primary targets were Iraqi airfields, air and missile defenses, and nuclear and poison gas facilities. Rather than challenge this formidable air armada, most of the Iraqi aircraft remained in underground bunkers; some attempted to slip away to Iran. During the next 43 days and nights allied airplanes, virtually unchallenged in the air, pounded Iraq's key military, government, and industrial installations.

Saddam, hoping to force Arab states into abandoning the coalition, fired Soviet-made missiles, called Scuds, at Israel. Riyadh, the Saudi capital, and Dharhan, the major coalition supply base, were also hit. The Scuds, which carried a small conventional warhead, were of little military significance. Moreover, many of the 86 Scuds were knocked out of the air by American Patriot missiles. Israel, though it sustained some losses, refrained from entering the war and the coalition held together.

While his troops were burrowing deep into the sand to escape allied bombs, Saddam clung to the hope that his forces could hold their own on the ground. During the Iran-Iraq war several years earlier, his army had succeeded in driving off repeated Iranian counterattacks. But Saddam miscalculated. The United States, having spent decades gearing up for a massive Soviet thrust into Europe, would prove a far more formidable foe than Iran.

With the allied bombing campaign experiencing diminishing returns against Iraq's limited military-industrial infrastructure, attention turned to the inevitable ground war. Colin Powell, Chairman of the U.S. Joint Chiefs of Staff, announced with chilling bravado the coalition strategy for defeating the Iraqi army: "First we're going to cut it off and then we're going to kill it."

General Schwartzkopf, however, seemed to be planning to bludgeon the Iraqi army with a frontal assault. In early February he made an elaborate show of massing ground forces immediately south of Kuwait. When Iraq reinforced and fortified these positions, Schwartzkopf surreptitiously shifted nearly a quarter of a million soldiers and thousands of tanks to positions nearly a hundred miles further west.

Early in the morning of February 24, U.S. and Saudi troops crashed through Iraqi lines into Kuwait. Naval and Marine units feinted at landing on the beaches of Kuwait City. While the Iraqis raced reinforcements to southern Kuwait and the coast, the main coalition offensive occurred far to the west as armored and airborne units roared northward across the desert toward the Euphrates River. Within 12 hours, the 101st Airborne Division had established a cluster of refueling and resupply depots 75 miles inside Iraq near the desert town of Salman. Within two days, allied forces had reached the Euphrates.

Allied bombers soon knocked out the bridges spanning the Euphrates, thereby trapping the entire Iraqi army. The only way out was a land bridge at Nasiriyah. The Republican Guard, the best of the Iraqi forces, fled in that direction, sustaining enormous losses from allied bombers and missile-firing helicopters along the way. About 50 miles west of Basra, the 300 tanks of the Republican Guard were intercepted by some 800 American tanks. The fighting began at dusk. When the sun rose the next morning, virtually all of the Iraqi tanks had been destroyed. Saddam then announced his willingness to comply with UN directives. In less than 100 hours, the allies had destroyed 3,700 Iraqi tanks, captured 175,000 Iraqi prisoners, and ousted the Iraqis from Kuwait. The ground war was over.

But Saddam remained in power, and his persistence gave notice that the post-Cold War era-would not necessarily be dominated by American military might.

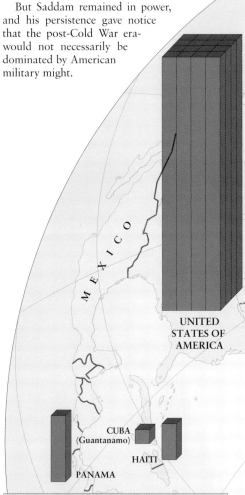

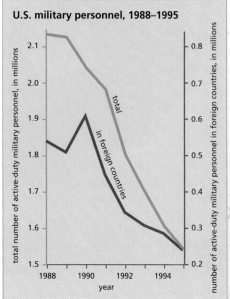

U.S. military personnel, 1988–1995

total number of active-duty military personnel, in millions

number of active-duty military personnel in foreign countries, in millions

year

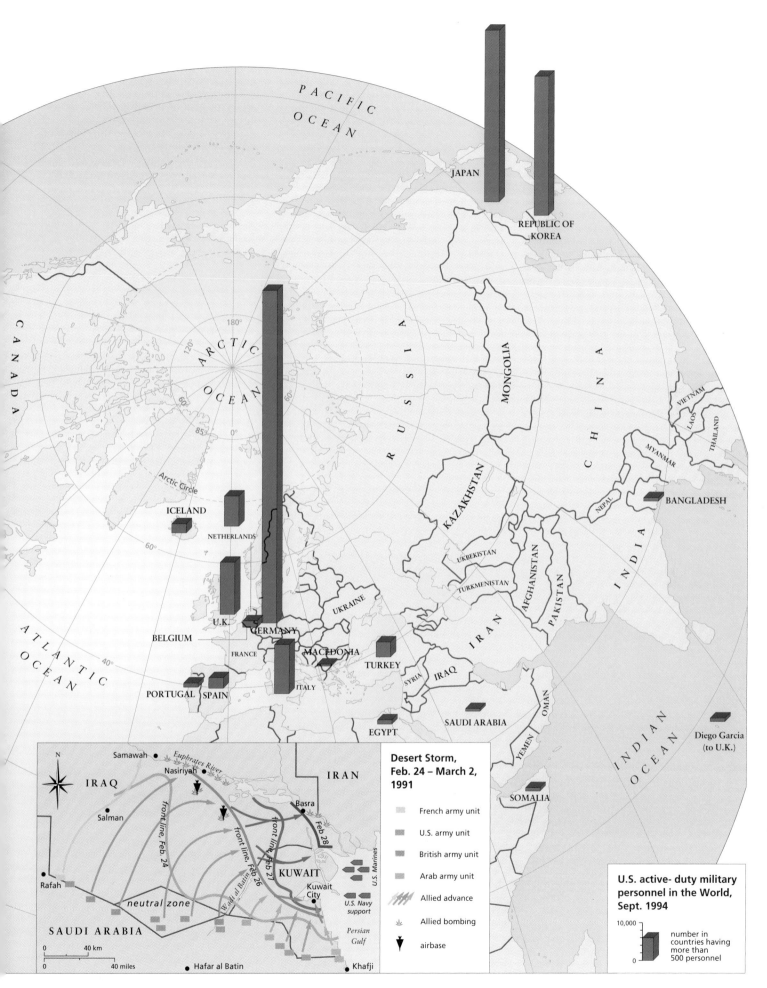

PACIFIC
OCEAN

JAPAN

REPUBLIC OF
KOREA

CANADA

ARCTIC
OCEAN

ICELAND

NETHERLANDS

Arctic Circle

ATLANTIC
OCEAN

U.K.

BELGIUM

GERMANY

FRANCE

PORTUGAL SPAIN

ITALY

MACEDONIA

TURKEY

SYRIA

IRAQ

EGYPT

SAUDI ARABIA

RUSSIA

MONGOLIA

CHINA

KAZAKHSTAN

UKRAINE

UKBEKISTAN

TURKMENISTAN

AFGHANISTAN

IRAN

PAKISTAN

NEPAL

INDIA

BANGLADESH

VIETNAM

LAOS

THAILAND

MYANMAR

OMAN

YEMEN

SOMALIA

INDIAN
OCEAN

Diego Garcia
(to U.K.)

**Desert Storm,
Feb. 24 – March 2,
1991**

Samawah

Euphrates River

Nasiriyah

IRAQ

IRAN

Basra

Feb 28

Salman

front line, Feb. 24

front line, Feb 26

front line, Feb 27

KUWAIT

Rafah

neutral zone

Wadi al Batin

Kuwait
City

U.S. Marines

SAUDI ARABIA

0   40 km

0   40 miles

Hafar al Batin

Khafji

Persian
Gulf

U.S. Navy
support

	French army unit
	U.S. army unit
	British army unit
	Arab army unit
	Allied advance
	Allied bombing
	airbase

**U.S. active- duty military
personnel in the World,
Sept. 1994**

10,000

0

number in
countries having
more than
500 personnel

THE ELECTIONS OF 1992 AND 1994
SHIFTING SANDS OR NEW FOUNDATIONS?

In the early 1990s, Republicans spoke confidently of their "lock" on the electoral college, believing that a secure base in the West and South would give their candidtates an enviable head start in all presidential contests (see Republicans Ascendant, p 224–225). Yet barely more than a year and a half after a Republican president orchestrated a military triumph in the Mideast, Democrat Bill Clinton won a thumping electoral victory. Voters had been angered by George Bush's aloofness and seeming lethargy in the face of an economic downturn, but were also disenchanted by record budget deficits, inadequate tax relief for most Americans, and assorted congressional shenanigans. This disenchantment did not, however, discriminate among the parties. Voters turned on Democrats as quickly as they had on Bush—such that in the mid-term elections of 1994, the GOP won a prize that had eluded it even during the heyday of the Reagan "Revolution," control of both houses of Congress.

As Democrats celebrated their 1992 victory, campaign strategist James Carville had warned that they had not broken the GOP "lock" but merely picked it. Clinton had selected another white southerner, Al Gore, as a running mate, probably helping him win a number of states which had not voted Democratic since 1976, including his native Arkansas, Tennessee (Gore's home state), Louisiana, and Kentucky. Promising to minister to the economy, Clinton had also won a number of midwestern states struggling not simply with recession, but a more fundamental decline of heavy industry. Most remarkable of all had been Clinton's capture of southern California, the wellspring of modern conservatism. As the Cold War eased, the economic dislocation attending reduced military spending and base closings had been focused,

like California's defense industries themselves, in the Los Angeles area. Clinton, like Michael Dukakis, won a majority in Los Angeles county but also pluralities in the other Southern California counties—with the decided exception of Orange—that so recently had been indispensable to GOP success in the state (see Republicans Ascendant, p 224–225).

Still, Carville had good reason to be cautious. Disenchantment with the political status quo, both in Southern California and nationwide, had manifested itself more in an unusually large third-party vote than a tidal surge toward the Democrats. Texas billionaire H. Ross Perot, despite his erratic campaigning, had won a bigger share of the popular vote than any third-party candidate since former President Theodore Roosevelt in 1912. Clinton's electoral college triumph had been based on the Democrat's simply running ahead of Bush in 33 states. Clinton had won actual majorities only in Arkansas and the inveterately Democratic District of Columbia.

The insecurity of Clinton's position quickly became evident. A 43 percent share of the popular vote hardly represented a ringing mandate, and, in any case, the voter disenchantment of the 1990s seemed to carry with it few positive prescriptions with respect to policy. The new adminstration committed various blunders while fractiousness within Congress prevented Democrats from making much of their majorities. But critics also scored Clinton —particularly in the case of health care reform—for overreaching, contending that he had attempted to give citizens more than many of them had asked for in electing him.

This sour mood set the stage for the Republican sweep in the congressional elections of 1994. The party won control of the Senate for the first time since 1986; not since Eisenhower's first term had it controlled the House. Republicans picked up seats across the nation but perhaps most notably in the South.

Southerners had been considerably slower to slough off their residual Democratic loyalties in voting for state, district, county, and municipal officers than for president. This election, though, demonstrated the GOP's growing success in building dynamic local organizations based on solid support among white southerners, particularly in the suburbs of Sunbelt metropolises like Atlanta, Houston, and Dallas.

Yet Republican congressmen, though they had spelled out their agenda in a pre-election "Contract with America," rather quickly found themselves in a position similar to Democrats' two years earlier. It was not clear how much more voters intended than simply to ring out the old. Like their predecessors, congressional Republicans were soon being accused of misreading the public and of overreaching in their efforts to cut spending and decentralize government.

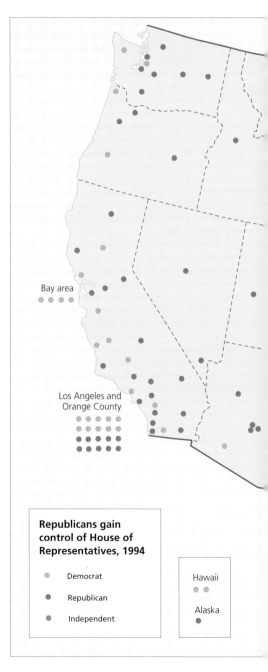

Bay area

Los Angeles and Orange County

Republicans gain control of House of Representatives, 1994

- Democrat
- Republican
- Independent

Hawaii

Alaska

Presidential election, 1992

- Clinton, Democrat
- Bush, Republican

Hawaii

Alaska

The voters of Macomb county, Michigan, illustrated the uncertain course of American politics in the 1990s—much as they had illustrated, through the 1970s and 1980s, important sources of GOP strength and of Democrats' declining fortunes. The sort of white ethnic voters who predominated in Macomb had been the working-class heart of the New Deal coalition and as they had moved into the suburbs voted by large margins for John Kennedy in 1960 and Lyndon Johnson in 1964. Their loyalty began to fade, however, as the national party's support for civil rights was translated into an endorsement of school busing to promote racial integration and as Democrats sometimes seemed more interested in embracing feminism and even the counterculture than in preserving the New Deal fundamentals of economic security. Macomb's alienation first expressed itself in a relatively large vote in 1968 for George Wallace, whose strident law and order rhetoric resonated not only in the South but in the white suburbs of crime-ridden cities like Detroit. By the 1970s, a majority of Macomb voters had identified with the culturally conservative GOP at the presidential level, though a large portion of the county continued to elect a Democratic congressman into the 1990s. Evidently, many wearied of the Republicanism of George Bush after 1988, but this hardly

redounded to the benefit of Democrats, who did not win a majority when Republicans lost theirs in 1992. Instead, Perot ran ahead of his nationwide 19 percent. Two years later, the county backtracked, voters in large number returning to the GOP. It is unclear whether this ebb and flow of party loyalties in Macomb county—and, indeed, across America —suggested simply that an era of Republican preeminence had been briefly interrupted in 1992 or, instead, signalled the beginning of some more fundamental realignment.

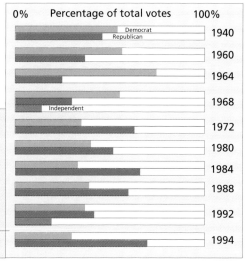

BIBLIOGRAPHICAL SOURCES, NOTES AND CREDITS

This historical atlas was a collaborative endeavor. Our greatest debt is to the historians, scholars and cartographers, listed below, whose ideas and materials served as the principal sources for the maps. The artists, mapmakers and graphics specialists at Arcadia Editions Limited translated our wayward notions and abstractions into visually coherent form. We especially thank Malcolm Swanston, the president of Arcadia, who served as art director and chief cartographer. We also thank Kenneth R. Wright of Henry Holt for his vision, enthusiasm and support. In addition to these, we thank the staff of Arcadia.

Research: Susanne Pichler; also, the reference departments of Butler Library, Columbia University, the New York Public Library, and the University of Arkansas. Fact-checking: Patricia Riordan
Senior editor, New York: Mary Elin Korchinsky.
Editors, United Kingdom: Rhonda Carrier and Nina E. E. Swanston.
Arcadia Editions Limited: art and design: Julian Baker, Peter Gamble, Elsa Gibert, Isabelle Lewis, Kevin Panton, Jeanne Radford, Peter Smith, Jonathan Young.

Part I: Pre-Columbian America

A Continent Adrift

John Gribben, *This Shaking Earth* (1978); Peter J. Smith, ed., *The Earth* (1986); B. Bolt, *Earthquakes: A Primer* (1978); David G. Smith, ed., *The Cambridge Encyclopedia of Earth Sciences* (1982); Robert S. Dietz, "Geosynclines, Mountains, and Continent-Building," Robert S. Dietz and John C. Holden, "The Breakup of Pangaea," Don L. Anderson, "The San Andreas Fault," and A. Hallam, "Alfred Wegener and the Hypothesis of Continental Drift," all in J. Tuzo Wilson, *Continents Adrift and Continents Aground* (1976).

The Climatic Challenge

Charles O. Paullin, *Atlas of the Historical Geography of the United States* (1932); U. S. Congress, 36th Congress "Effect of Storm on the Island and Main Ship Channel on Galveston, Texas" *House Document 134* (1900); Ivan R. Tannehill, *Hurricanes, Their Nature and History* (1938); Herbert M. Mason, *Death from the Sea; our greatest natural disaster* (1972).

Global Warming

American Heritage Pictorial Atlas of the United States History (1966); Charles O. Paullin, *Atlas of the Historical Geography of the United States* (1932); David Graham Smith, ed., *The Cambridge Encyclopedia of Earth Sciences* (1982); William C. Clark and R. E. Munn, eds., *Sustainable Development of the Biosphere*

(1986); W. R. Emanuel, H. H. Shugart, and M. P. Stevenson, "Climatic change and the broad-scale distribution of terrestrial ecosystem complexes," *Climatic Change* (1985); M. B. McElroy, "Change in the natural environment of the Earth: the historical record," in Clark, eds.; *Scientific American* (April, 1989); *Scientific American, Technology Review*, (April, 1990); Smithsonian Institution Traveling Exhibition Service, *Tropical Rainforests: A Disappearing Treasure* (1988); Natural History (1990).

First Peoples of North America

Brian Fagan, *The Great Journey: The Peopling of Ancient America* (1987); Karl W. Butzer, "The Indian legacy in the American landscape," in Michael P. Conzen, *The Making of the American Landscape* (1989); *Historical Atlas of Canada*, Vol 1 (1987); Norman Stone, ed., *Times Atlas of World History* (1989); Joseph H. Greenberg, Christy G. Turner II, and Stephen L. Zegura, "The Settlement of the Americas: A Comparison of the Linguistic, Dental, and Genetic Evidence," *Current Anthropology* 27 (December, 1986). The authors gratefully acknowledge the assistance of Wilcomb Washburn. Note: Nearly all scholars believe that the first Americans crossed over what is now the Bering Strait, although the time of the first passage is widely debated. In the late 1970s some scholars moved back the crossing date to perhaps as early as 70,000 BC (See especially Richard S. MacNeish, "Early Man in the New World," *American Scientist* 63 (1976) and Tom D. Dillehay, "A Late Ice-Age Settlement in Southern Chile," *Scientific American*, 251 [1984]). The dates mentioned in the text are now regarded as conservative, for the general trend in current archaeology is to date human skeletal remains at earlier and earlier periods.

Myth of the Mound Builders

Karl W. Butzer, "The Indian legacy in the American landscape," in Michael P. Conzen, ed., *The Making of the American Landscape* (1990); E. G. Squier and E. H. Davis *Ancient Monuments of the Mississippi Valley* (1848); Brian M. Fagan, *The Great Journey: The Peopling of Ancient America* (1987); Charles Hudson, Chester B. De Pratter and Marvin T. Smith, "Hernando de Soto's Expedition through the Southern United States," in Jerald T. Milanich and Susan Milbrath, eds., *First Encounters: Spanish Explorations in the Caribbean and the United States, 1492-1570* (1989); Marshall McKusick, *The Davenport Conspiracy* (1970); Robert Silverberg, *Mound Builders of Ancient America: The Archaeology of a Myth* (1968); M. Coe, D. Snow, and E. Benson, *Atlas of Ancient America* (1988); Melvin L. Fowler, "A Pre-Columbian Urban Center on the Mississippi," Scientific American (August, 1975).

Origins of Indian Languages

Harold E. Driver and William C. Massey, "Comparative Studies of North American Indians," *Transactions of the American Philosophical Society* (1957); J. W. Powell, Linguistic Stocks of American Indians (1891); Edward Sapir, "Languages of the World," *Encyclopedia Britannica* (1929); C. F. and F. M. Voegelin, *Map of North American Indian Languages* (1966); M. Ruhlen, *A Guide to the World's Languages* (1987); Joseph H. Greenberg, *Languages in the Americas* (1987); James Matisoff, "On Megalo-comparison," *Language* 66 (1990). Note: For reasons of graphical presentation, some of Powell's smaller linguistic categories have been combined.

Savage Tribes or Sovereign Nations?

Patricia Albers and Jeanne Kay, "Sharing the Land: A Study in American Indian Territoriality," in Thomas E. Ross and Tyrel G. Moore, eds., *A Cultural Geography of North American Indians* (1987); Harold E. Driver, *Indians of North America* (1969); William R. Swagerty, "Indian Trade in the Trans-Mississippi West to 1870," in Wilcomb E. Washburn, ed., *History of Indian-White Relations* (1988); C. Waldman and M. Broun, eds., *Atlas of the North American Indians* (1985); Amos Bad Heart Bull and Helen Blish, *A Pictographic History of the Aglala Sioux* (1987). The authors gratefully acknowledge the assistance of Wilcomb Washburn.

The World in 1500: I

Colin McEvedy and Richard Jones, *Atlas of World Population History* (1978). See also the sources for **Disease Devastates the Indians** (below).

The World in 1500: II

Norman Stone, ed., *Times Atlas of World History* (1989).

Part 2: Colonial America

Columbus Navigates to a "New" World

R. Shirley, *Mapping of the World* (1929); Alexander O. Vietor, "A Pre-Columbian map of the world, circa 1489," *Imago Mundi* 17; *American Heritage Pictorial Atlas of the United States History* (1966); J. B. Hewson, *A History of the Practice of Navigation* (1951); Carlo M. Cipolla, *Guns and Sails in the Early Phase of European Expansion, 1480-1700* (1965); G. L. Hosmer, *Navigation Then and Now* (1924).

European Ecological Imperialism

Charles O. Paullin, *Atlas of the Historical Geography of the United States* (1932); Norman Stone, ed., *Times Atlas of World History* (1989);

G. S. Elton, *The Ecology of Invasions* (1957); The U.S. Bureau of the Census, *Agricultural Atlas*, (1988); Percy Bidwell and J. Falconer, *History of Agriculture in Northern United States* (1973); Alfred W. Crosby, *The Columbian Exchange: Biological and Cultural Consequences of 1497* (1972) and *Ecological Imperialism: The Biological Expansion of Europe, 900-1900* (1986); Carl Waldman, *Atlas of the North American Indian* (1985); Kenneth F. Kiple, ed., *The Cambridge World History of Human Disease* (1993). Note: We refer to "European" ecological imperialism, because the carriers of the microbes into the Western Hemisphere were mostly Europeans; but the original microbes themselves washed throughout Europe, Asia and Africa; one might more precisely refer to them as "Old World" diseases; see also the notes for **Disease Devastates the Indians.**

European Footholds Along the Atlantic

U.S. Bureau of the Census, *Historical Statistics of the United States*, Table Z (1975); B. P. Gerhard, *The North Frontier of New Spain* (1982); *Historical Atlas of Canada* (1987).

Disease Devastates the Indians

Alfred W. Crosby, *The Columbian Exchange: Biological and Cultural Consequences of 1492* (1972) and *Ecological Imperialism: The Biological Expansion fo Europe, 900-1900* (1986); Carl Waldman, *Atlas of the North American Indian* (1985); A. L. Kroeber, *Cultural and Natural Areas of Native North America* (1939); James Mooney, *The Aboriginal Population of America North of Mexico* (1928); Henry F. Dobyns, *Their Number Become Thinned: Native American Population Dynamics in Eastern North America* (1983); Colin McEvedy, *The Penguin Atlas of North American History to 1870* (1988); Colin McEvedy, *Atlas of World Population History* (1978). Notes: No subject in this atlas is more hotly disputed than the pre-Columbian population of the Americas. Recent scholarship suggests far higher pre-Columbian population estimates than those shown here. The highest estimate is 145 million, with 18 million living in the region now defined by the continental United States and Canada. See Henry F. Dobyns, "Reassessing New World Populations at the Time of Contact," unpublished paper delivered at Institute for Early Contact Studies, University of Florida at Gainesville (April, 1988). In this and other layouts, we have chosen lower estimates, which are more consistent with data established for worldwide comparison. Whatever the pre-Columbian population, the losses from disease surely constituted one the greatest tragedies in history; for a summary, see David E. Stannard, *American Holocaust: Columbus and the Conquest of the New World* (1992).

The Great English Migration

Virginia Dejohn Anderson, "Migrants and Motives: Religion and the Settlement of New England, 1630-1640," *New England Quarterly* 58 (1985); David Grayson Allen, *In English Ways: The Movement of Societies and the Transferal of English Local Law and Custom to Massachusetts Bay in the Seventh Century* (1981); T. H. Breen and Stephen Foster, "Moving to the New World: The Character of Early Massachusetts Immigration," *William and Mary Quarterly* 30 (1973); Martin Gilbert, *The Dent Atlas of American History* (1993).

Spain's North American Frontier

Herbert Bolton, *The Spanish Borderlands* (1921); Peter Gerhard, *The North Frontier of New Spain* (1982); Oakah Jones, Los Paisanos: *Spanish Settler on the Northern Frontier of New Spain* (1919); John Kessell. Kiva, Cross, and Crown: *The Pecos Indians and New Mexico, 1540-1840* (1979); Alfred Kidder, *Pecos, New Mexico: Archaeological Notes* (1958); Max Moorhead, *The Presidio* (1975); David Weber, ed. *New Spain's Far Northern Frontier: Essays on Spain in the American West, 1540-1821* (1979); L. J. Cappon, ed., *Atlas of Early American History: The Revolutionary Era, 1760-1790* (1976).

African Slave Trade

Philip D. Curtin, *The Atlantic Slave Trade: A Census* (1969); A. W. Lawrence, *Trade Castles & Forts of West Africa* (1964); Norman Stone, ed., *Times Atlas of World History* (1989); J. Coughtry, *The Notorious Triangle* (1981); Verner Crane, ed., *A Rhode Island Slaver: Trade Book of the Sloop Adventure, 1773-1774* (1922); Gilman M. Ostrander, "The Colonial Molasses Trade," *Agricultural History* 30 (1956); Gilman M. Ostrander, "The Making of the Triangular Trade Myth," *William and Mary Quarterly* (1974).

Church Formation in Colonial America

This layout was designed and written by Jon Butler of Yale University. See especially his *Awash in a Sea of Faith: Christianizing the American People* (1990); also Edwin Scott Gaustad, *Historical Atlas of Religion in America* (1976).

Sacralizing the Landscape

This layout was designed and written by Jon Butler of Yale University. Sources include Sumner Chilton Powell, *Puritan Village: The Formation of a New England Town* (1963); Albert Simons and Samuel Lapham, *The Early Architecture of Charleston* (1970); Samuel G. Stoney, *Plantations of the Carolina Low Country* (1989); Dell Upton, *Holy Things and Profane: Anglican Parish Churches in Colonial Virginia* (1986);

Church Membership

This layout was designed and written by John Butler of Yale University. Sources on membership patterns include Frederick Lewis Weis, *The Colonial Churches and the Colonial Clergy of the Middle and Southern Colonies, 1607-1776* (1938) and his *The Colonial Clergy and the Colonial Churches of New England* (1936); Rodney Stark and Roger Finke, "American Religion in 1776: A Statistical Portrait," *Sociological Analysis*, 49 (1988); and Charles O. Paullin, *Atlas of the Historical Geography of the United States* (1932).

The Containment of France

New Cambridge Modern History (1974); *American Heritage Pictorial Atlas of the United States History* (1966).

Eighteenth-Century Warfare

Historical Atlas of Canada (1987); Christopher Duffy, *Fire & Stone: The Science of Fortress Warfare, 1660-1860* (1975); *American Heritage Pictorial Atlas of the United States History* (1966).

George Washington in the West

American Heritage Pictorial Atlas of the United States History (1966).

The Great War for the Empire

The most important source, and the one on which nearly all sources rely, is the *West Point Atlas of American Wars* (originally published 1959, reprinted, 1995).

Part 3: A New Nation

The American Revolution

The most important source for this, and subsequent layouts on the American Revolution is Vincent J. Esposito, ed., *West Point Atlas of American Wars* [vol. 1, 1689-1900], (1959). Robert H. Ferrell and Richard Natkiel, *Atlas of American History* (1987); David Hackett Fisher, *Paul Revere's Ride* (1994).

From New York to Princeton

Vincent J. Esposito, ed., *West Point Atlas of American Wars* [vol. 1, 1689-1900], (1959). Robert H. Ferrell and Richard Natkiel, *Atlas of American History* (1987).

The Battle of Saratoga

Vincent J. Esposito, ed., *West Point Atlas of American Wars* [vol. 1, 1689-1900], (1959). Robert H. Ferrell and Richard Natkiel, *Atlas of American History* (1987).

The War Moves South

Vincent J. Esposito, ed., *West Point Atlas of American Wars* [vol. 1, 1689-1900], (1959). Robert H. Ferrell and Richard Natkiel, *Atlas of American History* (1987).

The Battle of Yorktown

Vincent J. Esposito, ed., *West Point Atlas of American Wars* [vol. 1, 1689-1900], (1959). Robert H. Ferrell and Richard Natkiel, *Atlas of American History* (1987).

People of the New Nation

This layout was designed and written by Robert V. Wells. The demographic data was from the U.S. census; the county boundaries are from Lester Cappon, ed., *Atlas of Early American History* (1976); copies of the computer print-outs on which these maps and graphs were derived are available from Mark C. Carnes, Barnard College, Columbia University.

Political Conflict in the New Nation

The main source is Jackson Turner Main, *Political Parties before the Constitution* (1973). The maps in this atlas differ from Main's in several inconsequential points of detail; Main's maps were composite assessments, while these have been derived from legislators' votes on a single issue.

Claiming the West

Charles O. Paullin, *Atlas of the Historical Geography of the United States* (1932); Frederick Merk, *History of the Westward Movement* (1978); *American Heritage Pictorial Atlas of the United States History* (1966).

Lewis and Clark Reveal the Northwest

Bernard de Voto, *Journals of Lewis and Clark* (1953) and *Across the Wide Missouri* (1964); John Logan Allen, *Passage through the Garden: Lewis and Clark and the Image of the American Northwest* (1975).

The War of 1812

Vincent J. Esposito, ed., *West Point Atlas of American Wars* [vol. 1, 1689-1900], (1959); Charles O. Paullin, *Atlas of the Historical Geography of the United States* (1932).

Capitalism

Alan Pred, "Manufacturing in the American Mercantile City: 1800-1840," *Annals of the Association of American Geographers* 56 (1966, June); Paul Johnson, "A Shopkeeper's Millenium: Society and Revivals in Rochester, NY, 1815-1837," (UCLA dissertation, 1975); see also

Johnson's *A Shopkeeper's Millennium* (1978); Sam Bass Warner, *The Private City: Remainder of Title: Philadelphia in three periods of its growth* (1968). The authors gratefully acknowledge the assistance of Paul Johnson.

Politics in the Jacksonian Era

Charles O. Paullin, *Atlas of the Historical Geography of the United States* (1932).

Removal of the Indians

Francis Paul Prucha, *Atlas of American Indian Affairs* (1990). Charles O. Paullin, *Atlas of the Historical Geography of the United States* (1932); John Wesley Morris, et al., *Historical Atlas of Oklahoma* (1986).

Politics after Jackson

The Ohio and Mississippi maps are adapted from J. R. Sharp, *The Jacksonians versus the Bank* (1970). See also Dixon Ryan Fox, *Aristocracy in the Politics of New York* (1919); R. Ernst, *Immigrant Life in New York City, 1825-1863* (1949); Lee Benson, *The Concept of Jacksonian Democracy* (1961).

The Burned-Over District

Whitney R. Cross, *The Burned-Over District: The Social and Intellectual History of Enthusiastic Religion in Western New York, 1800-1850* (1950); Lois Kimball Mathews, *The Spread of New England Settlement and Institutions to the Mississippi River, 1620-1865* (1909); Delores Hayden, *Seven American Utopias: The Architecture of Communitarian Socialism, 1790-1975* (1976); Charles O. Paullin, *Atlas of the Historical Geography of the United States* (1932).

Utopian Communities

Dolores Hayden, *Seven American Utopias: The Architecture of Communitarian Socialism, 1790-1975* (1976); E. R. Hogan, *The Shaker Holy Land* (1980); Robert P. Emlen, *Shaker Village Views* (1987); E. D. Andrew, *The People Called Shakers* (1953); Louis J. Kern, *An Ordered Love: Sex Roles and Sexuality in Victorian Utopias— the Shakers, the Mormons, and the Oneida Community* (1981); Lawrence Foster, *Religion and Sexuality: Three American Communal Experiments of the Nineteenth Century* (1981).

Fertility and the Frontier

Yasukichi Yasuba, *Birth Rates of the White Population in the U.S., 1800-1860* (1962); Charles O. Paullin, *Atlas of the Historical Geography of the United States* (1932); John Modell, "Family and Fertility on the Indiana Frontier, 1820" *American Quarterly* XXIII (1971); Richard A. Easterlin, "Does Human Fertility Adjust to the Environment," *The American Economic Review*

LXI (1971); U.S. Bureau of the Census, *Historical Statistics of the U.S.*, Number of Children Under 5 Years Old Per 1,000 Women 20-44 Years Old by Race and Residence, by Geographic Divisions (1975).

Irish and German Immigration

Ruth Dudley Edwards, *Atlas of Irish History* (1981); O. MacDonagh, "Irish Famine Emigration to the U.S.," *Perspectives in American History* 10 (1976); S. H. Cousens, "The Regional Pattern of Emigration during the Great Irish Famine, 1846-51," in Institute of British Geographers, *Transactions and Papers* 28 (1960); S. H. Cousens, "Emigration and Demographic Change in Ireland, 1851-1861," *Economic History Review* 14 (1961-62); U.S. Bureau of the Census; "Migration: Imigrants, by Country, 1820-1970," (1975).

The War with Mexico

John Eisenhower, *So Far from God: The U.S. War with Mexico, 1846-1848* (1989); Marshall de Bruhl, *Sword of San Jacinto: A Life of Sam Houston* (1993).

Part 4: Slavery and the Civil War

The Slave System

C. L. Lord and E. H. Lord, *Historical Atlas of the United States* (1944); Martin Gilbert, *American History Atlas* (1968); Randolph Campbell, *An Empire for Slavery: The Peculiar Institution in Texas, 1821-1865* (1989).

Slavery in the Territories

Holman Hamilton, *Prologue to Conflict: The Crisis and Compromise of 1850* (1964); Kenneth Martis, *The Historical Atlas of United States Congressional Districts, 1789-1983* (1982); David M. Potter, *The Impending Crisis, 1848-1861* (1976).

Abolitionists and Runaways

For further information, please see the introduction to this book. The basic source is Wilbur Siebert, *The Underground Railroad* (1898); also Frederick Douglass, *Narrative of the Life of Frederick Douglass, an American Slave* (1845); William Craft & Ellen Craft, *Running a Thousand Miles for Freedom; or, the Escape of William and Ellen Craft from Slavery* (1860); *Four Fugitive Slave Narratives* (1969) [includes Josiah Henson and William Wells Brown]; Gilbert Osofsky, ed., *Puttin' on Ole Massa: The Slave Narratives of Henry Bibb, William Wells Brown, and Solomon Northup* (1969); Rayford Logan & Michael Winston, eds., *Dictionary of American Negro Biography* (1982); Charles E. Stevens, *Anthony Burns: A History* (1856); William Edward Farrison, *William Wells Brown: Author and Reformer* (1969); *The Reverend J. W.*

Loguen, as a Slave and as a Freeman; a Narrative of Real Life (1859); Joel Shor, *Henry Highland Garnet: A Voice of Black Radicalism in the Nineteenth Century* (1977).

The Coming of the Civil War

Charles O. Paullin, *Atlas of the Historical Geography of the United States* (1932).

Secession of the South

C. L. Lord and E. H. Lord, *Historical Atlas of the United States* (1944). Note: The map depicted here shows popular vote in secession referenda in Texas and Tennessee, but for the other states it indicates the position of counties' representatives in secession conventions.

The Civil War I: Resources and War Aims

James M. McPherson, *Battle Cry of Freedom: The Civil War Era* (1988); Peter J. Parish, *The American Civil War* (1975); Sam Hilliard, *Atlas of Antebellum Agriculture* (1984); Charles O. Paullin, *Atlas of the Historical Geography of the United States* (1932); *American Heritage Pictorial Atlas of the United States History* (1966); C. L. Lord and E. H. Lord, *Historical Atlas of the United States* (1944). Note: Southern and central Louisiana and coastal Texas produced significant amounts of sugar, information that has been omitted from this map to avoid cluttering it.

The Civil War II: 1861-1862

James McPherson, *Battle Cry of Freedom: The Civil War Era* (1988); Peter J. Parish, *The American Civil War* (1975); Vincent J. Esposito, ed., *The West Point Atlas of American Wars* [vol. 1, 1689-1900] (1959).

Emancipation and Black Military Service

Ira Berlin, et al., eds., *The Black Military Experience* [*Freedom: A Documentary History of Emancipation*, series 2] (1982); Ira Berlin, et. al., eds., *The Destruction of Slavery* [*Freedom: A Documentary History of Emancipation* series 1, vol. 1] (1985); *Congressional Globe*, 37th Congress, 11 July 1862 (pp.3267-3268); Kenneth Martis, *The Historical Atlas of United States Congressional Districts, 1789-1983* (1982); Eric Foner, *Reconstruction: America's Unfinished Revolution, 1863-1877* (1988); Eric Foner, "The South's Inner Civil War," *American Heritage* (March, 1989); James M. McPherson, *Battle Cry of Freedom: The Civil War Era* (1988); James M. McPherson, "Who Freed the Slaves?" *Proceedings of the American Philosophical Society* 139 (March, 1995); Peter J. Parish, *The American Civil War* (1975). Note for the Second Confiscation Act map: Paired votes have been identified as yea or nay of the sentiments of the congressman in question could be determined.

Day of Decision

James M. McPherson, *Battle Cry of Freedom: The Civil War Era* (1988); Peter J. Parish, *The American Civil War* (1975); Shelby Foote, *The Civil War, a Narrative: Fredericksburg to Meridian* (1963); Vincent J. Esposito, ed., *West Point Atlas of American Wars* [vol. 1, 1689-1900] (1959).

Total War: 1864-1865

Marion B. Lucas, *Sherman and the Burning of Columbia* (1976); James M. McPherson, *Battle Cry of Freedom: The Civil War Era* (1988); Vincent J. Esposito, ed., *West Point Atlas of American Wars* [vol. 1, 1689-1900] (1959); William C. Davis, *Death in the Trenches: Grant at Petersburg* (1986); Charles Royster, *The Destructive War: William Tecumseh Sherman, Stonewall Jackson, and the Americans* (1991).

The Politics of Reconstruction

Eric Foner, *Reconstruction: America's Unfinished Revolution, 1863-1877* (1988); Terry Seip, *The South Returns to Congress: Men, Economic Measures, and Intersectional Relationships, 1868-1879* (1983); Kenneth Martis, *The Historical Atlas of United States Congressional Districts, 1789-1983* (1982); *Biographical Director of the United States Congress, 1774-1989* (1989); R. Sobel & J. Raimo, *Biographical Director of the Governors of the United States, 1789-1978*, 4 vols. (1978). Note for Reconstruction and Redemption map: Redemption dated by the installation of Democratic governors or of governors elected with Democratic support.

Reconstruction: Land and Labor

Roger Ransom and Richard Sutch, *One Kind of Freedom: The Economic Consequences of Emancipation* (1977); Claude Oubre, *Forty Acres and a Mule: The Freedman's Bureau and Black Landownership* (1978); Eric Foner, *Reconstruction: America's Unfinished Revolution, 1863-1877* (1988); *Scribner's Monthly* 21 (April 1881); C. Vann Woodward, *Origins of the New South, 1877-1913* (1951); Barbara J. Fields, "The Advent of Capitalist Agriculture: The New South in a Bourgeois World" in *Essays on the Postbellum Southern Economy*, eds., Thavolia Glymph and John J. Kushma (1985).

Part 5: America in the Gilded Age

Toward a National Railway Network

The main map is adapted from George R. Taylor and Irene D. Neu, *The American Railroad Network, 1861-1890* (1956); Charles O. Paullin, *Atlas of the Historical Geography of the United States* (1932), Carl Condit, *The Railroad and the City* (1977).

Railroads, Canals, and Economic Growth

The main idea of this layout is from Robert Fogel, *Railroads and Economic Growth* (1964). Other information from the U.S. Department of Commerce, *Historical Statistics of the United States* (1975); Charles O. Paullin, *Atlas of the Historical Geography of the United States* (1932).

The Indians Crushed

American Heritage Pictorial Atlas of the United States History (1966); Norman Stone, ed., *Times Atlas of World History* (1989); Richard Natkiel, *Atlas of American Wars* (1986); Francis Paul Prucha, *Atlas of American Indian Affairs* (1990); Evan S. Connell, *Son of the Morning Star: Custer and the Little Bighorn* (1984).

Strangers at the City Gates

U.S. Bureau of the Census, *Historical Statistics of the United States* (1975); James D. B. DeBow, *Compendium of the Seventh Census 1850; Statistical Abstract of the U.S., 1918* (1919); *Statistical Abstract of the U.S., 1972* (1973); *Thirteenth census of the U.S., 1910: Abstract of the Census* (1913); *Fifteenth Census of the U.S., Population* (1930).

From Shtetl to Stoop

H. H. Ben-Sasson, ed., *A History of the Jewish People* (1976); Yitzhak Alperovitz, ed., *Gorzd Book: A Memorial to the Jewish Community of Gorzd* (1980); Moses Rischin, *The Promised City: New York's Jews, 1870-1914* (1962); Martin Gilbert, *Jewish History Atlas* (1977). The authors gratefully acknowledge the assistance of Jeffrey Shandler.

The Conquest of Cholera

John Snow, *On the Mode and Communication of Cholera* (1936) Forty-Third Congress, *House Executive Documents* 13 (1874-1875); *The Water Supply of the City of New York* (1938).

Prostitution in 19th-Century New York

This layout was designed and written by Timothy Gilfoyle, author of *City of Eros: New York City, Prostitution, and the Commercialization of Sex* (1992); Committee of Fifteen Papers (New York Public Library); Mayors' Papers (New York City Municipal Archives and Records Center); George S. Bromley, *Atlas of the City of New York* (1899).

Industrial Paternalism and Workers' Communities

Margaret Byington, *Homestead: The Households of a Mill Town* (1910); Richard T. Ely, "Pullman: A Social Study," *Harper's New Monthly Magazine* 70 (1885); Stanley Buder,

Pullman: An Experiment in Industrial Order and Community Planning, 1880-1930 (1967); U.S. Bureau of the Census, *Historical Statistics of the United States* (1974); Gwendolyn Wright, *Building the Dream: A Social History of Housing in America* (1981).

The Creation of U.S. Steel

The information on the location and ownership of the principal factories, mills, and furnaces of the steel industry is from the American Iron and Steel Association, Directory of the Iron and Steel Works of the United States (1901). See also Kenneth Warren, *The American Steel Industry, 1850-1970: A Geographical Interpretation* (1973); Carnegie Brothers and Co., *The Edgar Thomson Steel Works and Blast Furnaces* (n.d.); J. S. Jeans, *American Industrial Conditions and Competition* (1902). The authors gratefully acknowledge the research assistance of Andrew Sandoval-Strausz.

The Rise of Populism

Roscoe Martin, *The People's Party in Texas: A Study in Third Party Politics* (1933); Fred Shannon, *The Farmer's Last Frontier: Agriculture, 1860-1897* (1945); U.S. Bureau of the Census, *Historical Statistics of the United States, Colonial Times to 1970* (1975); U.S. Census Office, *Report on Wealth, Debt, and Taxation at the Eleventh Census, 1890* (1895); U.S. Department of Agriculture, *Atlas of American Agriculture* (1936); John Hicks, *The Populist Revolt: A History of the Farmers' Alliance and the People's Party* (1931); C. Vann Woodward, *Origins of the New South, 1877-1913* (1951); Lawrence Goodwyn, *Democratic Promise: The Populist Moment in America* (1976); James Turner, "Understanding the Populists," *Journal of American History* 67 (1980-81); Stanley Parsons, *The Populist Context: Rural Versus Urban Power on a Great Plains Frontier* (1973); Steven Hahn, *The Roots of Southern Populism: Yeoman Farmers and the Transformation of the Georgia Upcountry, 1850-1890* (1983).

Money and Power

Kenneth Martis, *The Historical Atlas of Political Parties in Congress, 1789-1989* (1989); Charles O. Paullin, *Atlas of the Historical Geography of the United States* (1932); Edgar E. Robinson, *The Presidential Vote, 1896-1932* (1934); William Diamond, "Urban and Rural Voting in 1896," 46 *American Historical Review* (1940-1941); Gilbert Fite, "The Election of 1896," in Arthur M. Schlesinger, Jr. and F. Israel, eds., *History of American Presidential Elections, 1789-1968*, vol. 2 (1971); Gilbert Fite, "Republican Strategy and the 1896 Farm Vote," *American Historical Review* 65 (1959-1960); Paul Glad, *McKinley, Bryan and the People* (1964); J. Rogers Hollingsworth, *The Whirligig of Politics: The Democracy of Cleveland and Bryan* (1963); Richard Jensen, *The Winning of the Midwest:*

Social and Political Conflict, 1888-1896 (1971); Stanley Jones, *The Presidential Election of 1896* (1964); Paul Kleppner, *Continuity and Change in Electoral Politics, 1893-1928* (1987); Paul Kleppner, *The Cross of Culture: A Social Analysis of Midwestern Politics, 1850-1900* (1970).

The Boundary Disputes of the 1890s

Charles O. Paullin, *Atlas of the Historical Geography of the United States* (1932); Thomas A. Bailey, *A Diplomatic History of the American People* (1940).

The Course of Empire

The scholarly debate is summarized in Robert L. Beisner, *From the Old Diplomacy to the New, 1865-1900* (1975); see especially Walter LaFeber, *The New Empire: An Interpretation of American Expansion, 1860-1898* (1963); and Thomas J. McCormick, *China Market: America's Quest for Informal Empire* (1967). Information for the maps is from James S. Dennis, et al., *World Atlas of Christian Missions* (1911); Norman Stone, ed., *Times Atlas of World History* (1989); Historical Statistics (1975).

The Spanish-American War

David F. Trask, *The War with Spain in 1898* (1981); West Point Atlas; G. J. A. O'Toole, *The Spanish War* (1984); A. C. M. Azoy, *Signal 250!* (1964); Vincent J. Esposito, ed., *West Point Atlas of American Wars* [vol. 1, 1689-1900] (1959).

The Fruits of Empire

The map of the House of Representatives vote on Hawaii is from the rollcall as cited in the *Congressional Record* (1898), pp.6015ff; Kenneth Martis, *The Historical Atlas of United States Congressional Districts, 1789-1983* (1982); See also J. C. Sitterson, *Sugar Country: The Cane Sugar Industry in the South, 1753-1950* (1953); U.S. Bureau of the Census, *Historical Statistics of the United States* (1975); Stanley M. Karnow, *In Our Image: America's Empire in the Philippines* (1989); David Haward Bain, *Sitting in Darkness: Americans in the Philippines* (19894); M. Wilcox, *Harper's History of the War in the Philippines* (1900); William Thaddeux Sexton, *Soldiers in the Sun* (1939); K. I. Faust, *Campaigning in the Philippines* (1899).

Part 6: America in the Early 20th Century

Panama

David McCullough, *The Path Between the Seas: The Creation of the Panama Canal, 1870-1914* (1977); Miles P. Duval, *Cadiz to Cathey Spanish* (1973); W. J. Abbot, *Panama and the Canal* (1914); M. L. McCarty, *Glimpses of Panama and of the Canal* (1913).

Women's Suffrage

Eleanor Flexner, *Century of Struggle: The Woman's Rights Movement in the United States* (1959); Rand McNally & Co's *California* (1896); *California Blue Book, or State Roster* (1911); *San Francisco Chronicle* (October 13, 1911; C. L. Lord and E. H. Lord, *Historical Atlas of the United States* (1944); Charles O. Paullin, *Atlas of the Historical Geography of the United States* (1932).

The United States in World War I

L. P. Ayres, *The War with Germany: A Statistical Summary* (1919); Vincent J. Esposito, ed., *West Point Atlas of American Wars* [vol. 1, 1689-1900] (1959); C. L. Lord and E. H. Lord, *Historical Atlas of the United States* (1944); Martin Gilbert, *American History Atlas* (1968).

The Geography of "Stupidity"

Robert M. Yerkes, "Psychological Examining in the United States Army," *Memoirs of the National Academy of Sciences* (1921); Clarence S. Yoakum and Robert M. Yerkes, ed., *Army Mental Tests* (1920); U.S. Bureau of the Census, *Abstract of the Census: Population* (1910); M. F. Ashley Montagu, "Intelligence of Northern Negroes and Southern Whites in the First World War," *The American Journal of Psychology* 58 (1945); Daniel J. Kevles, "Testing the Army's Intelligence: Psychologists and the Military in World War I," *Journal of American History* 55 (1968). Note: Yerkes graded the "intelligence tests" on an A, B, C, and D basis and gathered the data by state. "Least intelligent" represents the states that fell in the lowest quartile of his grading scheme.

The Spanish Influenza Pandemic

E. O. Jordan, *Epidemic Influenza: A Survey* (1927); W. I. B. Beveridge, *Influenza: The Last Great Plague* (1977); Warren T. Vaughan, *Influenza: An Epidemiologic Study* (1921); Alfred W. Crosby, Jr., *Epidemic and Peace, 1918* (1976); G. F. Pyle, *The Diffusion of Influenza* (1986); J. D. Robertson, *A Report of an Epidemic of Influenza in Chicago Occurring during the Fall of 1918* (1918).

The Crusade for Prohibition

Andrew Sinclair, *Era of Excess* (1962); Norman H. Clark, *The Dry Years: Prohibition and Social Change in Washington* (1965); Charles O. Paullin, *Atlas of the Historical Geography of the United States* (1932); F. B. Streetcar, "Michigan Prohibition Legislation," *Michigan History* 2 (1918); *Grand Rapids Press* (November 8, 1916); "Prohibition and Prosperity," *The Survey* 45 (1920); *Manual of the Common Council: City and Ward Boundaries* [Grand Rapids, 1910].

American Socialism in its Heyday

James Weinstein, *The Decline of Socialism in America, 1912-1925* (1967); Sally Miller, "Casting a Wide Net: The Milwaukee Movement to 1920" in *Socialism in the Heartland: The Midwestern Experience, 1900-1925*, ed. Donald Critchlow (1986); Sally Miller, "Milwaukee: Of Ethnicity and Labor" in *Socialism and the Cities*, ed. Bruce Stave (1975); James Green, *Grass-Roots Socialism: Radical Movements in the Southwest, 1895-1943* (1978); Steven Rosenstone et al., *Third Parties in America: Citizen Response to Major Party Failure* (1984); Garin Burbank, *When the Farmers Voted Red: The Gospel of Socialism in the Oklahoma Countryside, 1910-1924* (1976); David Shannon, *The Socialist Party of America: A History* (1955).

The Making of Black Harlem

Gilbert Osofsky, *Harlem, the Making of a Ghetto: negro New York, 1890-1930* (1971); Janes W. Johnson, *Black Manhattan* (1930); *New York Housing Authority, Harlem* (1934); Bureau of the Census, *Historical Statistics of the United States*, Series C25-75, (1975); Carter Goodrich, *Migration and Economic Opportunity* (1936); New York Department of City Planning, *Atlas of the Census: A Portrait of N. Y. C. from the 1980 Census* (1985).

Crime and Capital Punishment

Federal Bureau of Investigation, *Uniform Crime Reports* (1936-1940); *National Prisoner Statistics, Capital Punishment* (1979); William J. Bowers, *Legal Homicide: Death as Punishment in America, 1864-1982* (1984); Hugo Adam Bedau, ed. *The Death Penalty in America* (1982); U.S. Bureau of the Census, *Historical Statistics of the United States* (1960).

The Dust Bowl

U.S. Congress, Senate Special Committee to Investigate Unemployment and Relief, *Unemployment and Relief Hearings* (1938); U.S. Department of Agriculture, *Agricultural Statistics* (1934, 1936, 1938); D. Worster, *Dust Bowl* (1979); U.S. Bureau of the Census, *Historical Statistics of the United States* (1975); C. L. Lord and E. H. Lord, *Historical Atlas of the United States* (1944).

From New Era to New Deal

William Thorndale and William Dollarhide, *Map Guide to the U.S. Federal Censuses, 1790-1920* (1987); Edgar E. Robinson, *They Voted for Roosevelt, the Presidential Vote, 1932-1944* (1947).

The Great Depression

Works Projects Administration, *Report on the Progress of the WPA Program* (1939, 1941, 1942).

Materials for Erie, Pennsylvania were from the collections of the Erie County Historical Society in Erie, Pennsylvania.

Forging the Democratic Coalition

U.S. Bureau of the Census, "Population Characteristics by Census Tracts," *Census of 1930* (1931); K. L. Kusmer, *A Ghetto Takes Shape: Black Cleveland, 1870-1930* (1976); Howard W. Green, *Population Characteristics by Census Tracts* (1931); Board of Election, Ohio, *General Election, Nov. 6, 1928, Cuyahoga County* (1928, 1932, 1936).

Isolationism in the 1930s

Congressional Record, "Neutrality Act of 1936," (February 17, 1936; January 10, 1938); Kenneth Martis, *The Historical Atlas of United States Congressional Districts, 1789-1983* (1982); Charles O. Paullin, *Atlas of the Historical Geography of the United States* (1932).

America Enters World War II

J. G. Kirk and R. Natkiel, *Atlas of American Wars* (1986); H. N. Wallin, *Pearl Harbor: Why, How, Fleet Salvage, and Final Appraisal* (1968); *The Times Atlas of the Second World War* (1989).

The Battle of Midway

Charles Messenger, *Chronological Atlas of World War Two* (1989); John Keegan, ed., *The Times Atlas of the Second World War* (1989); J. Pimlott, *Historical Atlas of World War Two* (1995).

The United States in the European Theater

John Keegan, ed., *The Times Atlas of the Second World War* (1989).

The Allied Invasion of Northern Europe

John Keegan, ed., *The Times Atlas of the Second World War* (1989).

Pacific Counterattack

J. G. Kirk and R. Natkiel, *Atlas of American Wars* (1986); John Keegan, ed. *The Times Atlas of the Second World War* (1989); J. Pimlott, *Historical Atlas of World War Two* (1995); Vincent J. Esposito, ed., *West Point Atlas of American Wars* [vol. 1, 1689-1900] (1959).

The Manhattan Project and its Aftermath

U.S. Strategic Bombing Survey, Urban Areas Survey, *Effects of Air Attack on Urban Complex—Nagasaki* (1946); Peter Wyden, *Day One: Before Hiroshima and After* (1984); Takashi Nagai, *We of Nagasaki* (1951); Karen Dorn Steele, "Hanford's Bitter legacy," *Bulletin of Atomic Scientists* (January/February, 1988.

Japanese Immigrants, Japanese Internees

Yosaburo Yoshido, "Sources and Causes of Japanese Emigration," *The Annals of the American Academy of Political and Social Science* 34 (1909); Yuji Ichioka, *The Issei: The World of the First Generation Japanese Immigrants, 1885-1924* (1988); Yamato Ichihashi, *Japanese in the United States* (1932; 1969 reprint); *The Japanese-American Yearbook* (1909); U.S. Bureau of the Census, *Census for Population 1940*; also 1950; E. H. Spicer, et al, *Impounded People* (1969).

Part 7: Post-War America

White Flight

"St. Louis Area Residential Security Map, 19397," at Record Group 31, National Archives, Washington., D.C.; Kenneth T. Jackson, *Crabgrass Frontier: The Suburbanization of the United States* (1985); Barry Schwartz, ed., *The Changing Face of the Suburbs* (1976); J. T. Little, et. al., *The Contemporary Neighborhood Succession Process* (1969); U.S. Bureau of the Census, *Census of Population* (1950), (1960); B. Luckingham, *Phoenix: History of a Southwestern Metropolis* (1989); Department of Public Works, City of Dallas, *Map of Annexations, 1930-1960* (n.d.); W. N. Black, *"Empire of Consensus:" City Planning, Zoning, and Annexation in Dallas, 1900-1960* (1982).

The Suburban Dream

Levitt and Sons, "Map of Levittown, Pa," in G. A. Wissink, *American Cities in Perspective* (1962); Kenneth T. Jackson, *Crabgrass Frontier: The Suburbanization of the United States* (1985); *American Builder* (June, 1947); *Architectural Forum* (April, 1950); *House and Home* (December, 1952).

The Age of the Automobile

Dieter Hammerschlag, Brian K. Barber, and J. Michael Everett, *The Interstate Highway System and Urban Structure: A Force for Change in Rhode Island* (1976); State of California, *Traffic Volumes on California State Highways* (1961, 1989); George Webb and Karl Moskowitz, "California Freeway Capacity Study, 1956," *Highway Research Board, Proceedings* 36 (1957); Paul T. McElhiney, "Evaluating Freeway Performance in Los Angeles," *Traffic Quarterly* 14 (1960); David Brodsly, *LA Freeway* (1981). The authors gratefully acknowledge the assistance of Albert Proescholdt, Department of Transportation Survey Section, City of Los Angeles. Note: The California traffic volumes are approximations based on state data taken at peak time and hours.

The Brown Decision

Southern Education Reporting Service, *Statistical Summary of School Segregation—Desegregation in the Southern and Border States* (1967); Earl Black, *Southern Governors and Civil Rights: Racial Segregation as a Campaign Issue in the Second Reconstruction* (1976); Martin Gilbert, *American History Atlas* (1968).

Civil Rights

The New York Times (February 11, 1964); Kenneth Martis, *The Historical Atlas of United States Congressional Districts, 1789-1983* (1982).

The Struggle for Voting Rights

"U.S. Department of the Census, "Voting and Registration in the Election of November 1988: Population Characteristics, Series P-20, #440, Table 4"; Voter Education Project of the Southern Regional Council, *Negroes Holding Public Office in the South* (1968); *National Roster of Black Officials* (1977); *Black Elected Officials* (1987); *Mississippi House of Representatives by Districts*; *The New York Times* (July 10, 1965); U.S. Bureau of the Census, *Voting and Registration in the Election of November 1992* (1993); Joint Center for Political Studies, *Black Elected Officials* [1992-93 ed.] (1993).

The Race Riots of the 1960s

[Kerner Commission] *Report of the National Advisory Commission on Civil Disorders* (1968); "Civil Riot Chronology," *Congressional Quarterly Almanac* 23 (1967); R. J. Murphy and J. W. Watson, *The Structure of Discontent* (1967).

Integrating the Schools

U.S. Commission on Civil Rights, *Racial Isolation in the Public Schools* (1967); Little Rock School District, "Monthly Attendance Report, 1964"; U.S. Census, "Special Census, 1964: Series P-28, #1375, 1964"; E. H. Buell, *School Desegregation and Defended Neighborhoods* (1981); Judge Arthur Gerrity, "Morgan V. Hennigan," *379 Federal Supplement* 410 (1974); "Enrollment Report, October 1, 1980"; Center for Survey Research, *Boston Redevelopment Authority Household Survey* (1980); *New York Times*, September 14, 1974; Newburgh City School District, "Racial Analysis Report, 1971" and "Enrollment Analysis, 1989". The authors gratefully acknowledge the assistance of Leonard Thalmueller and Sterling Ingram of the Little Rock School District; and Ken Dewitt and Walter Millman of the Newburgh City School District and Jim Halpin of the Newburgh Free Library.

Restoration of Death

William J. Bowers, *Legal Homicide: Death as Punishment in America, 1864-1982* (1984); Hugo Adam Bedau, ed., *The Death Penalty in America* (1982); U.S. Department of Justice, *Capital Punishment* (1981); Federal Bureau of Investigation, *Crime in the United States* (1982, 1986); U.S. Bureau of Justice Statistics, *Sourcebook of Criminal Justice Statistics: 1994* (1995); *The Statistical Abstract of the United States: 1995* (1995).

Defeat of the Equal Rights Amendment

Data on Senate vote from Chicago Tribune, June 25, 1982; also *Chicago Tribune*, June 8, 12, 18 and 23, 1982 Legislative Districts from *Illinois Blue Book, 1981-1982*; *The New York Times* (April 15, 1980; April 28, 1980); B. G. Shortridge, *Atlas of American Women* (1987); Gilbert Steiner, *Constitutional Inequality: The Political Fortunes of the Equal Rights Amendment* (1985); Val Burris, "Who Opposed the ERA? An Analysis of the Social Bases of Antifeminism," *Social Science Quarterly* 64 (1983). Note: For reasons of graphical clarity, the vote in northeastern Illinois extends beyond the geographical limits of Cook County.

Republicans Ascendant

Kevin Phillips, *The Emerging Republican Majority* (1969); E. Black and M. Black, *Politics and Society in the South* (1987); Herbert B. Asher, *Presidential Elections and American Politics* (1976); Richard M. Scammon and Alice V. McGillivray [comp], *America at the Polls: A Handbook of American Presidential Election Statistics* (1994).

Part 8: America and the World After World War II

The Marshall Plan and the Cold War

The Statesman's Yearbook, 1945-1953; R. N. Tannahill, *The Communist Parties of Western Europe* (1978); R. Mayne, *The Recovery of Europe* (1970); H. B. Price, *The Marshall Plan and Its Meaning* (1955); R. J. Donovan, *The Second Victory: The Marshall Plan and the Postwar Revival of Europe* (1987); *Congressional Record-House* (April 2, 1948); Norman Stone, ed., *Times Atlas of World History* (1989); Kenneth Martis, *The Historical Atlas of United States Congressional Districts, 1789-1983* (1982).

Dropshot

The maps are based on the secret plan prepared by the Joint Chiefs of Staff in 1949, which was released through the United States' Freedom of Information Act in 1977 and originally published in Anthony Cave Brown, ed., *Dropshot: The United States Plan for War with the Soviet Union in 1957* (1978).

America's Frontline

John Keegan, ed., *The Times Atlas of the Second World War* (1989); Laurence Martin, *Before the Day After: Can NATO defend Europe?* (1985); George Rathjens, "How the use of nuclear weapons in Europe might arise," in Hylke Tromp, ed., *War in Europe: Nuclear and Conventional Perspectives* (1989); Eric Morris, *Blockade: Berlin and the Cold War* (1973); Frank R. Donovan, *Bridge in the Sky* (1968); J. M. Schick, *The Berlin Crisis, 1958-1962* (1971).

Korea: Defending the Periphery

J. G. Kirk and R. Natkiel, *Atlas of American Wars* (1986); Walt Sheldon, *Hell or High Water: MacArthur's Landing at Inchon* (1968); Donald Knox, *The Korean War: An Oral History* (1985).

Korean Stalemate

J. G. Kirk and R. Natkiel, *Atlas of American Wars* (1986); Donald Knox, *The Korean War: An Oral History* (1985).

The French in Vietnam

Phillip B. Davidson, *Vietnam at War: 1947-1975* (1988); William Westmoreland, *Report on Operations in Vietnam* (1968); George Herring, *America's Longest War* (1979).

The Battle of Ap Bac

The battle is described in searing detail by Neil Sheehan, *A Bright and Shining Lie: John Paul Vann and America in Vietnam* (1988), on which this reconstruction has been based.

The "Hearts and Minds" of the Vietnamese

William Momyer, *Air Power in Three Wars* (1978); Shelby L. Stanton, *Anatomy of a Division: 1st Cav in Vietnam* (1987); J. D. Coleman, *Pleiku: The Down of Helicopter Warfare in Vietnam* (1988); R. Michael Pearce, *Evolution of a Vietnamese Village: Part I: The Present, After Eight Months of Pacification* (1965); also Part III (1967).

Americanization of the War

William Westmoreland, *Report on Operations* (1965-1967); T. C. Thayer, *War Without Fronts: The American Experience in Vietnam* (1985); U.S. Congress Committee on the Judiciary, Subcommittee to Investigate Problems Concerned with Refugees and Escapees, *Civilian Casualty, Social Welfare, and Refugee Problems in South Vietnam* (1970); A. T. Rambo, et al, *Cultural Change in Rural Vietnam* (1973); Robert H. Ferrell and Richard Natkiel, *Atlas of American History* (1987); William Momyer, *Air Power in Three Wars* (1978).

The Tet Offensive

William Westmoreland, *Report on Operations in Vietnam, January 1964-June 1968* (1965, 1966, 1967, 1968); Don Oberdorfer, *Tet!* (1971); Robert Pisor, *The End of the Line: The Siege of Khe Sanh* (1982).

Ending the Vietnam War

The rollcall for the cutoff vote is from the *Congressional Record-House* (June 25, 1973); James Lawton Collins, Jr., *The Development and Training of the South Vietnamese Army, 1950-1972* (1975); Kenneth Martis, *The Historical Atlas of United States Congressional Districts, 1789-1983* (1982); William Westmoreland, *Report on Operations in Vietnam, January 1964-June 1968* (1968); Harrison Salisbury, *Vietnam Reconsidered: Lessons from a War* (1984); Robert H. Ferrell and Richard Natkiel, *Atlas of American History* (1987); R. D. Burns and M. Leitenberg, *The Wars in Vietnam, Cambodia and Laos, 1945-1982* (1988).

One Giant Leap for America

Staff Report of the Committee on Aeronautical and Space Sciences, *Manned Space Flight Program of the National Aeronautics and Space Administration: Projects Mercury, Gemini, and Apollo* (1962); Peter Ryan, *Invasion of the Moon, 1969* (1969); Kenneth F. Weaver, "The Flight of Apollo 11: 'One Great Leap for Mankind,'" *National Geographic* 136 (December, 1969).

Part 9: America, An Evolving Superpower

The First Information Revolution

Publisher's Weekly (1880); Charles Evans, *American Bibliography* (1903-1934); Roger Bristol, *Index of Printers, Publishers, and Booksellers Indicated by Charles Evans in his American Bibliography* (1961); *Literary Market Place* [1981 edition] (1980); *American Book Trade Directory* [1969-1970 edition] (1988); Hellmut Lehmann-Haupt, *The Book in America: A History of the Making and Selling of Books in the United States* (1951); John Tebbel, *Between Covers: The Rise and Transformation of Book Publishing in America* (1987); G. T. Tansell, "Some Statistics on American Printing, 1764-1783" in *The Press and the American Revolution*, eds. Bernard Bailyn and John Hency (1980). The authors gratefully acknowledge the assistance of the Austin History Center, Austin, Texas.

America's Hispanics

Frank Bean and Marta Tienda, *The Hispanic Population of the United States* (1987); Cary Davis, Carl Haub, and JoAnne Willette, "U.S. Hispanics: Changing the Face of America," *Population Bulletin* 38:2 (1983); Joan Moore and Harry Pachon, *Hispanics in the U.S.* (1987); Beth Anne Shelton, et. al., *Houston: Growth and Decline in a Sunbelt Boomtown* (1989); *Statistical Yearbook of the Immigration and Naturalization Service* (1989); Kal Wagenheim, *Puerto Ricans in the U.S* (1983); *New York Times* (February 21, February 22, and February 26, 1991); U.S. Census Bureau, *1990 Census of Population. Persons of Hispanic Origin in the United States* (1993); U.S. Census Bureau, *The Statistical Abstract of the United States: 1995* (1995); U.S. Census Bureau, *The Statistical Abstract of the United States: 1992* (1992); U.S. Immigration and Naturalization Service, *Factbook* (1995). The authors gratefully acknowledge the assistance of Peg Purser, Director of Community Research, University of Houston Center for Public Policy and Jacqueline M. Hagan of the Department of Sociology of the University of Houston.

Energy versus the Environment

Organization for Economic Cooperation and Development (OECD), *The State of the Environment* (1985); Walter H. Corson, *The Global Ecology Handbook: What You Can Do about the Environmental Crisis* (1990); R. Ostman, *Acid Rain* (1991); *Bulletin of Atomic Scientists* (August/September, 1986); Thomas H. Moss and D. L. Sills, eds., *Three Mile Island Accident* (1981); *The Economist World Atlas and Almanac* (1989); "In Harm's Way," *National Geographic* (January, 1990); R. Gould, *Going Sour: Science and Politics of Acid Rain* (1985); *The New York Times* (June 12, 1988; January 16, 1990); J. L. Regens & R. W. Rycroft, *The Acid Rain Controversy* (1988); "Pollutant Pathways," *Natural History* 7 (1986).

AIDS

The Statistical Abstract of the United States: 1995 (1995); U.S. Centers for Disease Control, *Summary of Notifiable Diseases, United States, 1994* (1995); idem, *Summary of Notifiable Diseases, United States, 1993* (1994); H. W. Jaffe, D. J. Bregman, & R. M. Selik, "Acquired Immune Deficiency Syndrome in the United States: the First 1,000 Cases," in *Journal of Infectious Diseases* (1983); Centers for Disease Control, *Human Immunodeficiency Virus Infection in the United States*, MMWR 36 (1987); Centers for Disease Control, *AIDS/HIV Record*, 3:2-3 (February 20, 1989); also same journal, vol. 4:1 (March 31, 1990); *Aids Information Sourcebook* (1991).

The Abortion Controversy

Alan Guttmacher Institute, *An Analysis of pre-1973 State Laws on Abortion* (March, 1989); Stanley K. Henshaw and Jennifer Van Vort, "Abortion Services in the United States, 1987 and 1988," *Family Planning Perspectives*, 22:3 (May/June, 1990); Pennsylvania Department of Health, "News Release: Health Department Releases 1987 Pennsylvania Abortion Data" (April 18, 1988); State Center for Health Statistics, *North Carolina Reported Abortions, 1987* (October, 1988); the *New York Manual/Members of Assembly, by District* (1970); *Statistical Abstract of the United States: 1995* (1995); David Garrow, *Liberty and Sexuality: The Right to Privacy and the Making of Roe v. Wade* (1994). The authors gratefully acknowledge the assistance of Stanley K. Henshaw of the Alan Guttmacher Institute.

A New World Order

U.S. Department of Defense, *Selected Manpower Statistics, Fiscal Year 1994*; U.S. Department of Defense, *Military Manpower Statistics, June 30 1995*; U.S. News and World Report (February 4, 1991); *Newsweek* (February 4, 1991).

The Elections of 1992 and 1994

The New York Times, November 10, 1994; *Congressional Quarterly, Guide to U.S. Elections*, Third Edition (1994); M. Barane and G. Ujifusa, *The Almanac of American Politics, 1996* (1995); R. Scammon and A. McGillivray, Congressional Quarterly, *America Votes* (1993).

Picture Credits

The publishers wish to thank the following:

Peter Newark's American Pictures

Pages 15, 23, 24, 25, 28, 33, 37, 38, 51, 58, 59, 63, 64, 66, 68, 70, 78, 80, 82, 83, 86, 87, 91, 96, 98, 106, 108, 115, 118, 120, 129, 131, 136, 151, 154, 155, 157, 161, 163, 165, 171, 173, 179, 181, 182, 189, 191, 193, 195, 197, 199, 209, 212, 213, 215, 221, 225, 237, 250, 251, 269.

Other sources:

British Library, London
Britsh Museum, Trustees, London
Carnegie Library, Pittsburgh
Chicago Tribune, Chicago
H. Josse
Hulton Deutsch Collection, London
National Archives, Washington, D.C.
National Portrait Gallery, London
San Francisco Museums of Art, San Francisco
Smithsonian Institute, Washington, D.C.
University of South Carolina, Columbia
Yale University Art Gallery, New Haven
and Private Collections

INDEX